FEDERAL TORT CLAIMS ACT

Contemporary Decisions

* * *

A LandMark Publication

Litigator Series

Federal Tort Claims Act
Contemporary Decisions

Published in the United States of America
 by LandMark Publications.
www.landmark-publications.com

Publication Date: May 2017;
Subject Heading: Federal Courts;
Audience: Law Professionals.

Character Set: ISO 8859-1 (Latin-1);
Language Code: EN;
Interior Type: Text; Monochrome.

Help us serve you better.
Write to landmarkpx@live.com with
your requests, comments and suggestions.

ISBN: 978-1521307236

Summary of Contents

PROLOGUE

"The concept of the immunity of government officers from personal liability springs from the same root considerations that generated the doctrine of sovereign immunity. While the latter doctrine — that the 'King can do no wrong' — did not protect all government officers from personal liability, the common law soon recognized the necessity of permitting officials to perform their official functions free from the threat of suits for personal liability." *Scheuer v. Rhodes,* 416 U.S. 232, 239, 94 S.Ct. 1683, 40 L.Ed.2d 90 (1974), *abrogated on other grounds by Harlow v. Fitzgerald,* 457 U.S. 800, 102 S.Ct. 2727, 73 L.Ed.2d 396 (1982). "[T]he scope of absolute official immunity afforded federal employees is a matter of federal law, to be formulated by the courts in the absence of legislative action by Congress." *Westfall v. Erwin,* 484 U.S. 292, 295, 108 S.Ct. 580, 98 L.Ed.2d 619 (1988) (internal quotation marks omitted), *superseded on other grounds by* Pub. L. No. 100-694, 102 Stat. 4563 (1988), codified at 28 U.S.C. § 2679(d). "The purpose of such official immunity is not to protect an erring official, but to insulate the decisionmaking process from the harassment of prospective litigation." *Id.*

The Westfall Act, which was enacted in response to the Supreme Court's decision in *Westfall,* "accords federal employees absolute immunity from common-law tort claims arising out of acts they undertake in the course of their official duties." *Osborn v. Haley,* 549 U.S. 225, 229, 127 S.Ct. 881, 166 L.Ed.2d 819 (2007). [Footnote omitted.] The immunity extends to both "negligent" and "wrongful" "act[s] or omission[s] of any employee ... acting within the scope of his office or employment." 28 U.S.C. § 2679(b)(1). The Act does not set out a test to determine whether an employee was "acting within the scope of his office or employment"; rather, Congress intended that courts would apply "the principles of *respondeat superior* of the state in which the alleged tort occurred" in analyzing the scope-of-employment issue. *Pelletier v. Fed. Home Loan Bank of S.F.,* 968 F.2d 865, 876 (9th Cir. 1992). The same analysis was employed before passage of the Westfall Act to determine whether the United States could be liable for an employee's torts under the FTCA. *Id.* at 875-76.

The Westfall Act does not provide immunity to an official from a suit "brought for a violation of the Constitution of the United States." *Id.* § 2679(b)(2)(A). That preserves claims against federal officers under *Bivens v. Six Unknown Named Agents of Federal Bureau of Narcotics,* 403 U.S. 388, 91 S.Ct. 1999, 29 L.Ed.2d 619 (1971). *Hui,* 559 U.S. at 807, 130 S.Ct. 1845. The Act also does not provide immunity from a suit "brought for a violation of a statute of the United States under which such action against an individual is otherwise authorized." 28 U.S.C. § 2679(b)(2)(B).

Saleh v. Bush, 848 F. 3d 880 (9th Cir. 2017)

FOREWORD

THIS CASEBOOK contains a selection of U. S. Court of Appeals decisions that analyze, discuss and interpret provisions of the Federal Tort Claims Act. The selection of decisions spans from 2013 to the date of publication.

Sovereign immunity precludes federal court jurisdiction. *FDIC v. Meyer,* 510 U.S. 471, 475 (1994). "[T]he United States can be sued only to the extent that it has waived its immunity." *United States v. Orleans,* 425 U.S. 807, 814 (1976); *see United States v. Mitchell,* 463 U.S. 206, 212 (1983) ("It is axiomatic that the United States may not be sued without its consent and that the existence of consent is a prerequisite for jurisdiction."); *Aviles v. Lutz,* 887 F.2d 1046, 1048 (10th Cir. 1989) (stating that, where Congress had not authorized suit under the FTCA, the district court was "without subject matter jurisdiction"). *Garling v. United States Environmental Protection Agency,* (10th Cir. 2017).

Through 28 U.S.C. § 1346(b)(1), the FTCA waives sovereign immunity for certain state law tort claims against the United States. This provision is subject to 28 U.S.C. § 2680(h), which lists exceptions to waiver for various intentional torts. But § 2680(h) also includes language that restores waiver for some of those torts. *Garling v. United States Environmental Protection Agency, ibid.*

The FTCA "is a limited waiver of sovereign immunity, making the Federal Government liable to the same extent as a private party for certain torts of federal employees acting within the scope of their employment." *Orleans,* 425 U.S. at 814. Subject to the exceptions listed in § 2680, the FTCA permits:

> civil actions on claims against the United States, for money damages . . . for injury or loss of property, or personal injury or death caused by the negligent or wrongful act or omission of any employee of the Government while acting within the scope of his office or employment, under circumstances where the United States, if a private person, would be liable to the claimant in accordance with the law of the place where the act or omission occurred.

28 U.S.C. § 1346(b)(1). "State substantive law applies to suits brought against the United States under the FTCA." *Hill v. SmithKline Beecham Corp.,* 393 F.3d 1111, 1117 (10th Cir. 2004). *Garling v. United States Environmental Protection Agency, ibid.*

Title 28 U.S.C. § 2680 lists exceptions to the FTCA's waiver of sovereign immunity. *Id.* § 2680(a)-(n). When an exception applies, sovereign immunity remains, and federal courts lack jurisdiction. *Aviles,* 887 F.2d at 1048; *see Franklin v. United States,* 992 F.2d 1492, 1495 (10th Cir. 1993) (stating that whether the FTCA exception in § 2680(h) applies was a "question of subject matter jurisdiction"); *see also Milligan v. United States,* 670 F.3d 686, 692 (6th Cir. 2012) ("Because the FTCA is a jurisdictional statute, if a case falls within the statutory exceptions of 28 U.S.C. § 2680, the court lacks subject matter jurisdiction. . . ." (brackets and quotations omitted)); *Hydrogen Tech. Corp. v. United States,* 831 F.2d 1155, 1161 (1st Cir. 1987) ("[B]ecause 28 U.S.C. § 1346(b) provides that federal courts shall have jurisdiction over FTCA claims '*subject to*' . . . section 2680 [and] the exceptions found in that section define the limits of federal subject matter jurisdiction in this area."). *Garling v. United States Environmental Protection Agency, ibid.*

* * *

A key FTCA requirement is that a person cannot sue under it unless he first presents his "claim" to the relevant administrative agency "within two years after such claim accrues" — failure to present a claim within that period "forever bar[s]" the claim. 28 U.S.C. § 2401(b). An essential element of a claim is "notification of the incident," via "an executed" SF 95 or "other written" document, "accompanied by" a demand "for money damages in a *sum certain.*" See 28 C.F.R. § 14.2(a) (emphasis added). The purpose behind the sum-certain requirement is to tip the government off as to its "possible liability" so that it can "'investigate the alleged negligent episode'" to see "'if settlement would be in the best interests of all.'" Coska v. United States, 114 F.3d 319, 322 (1st Cir. 1997) (*quoting Corte-Real v. United States,* 949 F.2d 484, 486 (1st Cir. 1991), in turn quoting *Lopez v. United States,* 758 F.2d 806, 809 (1st Cir. 1985)); *see also Reilly v. United States,* 863 F.2d 149, 173 (1st Cir. 1988) (noting that "[t]he goal of the administrative claim requirement is to let the government know what it is likely up against: mandating that a claimant propound a definite monetary demand ensures that '[t]he government will at all relevant times be aware of its maximum possible exposure to liability and will be in a position to make intelligent settlement decisions'" (*quoting Martinez v. United States,* 780 F.2d 525, 530 (5th Cir. 1986))). And because the FTCA ties "both the authority to settle a claim and the source of settlement funds to the amount of the underlying claim," [Footnote omitted.] not having a sum certain obviously makes it harder for the government to determine the claim's value and to "handl[e]" the claim "efficiently." *Kokotis,* 223 F.3d at 279. *Holloway v. US,* (1st Cir. 2017).

* * *

Courts consider whether an FTCA waiver of sovereign immunity applies via a Rule 12(b)(1) motion, because whether the government has waived its sovereign immunity goes to the court's subject matter jurisdiction. *Willoughby v. United States ex rel. U.S. Dep't of the Army,* 730 F.3d 476, 479 (5th Cir. 2013); *see also* 28 U.S.C. § 1346(b)(1). Waiver of sovereign immunity is strictly construed, meaning uncertainty is decided in favor of the government. *Willoughby,* 730 F.3d at 480. *Tsolmon v. US,* 841 F. 3d 378 (5th Cir. 2016).

* * *

The FTCA generally waives the United States' sovereign immunity from suits in tort, "render[ing] the Government liable in tort as a private individual would be under like circumstances." *Richards v. United States,* 369 U.S. 1, 6 (1962); *see also* 28

U.S.C. § 2674. But that waiver is subject to certain exceptions. *See generally* 28 U.S.C. § 2680. Under the foreign country exception, the FTCA's waiver of immunity does not apply to "[a]ny claim arising in a foreign country." *Id.* § 2680(k). *SH v. US*, (9th Cir. 2017).

In *Sosa*, the Supreme Court held that the foreign country exception to the FTCA "bars all claims based on any injury suffered in a foreign country, regardless of where the tortious act or omission occurred." *Sosa v. Alvarez-Machain*, 542 U.S. 692 (2004) at 712. *SH v. US*, (9th Cir. 2017), (discussing how to determine where an injury is "suffered.")

The foreign country exception codified Congress' "unwilling[ness] to subject the United States to liabilities depending upon the laws of a foreign power." *Id.* at 707 (alteration in original) (quoting *United States v. Spelar*, 338 U.S. 217, 221 (1949)). At the time the FTCA was passed, "the dominant principle in choice-of-law analysis for tort cases was *lex loci delicti*: courts generally applied the law of the place where the injury occurred." *Id.* at 705. Accordingly, the Court concluded that Congress likely intended the phrase "arising in" to have the same meaning in § 2680(k) as it did in state choice-of-law statutes: that is, to "express the position that a claim arises where the harm occurs." *Id.* at 711. [Footnote omitted.] *SH v. US*, (9th Cir. 2017).

The discretionary function exception is one of several limitations on the FTCA's waiver. The exception preserves the government's sovereign immunity when the plaintiff's claim is based on an act by a government employee that falls within that employee's discretionary authority. 28 U.S.C. § 2680(a). Whether an official's actions fall within the exception involves two inquiries: (1) "the conduct must be a 'matter of choice for the acting employee,'" *Spotts v. United States*, 613 F.3d 559, 567 (5th Cir. 2010) (quoting *Berkovitz ex rel. Berkovitz v. United States*, 486 U.S. 531, 536, 108 S.Ct. 1954, 100 L.Ed.2d 531 (1988)); and (2) "the judgment [must be] of the kind that the discretionary function exception was designed to shield,'" *id.* at 568 (quoting *United States v. Gaubert*, 499 U.S. 315, 322-23, 111 S.Ct. 1267, 113 L.Ed.2d 335 (1991)). The plaintiff has the burden of establishing that the discretionary function exception does not apply. *Spotts*, 613 F.3d at 569. *Tsolmon v. US, ibid.*

* * *

The *Feres* doctrine is a narrow exception to tort liability under federal statute: "[T]he Government is not liable under the FTCA for injuries to servicemen where the injuries arise out of or are in the course of activity incident to service." *Feres v. United States*, 340 U.S. 135, 146 (1950); *see also Meister v. Texas Adjutant Gen.'s Dep't*, 233 F.3d 332, 336 (5th Cir. 2000). The *Feres* Court held the FTCA waived sovereign immunity, "putting the United States government in the same position as any other defendant." *Meister*, 233 F.3d at 336.

After *Feres*, the Supreme Court "authorized a suit for damages against federal officials whose actions violated an individual's constitutional rights. . . ." *Chappell v. Wallace*, 462 U.S. 296, 298 (1983) (citing *Bivens v. Six Unknown Named Agents of Fed. Bureau of Narcotics*, 403 U.S. 388 (1970)). In *Chappell*, though, the Court limited the *Bivens* remedy by holding "that enlisted military personnel may not maintain a suit to recover damages from a superior officer for alleged constitutional violations." *Id.* at 305. The Court later reaffirmed the applicability of the *Feres* incident-to-service test, requiring courts to abstain from interfering in cases arising under such circumstances. *United States v. Stanley,* 483 U.S. 669, 683-84 (1987). *Morris v. Thompson,* (5th Cir. 2017).

* * *

In the FTCA, Congress waived sovereign immunity for claims brought against the United States based on the negligence or wrongful acts or omissions of its employees committed within the scope of employment, accepting liability in the same manner and to the same extent as a private individual would have under like circumstances. 28 U.S.C. §§ 1346(b)(1), 2671-2680. This waiver, however, is circumscribed by numerous exceptions, including an exception for claims "based upon the exercise or performance or the failure to exercise or perform a discretionary function or duty on the part of a federal agency or an employee of the Government, whether or not the discretion involved be abused." Id. § 2680(a) (emphasis added). Because waivers of sovereign immunity must be strictly construed, the plaintiff bears the burden of demonstrating jurisdiction and showing that none of the FTCA's exceptions apply. *See Welch v. United States,* 409 F.3d 646, 651 (4th Cir. 2005). *Wood v. US,* 845 F. 3d 123 (4th Cir. 2017).

* * *

The discretionary function exception "preserves the federal government's immunity . . . when an employee's acts involve the exercise of judgment or choice." The exception is found in 28 U.S.C. § 2680(a):

> Any claim based upon an act or omission of an employee of the Government, exercising due care, in the execution of a statute or regulation, whether or not such statute or regulation be valid, or based upon the exercise or performance or the failure to exercise or perform a discretionary function or duty on the part of a federal agency or an employee of the Government, whether or not the discretion involved be abused.

The Supreme Court has explained, "[t]he exception covers only acts that are discretionary in nature, acts that 'involv[e] an element of judgment or choice,' [] and 'it is the nature of the conduct, rather than the status of the actor' that governs whether the exception applies." "The basis for the discretionary function exception was Congress' desire to 'prevent judicial "second-guessing" of legislative and administrative decisions grounded in social, economic, and political policy through the medium of an action in tort.'" [Footnotes omitted.] *Wood v. US, ibid.*

A two-prong test determines whether the exception applies: (1) "the conduct must be a 'matter of choice for the acting employee[;]'" and (2) the "judgment [must be] of the kind that the discretionary function exception was designed to shield." Both prongs must be met for the exception to apply. With respect to the first prong, "[i]f a statute, regulation, or policy leaves it to a federal agency to determine when and how to take action, the agency is not bound to act in a particular manner and the exercise of its authority is discretionary." On the contrary, "[t]he requirement of judgment or choice is not satisfied if a 'federal statute, regulation, or policy specifically prescribes a course of action for an employee to follow,' because 'the employee has no rightful option but to adhere to the directive.'" Regarding the second prong, the court "consider[s] whether the actions taken are 'susceptible to policy analysis.'" "[T]he proper inquiry . . . is not whether [the official] *in fact* engaged in a policy analysis when reaching his decision but instead whether his decision was 'susceptible to policy analysis.'" In performing the two-prong test, "the question of *whether* the government was negligent is irrelevant." [Footnotes omitted.] *Gonzalez v. US*, (5th Cir. 2017).

* * *

To determine whether this discretionary function exception applies, courts apply a two-part test. The first step is to decide whether the conduct at issue involves "an element of judgment or choice" by the employee, rather than, for example, "when a federal statute, regulation, or policy specifically prescribes a course of action for an employee to follow." *Berkovitz v. United States,* 486 U.S. 531, 536, 108 S.Ct. 1954, 100 L.Ed.2d 531 (1988). The second step is to determine whether that judgment "is of the kind that the discretionary function exception was designed to shield" in that the judgment relates to a governmental action or decision "based on considerations of public policy." *Id.* at 536-37, 108 S.Ct. 1954; *see Suter,* 441 F.3d at 310-11. *Pornomo v. US*, 814 F. 3d 681 (4th Cir. 2016).

If an action is discretionary within the meaning of the exception, the exception applies "whether or not the discretion involved be abused." 28 U.S.C. § 2680(a); *United States v. Gaubert,* 499 U.S. 315, 323, 111 S.Ct. 1267, 113 L.Ed.2d 335 (1991) (noting that discretionary actions are "protected, even if those particular actions were negligent"). It applies "even if the discretion has been exercised erroneously" and is deemed to have frustrated the relevant policy purpose. *Holbrook v. United States,* 673 F.3d 341, 350 (4th Cir.2012). "The inquiry is thus whether the discretion exists, not whether in later litigation it is alleged to have been abused. Were it otherwise, Congress' intent to shield an agency's discretionary decisions from FTCA lawsuits would be set at naught." *Id. Pornomo v. US, ibid.*

* * *

"The FTCA bars claimants from bringing suit in federal court until they have exhausted their administrative remedies." *McNeil v. United States,* 508 U.S. 106, 113, 113 S.Ct. 1980, 124 L.Ed.2d 21 (1993). Specifically, the FTCA states, in pertinent part, that

> [a]n action shall not be instituted upon a claim against the United States for money damages for injury or loss of property or personal injury or death caused by the negligent or wrongful act or omission of any employee of the Government while acting within the scope of his office or employment, unless the claimant shall have first presented the claim to the appropriate Federal

agency and his claim shall have been finally denied by the agency in writing and sent by certified or registered mail.

28 U.S.C. § 2675(a). This exhaustion requirement is "jurisdictional and cannot be waived." [Footnote omitted.] *Bradley v. United States by Veterans Admin.,* 951 F.2d 268, 270 (10th Cir.1991). "In other words, the FTCA bars would-be tort plaintiffs from bringing suit against the government unless the claimant has previously submitted a claim for damages to the offending agency, because Congress wants agencies to have an opportunity to settle disputes before defending against litigation in court." *Smoke Shop, LLC v. United States,* 761 F.3d 779, 786 (7th Cir.2014) (citing *McNeil,* 508 U.S. at 112 & n. 7, 113 S.Ct. 1980). *Lopez v. US,* 823 F. 3d 970 (10th Cir. 2016).

The FTCA renders the United States liable for the torts of its employees, [ ]"in the same manner and to the same extent as a private individual under like circumstances." 28 U.S.C. § 2674. The FTCA requires a plaintiff pursuing a tort claim to follow a multi-step process. First, a plaintiff must file his claim with the appropriate federal agency, which then has the power to settle or deny it. 28 U.S.C. §§ 2401(b), 2675(a). The plaintiff may file a civil action against the United States only if the agency has denied the claim. 28 U.S.C. § 2675(a). *Raplee v. US,* 842 F. 3d 328 (4th Cir. 2016).

In *Shelton,* the court ruled that the plaintiff cannot establish a claim for negligence under the FTCA based on the alleged incident, because he did not exhaust his administrative remedies. *Shelton v. Bledsoe,* 775 F. 3d 554 (3rd Cir. 2015). The disctric court granted the defendants' motion to dismiss the FTCA claim based on its conclusion that the plaintiff's failure to exhaust deprived the court of jurisdiction to hear that claim. Affirmed. *Shelton v. Bledsoe,* 775 F. 3d 554 (3rd Cir. 2015).

No claim can be brought under the FTCA unless the plaintiff first presents the claim to the appropriate federal agency and the agency renders a final decision on the claim. 28 U.S.C. § 2675(a); *see also McNeil v. United States,* 508 U.S. 106, 112, 113 S.Ct. 1980, 124 L.Ed.2d 21 (1993); *Deutsch v. United States,* 67 F.3d 1080, 1091 (3d Cir. 1995) ("[A] claimant must have first presented the claim, in writing and within two years after its accrual, to the appropriate federal agency, and the claim must have been denied."). This requirement is jurisdictional and cannot be waived. *Rosario v. Am. Export-Isbrandtsen Lines, Inc.,* 531 F.2d 1227, 1231 (3d Cir. 1976). *Shelton v. Bledsoe, ibid.*

* * *

The FTCA permits suits against the government for torts caused by the wrongful acts of any government employee while acting within the scope of his office or employment. *See* 28 U.S.C. §§ 1346(b)(1), 2645. Plaintiffs have two years from the time of accrual to file a claim with the appropriate agency and then, if the claim is denied, six months after the denial to file suit. See id. § 2401(b). *Dominguez v. US,* 799 F. 3d 151 (1st Cir. 2015).

* * *

In *Dubose v. Kansas City Southern Railway Co.,* the court explained that the discovery rule governs the accrual of causes of action in federal cases where a plaintiff claims it was not aware of the injury or could not have discovered facts critical to ascertaining the injury's cause. *See* 729 F.2d 1026, 1030 (5th Cir.1984). Under the discovery rule, "a claim accrues when a plaintiff knows both her injury and its cause." *Trinity Marine Products, Inc. v. US,* 812 F. 3d 481 (5th Cir. 2016).

FEDERAL CIRCUIT DECISIONS
Federal Tort Claims Act

766 F.3d 576 (2014)

Walter J. HIMMELREICH, Plaintiff-Appellant,
v.
FEDERAL BUREAU OF PRISONS, et al., Defendants,
J. Fitzgerald, et al., Defendants-Appellees.

No. 13-4212.

United States Court of Appeals, Sixth Circuit.

Decided and Filed: September 9, 2014.

Himmelreich v. Federal Bureau of Prisons, 766 F. 3d 576 (6th Cir. 2014)

ON BRIEF: Lisa Hammond Johnson, United States Attorney's Office, Cleveland, Ohio, for Appellee. Walter Himmelreich, Danbury, Connecticut, pro se.

Before: COLE, Chief Judge; MOORE and GIBBONS, Circuit Judges.

OPINION

PER CURIAM.

In 2010, Walter J. Himmelreich—a federal prisoner—filed a complaint against numerous defendants, alleging several p.577 causes of action. The district court dismissed the complaint for failure to state a claim. On appeal, in Case No. 11-3474, we affirmed the dismissal of the majority of the claims and defendants, but we vacated and remanded two claims for further proceedings: a claim of retaliation in violation of the First Amendment based on Himmelreich's placement in administrative detention for sixty days in 2009, allegedly in retaliation for his filing of a claim under the Federal Tort Claims Act ("FTCA"); and a claim of failure to protect in violation of the Eighth Amendment based on an assault on Himmelreich by another inmate in 2008. On remand, the remaining defendants moved for summary judgment, arguing that Himmelreich had failed to exhaust his administrative remedies on the two claims at issue and that his Eighth Amendment claim was barred because he had elected to file a claim under the FTCA regarding the assault incident. The district court found the defendants' arguments to be valid and granted their motion for summary judgment. Himmelreich now appeals pro se, and we unanimously agree that oral argument is not needed. Fed. R.App. P. 34(a). For the reasons stated below, we conclude that Himmelreich's failure to exhaust his administrative remedies should have been excused and that the FTCA's judgment bar does not apply to this case. Consequently, we once again VACATE the district court's judgment and REMAND the case for further proceedings consistent with this opinion.

I.

The Prison Litigation Reform Act ("PLRA"), 110 Stat. 1321-71, 42 U.S.C. § 1997e(a), prevents a prisoner from filing suit "with respect to prison conditions ... until such administrative remedies as are available are exhausted." In *Woodford v. Ngo*, 548 U.S. 81, 126 S.Ct. 2378, 165 L.Ed.2d 368 (2006), the Supreme Court interpreted this language as requiring "proper exhaustion," meaning that a prisoner must "make full use of the prison grievance process" and "compl[y] with the system's critical procedural rules." *Id.* at 93-95, 126 S.Ct. 2378. There are few exceptions to this strict rule, but we have excused a prisoner's lack of complete compliance when the improper actions of prison officials render the administrative remedies functionally unavailable. *See generally Brock v. Kenton Cnty.,* 93 Fed. Appx. 793, 798 (6th Cir.2004) (collecting cases).

Himmelreich admits that he did not complete all of the steps in the prison grievance process, but he claims to have been "intimidated by Captain Fitzgerald... into not filing any more Administrative Remedies" with regard to his Eighth Amendment claim against the B-Unit Disciplinary Team. R. 47 at 10 (Pl.'s Resp. to Mot. for Summ. J.) (Page ID # 278). In determining whether Himmelreich fits within this exception, we must ask whether Captain Fitzgerald's threats and actions would "deter a person of ordinary firmness from [continuing with the grievance process]." *See Thaddeus-X v. Blatter,* 175 F.3d 378, 396 (6th Cir.1999) (en banc) (internal quotation marks omitted); *Bell v. Johnson,* 308 F.3d 594, 603 (6th Cir.2002).

Himmelreich alleges that Captain Fitzgerald told him that if Himmelreich continued with his grievances regarding the attack, "[she would] personally see that [Himmelreich was] transferred to a penitentiary and [he would] more than likely be attacked and not just beat up." R. 47 at 7 (Pl.'s Resp. to Mot. for Summ. J.) (Page ID # 275). When Himmelreich filed his FTCA lawsuit, he claimed that Captain Fitzgerald followed through with her threats and placed him in the Special Housing Unit ("SHU"). *Id.* at 11 (Page p.578 ID # 279). Once Himmelreich was put in the SHU, Captain Fitzgerald allegedly yelled, "'You want to know why you're in here? You're in here because of the fuckin' Tort Claim you filed! That's why you're in here!'" R. 1 at 15 (Compl. at ¶ 66) (Page ID # 15).

Unlike the vague and conclusory allegations at issue in *Boyd v. Corrections Corp. of America,* 380 F.3d 989, 997 (6th Cir.2004), Himmelreich's claims of intimidation are specific. If Himmelreich's allegations are true, which we must assume at this stage in the litigation, *Risher v. Lappin,* 639 F.3d 236, 240 (6th Cir.2011), a reasonable jury could conclude that Captain Fitzgerald's actions and statements would deter a person of ordinary firmness from continuing with the grievance process. Accordingly, we conclude that Himmelreich has demonstrated that a genuine issue of material fact exists as to whether Captain Fitzgerald improperly prevented Himmelreich from exhausting his administrative remedies.

In reaching this conclusion, we reject the government's argument that Himmelreich's filing of other administrative complaints and the FTCA lawsuit near the time that he claims to have been threatened prevents a finding of intimidation. We do not believe that minor complaints related to "requests to watch [the] *Passion of the Christ* movie," R. 45-4 at 2 (Grievance Record) (Page ID # 251), and to requests "to make a [weekly] call to [his] parents while in [the] SHU," *id.* at 11 (Page ID # 260), are relevant when Captain Fitzgerald purportedly told Himmelreich "that if he didn't stop [with his complaints about the assault] she would ship him to an ADX [higher-security prison], or better yet, to a [penitentiary] where she knows he will get shanked and probably killed," R. 1 at 14 (Compl. at ¶ 59) (Page ID # 14). Complaints and grievances related to petty requests and those related to prison-official misconduct are wholly different, particularly when there are specific allegations in the record that Captain Fitzgerald actually retaliated against

Himmelreich for filing grievances and lawsuits related to a specific assault. In our view, this retaliation and intimidation—if proven true—would render the grievance process functionally unavailable for a person of ordinary firmness. Thus, we VACATE the district court's grant of summary judgment on the basis of a failure to exhaust.

II.

The district court also found that the FTCA's judgment bar, 28 U.S.C. § 2676, applied in this case and, for this alternative reason, granted the government summary judgment with respect to Himmelreich's Eighth Amendment claim. Section 2676 states in full: "The judgment in an action under section 1346(b) of this title shall constitute a complete bar to any action by the claimant, by reason of the same subject matter, against the employee of the government whose act or omission gave rise to the claim." According to the district court, "[t]he plain language of section 2676 requires that the bar apply to all actions by the Plaintiff, not just judgments on the merits." R. 53 at 6-7 (D. Ct. Op.) (Page ID #436-37) (citing *Manning v. United States,* 546 F.3d 430, 437-38 (7th Cir.2008)). We disagree.

A careful reading of the record shows that the district court dismissed Himmelreich's FTCA action for a lack of subject-matter jurisdiction. R. 34 at 2-5 (D. Ct. Rule 12(b)(1) Op.) (Page ID #171-74) (Case Number 4:10-cv-307); *see also* R. 31 at 1 (Gov't Rule 12(b)(1) Mot.) (Page ID # 136) (Case Number 4:10-cv-307). Specifically, the district court found that the discretionary-function exception applied, which deprived the district court of subject-matter p.579 jurisdiction. Therefore, the district court granted the government's Rule 12(b)(1) motion and dismissed the action for a lack of jurisdiction. R. 34 at 2-5 (D. Ct. Rule 12(b)(1) Op.) (Page ID # 171-74) (Case Number 4:10-cv-307).

A dismissal for lack of subject-matter jurisdiction does not trigger the § 2676 judgment bar. Put bluntly, in the absence of jurisdiction, the court lacks the power to enter judgment. *See* 10A Charles Alan Wright, Arthur Miller, & Mary Kay Kane, *Federal Practice & Procedure* § 3713 (3d ed.1998) ("If the court has no jurisdiction, it has no power to enter a judgment on the merits and must dismiss the action."). Because we hold that district courts lack subject-matter jurisdiction over an FTCA claim when the discretionary-function exception applies, as it did here, *see Kohl v. United States,* 699 F.3d 935, 939-40 (6th Cir.2012), we do not view the district court's dismissal of Himmelreich's previous action as implicating the FTCA's judgment bar. Accordingly, we conclude that the district court erred in citing the judgment bar as an independent basis for granting summary judgment on Himmelreich's Eighth Amendment claim. *See* R. 53 at 6-7 (D. Ct. Op.) (Page ID # 436-37).

In reaching its conclusion, the district court relied upon *Harris v. United States,* 422 F.3d 322 (6th Cir.2005), and *Manning,* 546 F.3d 430, but it misreads both of these cases. In *Harris,* the plaintiff simultaneously filed *Bivens* and FTCA claims against the United States and government officials. 422 F.3d at 324. The district court "entered a 'judgment' on the merits of [the] FTCA claims," and we concluded that this judgment barred consideration of the plaintiff's *Bivens* claim. *Id.* at 334. Specifically, we held that § 2676 "fails to draw a distinction between a decision for or against the government" and that § 2676 bars a *Bivens* action regardless of which party prevailed on the merits of the FTCA claim. *Id.* at 334-35. Holding that a judgment on the merits, irrespective of who won, triggers the judgment bar is a far cry from holding that any disposition of an FTCA action prevents other suits, a distinction that the *Harris* panel explicitly recognized by citing *Hallock v. Bonner,* 387 F.3d 147, 155 (2d Cir.2004), *reversed on other grounds sub nom. Will v. Hallock,* 546 U.S. 345, 126 S.Ct. 952, 163 L.Ed.2d 836 (2006). *See Harris,* 422 F.3d at 335. In *Hallock,* the Second Circuit stated that "an action brought under the FTCA and dismissed for lack of subject matter jurisdiction because it falls within an exception to the restricted waiver of sovereign immunity provided by the FTCA does not result in a 'judgment in an action under section 1346(b) [the Federal Tort Claims Act].'" 387 F.3d at 155 (quoting 28 U.S.C. § 2676).[1] *Harris* described this precise holding in a parenthetical and cited the case approvingly. 422 F.3d at 335.

Manning does not hold to the contrary or support the district court's statement that "[t]he plain language of section 2676 requires that the bar apply to all actions by the Plaintiff, not just judgments on the merits." R. 53 at 6-7 (D. Ct. Op.) (Page ID # 436-37) (citing *Manning,* 546 F.3d at 437-38). In *Manning,* the plaintiff "concede[d] that the district court entered a 'judgment' on the merits of his FTCA claim" (a fact that we believe renders *Manning* completely irrelevant to this case). 546 F.3d at 433. Nonetheless, in that case, the plaintiff argued that the p.580 judgment bar could not be "appl[ied] retroactively to nullify a *previous Bivens* judgment." *Id.* The Seventh Circuit disagreed and applied the § 2676 judgment bar retroactively. *Id.* at 438. Nowhere did the Seventh Circuit hold in *Manning* that a dismissal of an FTCA claim for a lack of subject-matter jurisdiction qualifies as a judgment under § 2676. In *Williams v. Fleming,* 597 F.3d 820 (7th Cir.2010), the Seventh Circuit expressly punted on that question, the one before us now, stating: "[w]e need not address [the] contention [that any dismissal, whether or not on the merits, suffices for application of § 2676] today...." *Id.* at 822 n. 2.

Moreover, the Seventh Circuit's disposition of this question, in particular, is unhelpful. The Seventh Circuit treats the dismissal of an FTCA action due to the application of the discretionary-function exception as a decision on the merits. *See Collins v. United States,* 564 F.3d 833, 837-38 (7th Cir.2009). We have repeatedly taken the opposite view, which is that we lack subject-matter jurisdiction over an FTCA claim if the discretionary-function exception applies in a given case. *See, e.g., Kohl,* 699 F.3d at 939-40; *Milligan v. United States,* 670 F.3d 686, 695 (6th Cir. 2012) ("[I]t is evident that the discretionary function exception bars subject matter jurisdiction for the [plaintiffs'] claims."). In other cases, a dismissal for a lack of subject-matter jurisdiction carries no preclusive effect. *See, e.g., Marrese v. Am. Academy of Orthopaedic Surgeons,* 470 U.S. 373, 382, 105 S.Ct. 1327, 84 L.Ed.2d 274 (1985); *Wilkins v. Jakeway,* 183 F.3d 528, 533 n. 6 (6th Cir.1999); Restatement (Second) of Judgments § 26(1)(c) (1982). We see no reason to depart from that general rule in this situation.

In *Harris,* we also noted that the purpose of a judgment bar is to prevent the possibility of double recoveries and the cost of defending multiple suits regarding the same conduct for the government. 422 F.3d at 335-36. It is not punitive in nature. Holding that a plaintiff's filing of an FTCA action, when that statute does not permit recovery, prevents the plaintiff from alleging the correct cause of action furthers neither of these interests. Seeing no compelling reason in the text or purpose of § 2676 to conclude that a dismissal for a lack of jurisdiction triggers the judgment bar, we hold that the district court erred in applying the judgment bar here and VACATE its decision accordingly.

III.

For the forgoing reasons, we VACATE the district court's grant of summary judgment and REMAND for proceedings consistent with this opinion.

[1] *See also Pellegrino v. U.S. Transp. Sec. Admin.,* No. 09-5505, 2014 WL 1489939, at *8-9 (E.D.Pa. April 16, 2014); *Saleh v. Wiley,* No. 09-cv-02563-PAB-KLM, 2012 WL 4356224, at *3-4 (D.Colo. June 12, 2012); *Kyei v. Beebe,* No. CV 01-1266-PA, 2005 WL 3050442, at *2 n. 3 (D.Or. Nov. 13, 2005).

722 F.3d 1360 (2013)

UNITED STATES MARINE, INC., Plaintiff-Appellant,
v.
UNITED STATES, Defendant/Third Party Plaintiff-Appellee,
v.
VT Halter Marine, Inc., Third Party Defendant/Counterclaimant.

No. 2012-1678.

United States Court of Appeals, Federal Circuit.

July 15, 2013.

US Marine, Inc. v. US, 722 F. 3d 1360 (Fed. Cir. 2013)

p.1361 Charles L. Egan, Slater & Zeien, L.L.P., of Washington, DC, argued for plaintiff-appellant. With him on the brief were Marcus B. Slater, Jr. and Jennifer J. Zeien.

Domenique G. Kirchner, Senior Trial Counsel, Commercial Litigation Branch, Civil Division, United States Department of Justice, of Washington, DC, argued for defendant/third party plaintiff-appellee. With her on the brief were Stuart F. Delery, Principal Deputy Assistant Attorney General, Jeanne E. Davidson, Director, and Steven J. Gillingham, Assistant Director.

Before LOURIE, PLAGER, and TARANTO, Circuit Judges.

TARANTO, Circuit Judge.

United States Marine, Inc. (USM) sued the United States in the United States District Court for the Eastern District of Louisiana under the Federal Tort Claims Act (FTCA), 28 U.S.C. §§ 1346(b), 2674. USM alleged that the United States misappropriated USM's trade secrets. Specifically, USM claimed that the United States Navy, which had lawfully obtained USM's proprietary technical drawings under a contract (to which USM was not a party), owed USM a duty of secrecy that it breached by disclosing those drawings to a rival private firm for use in designing military boats for the government.

After the district court found the United States liable for trade-secret misappropriation and awarded USM damages, the United States Court of Appeals for the Fifth Circuit held that the district court lacked jurisdiction over USM's claims under the FTCA. The Fifth Circuit reasoned that (a) the Navy's liability and USM's recovery depended on the interpretation of a federal-government contract and (b) therefore the matter lay exclusively within the jurisdiction of the Court of Federal Claims under the Tucker Act, 28 U.S.C. p.1362 § 1491(a)(1). The Fifth Circuit vacated the district court's judgment and remanded for transfer of the case to the Claims Court under 28 U.S.C. § 1631. We review the district court's subsequent transfer order under 28 U.S.C. § 1292(d)(4)(A).

Given the decision of the transfer question in this case by the Fifth Circuit, we do not decide the question afresh. We ask only whether the Fifth Circuit decision was clearly in error. Unable to say that it was, we affirm.

BACKGROUND

USM is a Louisiana corporation that builds military boats. Sometime before mid-1993, working with VT Halter Marine, Inc., which was a subsidiary of Trinity Marine Group and also a shipbuilder, USM developed a design for a special-operations craft with a hull made out of composite materials. The companies developed the design — now called the "Mark V," a name covering several versions — for VT Halter to use in competing for the "MK V Special Operations Craft and Transporter System Contract" with the United States Navy. Before VT Halter submitted a bid to the Navy, USM and VT Halter built a prototype of the special-operations craft, an operational "parent craft" that they could modify to meet the Navy's requirements if VT Halter secured the contract. The district court in this case found that the design and development of the craft did not rely on government funds. VT Halter also designed a version of the craft with an aluminum hull. Although the working relationship between USM and VT Halter initially was informal, a letter from Trinity Marine Group to USM in 1995 stated that the companies shared ownership of the Mark V design, which was confirmed in a later agreement reached after corporate changes, bankruptcy, and other proceedings.

As part of its bid for two development contracts with the Navy in 1993, VT Halter submitted technical drawings of both the aluminum and composite versions of the Mark V design. VT Halter stamped the drawings with a "Limited Rights Legend" that invoked a specific provision of the Defense Federal Acquisition Regulations Supplement (DFARS), namely, Section 252.227-7013(a)(15), which states limitations on the government's use and outside disclosure of certain information. VT Halter's proposal also stated that, if it were awarded the contracts, any design data would be furnished subject to restrictions on the government's use and disclosure as provided for in the contracts.

On August 6, 1993, the Navy, through its Special Operations Command, awarded VT Halter two contracts to develop prototypes of (respectively) the aluminum- and composite-hull crafts. The development contracts incorporated by reference all of DFARS § 252.227-7013, which addresses "[r]ights in technical data and computer software." As required, VT Halter marked its submitted design drawings and technical data with a Limited Rights Legend as prescribed by the DFARS provision.

On November 30, 1994, after testing and evaluation of the prototypes, the Navy selected the Mark V aluminum-hull craft for actual construction and awarded VT Halter a production contract. VT Halter again submitted design drawings marked with the legend required by DFARS § 252.227-7013; but for whatever reason, the production contract did not incorporate that provision. Pursuant to the production contract, VT Halter built and delivered twenty-four Mark V special-operations craft to the Navy.

In 2004, a division of the Navy awarded a research grant to the University of p.1363 Maine to improve the ride and handling capabilities of the Mark V craft. Between 2004 and late 2006, the Navy provided numerous, detailed design drawings of the Mark V craft to firms that were acting as contractors for Maine Marine Manufacturing LLC, a joint venture between the University of Maine and a private shipbuilder. Although the design drawings were stamped with the DFARS

Limited Rights Legend, the Navy did not obtain VT Halter's consent for the Navy's disclosure to the firms. In 2006, the Navy awarded Maine Marine Manufacturing a contract to design and construct a prototype special-operations craft, known as the Mark V.1, intended to be as similar as possible to the Mark V craft, with only a few changes to improve ride and handling.

When USM discovered that the Navy had disclosed its Mark V design information outside the government, it took pre-suit steps prescribed by the FTCA and then sued the United States for misappropriation of trade secrets in the federal district court in Louisiana. The FTCA expressly declares the United States subject to liability on certain tort claims — using relevant state law to define the torts — and vests jurisdiction over such claims exclusively in the district courts, thus waiving sovereign immunity for such claims. 28 U.S.C. §§ 1346(b)(1), 2674. In its complaint, USM alleged that the United States owed it a duty to maintain the secrecy of its Mark V design information and to limit its use because of the confidentiality provisions in the contracts and the legends stamped on the design drawings. USM requested damages in the amount of $63,550,000 for the alleged wrongful disclosure by the Navy.

The government moved to dismiss USM's claim for lack of subject matter jurisdiction. Pointing to USM's allegation that the Navy's duty to protect the Mark V design information and drawings arose from the contracts between VT Halter and the Navy, the government argued that USM's claim should be treated as a claim of tortious breach of contract, which could be heard only by the Claims Court under the Tucker Act, 28 U.S.C. § 1491(a)(1). The district court denied the government's motion, concluding that although the contract "provide[d] the underpinnings of USM[]'s state law trade secret claim," the mere existence of potential non-FTCA claims did not eliminate the district court's jurisdiction over the FTCA claim that USM actually asserted.

After the district court also refused to find that VT Halter was a necessary party to the case, the government brought VT Halter into the case through a third-party complaint seeking to hold it liable for any damages the government might have to pay for the alleged trade-secret misappropriation. In response, VT Halter filed a counterclaim against the United States, adding its own FTCA-based claim for trade-secret misappropriation to USM's. The government moved to dismiss VT Halter's counterclaim on the jurisdictional ground that it already had unsuccessfully invoked against USM's suit, but the district court denied the motion. Despite arguing that jurisdiction was proper in the Claims Court in both motions to dismiss, at no point during the litigation did the government request a transfer of the case to the Claims Court.

In January 2010, the district court held a two-day bench trial on liability. On April 1, 2010, the court found that the Navy misappropriated Mark V design information by disclosing it to Maine Marine Manufacturing (and its contractors) without VT Halter's or USM's authorization. *U.S. Marine, Inc. v. United States,* No. 08-2571, 2010 WL 1403958, at *6 (E.D.La. Apr. 1, 2010). Regarding the source of the restriction on the government's use of the p.1364 design information — a necessary element of the tort — the court determined that "[b]oth the contractual provision and limited rights legends were sufficient notification to the government that disclosure of the [Mark V] design would violate a duty to its owners." *Id.* After a separate bench trial on damages, the court held that, although USM and VT Halter failed to prove actual losses or unjust enrichment, they were entitled to approximately $1.45 million in damages as a reasonable royalty for the government's use of the trade secrets.

The government appealed, challenging both the district court's jurisdiction over VT Halter's claim and the damages award. The government did not challenge the district court's jurisdiction over USM's claim. USM and VT Halter cross-appealed to challenge the damages award.

The Fifth Circuit held that the district court lacked jurisdiction over VT Halter's counterclaim under the FTCA. *U.S. Marine, Inc. v. United States,* 478 Fed.Appx. 106 (5th Cir.2012). Although VT Halter styled its counterclaim as a tort, the Fifth Circuit ruled that the Navy's alleged duty not to use or disclose the Mark V design information without permission "stem[med] directly from the 'limited rights' provisions found in the VT Halter-Navy contracts," and the district court had necessarily interpreted those contract provisions in order to determine the Navy's duties with respect to using and disclosing the design information. *Id.* at 110-11. Therefore, the Fifth Circuit reasoned, any claims stemming from the alleged breach of such provisions sounded in contract, not in tort, and were within the exclusive jurisdiction of the Claims Court. *Id.* at 107-08.

Although the government did not appeal the district court's jurisdiction over USM's claim, and indeed stated at oral argument that the Claims Court would not have jurisdiction over USM's claim, the Fifth Circuit *sua sponte* held USM's claim barred from district court for the same reason as VT Halter's. A majority of the panel held that USM's claim, like VT Halter's, was based on the contract between VT Halter and the Navy and was therefore within the exclusive jurisdiction of the Claims Court:

> Like VT Halter's counterclaim, the "limited rights" provisions of the contracts provide the essential basis for USM[]'s claim. We can find no basis for the Navy's potential liability independent of those terms and the duties of non-disclosure they placed upon the Navy.... The Tucker Act explicitly forbids such interpretation of federal contracts by the district courts, and there is no potential liability in this case without it.

Id. at 111. Perhaps reflecting uncertainty fostered by the changing positions of the government, the majority noted that the lack of privity between the Navy and USM might mean that USM would be denied the right to recover in the Claims Court. *Id.* at 111 n. 3. With no further analysis, the court left it to the Claims Court to consider whether USM qualified as an implied third-party beneficiary allowed to enforce the contracts' limited-rights provisions under the Tucker Act. *Id.* The Fifth Circuit vacated the district court's judgment and remanded with instructions to transfer the case to the Claims Court under 28 U.S.C. § 1631. 478 Fed.Appx. at 111.

Judge Elrod dissented in part, disagreeing with the majority's holding that the district court lacked jurisdiction over USM's claim. *Id.* at 112. According to Judge Elrod, because USM was neither a contracting party nor an implied third-party beneficiary to the contract with the Navy, there was no privity between USM and the United States and the claim could not sound in contract, but instead was a tort claim outside the Claims Court's jurisdiction under the Tucker Act and within p.1365 the district court's jurisdiction under the FTCA. *Id.*

The district court, acting pursuant to the Fifth Circuit's mandate, transferred the case to the Claims Court. USM appealed. This court has jurisdiction under 28 U.S.C. § 1292(d)(4)(A).[1]

DISCUSSION

For the transfer order to be correct under 28 U.S.C. § 1631, two conditions must be met, as the government expressly agrees: the district court must lack jurisdiction over USM's action, and the Claims Court must have jurisdiction over USM's action. *See* Appellee United States Br. at 30; *Jan's Helicopter Serv., Inc. v. Fed. Aviation Admin.*, 525 F.3d 1299, 1303 (Fed.Cir.2008) ("A case may be transferred under [S]ection 1631 only to a court that has subject matter jurisdiction."); *Christianson v. Colt Indus. Operating Corp.*, 486 U.S. 800, 818, 108 S.Ct. 2166, 100 L.Ed.2d 811 (1988) (understanding that only a court "that has jurisdiction" can receive a case by Section 1631 transfer); *United States v. U.S. Shoe Corp.*, 523 U.S. 360, 366 n. 3, 118 S.Ct. 1290, 140 L.Ed.2d 453 (1998) (Section 1631 "authorizes intercourt transfers, when 'in the interest of justice,' to *cure* want of jurisdiction") (emphasis added); S.Rep. No. 97-275, at 30 (1981), 1982 U.S.C.C.A.N. 11, 40 (new Section 1631 "would authorize the court in which a case is improperly filed to transfer it to a court *where subject matter jurisdiction is proper*") (emphasis added).

The Fifth Circuit is a coordinate court, not bound by any ruling this court might independently make on the question. If we were to disagree with that court's judgment requiring transfer, the case would seemingly be left without a forum, unless the Supreme Court intervened. In these circumstances, under the "law of the case" doctrine as explained in *Christianson,* we think that we must affirm the transfer order here unless we conclude that the Fifth Circuit's judgment requiring transfer was "clearly erroneous," *i.e.,* was not even "plausible." *See* 486 U.S. at 819, 108 S.Ct. 2166. Whatever result we would reach if we were considering the question de novo, we are not able to draw that conclusion.

A

If one were to look only at the statutory grants of jurisdiction, and start with the statute under which USM brought its claim, transfer here would be hard to support. That is so with regard to both requirements for the Section 1631 transfer: that the district court lack jurisdiction and the Claims Court have jurisdiction.

In the liability-imposing section of the FTCA, with exceptions not applicable here, Congress unequivocally imposed liability on the United States for torts, using state law to define the torts. 28 U.S.C. § 2674 ("The United States shall be liable, respecting the provisions of this title relating to tort claims, in the same manner and to the same extent as a private individual under like circumstances...."). There is no dispute here, and the Fifth Circuit recognized, that misappropriation of a trade secret is a form of liability-supporting tort that is recognized in Virginia (the relevant state in this case) and more generally. *See U.S. Marine,* 478 Fed.Appx. at

108-09; RESTATEMENT (FIRST) OF TORTS § 757 (1939); RESTATEMENT THIRD OF UNFAIR COMPETITION § 40 (1995); *Reingold v. Swiftships Inc.,* 210 F.3d 320, 322-23 (5th Cir. 2000) (noting widespread adoption of the Uniform Trade Secrets Act); *Kramer v.* p.1366 *Sec'y, United States Dep't of the Army,* 653 F.2d 726, 729-30 (2d Cir.1980). In 28 U.S.C. § 1346(b)(1), Congress expressly granted district courts, like the Louisiana district court here, jurisdiction to adjudicate such liability.

In contrast, the Claims Court cannot adjudicate USM's claim of tort liability for misappropriation of trade secrets under Virginia law standards made applicable to the United States by Section 2674. In Section 1346(b)(1), Congress committed the adjudication of Section 2674 liability to the *"exclusive* jurisdiction" of the district courts. (Emphasis added.) Nothing on the face of the Claims Court's jurisdictional statute, 28 U.S.C. § 1491, overrides that exclusive commitment. Indeed, as a textual matter, one possible reading of the terms of Section 1491(a)(1), though not the only possible reading, might suggest that the provision does not even apply if a claim both is founded upon on a contract and "sound[s] in" tort.[2]

In short, USM's expressly stated claim is an FTCA claim for liability based on the Virginia law of trade-secret misappropriation. That claim, on its face, is within the district court's jurisdiction and is not within the Claims Court's jurisdiction. Without further analysis, those conclusions would make the Fifth Circuit's order to transfer the case wrong on both of the premises required for transfer.

B

The basis for the Fifth Circuit's conclusion can be seen if one changes the analysis in two ways. The first is to begin with the Tucker Act, not with the FTCA. The second is to give prominence to the essential background principle of sovereign immunity and what it means for jurisdiction over claims against the United States.

As relevant here, the Tucker Act, in 28 U.S.C. § 1491(a)(1), grants the Claims Court jurisdiction over a claim "founded... upon any express or implied contract with the United States ...," and where the claim is for $10,000 or more, the Tucker Act grants jurisdiction over such a claim only to the Claims Court. A similar contract claim, if for less than $10,000, is within the concurrent jurisdiction of the Claims Court and district courts under the Little Tucker Act, 28 U.S.C. § 1346(a)(2). And regardless of the amount at issue, the statutes assign appeals involving such a claim exclusively to this court. 28 U.S.C. § 1295(a)(2), (a)(3); *United States v. Hohri,* 482 U.S. 64, 107 S.Ct. 2246, 96 L.Ed.2d 51 (1987).

The forum specification has particular significance in light of the principle of sovereign immunity, which makes the United States generally not amenable to a suit unless Congress has authorized the suit, *i.e.,* waived sovereign immunity. *See Dep't of the Army v. Blue Fox, Inc.,* 525 U.S. 255, 261, 119 S.Ct. 687, 142 L.Ed.2d 718 (1999); *Block v. North Dakota ex rel. Bd. of Univ. & School Lands,* 461 U.S. 273, 287, 103 S.Ct. 1811, 75 L.Ed.2d 840 (1983). Importantly, the principle of sovereign immunity restricts adjudication to the particular forums in which the sovereign has consented to suit. *United States v. Shaw,* 309 U.S. 495, 501, 60 S.Ct. 659, 84 L.Ed. 888 (1940); *Minnesota v. United States,* p.1367 305 U.S. 382, 388, 59 S.Ct. 292, 83 L.Ed.

235 (1939); *McElrath v. United States,* 102 U.S. 426, 440, 26 L.Ed. 189 (1880); *cf. Block,* 461 U.S. at 287, 103 S.Ct. 1811 ("[W]hen Congress attaches conditions to legislation waiving the sovereign immunity of the United States, those conditions must be strictly observed...."); *Irwin v. Dep't of Veterans Affairs,* 498 U.S. 89, 94, 111 S.Ct. 453, 112 L.Ed.2d 435 (1990) (same); *see also College Sav. Bank v. Fla. Prepaid Postsecondary Educ. Expense Bd.,* 527 U.S. 666, 676, 119 S.Ct. 2219, 144 L.Ed.2d 605 (1999) (forum specificity for state sovereign immunity waivers). Because of those principles, it is fair to say that when Congress limits the waiver to a particular forum, the limitation is an implied, presumptive commitment of the matter to that forum.

Even when Congress has enacted a statute presumptively restricting a matter to a particular forum, Congress can, of course, enact a second statute that modifies the effect of the first statute, routing such a matter either concurrently or exclusively to another forum. Deciding when that has occurred may require close statutory analysis, with particular attention, when the statutes involve sovereign-immunity waivers, to the policies behind the terms defining such waivers. In addition, and of special relevance here, it is a commonplace that a variety of legal claims can arise from the same conduct and involve closely related facts but have different elements and carry different labels like "contract" and "tort" that are used by Congress in different statutes. In that situation, a court may face challenging questions in determining the boundaries between one or more assertedly applicable jurisdictional statutes and deciding how to deal with any overlap of such statutes. When the statutes involve waivers of sovereign immunity, a court deciding where a particular claim may or must be litigated must consider the policies behind the several potentially applicable waivers.

Those principles apply to the Tucker Act, which both confers jurisdiction on the Claims Court and "waive[s] sovereign immunity for claims premised on other sources of law (*e.g.,* statutes and contracts)." *United States v. Navajo Nation,* 556 U.S. 287, 290, 129 S.Ct. 1547, 173 L.Ed.2d 429 (2009); *see United States v. Bormes,* ___ U.S. ___, 133 S.Ct. 12, 16-17, 184 L.Ed.2d 317 (2012). Courts have sometimes held that Congress assigned matters otherwise covered by the Tucker Act to other forums. *See, e.g., In re Liberty Constr.,* 9 F.3d 800, 801-02 (9th Cir. 1993) (discussing sue-and-be-sued provisions that might displace the Tucker Act commitment). But when there is no other jurisdictional grant covering a contract claim already covered by the Tucker Act, that Act's conferral of jurisdiction on the Claims Court is exclusive because no other grant exists. *Bowen v. Massachusetts,* 487 U.S. 879, 910 n. 48, 108 S.Ct. 2722, 101 L.Ed.2d 749 (1988) (With no express exclusivity language in the Tucker Act, the Claims Court's "jurisdiction is 'exclusive' only to the extent that Congress has not granted any other court authority to hear the claims that may be decided by" the Claims Court.). The Supreme Court has explained the policy underlying the presumptive exclusivity: to promote uniformity through forum specification, notably by providing for a single appellate tribunal. *See Hohri,* 482 U.S. at 71-73, 107 S.Ct. 2246.

The policy actually at stake has to do with the forum, not directly with choice of law. The Fifth Circuit quoted the Tenth Circuit's recognition of "the strong policy in favor of construing federal contracts under uniform federal law." *Union Pac. R.R. Co. v. United States,* 591 F.3d 1311, 1320 (10th Cir.2010), quoted at *U.S. Marine,* p.1368 478 Fed.Appx. at 110. But it is not clear why federal law would not govern the construction of federal contracts even in an FTCA case generally governed by state law; indeed, federal law is deemed a part of state law. *See Fidelity Fed. Sav. & Loan Ass'n v. de la Cuesta,* 458 U.S. 141, 157, 102 S.Ct. 3014, 73 L.Ed.2d 664 (1982). It is the tribunal doing the construing, not the law governing the construction, that clearly distinguishes an FTCA action — tried in district court, with appeal to the regional circuit — from a Tucker Act action — tried in the Claims Court (for claims of at least $10,000), with appeal to this court (regardless of amount).

Accordingly, if one begins with the Tucker Act grant, one must ask, in a case like this, whether the matter at issue falls within that grant and, if so, whether another statute should be read to grant a district court jurisdiction over the matter despite the Tucker Act. A court must consider whether the matter is within the policy underlying the presumptive congressional commitment to Claims Court/Federal Circuit exclusivity, whether it is within another congressionally enacted policy (*e.g.,* the FTCA's liability-imposing policy, 28 U.S.C. § 2674), and whether the latter displaces the former if both apply.

The Fifth Circuit in this case started with the Tucker Act and proceeded down this analytic path. It held that USM's claim depends on an adjudication of the government's contract obligation, which the Tucker Act presumptively limits to the Claims Court for claims of this magnitude.[3] USM does not dispute that characterization of its claim, which therefore brings into play the Tucker Act's forum policies. The Fifth Circuit must be understood as having then determined that there was no good enough reason to find a congressional displacement, for this case, of the Tucker Act's commitment of major contract-adjudication issues to particular forums.

C

In doing so, the Fifth Circuit followed a number of decisions, going back half a century, involving tort and other non-contract claims that arose out of conduct that also gave rise to contract claims. Those decisions hold that sometimes a party's tort claim in district court is so rooted in a contract-breach claim that its adjudication outside the Tucker Act's grant of jurisdiction would be an unjustified incursion on the presumptive commitment of contract matters to the forums designated in the Tucker Act. In those cases, any claim of liability under the FTCA, specifically 28 U.S.C. § 2674, was necessarily displaced, because that claim cannot be heard in the Claims Court.

In *Woodbury v. United States,* the Ninth Circuit ruled that a claim against the United States for breach of fiduciary duty, though styled as a tort, should be treated as claim for a breach of contract properly within the jurisdiction of the Claims Court. 313 F.2d 291 (9th Cir. 1963). Mr. Woodbury obtained financing from a federal agency for the construction of prefabricated housing for naval and civilian personnel at Kodiak Naval Base in Alaska. *Id.* at 292-93. He met with financial difficulties during the course of the project, and when the agency filed a foreclosure p.1369 action in district court, he sued the United States under the FTCA for breach of fiduciary duty for failure to arrange for or provide long-term financing. *Id.*

at 293-94. The district court dismissed the claim for lack of jurisdiction, and the Ninth Circuit agreed.

According to the Ninth Circuit, where an "action is essentially for breach of a contractual undertaking, and the liability, if any, depends wholly upon the government's alleged promise, the action must be under the Tucker Act, and cannot be under the [FTCA]." *Id.* at 296. The court explained:

> Many breaches of contract can also be treated as torts. But in cases such as this, where the "tort" complained of is based entirely upon breach by the government of a promise made by it in a contract, so that the claim is in substance a breach of contract claim, and only incidentally and conceptually also a tort claim, we do not think that the common law or local state law right to "waive the breach and sue in tort" brings the case within the Federal Tort Claims Act.

Id. at 295. The Ninth Circuit added that a different result threatened "the long established policy that government contracts are to be given a uniform interpretation and application under federal law." *Id.* The Ninth Circuit concluded that Mr. Woodbury's claim for breach of fiduciary duty had to be brought under the Tucker Act because liability depended entirely on the contractual promise by the federal agency and whether the agency breached it. *Id.* at 297.

Other cases followed *Woodbury*. In *Davis v. United States,* 961 F.2d 53, 55-57 (5th Cir.1991), Mr. Davis brought several tort claims against the United States under the FTCA after the Federal Deposit Insurance Corporation assigned his promissory note in alleged violation of the note's non-assignment clause. *Id.* at 55. The Fifth Circuit affirmed the district court's dismissal for lack of jurisdiction, concluding that each of the claims, though pleaded in tort, was "predicated upon the breach of [the] condition in the promissory note." *Id.* at 56. In *Wood v. United States,* 961 F.2d 195 (Fed.Cir.1992), this court considered whether the district court had properly transferred Mr. Wood's tort claims to the Claims Court. We held that, because Mr. Wood's primary complaint was that the government had failed to provide an allegedly promised certificate of airworthiness, and his only viable claims depended on that contract claim, jurisdiction lay only in the Claims Court under the Tucker Act. *Id.* at 198.

Several other cases have reached a similar conclusion. *See Blanchard v. St. Paul Fire & Marine Ins. Co.,* 341 F.2d 351, 359 (5th Cir.1965) (holding that the plaintiff's claim could not be brought under the FTCA where "the sole relationship between [plaintiff] and the United States was wholly contractual in character" and plaintiff's claims "relate[d] exclusively to the manner in which various government officials... performed their responsibilities with respect to the execution of the contract"); *Wilkerson v. United States,* 67 F.3d 112, 118 (5th Cir.1995) (claim for a taking under the Fifth Amendment of the United States Constitution must be brought in the Claims Court under the Tucker Act, "even though some other statute conferring jurisdiction would otherwise allow the district court to hear the case"); *Friedman v. United States,* 391 F.3d 1313 (11th Cir.2004) (affirming a determination that jurisdiction was proper in the Claims Court where the plaintiff included claims sounding in tort, but those tort claims were grounded in or turned on the interpretation of a settlement agreement with the United States). Other decisions have found particular contract connections insufficient p.1370 to require Claims

Court adjudication of particular matters. *E.g., Love v. United States,* 915 F.2d 1242, 1245-47 (9th Cir. 1989) (holding that a conversion claim sounded in tort, not contract); *Aleutco Corp. v. United States,* 244 F.2d 674, 678 (3rd Cir.1957) ("The fact that the claimant and the United States were in a contractual relationship does not convert an otherwise tortious claim into one in contract.").

This court in *Awad v. United States* held that certain tort claims arising out of an alleged agreement with the United States could be brought only in the Claims Court. 301 F.3d 1367, 1375 (Fed.Cir.2002). Upon entering the United States Marshals Service's Witness Security Program, Mr. Awad signed a Memorandum of Understanding in which the government stated that it would return his foreign-issued passport if he left the program. *Id.* at 1369. He also alleged that officials of the government told him that he would receive United States citizenship and a United States passport in return for his testimony against an alleged terrorist. *Id.* After cooperating with the government, Mr. Awad withdrew from the witness-protection program; but the government neither returned his foreign-issued passport, nor helped him to obtain a United States passport or United States citizenship. *Id.* at 1369-70.

Mr. Awad filed several tort claims against the United States in district court. The district court, after determining that his tort claims depended on the government's breach of its alleged contractual obligations, concluded that it lacked jurisdiction and transferred the case to the Claims Court. *Id.* at 1370-71. On appeal, we affirmed the transfer decision under the reasoning in the *Woodbury* line of cases. We explained that there was no "statutory or common law basis for a duty on the part of the government to provide [Mr. Awad] with U.S. citizenship and a passport"; rather, any duty the United States owed to Mr. Awad was purely contractual. *Id.* at 1373-74. Because Mr. Awad's action sounded in contract, and not in tort, and was for more than $10,000, jurisdiction could lie only in the Claims Court. *Id.* at 1375.

D

As already noted, in those cases the plaintiffs necessarily lost the ability to pursue FTCA tort claims when the matters were routed to the Claims Court. The fact that transfer of USM's case to the Claims Court will cause it to lose its tort claim as pleaded, therefore, does not distinguish this case from those. The argument over the application or distinction of the *Woodbury* line of cases, instead, focuses on what claims would be meaningfully available in the Claims Court upon transfer.

In at least most of the cases in the *Woodbury* line, the plaintiffs had the kind of asserted privity of contract with the United States that readily permits litigation of the issues of contract breach, injury, and damages under the Tucker Act (subject to generally applicable requirements such as timeliness). In that circumstance, transfer to the Claims Court, while depriving the plaintiff of the ability to press an FTCA tort claim, seemingly leaves the plaintiff with a cause of action that, upon proper proof, permits recovery of compensation for contract-related harm caused by the United States. USM's case is challenging for application of the *Woodbury* principle precisely because of the arguable difference in that respect. But for two reasons together, we are not prepared to say that the Fifth Circuit's reliance on the *Woodbury* principle is clearly in error.

1

It is not clear whether a meaningful opportunity for recovery in the Claims p.1371 Court is always a necessary requirement for application of the principle implemented in the *Woodbury* line of cases. The policy implicit in the Tucker Act's presumptive commitment of government-contract adjudications to the Claims Court (except for small claims) and to this court (for all claims) conceivably might be impaired by allowing another forum to construe a government-contract provision even if the Claims Court could not do so in the particular case. Such a construction might impair the government's interest in uniform construction of a provision, like a standard DFARS provision, that is widely used in the government's contracts. Perhaps, too, if a plaintiff's non-contract claim depends essentially on establishing a contract breach, and the applicable contract law deliberately withholds a right of enforcement from the particular plaintiff, the congressional policy implicit in the Tucker Act might be thought to bar that plaintiff's non-contract claim because allowing it would circumvent that enforcement limitation. More broadly, appeals to the idea that wrongs presumptively have remedies, which often has great force in resolving genuine uncertainties in statutory interpretation, require special caution where the wrongdoer is the United States, which, by virtue of sovereign immunity, generally cannot be sued even for harm it wrongfully inflicts except where it consents to suit. *See United States v. Testan,* 424 U.S. 392, 401-02, 96 S.Ct. 948, 47 L.Ed.2d 114 (1976). For these reasons, we cannot easily dismiss (while we need not affirmatively embrace) the notion that an apparent congressional bar on adjudication of the United States' contractual duties outside the Tucker Act forums can prevail even when the result is to preclude recovery for harm.

In fact, in not all of the *Woodbury* line of cases is it truly clear that a remedy was meaningfully available in the Claims Court. For example, in *Wood,* we noted the possibility that the plaintiff could face significant hurdles to recovery in the Claims Court: "remedies beyond damages, such as specific performance, are not available," and whether jurisdiction ultimately lay in the Claims Court required inquiry into whether there was "privity between Wood and the government." 961 F.2d at 199. And in *Awad,* although we affirmed the transfer order, we left it to the Claims Court to determine in the first instance whether the contract at issue subjected the government to monetary liability for a breach, a necessary prerequisite for Tucker Act jurisdiction. 301 F.3d at 1374-75.

2

This case, however, does not require us to adopt or to reject the starker potential view of a Tucker-Act-exclusivity principle, because we cannot say that USM itself lacks a meaningful remedy under the Tucker Act in the Claims Court. Unable to exclude the availability of a meaningful Tucker Act remedy for USM, we are not prepared to conclude that USM's position differs materially, in the respect USM rightly features as its strongest point, from that of most plaintiffs in the *Woodbury* line.

This is not because we recognize a meaningful possibility that USM can litigate a *tort* claim in the Claims Court. If a tort claim is brought under the FTCA, it plainly cannot be adjudicated in the Claims Court, because Section 1346(b)(1) gives the district court exclusive jurisdiction over such claims. But that conclusion does not itself exclude the possibility of recognizing non-FTCA tort claims as claims that are "founded ... upon an express or implied contract...." Indeed, as a purely textual matter, it is hardly unreasonable to conclude that, if the Tucker Act's "founded... upon" language displaces another court's jurisdiction over a tort claim because that tort claim is "founded ... upon" p.1372 a contract, that language must affirmatively embrace tort claims where they are "founded ... upon" a contract. In that view, the Tucker Act's language would have the same scope for what it affirmatively embraces as for what it impliedly excludes from other courts. But history counts strongly against allowing adjudication of any "tort" claims under the Tucker Act.

Based on the background principle of sovereign immunity, the familiarity of the contract/tort distinction, and the language of the Tucker Act, this court's predecessor long ago recognized: "Congress has always withheld from this court and from the Tucker Act original jurisdiction over tort claims against the government." *Eastport S.S. Corp. v. United States,* 372 F.2d 1002, 1010 (Ct.Cl.1967) (citing Supreme Court authorities). Ample authority supports that recognition. *See Keene Corp. v. United States,* 508 U.S. 200, 214, 113 S.Ct. 2035, 124 L.Ed.2d 118 (1993) ("tort cases are outside the jurisdiction of the Court of Federal Claims today") (footnote omitted); *Hohri,* 482 U.S. at 72 n. 4, 107 S.Ct. 2246 (relying on *Eastport's* discussion of noncontractual liability under the Tucker Act); *Gibbons v. United States,* 75 U.S. (8 Wall.) 269, 275, 19 L.Ed. 453 (1868) ("The language of the statutes which confer jurisdiction upon the Court of Claims, excludes by the strongest implication demands against the government founded on torts.").[4] That categorical view, limiting Tucker Act contract-based claims to claims allowed by contract law, fits the requirement that, for Tucker Act jurisdiction, "other sources of law (*e.g.,* statutes and contracts)" must authorize compensation to the plaintiff upon proof of the specified wrong and injury. *Navajo Nation,* 556 U.S. at 290, 129 S.Ct. 1547; *Bormes,* 133 S.Ct. at 16-17. Whereas a contract implicitly carries that authorization to the extent of contract-law remedies, *see Holmes v. United States,* 657 F.3d 1303, 1314 (Fed.Cir.2011), an additional tort remedy would seem to need separate congressional authorization outside the Tucker Act. In any event, we are not prepared to initiate what would be a sea-change in Tucker Act law to find a tort claim cognizable in the Claims Court.

Instead, we rest our conclusion about the possibility of a meaningful Tucker Act remedy for USM on other grounds. The first is that it now appears that USM can pursue a contract claim, in the specific sense that it can proceed directly to litigate whether the government breached a contract-based obligation (regarding USM's trade secrets), the harm caused, and the appropriate quantification of damages. The Fifth Circuit expressly ruled that "USM[] was a subcontractor to VT Halter with respect to the VT Halter-Navy contracts," while noting that it would ultimately be for the Claims Court to decide what contract-enforcement rights USM had. *U.S. Marine,* 478 Fed.Appx. at 111 & n. 3.[5] That ruling is subject to the law-of-the-case doctrine, with its protections and limitations, as to both USM and the government.

In any event, the government's jurisdictional position here, together with our acceptance of it, legally settles the threshold p.1373 question whether USM is among those authorized to recover upon proof of breach of contract, injury, and amount of damages. As in the district court (but not in the Fifth Circuit), the government has now affirmatively urged that the Claims Court has jurisdiction under the Tucker Act's "founded ... upon an express or implied contract" provision.[6] Under this court's precedents, that position requires — and if the position is now accepted by this court, as it is, thus legally establishes — the premise that USM is within the class of those authorized to recover upon proof of breach of contract, injury, and amount of damages.

Specifically, this court has expressly held that whether the plaintiff is among those who may recover upon proof of the asserted wrong is part of the jurisdictional inquiry for the Tucker Act: there is no jurisdiction unless the plaintiff is among such persons. *Greenlee Cnty. v. United States,* 487 F.3d 871, 876 & n. 2 (Fed.Cir. 2007); *see Jan's Helicopter Serv.,* 525 F.3d at 1308 (case cited "passim" by the United States in its brief here). That rule, though established in cases involving the Constitution-and-laws clause of the Tucker Act, must apply to the contract clause, which merely sets forth a source of compensation authorization parallel to those covered by the Constitution-and-laws clause. *See Navajo Nation,* 556 U.S. at 290, 129 S.Ct. 1547 (Tucker Act "waives sovereign immunity for claims premised on other sources of law (*e.g.,* statutes and contracts)"); *Bormes,* 133 S.Ct. at 16-17 (same); *see also United States v. Mitchell,* 463 U.S. 206, 216, 103 S.Ct. 2961, 77 L.Ed.2d 580 (1983) ("[T]he Act makes absolutely no distinction between claims founded upon contracts and claims founded upon other specified sources of law."). Given those principles, the government's assertion that the Claims Court has jurisdiction over USM's claim entails that USM is among those entitled to recover upon proof of the wrong at issue here, namely, the government's breach of contract, and proof of injury and amount of damages.

In short, the government's argument for the Claims Court's jurisdiction (made here and in the district court, but not in the Fifth Circuit) legally acknowledges that USM is entitled to get to the breach, injury, and damages questions, having cleared the threshold of being among those with a right to recover upon satisfactory proof on those questions. And it follows that this court's action in now adopting the government's argument and affirming the transfer order, which depends on the Claims Court's having jurisdiction, establishes that right, as a matter of binding precedent and judicial estoppel. *See New Hampshire v. Maine,* 532 U.S. 742, 121 S.Ct. 1808, 149 L.Ed.2d 968 (2001) (judicial estoppel). While USM has until now sought to deny its right to recover in contract in the Claims Court, it may well be able to do so once the case is transferred to the Claims Court based on the government's jurisdictional argument.

The second reason for our conclusion that USM may have a meaningful remedy in the Claims Court concerns the possibility that USM has a takings claim. The Supreme Court has held that a government p.1374 use or disclosure of a trade secret can constitute a taking for which, under the Fifth Amendment, the United States must pay just compensation. *Ruckelshaus v. Monsanto Co.,* 467 U.S. 986, 1001-04, 104 S.Ct. 2862, 81 L.Ed.2d 815 (1984) (trade secrets protected by Takings Clause); *id.* at 1011-14, 104 S.Ct. 2862 (disclosure or use by the government contrary to restrictions under which the government received trade-secret information may be a compensable taking). The Tucker Act, in 28 U.S.C. § 1491(a)(1), embraces takings claims within its coverage of claims "founded ... upon the Constitution...." *See Preseault v. I.C.C.,* 494 U.S. 1, 12, 110 S.Ct. 914, 108 L.Ed.2d 1 (1990); *Ruckelshaus,* 467 U.S. at 1016-17, 104 S.Ct. 2862; *Reg'l Rail Reorganization Act Cases,* 419 U.S. 102, 126, 95 S.Ct. 335, 42 L.Ed.2d 320 (1974); *United States v. Causby,* 328 U.S. 256, 267, 66 S.Ct. 1062, 90 L.Ed. 1206 (1946). In a recent nonprecedential opinion, this court has recognized the point, reversing a dismissal of a takings claim involving trade secrets. *Gal-Or v. United States,* 470 Fed.Appx. 879 (Fed.Cir.2012).

Under that authority, USM may have a claim for compensation under the Tucker Act, a claim that may, among other things, relate back to the original complaint for limitations purposes. We do not say that USM has such a claim, because the case has not been pled in that form (the case not having been in a forum where such pleading was possible), and the issue therefore has not been explored. Nor do we say anything about the merits of such a claim if USM can assert it. We say only that such a claim may be available to USM; if so, the claim might provide USM a meaningful compensatory remedy for the wrong and injury it alleges.

If USM has a meaningful remedy in the Claims Court, USM's strongest argument for seeking to distinguish the *Woodbury* line of cases, and for criticizing the Fifth Circuit's resolution of the boundary problem for the FTCA and Tucker Act in this case, weakens substantially. On that premise, the transfer question does not depend on the stark and much more problematic assertion that the interest in uniform Claims Court (and Federal Circuit) adjudication of government-contract obligations, an interest embodied in the Tucker Act, is so strong as to justify stripping an injured party of any right to compensation, including the right Congress expressly granted in the FTCA's Section 2674. If USM has a meaningful remedy in the Claims Court, both of the congressionally declared interests — the forum-specificity interest and the compensation interest — can be meaningfully preserved. We are not prepared to conclude that this case clearly requires sacrifice of the compensation interest.

CONCLUSION

We need not say whether we would draw a conclusion different from that of the Fifth Circuit if we were freshly conducting the analysis of the interaction of the FTCA and Tucker Act schemes. When the general Tucker Act's reach overlaps with that of another statutory regime, it is certainly possible that the other regime is the one that takes precedence. But we cannot say that the Fifth Circuit's determination, that in this case it is the FTCA that gives way, is clearly wrong.

The Fifth Circuit ruling that the case must be transferred to the Claims Court is law of the case. Applying that doctrine, we affirm the resulting transfer order. In doing so, we necessarily hold that the Claims Court has jurisdiction over USM's suit, with all that entails under this court's precedents about the issues thereby resolved. At this point, this case presents even more than the usual reasons for litigation p.1375 to proceed with expedition and with minimization of wasteful duplication.

No costs.

AFFIRMED.

[1] Only USM appeals to this court. USM informed us, without contradiction from the government, that VT Halter will not pursue its own claim and has agreed with USM about how to share any recovery. Appellant USM Br. at 3 n. 2; Oral Argument at 00:46-1:17.

[2] Section 1491(a)(1) covers "any claim against the United States founded either upon the Constitution, or any Act of Congress or any regulation of an executive department, or upon any express or implied contract with the United States, or for liquidated or unliquidated damages in cases not sounding in tort." The grammatical reach of the "cases not sounding in tort" phrase is not immediately apparent. If the phrase were read as attaching to all the enumerated matters ("founded... upon any ... contract ... in cases not sounding in tort"), it might suggest that Section 1491(a)(1) does not extend to claims with a contract basis if they also "sound[] in tort."

[3] This view comports with a possible reading of the text of Section 1491(a)(1), under which "in cases not sounding in tort" attaches only to the phrase "for liquidated or unliquidated damages." *See* note 2, *supra* (quoting text and noting alternative possible textual reading). The government seems to adopt this reading: in describing what Section 1491(a)(1) encompasses, it quotes the contract portion with a full stop, without including the "in cases not sounding in tort" phrase as a limitation. Appellee United States Br. at 11.

[4] Regardless of its precise grammatical role in Section 1491, the presence of the phrase "in cases not sounding in tort" suggests that tort claims are outside the enumeration of covered claims.

[5] Although the general rule is that "[a] plaintiff must be in privity with the United States to have standing to sue the sovereign on a contract claim," *First Annapolis Bancorp, Inc. v. United States,* 644 F.3d 1367, 1373 (Fed. Cir.2011) (citing authorities), a third party sometimes may recover damages for the government's breach of a contractual duty, *see, e.g., D & H Distrib. Co. v. United States,* 102 F.3d 542, 546-47 (Fed.Cir.1996).

[6] In the Fifth Circuit, the United States did not urge that USM's action was within the jurisdiction of the Claims Court or outside the district court's jurisdiction (although it had made a motion so arguing in the district court). Now it has made both arguments. In particular, it has argued that the Claims Court has "jurisdiction" over a contract claim by USM (directly under the Tucker Act, the government clarified at oral argument, not under the Contract Disputes Act, which applies only to "contractors"). Appellee United States Br. at 22, 25-26 (defending "subject matter jurisdiction in the Court of Federal Claims of this matter"), 27, 33-43; Oral Argument at 24:19-25:00, 26:32-52, 27:56-28:20.

DC CIRCUIT DECISIONS
Federal Tort Claims Act

828 F.3d 935 (2016)

Carlos LOUMIET, Esquire, Appellant
v.
UNITED STATES of America, et al., Appellees.

No. 15-5208.

United States Court of Appeals, District of Columbia Circuit.

Argued March 24, 2016.

Decided July 12, 2016.

Loumiet v. US, 828 F. 3d 935 (DC Cir. 2016)

p.938 Appeal from the United States District Court, for the District of Columbia, (No. 1:12-cv-01130).

Carlos Loumiet, pro se, argued the cause and filed the briefs for appellant.

Steve Frank, Attorney, U.S. Department of Justice, argued the cause for appellees. With him on the brief were Benjamin C. Mizer, Principal Deputy Assistant Attorney General, and Mark B. Stern, Attorney.

Before: ROGERS and PILLARD, Circuit Judges, and SENTELLE, Senior Circuit Judge.

PILLARD, Circuit Judge:

Appellant Carlos Loumiet's participation in a bank audit got him into trouble with the Office of the Comptroller of the Currency (OCC), a bureau within the Department of Treasury. Loumiet claims the OCC's enforcement action against him was trumped-up and retaliatory. On this appeal from the district court's dismissal of the case on the pleadings, we address only the timeliness of his claims, and whether the Constitution places any limit on the governmental policymaking discretion immunized by the discretionary-function exception to the Federal Tort Claims Act (FTCA or the Act).

After prosecuting Loumiet for nearly three years, culminating in a three-week trial, the OCC dismissed its enforcement action against him — an action which this court has since described as not "substantially justified." *Loumiet v. Office of Comptroller of Currency,* 650 F.3d 796, 797-98 (D.C. Cir. 2011). Loumiet then brought suit against the United States and four OCC employees, claiming that their enforcement action and related conduct were both tortious and unconstitutional. The district court dismissed Loumiet's tort claims against the United States under the p.939 FTCA's discretionary-function exception and dismissed his constitutional *Bivens* claims against the individual defendants as time-barred.

We conclude, in line with the majority of our sister circuits to have considered the question, that the discretionary-function exception does not categorically bar FTCA tort claims where the challenged exercise of discretion allegedly exceeded the government's constitutional authority to act. Nor are Loumiet's *Bivens* claims time-barred, because the continuing-violations doctrine applies to extend the applicable statute of limitations where, as here, a plaintiff alleges continuing conduct causing cumulative harm. Accordingly, we reverse the district court's dismissal order and remand for further proceedings.

I

We review the district court's dismissal of Loumiet's claims *de novo,* accepting as true the factual allegations in the complaint. *See Jerome Stevens Pharm., Inc. v. FDA,* 402 F.3d 1249, 1250 (D.C. Cir. 2005).

In the early 2000s, Loumiet was on a team of attorneys Hamilton Bank hired to prepare an audit report during a securities-fraud investigation of the bank by the OCC. The final audit report was unable to reach a conclusion as to whether the bank's executives had engaged in intentional wrongdoing. The OCC contested certain of the report's findings, but, after further investigation, Loumiet and his team declined to change their conclusions.

Around that time, Loumiet sent the Treasury Inspector General a series of letters in which he expressed concern that, while on site at Hamilton Bank during the OCC's investigation, OCC employees had made racist remarks regarding the bank's Hispanic employees. The bank filed suit against the OCC in 2002, alleging civil rights violations arising out of the investigation. Shortly thereafter, the OCC closed Hamilton Bank for operating in an unsafe manner — a closure Loumiet alleges was unjustified and incurred considerable unnecessary cost for the bank's receiver, the Federal Deposit Insurance Corporation.

On November 6, 2006, the Comptroller initiated an administrative enforcement proceeding against Loumiet under the Financial Institutions Reform, Recovery, and Enforcement Act, alleging that he was an "institution-affiliated party" who knowingly or recklessly breached his fiduciary duty to Hamilton Bank when preparing the audit and caused a "significant adverse effect" on the bank. 12 U.S.C. § 1813(u)(4). During the course of the enforcement action against him, Loumiet alleges, OCC personnel made unsubstantiated charges and false statements to the press. On June 18, 2008, after a three-week administrative trial, the presiding Administrative Law Judge recommended dismissal of the OCC's claims in their entirety, and on July 27, 2009, the Comptroller dismissed the action. Later, this court concluded the OCC's enforcement action was not "substantially justified" and awarded Loumiet attorney's fees. *Loumiet,* 650 F.3d at 797.

According to Loumiet's complaint in the action now before us, the OCC's frivolous enforcement proceeding caused significant damage: his banking-law practice evaporated, his income fell significantly, he dropped several partnership levels at his firm, and he suffered severe emotional distress. Seeking compensation for those harms, in 2011 Loumiet filed an administrative unlawful-retaliation claim, which the OCC denied in January 2012. Loumiet filed this suit in federal district court on July 9, 2012. He brought common-law tort claims under the FTCA against the government for intentional infliction of emotional distress, invasion of privacy, abuse of process, malicious prosecution, negligent p.940 supervision, and civil conspiracy.[1] He sued the individual government officials under *Bivens v. Six Unknown Named Agents of Federal Bureau of Narcotics,* 403 U.S. 388, 91 S.Ct. 1999, 29 L.Ed.2d 619 (1971), claiming retaliatory prosecution in violation of the First and Fifth Amendments. Loumiet alleged that the officials were "driven by a desire to retaliate" against him in bringing a baseless prosecution that interfered with his "right to communicate with his client free of Government intimidation and punishment." Compl. ¶¶ 138, 141.

The district court granted the defendants' motion to dismiss as to most of Loumiet's claims. *See Loumiet v. United States (Loumiet I)*, 968 F.Supp.2d 142, 144-45 (D.D.C. 2013). First, the court concluded that many of Loumiet's FTCA claims were "inextricably tied" to the OCC's decision to prosecute, so must be dismissed pursuant to the FTCA's discretionary-function exception, 28 U.S.C. § 2680(a). *See Loumiet I*, 968 F.Supp.2d at 156-58. A prosecutorial decision is a quintessential discretionary function even if, in the circumstances of a particular case, the prosecution proceeded unreasonably in light of the paucity of its evidence. *Id.* at 156-57. In the court's view, none of the authorities Loumiet cited "specifically prescribe[d] a course of action for an employee to follow" so as to bar application of the discretionary-function exception here. *Id.* at 157 (quoting *Berkovitz v. United States*, 486 U.S. 531, 536, 108 S.Ct. 1954, 100 L.Ed.2d 531 (1988)).

Before dismissing Loumiet's FTCA claims on that ground, however, the court explained that those claims, which he filed with the agency on July 20, 2011, were not barred by the FTCA's two-year statute of limitations. *Id.* at 153-55. The malicious-prosecution claim did not accrue until July 27, 2009, when the OCC dismissed the enforcement action, *id.* at 153, and the continuing-violations doctrine delayed accrual of his other FTCA claims until the same date because the enforcement action constituted a continuing harm until its final disposition, *id.* at 154-55 (citing *Whelan v. Abell*, 953 F.2d 663, 674 (D.C. Cir. 1992)).

Notwithstanding its application of the continuing-violations doctrine to Loumiet's FTCA claims and its characterization of the *Bivens* and FTCA claims as intertwined, the court held that Loumiet had forfeited that doctrine's applicability to his *Bivens* claims. *Id.* at 152 n. 3. The claims were barred by the applicable three-year statute of limitations, the court concluded, because the claims accrued when Loumiet knew or had reason to know that the enforcement action was retaliatory and was unsupported by probable cause, which was either when the OCC first filed the action or, at the latest, when the ALJ ruled in his favor four years before Loumiet filed his complaint. *Id.* at 150-51.

On Loumiet's motion for reconsideration, the district court addressed for the first time his allegations that the OCC's decision to prosecute him was unconstitutionally retaliatory and so beyond the governmental policymaking authority protected by the FTCA's discretionary-function exception. *Loumiet v. United States (Loumiet II)*, 65 F.Supp.3d 19, 25-26 (D.D.C. 2014). "[E]ven 'constitutionally defective' actions," the court held, "are in fact protected by the discretionary function exception." *Id.* at 25. The court eventually dismissed Loumiet's remaining p.941 claims on grounds not pressed before this court. Loumiet timely appealed.

II

We begin with the government's contention that the conduct Loumiet alleges to be tortious under the FTCA involved performance of a "discretionary function" and is therefore immune from liability under the Act. The FTCA provides a limited waiver of the federal government's sovereign immunity from damages liability for torts committed by federal employees acting within the scope of their employment. *See* 28 U.S.C. §§ 1346(b), 2674. The Act expressly retains immunity from some tort liability through a number of statutory exceptions. *See id.* § 2680. If one of those exceptions applies, the court lacks subject-matter jurisdiction to hear the plaintiff's claims. *See Simmons v. Himmelreich,* U.S. ___, 136 S.Ct. 1843, 1846, 195 L.Ed.2d 106 (2016).

At issue here is the discretionary-function exception, which provides that the Act's waiver of sovereign immunity "shall not apply to":

> Any claim ... based upon the exercise or performance or the failure to exercise or perform a discretionary function or duty on the part of a federal agency or an employee of the Government, whether or not the discretion involved be abused.

28 U.S.C. § 2680(a). "[T]he purpose of the exception is to 'prevent judicial second-guessing of legislative and administrative decisions grounded in social, economic, and political policy through the medium of an action in tort.'" *United States v. Gaubert,* 499 U.S. 315, 323, 111 S.Ct. 1267, 113 L.Ed.2d 335 (1991) (quoting *United States v. Varig Airlines,* 467 U.S. 797, 814, 104 S.Ct. 2755, 81 L.Ed.2d 660 (1984)). Congress enacted the FTCA to remedy and deter tortious conduct by federal personnel, but sought in the FTCA's discretionary-function exception to prevent such claims from impairing the government's legitimate exercises of policy discretion. *See Red Lake Band of Chippewa Indians v. United States,* 800 F.2d 1187, 1195-96 (D.C. Cir. 1986); *Gray v. Bell,* 712 F.2d 490, 506 (D.C. Cir. 1983). A factfinder's post-hoc determination in a lawsuit that governmental conduct fell short of standards of reasonable care, for example, should not be permitted to gainsay the contrary determination of officials vested with discretion to decide "how best to accommodate" conflicting policy goals "and the reality of finite agency resources." *Berkovitz,* 486 U.S. at 537, 108 S.Ct. 1954 (internal quotation marks omitted). Duly authorized government personnel, not judges or juries, decide what counts as reasonable public policy.

To determine whether governmental conduct falls within the discretionary-function exception, we look at the "nature of the conduct, rather than the status of the actor," *Gaubert,* 499 U.S. at 322, 111 S.Ct. 1267 (quoting *Varig Airlines,* 467 U.S. at 813, 104 S.Ct. 2755), and ask two questions:

First, we consider whether the challenged conduct "involves an element of judgment or choice." *Berkovitz,* 486 U.S. at 536, 108 S.Ct. 1954. If an exercise of discretion is involved, then, consistent with the last clause of the exception, "the discretionary function exception immunizes even government abuses of discretion." *Shuler v. United States,* 531 F.3d 930, 935 (D.C. Cir. 2008); *see* 28 U.S.C. § 2680(a) (excluding from the reach of the FTCA government exercises of discretion "whether or not the discretion involved be abused"). But the element of discretion is necessarily absent where "a federal statute, regulation, or policy specifically prescribes a course of action for an employee to follow." *Berkovitz,* 486 U.S. at 536, 108 S.Ct. 1954. The exception thus does not p.942 apply to a claim that an agency failed to "perform its clear duty" or to "act in accord with a specific mandatory directive." *Id.* at 545, 108 S.Ct. 1954.

Second, if the conduct does involve some element of judgment or choice, we must ask whether the "judgment is of the kind that the discretionary function exception was designed to shield," *Gaubert,* 499 U.S. at 322-23, 111 S.Ct. 1267 (quoting

Berkovitz, 486 U.S. at 536, 108 S.Ct. 1954), that is, whether the actions or decisions "were within the range of choice accorded by federal policy and law and were the results of policy determinations," *Berkovitz,* 486 U.S. at 538, 108 S.Ct. 1954. Even a discretionary act within the scope of a federal official's employment is not within the exception if it "cannot be said to be based on the purposes that the regulatory regime seeks to accomplish." *Gaubert,* 499 U.S. at 325 n. 7, 111 S.Ct. 1267. The exception thus "insulates the Government from liability if the action challenged in the case involves the permissible exercise of policy judgment," *Berkovitz,* 486 U.S. at 537, 108 S.Ct. 1954, but "[a]n employee of the government acting beyond his authority is not exercising the sort of discretion the discretionary function exception was enacted to protect," *Red Lake,* 800 F.2d at 1196.

This court has long held that the decision "whether to prosecute" is typically a "quintessentially discretionary" function that involves judgment and requires balancing policy goals and finite agency resources, thus meriting protection under the discretionary-function exception. *Moore v. Valder,* 65 F.3d 189, 197 (D.C. Cir. 1995); *see Gray,* 712 F.2d at 514. In determining whether the exception applies, we have treated the decision to initiate an administrative proceeding as we do a decision to pursue a criminal prosecution. *See Sloan v. U.S. Dep't of Hous. & Urban Dev.,* 236 F.3d 756, 760 (D.C. Cir. 2001). A decision by the OCC to bring an action pursuant to its broad statutory enforcement authority, 12 U.S.C. § 1818(b), (i), therefore ordinarily would appear to qualify for the discretionary-function exception, even if a factfinder considering a tort claim arising out of the enforcement decision might conclude that the prosecution was unreasonable or otherwise amounted to an abuse of the OCC's enforcement discretion.

But our inquiry into the viability of Loumiet's FTCA claims does not end there. This case raises the additional, thorny question — novel in our circuit — whether the FTCA's discretionary-function exception shields the United States from common-law tort liability under the Act even when the otherwise discretionary conduct the plaintiff challenges exceeds constitutional limits on the government's authority to act. Loumiet alleges FTCA tort claims, including claims of intentional infliction of emotional distress and malicious prosecution, based on conduct generally subject to the agency's enforcement discretion. But he also alleges that the OCC's retaliatory enforcement action violated his First and Fifth Amendment rights and thus was not an exercise of the sort of discretion the exception shields. *See* Compl. ¶ 111, App. Tab 2 at 64 ("Because the defendants' behavior failed to comply with the internal rules and procedures of the OCC itself, and also grossly offended the First and Fifth Amendments to our Constitution, the 'discretionary activity' exclusion under the FTCA does not apply.").

The government responds that the challenged prosecution was, at bottom, discretionary, and that Loumiet's constitutional allegations do not affect the applicability of the discretionary-function exception to bar the FTCA claims. Because the FTCA does not waive sovereign immunity for constitutional torts, the government objects, there can be no unconstitutional-discretion limitation p.943 on the exception. In any event, it contends, Loumiet alleges no violation of any clearly established constitutional directive — the only type of constitutional violation that, in the government's view, might render the discretionary-function exception inapplicable.

We hold that the FTCA's discretionary-function exception does not provide a blanket immunity against tortious conduct that a plaintiff plausibly alleges also flouts a constitutional prescription. At least seven circuits, including the First, Second, Third, Fourth, Fifth, Eighth, and Ninth, have either held or stated in dictum that the discretionary-function exception does not shield government officials from FTCA liability when they exceed the scope of their constitutional authority. In *Nurse v. United States,* for example, the Ninth Circuit held that "[i]n general, governmental conduct cannot be discretionary if it violates a legal mandate," including a constitutional mandate. 226 F.3d 996, 1002 (9th Cir. 2000). The discretionary-function exception was inapplicable, that court explained, because the plaintiff had alleged tort claims based on "discriminatory, unconstitutional policies which the[] [defendants] had no discretion to create." *Id.* Likewise, the Eighth Circuit in *Raz v. United States* held that the FBI's "alleged surveillance activities f[e]ll outside the FTCA's discretionary-function exception" where the plaintiff had "alleged they were conducted in violation of his First and Fourth Amendment rights." 343 F.3d 945, 948 (8th Cir. 2003); *see also, e.g., Limone v. United States,* 579 F.3d 79, 102 (1st Cir. 2009) (holding that challenged "conduct was unconstitutional and, therefore, not within the sweep of the discretionary function exception"); *Medina v. United States,* 259 F.3d 220, 225 (4th Cir. 2001) (In "determin[ing] the bounds of the discretionary function exception ... we begin with the principle that federal officials do not possess discretion to violate constitutional rights or federal statutes." (internal quotation marks, alterations, and citations omitted)); *U.S. Fid. & Guar. Co. v. United States,* 837 F.2d 116, 120 (3d Cir. 1988) ("[C]onduct cannot be discretionary if it violates the Constitution, a statute, or an applicable regulation. Federal officials do not possess discretion to violate constitutional rights or federal statutes."); *Sutton v. United States,* 819 F.2d 1289, 1293 (5th Cir. 1987) ("[A]ction does not fall within the discretionary function exception of § 2680(a) when governmental agents exceed the scope of their authority as designated by statute or the Constitution.");[2] *Myers & Myers Inc. v. USPS,* 527 F.2d 1252, 1261 (2d Cir. 1975) ("It is, of course, a tautology that a federal official cannot have discretion to behave unconstitutionally or outside the scope of his delegated authority.").[3]

p.944 To this court's knowledge, only the Seventh Circuit has held otherwise. *Küskila v. United States,* 466 F.2d 626, 627-28 (7th Cir. 1972). That court applied the discretionary-function exception to immunize the government from FTCA liability arising from the decision of a military-base commander to exclude the plaintiff, a civilian manager at the base's credit union, from entering the base because she carried antiwar literature and planned an off-site antiwar rally — an exclusion the court had already determined violated the First Amendment. *Id.; see Küskila v. Nichols,* 433 F.2d 745, 746-51 (7th Cir. 1970) (en banc). The bank manager sought damages under the FTCA, but the court of appeals sustained dismissal of that claim as deriving from an FTCA-excepted governmental "exercise of discretion, albeit constitutionally repugnant." *Küskila,* 466 F.2d at 627-28.

This circuit has yet to decide whether the FTCA's discretionary-function exception generally immunizes allegedly unconstitutional abuses of discretion by the government. In deciding that it does not, we follow the clear weight of circuit authority. By the same token that the government has no policymaking discretion to violate "a federal statute, regulation, or policy specifically prescrib[ing] a course of action for [its] employee to follow," *Berkovitz,* 486 U.S. at 536, 108 S.Ct. 1954, the government lacks discretion to make unconstitutional policy choices. Although the discretionary-function exception shields government policymakers' lawful discretion to set social, economic, and political policy priorities from judicial second-guessing via tort law, there is no blanket exception for discretion that exceeds constitutional bounds.

As we have previously held, the policy discretion of federal personnel acting in their official capacity is necessarily "circumscribed by the rules that limit the bounds of [their] authority." *Red Lake,* 800 F.2d at 1197. Thus, in *Red Lake,* we concluded that an FBI agent who, due to FBI policy, lacked authority over non-FBI officials at a hostage situation was unprotected by the discretionary-function exception from a suit challenging orders he gave to officials not under his lawful command. *Id.* at 1196-97. The exception did not apply, we explained, because "[a] government official has no discretion to violate the binding laws, regulations, or policies that define the extent of his official powers. An employee of the government acting beyond his authority is not exercising the sort of discretion the discretionary function exception was enacted to protect." *Id.* at 1196.

The discretionary-function exception likewise does not shield decisions that exceed constitutional bounds, even if such decisions are imbued with policy considerations. *See Medina,* 259 F.3d at 225 (acknowledging, in reliance on *Berkovitz,* 486 U.S. at 536, 108 S.Ct. 1954, and *Red Lake,* 800 F.2d at 1196, that federal officials lack discretion to violate constitutional rights). A constitutional limit on governmental power, no less than a federal statutory or regulatory one like the FBI policy in *Red Lake,* circumscribes the government's authority even on decisions that otherwise would fall within its lawful discretion. The government "has no 'discretion' to violate the Federal Constitution; its dictates are absolute and imperative." *Owen v. City of Independence, Mo.,* 445 U.S. 622, 649, 100 S.Ct. 1398, 63 L.Ed.2d 673 (1980). Indeed, the absence of a limitation on the discretionary-function exception for constitutionally ultra vires conduct would yield an illogical result: the FTCA would authorize tort claims against the government for conduct that violates the mandates of a statute, rule, or policy, while insulating the government from claims alleging on-duty conduct so egregious that it violates the p.945 more fundamental requirements of the Constitution.

Neither *Moore,* 65 F.3d 189, nor *Gray,* 712 F.2d 490, on which the government relies, addressed whether the discretionary-function exception immunizes even unconstitutional decisions to prosecute. In those cases, as here, we considered FTCA common-law tort claims against the government premised on conduct also alleged to be unconstitutional. *Moore,* 65 F.3d at 191; *Gray,* 712 F.2d at 495. The parties in *Moore* disputed the scope of the discretionary-function exception as applied to various alleged misdeeds relating to investigation and prosecution. We drew the line between conduct tied to the "quintessentially discretionary" decision to prosecute, which we held was immunized, and "discrete" and "separable" activity such as "disclosing grand jury testimony to unauthorized third parties," which we held was not. *Id.* at 196-97. The plaintiff in *Moore* did not argue, nor did we consider, whether constitutional limits on a prosecutor's discretion affected the discretionary-function exception's applicability. *See id.; see also* Br. of Plaintiff-

Appellant, *Moore v. United States,* Nos. 99-5197, 1999 WL 34834283 (D.C. Cir. Dec. 17, 1999). Similarly in *Gray,* the focus of dispute was whether the prosecutors' pre-indictment investigatory actions were distinct from their clearly discretionary — and thus, all assumed, immunized — decision to prosecute. 712 F.2d at 515-16. In holding that they were not, we nowhere discussed any effect the alleged unconstitutionality of the prosecutors' actions might have on the availability of the discretionary-function exception. *Id.*

The government also contends that recognition of constitutional limitations on the FTCA's discretionary-function exception would run counter to the Supreme Court's statement in *FDIC v. Meyer,* 510 U.S. 471, 478, 114 S.Ct. 996, 127 L.Ed.2d 308 (1994), that "the United States simply has not rendered itself liable under [the FTCA] for constitutional tort claims," which are actionable only against individual officials under *Bivens,* Br. of the United States 18-19. Judge Smith voiced a similar concern in his dissent from the Fifth Circuit panel decision in *Castro* when he worried that, "by a plaintiff's artful pleading, the United States c[ould] be liable whenever the Constitution is violated even though, under *Meyer,* the sovereign is not subject to liability for constitutional torts." *Castro v. United States,* 560 F.3d 381, 394 (5th Cir. 2009) (Smith, J., dissenting), *rev'd on reh'g en banc,* 608 F.3d 266 (5th Cir. 2010).

But those contentions miscast the relationship between FTCA state-law torts and *Bivens* constitutional claims. The state-law substance of an FTCA claim is unchanged by courts' recognition of constitutional bounds to the legitimate discretion that the FTCA immunizes. Federal constitutional claims for damages are cognizable only under *Bivens,* which runs against individual governmental officials personally. *See Meyer,* 510 U.S. at 482, 485-86, 114 S.Ct. 996. The FTCA, in contrast, provides a method to enforce state tort law against the federal government itself. *See* 28 U.S.C. § 1346(b)(1); *cf. Carlson v. Green,* 446 U.S. 14, 20-21, 100 S.Ct. 1468, 64 L.Ed.2d 15 (1980) (describing distinct goals and characteristics of FTCA and *Bivens* claims and concluding that "Congress views FTCA and *Bivens* as parallel, complementary causes of action"). A plaintiff who identifies constitutional defects in the conduct underlying her FTCA tort claim — whether or not she advances a *Bivens* claim against the individual official involved — may affect the availability of the discretionary-function defense, but she does not thereby convert an FTCA claim into a constitutional damages claim against the government; state law is necessarily still the source of the substantive standard p.946 of FTCA liability. The First Circuit has similarly emphasized, in holding unconstitutional conduct to fall outside of "the sweep of the discretionary function exception," that it does not view the government's "constitutional transgressions as corresponding to the plaintiffs' causes of action — after all, the plaintiffs' claims are not *Bivens* claims — but rather, as negating the discretionary function defense." *Limone,* 579 F.3d at 102 & n. 12.

The question remains whether or to what degree a constitutional mandate must be specific or clearly established to render the discretionary-function exception inapplicable. Contending that the exception should at least immunize governmental policy discretion that is not clearly unconstitutional, the government adverts to the qualified-immunity doctrine of *Harlow v. Fitzgerald,* 457 U.S. 800, 818, 102 S.Ct. 2727, 73 L.Ed.2d 396 (1982), under which a constitutional tort plaintiff seeking to defeat an individual official's qualified-immunity defense must show that the claimed constitutional rights were "clearly established," Br. of the United States 19. The government appreciates that qualified immunity as such applies only to governmental officials sued in their individual capacities, not to the government as an entity. *Harlow,* 457 U.S. at 818, 102 S.Ct. 2727. Qualified immunity — a form of official immunity — is directly tied to "the risk that fear of personal monetary liability and harassing litigation will unduly inhibit officials in the discharge of their duties," to the detriment of the public interest. *Anderson v. Creighton,* 483 U.S. 635, 638, 107 S.Ct. 3034, 97 L.Ed.2d 523 (1987); *see also Harlow,* 457 U.S. at 816, 819, 102 S.Ct. 2727.

We take the government to be arguing by analogy that principles similar to those that undergird qualified immunity should extend to preserve discretionary-function immunity for some unconstitutional acts. We have found no precedent in any circuit holding as the government urges, nor does it cite any. At this juncture we see no cause to make this the first. Indeed, the district court on remand might allow Loumiet's FTCA claims to proceed under a narrow standard such as the government suggests.[4] That would leave for another day the question whether the FTCA immunizes exercises of policy discretion in violation of constitutional constraints that are not already clear.

To resolve this appeal, we need go no further than to hold that the district court erred as a matter of law in barring Loumiet's FTCA claims on the ground that, as a general matter, "even constitutionally defective" exercises of discretion fall within the Act's discretionary-function exception. *Loumiet II,* 65 F.Supp.3d at 25. That broad-brush approach is foreclosed by our holding today. The district court should determine in the first instance whether Loumiet's complaint plausibly alleges that the OCC's conduct exceeded the scope of its constitutional authority so as to vitiate discretionary-function immunity.

III

Loumiet also asserts that the district court erred in dismissing his First and Fifth Amendment *Bivens* claims as time-barred.[5] Those claims did not accrue, p.947 he contends, until the OCC finally dismissed its enforcement action on July 27, 2009, because the agency's ongoing prosecution of that action inflicted continuing harm until its final dismissal. The defendants counter that Loumiet failed to raise that continuing-violations argument before the district court and that the doctrine in any event does not assist him. For the following reasons, we conclude that Loumiet adequately advanced the continuing-violations doctrine before the district court, and that his *Bivens* claims, staked on continuing, harmful conduct, were timely.

"When a federal action contains no statute of limitations, courts will ordinarily look to analogous provisions in state law as a source of a federal limitations period." *Doe v. Dep't of Justice,* 753 F.2d 1092, 1114 (D.C. Cir. 1985); *see id.* at 1114-15 (applying state limitations period in *Bivens* action). In this case, there is no dispute that the District of Columbia's general three-year statute of limitations applies to Loumiet's *Bivens* claims. *See* D.C. Code § 12-301(8). Therefore, if Loumiet's claims accrued before July 9, 2009 — more than three years before he filed his July 9, 2012, complaint — they would be barred by the statute of limitations.

State law dictates the statute of limitations, but the timing of the accrual of Loumiet's claims is a question of federal law. *Cf. Wallace v. Kato,* 549 U.S. 384, 388, 127 S.Ct. 1091, 166 L.Ed.2d 973 (2007) ("[T]he accrual date of a § 1983 cause of action is a question of federal law that is *not* resolved by reference to state law."). Ordinarily, "accrual occurs when the plaintiff has a complete and present cause of action, that is, when the plaintiff can file suit and obtain relief." *Id.* (internal quotation marks, alterations, and citations omitted). In other words, "[a] claim normally accrues when the factual and legal prerequisites for filing suit are in place." *Earle v. District of Columbia,* 707 F.3d 299, 306 (D.C. Cir. 2012) (quoting *Norwest Bank Minn. Nat'l Ass'n v. FDIC,* 312 F.3d 447, 451 (D.C. Cir. 2002)).

The defendants contend, and the district court agreed, *Loumiet I,* 968 F.Supp.2d at 149-53, that under that general accrual rule, Loumiet's First and Fifth Amendment retaliatory prosecution claims are time-barred because all of the events underpinning each of the elements of those claims took place well before the statute-of-limitations cutoff of July 9, 2009. We need not decide whether Loumiet's claims would have been untimely under the general accrual rule, however, because we agree with Loumiet's contention that the continuing-violations doctrine displaced it here to render his claims timely filed.

As an initial matter, Loumiet adequately raised, and thus preserved for our review, his continuing-violations argument. The district court relied on that argument in holding that the FTCA claims were timely, but treated it as forfeited for the *Bivens* claims. *See Loumiet I,* 968 F.Supp.2d at 152 n. 3, 155; *Loumiet II,* 65 F.Supp.3d at 24-25. In addressing the timeliness of his claims before the district court, however, Loumiet expressly analogized his *Bivens* retaliatory prosecution claims to his FTCA tort claims, characterizing the former as "simply an offspring of the OCC's malicious prosecution." Pl. Opp. to Mot. to Dismiss, App. Tab 3 at 35. Loumiet thus adequately incorporated by reference his invocation of the continuing-violations theory as to his FTCA claims. *Compare id.* at 35-36, *with id.* at 49-51. We therefore consider the argument.

Even while this court "do[es] not lightly create exceptions to the general p.948 rule of claim accrual," *Earle,* 707 F.3d at 306 n. 9, it has "recognized various exceptions to, and glosses on, the rule" including the "muddled, ... intricate[,] and somewhat confusing" continuing-violations, or continuing-tort, doctrine, *id.* at 309 (internal quotation marks omitted). The continuing-violations doctrine applies where "no single incident in a continuous chain of tortious activity can 'fairly or realistically be identified as the cause of significant harm,'" and so it is "proper to regard the cumulative effect of the conduct as actionable." *Page v. United States,* 729 F.2d 818, 821-22 (D.C. Cir. 1984) (quoting *Fowkes v. Penn. R.R. Co.,* 264 F.2d 397, 399 (3d Cir. 1959)). The court has recognized two types of continuing violations, only the second of which is implicated here: (1) where defendants violated a statutorily imposed continuing obligation, *Earle,* 707 F.3d at 307; or (2) where the "character [of the challenged conduct] as a violation did not become clear until it was repeated during the limitations period, typically because it is only its cumulative impact (as in the case of a hostile work environment) that reveals its illegality," *id.* at 306 (quoting *Taylor v. FDIC,* 132 F.3d 753, 765 (D.C. Cir. 1997)).

In *Page,* we recognized the latter type of continuing violation in the context of an FTCA claim alleging a "gradual" injury "resulting from the cumulative impact of years of allegedly tortious drug treatment." 729 F.2d at 822. It "seem[ed] unrealistic," we explained, "to regard each prescription of drugs as the cause of a separate injury, or as a separate tortious act triggering a new limitation period." *Id.* at 822-23. Accordingly, we held that the plaintiff's claim did not accrue until the conclusion of what was alleged to have been nearly twenty years of tortious drug treatment. *Id.* at 819, 822-23.

Under our decision in *Whelan,* that reasoning holds true where a plaintiff has alleged that the full course of legal proceedings effected a single, cumulative harm. We held there that a claim of tortious interference with business opportunities could proceed even if the business opportunities did not exist at the time of the allegedly interfering lawsuit, because under the continuing-violations doctrine, "a lawsuit is a continuous, not an isolated event," the effects of which "persist from the initial filing to the final disposition of the case." 953 F.2d at 673. Put another way, a lawsuit "is repetitive in that it represents the assertion, every day, of the plaintiff's claim," and "[a] defendant subject to a lawsuit is likely to suffer damage not so much from the initial complaint but from the cumulative costs of defense and the reputational harm caused by an unresolved claim." *Id.* A lawsuit is thus different from the typical case of a "mere failure to right a wrong and make the plaintiff whole." *Id.* (quoting *Fitzgerald v. Seamans,* 553 F.2d 220, 230 (D.C. Cir. 1977)).

Page and *Whelan* are dispositive here. Loumiet alleges continuing harm resulting not only from the filing of the OCC's frivolous, retaliatory legal proceedings against him, but also from the agency's continued prosecution of Loumiet and associated publicity over a period of many years. It is not only the initiation of the OCC's action that Loumiet identified as harmful; he also cited, among other things, the experts the OCC sought to put on the stand, Compl. ¶¶ 93-94, App. Tab 2 at 52-54, statements made to the press, *id.* ¶¶ 15-16, 85, 91, App. Tab 2 at 4-5, 48-49, 51-52, the three-week trial in which Loumiet had to defend himself against baseless allegations, *id.* ¶¶ 94-105, App. Tab 2 at 59-60, the testimony levelled against him, *id.* ¶¶ 94-95, 98-105, App. Tab 2 at 53-54, 56-60, and the four years of decreased income, downgraded partnership stake, and continuing emotional distress he alleges he suffered throughout the pendency of the OCC enforcement action, *id.* ¶ 106, App. Tab 2 at p.949 60-61. As with the ongoing tort in *Whelan,* the commencement of the OCC action at issue here was but "the first link in a chain of conduct that d[id] not end until the [OCC] cease[d] prosecution of the suit." 953 F.2d at 674 (citing *Page,* 729 F.2d at 821-22).

The defendants contend that neither *Page* nor *Whelan* applies because neither case involved a *Bivens* claim. Limitations doctrines are typically trans-substantive, however, and this one is no exception. *Whelan* places squarely within the scope of the continuing-violations doctrine ongoing legal proceedings that cause continuing harm. 953 F.2d at 673-74. The defendants offer no reason why that rule should differ in the *Bivens* context. *Cf. Va. Hosp. Ass'n v. Baliles,* 868 F.2d 653, 663 (4th Cir. 1989), *aff'd sub nom. Wilder v. Va. Hosp. Ass'n,* 496 U.S. 498, 110 S.Ct. 2510, 110 L.Ed.2d 455 (1990) (applying continuing-violations doctrine to delay accrual in § 1983 case). Loumiet filed his *Bivens* claims on July 9, 2012, within three years of the

OCC's July 27, 2009, dismissal of its enforcement action against him. Those claims were therefore timely. Accordingly, we remand to the district court for its consideration of the remaining defenses raised but not yet decided in the district court. *See Loumiet I,* 968 F.Supp.2d at 149.[6]

* * *

For the foregoing reasons, we reverse the dismissal order of the district court and remand for further proceedings consistent with this opinion.

So ordered.

[1] Loumiet also asserted many of these same common-law tort claims under the FTCA against the individual defendants, which the district court dismissed pursuant to the Westfall Act, 28 U.S.C. § 2679(d)(1). *See Loumiet v. United States (Loumiet I)*, 968 F.Supp.2d 142, 153 (D.D.C. 2013). Loumiet has not appealed that ruling.

[2] A panel of the Fifth Circuit later relied on *Sutton* to hold the discretionary-function exception inapplicable to conduct a plaintiff had alleged to violate the Fourth and Fifth Amendments. *See Castro v. United States,* 560 F.3d 381, 389-90 (5th Cir. 2009) (subsequent history omitted). The en banc Fifth Circuit summarily vacated the *Castro* panel decision, but in so doing did not address the interplay between constitutional allegations and the discretionary-function exception. *See Castro v. United States,* 608 F.3d 266, 268-69 (5th Cir. 2010) (en banc). Instead, it adopted the prior district court opinion, *id.* which also was silent on the import of the plaintiff's constitutional allegations, *see Castro v. United States,* No. CIV.A. C-06-61, 2007 WL 471095, at *79 (S.D. Tex. Feb. 9, 2007) (subsequent history omitted). Notwithstanding *Sutton,* the Fifth Circuit has since observed that the circuit has "not yet determined whether a constitutional violation, as opposed to a statutory, regulatory, or policy violation, precludes the application of the discretionary function exception." *Spotts v. United States,* 613 F.3d 559, 569 (5th Cir. 2010) (citing *Castro,* 608 F.3d 266).

[3] The government's briefing not only failed to distinguish this great weight of authority, but did not even acknowledge it.

[4] *Cf. Moore v. Hartman,* 704 F.3d 1003, 1004 (D.C. Cir. 2013) (noting that "the precedent in this Circuit clearly established in 1988 ... the contours of the First Amendment right to be free from retaliatory prosecution"); *Moore v. Valder,* 65 F.3d at 196 (holding that a "retaliatory prosecution claim ... does allege the violation of clearly established law").

[5] Loumiet's Fifth Amendment due-process and First Amendment speech-based retaliation claims are premised on identical allegations, and Loumiet does not argue that they should have different dates of accrual. Accordingly, like the district court, we do not differentiate between those claims in assessing their timeliness. *See Loumiet I,* 968 F.Supp.2d at 150 n. 2.

[6] Because we reverse the dismissal of Loumiet's *Bivens* claims, we need not reach the question whether the district court abused its discretion in denying Loumiet's motion for reconsideration as to those claims.

PERRY CAPITAL LLC, FOR AND ON BEHALF OF INVESTMENT FUNDS FOR WHICH IT ACTS AS INVESTMENT MANAGER, Appellant,
v.
STEVEN T. MNUCHIN, IN HIS OFFICIAL CAPACITY AS THE SECRETARY OF THE DEPARTMENT OF THE TREASURY, ET AL., Appellees.

Nos. 14-5243 Consolidated with 14-5254, 14-5260, 14-5262.

United States Court of Appeals, District of Columbia Circuit.

Argued April 15, 2016.

Decided February 21, 2017.

Perry Capital LLC v. Mnuchin, (DC Cir. 2017)

Appeals from the United States District Court for the District of Columbia, Nos. 1:13-cv-01025, 1:13-cv-01053, 1:13-cv-01439, 1:13-cv-01288.

Theodore B. Olson argued the cause for Perry Capital LLC, et al. With him on the briefs were Douglas R. Cox, Matthew D. McGill, Charles J. Cooper, David H. Thompson, Peter A. Patterson, Brian W. Barnes, Drew W. Marrocco, Michael H. Barr, Richard M. Zuckerman, Sandra Hauser, and Janet M. Weiss.

Hamish P.M. Hume argued the cause for American European Insurance Company, *et al.* With him on the briefs were *Matthew A. Goldstein, David R. Kaplan,* and *Geoffrey C. Jarvis.*

Thomas P. Vartanian, Steven G. Bradbury, Robert L. Ledig, and *Robert J. Rhatigan* were on the brief for *amici curiae* the Independent Community Bankers of America, the Association of Mortgage Investors, Mr. William M. Isaac, and Mr. Robert H. Hartheimer in support of appellants.

Thomas F. Cullen, Jr., Michael A. Carvin, James E. Gauch, Lawrence D. Rosenberg, and *Paul V. Lettow* were on the brief for *amici curiae* Louise Rafter, Josephine and Stephen Rattien, and Pershing Square Capital Management, L.P. in support of appellants and reversal.

Jerrold J. Ganzfried and *Bruce S. Ross* were on the brief for *amici curiae* 60 Plus Association, Inc. in support of reversal.

Eric Grant was on the brief for *amicus curiae* Jonathan R. Macey in support of appellants and reversal.

Thomas R. McCarthy was on the brief for *amici curiae* Timothy Howard and The Coalition for Mortgage Security in support of appellants.

Myron T. Steele was on the brief for *amicus curiae* Center for Individual Freedom in support of appellants.

Michael H. Krimminger was on the brief for *amicus curiae* Investors Unite in support of appellants for reversal.

Howard N. Cayne argued the cause for appellees Federal Housing Finance Agency, et al. With him on the brief were Paul D. Clement, D. Zachary Hudson, Michael J. Ciatti, Graciela Maria Rodriguez, David B. Bergman, Michael A.F. Johnson, Dirk C. Phillips, and Ian S. Hoffman.

Mark B. Stern, Attorney, U.S. Department of Justice, argued the cause for appellee Steven T. Mnuchin. With him on the brief were *Benjamin C. Mizer*, Principal Deputy

Assistant Attorney General, *Beth S. Brinkmann,* Deputy Assistant Attorney General, *Alisa B. Klein, Abby C. Wright,* and *Gerard Sinzdak,* Attorneys.

Dennis M. Kelleher was on the brief for *amicus curiae* Better Markets, Inc. in support of appellees and affirmance.

Pierre H. Bergeron was on the brief for *amicus curiae* Black Chamber of Commerce in support of neither party.

Before: BROWN and MILLETT, *Circuit Judges,* and GINSBURG, *Senior Circuit Judge.*

Opinion for the Court filed by *Circuit Judge* MILLETT and *Senior Circuit Judge* GINSBURG.

Dissenting opinion filed by *Circuit Judge* BROWN.

MILLETT, Circuit Judge, and GINSBURG, Senior Circuit Judge.

In 2007-2008, the national economy went into a severe recession due in significant part to a dramatic decline in the housing market. That downturn pushed two central players in the United States' housing mortgage market—the Federal National Mortgage Association ("Fannie Mae" or "Fannie") and the Federal Home Loan Mortgage Corporation ("Freddie Mac" or "Freddie")—to the brink of collapse. Congress concluded that resuscitating Fannie Mae and Freddie Mac was vital for the Nation's economic health, and to that end passed the Housing and Economic Recovery Act of 2008 ("Recovery Act"), Pub. L. No. 110-289, 122 Stat. 2654 (codified, as relevant here, in various sections of 12 U.S.C.). Under the Recovery Act, the Federal Housing Finance Agency ("FHFA") became the conservator of Fannie Mae and Freddie Mac.

In an effort to keep Fannie Mae and Freddie Mac afloat, FHFA promptly concluded on their behalf a stock purchase agreement with the Treasury Department, under which Treasury made billions of dollars in emergency capital available to Fannie Mae and Freddie Mac (collectively, "the Companies") in exchange for preferred shares of their stock. In return, Fannie and Freddie agreed to pay Treasury a quarterly dividend in the amount of 10% of the total amount of funds drawn from Treasury. Fannie's and Freddie's frequent inability to make those dividend payments, however, meant that they often borrowed more cash from Treasury just to pay the dividends, which in turn increased the dividends that Fannie and Freddie were obligated to pay in future quarters. In 2012, FHFA and Treasury adopted the Third Amendment to their stock purchase agreement, which replaced the fixed 10% dividend with a formula by which Fannie and Freddie just paid to Treasury an amount (roughly) equal to their quarterly net worth, however much or little that may be.

A number of Fannie Mae and Freddie Mac stockholders filed suit alleging that FHFA's and Treasury's alteration of the dividend formula through the Third Amendment exceeded their statutory authority under the Recovery Act, and constituted arbitrary and capricious agency action in violation of the Administrative Procedure Act, 5 U.S.C. § 706(2)(A). They also claimed that FHFA, Treasury, and the Companies committed various common-law torts and breaches of contract by restructuring the dividend formula.

We hold that the stockholders' statutory claims are barred by the Recovery Act's strict limitation on judicial review. *See* 12 U.S.C. § 4617(f). We also reject most of the stockholders' common-law claims. Insofar as we have subject matter jurisdiction over the stockholders' common-law claims against Treasury, and Congress has waived the agency's immunity from suit, those claims, too, are barred by the Recovery Act's limitation on judicial review. *Id.* As for the claims against FHFA and the Companies, some are barred because FHFA succeeded to all rights, powers, and privileges of the stockholders under the Recovery Act, *id.* § 4617(b)(2)(A); others fail to state a claim upon which relief can be granted. The remaining claims, which are contract-based claims regarding liquidation preferences and dividend rights, are remanded to the district court for further proceedings.

I. Background

A. Statutory Framework

1. The Origins of Fannie Mae and Freddie Mac

Created by federal statute in 1938, Fannie Mae originated as a government-owned entity designed to "provide stability in the secondary market for residential mortgages," to "increas[e] the liquidity of mortgage investments," and to "promote access to mortgage credit throughout the Nation." 12 U.S.C. § 1716; *see id.* § 1717. To accomplish those goals, Fannie Mae (i) purchases mortgage loans from commercial banks, which frees up those lenders to make additional loans, (ii) finances those purchases by packaging the mortgage loans into mortgage-backed securities, and (iii) then sells those securities to investors. In 1968, Congress made Fannie Mae a publicly traded, stockholder-owned corporation. *See* Housing and Urban Development Act, Pub. L. No. 90-448, § 801, 82 Stat. 476, 536 (1968) (codified at 12 U.S.C. § 1716b).

Congress created Freddie Mac in 1970 to "increase the availability of mortgage credit for the financing of urgently needed housing." Federal Home Loan Mortgage Corporation Act, Pub. L. No. 91-351, preamble, 84 Stat. 450 (1970). Much like Fannie Mae, Freddie Mac buys mortgage loans from a broad variety of lenders, bundles them together into mortgage-backed securities, and then sells those mortgage-backed securities to investors. In 1989, Freddie Mac became a publicly traded, stockholder-owned corporation. *See* Financial Institutions Reform, Recovery, and Enforcement Act of 1989, Pub. L. No. 101-73, § 731, 103 Stat. 183, 429-436.

Fannie Mae and Freddie Mac became major players in the United States' housing market. Indeed, in the lead up to 2008, Fannie Mae's and Freddie Mac's mortgage portfolios had a combined value of $5 trillion and accounted for nearly half of the United States mortgage market. But in 2008, the United States economy fell into a severe recession, in large part due to a sharp decline in the national housing market. Fannie Mae and Freddie Mac suffered a precipitous drop in the value of their mortgage portfolios, pushing the Companies to the brink of default.

2. The 2008 Housing and Economic Recovery Act

Concerned that a default by Fannie and Freddie would imperil the already fragile national economy, Congress enacted the Recovery Act, which established FHFA and authorized it to undertake extraordinary economic measures to resuscitate the Companies. To begin with, the Recovery Act denominated Fannie and Freddie "regulated entit[ies]" subject to the direct "supervision" of FHFA, 12 U.S.C. § 4511(b)(1), and the "general regulatory authority" of FHFA's Director, *id.* § 4511(b)(1), (2). The Recovery Act charged FHFA's Director with "oversee[ing] the prudential operations" of Fannie Mae and Freddie Mac and "ensur[ing] that" they "operate[] in a safe and sound manner," "consistent with the public interest." *Id.* § 4513(a)(1)(A), (B)(i), (B)(v).

The Recovery Act further authorized the Director of FHFA to appoint FHFA as either conservator or receiver for Fannie Mae and Freddie Mac "for the purpose of reorganizing, rehabilitating, or winding up the[ir] affairs." 12 U.S.C. § 4617(a)(2). The Recovery Act invests FHFA as conservator with broad authority and discretion over the operation of Fannie Mae and Freddie Mac. For example, upon appointment as conservator, FHFA "shall * * * immediately succeed to * * * all rights, titles, powers, and privileges of the regulated entity, and of any stockholder, officer, or director of such regulated entity with respect to the regulated entity and the assets of the regulated entity." *Id.* § 4617(b)(2)(A). In addition, FHFA "may * * * take over the assets of and operate the regulated entity," and "may * * * preserve and conserve the assets and property of the regulated entity." *Id.* § 4617(b)(2)(B)(i), (iv).

The Recovery Act further invests FHFA with expansive "[g]eneral powers," explaining that FHFA "may," among other things, "take such action as may be * * * necessary to put the regulated entity in a sound and solvent condition" and "appropriate to carry on the business of the regulated entity and preserve and conserve [its] assets and property[.]" 12 U.S.C. § 4617(b)(2), (2)(D). FHFA's powers also include the discretion to "transfer or sell any asset or liability of the regulated entity in default * * * without any approval, assignment, or consent," *id.* § 4617(b)(2)(G), and to "disaffirm or repudiate [certain] contract[s] or lease[s]," *id.* § 4617(d)(1). *See also id.* § 4617(b)(2)(H) (power to pay the regulated entity's obligations); *id.* § 4617(b)(2)(I) (investing the conservator with subpoena power).

Consistent with Congress's mandate that FHFA's Director protect the "public interest," 12 U.S.C. § 4513(a)(1)(B)(v), the Recovery Act invested FHFA as conservator with the authority to exercise its statutory authority and any "necessary" "incidental powers" in the manner that "the Agency [FHFA] determines is in the best interests of the regulated entity *or the Agency*." *Id.* § 4617(b)(2)(J) (emphasis added).

The Recovery Act separately granted the Treasury Department "temporary" authority to "purchase any obligations and other securities issued by" Fannie and Freddie. 12 U.S.C. §§ 1455(*l*)(1)(A), 1719. That provision made it possible for Treasury to buy large amounts of Fannie and Freddie stock, and thereby infuse them with massive amounts of capital to ensure their continued liquidity and stability.

Continuing Congress's concern for protecting the public interest, however, the Recovery Act conditioned such purchases on Treasury's specific determination that the terms of the purchase would "protect the taxpayer," 12 U.S.C. § 1719(g)(1)(B)(iii), and to that end specifically authorized "limitations on the payment of dividends," *id.* § 1719(g)(1)(C)(vi). A sunset provision terminated Treasury's authority to purchase such securities after December 31, 2009. *Id.* § 1719(g)(4). After that, Treasury was authorized only "to hold, exercise any rights received in connection with, or sell, any obligations or securities purchased." *Id.* § 1719(g)(2)(D).

Lastly, the Recovery Act sharply limits judicial review of FHFA's conservatorship activities, directing that "no court may take any action to restrain or affect the exercise of powers or functions of the Agency as a conservator." 12 U.S.C. § 4617(f).

B. Factual Background

On September 6, 2008, FHFA's Director placed both Fannie Mae and Freddie Mac into conservatorship. The next day, Treasury entered into Senior Preferred Stock Purchase Agreements ("Stock Agreements") with Fannie and Freddie, under which Treasury committed to promptly invest billions of dollars in Fannie and Freddie to keep them from defaulting. Fannie and Freddie had been "unable to access [private] capital markets" to shore up their financial condition, "and the only way they could [raise capital] was with Treasury support." *Oversight Hearing to Examine Recent Treasury and FHFA Actions Regarding the Housing GSEs Before the H. Comm. on Fin. Servs.,* 110th Cong. 12 (2008) (Statement of James B. Lockhart III, Director, FHFA).

In exchange for that extraordinary capital infusion, Treasury received one million senior preferred shares in each company. Those shares entitled Treasury to: (i) a $1 billion senior liquidation preference—a priority right above all other stockholders, whether preferred or otherwise, to receive distributions from assets if the entities were dissolved; (ii) a dollar-for-dollar increase in that liquidation preference each time Fannie and Freddie drew upon Treasury's funding commitment; (iii) quarterly dividends that the Companies could either pay at a rate of 10% of Treasury's liquidation preference or a commitment to increase the liquidation preference by 12%; (iv) warrants allowing Treasury to purchase up to 79.9% of Fannie's and Freddie's common stock; and (v) the possibility of periodic commitment fees over and above any dividends.[1]

The Stock Agreements also included a variety of covenants. Of most relevance here, the Stock Agreements included a flat prohibition on Fannie and Freddie "declar[ing] or pay[ing] any dividend (preferred or otherwise) or mak[ing] any other distribution (by reduction of capital or otherwise), whether in cash, property, securities or a combination thereof" without Treasury's advance consent (unless the dividend or distribution was for Treasury's Senior Preferred Stock or warrants). J.A. 2451.

The Stock Agreements initially capped Treasury's commitment to invest capital at $100 billion per company. It quickly became clear, however, that Fannie and Freddie were in a deeper financial quagmire than first anticipated. So their survival would require even greater capital infusions by Treasury, as sufficient private investors were still nowhere to be found. Consequently, FHFA and Treasury adopted the First Amendment to the Stock Agreements in May 2009, under which Treasury agreed to double the funding commitment to $200 billion for each company.

Seven months later, in a Second Amendment to the Stock Agreements, FHFA and Treasury again agreed to raise the cap, this time to an adjustable figure determined in part by the amount of Fannie's and Freddie's quarterly cumulative losses between 2010 and 2012. As of June 30, 2012, Fannie and Freddie together had drawn $187.5 billion from Treasury's funding commitment.

Through the first quarter of 2012, Fannie and Freddie repeatedly struggled to generate enough capital to pay the 10% dividend they owed to Treasury under the amended Stock Agreements.[2] FHFA and Treasury stated publicly that they worried about perpetuating the "circular practice of the Treasury advancing funds to [Fannie and Freddie] simply to pay dividends back to Treasury," and thereby increasing their debt loads in the process.[3]

Accordingly, FHFA and Treasury adopted the Third Amendment to the Stock Agreements on August 17, 2012. The Third Amendment to the Stock Agreements replaced the previous quarterly 10% dividend formula with a requirement that Fannie and Freddie pay as dividends only the amount, if any, by which their net worth for the quarter exceeded a capital buffer of $3 billion, with that buffer decreasing annually down to zero by 2018. In simple terms, the Third Amendment requires Fannie and Freddie to pay quarterly to Treasury a dividend equal to their net worth—however much or little that might be. Through that new dividend formula, Fannie and Freddie would never again incur more debt just to make their quarterly dividend payments, thereby precluding any dividend-driven downward debt spiral. But neither would Fannie or Freddie be able to accrue capital in good quarters.

Under the Third Amendment, Fannie Mae and Freddie Mac together paid Treasury $130 billion in dividends in 2013, and another $40 billion in 2014. The next year, however, Fannie's and Freddie's quarterly net worth was far lower: Fannie paid Treasury $10.3 billion and Freddie paid Treasury $5.5 billion. *See* FANNIE MAE, FORM 10-K FOR THE FISCAL YEAR ENDED DECEMBER 31, 2015 (Feb. 19, 2016); FREDDIE MAC, FORM 10-K FOR THE FISCAL YEAR ENDED DECEMBER 31, 2015 (Feb. 18, 2016). By comparison, without the Third Amendment, Fannie and Freddie together would have had to pay Treasury $19 billion in 2015 or else draw once again on Treasury's commitment of funds and thereby increase Treasury's liquidation preference. In the first quarter of 2016, Fannie paid Treasury $2.9 billion and Freddie paid Treasury no dividend at all. *See* FANNIE MAE, FORM 10-Q FOR THE QUARTERLY PERIOD ENDED MARCH 31, 2016 (May 5, 2016); FREDDIE MAC, FORM 10-Q FOR THE QUARTERLY PERIOD ENDED MARCH 31, 2016 (May 3, 2016).

Under the Third Amendment, and FHFA's conservatorship, Fannie and Freddie have continued their operations for more than four years. During that time, Fannie and Freddie, among other things, collectively purchased at least 11 million mortgages on single-family owner-occupied properties, and Fannie issued over $1.5 trillion in single-family mortgage-backed securities.[4]

C. Procedural History

In 2013, a number of Fannie Mae and Freddie Mac stockholders filed suit challenging the Third Amendment. Different groups of plaintiffs have pressed different claims. First, various hedge funds, mutual funds, and insurance companies (collectively, "institutional stockholders") argued that (i) FHFA's and Treasury's adoption of the Third Amendment exceeded their authority under the Recovery Act, and (ii) FHFA and Treasury each engaged in arbitrary and capricious conduct, in violation of the Administrative Procedure Act ("APA"). The institutional stockholders requested declaratory and injunctive relief, but no damages.[5]

Second, a class of stockholders ("class plaintiffs") and a few of the institutional stockholders alleged that, in adopting the Third Amendment, FHFA and the Companies breached the terms governing dividends, liquidation preferences, and voting rights in the stock certificates for Freddie's Common Stock and for both Fannie's and Freddie's Preferred Stock. They further alleged that those defendants breached the implied covenants of good faith and fair dealing in those certificates. The class plaintiffs also alleged that FHFA and Treasury breached state-law fiduciary duties owed by a corporation's management and controlling shareholder, respectively. Some of the institutional stockholders asserted similar claims against FHFA. The class plaintiffs asked the court to declare their lawsuit a "proper derivative action," J.A. 277, and to award damages as well as injunctive and declaratory relief.

The district court granted FHFA's and Treasury's motions to dismiss both complaints for failure to state a claim under Federal Rule of Civil Procedure 12(b)(6). *See Perry Capital LLC v. Lew*, 70 F. Supp. 3d 208, 246 (D.D.C. 2014). Specifically, the court dismissed the Recovery Act and APA claims as barred by the Recovery Act's express limitation on judicial review, 12 U.S.C. § 4617(f). The court dismissed the APA claims against Treasury on the same statutory ground, reasoning that Treasury's "interdependent, contractual conduct is directly connected to FHFA's activities as a conservator." *Id.* at 222. The district court explained that "enjoining Treasury from partaking in the Third Amendment would restrain FHFA's uncontested authority to determine how to conserve the viability of [Fannie and Freddie]." *Id.* at 222-223.

Turning to the class plaintiffs' claims for breach of fiduciary duty, the court dismissed those as barred by FHFA's statutory succession to all rights and interests held by Fannie's and Freddie's stockholders, 12 U.S.C. § 4617(b)(2)(A). The court then dismissed the breach of contract and breach of the implied covenant of good faith and fair dealing claims based on liquidation preferences as not ripe because Fannie and Freddie had not been liquidated. Finally, the district court dismissed the dividend-rights claims, reasoning that no such rights exist.[6]

II. Jurisdiction

Before delving into the merits, we pause to assure ourselves of our jurisdiction, as is our duty. *See Steel Co. v. Citizens for a Better Environment,* 523 U.S. 83, 94 (1998) ("On every writ of error or appeal, the first and fundamental question is that of jurisdiction[.]") (citation omitted). A provision of the Recovery Act deprives courts of jurisdiction "to affect, by injunction or otherwise, the issuance or effectiveness of any classification or action of the Director under this subchapter * * * or to review, modify, suspend, terminate, or set aside such classification or action." 12 U.S.C. § 4623(d).

That language does not strip this court of jurisdiction to hear this case. By its terms, Section 4623(d) applies only to "any classification or action of the Director." 12 U.S.C. § 4623(d). Thus, Section 4623(d) prohibits review of the Director's establishment of "risk-based capital requirements * * * to ensure that the enterprises operate in a safe and sound manner, maintaining sufficient capital and reserves to support the risks that arise in the operations and management of the enterprises." *Id.* § 4611(a)(1). In particular, Section 4614 requires "the Director" to "classify" Fannie and Freddie as "adequately capitalized," "undercapitalized," "significantly undercapitalized," or "critically undercapitalized." *Id.* § 4614(a). Classification as undercapitalized or significantly undercapitalized in turn subjects Fannie and Freddie to a host of supervisory actions by "the Director." *See id.* §§ 4615-4616. It is those capital-classification decisions that Section 4623(d) insulates from judicial review.

The Third Amendment was not a "classification or action of the Director" of FHFA. Rather, it was an action taken by FHFA acting as Fannie's and Freddie's conservator. Judicial review of the actions of the agency as *conservator* is addressed by Section 4617(f), not by Section 4623(d)'s particular focus on the Director's own actions. *Compare* 12 U.S.C. § 4617(f) (referencing "powers or functions of *the Agency*") (emphasis added), *with id.* § 4623(d) (referencing "any classification or action of *the Director*") (emphasis added).

FHFA argues that the Director's decision in 2008 to suspend capital classifications of Fannie Mae and Freddie Mac during the conservatorship could be a "classification or action of the Director." FHFA Suppl. Br. at 6-8 (quoting 12 U.S.C. § 4623(d)). Perhaps. But those are not the actions that the institutional stockholders and the class plaintiffs challenge. Instead, they challenge FHFA's decision as conservator to agree to changes in the Stock Agreement and to how Fannie and Freddie will compensate Treasury for its extensive past and promised future infusions of needed capital. Those actions do not fall within Section 4623(d)'s jurisdictional bar for Director-specific actions.

III. Statutory Challenges to the Third Amendment

Turning to the merits, we address first the institutional stockholders' claims that FHFA's and Treasury's adoption of the Third Amendment violated both the Recovery Act and the APA. Both of those statutory claims founder on the Recovery Act's far-reaching limitation on judicial review. Congress was explicit in Section 4617(f) that "no court" can take "any action" that would "restrain or affect"

FHFA's exercise of its "powers or functions * * * as a conservator or a receiver." 12 U.S.C. § 4617(f). We take that law at its word, and affirm dismissal of the institutional stockholders' claims for injunctive and declaratory relief designed to unravel FHFA's adoption of the Third Amendment.

A. Section 4617(f) Bars the Challenges to FHFA Based on the Recovery Act

1. Section 4617(f)'s Textual Barrier to Plaintiffs' Claims for Relief

The institutional stockholders' complaints ask the district court to declare the Third Amendment invalid, to vacate the Third Amendment, and to enjoin FHFA from implementing it. Those prayers for relief fall squarely within Section 4617(f)'s plain textual compass. The institutional stockholders seek to "restrain [and] affect" FHFA's "exercise of powers" "as a conservator" in amending the terms of Fannie's and Freddie's contractual funding agreement with Treasury to guarantee the Companies' continued access to taxpayer-financed capital without risk of incurring new debt just to pay dividends to Treasury. Such management of Fannie's and Freddie's assets, debt load, and contractual dividend obligations during their ongoing business operation sits at the core of FHFA's conservatorship function.

This court has interpreted a nearly identical statutory limitation on judicial review to prohibit claims for declaratory, injunctive, and other forms of equitable relief as long as the agency is acting within its statutory conservatorship authority. The Financial Institutions Reform, Recovery, and Enforcement Act of 1989 ("FIRREA"), Pub. L. No. 101-73, 103 Stat. 183, governs the Federal Deposit Insurance Corporation ("FDIC") when it serves as a conservator or receiver for troubled financial institutions. Section 1821(j) of that Act prohibits courts from "tak[ing] any action * * * to restrain or affect the exercise of powers or functions of [the FDIC] as a conservator or a receiver." 12 U.S.C. § 1821(j).

In multiple decisions, we have held that Section 1821(j) shields from a court's declaratory and other equitable powers a broad swath of the FDIC's conduct as conservator or receiver when exercising its statutory authority. To start with, in *National Trust for Historic Preservation in the United States v. FDIC* (*National Trust I*), 995 F.2d 238 (D.C. Cir. 1993) (per curiam), *aff'd in relevant part,* 21 F.3d 469 (D.C. Cir. 1994), we held that Section 1821(j) "bars the [plaintiff's] suit for injunctive relief" seeking to halt the sale of a building as violating the National Historic Preservation Act, 16 U.S.C. § 470 *et seq.* (repealed December 19, 2014). *See* 995 F.2d at 239. We explained that, because "the powers and functions the FDIC is exercising are, by statute, deemed to be those of a receiver," an injunction against the sale "would surely 'restrain or affect' the FDIC's exercise of those powers or functions." *Id.* Given Section 1821(j)'s "strong language," we continued, it would be "[im]possible * * * to interpret the FDIC's 'powers' and 'authorities' to include the limitation that those powers be subject to—and hence enjoinable for non-compliance with—any and all other federal laws." *Id.* at 240. Indeed, "given the breadth of the statutory language," Section 1821(j) "would appear to bar a court from acting" notwithstanding a "parade of possible violations of existing laws." *National Trust for Historic Preservation in the United States v. FDIC* (*National Trust II*), 21 F.3d 469, 472 (D.C. Cir. 1994) (per curiam) (Wald, J., joined by Silberman, J., concurring).

Again in *Freeman v. FDIC,* 56 F.3d 1394 (D.C. Cir. 1995), this court rejected the plaintiffs' attempt to enjoin the FDIC, as receiver of a bank, from foreclosing on their home, *id.* at 1396. We acknowledged that Section 1821(j)'s stringent limitation on judicial review "may appear drastic," but that "it fully accords with the intent of Congress at the time it enacted FIRREA in the midst of the savings and loan insolvency crisis to enable the FDIC" to act "expeditiously" in its role as conservator or receiver. *Id.* at 1398. Given those exigent financial circumstances, "Section 1821(j) does indeed effect a sweeping ouster of courts' power to grant equitable remedies[.]" *Id.* at 1399; *see also MBIA Ins. Corp. v. FDIC,* 708 F.3d 234, 247 (D.C. Cir. 2013) (In Section 1821(j), "Congress placed 'drastic' restrictions on a court's ability to institute equitable remedies[.]") (quoting *Freeman,* 56 F.3d at 1398).

The rationale of those decisions applies with equal force to Section 4617(f)'s indistinguishable operative language. The plain statutory text draws a sharp line in the sand against litigative interference—through judicial injunctions, declaratory judgments, or other equitable relief—with FHFA's statutorily permitted actions as conservator or receiver. And, as with FIRREA, Congress adopted Section 4617(f) to protect FHFA as it addressed a critical aspect of one of the greatest financial crises in the Nation's modern history.

2. FHFA's Actions Fall Within its Statutory Authority

The institutional stockholders cite language in *National Trust I,* which states that FIRREA's—and by analogy the Recovery Act's—prohibition on injunctive and declaratory relief would not apply if the agency "has acted or proposes to act beyond, or contrary to, its statutorily prescribed, constitutionally permitted, powers or functions," *National Trust I,* 995 F.2d at 240. They then argue that FHFA's adoption of the Third Amendment was out of bounds because, in their view, the Recovery Act "*requires* FHFA as conservator to act independently to conserve and preserve the Companies' assets, to put the Companies in a sound and solvent condition, and to rehabilitate them." Institutional Pls. Br. at 26 (emphasis added). As the institutional stockholders see it, by committing Fannie's and Freddie's quarterly net worth—if any—to Treasury in exchange for continued access to Treasury's taxpayer-funded financial lifelines, FHFA acted like a *de facto* receiver functionally liquidating Fannie's and Freddie's businesses. And FHFA did so, they add, without following the procedural preconditions that the Recovery Act imposes on a receivership, such as publishing notice and providing an alternative dispute resolution process to resolve liquidation claims, *see* 12 U.S.C. § 4617(b)(3)(B)(i), (b)(7)(A)(i).[7]

That exception to the bar on judicial review has no application here because adoption of the Third Amendment falls within FHFA's statutory conservatorship powers, for four reasons.

(i) The Recovery Act endows FHFA with extraordinarily broad flexibility to carry out its role as conservator. Upon appointment as conservator, FHFA "immediately succeed[ed] to * * * all rights, titles, powers, and privileges" not only of Fannie Mae and Freddie Mac, but also "of any stockholder, officer, or director of such regulated entit[ies] with respect to the regulated entit[ies] and the assets of the regulated entit[ies.]" 12 U.S.C. § 4617(b)(2)(A)(i). In addition, among FHFA's many "[g]eneral powers" is its authority to "[o]perate the regulated entity," pursuant to which FHFA "*may,* as conservator or receiver * * * take over the assets of and operate * * * and conduct all business of the regulated entity; * * * collect all obligations and money due the regulated entity; * * * perform all functions of the regulated entity * * *; preserve and conserve the assets and property of the regulated entity; and * * * provide by contract for assistance in fulfilling any function, activity, action, or duty of the Agency as conservator or receiver." *Id.* § 4617(b)(2), (2)(B) (emphasis added). The Recovery Act further provides that FHFA "*may,* as conservator, take such action as may be * * * necessary to put the regulated entity in a sound and solvent condition; and * * * appropriate to carry on the business of the regulated entity and preserve and conserve the assets and property of the regulated entity." *Id.* § 4617(b)(2)(D) (emphasis added). FHFA also "*may* disaffirm or repudiate [certain] contract[s] or lease[s]." *Id.* § 4617(d)(1) (emphasis added); *see also id.* § 4617(b)(2)(G) (providing that FHFA "*may,* as conservator or receiver, transfer or sell any asset or liability of the regulated entity in default" without consent) (emphasis added).

Accordingly, time and again, the Act outlines what FHFA as conservator "may" do and what actions it "may" take. The statute is thus framed in terms of expansive grants of permissive, discretionary authority for FHFA to exercise as the "Agency determines is in the best interests of the regulated entity or the Agency." 12 U.S.C. § 4617(b)(2)(J). "It should go without saying that 'may means may.'" *United States Sugar Corp. v. EPA,* 830 F.3d 579, 608 (D.C. Cir. 2016) (quoting *McCreary v. Offner,* 172 F.3d 76, 83 (D.C. Cir. 1999)). And "may" is, of course, "permissive rather than obligatory." *Baptist Memorial Hosp. v. Sebelius,* 603 F.3d 57, 63 (D.C. Cir. 2010).

Entirely absent from the Recovery Act's text is any mandate, command, or directive to build up capital for the financial benefit of the Companies' stockholders. That is noteworthy because, when Congress wanted to compel FHFA to take specific measures as conservator or receiver, it switched to language of command, employing "shall" rather than "may." *Compare* 12 U.S.C. § 4617(b)(2)(B) (listing actions that FHFA "may" take "as conservator or receiver" to "[o]perate the regulated entity"), *and id.* § 4617(b)(2)(D) (specifying actions that FHFA "may, as conservator" take), *with id.* § 4617(b)(2)(E) (specifying actions that FHFA "shall" take when "acting as receiver"), *and id.* § 4617(b)(14)(A) (specifying that FHFA as conservator or receiver "shall * * * maintain a full accounting"). "[W]hen a statute uses both 'may' and 'shall,' the normal inference is that each is used in its usual sense—the one act being permissive, the other mandatory." *Sierra Club v. Jackson,* 648 F.3d 848, 856 (D.C. Cir. 2011) (internal quotation marks and citation omitted).

In short, the most natural reading of the Recovery Act is that it permits FHFA, but does not compel it in any judicially enforceable sense, to preserve and conserve Fannie's and Freddie's assets and to return the Companies to private operation. And, more to the point, the Act imposes no precise order in which FHFA must exercise its multi-faceted conservatorship powers.

FHFA's execution of the Third Amendment falls squarely within its statutory authority to "[o]perate the [Companies]," 12 U.S.C. § 4617(b)(2)(B); to "reorganiz[e]" their affairs, *id.* § 4617(a)(2); and to "take such action as may be * * * appropriate to carry on the[ir] business," *id.* § 4617(b)(2)(D)(ii). Renegotiating dividend agreements, managing heavy debt and other financial obligations, and ensuring ongoing access to vital yet hard-to-come-by capital are quintessential conservatorship tasks designed to keep the Companies operational. The institutional stockholders no doubt disagree about the necessity and fiscal wisdom of the Third Amendment. But Congress could not have been clearer about leaving those hard operational calls to FHFA's managerial judgment.

That, indeed, is why Congress provided that, in exercising its statutory authority, FHFA "may" "take any action * * * which *the Agency determines* is in the best interests of the regulated entity or the Agency." 12 U.S.C. § 4617(b)(2)(J) (emphasis added). Notably, while FIRREA explicitly permits FDIC to factor the best interests of depositors into its conservatorship judgments, *id.* § 1821(d)(2)(J)(ii), the Recovery Act refers only to the best interests of FHFA and the Companies—and *not* those of the Companies' shareholders or creditors. Congress, consistent with its concern to protect the public interest, thus made a deliberate choice in the Recovery Act to permit FHFA to act in its own best governmental interests, which may include the taxpaying public's interest.

The dissenting opinion (at 8) views Sections 4617(b)(2)(D) and (E) as "mark[ing] the bounds of FHFA's conservator or receiver powers." Not so. As a plain textual matter, the Recovery Act expressly provides FHFA many "[g]eneral powers" "as conservator or receiver," 12 U.S.C. § 4617(b)(2), that are not delineated in Section 4617(b)(2)(D) or (E). *See id.* § 4617(b)(2)(A) (assuming "all rights, titles, powers, and privileges of the regulated entity, and of any stockholder, officer, or director of such regulated entity with respect to the regulated entity and the assets of the regulated entity"); *id.* § 4617(b)(2)(B) (power to "[o]perate the regulated entity"); *id.* § 4617(b)(2)(C) (power to "provide for the exercise of any function by any stockholder, director, or officer of any regulated entity"); *id.* § 4617(b)(2)(G) (power to "transfer or sell any asset or liability of the regulated entity in default"); *id.* § 4617(b)(2)(H) (power to "pay [certain] valid obligations of the regulated entity"); *id.* § 4617(b)(2)(I) (power to issue subpoenas and take testimony under oath). *See also id.* § 4617(d)(1) (granting FHFA as the conservator or receiver the power to "repudiate [certain] contract[s] or lease[s]").

The institutional stockholders also argue that, because Section 4617(b)(2)(D) describes FHFA's "[p]owers as conservator" by providing that FHFA "may * * * take such action as may be" "necessary to put the [Companies] in a sound and solvent condition" and "appropriate to * * * preserve and conserve [their] assets," FHFA may act only when those two conditions are satisfied. Institutional Pls. Reply Br. at 13. In their view, FHFA "does not have other powers as conservator." *Id.*

The short answer is that the Recovery Act says nothing like that. It contains no such language of precondition or mandate. Indeed, if that is what Congress meant, it would have said FHFA "may only" act as necessary or appropriate to those tasks. Not only is that language missing from the Recovery Act, but Congress did not even say that FHFA "should"—let alone, "should first"—preserve and conserve assets or "should" first put the Companies in a sound and solvent condition. Nor did it articulate FHFA's power directly in terms of asset preservation or sound and solvent company operations. What the statute says is that FHFA "*may* * * * take such action as *may* be" "necessary to put the [Companies] in a sound and solvent condition" and "*may* be" "appropriate to * * * preserve or conserve [the Companies'] assets." 12 U.S.C. § 4617(b)(2)(D) (emphases added). So at most, the Recovery Act empowers FHFA to "take such action" as may be necessary or appropriate to fulfill several goals. That is how Congress wrote the law, and that is the law we must apply. *See Barnhart v. Sigmon Coal Co.,* 534 U.S. 438, 461-462 (2002) ("[C]ourts must presume that a legislature says in a statute what it means and means in a statute what it says there.") (quoting *Connecticut Nat'l Bank v. Germain,* 503 U.S. 249, 253-254 (1992)); *Klayman v. Zuckerberg,* 753 F.3d 1354, 1358 (D.C. Cir. 2014) ("[I]t is this court's obligation to enforce statutes as Congress wrote them.").[8]

(ii) Even if the Recovery Act did impose a primary duty to preserve and conserve assets, nothing in the Recovery Act says that FHFA must do that in a manner that returns them to their prior private, capital-accumulating, and dividend-paying condition for all stockholders. *See* Institutional Pls. Br. at 44. Tellingly, the institutional stockholders and dissenting opinion accept that the original Stock Agreements and the First and Second Amendments fit comfortably within FHFA's statutory authority as conservator. *See* Dissenting Op. at 21 (acknowledging that FHFA "manage[d] the Companies within the conservator role" until "the tide turned * * * with the Third Amendment"). But the Stock Agreements and First and Second Amendments themselves both obligated the Companies to pay large dividends to Treasury and prohibited them, without Treasury's approval, from "declar[ing] or pay[ing] any dividend (preferred or otherwise) or mak[ing] any other distribution (by reduction of capital or otherwise), whether in cash, property, securities or a combination thereof." *E.g.,* J.A. 2451; *cf.* 12 U.S.C. § 1719(g)(1)(C)(vi) ("To protect the taxpayers, the Secretary of the Treasury shall take into consideration," *inter alia,* "[r]estrictions on the use of corporation resources, including limitations on the payment of dividends[.]").

That means that FHFA's ability as conservator to give Treasury (and, by extension, the taxpayers) a preferential right to dividends, to the effective exclusion of other stockholders, was already put in place by the unchallenged and thus presumptively proper Stock Agreements and Amendments that predated the Third Amendment. The Third Amendment just locked in an exclusive allocation of dividends to Treasury that was already made possible by—and had been in practice under—the previous agreements, in exchange for continuing the Companies' unprecedented access to guaranteed capital.

The institutional stockholders point to Section 4617(a)(2) as a purported source of FHFA's mandatory duty to return the Companies to their old financial ways. But that Section provides only that FHFA's Director has the power to appoint FHFA as "conservator or receiver for the purpose of reorganizing, rehabilitating, or winding up the affairs of a regulated entity." 12 U.S.C. § 4617(a)(2). It is then the multi-paged remaining portion of Section 4617 that details at substantial length FHFA's many "[g]eneral powers" as conservator or receiver. *Id.* § 4617(b)(2).

Furthermore, that explicit power to "reorganiz[e]" supports FHFA's action because the Third Amendment reorganized the Companies' financial operations in a manner that ensures that quarterly dividend obligations are met without drawing upon Treasury's commitment and thereby increasing Treasury's liquidation preference. FHFA's textual authority to reorganize and rehabilitate the Companies, in other words, forecloses any argument that the Recovery Act made the *status quo ante* a statutorily compelled end game.

In addition, the Recovery Act openly recognizes that sometimes conservatorship will involve managing the regulated entity in the lead up to the appointment of a liquidating receiver. *See* 12 U.S.C. § 4617(a)(4)(D) (providing that appointment of FHFA as a receiver automatically terminates a conservatorship under the Act). The authority accorded FHFA as a conservator to reorganize or rehabilitate the affairs of a regulated entity thus must include taking measures to prepare a company for a variety of financial scenarios, including possible liquidation. Contrary to the dissenting opinion (at 11), that does not make FHFA a "hybrid" conservator-receiver. It makes FHFA a fully armed conservator empowered to address all potential aspects of the Companies' financial condition and operations at all stages when confronting a threatened business collapse of truly unprecedented magnitude and with national economic repercussions.

The institutional stockholders nonetheless argue that, rather than adopt the Third Amendment's dividend allocation, FHFA could instead have adopted a payment-in-kind dividend option that would have increased Treasury's liquidation preference by 12% in return for avoiding a 10% dividend payment. Perhaps. But the Recovery Act does not compel that choice over the variable dividend to Treasury put in place by the Third Amendment. Either way, Section 4617(f) flatly forbids declaratory and injunctive relief aimed at superintending to that degree FHFA's conservatorship or receivership judgments.[9]

The dissenting opinion claims that the Third Amendment's prevention of capital accumulation went too far because it constitutes a "*de facto* receiver[ship]" or "*de facto* liquidation," and thus could not possibly constitute a permissible "conservator" measure. *See* Dissenting Op. at 10, 17, 25. That position presumes the existence of a rigid boundary between the conservator and receiver roles that even the dissenting opinion seems to admit may not exist. *See* Dissenting Op. at 7 (acknowledging that "the line between a conservator and a receiver may not be completely impermeable"). Wherever that line may be, it is not crossed just because an agreement that ensures continued access to vital capital diverts all dividends to the lender, who had singlehandedly saved the Companies from collapse, even if the dividend payments under that agreement may at times be greater than the dividend payments under previous agreements. The proof that no *de facto* liquidation occurred is in the pudding: non-capital-accumulating entities that continue to operate long-term, purchasing more than 11 million mortgages and issuing more than $1.5 trillion in single-family mortgage-backed securities over four years, are not the same thing as liquidating entities.

The argument also overlooks that the Third Amendment's redirection of dividends to Treasury came in exchange for a promise of continued access to necessary capital free of the preexisting risk of accumulating more debt simply to pay dividends to Treasury. Now, after more than eight years of conservatorship—four of which have been under the Third Amendment—Fannie and Freddie have gone from a state of near-collapse to fluctuating levels of profitability. FHFA thus has "carr[ied] on the business of" Fannie and Freddie, 12 U.S.C. § 4617(b)(2)(D)(ii), in that they remain fully operational entities with combined operating assets of $5 trillion, *see* Treasury Resp. Br. at 35. While the dissenting opinion worries that the Companies have "no hope of survival past 2018," Dissenting Op. at 27, the Third

Amendment allows the Companies after 2018 to draw upon Treasury's remaining funding commitment if needed to remedy any negative net worth.[10]

(iii) The institutional stockholders argue that the Third Amendment violated FHFA's "fiduciary and statutory obligations to * * * rehabilitate [the Companies] to normal business operations," Institutional Pls. Br. at 34, because the Amendment was as a factual matter not needed to prevent further indebtedness, and was instead intended to secure a windfall for Treasury (and indirectly taxpayers) at the expense of the stockholders. They likewise contend that FHFA's motivation for adopting the Third Amendment all along has been to liquidate the Companies. They rest those arguments on factual allegations that FHFA and Treasury knew Fannie and Freddie had just turned an economic corner, and had experienced substantial increases in their net worth. In that regard, the institutional stockholders cite evidence that FHFA and Treasury were aware before they adopted the Third Amendment that Fannie and Freddie might each experience a substantial one-time increase in net worth in 2013 and 2014 due to the realization of certain deferred tax assets. They also point to presentations Fannie Mae made to FHFA and Treasury in July and August before the Third Amendment was executed, predicting that Fannie Mae and Freddie Mac would need only small draws from Treasury's commitment (totaling less than $9 billion) to pay Treasury its dividend through the year 2022. In the institutional stockholders' view, FHFA's alleged knowledge that rosier days were dawning shows that FHFA had no legitimate conservatorship reason to adopt the Third Amendment rather than to pursue measures that would allow the Companies to accumulate capital and return to the dividend-paying *status quo ante*.

To be clear, though, the institutional stockholders argue that the Third Amendment would be just as flawed in their view even if Fannie and Freddie had made *no* profits, were badly hemorrhaging money in 2013 and 2014, and thus were in dire need of the Third Amendment's promise of continued access to capital, free from dividend obligations that would have increased still further Treasury's liquidation preference. *See* Oral Arg. Tr. 22-24 (Q: "[D]oes the argument that they were not acting as a proper conservator depend on the fact that they were in fact profitable? A: "[N]o, it doesn't.").[11]

Treasury argues, by contrast, that FHFA was taking a broader and longer-term view of the Companies' financial condition. In almost every quarter before the Third Amendment was adopted, Fannie and Freddie had been unable to make their dividend payments to Treasury without taking on more debt to Treasury. In SEC filings, Fannie and Freddie themselves predicted that they would be unable to pay the 10% dividend over the long term. *See, e.g.,* J.A. 1983 (Fannie Mae statement that it "do[es] not expect to generate net income or comprehensive income in excess of [its] annual dividend obligation to Treasury over the long term[,]" so its "dividend obligation to Treasury will increasingly drive [its] future draws under the senior [Stock Agreement]"); *id.* at 2160 (similar for Freddie Mac). Other market participants shared that view. *See, e.g., id.* at 655 (Moody's report).

According to Treasury, the Third Amendment put a structural end to "the circular practice of the Treasury advancing funds to [Fannie and Freddie] simply to pay dividends back to Treasury." Treasury Press Release, *supra.* Said another way, the Third Amendment changed the dividend formula to require Fannie and Freddie to pay whatever dividend they could afford—however little, however much— to prevent them from ever again having to fruitlessly borrow from Treasury to pay Treasury. If Fannie and Freddie made profits, Treasury would reap the rewards; if they suffered losses, Treasury would have to forgo payment entirely.

The problem with the institutional stockholders' argument is that the factual question of whether FHFA adopted the Third Amendment to arrest a "debt spiral" or whether it was intended to be a step in furthering the Companies' return to "normal business operations" is not dispositive of FHFA's authority to adopt the Third Amendment. Nothing in the Recovery Act confines FHFA's conservatorship judgments to those measures that are driven by financial necessity. And for purposes of applying Section 4617(f)'s strict limitation on judicial relief, allegations of motive are neither here nor there, as the dissenting opinion agrees (at 20). The stockholders cite nothing—nor can we find anything—in the Recovery Act that hinges FHFA's exercise of its conservatorship discretion on particular motivations. *See Leon County, Fla. v. FHFA*, 816 F. Supp. 2d 1205, 1208 (N.D. Fla. 2011) ("Congress barred judicial review of the conservator's actions without making an exception for actions said to be taken from an improper motive.").

Likewise, the duty that the Recovery Act imposes on FHFA to comply with receivership procedural protections textually turns on FHFA actually liquidating the Companies. *See, e.g.,* 12 U.S.C. § 4617(b)(3)(B) ("The receiver, in any case involving the liquidation or winding up of the affairs of [Fannie or Freddie], shall * * * promptly publish a notice to the creditors of the regulated entity to present their claims, together with proof, to the receiver[.]"). Undertaking permissible conservatorship measures even with a receivership mind would not be out of statutory bounds.

The institutional stockholders' burden instead is to show that FHFA's actions were frolicking outside of statutory limits as a matter of law. What matters then is the substantive measures that FHFA took, and nothing in the Recovery Act mandated that FHFA take steps to return Fannie Mae and Freddie Mac at the first sign of financial improvement to the old economic model that got them into so much trouble in the first place. Nor did anything in the Recovery Act forbid FHFA from adopting measures that took a more comprehensive, wait-and-see view of the Companies' long-term financial condition, or simply kept the Companies' heads above water while FHFA observed their economic performance over time and through ever-changing market conditions. *See, e.g., supra* note 11.[12]

(iv) The institutional stockholders cite state-law and historical sources to suggest that FHFA was not acting as a common-law conservator normally would when it adopted the Third Amendment. *See* Institutional Pls. Br. at 29-33. The problem for the plaintiffs is that arguments about the contours of common-law conservatorship do nothing to show that FHFA exceeded *statutory* bounds, which is what *National Trust I* referenced. Under the Recovery Act, FHFA as conservator may "take any action authorized by this section, which the Agency determines is in the best interests of the regulated entity *or the Agency.*" 12 U.S.C. § 4617(b)(2)(J)(ii) (emphasis added). That explicit statutory authority to take conservatorship actions in the conservator's own interest, which here includes the public and governmental interests, directly undermines the dissenting opinion's supposition that Congress intended FHFA to be nothing more than a common-law conservator. *See*

Dissenting Op. at 16 (asserting that, in the common-law probate context, a conservator is generally "forbid[den] * * * from acting for the benefit of the conservator himself or a third party").

On top of that, Congress in the Recovery Act gave FHFA the ability to obtain from Treasury capital infusions of unprecedented proportions, as long as the deal FHFA struck with Treasury "protect[ed] the taxpayer" and "provide[d] stability to the financial markets." 12 U.S.C. §§ 1455, 1719(g)(1)(B)(i), (iii). That $200 billion-plus lifeline is what saved the Companies—none of the institutional stockholders were willing to infuse that kind of capital during desperate economic times—and bears no resemblance to the type of conservatorship measures that a private common-law conservator would be able to undertake. Indeed, the dissenting opinion acknowledges that FHFA "operating as a conservator may act in its own interests to protect both the Companies and the taxpayers from whom [FHFA] was ultimately forced to borrow[.]" Dissenting Op. at 19. To paraphrase the dissenting opinion (at 27), Congress made clear in the Recovery Act that FHFA is not your grandparents' conservator. For good reason.

The dissenting opinion asserts that our reading of Section 4617(b)(2)(J)(ii) effectively "forecloses *any* opportunity for meaningful judicial review of FHFA's actions," Dissenting Op. at 18, and decries the abandonment of the "rule of law," *see id.* at 2. That is quite surprising to hear. As the balance of our opinion makes clear—much of which the dissenting opinion joins—the Recovery Act only limits judicial *remedies* (banning injunctive, declaratory, and other equitable relief) after a court determines that the actions taken fall within the scope of statutory authority. The Act does not prevent either constitutional claims (none are raised here) or judicial review through cognizable actions for damages like breach of contract.

The dissenting opinion also argues that the court's holding is inconsistent with Congress's provision of judicial review for FHFA's actions in Section 4617(a)(5). Dissenting Op. at 18. But Section 4617(a)(5) permits judicial review *only* at the behest of a regulated entity itself and even then *only* of the Director's decision to appoint FHFA as a conservator or receiver.[13] That narrow focus of the provision is underscored by the requirement that the lawsuit must be promptly filed within thirty days of the appointment decision (a deadline that none of the plaintiffs here met). We thus beg to differ with the dissenting opinion's claim (at 18, 22) that Section 4617(a)(5) provides more intrusive judicial review for actions FHFA takes when acting as a receiver, many of which would presumably occur outside of that thirty-day filing window. *Cf. James Madison Ltd. by Hecht v. Ludwig,* 82 F.3d 1085, 1092-1094 (D.C. Cir. 1996) (distinguishing between provisions in FIRREA for judicial review of the appointment of FDIC as conservator or receiver and those governing judicial review of the FDIC's exercise of its powers as conservator or receiver). Nothing in our reading of Section 4617(b)(2)(J)(ii), which governs what decisions a properly appointed conservator or receiver makes, undermines the sharply cabined opportunity for early-stage judicial review of the appointment decision itself.

* * * * *

In short, for all of their arguments that FHFA has exceeded the bounds of conservatorship, the institutional stockholders have no textual hook on which to hang their hats. Indeed, they do not dispute that FHFA had the authority as conservator to enter the Companies into the Stock Agreements with Treasury to raise vitally needed capital, to agree to pay dividends to Treasury on the stocks sold as part of that capital-raising bargain, to foreclose dividend payments to private stockholders in that process, *cf.* 12 U.S.C. § 1719(g)(1)(C)(vi), or to amend the terms of the Stock Agreements. The dissenting opinion even admits that FHFA's actions prior to the Third Amendment—which include the debt-inducing dividends paid under the First and Second Amendments as well as the original Stock Agreements—were "within the conservator role." *See* Dissenting Op. at 21.

What the institutional stockholders and dissenting opinion take issue with, then, is the allocated amount of dividends that FHFA negotiated to pay its financial-lifeline stockholder— Treasury—to the exclusion of other stockholders, and that decision's feared impact on business operations in the future. But Section 4617(f) prohibits us from wielding our equitable relief to second-guess either the dividend-allocating terms that FHFA negotiated on behalf of the Companies, or FHFA's business judgment that the Third Amendment better balances the interests of all parties involved, including the taxpaying public, than earlier approaches had. *See County of Sonoma v. FHFA,* 710 F.3d 987, 993 (9th Cir. 2013) ("[I]t is not our place to substitute our judgment for FHFA's[.]"). Because the Third Amendment falls within FHFA's broad conservatorship authority under the Recovery Act, we must enforce Section 4617(f)'s explicit prohibition on the equitable relief that the institutional stockholders seek.

B. Section 4617(f) Bars the Challenges to FHFA's Compliance with the APA

The institutional stockholders also claim that FHFA's adoption of the Third Amendment amounted to arbitrary and capricious agency action in violation of the APA. That argument cannot surmount Section 4617(f)'s barrier to equitable relief—the only form of relief statutorily authorized for an APA violation. *See* 5 U.S.C. § 702 (allowing "action in a court * * * seeking relief other than money damages"); *Cohen v. United States,* 650 F.3d 717, 723 (D.C. Cir. 2011) (en banc). Indeed, Section 4617(f)'s strict limitation on judicial review would be an empty promise if it evaporated upon the assertion that FHFA's actions ran afoul of some other statute.

We accordingly "do not think it possible, in light of the strong language of" Section 4617(f) to read the Recovery Act's grant of "'powers' and 'authorities' to include the limitation that those powers be subject to—and hence enjoinable for non-compliance with—any and all other federal laws." *See National Trust I,* 995 F.2d at 240. Just as we cannot second-guess FHFA's conservatorship decisions under the Recovery Act, we cannot quarterback those actions under the APA either.

C. Section 4617(f) Bars the Challenges to Treasury's Compliance with the Recovery Act and the APA

Lastly, the institutional stockholders argue that declaratory and injunctive relief should be available against Treasury because its own actions in signing on to the Third Amendment both violated the Recovery Act and were arbitrary and capricious in violation of the APA. Those claims fall within Section 4617(f)'s sweep as well.

To be sure, Section 4617(f) most explicitly bars judicial relief against FHFA, and not Treasury. But Section 4617(f) also forecloses judicial relief that would "affect" the exercise of FHFA's "powers or functions" as conservator or receiver. 12 U.S.C. § 4617(f). An action "can 'affect' the exercise of powers by an agency without being aimed directly at [that agency]." *Hindes v. FDIC,* 137 F.3d 148, 160 (3d Cir. 1998); *see also Telematics Int'l, Inc. v. NEMLC Leasing Corp.,* 967 F.2d 703, 707 (1st Cir. 1992) (Enjoining a third party "would have the same effect, from the FDIC's perspective, as directly enjoining the FDIC[.]").

In this case, the effect of any injunction or declaratory judgment aimed at Treasury's adoption of the Third Amendment would have just as direct and immediate an effect as if the injunction operated directly on FHFA. After all, it takes (at least) two to contract, and the Companies, under FHFA's conservatorship, are just as much parties to the Third Amendment as Treasury. One side of the agreement cannot exist without the other.

Accordingly, Section 4617(f)'s prohibition on relief that "affect[s]" FHFA applies here because the requested injunction's operation would have exactly the same force and effect as enjoining FHFA directly. *See Dittmer Properties, L.P. v. FDIC,* 708 F.3d 1011, 1017 (8th Cir. 2013) ("Dittmer's request for injunctive relief is barred by § 1821(j), even though the FDIC is no longer the holder of the note, because the relief requested—a declaration that the note is void as to Dittmer— affects the FDIC's ability to function as receiver in th[is] case.").[14]

The institutional stockholders argue that this case is different because they claim Treasury "violated a provision of federal law unrelated to the conduct of a receivership." Institutional Pls. Reply Br. at 25. But Section 4617(f)'s plain language focuses on the "[e]ffect" of "any action" on FHFA's exercise of its powers; the cause of that effect is textually irrelevant. What matters here is that the institutional stockholders' claims against Treasury are integrally and inextricably interwoven with FHFA's conduct as conservator. Specifically, the complaint alleges that Treasury violated a provision of the Recovery Act—the very same law that governs FHFA's conservatorship activities—and that the Recovery Act prevented Treasury from entering into the Third Amendment with the Companies, operating at the direction of FHFA as conservator. Such a holding would just be another way of declaring that the Recovery Act barred FHFA from entering the Companies into the Third Amendment with Treasury. Treasury's action thus cannot be enjoined without simultaneously unraveling FHFA's own exercise of its powers and functions.

In so holding, we have no occasion to decide whether or how Section 4617(f) might apply to "an order against a third party [that] would be of little consequence to [FHFA's] overall functioning as receiver" or conservator, *Hindes,* 137 F.3d at 161, or to third-party activities that are by their nature less interwoven with FHFA's judgments as conservator or receiver. It is enough that, in this case, the direct and unavoidable effect of invalidating Treasury's contract with the Companies would be to void the contract with Treasury that FHFA concluded on the Companies' behalf. That would be a "dramatic and fundamental" incursion on FHFA's exercise of its conservatorship authority. *Id.*[15]

IV. The Class Plaintiffs' Claims

The class plaintiffs appeal the dismissal of their claims against Treasury, the FHFA, and the Companies (as nominal defendants) for breach of fiduciary duty,[16] and against the FHFA and the Companies for breach of contract and for breach of the implied covenant of good faith and fair dealing.[17] Two groups of institutional shareholders — namely, the Arrowood plaintiffs and the Fairholme plaintiffs — likewise asserted common-law claims in district court (in addition to their APA claims), but they did not preserve their appeal against the dismissal of those claims: They did not raise in their opening brief their claims for breach of contract. The Fairholme plaintiffs also forfeited their claim for breach of fiduciary duty against the FHFA by failing to raise in their opening brief the district court's alternative holding that the "claim is derivative. . . and, therefore, barred under § 4617(b)(2)(A)(i)," *Perry Capital LLC,* 70 F. Supp. 3d at 229 n.24. *See Jankovic v. Int'l Crisis Grp.,* 494 F.3d 1080, 1086 (D.C. Cir. 2007).

A. The Claims Against Treasury

The class plaintiffs alleged that by executing the Third Amendment Treasury violated fiduciary duties to the Companies and their shareholders that are imposed by state corporate law because it is a controlling shareholder in the Companies. We have subject matter jurisdiction over the class plaintiffs' claims for breach of fiduciary duty against Treasury because "all civil actions to which [Freddie Mac] is a party shall be deemed to arise under the laws of the United States, and the district courts of the United States shall have original jurisdiction of all such actions." 12 U.S.C. § 1452(f); *see also Lackey v. Wells Fargo Bank, N.A.,* 747 F.3d 1033, 1035 n.2 (8th Cir. 2014) ("Because Freddie Mac is a party to this case, the district court had original jurisdiction pursuant to 12 U.S.C. § 1452(f)").[18]

Whether sovereign immunity shields Treasury from suit is a trickier question because the class plaintiffs forfeited any argument under the Federal Tort Claims Act, 28 U.S.C. § 1346(b), by failing to respond to Treasury's contention that the FTCA is inapplicable. *Cf. NetworkIP, LLC v. FCC,* 548 F.3d 116, 120 (D.C. Cir. 2008) ("[A]rguments in favor of subject matter jurisdiction can be waived by inattention or deliberate choice"). The class plaintiffs argue the APA provides an alternate waiver of sovereign immunity for their claims for breach of fiduciary duty against Treasury. Under 5 U.S.C. § 702,

> An action in a court of the United States seeking relief other than money damages and stating a claim that an agency or an officer or employee thereof acted or failed to act in an official capacity or under color of legal authority shall

not be dismissed nor relief therein be denied on the ground that it is against the United States. . . .

We agree with the class plaintiffs with respect to their pleas for declaratory relief against Treasury for several reasons.

First, the class plaintiffs sought "relief other than money damages," to which the waiver of § 702 is limited, by requesting a declaration that Treasury breached its fiduciary duties. *Bowen v. Massachusetts,* 487 U.S. 879, 892 (1988) (holding declaratory relief is not "money damages").[19] Therefore, § 702 waives immunity for the class plaintiffs' claims for breach of fiduciary duty insofar as they seek declaratory relief.

Second, § 702 waives Treasury's immunity for the claims for breach of fiduciary duty because they are not founded upon a contract. The waiver in § 702 does not apply "if any other statute that grants consent to suit expressly or impliedly forbids the relief which is sought." *See also Albrecht v. Comm. on Emp. Benefits,* 357 F.3d 62, 67-68 (D.C. Cir. 2004). We have interpreted the Tucker Act, 28 U.S.C. § 1491(a)(1), which waives sovereign immunity for some claims "founded . . . upon" a contract and brought in the U.S. Court of Federal Claims, to "impliedly forbid[]" contract claims against the Government from being brought in district court under the waiver in the APA. *Albrecht,* 357 F.3d at 67-68. Treasury on appeal does not dispute the class plaintiffs' characterization of their claims as not contractual, though the agency argued in district court that the claims were in essence a contract action because it "assumed [any fiduciary duties] in entering into the [Stock Agreements]" with Fannie Mae and Freddie Mac. Treasury Defs. Mem. in Support of Mot. To Dismiss or for Summ. J., Doc. No. 19-1, at 44 *In re Fannie Mae/Freddie Mac Senior Preferred Stock Purchase Agreement Class Action Litigs.,* 1:13-mc-01288 (Jan. 17, 2014). That Treasury has not briefed the issue on appeal does not, however, relieve us of our obligation to assure ourselves we have jurisdiction, *see Steel Co.,* 523 U.S. at 94; this obligation extends to sovereign immunity because it is "jurisdictional in nature," *FDIC v. Meyer,* 510 U.S. 471, 475 (1994), and may not be waived by an agency's conduct of a lawsuit, *Dep't of the Army v. FLRA,* 56 F.3d 273, 275 (D.C. Cir. 1995).

In order to determine whether an action is in "its essence" contractual, we examine "the source of the rights upon which the plaintiff bases its claims" and "the type of relief sought (or appropriate)." *Megapulse, Inc. v. Lewis,* 672 F.2d 959, 968 (D.C. Cir. 1982); *see also Albrecht,* 357 F.3d at 68-69. The class plaintiffs claim that, because it is the controlling shareholder, Treasury owes the Companies and their shareholders "fiduciary duties of due care, good faith, loyalty, and candor." J.A. 275 ¶ 177; *see also* Derivative Compl., Doc. No. 39, at 27 ¶ 74 *In re Fannie Mae/Freddie Mac,* 1:13-mc-01288 (July 30, 2014). These claims against Treasury are not "a disguised contract action," *Megapulse, Inc.,* 672 F.2d at 968, because they do not seek to enforce any duty imposed upon Treasury by the Stock Agreements — the only relevant contracts to which Treasury is a party. Although any fiduciary duty allegedly owed by Treasury as a controlling shareholder in the Companies arose from its purchase of shares pursuant to the Stock Agreements, we do not think that "*any* case requiring *some* reference to . . . a contract is necessarily *on the contract* and therefore directly within the Tucker Act." *Id.* at 967-68. The class plaintiffs do not contend Treasury breached the terms of the Stock Agreements nor otherwise invoke them except to establish that Treasury is a controlling shareholder.

The relief the class plaintiffs seek does not further illuminate whether their claims are essentially contractual. In *Megapulse,* we held the action was not founded upon a contract in part because the plaintiffs sought no specific performance of the contract and no damages, 672 F.2d at 969, presumably because specific performance is an explicitly contractual remedy and because "damages are a prototypical contract remedy," *A & S Council Oil Co. v. Lader,* 56 F.3d 234, 240 (D.C. Cir. 1995). Here, the class plaintiffs seek a declaration that Treasury breached its fiduciary duties and an award of "compensatory damages" in favor of the Companies. These forms of relief are not specific to actions that sound in contract, *cf. Spectrum Leasing Corp. v. United States,* 764 F.2d 891, 894-95 (D.C. Cir. 1985) (concluding a claim was essentially contractual in part because the relief sought amounted to "the classic contractual remedy of specific performance"), and any relief would not be determined by reference to the terms of the contract, *cf. Albrecht,* 357 F.3d at 69 (concluding a claim was essentially contractual in part because a contract would "determine whether the relief sought . . . is available").[20] The plaintiffs also seek rescission with respect to their claim regarding Fannie Mae. This plea does not render the claim essentially contractual even though rescission is typically a remedy for breach of contract because there is no question that any breach of contract claim would concern the Purchase Agreement and the class plaintiffs seek rescission of only the Third Amendment. In sum, the Tucker Act does not "impliedly forbid[]" us from awarding relief against Treasury based on the waiver of immunity in § 702 because the class plaintiffs' claims are not founded upon a contract.

Third, Treasury's argument that § 702 does not waive its immunity from suit for state law claims is foreclosed by our precedent. We have "repeatedly" and "expressly" held in the broadest terms that "the APA's waiver of sovereign immunity applies to any suit whether under the APA or not." *Trudeau v. FTC,* 456 F.3d 178, 186 (D.C. Cir. 2006) (internal quotation marks omitted). Furthermore, we concluded in *United States Information Agency v. Krc,* 989 F.2d 1211 (D.C. Cir. 1993), that § 702 waived sovereign immunity for a (presumably) state tort claim against the Government because the FTCA did not "impliedly forbid" the non-monetary relief the plaintiff sought. *Id.* at 1216 (citing § 702).

Fourth, the class plaintiffs forthrightly point out that we have held "the waiver of sovereign immunity under § 702 is limited by the 'adequate remedy' bar of § 704," *Nat'l Wrestling Coaches Ass'n v. Dep't of Educ.,* 366 F.3d 930, 947 (D.C. Cir. 2004) (quoting 5 U.S.C. § 704); *see also Transohio Sav. Bank v. Dir., OTS,* 967 F.2d 598, 607 (D.C. Cir. 1992), and go on to argue we should look to more recent authority that contradicts those holdings, *see Trudeau,* 456 F.3d at 187-89. Again, that Treasury has no response to this point does not relieve us of our duty to ascertain whether Treasury's immunity has been waived. We agree with the class plaintiffs that the holdings in *National Wrestling* and *Transohio Savings* are no longer good law.

Section 704 provides that "final agency action for which there is no other adequate remedy in a court [is] subject to judicial review." 5 U.S.C. § 704. In *Cohen v. United States,* 650 F.3d 717 (D.C. Cir. 2011) (en banc), after first concluding that immunity from suit was waived by § 702 with nary a mention of the adequate remedy bar of § 704, *id.* at 722-31, we held that whether there is an "other adequate remedy" for the purpose of § 704 determines whether a litigant states "a valid cause of action" under the APA. *Id.* at 731. We did not expressly speak to whether the adequate remedy bar limits immunity, but it strains credulity to think the choice to address the adequate remedy bar not as a condition of immunity, but instead as a requirement for a cause of action, was not deliberate in that case.

A further reason for this reading of *Cohen* is that we there cited approvingly, *id.* at 723, our prior holding in *Trudeau,* 456 F.3d 178, that the requirement of final agency action in § 704 is not a condition of the waiver of immunity in § 702, but instead limits the cause of action created by the APA, *id.* at 187-89. The holding of *Trudeau* and its endorsement in *Cohen* clearly override *National Wrestling* and *Transohio Savings:* We see no textual or logical basis for construing § 704 — which limits judicial review to "final agency action for which there is no other adequate remedy" — to condition a waiver of sovereign immunity on the absence of an adequate remedy but not on the presence of final agency action. In *Trudeau* we concluded the finality requirement does not bear upon the waiver of immunity in § 702 because the waiver "is not limited to APA cases — and hence . . . it applies regardless of whether the elements of an APA cause of action [under § 704] are satisfied." *Id.* at 187. This reasoning applies equally to the adequate remedy bar. *See Viet. Veterans of Am. v. Shinseki,* 599 F.3d 654, 661 (D.C. Cir. 2010) (relying in part upon our holding that the finality requirement no longer limits a court's subject matter jurisdiction to reach the same conclusion for the adequate remedy bar and referring to them collectively as the "the APA's reviewability provisions").

Furthermore, in a departure from prior cases, we have several times recognized that the finality requirement and adequate remedy bar of § 704 determine whether there is a cause of action under the APA, not whether there is federal subject matter jurisdiction. *Cent. for Auto Safety v. Nat'l Highway Traffic Safety Admin.,* 452 F.3d 798, 805-06 (D.C. Cir. 2006); *Trudeau,* 456 F.3d at 183-85; *Shinseki,* 599 F.3d at 661; *Cohen,* 650 F.3d at 731 & n.10. Reading § 704 to limit only the cause of action that may be brought under the APA and not the grant of immunity in § 702 is in line with our new understanding of § 704 as narrowly focused upon the requirements for the APA cause of action. We therefore hold that § 702 waives Treasury's immunity regardless whether there is another adequate remedy under § 704 because the absence of such a remedy is instead an element of the cause of action created by the APA.

In sum, pursuant to 12 U.S.C. § 1452(f) and 28 U.S.C. § 1291, we have subject matter jurisdiction over the class plaintiffs' claims against Treasury for breach of fiduciary duty, and the Congress waived the agency's immunity from suit for these claims, insofar as they are for declaratory relief, in the APA, 5 U.S.C. § 702. We nonetheless affirm the district court's dismissal of the claims for a declaratory judgment. As discussed in greater detail above, *supra* at 38-40, 12 U.S.C. § 4617(f) bars us from awarding equitable relief against Treasury with respect to the Third Amendment because doing so would impermissibly "restrain or affect the exercise of powers or functions of the [FHFA] as a conservator."

B. The Claims Against the FHFA and the Companies

The class plaintiffs sued the FHFA (and the Companies, as nominal defendants) for breach of fiduciary duties imposed on a corporation's management under state law. They also alleged claims against the FHFA and the Companies for breach of contract and breach of the implied covenant of good faith and fair dealing. We have subject matter jurisdiction over the class plaintiffs' claims under 12 U.S.C. § 1452(f). As mentioned above, our obligation to assure ourselves we have jurisdiction, *see Steel Co.,* 523 U.S. at 94, extends to sovereign immunity because it is jurisdictional, *Meyer,* 510 U.S. at 475. "A waiver. . . must be unequivocally expressed in statutory text," *Lane v. Pena,* 518 U.S. 187, 192 (1996), so the Government may not waive immunity merely by its conduct in a lawsuit, *Dep't of the Army,* 56 F.3d at 275. We therefore disregard FHFA's point that the agency, "in its capacity as Conservator, has not asserted sovereign immunity with respect to [its] execution of the Third Amendment." FHFA July 2016 Supp. Br. at 4.

Assuming the FHFA has sovereign immunity when it acts on behalf of the Companies as conservator, *cf. Auction Co. of Am. v. FDIC,* 141 F.3d 1198, 1201-02 (D.C. Cir. 1998) (holding a suit against the FDIC was a suit against the United States for purposes of jurisdiction and sovereign immunity where the FDIC "did not act as receiver for any particular depository"), the Congress has waived the agency's immunity by consenting to suit. The Congress has granted Freddie Mac "power . . . to sue and be sued . . . in any State, Federal, or other court," 12 U.S.C. § 1452(c)(7), and has granted Fannie Mae the same "power . . . to sue and to be sued . . . in any court of competent jurisdiction, State or Federal," *id.* § 1723a(a). The FHFA "by operation of law[] immediately succeed[ed] to . . . all . . . powers" of the Companies upon its appointment as conservator — including the Companies' power to sue and be sued — under the so-called Succession Clause of the Recovery Act. *Id.* § 4617(b)(2)(A)(i). Such a statutory grant of power to "sue and be sued" constitutes an "unequivocally expressed" waiver of sovereign immunity. *United States v. Nordic Vill. Inc.,* 503 U.S. 30, 33-34 (1992); *see also Meyer,* 510 U.S. at 475.[21]

By providing for the FHFA to succeed to the Companies' power to sue and be sued, the Congress has given its express consent that the FHFA is subject to suit in the same way the Companies would otherwise be when the agency acts on their behalf as conservator. This understanding is borne out by the FHFA's other functions under the Succession Clause, which further provides that the FHFA succeeds to "all rights, titles, powers, and privileges of the regulated entity." § 4617(b)(2)(A)(i). The Supreme Court interpreted the nearly identical provision in FIRREA to "place[] the FDIC in the shoes of the [entity in receivership], to work out its claims under state law." *O'Melveny & Myers v. FDIC,* 512 U.S. 79, 86-87 (1994) (interpreting 12 U.S.C. § 1821(d)(2)(A)(i)). The Recovery Act further empowers the FHFA, as conservator, to "take over the assets of and operate the [Companies] with all the powers of [their] shareholders, . . . directors, and . . . officers" and to "perform all functions of the [Companies] in the name of the [Companies]." 12 U.S.C. § 4617(b)(2)(B)(i), (iii).

What if the class plaintiffs' claims for breach of fiduciary duty are cognizable under the FTCA, 28 U.S.C. § 1346(b)? The FTCA does not withdraw the Congress's waiver of immunity in this case, for the FTCA provides:

> The authority of any federal agency to sue and be sued in its own name shall not be construed to authorize suits against such federal agency on claims which are cognizable under [the FTCA], and the remedies provided by this title in such cases shall be exclusive.

28 U.S.C. § 2679(a). The Congress has not, however, authorized the FHFA to be sued "in its own name" by enacting a "sue and be sued" clause specifically for the agency. Instead, the Congress has granted the FHFA the power to be sued just as the Companies would be absent a conservatorship insofar as the agency steps into the shoes of the Companies and acts on their behalf to defend alleged breaches of their obligations. Because the Companies, pre-conservatorship, were not affected by the FTCA proviso cited above, neither is the FHFA when it is sued for an action taken on their behalf — in this case, the Third Amendment.[22] Nor would the Tucker Act, 28 U.S.C. § 1491(a)(1), require the class plaintiffs to file their claims for breach of contract in the Court of Federal Claims. "If a separate waiver of sovereign immunity and grant of jurisdiction exist, district courts may hear cases over which, under the Tucker Act alone, the Court of Federal Claims would have exclusive jurisdiction." *Auction Co. of Am. v. FDIC*, 132 F.3d 746, 752 n.4 (D.C. Cir. 1997) (suit for breach of contract), *clarified on denial of reh'g*, 141 F.3d 1198 (1998).

1. The Succession Clause

The FHFA and the class plaintiffs dispute whether the common-law claims against the agency are barred by the so-called Succession Clause, which provides that the FHFA, as conservator, "succeed[s] to" the stockholders' rights "with respect to" the Companies and their assets, 12 U.S.C. § 4617(b)(2)(A)(i). In *Kellmer v. Raines*, 674 F.3d 848 (D.C. Cir. 2012), we held the Succession Clause "plainly transfers [to the FHFA the] shareholders' ability to bring derivative suits" on behalf of the Companies, but left open whether it transfers claims as to which the FHFA would face a manifest conflict of interest. *Id.* at 850.

The class plaintiffs argue the Succession Clause should not be read to bar their derivative claims for breach of fiduciary duty because the FHFA would face a conflict of interest in pursuing, on behalf of the Companies, claims against itself. They also argue the Succession Clause does not apply to their direct claims for breach of contract and for breach of fiduciary duty. The FHFA responds that the Succession Clause transfers to it the right to bring derivative suits without exception, that all the claims of the class plaintiffs are derivative, and that the Succession Clause also transfers any direct claims to the agency.

The district court held the statute bars all the class plaintiffs' claims and dismissed them "pursuant to [Federal Rule of Civil Procedure] 12(b)(1) for lack of standing," *Perry Capital LLC*, 70 F. Supp. 3d at 233, 235 n.39, 239 n.45, but whether the Succession Clause bars the claims has no bearing upon standing under Article III of the Constitution of the United States. *See Lujan v. Defs. of Wildlife*, 504 U.S. 555, 560-61 (1992). The district court's error, however, is of no moment; we simply examine the issue under Rule 12(b)(6). *EEOC v. St. Francis Xavier Parochial Sch.*, 117 F.3d 621, 624 (D.C. Cir. 1997) ("Although the district court erroneously dismissed the action pursuant to Rule 12(b)(1), we could nonetheless affirm the dismissal if dismissal were otherwise proper based on failure to state a claim under Federal Rule of Civil Procedure 12(b)(6)").

We conclude the Succession Clause transfers to the FHFA without exception the right to bring derivative suits but not direct suits. The class plaintiffs' claims for breach of fiduciary duty are derivative and therefore barred, but their contract-based claims are direct and may therefore proceed.

a. The Succession Clause bars derivative suits, but not direct suits

The Recovery Act transfers some of the shareholders' rights to the FHFA during conservatorship and receivership and provides that others are retained by the shareholders during conservatorship but terminated during receivership. Specifically, the Succession Clause provides that "as conservator or receiver" the FHFA "shall . . . by operation of law, immediately succeed to . . . all rights, titles, powers, and privileges of the regulated entity, and of any stockholder . . . with respect to the regulated entity and [its] assets." § 4617(b)(2)(A)(i). The Recovery Act further limits shareholders' rights during receivership by providing that the FHFA's appointment as receiver and consequent succession to the shareholders' rights "terminate[s] all rights and claims that the stockholders . . . of the regulated entity may have against the assets or charter of the regulated entity or the [FHFA] . . . except for their right to payment, resolution, or other satisfaction of their claims" in the administrative claims process. § 4617(b)(2)(K)(i).

The Recovery Act thereby transfers to the FHFA all claims a shareholder may bring derivatively on behalf of a Company whilst claims a shareholder may lodge directly against the Company are retained by the shareholder in conservatorship but terminated during receivership. The Act distinguishes between the transfer of rights "with respect to the regulated entity and [its] assets" in the Succession Clause and the termination of rights "against the assets or charter of the regulated entity" in § 4617(b)(2)(K)(i). Rights "with respect to" a Company and its assets are only those an investor asserts derivatively on the Company's behalf. *Cf. Levin v. Miller,* 763 F.3d 667, 672 (7th Cir. 2014) (so interpreting the analogous provision of FIRREA, 12 U.S.C. § 1821(d)(2)(A)(i)). Rights and claims "against the assets or charter of the regulated entity" are an investor's direct claims against and rights to the assets of the Company once it is placed in receivership in order to be liquidated, *see* 12 U.S.C. § 4617(b)(2)(E); that the Recovery Act terminates such rights and claims in receivership indicates that shareholders' direct claims against and rights in the Companies survive during conservatorship.[23]

This reading is borne out by the statutory context. If the Succession Clause transferred all of the stockholders' rights to the FHFA in conservatorship and receivership, as the FHFA contends, then they would have no rights left to assert during the administrative claims process should a Company be liquidated. That result is plainly precluded by § 4617(b)(2)(K)(i), which excepts from termination upon the FHFA's appointment as receiver a shareholder's "right to payment, resolution, or other satisfaction of [his or her] claims." Furthermore, we see the logic in permitting the shareholders to retain their rights to bring suit against a Company during conservatorship and terminating those rights when the Agency institutes an administrative claims process as required when it becomes a receiver. *See* 12 U.S.C. § 4617(b)(3)-(5). We note that the Federal Circuit recently held, albeit without considering the Succession Clause, that Fannie Mae's former Chief Financial Officer had no takings claim based on the company's failure — pursuant to FHFA's regulations — to pay severance benefits as mandated by his employment contract because the CFO "was left with the right to enforce his contract against Freddie Mac in a breach of contract action . . . under state contract law." *Piszel v. United States,* 833 F.3d 1366, 1377 (Fed. Cir. 2016).

The class plaintiffs argue that because, as shareholders, they retain rights in the Companies during a conservatorship, the Succession Clause should be read to permit them to sue derivatively to protect those rights when the FHFA has a conflict of interest. They point to the decisions of two other circuits interpreting 12 U.S.C. § 1821(d)(2)(A), a nearly identical provision in FIRREA, to permit such an exception. *See First Hartford Corp. Pension Plan & Tr. v. United States,* 194 F.3d 1279, 1295 (Fed. Cir. 1999); *Delta Sav. Bank v. United States,* 265 F.3d 1017, 1022-23 (9th Cir. 2001). Contrary to the class plaintiffs' assertions, two circuit court decisions do not so clearly "settle[] the meaning of [the] existing statutory provision" in FIRREA that we must conclude the Congress intended *sub silentio* to incorporate those rulings into the Recovery Act. *Merrill Lynch v. Dabit,* 547 U.S. 71, 85 (2006).

Nor are we convinced by the reasoning of those two cases that the Succession Clause implicitly excepts derivative suits where the FHFA would have a conflict of interest. The courts in those cases thought it would be irrational to transfer to an agency the right to sue itself derivatively because "the very object of the derivative suit mechanism is to permit shareholders to file suit on behalf of a corporation when the managers or directors of the corporation, perhaps due to a conflict of interest, are unable or unwilling to do so." *First Hartford,* 194 F.3d at 1295; *see also Delta Sav.,* 265 F.3d at 1022-23 (extending the exception to suits against certain agencies with which the conservator or receiver has an "interdependent" relationship and "managerial and operational overlap"). As the district court in this case noted, however, it makes little sense to base an exception to the rule against derivative suits in the Succession Clause "on the purpose of the 'derivative suit mechanism,'" rather than the plain statutory text to the contrary. *See Perry Capital LLC,* 70 F. Supp. 3d at 230-31. We therefore conclude the Succession Clause does not permit shareholders to bring derivative suits on behalf of the Companies even where the FHFA will not bring a derivative suit due to a conflict of interest.

b. The class plaintiffs' claims for breach of fiduciary duty are derivative but their contract-based claims are direct and may proceed

Having concluded the Succession Clause extends to derivative, but not direct, claims, it follows that the class plaintiffs' claims for breach of fiduciary duty are barred but their contract-based claims may proceed. The class plaintiffs contend they asserted both direct and derivative claims for breach of fiduciary duty, alleging a direct claim against the FHFA "with respect to . . . Fannie Mae" under Delaware law.[24] Class Pls. Br. at 21-22. In order to determine whether these claims are direct or derivative, we must examine (1) "[w]ho suffered the alleged harm" and (2) "who would receive the benefit of the recovery." *Tooley v. Donaldson, Lufkin & Jenrette, Inc.,* 845 A.2d 1031, 1035 (Del. 2004); *see also Gentile v. Rossette,* 906 A.2d 91, 99-101 (Del. 2006). A suit is direct if "[t]he stockholder . . . demonstrate[s] that the duty breached was owed to the stockholder" and that "[t]he stockholder's claimed direct injury [is] independent of any alleged injury to the corporation." *Tooley,* 845 A.2d at 1039.

The class plaintiffs did not plead a direct claim for breach of fiduciary duty because they did not seek relief that would accrue directly to them. They instead requested a declaration that, "through the Third Amendment, Defendant[] FHFA ... breached [its] ... fiduciary dut[y] to Fannie Mae," and sought an award of "compensatory damages and disgorgement in favor of Fannie Mae." J.A. 278 ¶¶ 4-5. Both forms of relief would benefit Fannie Mae directly and the shareholders only derivatively. *See Tooley,* 845 A.2d at 1035. The class plaintiffs also asked the district court to declare the Third Amendment was not "in the best interests of Fannie Mae or its shareholders, and constituted waste and a gross abuse of discretion," J.A. 278 ¶ 3, but a declaration that only partially resolves a cause of action does not remedy any injury. *Cf. Calderon v. Ashmus,* 523 U.S. 740, 746-47 (1998) (holding that the case or controversy requirement of Article III was not satisfied where a prisoner sought a declaratory judgment as to the validity of a defense a state was likely to raise in his habeas action). In the introductory portion of their complaint, the class plaintiffs also sought rescission of the Third Amendment to remedy the alleged breach of fiduciary duty, but the class plaintiffs requested this relief only for their derivative claim. J.A. 215 ¶ 3 ("This is also a derivative action brought by Plaintiffs on behalf of Fannie Mae, seeking . . . equitable relief, including rescission, for breach of fiduciary duty"), 226 ¶ 27 ("[T]his action also seeks, derivatively on behalf of Fannie Mae, an award of . . . equitable relief with respect to such breach, including rescission of the Third Amendment").

In any event, the class plaintiffs forfeited in district court any argument that their claim for breach of fiduciary duty is direct. In its motion to dismiss, the FHFA contended the class plaintiffs' claims for breach of fiduciary duty were derivative, but the class plaintiffs did not respond by arguing they asserted a direct claim. Although they occasionally referred to the FHFA's fiduciary duties to the shareholders, the class plaintiffs did not develop any argument that the claims are direct and instead discussed separately why the Succession Clause does not bar "Their Direct Contract-Based Claims," Mem. in Opp'n to Mot. to Dismiss, Doc. No. 33 at 25 *In re Fannie Mae/Freddie Mac,* 1:13-mc-01288 (Mar. 21, 2014) (hereinafter Class Pls. Opp'n to Mot. to Dismiss), and "Their Derivative Claims" for breach of fiduciary duty, *id.* at 32. The class plaintiffs then characterize their only count of breach of fiduciary duty as asserting "derivative claims." *Id.*

The class plaintiffs ask for a "remand to allow [them] to pursue their direct fiduciary breach claims regarding the Fannie Mae Third Amendment." Class Pls. Br. at 23. At oral argument they cited *DKT Memorial Fund v. Agency for International Development,* 810 F.2d 1236 (D.C. Cir. 1987), in which this court, "in the interest of justice," granted counsel's motion at oral argument to amend the complaint in order to correct an inadvertent error and then ruled the claims, as amended, were not subject to dismissal upon the grounds asserted by the defendants. *Id.* at 1239. In this case the class plaintiffs ask us to grant them leave to amend the complaint to add a new claim they are not asking us to rule on but instead want to pursue in district court. We see no reason to oust the district judge from making that decision in the first instance when the case returns to district court for further proceedings on certain of the plaintiffs' contract-based claims.

The district court also held the class plaintiffs' contract-based claims were derivative. *Perry Capital LLC,* 70 F. Supp. 3d at 235 & n.39, 239 n.45. Contrary to the FHFA's assertions, the class plaintiffs sufficiently appealed this ruling. Their statement of issues on appeal comprises whether the Succession Clause "bars any of Appellants' claims in this action." Furthermore, that the class plaintiffs' contract-based claims are direct is apparent from their extensive discussion of the FHFA's alleged breach of their contractual rights and the harm the alleged breach caused them.

Indeed, the contract-based claims are obviously direct "because they belong to" the class plaintiffs "and are ones that only [the class plaintiffs] can assert." *Citigroup Inc. v. AHW Inv. P'ship,* 140 A.3d 1125, 1138 (Del. 2016). These are "not claims that could plausibly belong to" the Companies because they assert that the Companies breached contractual duties owed to the class plaintiffs by virtue of their stock certificates. *Id.* We therefore do not subject them to the two-part test set forth in *Tooley,* which determines "when a cause of action for breach of fiduciary duty or to enforce rights belonging to the corporation itself must be asserted derivatively." *NAF Holdings, LLC v. Li & Fung (Trading) Ltd.,* 118 A.3d 175, 176 (Del. 2015). The two-part test is necessary "[b]ecause directors owe fiduciary duties to the corporation and its stockholders, [and] there must be some way of determining whether stockholders can bring a claim for breach of fiduciary duty directly, or whether a particular fiduciary duty claim must be brought derivatively." *Citigroup Inc.,* 140 A.3d at 1139 (footnote omitted). *Tooley* has no application "when a plaintiff asserts a claim based on the plaintiff's own right." *Id.* at 1139-40; *El Paso Pipeline GP Co. v. Brinckerhoff,* 2016 WL 7380418, at *9 (Del. Dec. 20, 2016) ("[W]hen a plaintiff asserts a claim based upon the plaintiff's own right . . . *Tooley* does not apply").[25]

2. The Class Plaintiffs' contract-based claims

As a preliminary matter, the class plaintiffs assert the bar to equitable relief of 12 U.S.C. § 4617(f), discussed above, does not apply "to equitable claims related to contractual breaches," Class Pls. Br. at 34-35, but this argument is forfeit because it was not raised in district court. *Bennett v. Islamic Republic of Iran,* 618 F.3d 19, 22 (D.C. Cir. 2010). Accordingly, we evaluate the class plaintiffs' contract-based claims only insofar as they seek damages. As discussed in greater detail above, *supra* at 17-37, an award of equitable relief against the FHFA with respect to the Third Amendment would impermissibly "restrain or affect the exercise of powers or functions of the [FHFA] as a conservator," § 4617(f), and a similar award against the Companies would plainly achieve the same result. The class plaintiffs next challenge the district court's dismissal under Rules 12(b)(1) and (6) of their claims against the FHFA and the Companies for breach of contract and breach of the implied covenant as to the provisions in the stock certificates dealing with voting and dividend rights and liquidation preferences. Upon *de novo* review, *Kim v. United States,* 632 F.3d 713, 715 (D.C. Cir. 2011), we affirm the dismissal of all claims except for those regarding the liquidation preferences and the claim for breach of implied covenant regarding dividend rights.

a. Voting rights

The class plaintiffs contend the Third Amendment violates their stock certificates that, with some variations not relevant here, provide that a vote of two thirds of the stockholders is required "to authoriz[e], effect[] or validat[e] the amendment, alteration, supplementation or repeal of any of the provisions of [the] Certificate if such [action] would materially and adversely affect the . . . terms or conditions of the [stock]." J.A. 251. The class plaintiffs claim they were entitled to vote on the Third Amendment because it "nullif[ied] their right ever to receive a dividend or liquidation distribution," and thereby "materially and adversely affect[ed]" them. Class Pls. Reply Br. at 11. The FHFA does not respond to this argument on appeal, and the district court nowhere addressed it in dismissing the contract-based claims. We nonetheless affirm the district court's dismissal. Although the Third Amendment makes it impossible for the class plaintiffs to receive dividends or a liquidation preference, it was not an "alteration, supplementation or repeal of . . . provisions" in the certificates. Those provisions guarantee only the right to vote on certain changes to the certificates, not on any corporate action that affects the rights guaranteed by the certificates.

b. Dividend rights

The class plaintiffs' various stock certificates provide (with irrelevant variations in wording) that stockholders will "be entitled to receive, ratably, when, as and if declared by the Board of Directors, in its sole discretion . . . [,] non-cumulative cash dividends," J.A. 248, or "shall be entitled to receive, ratably, dividends . . . when, as and if declared by the Board," J.A. 250. According to the class plaintiffs, the certificates thereby guarantee them a right to dividends, discretionary though they may be. We agree with the FHFA's response that the class plaintiffs have no enforceable right to dividends because the certificates accord the Companies complete discretion to declare or withhold dividends.

The class plaintiffs argue they nonetheless have a contractual right to discretionary dividends because Delaware and Virginia limit directors' discretion to withhold dividends. This limit upon a board's discretion stems from its fiduciary duties to shareholders, not from the terms of their stock certificates. *See Gabelli & Co. v. Liggett Grp. Inc.,* 479 A.2d 276, 280 (Del. 1984) (Dividends may not be withheld as a result of "fraud or gross abuse of discretion"); *Penn v. Pemberton & Penn, Inc.,* 189 Va. 649, 658, 53 S.E.2d 823, 828 (Va. 1949) (Failure to declare dividends is actionable if it "is so arbitrary, or so unreasonable, as to amount to a breach of trust"). Such fiduciary duties have no bearing upon whether the terms of the contracts imposed a duty to declare dividends, as the class plaintiffs alleged.

Lastly, the class plaintiffs advance a convoluted argument that the Third Amendment violated their rights to receive mandatory dividends (1) for their preferred stock before any distributions on common stock, and (2) for their common stock "ratably," along with other holders of such stock. Before the Third Amendment, the class plaintiffs assert, Treasury could have received a dividend exceeding the 10% coupon on its liquidation preference only by exercising its option to purchase up to 79.9% of the Companies' common stock, and the payment of any dividend on that common stock would have required distributions to the class plaintiffs as well. To the class plaintiffs, it follows that their right to mandatory dividends was breached by the provision of the Third Amendment for dividends to be paid to Treasury that could (and at times did) exceed the 10% coupon. This argument fails because the plaintiffs have not shown their certificates guarantee that more senior shareholders will not exhaust the funds available for distribution as dividends. The class plaintiffs contend the Third Amendment "was a fiduciary breach, and hence cannot be relied on as the basis for nullifying the *mandatory* priority and ratability rights," Class Pls. Br. at 39, but this argument goes to their claims for breach of fiduciary duty, addressed above.

The class plaintiffs next challenge the district court's dismissal of their claim that the implied covenant prohibited the FHFA from depriving them of the opportunity to receive dividends. The class plaintiffs argue the district court wrongly concluded the FHFA did not breach the implied covenant because it acted within its statutory authority. *See Perry Capital LLC,* 70 F. Supp. 3d at 238-39. The FHFA contends the plaintiffs "try to impose fiduciary and other duties on the Conservator to always act in the best interests of shareholders, when [the Recovery Act] instead authorizes the Conservator to '[act] in the best interests of the [Companies] or the Agency,'" FHFA Br. at 18 (citing § 4617(b)(2)(J)(ii)) (second alteration in original), and that "the Conservator's discretion to declare dividends, unlike that of a corporate board, is without limitation," *id.* at 56 n.21. Insofar as the FHFA argues (and the district court held) that the Recovery Act preempts state law imposing an implied covenant, this approach is foreclosed by the plain text of the Recovery Act and by our precedent.

Virginia and Delaware law imposing an implied covenant of good faith and fair dealing is not "an obstacle to the accomplishment and execution of the full purposes and objectives of Congress," *Hillman v. Maretta,* 133 S. Ct. 1943, 1949-50 (2013), and is therefore not preempted by the Recovery Act. The Recovery Act provides that the FHFA, as conservator, "may disaffirm or repudiate any contract" the Companies executed before the conservatorship "the performance of which the conservator . . . determines to be burdensome," 12 U.S.C. § 4617(d)(1), "within a reasonable period following" the agency's appointment as conservator, *id.* § 4617(d)(2). That the Recovery Act permits the FHFA in some circumstances to repudiate contracts the Companies concluded before the conservatorship indicates that the Companies' contractual obligations otherwise remain in force. *Cf. Waterview Mgmt. Co. v. FDIC,* 105 F.3d 696, 700-01 (D.C. Cir. 1997) (so interpreting a nearly identical provision in FIRREA, 12 U.S.C. § 1821(e)). Furthermore, by providing for the FHFA to succeed to "all rights, titles, powers, and privileges of the [Companies]," 12 U.S.C. § 4617(b)(2)(A)(i), the Recovery Act places the FHFA "'in the shoes'" of the Companies and "does not permit [the agency] to increase the value of the [contract] in its hands by simply 'preempting' out of existence pre-receivership contractual obligations." *Waterview Mgmt. Co.,* 105 F.3d at 701 (quoting *O'Melveny & Myers,* 512 U.S. at 87, in reaching the same conclusion for the Succession Clause of FIRREA, 12 U.S.C. § 1821(d)(2)(A)(i)).

The class plaintiffs next challenge the district court's conclusion that they failed to state a claim for breach of the implied covenant, which they contend required the

Companies — and, therefore, their conservator — to act reasonably and not to deprive them of the fruits of their bargain, namely the opportunity to receive dividends. The FHFA urges us to affirm the district court's determination that the class plaintiffs' lack of an enforceable contractual right to dividends foreclosed the claim that the implied covenant instead provided such a right. *See Perry Capital LLC,* 70 F. Supp. 3d at 238.

Under Delaware law, "[e]xpress contractual provisions always supersede the implied covenant," *Gerber v. Enter. Prod. Holdings, LLC,* 67 A.3d 400, 419 (Del. 2013), *overruled on other grounds by Winshall v. Viacom Int'l Inc.,* 76 A.3d 808, 815 n.13 (Del. 2013), and "one generally cannot base a claim for breach of the implied covenant on conduct authorized by the terms of the agreement," *Dunlap v. State Farm Fire & Cas. Co.,* 878 A.2d 434, 441 (Del. 2005). Here, however, the stock certificates upon which the class plaintiffs rely provide for dividends "if declared by the Board of Directors, in its sole discretion." J.A. 248. A party to a contract providing for such discretion violates the implied covenant if it "act[s] arbitrarily or unreasonably." *Nemec v. Shrader,* 991 A.2d 1120, 1126 (Del. 2010); *see also Gerber,* 67 A.3d at 419 ("When exercising a discretionary right, a party to the contract must exercise its discretion reasonably" (emphasis omitted)). What is arbitrary or unreasonable depends upon "the parties' reasonable expectations at the time of contracting." *Nemec,* 991 A.2d at 1126; *see also Gerber,* 67 A.3d at 419. Virginia law similarly provides "where discretion is lodged in one of two parties to a contract . . . such discretion must, of course, be exercised in good faith." *Historic Green Springs, Inc. v. Brandy Farm, Ltd.,* 32 Va. Cir. 98, at *3 (Va. Cir. 1993) (alteration in original); *see also Va. Vermiculite, Ltd. v. W.R. Grace & Co.—Conn.,* 156 F.3d 535, 542 (4th Cir. 1998).

We remand this claim, insofar as it seeks damages, for the district court to evaluate it under the correct legal standard, namely, whether the Third Amendment violated the reasonable expectations of the parties at the various times the class plaintiffs purchased their shares. We note that the class plaintiffs specifically allege that some class members purchased their shares before the Recovery Act was enacted in July 2008 and the FHFA was appointed conservator the following September, while others purchased their shares later, but the class plaintiffs define their class action to include more broadly "all persons and entities who held shares . . . and who were damaged thereby," J.A. 262-63. The district court may need to redefine or subdivide the class depending upon what the various plaintiffs could reasonably have expected when they purchased their shares. For those who purchased their shares after the enactment of the Recovery Act and the FHFA's appointment as conservator, the analysis should consider, *inter alia,* (1) Section 4617(b)(2)(J)(ii) (authorizing the FHFA to act "in the best interests of the [Companies] or the Agency"), (2) Provision 5.1 of the Stock Agreements, J.A. 2451, 2465 (permitting the Companies to declare dividends and make other distributions only with Treasury's consent), and (3) pertinent statements by the FHFA, *e.g.,* J.A. 217 ¶ 8, referencing *Statement of FHFA Director James B. Lockhart at News Conference Announcing Conservatorship of Fannie Mae and Freddie Mac* (Sept. 7, 2008) (The "FHFA has placed Fannie Mae and Freddie Mac into conservatorship. That is a statutory process designed to stabilize a troubled institution with the objective of returning the entities to normal business operations. FHFA will act as the conservator to operate the Enterprises until they are stabilized.").

The district court also held the class plaintiffs "fail to plead claims of breach of the implied covenant against the [Companies]" because they allege only that the FHFA's actions were arbitrary and unreasonable. *Perry Capital LLC,* 70 F. Supp. 3d at 239. This is a distinction without a difference because the action they challenge — the FHFA's adoption of the Third Amendment — was taken on behalf of the Companies. The Companies and the FHFA are thus identically situated for purposes of this claim.

c. Liquidation preferences

The class plaintiffs also allege the FHFA, by adopting the Third Amendment, breached the guarantees in their stock certificates and in the implied covenant to a share of the Companies' assets upon liquidation because it ensured there would be no assets to distribute. The FHFA urges us to affirm the district court's dismissal of these claims as unripe. *See Perry Capital LLC,* 70 F. Supp. 3d at 234-35.

"The ripeness doctrine generally deals with when a federal court can or should decide a case," *Am. Petrol. Inst. v. EPA,* 683 F.3d 382, 386 (D.C. Cir. 2012), and has both constitutional and prudential facets. Ripeness "shares the constitutional requirement of standing that an injury in fact be certainly impending." *Nat'l Treasury Emps. Union v. United States,* 101 F.3d 1423, 1427 (D.C. Cir. 1996). We decide whether to defer resolving a case for prudential reasons by "evaluat[ing] (1) the fitness of the issues for judicial decision and (2) the hardship to the parties of withholding court consideration." *Nat'l Park Hosp. Ass'n v. Dep't of Interior,* 538 U.S. 803, 808 (2003); *see Am. Petrol.,* 683 F.3d at 386.

These claims satisfy the constitutional requirement because the class plaintiffs allege not only that the Third Amendment poses a "certainly impending" injury, *Nat'l Treasury,* 101 F.3d at 1427, but that it immediately harmed them by diminishing the value of their shares. *Cf. State Nat'l Bank v. Lew,* 795 F.3d 48, 56 (D.C. Cir. 2015) (holding unripe a claim seeking recovery for a present loss in share-price in part because the plaintiffs failed to allege "their current investments are worth less now, or have been otherwise adversely affected now"). The class plaintiffs allege the Third Amendment, by depriving them of their right to share in the Companies' assets when and if they are liquidated, immediately diminished the value of their shares. The case or controversy requirement of Article III of the U.S. Constitution is therefore met.

The FHFA (like the district court) says the claims are not prudentially ripe because there can be no breach of any contractual obligation to distribute assets until the Companies are required to perform, namely, upon liquidation. Not so. Under the doctrine of anticipatory breach, "a voluntary affirmative act which renders the obligor unable . . . to perform" is a repudiation, RESTATEMENT (SECOND) OF CONTRACTS § 250(b), that "ripens into a breach prior to the time for performance . . . if the promisee elects to treat it as such" by, for instance, suing for damages, *Franconia Assocs. v. United States,* 536 U.S. 129, 143 (2002) (internal quotation marks omitted); RESTATEMENT (SECOND) OF

CONTRACTS §§ 253(1), 256 cmt. c. *Accord Lenders Fin. Corp. v. Talton,* 249 Va. 182, 189, 455 S.E.2d 232, 236 (Va. 1995); *W. Willow-Bay Court, LLC v. Robino-Bay Court Plaza, LLC,* C.A. No. 2742-VCN, 2009 WL 458779, at *5 & n.37 (Del. Ch. Feb. 23, 2009). An anticipatory breach satisfies prudential ripeness and therefore enables the promisee to seek damages immediately upon repudiation, *Sys. Council EM-3 v. AT&T Corp.,* 159 F.3d 1376, 1383 (D.C. Cir. 1998) ("[I]f a performing party unequivocally signifies its intent to breach a contract, the other party may seek damages immediately under the doctrine of anticipatory repudiation"). In other words, anticipatory breach is "a doctrine of accelerated ripeness" because it "gives the plaintiff the option to have the law treat the promise to breach [or the act rendering performance impossible] as a breach itself." *Homeland Training Ctr., LLC v. Summit Point Auto. Research Ctr.,* 594 F.3d 285, 294 (4th Cir. 2010) (citing *Franconia Assocs.,* 536 U.S. at 143).

The class plaintiffs' claims for breach of contract with respect to liquidation preferences are better understood as claims for anticipatory breach, so there is no prudential reason to defer their resolution.[26] Nor do we see any prudential obstacle to adjudicating the class plaintiffs' claim that repudiating the guarantee of liquidation preferences constitutes a breach of the implied covenant. Our holding that the claims are ripe sheds no light on the merit of those claims and, contrary to the assertions in the dissenting opinion (at 17), has no bearing upon the scope of the FHFA's statutory authority as conservator under the Recovery Act. Whether the class plaintiffs stated claims for breach of contract and breach of the implied covenant is best addressed by the district court in the first instance.[27] That court's earlier conclusion in the negative was made for "largely the same reasons" that it had held the claims unripe, *Perry Capital LLC,* 70 F. Supp. 3d at 236, and so must be reconsidered in light of our reversal of the court's holding on ripeness.

V. Conclusion

We affirm the judgment of the district court that the institutional plaintiffs' claims against the FHFA and Treasury alleging arbitrary and capricious conduct and conduct in excess of their statutory authority are barred by 12 U.S.C. § 4617(f). We affirm the district court's dismissal of their common-law claims because they were not properly appealed. With respect to the class plaintiffs' claims, we affirm the judgment of the district court on all claims except for the claims alleging breach of contract and breach of the implied covenant of good faith and fair dealing regarding liquidation preferences and the claim for breach of the implied covenant with respect to dividend rights, which claims we remand for further proceedings consistent with this opinion.

So ordered.

BROWN, Circuit Judge, dissenting in part.

One critic has called it "wrecking-ball benevolence," James Bovard, Editorial, *Nothing Down: The Bush Administration's Wrecking-Ball Benevolence,* BARRON'S, Aug. 23, 2004, http://tinyurl.com/Barrons-Bovard; while another, dismissing the compassionate rhetoric, dubs it "crony capitalism," Gerald P. O'Driscoll, Jr., Commentary, *Fannie/Freddie Bailout Baloney,* CATO INST., http://tinyurl.com/Cato-O-Driscoll (last visited Feb. 13, 2017). But whether the road was paved with good intentions or greased by greed and indifference, affordable housing turned out to be the path to perdition for the U.S. mortgage market. And, because of the dominance of two so-called Government Sponsored Entities ("GSE"s)—the Federal National Mortgage Association ("Fannie Mae" or "Fannie") and the Federal Home Loan Mortgage Corporation ("Freddie Mac" or "Freddie," collectively with Fannie Mae, the "Companies")—the trouble that began in the subprime mortgage market metastasized until it began to affect most debt markets, both domestic and international.

By 2008, the melt-down had become a crisis. A decade earlier, government policies and regulations encouraging greater home ownership pushed banks to underwrite mortgages to allow low-income borrowers with poor credit history to purchase homes they could not afford. Banks then used these risky mortgages to underwrite highly-profitable mortgage-backed securities—bundled mortgages—which hedge funds and other investors later bought and sold, further stoking demand for ever-riskier mortgages at ever-higher interest rates. Despite repeated warnings from regulators and economists, the GSEs' eagerness to buy these loans meant lenders had a strong incentive to make risky loans and then pass the risk off to Fannie and Freddie. By 2007, Fannie and Freddie had acquired roughly a trillion dollars' worth of subprime and nontraditional mortgages—approximately 40 percent of the value of all mortgages purchased. And since more risk meant more profit and the GSEs knew they could count on the federal government to cover their losses, their appetite for riskier mortgages was entirely rational.

The housing boom generated tremendous profit for Fannie and Freddie. But then the bubble burst. Individuals began to default on their loans, wrecking neighborhoods, wiping out the equity of prudent homeowners, and threatening the stability of banks and those who held or guaranteed mortgage-backed assets. In March 2008, Bear Sterns collapsed, requiring government funds to finance a takeover by J.P. Morgan Chase. In July, the Federal Deposit Insurance Corporation (the "FDIC") seized IndyMac. But Bear Sterns and IndyMac—huge companies, to be sure—paled in comparison to Fannie and Freddie, which together backed $5 trillion in outstanding mortgages, or nearly half of the $12 trillion U.S. mortgage market. In late-July 2008, Congress passed and President Bush signed the Housing and Economic Recovery Act of 2008, authorizing a new government agency, the Federal Housing Finance Agency ("FHFA" or the "Agency"), to serve as conservator or receiver for Fannie and Freddie if certain conditions were met; Fannie and Freddie were placed into FHFA conservatorship the following month. Only weeks thereafter, Lehman Brothers failed, the government bailed out A.I.G., Washington Mutual declared bankruptcy, and Wells Fargo obtained government assistance for its buy-out of Wachovia.

There is no question that FHFA was created to confront a serious problem for U.S. financial markets. The Court apparently concludes a crisis of this magnitude justifies extraordinary actions by Congress. Perhaps it might. But even in a time of exigency, a nation governed by the rule of law cannot transfer broad and unreviewable power to a government entity to do whatsoever it wishes with the assets of these Companies. Moreover, to remain within constitutional parameters, even a less-sweeping delegation of authority would require an explicit and comprehensive framework. *See Whitman v. Am. Trucking Ass'ns, Inc.,* 531 U.S. 457, 468 (2001) ("Congress . . . does not alter the fundamental details of a regulatory scheme in vague terms or ancillary provisions—it does not, one might say, hide elephants in mouseholes.") Here, Congress did *not* endow FHFA with unlimited authority to pursue its own ends; rather, it seized upon the statutory text that had governed the FDIC for decades and adapted it ever so slightly to confront the new challenge posed by Fannie and Freddie.

Perhaps this was a bad idea. The perils of massive GSEs had been indisputably demonstrated. Congress could have faced up to the mess forthrightly. Had both Companies been placed into immediate receivership, the machinations that led to this litigation might have been avoided. *See* Thomas H. Stanton, *The Failure of Fannie Mae and Freddie Mac and the Future of Government Support for the Housing Finance System,* 14-15 (Brooklyn L. Sch., Conference Draft, Mar. 27, 2009), http://tinyurl.com/Stanton-Conference (arguing Fannie and Freddie could have been converted into wholly owned government corporations with limited lifespans in order to stabilize the mortgage market). But the question before the Court is not whether the good guys have stumbled upon a solution. There are no good guys. The question is whether the government has violated the legal limits imposed on its own authority.

Regardless of whether Congress had many options or very few, it chose a well-understood and clearly-defined statutory framework—one that drew upon the common law to clearly delineate the outer boundaries of the Agency's conservator or, alternatively, receiver powers. FHFA pole vaulted over those boundaries, disregarding the plain text of its authorizing statute and engaging in *ultra vires* conduct. Even now, FHFA continues to insist its authority is *entirely without limit* and argues for a complete ouster of federal courts' power to grant injunctive relief to redress *any action* it takes while purporting to serve in the conservator role. *See* FHFA Br. 21. While I agree with much of the Court's reasoning, I cannot conclude the anti-injunction provision protects FHFA's actions here or, more generally, endorses FHFA's stunningly broad view of its own power. Plaintiffs— not all innocent and ill-informed investors, to be sure—are betting the rule of law will prevail. In this country, *everyone* is entitled to win that bet. Therefore, I respectfully dissent from the portion of the Court's opinion rejecting the Institutional and Class Plaintiffs' claims as barred by the anti-injunction provision and all resulting legal conclusions.

I.

The Housing and Economic Recovery Act of 2008 ("HERA" or the "Act"), Pub. L. No. 110-289, 122 Stat. 2654 (codified at 12 U.S.C. § 4511, *et seq.*), established a new financial regulator, FHFA, and endowed it with the authority to act as conservator or receiver for Fannie and Freddie. The Act also temporarily expanded the United States Treasury's ("Treasury") authority to extend credit to Fannie and Freddie as well as purchase stock or debt from the Companies. My disagreement with the Court turns entirely on its interpretation of HERA's text.

Pursuant to HERA, FHFA may supervise and, if needed, operate Fannie and Freddie in a "safe and sound manner," "consistent with the public interest," while "foster[ing] liquid, efficient, competitive, and resilient national housing finance markets." 12 U.S.C. § 4513(a)(1)(B). The statute further authorizes the FHFA Director to "appoint [FHFA] as conservator *or* receiver" for Fannie and Freddie "for the purpose of reorganizing, rehabilitating, or winding up [their] affairs." *Id.* § 4617(a)(1), (2) (emphasis added). In order to ensure FHFA would be able to act quickly to prevent the effects of the subprime mortgage crisis from cascading further through the United States and global economies, HERA also provided "no court may take any action to restrain or affect *the exercise of powers or functions* of [FHFA] as a conservator or a receiver." *Id.* § 4617(f) (emphasis added).

By its plain terms, HERA's broad anti-injunction provision bars equitable relief against FHFA only when the Agency acts within its statutory authority—*i.e.* when it performs its "powers or functions." *See New York v. FERC,* 535 U.S. 1, 18 (2002) ("[A]n agency literally has no power to act . . . unless and until Congress confers power upon it."). Accordingly, having been appointed as "conservator" for the Companies, FHFA was obligated to behave in a manner consistent with the conservator role as it is defined in HERA or risk intervention by courts. Indeed, this conclusion is consistent with judicial interpretations of HERA's sister statute and, more broadly, with the common law.

A.

FHFA's general authorization to act appears in HERA's "[d]iscretionary appointment" provision, which states, "The Agency may, at the discretion of the Director, be appointed conservator *or* receiver" for Fannie and Freddie. 12 U.S.C. § 4617(a)(2) (emphasis added). The disjunctive "or" clearly indicates FHFA may choose to behave either as a conservator or as a receiver, but it may not do both simultaneously. *See also id.* § 4617(a)(4)(D) ("The appointment of the Agency as receiver of a regulated entity under this section shall immediately terminate any conservatorship established for the regulated entity under this chapter."). The Agency chose the first option, publicly announcing it had placed Fannie and Freddie into conservatorship on September 6, 2008 after a series of unsuccessful efforts to capitalize the Companies. They remain in FHFA conservatorship today. Accordingly, we must determine the statutory boundaries of power, if any, placed on FHFA when it functions as a conservator and determine whether FHFA stepped out of bounds.

The Court emphasizes Subsection 4617(b)(2)(B)'s general overview of the Agency's purview:

> The Agency may, as conservator or receiver—
>
> (i) take over the assets of and operate the regulated entity with all the powers of the shareholders, the directors, and the officers of the regulated entity and conduct all business of the regulated entity;
>
> (ii) collect all obligations and money due the regulated entity;
>
> (iii) perform all functions of the regulated entity in the name of the regulated entity which are consistent with the appointment as conservator or receiver;
>
> (iv) preserve and conserve the assets and property of the regulated entity; and

(v) provide by contract for assistance in fulfilling any function, activity, action, or duty of the Agency as conservator or receiver.

Id. § 4617(b)(2)(B). From this text, the Court intuits a general statutory mission to behave as a "conservator" in virtually all corporate actions, presumably transitioning to a "receiver" only at the moment of liquidation. Op. 27 ("[HERA] openly recognizes that sometimes conservatorship will involve managing the regulated entity in the lead up to the appointment of a liquidating receiver."); 32 ("[T]he duty that [HERA] imposes on FHFA to comply with receivership procedural protections textually turns on FHFA actually liquidating the Companies."). In essence, the Court's position holds that because there was a financial crisis and only Treasury offered to serve as White Knight, both FHFA and Treasury may take any action they wish, apart from formal liquidation, without judicial oversight. This analysis is dangerously far-reaching. *See generally* 2 James Wilson, *Of the Natural Rights of Individuals, in* THE WORKS OF JAMES WILSON 587 (1967) (warning it is not "part of natural liberty. . . to do mischief to anyone" and suggesting such a nonexistent right can hardly be given to the state to impose by fiat). While the line between a conservator and a receiver may not be completely impermeable, the roles' heartlands are discrete, well-anchored, and authorize essentially distinct and specific conduct.

For clarification of the general mission statement appearing in Subsection (B), the reader need only continue to read through Subsection 4617(b)(2). *See Kellmer v. Raines,* 674 F.3d 848, 850 (D.C. Cir. 2012) ("[T]o resolve this [statutory interpretation of HERA] issue, we need only heed Professor Frankfurter's timeless advice: '(1) Read the statute; (2) read the statute; (3) read the statute!'" (quoting Henry J. Friendly, *Mr. Justice Frankfurter and the Reading of Statutes, in* BENCHMARKS 196, 202 (1967))).

A mere two subsections later, HERA helpfully lists the specific "powers" that FHFA possesses once appointed conservator:

The Agency may, as *conservator,* take such action as may be—

(i) necessary to put the regulated entity in a sound and solvent condition; and

(ii) appropriate to carry on the business of the regulated entity and preserve and conserve the assets and property of the regulated entity.

12 U.S.C. § 4617(b)(2)(D) (emphasis added). The next subsection defines FHFA's "[a]dditional powers *as receiver:*"

In any case in which the Agency is acting as receiver, the Agency shall place the regulated entity in liquidation and proceed to realize upon the assets of the regulated entity in such manner as the Agency deems appropriate, including through the sale of assets, the transfer of assets to a limited-life regulated entity[,] . . . or the exercise of any other rights or privileges granted to the Agency under this paragraph.

Id. § 4617(b)(2)(E) (emphasis added). Apparently, when the Court asserts "for all of their arguments that FHFA has exceeded the bounds of conservatorship, the institutional stockholders have no textual hook on which to hang their hats," Op. 36, it refers solely to the limited confines of Subsection 4617(b)(2)(B).

Plainly the text of Subsections 4617(b)(2)(D) and (b)(2)(E) mark the bounds of FHFA's conservator or receiver powers, respectively, if and when the Agency chooses to exercise them in a manner consistent with its general authority to "operate the regulated entity" appearing in Subsection 4617(b)(2)(B).[1] Of course, this is not to say FHFA may take action *if and only if* the preconditions listed in the statute are met. Indeed, in provisions *following the specific articulation of powers contained in Subsections (D) and (E),* and thus drafted in contemplation of the distinctions articulated in those earlier subsections, the statute lists certain powers that may be exercised by FHFA as either a "conservator or receiver." 12 U.S.C. § 4617(b)(2)(G) (power to "transfer or sell any asset or liability of the regulated entity in default" without prior approval by the regulated entity); *id.* § 4617(b)(2)(H) (power to "pay [certain] valid obligations of the regulated entity"). Indeed, each of these powers is entirely consistent with *either* the Subsection (D) conservator role or the Subsection (E) receiver role, and they do not override the distinctions between them. Congress cannot be expected to specifically address an entire universe of possible actions in its enacted text—assigning each to a "conservator," a "receiver," or both. *See, e.g., id.* § 4617(b)(2)(C) (joint conservator/receiver power to "provide for the exercise of any function by any stockholder, director, or officer of any regulated entity"). But if a power is enumerated as that of a "receiver" (or fairly read to be a "receiver" power), FHFA cannot exercise that power while calling itself a "conservator." The statute confirms as much: the Agency "as conservator or receiver" may "exercise all powers and authorities *specifically granted to conservators or receivers, respectively,* under [Section 4617], and such *incidental powers* as shall be necessary to carry out such powers." *Id.* § 4617(J)(i) (emphasis added).

A conservator endeavors to "put the regulated entity in a sound and solvent condition" by "reorganizing [and] rehabilitating" it, and a receiver takes steps towards "liquidat[ing]" the regulated entity by "winding up [its] affairs." 12 U.S.C. § 4617(a)(2), (b)(2)(D)-(E).[2] In short, FHFA may choose whether it intends to serve as a conservator or receiver; once the choice is made, however, its "hard operational calls" consistent with its "managerial judgment" are statutorily confined to acts within its chosen role. *See* Op. 23. There is no such thing as a hybrid conservator-receiver capable of governing the Companies in any manner it chooses up to the very moment of liquidation. *See* Op. 55-56 (noting HERA "terminates [shareholders] rights and claims" in receivership and acknowledging shareholders' direct claims against and rights in the Companies survive during conservatorship).[3]

Moreover, it is the proper role of courts to determine whether FHFA's challenged actions fell within its statutorily-defined conservator role. In *County of Sonoma v. FHFA,* for example, when our sister circuit undertook this inquiry, it observed, "If the [relevant] directive falls within FHFA's conservator powers, it is insulated from review and this case must be dismissed," but "[c]onversely, the anti-judicial review provision is inapplicable when FHFA acts beyond the scope of its conservator power." 710 F.3d 987, 992 (9th Cir. 2013); *see also Leon Cty. v. FHFA,* 700 F.3d 1273, 1278 (11th Cir. 2012) ("FHFA cannot evade judicial scrutiny by merely labeling its actions with a conservator stamp."). Here, the Court abdicates this crucial responsibility, blessing FHFA with unreviewable discretion over any action—short of formal liquidation—it takes towards its wards.

B.

But HERA does not exist in an interpretive vacuum. Congress imported the powers and limitations FHFA enjoys in its "conservator" and "receiver" roles, as well as the insulation from judicial review that accompanies them, directly from the Financial Institutions Reform, Recovery, and Enforcement Act of 1989 ("FIRREA"), Pub. L. No. 101-73, 103 Stat. 183, which governs the FDIC. *See* Mark A. Calabria, *The Resolution of Systemically Important Financial Institutions: Lessons from Fannie and Freddie* 10 (Cato Inst., Working Paper No. 25, 2015), http://tinyurl.com/Cato-Working-Paper ("In crafting the conservator and receivership provisions . . . the Committee staff . . . quite literally 'marked up' Sections 11 and 13 of the [Federal Deposit Insurance Act ("FDIA"), FIRREA's predecessor statute] . . . . The presumption was that FDIA powers would apply to a GSE resolution, unless there was a compelling reason otherwise."). Our interpretation of conservator powers and the judiciary's role in policing their boundaries under HERA is, therefore, guided by congressional intent expressed in FIRREA and the case law interpreting it. *See Lorillard v. Pons,* 434 U.S. 575, 580-81 (1978) (noting when "Congress adopts a new law incorporating sections of a prior law, Congress normally can be presumed to have had knowledge of the interpretation given to the incorporated law" and to have "adopte[d] that interpretation"); *Motion Picture Ass'n of Am., Inc. v. FCC,* 309 F.3d 796, 801 (D.C. Cir. 2002) ("Statutory provisions *in pari materia* normally are construed together to discern their meaning."); *see also* Felix Frankfurter, *Some Reflections on the Reading of Statutes,* 47 COLUM. L. REV. 527, 537 (1947) [hereinafter *Reading of Statutes*] ("[I]f a word is obviously transplanted from another legal source, whether the common law or other legislation, it brings the old soil with it.").

In language later copied word-for-word into HERA, FIRREA lists the FDIC's powers "as conservator or receiver," 12 U.S.C. § 1821(d)(2)(A)-(B), and it later lists the FDIC's "[p]owers as conservator" alone, *id.* § 1821(d)(2)(D). Save for references to a "regulated entity" in place of a "depository institution," the conservator powers delineated in the two statutes are *identical.* In fact, FIRREA's text demonstrates the Legislature's clear intent to create a textual distinction between conservator and receiver powers:

> The FDIC is authorized to act as conservator or receiver for insured banks and insured savings associations that are chartered under Federal or State law. The title also distinguishes between the powers of a conservator and receiver, *making clear that a conservator operates or disposes of an institution as a going concern while a receiver has the power to liquidate and wind up the affairs of an institution.*

H.R. REP. NO. 101-209, at 398 (1989) (Conf. Rep.) (emphasis added). Courts have respected this delineation, noting "Congress did not use the phrase 'conservator or receiver' loosely." *1185 Ave. of Americas Assocs. v. RTC,* 22 F.3d 494, 497 (2d Cir. 1994) ("Throughout FIRREA, Congress used 'conservator or receiver' where it granted rights to both conservators and receivers, and it used 'conservator' or 'receiver' individually where it granted rights to the [agency] in only one capacity.").

FIRREA had assigned to "conservators" responsibility for taking "such action as may be . . . necessary to put the insured depository institution in a sound and solvent condition; and . . . appropriate to carry on the business of the institution and preserve and conserve [its] assets," 12 U.S.C. § 1821(d)(2)(D), and it imposed upon them a "fiduciary duty to minimize the institution's losses," 12 U.S.C. § 1831f(d)(3). "Receivers," on the other hand, "place the insured depository institution in liquidation and proceed to realize upon the assets of the institution." *Id.* § 1821(d)(2)(E). The proper interpretation of the text is unmistakable: "a conservator may operate and dispose of a bank as a going concern, while a receiver has the power to liquidate and wind up the affairs of an institution." *James Madison Ltd. ex rel. Hecht v. Ludwig*, 82 F.3d 1085, 1090 (D.C. Cir. 1996); *see also, e.g., Del E. Webb McQueen Dev. Corp. v. RTC*, 69 F.3d 355, 361 (9th Cir. 1995) ("The RTC [a government agency similar to the FDIC], as conservator, operates an institution with the hope that it might someday be rehabilitated. The RTC, as receiver, liquidates an institution and distributes its proceeds to creditors according to the priority rules set out in the regulations."); *RTC v. United Tr. Fund, Inc.*, 57 F.3d 1025, 1033 (11th Cir. 1995) ("The conservator's mission is to conserve assets[,] which often involves continuing an ongoing business. The receiver's mission is to shut a business down and sell off its assets. A receiver and conservator consider different interests when making . . . strategic decision[s]."). The two roles simply do not overlap, and any conservator who "winds up the affairs of an institution" rather than operate it "as a going concern"—within the context of a formal liquidation or not—does so outside its authority as conservator under the statute.

Of course, parameters for the "conservator" and "receiver" roles are not the only things HERA lifted directly from FIRREA. The anti-injunction clause at issue here came too. Section 1821(j) of FIRREA provided, "[N]o court may take any action, except at the request of the Board of Directors by regulation or order, to restrain or affect the exercise of powers or functions of the [FDIC] as a conservator or a receiver." 12 U.S.C. § 1821(j). Another near-perfect fit.

Indeed, *National Trust for Historic Preservation in the United States v. FDIC* emphasized that, while FIRREA's anti-injunction clause prevented review of the FDIC's actions where it had "exercise[d the] powers or functions" granted to it as "conservator or receiver," the Court retained the ability to decide claims alleging the agency "ha[d] acted or propose[d] to act beyond, or contrary to, its statutorily prescribed, constitutionally permitted, powers or functions." 21 F.3d 469, 472 (D.C. Cir. 1994) (Wald, J., concurring); *see also Freeman v. FDIC*, 56 F.3d 1394, 1398 (D.C. Cir. 1995) ("'[Section] 1821(j) does indeed bar courts from restraining or affecting the exercise of powers or functions of the FDIC as a conservator or a receiver . . . unless it has acted or proposed to act beyond, or contrary to, its statutorily prescribed, constitutionally permitted, powers or functions.'" (quoting *Nat'l Tr. for Historic Pres.*, 21 F.3d at 472 (Wald, J., concurring))). Insulating all actions *within* the conservator role is an entirely different proposition from exempting actions *outside* that role, and this Circuit's precedent leaves no doubt that a thorough analysis is required to determine where on the continuum an agency stands before applying FIRREA's— or HERA's—anti-injunction clause to bar a plaintiff's claims.

C.

When Congress lifted HERA's conservatorship standards verbatim from FIRREA, it also incorporated the long history of fiduciary conservatorships at common law baked into that statute. Indeed, "[i]t is a familiar maxim that a statutory term is generally presumed to have its common-law meaning." *Evans v. United States*, 504 U.S. 255, 259 (1992); *see Morissette v. United States*, 342 U.S. 246, 263 (1952) ("[W]here Congress borrows terms of art in which are accumulated the legal tradition and meaning of centuries of practice, it presumably knows and adopts the cluster of ideas that were attached to each borrowed word in the body of learning from which it was taken and the meaning its use will convey to the judicial mind unless otherwise instructed. In such case, absence of contrary direction may be taken as satisfaction with widely accepted definitions, not as a departure from them."); *see generally* Roger J. Traynor, *Statutes Revolving in Common-Law Orbits*, 17 CATH. U. L. REV. 401 (1968) (discussing the interaction between statutes and judicial decisions across a number of fields, including commercial law). As Justice Frankfurter colorfully put it, "[I]f a word is obviously transplanted from another legal source, whether the common law or other legislation, it brings the old soil with it." *Reading of Statutes, supra,* at 537.

We have an obvious transplant here. At common law, "conservators" were appointed to protect the legal interests of those unable to protect themselves. In the probate context, for example, a conservator was bound to act as the fiduciary of his ward. *See In re Kosmadakes*, 444 F.2d 999, 1004 (D.C. Cir. 1971). This duty forbade the conservator—whether overseeing a human or corporate person—from acting for the benefit of the conservator himself or a third party. *See RTC v. CedarMinn Bldg. Ltd. P'ship*, 956 F.2d 1446, 1453-54 (8th Cir. 1992) (observing "[a]t least as early as the 1930s, it was recognized that the purpose of a conservator was to maintain the institution as an ongoing concern," and holding "the distinction in duties between [RTC] conservators and receivers" is thus not "more theoretical than real").[4]

Consequently, today's *Black's Law Dictionary* defines a "conservator" as a "guardian, protector, or preserver," while a "receiver" is a "disinterested person appointed . . . for the protection or collection of property that is the subject of diverse claims (for example, because it belongs to a bankrupt [entity] or is otherwise being litigated)." BLACK'S LAW DICTIONARY 370, 1460 (10th ed. 2014). These "[w]ords that have acquired a specialized meaning in the legal context must be accorded their *legal* meaning." *Buckhannon Bd. & Care Home, Inc. v. W.V. Dep't of Health & Human Res.,* 532 U.S. 598, 615 (2001) (Scalia, J., concurring).[5] They comprise the common law vocabulary that Congress chose to employ in FIRREA and, later, in HERA to authorize the FDIC and FHFA to serve as "conservators" in order to "preserve and conserve [an institution's] assets" and operate that institution in a "sound and solvent" manner. 12 U.S.C. § 1821(d)(2)(D).

The word "conservator," therefore, is not an infinitely malleable term that may be stretched and contorted to encompass FHFA's conduct here and insulate Plaintiffs' APA claims from judicial review. Indeed, the Court implicitly acknowledges this fact in permitting the Class Plaintiffs to mount a claim for anticipatory breach of the promises in their shareholder agreements. *See* Op. 71-73. A proper reading of the statute prevents FHFA from exceeding the bounds of the conservator role and behaving as a *de facto* receiver.

The Court suggests FHFA's incidental power to, "as conservator or receiver[,] . . . take any action authorized by [Section 4617], which the Agency determines is in the best interests of the regulated entity *or the Agency*" in 12 U.S.C. § 4617(b)(2)(J)(ii) erases any outer limit to FHFA's statutory powers despite the common law definition of "conservator" and, therefore, forecloses *any* opportunity for meaningful judicial review of FHFA's actions in conducting its so-called conservatorship at the time of the Third Amendment. *See* Op. 33-34. Of course, the Court's reading of Subsection 4617(b)(2)(J)(ii) directly contradicts the immediately-preceding subsection's authorization of FHFA "as conservator or receiver" to "exercise all powers and authorities specifically granted *to conservators or receivers, respectively*." 12 U.S.C. § 4617(b)(2)(J)(i) (emphasis added). It also upends Subsection 4617(a)(5)'s provision of judicial review for actions FHFA may take in certain facets of its receiver role. But even if that were not the case, Supreme Court precedent requires *an affirmative act by Congress*—an explicit "instruct[ion]" that review should proceed in a "contrary" manner—to authorize departure from a common law definition. *Morissette,* 342 U.S. at 263. And given the potential for disruption in the financial markets discussed in Part III *infra,* one would expect Congress to express itself explicitly in this matter. *See FDA v. Brown & Williamson Tobacco Corp.,* 529 U.S. 120, 160 (2000) ("[W]e are confident that Congress could not have intended to delegate a decision of such economic and political significance to an agency in so cryptic a fashion."). Congress offered no such statement here.

Rather, the more appropriate reading of the relevant text merely permits FHFA to engage in self-dealing transactions, an authorization otherwise inconsistent with the conservator role. *See Gov't of Rwanda v. Johnson,* 409 F.3d 368, 373 (D.C. Cir. 2005) (discussing "the age-old principle applicable to fiduciary relationships that, unless there is a full disclosure by the agent, trustee, or attorney of his activity and interest in the transaction to the party he represents and the obtaining of the consent of the party represented, the party serving in the fiduciary capacity cannot receive any profit or emolument from the transaction"); *see also* 7 COLLIER ON BANKRUPTCY ¶ 1108.09 (16th ed.) (noting a trustee's duty of loyalty in bankruptcy law requires a "single-minded devotion to the interests of those on whose behalf the trustee acts"). FHFA operating as a conservator may act in its own interests to protect both the Companies and the taxpayers from whom the Agency was ultimately forced to borrow, but FHFA is not empowered to jettison every duty a conservator owes its ward, and it is certainly not entitled to disregard the statute's own clearly defined limits on conservator power.

In fact, FIRREA contains a nearly identical self-dealing provision, which provides, "The [FDIC] may, as conservator or receiver . . . take any action authorized by this chapter, which the [FDIC] determines is in the best interests of the depository institution, its depositors, or the [FDIC]." 12 U.S.C. § 1821(d)(2)(J)(ii). This authorization has not given courts pause in interpreting FIRREA to require the FDIC to behave within its statutory role. *See Nat'l Tr. for Historic Pres.,* 21 F.3d at 472 (Wald, J., concurring) ("[Section] 1821(j) does indeed bar courts from restraining or affecting the exercise of powers or functions of the FDIC as a conservator or a receiver, unless it has acted or proposes to act beyond, or contrary to, its statutorily prescribed, constitutionally permitted, powers or functions."); *see also Sharpe v. FDIC,* 126 F.3d 1147, 1155 (9th Cir. 1997) (holding the statutory bar on judicial review of the FDIC's actions taken as a conservator or receiver "does not bar injunctive relief when the FDIC has acted beyond, or contrary to, its statutorily prescribed, constitutionally permitted, powers or functions").[6]

II.

Having determined this Court may enjoin FHFA if it exceeded its powers as conservator of Fannie and Freddie, I now examine FHFA's conduct. It is important to note at the outset the *motives* behind any actions taken by FHFA are irrelevant to this inquiry, as no portion of HERA's text invites such an analysis. Rather, I examine whether or not FHFA acted beyond its authority, looking only to whether its actions are consistent either with (1) "put[ting] the regulated entity in a sound and solvent condition" by "reorganizing [and] rehabilitating" it as a conservator or (2) taking steps towards "liquidat[ing]" it by "winding up [its] affairs" as a receiver. 12 U.S.C. § 4617(a)(2), (b)(2)(D)-(E).

In September 2008, FHFA placed Fannie and Freddie into conservatorship; Director James Lockhart explained the conservatorship as "a statutory process designed to stabilize a troubled institution with the objective of returning the entities to normal business operations" and promised FHFA would "act as the conservator to operate [Fannie and Freddie] until they are stabilized." Press Release, Fed. Hous. Fin. Agency, Statement of FHFA Director James B. Lockhart at News Conference Announcing Conservatorship of Fannie Mae and Freddie Mac (Sept. 7, 2008), http://tinyurl.com/Lockhart-Statement. FHFA even promised it would "continue to retain all rights in the [Fannie and Freddie] stock's financial worth; as such worth is determined by the market." JA 2443 (FHFA Fact Sheet containing "Questions and Answers on Conservatorship"). And, for a period of time thereafter, FHFA did in fact manage the Companies within the conservator role. It even enlisted Treasury to provide cash infusions that, while costly, preserved at least a portion of the value of the market-held shares in the corporations.

But the tide turned in August 2012 with the Third Amendment and its "Net Worth Sweep," transferring nearly all of the Companies' profits into Treasury's coffers. Specifically, the Third Amendment replaced Treasury's right to a fixed-rate 10 percent dividend with the right to sweep Fannie and Freddie's entire quarterly net worth (except for an initial capital reserve, which initially totaled $3 billion and will decline to zero by 2018). Additionally, the agreement provided that, regardless of the amount of money paid to Treasury as part of this Net Worth Sweep dividend, Fannie and Freddie would continue to owe Treasury the $187.5 billion it had originally loaned the Companies. It was, to say the least, a highly unusual transaction. Treasury was no longer another, admittedly very important, investor entitled to a preferred share of the Companies' profits; it had received a contractual right from FHFA to loot the Companies to the guaranteed exclusion of all other investors.

In an August 2012 press release summarizing the Third Amendment's terms, Treasury took a very different tone from Lockhart's 2008 statement: "[W]e are taking the next step toward responsibly *winding down* Fannie Mae and Freddie Mac, while continuing to support the necessary process of repair and recovery in the housing market." Press Release, Dep't of Treasury, Treasury Department Announces Further Steps To Expedite Wind Down of Fannie Mae and Freddie Mac (Aug. 17, 2012), http://tinyurl.com/Treasury-Press-Release (emphasis added). Treasury further noted the Third Amendment would achieve the "important objective[]" of "[a]cting upon the commitment made in the Administration's 2011 White Paper that the GSEs will be wound down and will not be allowed to retain profits, rebuild capital, and return to the market in their prior form." *Id.* The Acting FHFA Director echoed Treasury's sentiment in April 2013, explaining to Congress the following year the Net Worth Sweep would "wind down" Fannie and Freddie and "reinforce the notion that [they] will not be building capital as a potential step to regaining their former corporate status." Statement of Edward J. DeMarco, Acting Director, FHFA, Before the S. Comm. on Banking, Hous. & Urban Affairs (Apr. 18, 2013), http://tinyurl.com/DeMarco-Statement.

The evolution of FHFA's position from 2008 to 2013 is remarkable; it had functionally removed itself from the role of a HERA conservator. FHFA and Treasury even described their actions using HERA's *exact phrase defining a receiver's conduct,* yet FHFA still purported to exercise only its power as a conservator and operated free from HERA's constraints on receivers. *See* 12 U.S.C. § 4617(a)(4)(D), (b)(2)(E), (b)(3), (c) (establishing liquidation procedures and priority requirements); *id.* § 4617(a)(5) (providing for judicial review).

The shift in policy was borne out in FHFA's and Treasury's actions. Indeed, all parties agree the Net Worth Sweep had the effect of replacing a fixed-rate dividend with a quarterly transfer of each company's net worth above an initial (and declining) capital reserve of $3 billion. There is similarly no dispute that Treasury collected a $130 billion dividend in 2013, $40 billion in 2014, and $15.8 billion in 2015. In fact, during the period from 2008 to 2015, Fannie and Freddie together paid Treasury $241.2 billion, an amount well in excess of the $187.5 billion Treasury loaned the Companies. FHFA's decision to strip these cash reserves from Fannie and Freddie, consistently divesting the Companies of their near-entire net worth, is plainly antithetical to a conservator's charge to "preserve and conserve" the Companies' assets.

Of course, and as the Court observes, Op. 29-31, Fannie and Freddie continue to operate at a profit. Indeed, as early as the second quarter of 2012, the Companies had outearned Treasury's 10 percent cash dividend. Nonetheless, the Net Worth Sweep imposed through the Third Amendment— which was executed shortly after the second quarter 2012 earnings were released—confiscated all but a small portion of Fannie's and Freddie's profits. The maximum reserve of $3 billion, given the Companies' enormous size, rendered them extremely vulnerable to market fluctuations and risked triggering a need to once again infuse Fannie and Freddie with taxpayer money. *See* JA 1983 (2012 SEC filing stating "there is significant uncertainty in the current market environment, and any changes in the trends in macroeconomic factors that [Fannie] currently anticipate[s], such as home prices and unemployment, may cause [its] future credit-related expenses or income and credit losses to vary significantly from [its then-]current expectations"). In fact, FHFA has since referred to the Companies, even with their several-billion-dollar cushion, as "effectively balance-sheet insolvent" and "a textbook illustration of instability." Defs. Mot. to Dismiss at 19, *Samuels v. FHFA*, No. 13-cv-22399 (S.D. Fla. Dec. 6, 2013), ECF No. 38; *see also generally*, Statement of Melvin L. Watt, Director, FHFA, Statement Before the H. Comm. on Fin. Servs., at 3 (Jan. 27, 2015), http://tinyurl.com/Watt-Statement ("[U]nder the terms of the [contracts with Treasury], the [Companies] do not have the ability to build capital internally while they remain in conservatorship."). As time went on, and the maximum reserve decreased, the situation only deteriorated. Given the task of replicating their successful rise each quarter amid volatile market conditions, it is surprising the Companies managed to maintain consistent profitability until 2016, when Freddie Mac posted a $200 million loss in the first quarter. *See* FREDDIE MAC, FORM 10-Q FOR THE QUARTERLY PERIOD ENDED MARCH 31, 2016, at 7 (May 3, 2016). Under the circumstances, it strains credulity to argue FHFA was acting as a conservator to "observe[Fannie's and Freddie's] economic performance over time" and consider other regulatory options when it executed the Third Amendment. Op. 33. FHFA and Treasury are not "studying" the Companies, they are profiting off of them![7]

Nonetheless, the Court suggests the Third Amendment was simply a logical extension of the principles articulated in the prior two agreements. Op. 25-26. This is incorrect; the Net Worth Sweep fundamentally transformed the relationship between the Companies and Treasury: a 10 percent dividend became a sweep of the Companies' near-entire net worth; an in-kind dividend option disappeared in favor of cash payments; the ability to retain capital above and beyond the required dividend payment evaporated; and, most importantly, the Companies lost any hope of repaying Treasury's liquidation preference and freeing themselves from its debt. Indeed, the capital depletion accomplished in the Third Amendment, regardless of motive, is patently incompatible with any definition of the conservator role. Outside the litigation context, even FHFA agrees: "As one of the primary objectives of conservatorship of a regulated entity would be restoring that regulated entity to a sound and solvent condition, allowing capital distributions to deplete the entity's conservatorship assets would be inconsistent with the agency's statutory goals, as they would result in removing capital at a time when the Conservator is charged with rehabilitating the regulated entity." 76 Fed. Reg. 35,724, 35,727 (June 20, 2011). But rendering Fannie and Freddie mere pass-through entities for huge amounts of money destined for Treasury does exactly that which FHFA has deemed impermissible. Even Congress, in debating the Consolidated Appropriations Act of 2016, H.R. 2029, 114th Cong. § 702 (2015), acknowledged such action would require additional congressional authorization. *See* 161 Cong. Rec. S8760 (daily ed. Dec. 17, 2015) (statement of Sen. Corker) (noting the Senate Banking Committee passed a bipartisan bill to "protect taxpayers from future economic down-turns by replacing Fannie and Freddie with a privately capitalized system" that ultimately did not receive a vote by the full Senate).

Here, FHFA placed the Companies in *de facto* liquidation—inconsistent even with "managing the regulated entit[ies] in the lead up to the appointment of a liquidating receiver," as the Court incorrectly, and obliquely, defines the outer limits of the conservator role, Op. 27—when it entered into the Third Amendment and captured nearly all of the Companies' profits for Treasury. To paraphrase an aphorism usually attributed to Everett Dirksen, a hundred billion here, a hundred billion there, and pretty soon you're talking about real money. But instead of acknowledging the reality of the Companies' situation, the Court hides behind a false formalism, establishing a dangerous precedent for future acts of FHFA, the FDIC, and even common law conservators.

III.

Finally, the practical effect of the Court's ruling is pernicious. By holding, contrary to the Act's text, FHFA need not declare itself as either a conservator or receiver and then act in a manner consistent with the well-defined powers associated with its chosen role, the Court has disrupted settled expectations about financial markets in a manner likely to negatively affect the nation's overall financial health.

Congress originally established the FDIC to rebuild confidence in our nation's banking system following the Great Depression, *see* Banking Act of 1933, Pub. L. No. 73-66, 48 Stat. 162, and in the years that followed it has empowered the institution to insure deposits and serve as a conservator or receiver for failed banks, *see* Federal Deposit Insurance Act of 1950, Pub. L. No. 81-979, 64 Stat. 873 (FIRREA's predecessor statute, which incorporated the conservator and receiver roles). Consistent with its mission, the FDIC has provided assistance, up to and including conservatorship and receivership, for thousands of financial institutions over numerous periods of economic stress. For decades, investors relied on the common law's conservator/receiver distinction, maintained by the FDIC and enforced by courts, to evaluate their investments and guide judicial review.

Congress chose to import this effective statutory scheme into HERA in an effort to combat our most recent financial crisis, evidencing its belief that FIRREA's terms were equal to the task confronting FHFA. But FHFA's actions in implementing the Net Worth Sweep "bear no resemblance to actions taken in conservatorships or receiverships overseen by the FDIC." Amicus Br. for Indep. Comm. Bankers of Am. 6 (reflecting the views of former high-ranking officials of the FDIC). Yet today the Court holds that, in the context of HERA—and FIRREA by extension—any action taken by a regulator claiming to be a conservator (short of officially liquidating the company) is immunized from meaningful judicial scrutiny. All this in the context of the Third Amendment's Net Worth Sweep, which comes perilously close to liquidating Fannie and Freddie by ensuring they have no hope of survival past 2018. The Court's conservator is not your grandfather's, or even your father's, conservator. Rather, the Court adopts a dangerous and radical new regime that introduces great uncertainty into the already-volatile market for debt and equity in distressed financial institutions.

Now investors in regulated industries must invest cognizant of the risk that some conservators may abrogate their property rights entirely in a process that circumvents the clear procedures of bankruptcy law, FIRREA, and HERA. Consequently, equity in these corporations will decrease as investors discount their expected value to account for the increased uncertainty—indeed if allegations of regulatory overreach are entirely insulated from judicial review, private capital may even become sparse. Certainly, capital will become more expensive, and potentially *prohibitively* expensive during times of financial distress, for all regulated financial institutions.

More ominously, the existence of a predictable rule of law has made America's enviable economic progress possible. *See, e.g.,* TOM BETHELL, THE NOBLEST TRIUMPH: PROPERTY AND PROSPERITY THROUGH THE AGES 3 (1998) ("When property is privatized, and the rule of law is established, in such a way that all including the rulers themselves are subject to the same law, economies will prosper and civilization will blossom."). Private individual and institutional investors in regulated industries rightly expect the law will protect their financial rights—either through an agency interpreting statutory text or a court reviewing agency action thereafter. They are also entitled to expect a conservator will act to conserve and preserve the value of the company in which they have invested, honoring the capital and investment conventions of governing law. A rational investor contemplating the terms of HERA would not conclude Congress had changed these prevailing norms. *See generally Yates v. United States,* 135 S. Ct. 1074, 1096 (2015) (Kagan, J., dissenting) (noting statutory text may be drafted "to satisfy audiences other than courts"). Today, however, the Court explains this rational investor was wrong. And its bold and incorrect statutory interpretation could dramatically affect investor and public confidence in the fairness and predictability of the government's participation in conservatorship and insolvency proceedings.

When assessing responsibility for the mortgage mess there is, as economist Tom Sowell notes, plenty of blame to be shared. Who was at fault? "The borrowers? The lenders? The government? The financial markets? The answer is yes. All were responsible and many were irresponsible." THOMAS SOWELL, THE HOUSING BOOM AND BUST 28 (2009). But that does not mean more irresponsibility is the solution. Conservation is not a synonym for nationalization. Confiscation may be. But HERA did not authorize either, and FHFA may not do covertly what Congress did not authorize explicitly. What might serve in a banana republic will not do in a constitutional one.

* * *

FHFA, like the FDIC before it, was given broad powers to enable it to respond in a perilous time in U.S. financial history. But with great power comes great responsibility. Here, those responsibilities and the authority FHFA received to address them were well-defined, and yet FHFA disregarded them. In so doing, FHFA abandoned the protection of the anti-injunction provision, and it should be required to defend against the Institutional and Class Plaintiffs' claims.

[1] Thus far, Treasury has not asked Fannie and Freddie to pay any commitment fees.

[2] Neither company drew upon Treasury's commitment in the second quarter of 2012 though.

[3] Press Release, United States Dep't of the Treasury, *Treasury Department Announces Further Steps to Expedite Wind Down of Fannie Mae and Freddie Mac* (August 17, 2012), https://www.treasury.gov/press-center/press-releases/Pages/tg 1684. aspx ("Treasury Press Release").

[4] *See* FANNIE MAE, FORM 10-K FOR THE FISCAL YEAR ENDED DECEMBER 31, 2015 (Feb. 19, 2016); FREDDIE MAC, ANNUAL HOUSING ACTIVITIES REPORT FOR 2015, at 1 (March 15, 2016); FANNIE MAE, 2015 ANNUAL HOUSING ACTIVITIES REPORT AND ANNUAL MORTGAGE REPORT, tbl. 1A (March 14, 2016); FANNIE MAE, 2014 ANNUAL HOUSING ACTIVITIES REPORT AND ANNUAL MORTGAGE REPORT, tbl. 1A (March 13, 2015); FREDDIE MAC, ANNUAL HOUSING ACTIVITIES REPORT FOR 2014, at 1 (March 11, 2015); FANNIE MAE, 2013 ANNUAL HOUSING ACTIVITIES REPORT AND ANNUAL MORTGAGE REPORT, tbl. 1A (March 13, 2014); FREDDIE MAC, ANNUAL HOUSING ACTIVITIES REPORT FOR 2013, at 1 (March 12, 2014).

[5] One of the institutional stockholders—Arrowood—does not identify the claims for which it seeks damages in its prayer for relief. However, looking at the description of each claim, Arrowood alleges that it sustained damages only in its breach of contract and breach of implied covenant claims. For the Recovery Act and APA claims, Arrowood alleges only that it is entitled to relief "under 5 U.S.C. §§ 702, 706(2)(C)," J.A. 208, provisions of the APA that do not authorize money damages.

[6] The class plaintiffs had also alleged that the failure of FHFA and Treasury to provide just compensation for taking private property violated the Takings Clause of the Fifth Amendment. The district court dismissed that challenge for failure to state a legally cognizable claim, Fed. R. Civ. P. 12(b)(6), and the class plaintiffs have not challenged that ruling on appeal.

[7] The institutional stockholders do not argue that FHFA or Treasury transgressed constitutional bounds in any respect.

[8] The dissenting opinion suggests that Congress's use of permissive "may" terminology is "a simple concession to the practical reality that a conservator may not always succeed in rehabilitating its ward." Dissenting Op. at 9 n.1. Not so. Even with the hypothesized addition of mandatory terms to the statute, the Act would at most command FHFA to take actions "necessary to put the [Companies] in a sound and solvent condition" and "appropriate to * * * preserve and conserve [their] assets." 12 U.S.C. § 4617(b)(2)(D). FHFA's compliance thus would turn on its actions, not on their outcome.

[9] The institutional stockholders also contend that FHFA's adoption of the Third Amendment violated Section 4617(a)(7), which provides that FHFA "shall not be subject to the direction or supervision of any other agency." 12 U.S.C. § 4617(a)(7). The institutional stockholders pleaded, however, only that "on information and belief, FHFA agreed to the [Third Amendment] * * * at the insistence and under the direction and supervision of Treasury." J.A. 122, ¶ 70. On a motion to dismiss for failure to state a claim, we are not required to credit a bald legal conclusion that is devoid of factual allegations and that simply parrots the terms of the statute. *See Ashcroft v. Iqbal,* 556 U.S. 662, 678 (2009) ("A pleading that offers labels and conclusions or a formulaic recitation of the elements of a cause of action will not do. Nor does a complaint suffice if it tenders naked assertions devoid of further factual enhancement.") (citations, internal quotation marks, and alterations omitted).

[10] The dissenting opinion comments that the dividend payments under the Third Amendment did not go towards paying off what the Companies borrowed from Treasury. *See* Dissenting Op. at 21, 23. Yet the Stock Agreements and the First and Second Amendments, which the dissenting opinion acknowledges were lawful, *id.* at 21, similarly did not provide for the Companies' dividends to pay down Treasury's liquidation preference.

[11] After the large dividends in 2013 and 2014, Fannie and Freddie made a far smaller dividend payment—a combined $15.8 billion— in 2015. In the first quarter of 2016, Freddie Mac had a comprehensive loss of $200 million and paid no dividend at all. *See* FREDDIE MAC, FORM 10-Q FOR THE QUARTERLY PERIOD ENDED MARCH 31, 2016 (May 3, 2016). That loss was due to market forces such as interest-rate volatility and widening spreads between interest rates and benchmark rates. *Id.* at 1-2.

[12] We grant the plaintiffs' various motions to supplement the record with evidence of what FHFA and Treasury officials knew about the Companies' predicted financial performance and when. That evidence does not affect our analysis, and we see no need to remand the claims for the district court to consider a fuller administrative record because the Recovery Act simply does not impose upon FHFA the precise duties that the institutional plaintiffs' factual arguments suppose.

[13] Section 4617(a)(5) provides in full:

(A) In general

If the Agency is appointed conservator or receiver under this section, the regulated entity may, within 30 days of such appointment, bring an action in the United States district court for the judicial district in which the home office of such regulated entity is located, or in the United States District Court for the District of Columbia, for an order requiring the Agency to remove itself as conservator or receiver.

(B) Review

Upon the filing of an action under subparagraph (A), the court shall, upon the merits, dismiss such action or direct the Agency to remove itself as such conservator or receiver.

12 U.S.C. § 4617(a)(5).

[14] *See also Kuriakose v. Federal Home Loan Mortgage Corp.,* 674 F. Supp. 2d 483, 494 (S.D.N.Y. 2009) ("By moving to declare unenforceable the non-participation clause in Freddie Mac severance agreements, in essence Plaintiffs are seeking an order which restrains the FHFA from enforcing this contractual provision in the future. * * * [The Recovery Act] clearly provides that this Court does not have the jurisdiction to interfere with such authority.").

[15] None of the cases that plaintiffs cite has anything to do with third-party claims that would directly restrain or affect the actions of a conservator. *See, e.g., Ecco Plains, LLC v. United States,* 728 F.3d 1190, 1202 n.17 (10th Cir. 2013) (stating that Section 1821(j) does not apply to a claim for money damages); *National Trust II,* 995 F.2d at 241 (characterizing Section 1821(j) as "[t]he prohibition against restraining the FDIC" in a case that only sought to restrain the FDIC itself).

[16] The class plaintiffs named the Companies as nominal defendants to their derivative claims on behalf of the Companies for breach of fiduciary duty because "the corporation in a shareholder derivative suit should be aligned as a defendant when the corporation is under the control of officers who are the target of the derivative suit." *Knop v. Mackall,* 645 F.3d 381, 382 (D.C. Cir. 2011).

[17] The FHFA and the Companies submitted a joint brief. When describing their arguments on appeal, therefore, we will refer to them collectively as the FHFA.

[18] We previously have interpreted a so-called "Deemer Clause" to provide jurisdiction under 28 U.S.C. § 1331, *Auction Co. of Am. v. FDIC,* 132 F.3d 746, 751 (D.C. Cir. 1997), *clarified on denial of reh'g,* 141 F.3d 1198 (1998), but have also held a Deemer Clause instead grants jurisdiction "directly" under Article III, § 2 of the Constitution, *A.I. Trade Fin., Inc. v. Petra Int'l Banking Corp.,* 62 F.3d 1454, 1460 (D.C. Cir. 1995). Although we need not decide which is the correct approach, we must assure ourselves the Congress has "not expand[ed] the jurisdiction of the federal courts beyond the bounds established by the Constitution." *Verlinden B.V. v. Cent. Bank of Nigeria,* 461 U.S. 480, 491 (1983). For federally chartered organizations such as Freddie Mac, the Congress may grant federal jurisdiction "so long as the legislature does more than merely confer a new jurisdiction," but also "ensure[s] the proper administration of some federal law (although the disputed issues in any specific case may be confined to matters of state law)." *A.I. Trade,* 62 F.3d at 1461-62 (internal quotation marks and brackets omitted).

Whether the Deemer Clause is constitutional depends upon the substantive law anchoring that grant of federal jurisdiction today, not just the legislation extant when the clause was enacted, viz., the Emergency Home Finance Act of 1970, Pub. L. No. 91-351, § 303(e)(2), 84 Stat. 450, 453. Federal law today governs the composition and election of Freddie Mac's board of directors, 12 U.S.C. § 1452(a)(2), limits its capital distributions, § 1452(b), sets forth in detail both the powers of and limitations upon Freddie Mac with respect to its purchase and disposition of mortgages, §§ 1452(c), 1454(a), exempts the company from certain taxes, § 1452(e), and provides for conservatorship or receivership by the FHFA, § 4617. *Cf. A.I. Trade,* 62 F.3d at 1463. An issue of federal law may well arise in a suit involving Freddie Mac and "the potential application of that law provides a sufficient predicate for the exercise of the federal judicial power." *Id.* at 1462. The Congress may, "by bringing all such disputes within the unifying jurisdiction of the federal courts," avoid or ameliorate the potential for "diverse interpretations of those substantive provisions" that may prove "vexing to the very commerce" the provisions were undoubtedly "enacted to promote." *Id.* at 1463.

[19] Contrary to the class plaintiffs' assertions, however, their request for "[s]uch other and further relief as the Court may deem just and proper" does not qualify as non-monetary relief. J.A. 279 ¶ 12. Such boilerplate requests — which refer to the proviso of Federal Rule of Civil Procedure 54(c) that a "final judgment should grant the relief to which each party is entitled, even if the party has not demanded that relief in its pleadings" — "come[] into play only after the court determines it has jurisdiction." *See Hedgepeth ex rel. Hedgepeth v. Wash. Metro. Area Transit Auth.,* 386 F.3d 1148, 1152 n.2 (D.C. Cir. 2004) (Roberts, J.). The class plaintiffs do not argue that their request for "disgorgement," J.A. 278 ¶ 5, is not "money damages." Nor

do they invoke the request for rescission of the Third Amendment that appears outside of the prayer for relief in their complaint.

[20] The class plaintiffs also request "disgorgement" in favor of the Companies, but they do not explain further what measure of relief they seek and on appeal they appear to characterize the plea as one for damages. We do not take the class plaintiffs to seek more than restitution of the dividends paid to Treasury pursuant to the Third Amendment and in excess of the 10% dividend, because they have not alleged that Treasury has otherwise profited from its execution of the Third Amendment. Restitution of the benefits conferred by a plaintiff is not specific to claims for breach of contract, 1 DAN B. DOBBS, LAW OF REMEDIES § 4.1(1), pp. 552-53 (2d ed. 1993), so the plea for disgorgement does not alter our analysis.

[21] We need not reach the question whether the FHFA's conservatorship of Fannie Mae and Freddie Mac endows the Companies with sovereign immunity because their "sue and be sued" clauses would waive any immunity.

[22] It follows that the FTCA does not apply to Fannie Mae or Freddie Mac either, even though the FHFA, as conservator, exercises complete control over the Companies. The statute provides that the remedies set forth in the FTCA "shall be exclusive" despite any "sue and be sued" clause of a "federal agency," 28 U.S.C. § 2679(a), which includes "corporations primarily acting as instrumentalities or agencies of the United States, but does not include any contractor with the United States," *id.* § 2671. Generally, we determine whether a defendant is such a corporation that is subject to the FTCA by examining whether the Federal Government has the power "'to control the detailed physical performance of the [corporation].'" *Macharia v. United States,* 334 F.3d 61, 68 (D.C. Cir. 2003) (quoting *United States v. Orleans,* 425 U.S. 807, 814 (1976)). As we have just concluded, however, the Recovery Act evinces the Congress's intention to "place[]" the FHFA "in the shoes" of the Companies, *O'Melveny & Myers,* 512 U.S. at 86-87, which become wards of the Government. The Companies therefore remain subject to suit as private corporations for violations of state law just as they were before the FHFA was appointed conservator.

[23] The FHFA argues that "[b]ecause the Conservator already can pursue derivative claims belonging to the Enterprises, the statutory phrase 'rights . . . of any stockholder' only has meaning if it encompasses direct claims." FHFA Br. at 48. This argument is foreclosed by *Kellmer,* where we determined the Succession Clause "plainly transfers [to the FHFA the] shareholders' ability to bring derivative suits," 674 F.3d at 850, and it overlooks that, when the Companies are in conservatorship, the Succession Clause functions not only to grant the FHFA powers, but also to take powers from the shareholders.

[24] The district court applied Delaware law to the class plaintiffs' common-law claims. *See Perry Capital LLC,* 70 F. Supp. 3d at 235 n.39, 236, 238, 239 n.45. On appeal, all parties agree we should apply Delaware law to claims regarding Fannie Mae and Virginia law to those regarding Freddie Mac. The parties have thereby waived any objection to the district court's application of Delaware law to claims regarding Fannie Mae. *See A-L Assocs., Inc. v. Jorden,* 963 F.2d 1529, 1530 (D.C. Cir. 1992) (applying law "[t]he court below held, and the parties agree," was applicable); *Patton Boggs LLP v. Chevron Corp.,* 683 F.3d 397, 403 (D.C. Cir. 2012); *Jannenga v. Nationwide Life Ins. Co.,* 288 F.2d 169, 172 (D.C. Cir. 1961); *cf. Milanovich v. Costa*

Crociere, S.p.A., 954 F.2d 763, 766 (D.C. Cir. 1992) (applying U.S. contract principles to determine whether a contractual choice-of-law provision was valid where the district court had applied those principles because "both parties here have assumed that American contract law principles control"). *Accord, e.g., Williams v. BASF Catalysts LLC,* 765 F.3d 306, 316 (3d Cir. 2014) (holding that "parties may waive choice-of-law issues" in part because "choice-of-law questions do not go to the court's jurisdiction"). We have occasionally held a party forfeited any objection to the district court's choice of law in part because we could detect no "error," *Wash. Metro. Area Transit Auth. v. Georgetown Univ.,* 347 F.3d 941, 945 (D.C. Cir. 2003); *Nello L. Teer Co. v. Wash. Metro. Area Transit Auth.,* 921 F.2d 300, 302 n.2 (D.C. Cir. 1990), or "apparent error" in the district court's choice, *Burke v. Air Serv Int'l, Inc.,* 685 F.3d 1102, 1105 (D.C. Cir. 2012). We do not read these cases to have established a standard for forfeiture or waiver particular to choice of law, especially considering none indicated that the absence of an error or "apparent" error was necessary to the outcome. In this case, we see no reason to deviate from the district court's selection of Delaware law for the claims regarding Fannie Mae.

We need not address whether the district court should have applied Virginia law to the claims regarding Freddie Mac because, for purposes of this appeal, Delaware and Virginia law dictate the same result, *see Aref v. Lynch,* 833 F.3d 242, 262 (D.C. Cir. 2016) ("We need not determine which state's law applies . . . because the result is the same under all three" potentially applicable laws); *Skirlick v. Fid. & Deposit Co. of Md.,* 852 F.2d 1376, 1377 (D.C. Cir. 1988) (same), and the parties have waived any contention that yet another law should displace the district court's choice. The district court also cited federal case law in evaluating whether the class plaintiffs had a contractual right to dividends, *Perry Capital LLC,* 70 F. Supp. 3d at 237 & n.41, but the cited federal decisions do not displace state contract law, *cf. O'Melveny & Myers,* 512 U.S. at 85-89 (rejecting the argument that federal common law should govern tort claims lodged by the FDIC).

[25] The class plaintiffs (the only party to address on the merits whether the contract-based claims are direct or derivative) cite only Delaware law in addressing the claims for breach of contract as to both Fannie Mae and Freddie Mac despite their assumption that Virginia law governs claims against Freddie Mac. The issue need detain us no further because we have found no indication Virginia would classify the breach of contract claims as derivative. *Cf. Simmons v. Miller,* 261 Va. 561, 573, 544 S.E.2d 666, 674 (2001) ("A derivative action is an equitable proceeding in which a shareholder asserts, on behalf of the corporation, a claim that belongs to the corporation rather than the shareholder . . . . [A]n action for injuries to a corporation cannot be maintained by a shareholder on an individual basis and must be brought derivatively.").

[26] Although the class plaintiffs do not describe the Third Amendment as "an anticipatory repudiation" until their reply brief, Class Pls. Reply Br. at 13, they have emphasized throughout this litigation that it "nullified — and thereby breached — the contractual rights to a liquidation distribution" by rendering performance impossible. Class Pls. Br. at 40-41; *see also, e.g.,* J.A. 223 ¶ 22 (alleging the Third Amendment "effectively eliminated the property and contractual rights of Plaintiffs and the Classes to receive their liquidation preference upon the dissolution, liquidation or winding up of Fannie Mae and Freddie Mac"); Class Pls. Opp'n to

Mot. to Dismiss at 37 ("[T]he Third Amendment has made it impossible for [the Companies] ever to have . . . assets available for distribution to stockholders other than Treasury" and thereby "eliminated Plaintiffs' present . . . liquidation rights in breach of the Certificates" (internal quotation marks omitted)). The class plaintiffs allege they "paid valuable consideration in exchange for these contractual rights," which rights "had substantial market value . . . that [was] swiftly dissipated in the wake of the Third Amendment," J.A. 224 ¶ 23, causing the class plaintiffs to "suffer[] damages," *e.g.,* J.A. 269 ¶ 144.

[27] We remand the contract-based claims only insofar as they seek damages because the pleas for equitable relief are barred by 12 U.S.C. § 4617(f). "Because ripeness is a justiciability doctrine that is drawn both from Article III limitations on judicial power and from prudential reasons for refusing to exercise jurisdiction, we consider it first." *La. Pub. Serv. Comm'n v. FERC,* 522 F.3d 378, 397 (D.C. Cir. 2008) (internal quotation marks and brackets omitted); *see also In re Aiken Cty.,* 645 F.3d 428, 434 (D.C. Cir. 2011) ("The ripeness doctrine, even in its prudential aspect, is a threshold inquiry that does not involve adjudication on the merits"). We therefore first determined the claims are ripe, *supra* at 70-73, and only then concluded the requests for equitable relief are barred by § 4617(f).

[1] The Court makes much of the statute's statement that a conservator "*may*" take action to operate the company in a sound and solvent condition and preserve and conserve its assets while a receiver "*shall*" liquidate the company. It concludes the statute permits, but does not compel in any judicially enforceable sense, FHFA to preserve and conserve Fannie's and Freddie's assets however it sees fit. *See* Op. 21-25. I disagree. Rather, read in the context of the larger statute—especially the specifically defined powers of a conservator and receiver set forth in Subsections 4617(b)(2)(D) and (b)(2)(E)—Congress's decision to use permissive language with respect to a conservator's duties is best understood as a simple concession to the practical reality that a conservator may not always succeed in rehabilitating its ward. The statute wisely acknowledges that it is "not in the power of any man to command success" and does not convert failure into a legal wrong. *See* Letter from George Washington to Benedict Arnold (Dec. 5, 1775), *in* 3 THE WRITINGS OF GEORGE WASHINGTON, 192 (Jared Sparks, ed., 1834). Of course, this does not mean the Agency may affirmatively sabotage the Companies' recovery by confiscating their assets quarterly to ensure they cannot pay off their crippling indebtedness. There is a vast difference between recognizing that flexibility is necessary to permit a conservator to address evolving circumstances and authorizing a conservator to undermine the interests and destroy the assets of its ward without meaningful limit.

[2] The Director's discretion to appoint FHFA as "'conservator or receiver for the purpose of reorganizing, rehabilitating, or winding up the affairs of a regulated entity'" does not suggest slippage between the roles. *See* FHFA Br. 41 (quoting 12 U.S.C. § 4617(a)(2)). Between the conservator and receiver roles, FHFA surely has the power to accomplish each of the enumerated functions; nonetheless, a conservator can no more "wind[] up" a company than a receiver can "rehabilitat[e]" it. *See* 12 U.S.C. § 4617(b)(3)(B) (using "liquidation" and "winding up" as synonyms).

[3] HERA's provision for judicial review over a claim promptly filed "within 30 days" of the Director's decision to appoint a conservator or receiver further

indicates Congress contemplated continuity of the conservator or receiver role during the period the conservatorship or receivership endured. 12 U.S.C. § 4617(a)(5). Here, therefore, in transitioning *sub silencio* from the conservator to receiver role, FHFA has escaped the statute's contemplated, though admittedly brief, period for judicial review following the transition.

[4] While the execution of multiple contracts with Treasury "bears no resemblance to the type of conservatorship measures that a private common-law conservator would be able to undertake," Op. 34, that is a distinction in degree, not in kind.

[5] These legal definitions are reflected in the terms' ordinary meaning. For example, the *Oxford English Dictionary* defines a "conservator" as "[a]n officer appointed to conserve or manage something; a keeper, administrator, trustee of some organization, interest, right, or resource." 3 OXFORD ENGLISH DICTIONARY 766 (2d ed. 1989). In contrast, it defines a "receiver" as "[a]n official appointed by a government . . . to receive . . . monies due; a collector." 13 OXFORD ENGLISH DICTIONARY 317-18 (2d ed. 1989). Regardless of the terms' audience, therefore, a "conservator" protects and preserves assets for an entity while a "receiver" operates as a collection agent for creditors.

[6] The Court also suggests the authority to act "'in the best interests of the regulated entity or *the Agency*'" is consistent with the Director's mandate to protect the "'public interest.'" Op. 8 (quoting 12 U.S.C. § 4513(a)(1)(B)(v)). Of course, the FHFA Director is also bound to "carr[y] out [FHFA's] statutory mission only through activities that are authorized under and consistent with this chapter and the authorizing statutes." *Id.* § 4513(a)(1)(B)(iv). Indeed, this text only confirms what should have been evident: the availability of meaningful judicial review cannot bend to exigency, especially since Congress clearly did not believe the 2008 financial crisis required a more far-reaching statutory authorization than prior occasions of financial distress had commanded.

[7] Similarly, any argument that the Third Amendment was executed to avoid a downward spiral hardly saves FHFA at this juncture. *See, e.g.,* Op. 31-32. As an initial matter, the contention rests entirely upon an examination of motives. *But see id.* 32 (confirming motives are irrelevant to the legal inquiry). Second, even if one were to consider motives, the availability of an in-kind dividend and information recently obtained in this litigation creates, to put it mildly, a dispute of fact regarding the motivations behind FHFA and Treasury's decision to execute the Third Amendment.

776 F.3d 907 (2015)

Wilbert HARRIS, Appellant

v.

UNITED STATES DEPARTMENT OF VETERANS AFFAIRS, Appellee.

No. 13-5207.

United States Court of Appeals, District of Columbia Circuit.

Argued October 15, 2014.

Decided January 23, 2015.

Harris v. US Department of Veterans Affairs, 776 F. 3d 907 (DC Cir. 2015)

p.909 Donald M. Temple argued the cause and filed the brief for appellant.

R. Craig Lawrence, Assistant U.S. Attorney, argued the cause for appellee. With him on the brief were Ronald C. Machen Jr., U.S. Attorney, and Wyneva Johnson, Assistant U.S. Attorney.

Before: ROGERS and WILKINS, Circuit Judges, and RANDOLPH, Senior Circuit Judge.

Opinion for the Court filed by Senior Circuit Judge RANDOLPH.

RANDOLPH, Senior Circuit Judge.

Wilbert Harris brought an action against the United States Department of Veterans Affairs ("VA") seeking damages p.910 under the Federal Tort Claims Act ("FTCA"), 28 U.S.C. §§ 2671, *et seq.,* for false arrest and false imprisonment, assault and battery, negligence, negligent infliction of emotional distress, and intentional infliction of emotional distress. The district court granted the VA's motion for summary judgment on all claims. For the reasons that follow, we reverse the grant of summary judgment on Harris' assault and battery claim and on his claim of intentional infliction of emotional distress to the extent that it is based on his assault and battery claim. We affirm the grant of summary judgment on all other claims.

I.

Harris is a Vietnam War veteran who suffers from post-traumatic stress disorder ("PTSD"). On November 6, 2008, two days after the election of President Obama, Harris attended a group therapy session for veterans suffering from PTSD at the VA Medical Center in Washington, D.C.[1] David Sheets, a clinical social worker, ran the session. Harris had with him a newspaper announcing President Obama's election, and he displayed it proudly at the beginning of the session.

Harris and Sheets disagree on what occurred next, but Harris does not dispute that Sheets asked him not to discuss political issues during the session and, when he refused, Sheets asked him to leave. When Harris did not, Sheets left the room and returned a few minutes later with three VA police officers, Lieutenant William N. Nesbitt, Sergeant Denise G. Gentry, and Corporal Donald R. Christmas. As Harris left the room with the officers, Sheets told the officers that Harris had caused a "disturbance." Sheets said Harris could not return to the group therapy session. According to Harris, Harris asked for a patient advocate, was "never violent [or] combative," and attempted to re-enter the therapy room to recover his personal items, whereupon he was forced to the floor by the officers, handcuffed, and placed under arrest. Harris contends that during the arrest, one of the officers punched him in the ribs, fracturing one of them.

The parties agree that two officers then took Harris to the hospital's emergency department, where he was treated for a scrape on his left hand. After he was discharged from the emergency department, Harris was placed in a holding cell and issued a citation for "[d]isorderly [c]onduct which creates loud, boisterous, unusual noise." J.A. 55; *see* 38 C.F.R. § 1.218(b)(11). The citation was later dismissed without a hearing. Harris states that he "endured multiple hospital visits related to the injuries incurred" during the arrest, which included a fractured rib and permanent nerve damage in his left arm. He also claims that the attendant mental and emotional trauma further aggravated his PTSD.

Harris' amended complaint against the VA alleged false arrest and false imprisonment, assault and battery, negligence, negligent infliction of emotional distress, and intentional infliction of emotional distress under the FTCA. *See* 28 U.S.C. § 1346(b)(1). The VA moved for dismissal, or, in the alternative, for summary judgment. *See* Fed.R.Civ.P. 12(b)(1), (b)(6), 56. Harris opposed the VA's motion, arguing that "absent discovery" the VA's motion was "premature and should be denied." Pursuant to the Rules of the District Court for the District of Columbia, Harris included a "concise statement" of "all material facts" that he thought necessary p.911 to be litigated and "references to the parts of the record relied on to support [his] statement." Rule 7(h), Rules of the U.S. District Court for the District of Columbia. His statement included citations to affidavits and medical documents and referred to disputes over Harris' behavior during the confrontation, whether he acted aggressively toward the police or forcefully tried to re-enter the therapy room, how the police effected the arrest (specifically, whether they struck Harris once he was handcuffed), and whether Harris suffered a fractured rib and other injuries because of the arrest, among other disputes. Harris did not request discovery pursuant to Federal Rule of Civil Procedure 56(d).

The district court granted summary judgment to the VA on all claims. It concluded that "no reasonable jury could find that the arresting officers engaged in conduct amounting to false arrest and false imprisonment, assault and battery, negligence, negligent infliction of emotional distress, or intentional infliction of emotional distress." The court determined that the officers had probable cause to arrest Harris for disorderly conduct "because he attempted to re-enter the group therapy room against the officers' unequivocal directive not to do so." The court also held that the officers' use of force was reasonably necessary under the circumstances, ignoring Harris' later professions of numbness and weakness in his left hand because he had been diagnosed with carpal tunnel syndrome before his arrest. The court made no mention of Harris' alleged rib injury. Because Harris' arrest was secured with probable cause and reasonably necessary force, his claims of intentional infliction of emotional distress and negligent infliction of emotional distress also failed.

II.

We review a district court's decision to grant summary judgment *de novo* and consider the evidence in the light most favorable to the non-moving party. *See Ayissi-Etoh v. Fannie Mae,* 712 F.3d 572, 576 (D.C.Cir.2013) (per curiam). Summary judgment may be granted when "the pleadings, depositions, answers to interrogatories, and admissions on file, together with the affidavits, if any, show that there is no genuine issue as to any material fact and that the moving party is entitled to a judgment as a matter of law." *Anderson v. Liberty Lobby, Inc.,* 477 U.S. 242, 247, 106 S.Ct. 2505, 91 L.Ed.2d 202 (1986); *see* Fed.R.Civ.P. 56(a), (c). "A dispute over a material fact is 'genuine' if 'the evidence is such that a reasonable jury could return a verdict for the nonmoving party.'" *Arrington v. United States,* 473 F.3d 329, 333 (D.C.Cir.2006) (quoting *Anderson,* 477 U.S. at 248, 106 S.Ct. 2505). A fact is material if it "might affect the outcome of the suit under the governing law." *Id.* (quoting *Anderson,* 477 U.S. at 248, 106 S.Ct. 2505). A party opposing summary judgment must point the district court to disputed facts "with the requisite specificity and support them with appropriate references to the record." *Frito-Lay, Inc. v. Willoughby,* 863 F.2d 1029, 1034 (D.C.Cir. 1988). We may affirm summary judgment on any ground supported by the record. *Jones v. Bernanke,* 557 F.3d 670, 676 (D.C.Cir.2009).

III.

Tort liability under the FTCA is determined according to the law of the place where the alleged acts or omissions occurred—in this case, the District of Columbia. *Tarpeh-Doe v. United States,* 28 F.3d 120, 123 (D.C.Cir.1994). Applying D.C. tort law, we consider each of Harris' claims in turn.

1. False Arrest and False Imprisonment

The elements of the torts of false arrest and false imprisonment are: (1) detention p.912 or restraint against one's will within boundaries fixed by the defendant, and (2) the unlawfulness of such restraint. *Edwards v. Okie Dokie, Inc.,* 473 F.Supp.2d 31, 44 (D.D.C.2007).[2] The existence of probable cause for arrest defeats claims for false arrest and imprisonment. *See id.; Gabrou v. May Dep't Stores Co.,* 462 A.2d 1102, 1104 (D.C.1983) (per curiam).

Congress authorized the Secretary of Veterans Affairs to "prescribe regulations to provide for the maintenance of law and order and the protection of persons and property on [VA] property." 38 U.S.C. § 901(a)(1). Violations of such regulations may be punished by fines or imprisonment for not more than six months, or both. *Id.* § 901(c). One such regulation, codified at 38 C.F.R. § 1.218, establishes the rules of conduct "at all property under the charge and control of [the] VA." *Id.* § 1.218(a). Under § 1.218(a)(5), all persons on VA property are barred from (among other things) engaging in conduct "which creates loud or unusual noise . . . which otherwise impedes or disrupts the performance of official duties . . . [and] which prevents one from obtaining medical or other services." *Id.* A disturbance can also include the "[f]ailure to leave the premises when so ordered," whereupon "the offender is subject to arrest and removal from the premises." *Id.; see also id.* § 1.218(b)(11) (specifying schedule of offenses for disorderly conduct punishable pursuant to paragraph (a)).[3]

This regulation has been read to include causing a commotion that drew VA employees away from their ordinary duties, *United States v. Agront,* 773 F.3d 192, 199-200 (9th Cir.2014), and that "tended to 'impede or prevent the normal operation of a service'" at a VA facility. *United States v. Encinger,* 4:10CR3027, 2010 WL 2771884, at *4 (D.Neb. Jul. 13, 2010) (quoting 38 C.F.R. § 1.218(11)); *see also United States v. Shepard,* 362 Fed.Appx. 107, 112 (11th Cir.2010) (unpublished).

Harris emphasizes that there is a factual dispute over who ordered Harris not to reenter the group therapy room—he says it was Sheets while the district court stated it was the police. Appellant Br. at 10. But the dispute is of no moment. Undisputed evidence suffices to establish probable cause. In his amended complaint, Harris concedes that Sheets expelled him from group therapy and told the police that Harris caused a "disturbance" and "could not return to [the] group or continue treatment." Harris states that he acted calmly, that he "did not refuse to leave the [group therapy] room," and that he "never attempted to forcefully reenter the [group therapy] room and never disobeyed a police officer's statement." But Harris acknowledges that even after Sheets asked him to leave group therapy, he remained in the room and only left when Sheets returned with three VA police officers, and, once outside the room, he attempted to reenter, whether "forcefully" or not.

Taken together, these undisputed facts were sufficient to justify arrest. Sheets had ordered Harris to leave group therapy, p.913 and the police observed Harris' failure to comply when they entered the room. "Failure to leave the premises when so ordered constitute[d] a[] disturbance" that subjected Harris "to arrest and removal from the premises" under VA regulations. 38 C.F.R. § 1.218(a)(5). Sheets also interrupted the therapy session he was running to address Harris' alleged "disturbance." Conduct that "tend[s] to disturb the routine operations of a VA hospital . . . is prohibited" under § 1.218(b)(11). *Fentress,* 241 F.Supp.2d at 530 (quoting *United States v. Williams,* 892 F.2d 1044, 1990 WL 811, at *2 (6th Cir.1990) (per curiam) (unpublished)); *see also Agront,* 773 F.3d at 200.

Although Harris was charged only with "[d]isorderly [c]onduct which creates loud, boisterous, unusual noise," J.A. 55, under 38 C.F.R. § 1.218(b)(11), probable cause may exist "to arrest for any offense, even if it differs from the offense for which the arrest was actually made." *Enders v. District of Columbia,* 4 A.3d 457, 469 (D.C. 2010). The undisputed evidence in this case revealed the probability of several offenses: failing to leave the premises after being so ordered, distracting a VA employee (Sheets), and inhibiting medical treatment (group therapy). *See United States v. Prandy-Binett,* 995 F.2d 1069, 1073-74 (D.C.Cir.1993).

The evidence may have been insufficient to convict Harris, but the only question before us is whether the police had probable cause to arrest him, which the undisputed facts show that they did. Accordingly, we affirm the grant of summary judgment as to this claim.

2. Assault and Battery

An assault is an intentional attempt or threat to do physical harm to another. A battery is an intentional act that causes harmful or offensive bodily contact. *See Evans-Reid v. District of Columbia,* 930 A.2d 930, 937 (D.C.2007). The police have a qualified privilege to commit both torts when using "reasonable force to effect an arrest, provided that the means employed are not in excess of those which the actor reasonably believes to be necessary." *Arrington,* 473 F.3d at 335 (quoting *Etheredge v. District of Columbia,* 635 A.2d 908, 916 (D.C.1993)). "The 'reasonableness' of a particular use of force must be judged from the perspective of a reasonable officer on the scene, rather than with the 20/20 vision of hindsight." *Graham v. Connor,* 490 U.S. 386, 396, 109 S.Ct. 1865, 104 L.Ed.2d 443 (1989); *see also Plumhoff v. Rickard,* ___ U.S. ___, 134 S.Ct. 2012, 2020, 188 L.Ed.2d 1056 (2014). Accordingly, "a defendant's motion for summary judgment is to be denied only when . . . a reasonable jury could conclude that the excessiveness of the force is so apparent that no reasonable officer could have believed in the lawfulness of his actions." *Wardlaw v. Pickett,* 1 F.3d 1297, 1303 (D.C.Cir.1993).

The district court concluded that "there is no basis for a trier of fact to conclude that the officers used excessive force in executing the lawful arrest of [Harris]." But this conclusion overlooks genuine issues of material fact about what occurred during Harris' arrest, issues brought to the district court's attention with reasonable specificity in Harris' Statement of Material Facts in Dispute. *See Frito-Lay,* 863 F.2d at 1033-34.

Sheets stated that during Harris' confrontation with the officers outside of the therapy room, Harris became "verbally and emotionally out of control, resisting compliance." Harris then "appeared to attack one officer and was then taken to the ground and handcuffed by the police. He did not appear to be injured but he did appear to be a danger to others." The Uniform Offense Report filed the day of the incident and signed by one of the p.914 responding officers, Donald Christmas, describes how Harris "refuse[d] to comply" with the officers and "went towards LT. NESBIT [sic] and [sic] an aggressive way and got combatant [sic] with police officers," whereupon "he was then taken to the ground and put into restraints." However, the Use of Force Report Event Record that Nesbitt filed the day of the incident makes no mention of Harris coming toward him. It reported only that Harris "failed to comply with the police officers['] directives . . . became distributive [sic] and tried to enter a group session room forcefully," whereupon he "was taken down to the floor[,] [h]andcuffed[,] and escorted to the ER for treatment for difficulty breathing."

In a declaration Nesbitt executed in May 2012, he states that Harris "failed to comply with police directives and attempted to enter a room forcefully. I then assisted with a take-down and restraint." This declaration makes no mention of Harris' difficulty breathing.

Gentry's contemporaneous Use of Force Event Record states that Harris "failed to comply with directives, [and] he tried to enter a room forcefully," and that Gentry "assisted Cpl. Christmas and Lt. Nesbitt with a takedown to restrain and escort." Her later declaration relates essentially the same sequence of events.

Christmas' handwritten Use of Force Report states that Christmas "grab[b]ed [Harris'] left hand and put him in a[n] arm lock back down w[h]ere he then was put in restraint[s] and escorted to the E.R." Christmas' declaration repeats the declarations of the other officers, stating: "Harris failed to comply with police directives and attempted to enter a room forcefully. I then assisted with a take-down and restraint and, along with Sergeant Gentry, I escorted Mr. Harris to the [VA Medical Center] Emergency Department."

Harris has a quite different story. His affidavit states that he acted and spoke calmly, "never attempted to forcefully reenter the room and never disobeyed a police officer's statement." But, according to Harris' Statement of Material Facts in Dispute, "[r]egardless, the VA police officers forcefully threw [Harris] to the ground, placed him in a lock, and handcuffed him." Corporal Christmas "punched [him] in the rib after he was . . . handcuffed." Harris claims his physical injuries included "a fractured rib, scrapes to his forehead and left hand, ongoing neuropathy in his left fingers, [ ] bursitis in his left and right arms," and increased PTSD-related disability. Harris' medical records show that he complained of pain to his chest immediately after being brought to the emergency department and that he returned to the hospital two days after the incident complaining of sharp chest pain and was diagnosed with a rib fracture.

Whether the police officers' use of force in restraining Harris was reasonable turns on contested questions of fact—including whether Harris was "actively resisting arrest or attempting to evade arrest by flight," *Graham,* 490 U.S. at 396, 109 S.Ct. 1865, whether he "pose[d] an immediate threat to the safety of the officers or others," *id.,* and whether the police struck him after he was in restraints, *see Arrington,* 473 F.3d at 336-37; *Tafler v. District of Columbia,* 539 F.Supp.2d 385, 390-91 (D.D.C.2008); *see also DeGraff v. District of Columbia,* 120 F.3d 298, 302 (D.C.Cir. 1997).

"[A] plaintiff may defeat a summary judgment granted to a defendant if the parties' sworn statements are materially different." *Arrington,* 473 F.3d at 337.[4] p.915 Here, the affidavits, declarations, pleadings, and other evidence show that there are factual disputes that could affect the outcome of the suit. *See Anderson,* 477 U.S. at 247-49, 106 S.Ct. 2505. First, it is disputed what happened immediately before Harris was taken to the ground and handcuffed. Sheets and the Uniform Offense Report state that Harris "attack[ed]" one of the officers, but Nesbitt, Gentry, and Christmas state only that Harris attempted to enter the room "forcefully." Harris claims that he calmly turned to reenter the room to collect his belongings. Second, it is disputed whether Harris was struck in the chest during the arrest, as he claims and as Nesbitt's contemporaneous Use of Force Report Event Record (which said Harris had trouble breathing) could suggest. Third, it is disputed whether Harris' rib was fractured as a result of the arrest, as he claims and as the doctor's reports could suggest. Fourth, it is disputed whether Harris suffered permanent nerve damage as a result of the arrest, as he claims, but as some medical documentation disputes. Fifth, it is disputed whether Harris' arrest contributed to an increase in his PTSD disability rating, as he claims, or if it merely correlated with it, as a declaration from a VA Service Center Manager states.

Weighing credibility, resolving factual disputes, and drawing legitimate inferences are matters for the fact-finder; thus, summary judgment is inappropriate. *See Pardo-*

Kronemann v. Donovan, 601 F.3d 599, 604 (D.C.Cir.2010). Accordingly, we reverse the grant of summary judgment on Harris' assault and battery claim.

3. Negligence

Harris' third claim is for negligence. He claims that Sheets had a duty to treat him "in a manner that was sensitive to his victimization" and that "Sheets became mean spirited and vindictive," caused the confrontation with police, and, consequently, caused "unnecessary harm to Harris." The district court held that no reasonable jury could find that the arresting officers acted negligently. Because Harris advanced no argument in his brief before us about why the district court erred, we do not consider this claim. *See U.S. ex rel. Totten v. Bombardier Corp.,* 380 F.3d 488, 497 (D.C.Cir.2004). We therefore affirm the district court's grant of summary judgment on Harris' negligence claim.

4. Negligent Infliction of Emotional Distress

To make out a claim for negligent infliction of emotional distress, a plaintiff must show that "(1) the plaintiff was in the zone of physical danger, which was (2) created by the defendant's negligence, (3) the plaintiff feared for his own safety, and (4) the emotional distress so caused was serious and verifiable." *Rice v. District of Columbia,* 774 F.Supp.2d 25, 33 (D.D.C. 2011).

Harris argues that "Sheets was entrusted with the care of Veterans who were significantly mentally and emotionally ill," and that "he knew there was no basis to arrest Harris" but "called security . . . and recklessly caused them to become involved in the unnecessary arrest and detention thereby breaching his duty to Harris." p.916 Harris concludes: "As a direct and proximate result of the intentional and wrongful actions of [Sheets], [Harris] suffered physical harm, emotional distress and mental anguish."

The district court did not directly address the negligent infliction of emotional distress claim; instead, the court considered it with the claim of intentional infliction of emotional distress, concluding that both claims failed because the VA police arrested Harris with probable cause and reasonably necessary force.

We affirm the grant of summary judgment on the negligent infliction of emotional distress claim without reaching its merits because Harris did not properly plead the claim in his amended complaint. Harris describes Sheets' actions as knowing and "intentional," and "[i]ntent and negligence are regarded as mutually exclusive grounds for liability." *District of Columbia v. Chinn,* 839 A.2d 701, 706 (D.C. 2003) (internal quotation marks and citation omitted); *see also* DAN B. DOBBS ET AL., THE LAW OF TORTS § 31 (2d ed. 2011) ("Any given act may be intentional or it may be negligent, but it cannot be both."). Merely using the term negligence does "not raise a cognizable claim of negligence." *Chinn,* 839 A.2d at 708. Here, as in *Rice,* Harris "fail[ed] to distinguish the bases for [his] claims." *Rice,* 774 F.Supp.2d at 33. Because the amended complaint "does not distinguish between negligent and intentional acts, does not identify any specific act that was allegedly negligent, and fails to make out a claim of negligent infliction of emotional distress," *id.* at 33-34, we affirm the district court's grant of summary judgment on this claim.

5. Intentional Infliction of Emotional Distress

To make out a claim for intentional infliction of emotional distress, Harris "must show that the [VA] acted in an (1) extreme and outrageous manner (2) which was intentionally or recklessly calculated to cause [Harris] (3) severe emotional distress." *Joyce,* 795 F.Supp. at 5 (citing *Green v. Am. Broad. Co.,* 647 F.Supp. 1359, 1362 (D.D.C.1986)). Generally, "[l]iability has been found only where the conduct has been so outrageous in character, and so extreme in degree, as to go beyond all possible bounds of decency, and to be regarded as atrocious, and utterly intolerable in a civilized community." *Abourezk v. N.Y. Airlines, Inc.,* 895 F.2d 1456, 1459 (D.C.Cir.1990) (quoting *Sere v. Grp. Hospitalization, Inc.,* 443 A.2d 33, 37 (D.C. 1982)) (alteration in original); *see also* RESTATEMENT (SECOND) OF TORTS § 46 cmt. d (1965).

In his amended complaint, Harris alleged that Sheets "acted in a manner that he hoped would cause intentional harm to [Harris], including physical harm." Sheets allegedly "knew or should have known that his calling of security and excluding [Harris] from the class would result in further emotional and mental harm to [Harris]," and, as a result of Sheets' "intentional and wrongful actions [Harris] suffered physical harm, emotional distress and mental anguish." In his opposition to the VA's motion for summary judgment, Harris stated that he based his intentional infliction of emotional distress claim on both the VA officers' alleged use of excessive force and the allegedly unjustified arrest. He distinguished his case from *Gabrou v. May Department Stores,* 462 A.2d at 1102, on which the VA's motion for summary judgment relied, by noting that the plaintiff in *Gabrou* failed to plead assault and battery in his complaint, whereas "Harris's claim of excessive force is at the heart of his Amended Complaint and is sufficiently pled with facts that support his claim." He argues that the fact that he was "arrested, beaten, and brutalized could result in a jury concluding that the officers' behavior p.917 was 'outrageous,'" and, thus, his claim for intentional infliction of emotional distress should survive summary judgment.

As an initial matter, while Harris describes Sheets' actions in his amended complaint, the VA is the defendant and its agents (the police officers) allegedly committed the assault and battery. As the VA concedes in its papers before the district court and as the district court recognized in its decision, the issue here is whether the officers' actions constituted intentional infliction of emotional distress. The VA, through the doctrine of *respondeat superior,* would be liable for torts committed by the VA police officers acting in their scope of employment. *See Holder v. District of Columbia,* 700 A.2d 738, 741-42 (D.C. 1997). Accordingly, like the district court, we construe Harris' claim as against the defendant, the VA, and not Sheets.

As discussed, we hold that the VA had probable cause to arrest Harris. To the extent that Harris' claim of intentional infliction of emotional distress arises from the mere fact of his arrest, we agree with the district court that the probable cause for arrest defeats those claims. *See Joyce,* 795 F.Supp. at 5. But insofar as Harris' emotional distress claim relates to his assault and battery claim (and to the underlying allegations of excessive force), we reverse.

The district court predicated its ruling on the basis that Harris' arrest was effectuated with reasonable force. But that conclusion involves disputed factual issues, such as whether the police struck Harris once he was restrained, fracturing his rib and causing other injuries.

Applying the established three-part standard for intentional infliction of emotional distress, we note, first, that "a serious case of excessive force" can constitute outrageous behavior such that it satisfies a claim of intentional infliction of emotional distress. *Gabrou,* 462 A.2d at 1105 (internal quotation marks and citation omitted); *see Jackson v. District of Columbia,* 412 A.2d 948, 955 (D.C.1980); *see also Bender v. City of New York,* 78 F.3d 787, 791 (2d Cir.1996) (applying New York law); *Robins v. Harum,* 773 F.2d 1004, 1011 (9th Cir.1985) (applying Washington state law).

Second, the requisite intent of the defendant can be "inferred, either from the very outrageousness of the defendant's acts or . . . when the circumstances are such that 'any reasonable person would have known that (emotional distress and physical harm) would result.'" *Waldon v. Covington,* 415 A.2d 1070, 1077 (D.C.1980) (citation omitted); *see also Kotsch v. District of Columbia,* 924 A.2d 1040, 1046 (D.C.2007). Such an inquiry "is normally a factual question for the jury." *Ross v. DynCorp,* 362 F.Supp.2d 344, 360 (D.D.C. 2005) (quoting *Waldon,* 415 A.2d at 1078).

Third, with regard to the required showing of severe emotional distress, "[w]hile tort law historically required some physical manifestation or symptom of the alleged emotional distress as a condition for recovery, current D.C. law allows 'an action for intentional infliction [of emotional distress to] be made out even in the absence of physical injury or impact.'" *Id.* at 360-61 (alteration in original) (quoting *Waldon,* 415 A.2d at 1076). Harris states that he "endured multiple hospital visits," "suffered substantial mental and emotional trauma," and "aggravated [his] PTSD" as a result of the incident. The VA contests the degree to which his PTSD worsened and its cause. Harris' alleged injuries, including a fractured rib and worsened PTSD, might suffice to establish severe emotional distress. *See* RESTATEMENT (SECOND) OF TORTS § 46 cmt. k ("Normally, severe emotional distress is accompanied or followed by shock, illness, or p.918 other bodily harm, which in itself affords evidence that the distress is genuine and severe."); *see also District of Columbia v. Tulin,* 994 A.2d 788, 801 (D.C.2010) ("aggravation of a pre-existing depression" could support emotional distress claim).

Given how little is actually established about the VA police's arrest of Harris and its consequences on his health, we reverse the grant of summary judgment on this claim. *See Tulin,* 994 A.2d at 803.

IV.

We reverse the grant of summary judgment on Harris' assault and battery claim and on his claim of intentional infliction of emotional distress to the extent that it is based on his assault and battery claim. We affirm the grant of summary judgment on all other claims.

So ordered.

[1] Harris' amended complaint states that the incident in question occurred "[o]n or about November 5, 2008," although all other record evidence, including Harris' own Statement of Material Facts in Dispute, states it occurred on November 6, 2008.

[2] "In the District of Columbia, the torts of false arrest and false imprisonment are indistinguishable." *Joyce v. United States,* 795 F.Supp. 1, 4 (D.D.C.1992), *aff'd,* 986 F.2d 546 (D.C.Cir.1993) (unpublished) (citing *Shaw v. May Dep't Stores Co.,* 268 A.2d 607 (D.C.App. 1970)).

[3] Harris was cited only for a violation of the portion of the regulation that lists the schedule of offenses. 38 C.F.R. § 1.218(b)(11). We note, as have other courts, that a violation of § 1.218(b)(11) is tantamount to a violation of the offenses prohibited by § 1.218(a)(5). *See United States v. Dyers,* No. 1:06-MJ-455-AJB, 2007 WL 397109, at *1-2 (N.D.Ga. Jan. 30, 2007); *United States v. Fentress,* 241 F.Supp.2d 526, 529 (D.Md.2003), *aff'd,* 69 Fed.Appx. 643 (4th Cir.2003).

[4] The VA argues that we should not rely on *Arrington* for the proposition that a plaintiff's sworn statement, contradicting the defendant's version of the facts, is sufficient to create a genuine issue in dispute, because "unlike Arrington, Harris' affidavit appears to contradict his own complaints and the authrotiative [sic] medical evidence." Appellee Br. at 17 n. 2.

The VA has misread the sealed medical records. The VA writes in its brief that Harris did not complain of rib pain resulting from the incident "until over a year later." *Id.* at 17. That statement is not accurate. Harris' statements and the medical evidence are not contradictory.

FIRST CIRCUIT DECISIONS
Federal Tort Claims Act

845 F.3d 487 (2017)

Errol HOLLOWAY, Plaintiff, Appellant,
v.
UNITED STATES of America, Defendant, Appellee.

No. 16-1402.

United States Court of Appeals, First Circuit.

January 11, 2017.

Holloway v. US, 845 F. 3d 487 (1st Cir. 2017)

p.488 Appeal from the United States District Court for the District of Massachusetts, [Hon. Mark G. Mastroianni, *U.S. District Judge*].

Thomas M. Libbos, Springfield, MA, Katherine L. Lamondia-Wrinkle, and Thomas M. Libbos PC on brief for appellant.

Carmen M. Ortiz, United States Attorney, and Karen L. Goodwin, Assistant United States Attorney, on brief for appellee.

Before Lynch, Selya, and Thompson, Circuit Judges.

THOMPSON, Circuit Judge.

Preface

Errol Holloway appeals the grant of summary judgment to the United States in this action under the Federal Tort Claims Act ("FTCA"). Spying no reversible error, we affirm.

How the Case Got Here[1]

We reconstruct the chronology of events giving rise to this litigation:

• *June 22, 2012.* Holloway is injured while receiving treatment at Caring Health Center, Inc., a federally funded healthcare facility in Springfield, Massachusetts.

• *April 8, 2014.* Holloway — through his lawyer — files an administrative claim with the Department of Health and Human Services ("HHS"), using a Standard Form 95 ("SF 95"). But he fails to fill out the box for a sum certain. Text in that box warns that "[f]ailure to specify may cause forfeiture of your rights." Elsewhere the form — occasionally using boldface, underlining, and capitalized text — says that he had to provide a sum certain for the claim to be considered "presented," that he had "two years" to present the claim, and that "[f]ailure to completely execute this form or to supply the requested material within two years from the date the claim accrued may render your claim invalid."

• *April 17, 2014.* HHS acknowledges receiving Holloway's SF 95 and requests medical records, itemized bills, evidence of lost wages, and the like.

• *June 25, 2014.* More than two years after the incident at Caring Health Center, Holloway's lawyer submits medical bills, employment records, and other documents.

- *August 14, 2014.* A paralegal in the HHS general counsel's office calls Holloway's attorney, mentions the missing sum certain, and asks counsel to submit an amended SF 95 with the required sum certain. HHS then gets an p.489 amended form requesting a sum certain in the amount of $3,000,000 for personal injuries.

- *August 21, 2014.* HHS denies Holloway's claim, saying "[t]he evidence fails to establish that the alleged injuries were due to the negligent or wrongful act or omission of a federal employee acting within the scope of employment."

An unhappy Holloway sued the United States in federal court in February 2015, seeking damages under the FTCA. Convinced that Holloway's failure to provide a timely sum-certain demand deprived the court of jurisdiction, the United States moved to dismiss the case for lack of subject-matter jurisdiction. Holloway responded with a double-pronged argument: first, that he timely presented his claim because his submissions satisfied HHS's investigatory needs; second, and alternatively, that the limitations period should be tolled. The district judge referred the motion to a magistrate judge.

After noting that the Supreme Court had recently held that the FTCA's limitations period is nonjurisdictional and subject to equitable tolling, see United States v. Kwai Fun Wong, ___ U.S. ___, 135 S.Ct. 1625, 1638, 191 L.Ed.2d 533 (2015), the magistrate judge treated the motion as one for summary judgment and recommended that judgment enter for the United States. Her reasoning ran this way. For starters, she concluded that Holloway had neither timely specified a sum certain nor timely provided documents from which "such a sum could be ascertained" and so had not properly presented his claim to HHS. And then she found that nothing that took place here qualified as extraordinary circumstances meriting equitable tolling, particularly since Holloway conceded that he did have constructive or actual knowledge of the filing requirements. Holloway objected, attacking only the magistrate judge's untimeliness conclusion. Agreeing that Holloway "did not timely satisfy" the FTCA's requirements, the district judge later adopted the magistrate judge's recommendation on *de novo* review.

Which brings us to today, with Holloway asking us to reverse and send the matter to trial. But before tackling his many arguments, we pause to give a quick tutorial on the relevant aspects of the FTCA.

The FTCA

The FTCA waives sovereign immunity for certain tortious acts and omissions of federal employees. See 28 U.S.C. §§ 1346(b)(1), 2674. And like other sovereign-immunity waivers, the FTCA gets a strict reading. See, e.g., Donahue v. United States, 634 F.3d 615, 622 (1st Cir. 2011). What that means is that judges "must faithfully enforce" the FTCA's "requirements, neither 'extend[ing] the waiver beyond that which Congress intended [nor assuming] authority to narrow the waiver.'" Id. (quoting United States v. Kubrick, 444 U.S. 111, 118, 100 S.Ct. 352, 62 L.Ed.2d 259 (1979)).

A key FTCA requirement is that a person cannot sue under it unless he first presents his "claim" to the relevant administrative agency "within two years after such claim accrues" — failure to present a claim within that period "forever bar[s]" the claim. 28 U.S.C. § 2401(b). An essential element of a claim is "notification of the incident," via "an executed" SF 95 or "other written" document, "accompanied by" a demand "for money damages in a *sum certain.*" See 28 C.F.R. § 14.2(a) (emphasis added). The purpose behind the sum-certain requirement is to tip the government off as to its "possible liability" so that it can "'investigate the alleged negligent episode'" to see "'if settlement would p.490 be in the best interests of all.'" Coska v. United States, 114 F.3d 319, 322 (1st Cir. 1997) (quoting Corte-Real v. United States, 949 F.2d 484, 486 (1st Cir. 1991), in turn quoting Lopez v. United States, 758 F.2d 806, 809 (1st Cir. 1985)); see also Reilly v. United States, 863 F.2d 149, 173 (1st Cir. 1988) (noting that "[t]he goal of the administrative claim requirement is to let the government know what it is likely up against: mandating that a claimant propound a definite monetary demand ensures that '[t]he government will at all relevant times be aware of its maximum possible exposure to liability and will be in a position to make intelligent settlement decisions'" (quoting Martinez v. United States, 780 F.2d 525, 530 (5th Cir. 1986))). And because the FTCA ties "both the authority to settle a claim and the source of settlement funds to the amount of the underlying claim,"[2] not having a sum certain obviously makes it harder for the government to determine the claim's value and to "handl[e]" the claim "efficiently." Kokotis, 223 F.3d at 279.

Having said all this, we must acknowledge that we "approach[] the notice requirement leniently, 'recognizing that individuals wishing to sue the government must comply with the details of the law, but also keeping in mind that the law was not intended to put up a barrier of technicalities to defeat their claims.'" Santiago-Ramírez v. Sec'y of Dept. of Def., 984 F.2d 16, 19 (1st Cir. 1993) (quoting Lopez, 758 F.2d at 809). Perhaps that is why our cases suggest that the failure to specify a sum certain on the SF 95 may not be fatal if the claimant provides documents (*e.g.,* medical bills) that "lend" themselves "to determination of a sum certain or even an approximate total of damages claimed." See Kokaras v. United States, 980 F.2d 20, 22 (1st Cir. 1992); see also Coska, 114 F.3d at 323 (noting that "[i]t is the information available rather than the form in which it is presented that is crucial," but finding dismissal of plaintiff's claim appropriate where (among other things) "there was essential information missing from the packet and the letters" submitted there, "namely, the amount of damages being sought from the United States").

With this legal primer in place, we turn to the particulars of Holloway's challenges.

Arguments and Analysis[3]

Conceding — as he must — that his SF 95 did not include a sum certain, Holloway raises several arguments for reversal. None has merit, as the United States is quick to point out.

Quoting Santiago-Ramírez's language about our taking a "lenient" view of the FTCA's claim-presentment requirements, Holloway argues first that we should reverse the lower court's untimeliness ruling because his sum-certain omission was (emphasis his) "*inadvertent*": as he sees things, an inadvertent omission — in and of p.491 itself — excuses him from having to satisfy the sum-certain requirement. But the cases of ours that he talks about, — Kokaras and Corte-Real, for example — do not support his argument.

The Kokaras plaintiffs filed an SF 95 with the United States Post Office following a collision with a mail truck. See 980 F.2d at 21. In box A of the form, labeled "Property Damage," plaintiffs wrote "$2,906.61" and in box B, labeled "Personal Injury," they wrote "to be determined." Id. They left box C, labeled "Total," blank. Id. Later — but still within the two-year statute of limitations — they hired a lawyer who, during unsuccessful settlement talks, handed over medical records and bills. Id. Ultimately, we upheld the dismissal of the personal-injury claim, holding that plaintiffs did not timely state a sum certain — "[n]owhere on form SF 95 is a sum certain for the personal injuries stated," we wrote. Id. at 22-23. We also held that they did not timely provide the agency with documents with enough info to otherwise satisfy the sum-certain requirement (we did let the property-damages claim proceed because their SF 95 did *specify* a sum certain). Id.

The Corte-Real plaintiff filed an SF 95 that had "$100,000 plus because still treating and out of work" written in the box requiring him to state the dollar amount attributable to his personal injury. See 949 F.2d at 485. But he wrote "$100,000" — without any qualifying language — in the box requiring him to list the total dollar amount of his claims. Id. Emphasizing "the importance and absolute necessity of adher[ing] to the sum certain requirement," we said:

> Where as here a claim clearly states a specific sum and meets the sum certain requirement in all respects but for concern over the possible detraction of improper surplusage of this insubstantial variety, we see no reason not to strike the surplusage rather than the claim itself.

Id. at 486-87.

From all of this it is clear that Holloway's talk about inadvertent omissions is a distraction: Kokaras and Corte-Real whisper no hint of a suggestion that their outcomes turned on whether the plaintiffs accidently or intentionally failed to fill in the sum-certain box. As always in this type of case — given the FTCA's goal of efficiently handling claims and our desire not to promote "bureaucratic overkill," see Corte-Real, 949 F.2d at 486 — what matters is whether the plaintiff timely specified a sum certain on the SF 95 or otherwise timely provided documents from which a sum certain could be ascertained. And keeping our eyes firmly fixed on that standard, we trudge on.[4]

Perhaps sensing the grave problem with his inadvertent-omission argument, Holloway fashions a fallback position — namely, that despite his accidently omitting a sum certain from his SF 95, HHS's "investigatory needs were satisfied" in the end and so dismissal on timeliness grounds was not called for. To give his position a patina of plausibility, he contends that the documents he provided in response to HHS's request disclosed "enough" information to satisfy the sum-certain requirement and thus he should be deemed to have fully complied with his FTCA obligations. More, he believes that HHS's rejection of his p.492 FTCA claim "on the merits" shows that he in no way crippled "the agency's investigatory purpose." Call us unconvinced.

As for the "documents" facet of Holloway's argument, we see two problems. One is that he submitted those papers *after* the limitations period had run. The other is that those documents — like the documents considered insufficient in Coska and Kokotis — lack the necessary info to calculate a sum certain. The magistrate judge here did a fine job of listing the documents' shortcomings. "Plaintiff's medical bills," she wrote (as a for-instance), "d[o] not consistently identify the service provided, the total cost of the service, the amount of the cost covered by insurance, or the amount of the cost covered by Plaintiff," and "the employment records" contain no "indication as to the amount in lost wages Plaintiff might be claiming." Our own review of the records leads us to the same conclusion. If more were needed — and it plainly is not — Holloway's brief spends no time trying to explain away the flaws spotlighted below. And we will not do counsel's work for them. See Ondine Shipping Corp. v. Cataldo, 24 F.3d 353, 356 (1st Cir. 1994).

As for the "merits" facet of Holloway's argument, we note that even if HHS had enough info to conclude that a federal employee's negligence did not cause his injuries, all of HHS's investigatory needs were *not* satisfied without a sum certain. Remember, a sum certain helps the appropriate decisionmakers to decide whether settlement is the best option and, if it is, to also determine where to get the settlement funds from. See, e.g., Coska, 114 F.3d at 322; Reilly, 863 F.2d at 173. Holloway's brief does not say anything about these important needs.

Taking a different tack, Holloway argues that, if nothing else, HHS *misled* him into thinking that its investigatory needs were satisfied and so the United States should not have been allowed to seek dismissal on timeliness grounds. But this argument has no oomph. Recall how the SF 95 let him know — as plain as day — that he had two years to present his claim, that for a claim to be considered presented a sum-certain dollar amount had to be included, and that he may forfeit his rights by failing to comply. Recall too how our caselaw highlights how important a timely-stated sum certain is. Well, Holloway makes no effort to explain how his theory about being misled can fly given the clarity of the SF 95 and our caselaw. Cf. United States v. Dwyer, 843 F.2d 60, 64 (1st Cir. 1988) (emphasizing that courts "publish" opinions "so that future lawyers" will "know the law"). Also and critically, because (as we just said) he does not address all of the agency's important investigatory needs, he never explains how any HHS action implied that these needs had been met here — which further undermines his I-was-misled argument.[5]

In a parting shot, Holloway argues that he is entitled to equitable tolling of the FTCA's limitations period. But he did not raise this argument in his objection to the magistrate judge's recommended decision. And our waiver rule bars any consideration of this issue. See Sch. Union No. 37 p.493 v. United Nat'l Ins. Co., 617 F.3d 554, 564 (1st Cir. 2010).

Conclusion

For the reasons expressed above, we affirm the judgment entered below.

[1] We summarize the background facts in the light most agreeable to Holloway, as required on *de novo* review of a summary-judgment ruling. See Baltodano v. Merck, Sharp, & Dohme (I.A.) Corp., 637 F.3d 38, 41 (1st Cir. 2011).

[2] "[C]laims of $2,500 or less," for example, "can be settled on the authority of '[t]he head of each Federal agency or his designee' and are paid 'out of

appropriations available to that agency'"; "[c]laims of between $2,500 and $25,000 can be settled on the same authority, but are paid out of a separate appropriation"; and "claims in excess of $25,000 can only be settled 'with the prior written approval of the Attorney General or his designee.'" Kokotis v. USPS, 223 F.3d 275, 279 (4th Cir. 2000) (quoting 28 U.S.C. § 2672).

[3] Keep in mind, please, that we give fresh review to the grant of summary judgment, affirming if — after giving Holloway the benefit of all reasonable inferences in the record — there is no "genuine dispute" of "material fact" and the United States "is entitled to judgment as a matter of law." See Fed. R. Civ. P. 56(a); Tutor Perini Corp. v. Banc Am. Sec. LLC, 842 F.3d 71, 84 (1st Cir. 2016).

[4] After marching us through our caselaw, Holloway insists that other "circuit courts" have "refused to order dismissal" in "factually analogous situations." But he does not point to a single case from another circuit court to back up his statement. So we consider his other-circuits-support-my-position argument waived for lack of development. See United States v. Zannino, 895 F.2d 1, 17 (1st Cir. 1990).

[5] Holloway's argument kind of sort of has a whiff of equitable estoppel — a "doctrine ... used sparingly against the government." United States v. Ledée, 772 F.3d 21, 29 (1st Cir. 2014); see also Nagle v. Acton-Boxborough Reg'l Sch. Dist., 576 F.3d 1, 3 (1st Cir. 2009) (explaining that "under federal precedent, governments in the past have not been subject to estoppel or, more recently, have been held not subject to estoppel, save [in] exceptional situations that we have called 'hen's-teeth rare'" (quoting Costa v. INS, 233 F.3d 31, 38 (1st Cir. 2000))). But he does not develop the equitable-estoppel point, meaning any such argument is waived. See Zannino, 895 F.2d at 17.

799 F.3d 151 (2015)

Roberto Carlos DOMINGUEZ, Plaintiff, Appellant,
v.
UNITED STATES of America, Defendant, Appellee.

No. 13-2266.

United States Court of Appeals, First Circuit.

August 27, 2015.

Dominguez v. US, 799 F. 3d 151 (1st Cir. 2015)

p.152 Gerald A. Phelps for appellant.

Brian Pérez-Daple, Assistant United States Attorney, with whom Carmen M. Ortiz, United States Attorney, was on brief, for appellee.

Before HOWARD, Chief Judge, LYNCH and THOMPSON, Circuit Judges.

HOWARD, Chief Judge.

Plaintiff-appellant Roberto Carlos Dominguez filed suit seeking money damages against the United States under the Federal Tort Claims Act ("FTCA"), 28 U.S.C. §§ 1346(b)(1), 2671 et seq. Dominguez alleged that in 1998 and 1999 he was wrongfully detained and deported as an unauthorized alien despite his true status as a United States citizen. The district court dismissed the case as time barred on the government's motion, thereby rejecting Dominguez's attempt to use the discovery rule as shelter for his claims. Concluding that delayed accrual is foreclosed by the factual allegations in Dominguez's complaint, we affirm.

We construe the facts alleged favorably to the plaintiff, and, viewed through that lens, the complaint and attached exhibits present the following facts. *See Yacubian v. United States,* 750 F.3d 100, 107-08 (1st Cir.2014). Federal immigration authorities detained Dominguez from July 1998 through September 1999. In the course of numerous interrogations, Dominguez told Immigration and Customs Enforcement ("ICE") agents that he was born in Lawrence, Massachusetts, but the agents failed to investigate his citizenship status beyond the immigration file and ignored his claim of a United States birthplace. After an administrative hearing before an Immigration Judge ("IJ") in September 1999, Dominguez was ordered removed to the Dominican Republic. ICE agents told him that if he ever returned to America he would be incarcerated.

Dominguez lived in the Dominican Republic for the next ten years. At some point, friends and family told him to go to the United States Embassy to see what, if any, paperwork he could obtain in order to return to the United States. Dominguez did so, and after submitting a United States birth certificate and other documentation, he was granted a U.S. passport. He returned to this country in September 2009, and for about a year he lived in fear that he again would be deported or thrown in jail. In November 2010, Dominguez met with a lawyer to "give himself up" but instead allegedly learned that his detention and deportation at the hands of the federal government had been illegal. Dominguez did not pursue relief until February 2012 when he first filed a damages claim through administrative channels as required under the FTCA. *See* 28 U.S.C. § 2675(a). Meanwhile, in October 2011, federal authorities had asked the Commonwealth of

Massachusetts to detain him and also had required Dominguez to surrender his U.S. passport.[1]

p.153 In his complaint, Dominguez faults the government for, among other things, failing to investigate his claims of U.S. citizenship in 1998-1999 thereby causing his illegal detention and removal as a United States citizen. He attached to the complaint a purported Massachusetts birth certificate showing that he had been born in Lawrence, Massachusetts on November 9, 1979.[2] Dominguez asserted claims against the United States and three individual federal employees who had been involved in his detention and deportation or in issuing the 2011 detention letter. The individual defendants later were dismissed from the case, leaving the federal government as the sole defending party.

After conducting a hearing on the government's motion to dismiss, the district court granted the motion and entered a final judgment of dismissal in September 2013. We review the court's decision de novo. *Sanchez v. United States,* 740 F.3d 47, 52 (1st Cir.2014).

The FTCA permits suits against the government for torts caused by the wrongful acts of any government employee while acting within the scope of his office or employment. *See* 28 U.S.C. §§ 1346(b)(1), 2645. Plaintiffs have two years from the time of accrual to file a claim with the appropriate agency and then, if the claim is denied, six months after the denial to file suit. *See id.* § 2401(b). Therefore, if Dominguez's detention and deportation in 1998 and 1999 constituted the accrual conduct, his decade-plus delay in filing an agency claim in February 2012 would, of course, bar his federal suit. Application of the federal discovery rule is Dominguez's only hope, and it quickly fades.

The discovery rule applies to certain FTCA claims "under circumstances where the fact or cause of an injury is unknown to (and perhaps unknowable by) a plaintiff for some time after the injury occurs, and which will sometimes dictate that a claim accrues well after the time of the injury." *Rakes v. United States,* 442 F.3d 7, 19 (1st Cir.2006); *see Sanchez,* 740 F.3d at 52. For such claims, the cause of action accrues once the plaintiff knows, or in the exercise of reasonable diligence should have known, the factual basis of the cause of action, which includes the existence of an injury and its probable causal connection to the federal government. *McIntyre v. United States,* 367 F.3d 38, 52 (1st Cir.2004); *Callahan v. United States,* 426 F.3d 444, 451 (1st Cir.2005). This objective inquiry focuses on when a person similarly situated to the plaintiff would have discovered necessary facts in the exercise of reasonable diligence. *See Sanchez,* 740 F.3d at 52; *McIntyre,* 367 F.3d at 59.

Dominguez's own factual allegations in his complaint place the time of accrual well before February 2010, the date that is two years prior to his agency filing. He alleges that he knew of his United States birthplace at the time of his deportation in 1999 and also that his detention and deportation by the United States government were based on his status as an unauthorized alien. He alleges that he knew that, even though he had told federal officials of his United States citizenship status, the immigration proceedings p.154 continued and resulted in his removal from this country as a foreigner. Dominguez further alleges that, while in the Dominican Republic, he took steps to return to his alleged homeland and even acquired and delivered a Massachusetts birth certificate to the embassy. All of this he knew prior to September 2009 when he returned to the United States.

These are more than enough facts to charge a reasonable person with knowledge, and certainly would put a person on at least inquiry notice, in 1999 or soon thereafter of the putative injury and its probable causal connection to the federal government. Under any accounting, accrual occurred before September 2009 when Dominguez returned to the United States with a U.S. passport and birth certificate in hand. This dooms his federal lawsuit.

Dominguez asserts, however, that while he knew he had been deported in 1999, he remained in the dark about the illegal nature of his deportation and its probable connection to the failures of ICE agents. He contends that it was not until November 2010 when he met with a lawyer for the first time that the necessary basis for the cause of action became known to him. This argument goes nowhere. Federal law does not allow a potential plaintiff to await confirmation from an attorney before the limitations period begins to run. *See Sanchez,* 740 F.3d at 52; *Rakes,* 442 F.3d at 20 n. 8; *Callahan,* 426 F.3d at 451.

In an attempt to keep the door slightly ajar, Dominguez asserts a type of duress or fraud argument that skews application of the reasonable person inquiry under the federal discovery rule. He claims that the 1999 threats of imprisonment should he return to the United States (and other vague allusions of "negligence, fraud, threats, and intimidation" by ICE agents) overpowered his mind and rendered him unable to link the government misconduct to his injury until 2010 when legal counsel cleared the cloud. The trouble is, he relies on Massachusetts law (a single case) to advance his anemic argument, *see Riley v. Presnell,* 409 Mass. 239, 565 N.E.2d 780 (1991), when it is federal law that governs the statute of limitations accrual question for FTCA claims. *See, e.g., United States v. Kubrick,* 444 U.S. 111, 123, 100 S.Ct. 352, 62 L.Ed.2d 259 (1979); *Sanchez,* 740 F.3d at 52; *see also Rakes,* 442 F.3d at 19 n. 7 (collecting cases). And, federal law is to the contrary. *Cf. Rakes,* 442 F.3d at 24-27 (demonstrating that the concepts of duress and fraudulent concealment pertain to tolling doctrines under federal law and are not part of the discovery rule calculus).

Dominguez also contends that the government's ongoing refusal to acknowledge his citizenship status constitutes a continuing tort that delays accrual of his FTCA claim until he is adjudicated a United States citizen. However, not only was his administrative complaint based only on the government's conduct in 1998-1999, but also he offers no argument as to how he could possibly be entitled to such an adjudication of his citizenship in the face of the IJ's 1999 deportation ruling that he neither appealed to the Board of Immigration Appeals nor sought to reopen. With this essential link lacking, Dominguez's continuing violation theory is a nonstarter. *Cf., Fisher v. United States,* 959 F.2d 230, 1992 WL 63516, at *4 (1st Cir.1992) (per curiam) (unpublished disposition) (holding that false arrest with its ongoing effects is not a continuing tort and thus accrues at the time of arrest).

Finally, we note that any peripheral argument based on equitable tolling, *see United States v. Kwai Fun Wong,* 575 U.S. ___, 135 S.Ct. 1625, 191 L.Ed.2d 533 (2015), either has been waived for lack of p.155 development, *see United States v. Zannino,* 895 F.2d 1, 17 (1st Cir.1990), or is so embedded in his discovery rule arguments such that they fall together, *see, e.g., Sanchez,* 740 F.3d at 53-54 (holding that the plaintiff's patent lack of diligence forecloses equitable tolling of FTCA claim).

Because we resolve this case on statute of limitations grounds, we do not reach the government's other assorted bases for dismissal. The judgment of the district court is *affirmed*.

Costs are awarded to the appellee.

[1] At argument before us, the government represented that Dominguez is not in custody and that no removal proceedings are pending against him.

[2] The government identifies several discrepancies which, it claims, undermine the validity of the Massachusetts birth certificate document and stands by its initial reliance on documents in the immigration file to show Dominguez's Dominican Republic citizenship. It is unnecessary for us to decide the validity of the document.

Second Circuit Decisions
Federal Tort Claims Act

825 F.3d 118 (2016)

Daniel MCGOWAN, Plaintiff-Appellant,

v.

UNITED STATES of America, Tracy Rivers, Residential Reentry Manager,
Defendants-Appellees,

Core Service Group, Inc., Community First Services, Inc., Grace Terry, Facility
Director, Massiel Suriel, Case Manager, Unknown United States Marshals,
Defendants.[1]

Docket No. 15-1786 August Term, 2015.

United States Court of Appeals, Second Circuit.

Argued: March 2, 2016.

Decided: June 7, 2016.

McGowan v. US, 825 F. 3d 118 (2nd Cir. 2016)

Appeal from a final judgment, entered on April 7, 2015, in the United States District Court for the Eastern District of New York (Cogan, J.), dismissing plaintiff Daniel McGowan's complaint. McGowan alleged that, while serving a federal sentence of incarceration, he was placed in solitary confinement for approximately twenty-two hours in retaliation for publishing an article online. As relevant here, he asserted claims for violation of his First Amendment rights against Tracy Rivers, a Bureau of Prisons employee, under *Bivens v. Six Unknown Named Agents,* 403 U.S. 388 (1971), and for false imprisonment and negligence against the United States under the Federal Tort Claims Act ("FTCA"), 28 U.S.C. §§ 1346(b), 2671-2680.

We hold that: (1) Rivers is entitled to qualified immunity from McGowan's Bivens claim because the asserted First Amendment right was not clearly established at the time of the challenged conduct; and (2) the district court lacked subject-matter jurisdiction of McGowan's FTCA claims because they have no private analogue. Accordingly, we AFFIRM the judgment of the district court.

ALEXANDER A. REINERT, New York, NY (David B. Rankin, Rankin & Taylor PLLC, New York, NY, on the brief), for Plaintiff-Appellant.

ELLIOT M. SCHACHNER, Assistant United States Attorney (Varuni Nelson, Assistant United States Attorney, on the brief), for Robert L. Capers, United States Attorney for the Eastern District of New York, Brooklyn, NY, for Defendants-Appellees.

Before: Katzmann, Chief Judge, Sack and Lohier, Circuit Judges.

Per Curiam:

p.121Plaintiff Daniel McGowan appeals from a judgment of the United States District Court for the Eastern District of New York (Cogan, J.), entered on April 7, 2015, dismissing his complaint. As relevant here, McGowan asserted claims for violation of his First Amendment rights under *Bivens v. Six Unknown Named Agents,* 403 U.S. 388, 91 S.Ct. 1999, 29 L.Ed.2d 619 (1971), and for false imprisonment and negligence under the Federal Tort Claims Act ("FTCA"), 28 U.S.C. §§ 1346(b), 2671-2680. The district court dismissed McGowan's *Bivens* claim on the ground that there is no private right of action for violation of a federal prisoner's First Amendment rights. It dismissed McGowan's false imprisonment claim for failure to state a claim upon which relief may be granted and dismissed his negligence claim for lack of subject-matter jurisdiction. We affirm p.122 the dismissal of McGowan's negligence claim for lack of subject-matter jurisdiction, and we affirm the dismissal of his remaining claims on alternative grounds.

BACKGROUND

On June 4, 2007, following his conviction in the United States District Court for the District of Oregon on multiple counts of arson, attempted arson, and conspiracy to commit arson, McGowan was sentenced principally to eighty-four months' incarceration. On December 11, 2012, he was transferred to Brooklyn House Residential Reentry Center ("RRC") to serve the remainder of his sentence. McGowan alleges that, at Brooklyn House RRC, he received daily work passes, which allowed him to maintain full-time employment as a receptionist, and enjoyed privileges such as weekend home visits, unrestricted use of the internet, a shopping pass, and the opportunity to apply to attend social events.

On April 1, 2013, McGowan published an article on the Huffington Post website under his own byline. *See* Daniel McGowan, *Court Documents Prove I was Sent to a Communications Management Unit (CMU) for my Political Speech,* Huffington Post (Apr. 1, 2013, 8:36 AM), http:// www.huffingtonpost.com/daniel-mcgowan/ communication-management-units_b_ 2944580.html. In the article, McGowan asserted that, while serving his federal sentence, he had been placed in a highly restrictive Communication Management Unit in retaliation for publishing political opinion pieces. *Id.*

McGowan alleges that, shortly after his article appeared online, defendant Tracy Rivers, the Residential Reentry Manager at the New York Residential Reentry Management Office of the Bureau of Prisons ("BOP"), determined that he should be issued an incident report and remanded to a federal detention center. The incident report stated that McGowan had violated "BOP Program Statement no. 1480.05 dated September 21, 2000; 540.62 page 5, section (d)," which provided that "an inmate currently confined in an institution may not be employed or act as a reporter or publish under a byline" (the "Byline Regulation").

However, unbeknownst to Rivers, by the time these events occurred, the Byline Regulation had been rescinded. Specifically, in August 2007, a district court in Colorado held that the Byline Regulation was unconstitutional under the First Amendment. *See Jordan v. Pugh,* 504 F.Supp.2d 1109, 1124 (D. Colo. 2007). On November 27, 2007, the BOP issued mandatory guidance to its staff instructing them not to enforce it. On April 23, 2010, the BOP published an interim rule rescinding the Byline Regulation, and finalized that rule on May 3, 2012.

McGowan alleges that on April 4, 2013, he was taken from Brooklyn House RRC to the Metropolitan Detention Center and placed in the Special Housing Unit ("SHU"). After McGowan's lawyers contacted the BOP, Kerry P. Kemble, Assistant Administrator of the Residential Reentry Management Branch of the BOP, informed Rivers that the Byline Regulation had been rescinded. Kemble and Rivers agreed to expunge the incident report and return McGowan to Brooklyn House RRC. McGowan returned to Brooklyn House RRC on April 5, 2013, having spent approximately twenty-two hours in the SHU.

McGowan commenced this action on August 20, 2014, and filed his Amended Complaint on November 12, 2014. As relevant here, he asserted claims for: (1) violation of his First Amendment rights against Tracy Rivers under *Bivens v. Six Unknown Named Agents,* 403 U.S. 388, 91 S.Ct. 1999, 29 L.Ed.2d 619 (1971); (2) false imprisonment p.123 against the United States under the FTCA; and (3) negligence against the United States under the FTCA. McGowan also brought state law claims against Core Services Group, Inc. d/b/a Community First Services, Inc., the private operator of Brooklyn House RRC; those claims are not at issue in this appeal.[2]

On March 23, 2015, the district court granted the defendants' motion to dismiss McGowan's Amended Complaint. First, it declined to recognize a *Bivens* remedy for violations of federal prisoners' First Amendment rights. *McGowan v. United States,* 94 F.Supp.3d 382, 387-90 (E.D.N.Y. 2015). Second, it held that McGowan failed to state a claim for false imprisonment because, as an inmate serving a lawful sentence, his confinement was "uncategorically privileged." *Id.* at 390. Third, it held that it lacked subject-matter jurisdiction to hear McGowan's FTCA negligence claim because there was no "private analogue" to the BOP's allegedly negligent failure to follow its own regulation. *Id.* at 392-94. Having dismissed all of McGowan's federal claims, the district court declined to exercise supplemental jurisdiction over his state law claims. *Id.* at 394. This appeal followed.

DISCUSSION

I. Bivens Claim

In *Bivens,* the Supreme Court recognized "an implied private action for damages against federal officers alleged to have violated a citizen's constitutional rights." *Corr. Servs. Corp. v. Malesko,* 534 U.S. 61, 66, 122 S.Ct. 515, 151 L.Ed.2d 456 (2001) (citing *Bivens v. Six Unknown Named Agents,* 403 U.S. 388, 91 S.Ct. 1999, 29 L.Ed.2d 619 (1971)). We have established a two-step process for determining whether a *Bivens* remedy is available for an alleged constitutional injury. "First, the court must determine whether the underlying claims extend *Bivens* into a 'new context.'" *Turkmen v. Hasty,* 789 F.3d 218, 234 (2d Cir. 2015) (quoting *Arar v. Ashcroft,* 585 F.3d 559, 572 (2d Cir. 2009)). If the plaintiff's claims arise in a new context, the court then asks "(a) 'whether there is an alternative remedial scheme available to the plaintiff,' and, even if there is not, (b) 'whether special factors counsel hesitation in creating a *Bivens* remedy.'" *Id.* (quoting *Arar,* 585 F.3d at 572).

McGowan argues that his claim does not require us to extend *Bivens* to a new context, and, even if it did, that there is no adequate "alternative remedial scheme" and no "special factor[] counsel[ing] hesitation." *Id.* Accordingly, he argues, the district court erred in refusing to recognize a *Bivens* remedy. We need not decide this difficult issue, however, because we conclude that McGowan's *Bivens* claim fails for the independent reason that defendant Rivers is entitled to qualified immunity.

Although we generally decline to consider arguments that were not passed on by the district court, this principle is prudential, not jurisdictional. *See Fabrikant v. French,* 691 F.3d 193, 212 (2d Cir. 2012). We retain discretion to consider such arguments based on factors such as "the interests of judicial economy" and "whether the unaddressed issues present pure questions of law." *Bacolitsas v. 86th & 3rd Owner, LLC,* 702 F.3d 673, 681 (2d Cir. 2012). Both of these factors are present here. The issue of qualified immunity was presented in the district court, has been fully briefed on appeal, and turns on p.124 the purely legal question of whether McGowan alleged a violation of a clearly established right. *See Fabrikant,* 691 F.3d at 212 ("The matter of whether a right was clearly established at the pertinent time is a question of law." (quoting *Dean v. Blumenthal,* 577 F.3d 60, 67 n.6 (2d Cir. 2009))). It is therefore appropriate for us to consider the defense of qualified immunity on appeal.

"The doctrine of qualified immunity protects government officials from liability for civil damages 'unless a plaintiff pleads facts showing (1) that the official violated a statutory or constitutional right, and (2) that the right was "clearly established" at the time of the challenged conduct.'" *Wood v. Moss,* ___ U.S. ___, 134 S.Ct. 2056, 2066-67, 188 L.Ed.2d 1039 (2014) (quoting *Ashcroft v. al-Kidd,* 563 U.S. 731, 735, 131 S.Ct. 2074, 179 L.Ed.2d 1149 (2011)). For a right to be "clearly established," the "contours of the right must be sufficiently clear that a reasonable official would understand that what he is doing violates that right." *Anderson v. Creighton,* 483 U.S. 635, 640, 107 S.Ct. 3034, 97 L.Ed.2d 523 (1987). In making this determination, we consider Supreme Court and Second Circuit precedent as it existed at the time of the challenged conduct. *See Garcia v. Does,* 779 F.3d 84, 92 (2d Cir. 2014). Nonetheless, the "'absence of a decision by this Court or the Supreme Court directly addressing the right at issue will not preclude a finding that the law was clearly established' so long as preexisting law 'clearly foreshadow[s] a particular ruling on the issue.'" *Id.* (quoting *Tellier v. Fields,* 280 F.3d 69, 84 (2d Cir. 2000)). A court may "grant qualified immunity on the ground that a purported right was not 'clearly established' by prior case law, without resolving the often more difficult question whether the purported right exists at all." *Reichle v. Howards,* ___ U.S. ___, 132 S.Ct. 2088, 2093, 182 L.Ed.2d 985 (2012).

We conclude that, at the time the alleged violation occurred, our case law did not clearly establish that McGowan had a First Amendment right to publish his article. The Supreme Court has held that "when a prison regulation impinges on inmates' constitutional rights, the regulation is valid if it is reasonably related to legitimate penological interests." *Turner v. Safley,* 482 U.S. 78, 89, 107 S.Ct. 2254, 96 L.Ed.2d 64 (1987). This test is "particularly deferential to the informed discretion of corrections officials" where "accommodation of an asserted right will have a significant 'ripple effect' on fellow inmates or on prison staff." *Id.* at 90, 107 S.Ct. 2254. For example, the Supreme Court has upheld "proscriptions of media interviews with individual inmates, prohibitions on the activities of a prisoners' labor union, and restrictions on inmate-to-inmate written correspondence." *Shaw v. Murphy,* 532 U.S. 223, 229, 121 S.Ct. 1475, 149 L.Ed.2d 420 (2001) (citations omitted).

We have not identified any binding authority in existence at the relevant time that either "directly address[ed]" the reasonableness of the challenged conduct or "clearly foreshadow[ed]" a ruling in McGowan's favor, *Garcia,* 779 F.3d at 92, nor has McGowan cited any such case. McGowan relies instead on cases establishing the right of a prisoner to be free from retaliation for filing a lawsuit or grievance.

See Espinal v. Goord, 558 F.3d 119, 128-29 (2d Cir. 2009); *Davis v. Goord,* 320 F.3d 346, 352-53 (2d Cir. 2003); *Gayle v. Gonyea,* 313 F.3d 677, 683 (2d Cir. 2002).[3] p.125 But a prisoner's publishing a bylined article may implicate different penological interests from those implicated by his filing a lawsuit or grievance. For example, in litigating the constitutionality of the Byline Regulation in the District of Colorado, the government took the position that allowing inmates to publish bylined articles could create security problems by permitting such inmates to become "big wheels" in the prison community, or could incite violence, or could intimidate prison staff members. *See Jordan,* 504 F.Supp.2d at 1120-23. Whether or not we would agree with that analysis is beside the point. We conclude only that, in light of the different interests at stake, our case law establishing a prisoner's right to file a lawsuit or grievance does not clearly establish a prisoner's right to publish an article under a byline. Indeed, the only authority that McGowan has identified that involved expression similar to that at issue in this case is a district court opinion, which, of course, is not binding. *See Shaheen v. Filion,* No. 9:04-CV-625 (FJS/DRH), 2006 WL 2792739, at *3 (N.D.N.Y. Sept. 17, 2006).

Thus, in light of the absence of authority clearly establishing the claimed right, we are constrained to hold that Rivers is entitled to qualified immunity from McGowan's *Bivens* claim. In so holding, we do not reach the question of whether Rivers violated McGowan's First Amendment rights.

II. FTCA Claims

"The United States, as sovereign, is immune from suit save as it consents to be sued ..., and the terms of its consent to be sued in any court define that court's jurisdiction to entertain the suit." *Liranzo v. United States,* 690 F.3d 78, 84 (2d Cir. 2012) (quoting *United States v. Mitchell,* 445 U.S. 535, 538, 100 S.Ct. 1349, 63 L.Ed.2d 607 (1980)). Subject to certain exceptions, *see* 28 U.S.C. § 2680, the FTCA waives the sovereign immunity of the United States against claims for property damage or personal injury "caused by the negligent or wrongful act or omission of any employee of the Government while acting within the scope of his office or employment, under circumstances where the United States, if a private person, would be liable to the claimant in accordance with the law of the place where the act or omission occurred." *Id.* § 1346(b)(1); *see also id.* § 2674. Accordingly, "for liability to arise under the FTCA, a plaintiff's cause of action must be 'comparable' to a 'cause of action against a private citizen' recognized in the jurisdiction where the tort occurred." *Chen v. United States,* 854 F.2d 622, 626 (2d Cir. 1988) (quoting *C.P. Chem. v. United States,* 810 F.2d 34, 37 (2d Cir. 1987)). This "private analogue" requirement asks "whether a private person would be responsible for similar negligence under the laws of the State where the acts occurred." *Dorking Genetics v. United States,* 76 F.3d 1261, 1266 (2d Cir. 1996) (quoting *Rayonier Inc. v. United States,* 352 U.S. 315, 319, 77 S.Ct. 374, 1 L.Ed.2d 354 (1957)).

"When reviewing the dismissal of a complaint for lack of subject matter jurisdiction, we review factual findings for clear error and legal conclusions *de novo,* accepting all material facts alleged in the complaint as true and drawing all reasonable inferences in the plaintiff's favor." *Liranzo,* 690 F.3d at 84. "The plaintiff bears the burden of proving subject matter jurisdiction by a preponderance of the evidence." *Aurecchione v. Schoolman* p.126 *Transp. Sys., Inc.,* 426 F.3d 635, 638 (2d Cir. 2005). The United States' waiver of immunity under the FTCA "is to be strictly construed in favor of the government." *Long Island Radio Co. v. NLRB,* 841 F.2d 474, 477 (2d Cir. 1988).

McGowan asserts claims under the FTCA for false imprisonment and negligence. Under New York law, the elements of the tort of false imprisonment are: "(1) the defendant intended to confine [the plaintiff], (2) the plaintiff was conscious of the confinement, (3) the plaintiff did not consent to the confinement and (4) the confinement was not otherwise privileged." *Broughton v. State,* 37 N.Y.2d 451, 373 N.Y.S.2d 87, 335 N.E.2d 310, 314 (1975). The district court held that McGowan failed to state a claim for false imprisonment on the ground that the government's confinement of an inmate pursuant to a lawful judgment is "uncategorically privileged." *McGowan v. United States,* 94 F.Supp.3d 382, 390 (E.D.N.Y. 2015). It also noted that the government argued that McGowan's false imprisonment claim lacked a private analogue, but declined to rely on that ground. *See id.* at 392.

On appeal, McGowan argues that the district court erred in concluding that his confinement was "uncategorically privileged" because New York law recognizes a tort of "wrongful confinement" of an inmate within solitary confinement or keeplock. *See Ramirez v. State,* 171 Misc.2d 677, 655 N.Y.S.2d 791, 794 (N.Y. Ct. Cl. 1997). Some New York courts have described the tort of wrongful confinement as a "species of false imprisonment." *Gittens v. State,* 132 Misc.2d 399, 504 N.Y.S.2d 969, 974 (N.Y. Ct. Cl. 1986). To recover for wrongful confinement, a prisoner must demonstrate that "he had been subjected to punitive segregation for no legitimate reason and without the rudimentary protections of due process." *Willey v. Kirkpatrick,* 801 F.3d 51, 71 (2d Cir. 2015) (quoting *Gittens,* 504 N.Y.S.2d at 972). McGowan argues that he adequately stated a claim for wrongful confinement under New York law.[4]

The parties dispute whether McGowan forfeited his wrongful confinement argument by failing to raise it in the district court. Whether or not this argument has been forfeited, however, it fails for the independent reason that the tort of wrongful confinement lacks a private analogue. McGowan asserts, without citation, that the tort of wrongful confinement could run against municipalities and their employees. Even assuming that he is correct, the Supreme Court has made clear that the relevant inquiry is the liability of a "private person" under State law, not that of a "state or municipal entity." *United States v. Olson,* 546 U.S. 43, 45-46, 126 S.Ct. 510, 163 L.Ed.2d 306 (2005). Accordingly, the liability of municipalities or municipal actors performing governmental functions cannot serve as a private analogue.

McGowan further posits that private contractors operating local, state, or federal detention facilities could provide the requisite private analogue. He cites no authority for the proposition that private contractors can be held liable for wrongful confinement under New York law. Even assuming that they can, when private prison contractors perform governmental functions pursuant to contracts with governmental entities, they are not similarly situated to any private actor. The private analogue inquiry asks whether "[p]rivate p.127 individuals ... may create a relationship with third parties that is similar to the relationship between" a governmental actor and a citizen, not whether a government contractor could create such a relationship. *Olson,* 546 U.S. at 47, 126 S.Ct. 510; *cf. Liranzo,* 690 F.3d at 94-95 (focusing on state-law liability of a person acting "entirely in his or her private capacity"). Private persons cannot establish facilities to detain other persons — only the government can, either on its own or through a governmental contractor. In short, there is no circumstance in state tort law that is analogous to the situation here. Accordingly, there is no private analogue to McGowan's claim.[5]

McGowan's FTCA negligence claim also fails. McGowan alleges that the BOP negligently failed to follow its own disciplinary regulations. We addressed a similar claim in *Chen v. United States,* in which the plaintiff, a federal contractor, alleged that the General Services Administration negligently misapplied federal procurement regulations, causing him to lose a lucrative contract. *See* 854 F.2d at 624-25. We held that the plaintiff's claim was not actionable under the FTCA. First, we held that "violation of the government's duties under federal procurement regulations 'is action of the type that private persons could not engage in and hence could not be liable for under local law.'" *Id.* at 626 (quoting *Jayvee Brand v. United States,* 721 F.2d 385, 390 (D.C. Cir. 1983)). Second, we held that, even if the plaintiff's proposed private analogue — "wrongful sanctions by private associations against individual members" — were analogous to the government's alleged conduct, the plaintiff failed to demonstrate that New York law "recognizes a cause of action *in tort*" for such conduct. *Id.* at 626-27.

McGowan's claim, like Chen's, is grounded solely on the government's failure to follow applicable regulations. *See id.* He contends that the relevant private analogue is a private party's failure to follow its own internal regulations. Even if that situation were analogous to the one presented here, however, McGowan has failed to establish that New York law recognizes a freestanding duty to abide by private regulations. The cases on which he relies establish only that failure to do so constitutes *evidence* of negligence, not negligence in itself. *See Cruz v. Madison Detective Bureau, Inc.,* 137 A.D.2d 86, 91, 528 N.Y.S.2d 372 (1st Dep't 1988) (holding that security company's failure to follow procedures was evidence of negligence); *Haber v. Cross County Hosp.,* 37 N.Y.2d 888, 889, 378 N.Y.S.2d 369, 340 N.E.2d 734 (N.Y. Ct. App. 1975) ("[T]he hospital's failure to abide by its own rule is some evidence of negligence."); *see also Florence v. Goldberg,* 44 N.Y.2d 189, 404 N.Y.S.2d 583, 375 N.E.2d 763, 767 (1978) (suggesting that police department's adoption of rules and regulations relating to provision of crossing guards was evidence that it assumed a duty to supervise school crossings); p.128 *Danbois v. N.Y. Cent. R. Co.,* 12 N.Y.2d 234, 238 N.Y.S.2d 921, 189 N.E.2d 468, 471 (1963) ("Violation of [company rules] ... is not negligence in itself but under certain circumstances may be regarded by the trier of fact as some evidence of negligence."). Accordingly, McGowan has not "show[n] a violation of a duty for which the applicable state law would provide recovery." *Chen,* 854 F.2d at 627 (quoting *Myers & Myers, Inc. v. U.S.P.S.,* 527 F.2d 1252, 1261 (2d Cir. 1975)).

Finally, to the extent that McGowan asserts a theory of negligence *per se,* it is well established in New York law that "violation of a rule of an administrative agency is merely some evidence of negligence but does not establish negligence as a matter of law because a regulation lacks the force and effect of a statute." *Chen,* 854 F.2d at 627 (alterations and internal quotation marks omitted).

Accordingly, we conclude that the district court correctly dismissed McGowan's negligence claim on the ground that it lacks a private analogue.

CONCLUSION

For the reasons stated herein, we AFFIRM the judgment of the district court.

[1] The Clerk of the Court is directed to amend the caption to conform to the above.

[2] Defendants Grace Terry, Massiel Suriel, and Unknown United States Marshals were not named in the Amended Complaint and also are not parties to this appeal.

[3] McGowan also cites a case relating to a prisoner's free exercise rights. *See Holland v. Goord,* 758 F.3d 215, 225-26 (2d Cir. 2014). That case was decided over a year after the conduct at issue in this case, and therefore is not relevant to the state of clearly established law at that time.

[4] McGowan does not, on appeal, challenge the district court's conclusion as it applies to ordinary claims of false imprisonment, as distinct from prisoners' claims of wrongful confinement. Accordingly, he has abandoned such challenge.

[5] The FTCA does not waive sovereign immunity for claims of false imprisonment, excepting those false imprisonment claims arising from the "acts or omissions of investigative or law enforcement officers of the United States Government," which are defined as "any officer of the United States who is empowered by law to execute searches, to seize evidence, or to make arrests for violations of Federal law." 28 U.S.C. § 2680(h). The government does not challenge Rivers' status as an "investigative or law enforcement officer[]," and we have previously recognized that BOP employees so qualify based on their authority to make arrests under 18 U.S.C. § 3050. *See Hernandez v. Lattimore,* 612 F.2d 61, 64 n.7 (2d Cir. 1979). Nonetheless, the record is silent on this issue, so we assume without deciding that Rivers is an "investigative or law enforcement officer[]" within the meaning of 28 U.S.C. § 2680(h).

THIRD CIRCUIT DECISIONS
Federal Tort Claims Act

775 F.3d 554 (2015)

Norman SHELTON, Appellant,

v.

Bryan A. BLEDSOE, Warden of USP Lewisburg; Thomas A. Kane, Acting Director of Bureau of Prisons; et al. p.555

No. 12-4226.

United States Court of Appeals, Third Circuit.

Argued September 11, 2013.

Opinion Filed: January 7, 2015.

Shelton v. Bledsoe, 775 F. 3d 554 (3rd Cir. 2015)

p.557 Stephen D. Brown, Esq., Christine C. Levin, Esq. (argued), Jennifer L. Burdick, Esq., Francis J. Demody, Esq., Sean P. McConnell, Dechert LLP, Philadelphia, PA, for Plaintiff-Appellant.

Michael J. Butler, Esq. (argued), Office of United States Attorney, Harrisburg, PA, for Defendants-Appellees.

Before: McKEE, Chief Judge, SMITH and SLOVITER, Circuit Judge.

OPINION OF THE COURT

McKEE, Chief Judge.

Norman Shelton appeals the district court's denial of class certification and grant of summary judgment in favor of defendants on Shelton's claims for alleged violations of the Eighth Amendment and the Federal Tort Claims Act ("FTCA"). For the reasons that follow, we will vacate the order denying class certification and granting summary judgment to defendants on Shelton's Eighth Amendment claim. We will affirm the district court's dismissal of Shelton's FTCA claim.

I. FACTS AND PROCEDURAL HISTORY

The Special Management Unit, or "SMU," is a housing unit within the United States Penitentiary at Lewisburg, Pennsylvania ("USP-Lewisburg"). The SMU houses inmates who have been identified as having violent tendencies or who have a history of gang involvement during their incarceration. Inmates assigned to the SMU are confined to their cells for 23 hours a day, but they can spend the remaining hour in a recreation cage if they choose. SMU officials (including several of the defendants) are responsible for assigning cellmates in a manner that ensures the safety and security of the prison. When first assigned to the SMU, inmates are interviewed by prison officials. Information obtained during the interview is used to ensure that inmates who may be hostile to each other are not housed in the same cell.

Shelton, an inmate at USP-Lewisburg, brought this action on behalf of himself and other inmates housed in the SMU. He alleges that the defendants have engaged in a pattern, practice, or policy of improperly placing inmates who are known to be hostile to each other in the same cell. He also claims that the defendants fail to intervene when the predictable inmate-on-inmate violence erupts, and that defendants improperly restrain inmates who refuse cell assignments with inmates who are known to be hostile to them. The complaint seeks damages for Shelton personally, but it seeks only injunctive and declaratory relief on behalf of the class. Appendix ("A A.") 88-89.

Shelton's individual claims under the Eighth Amendment and the FTCA were initially based on two separate incidents in 2009, one of which occurred in August, and the other in November. However, Shelton voluntarily dismissed claims arising from p.558 the August incident. We are therefore only concerned with the November incident, which occurred when Shelton was scheduled to be moved to another cell and housed with an inmate named Carr. According to Shelton, Carr had previously told a prison official, defendant Raup, that he would attack Shelton if they were housed in the same cell.

Raup purportedly threatened Shelton with punitive restraints when Shelton asked not to be housed with Carr. Shelton alleges that he was nevertheless physically forced into the cell by defendants Raup, Zelder, and two John Doe corrections officers. The next day, while Shelton was bending over to retrieve a food tray, Carr purportedly assaulted him. Shelton alleges that defendants Fisher, Raup, Kulago, Zelder, Moffit and Combe were outside his cell during the attack but did not attempt to intervene. The defendants claim that they responded in accordance with applicable policies that are designed to protect both inmates and guards.

Shelton's Eighth Amendment claims on behalf of the class are based on allegations that prison officials improperly placed inmates in cells with inmates known to be hostile to them. He alleges that the committee that makes the cell assignments places hostile inmates in the same cell despite committee's knowledge of prior violence between the inmates and its knowledge of the obvious risk the cell assignments create. According to Shelton, the injurious effects of this practice are exacerbated by a prison policy which prevents guards from promptly intervening when inmate-on-inmate violence erupts. This policy purportedly requires corrections officers to stand outside a cell and use only verbal warnings until a lieutenant arrives when inmate violence erupts inside a cell.

Shelton defined the class for which he sought injunctive and declaratory relief as:

> [a]ll persons who are currently or will be imprisoned in the SMU program at USP Lewisburg. The class period commences from the time of this filing, and continues so long as USP Lewisburg Officials and Corrections Officers persist in the unconstitutional patterns, practices, or policies of (1) placing hostile inmates together in cells or recreation cages, and enforcing this placement through the use of punitive restraints, and (2) failing to take any reasonable measures to protect the inmates from inmate-on-inmate violence by hostile inmates.

A A. 77 (Compl. ¶ 119).

Shelton filed his motion for class certification 90 days after he filed the complaint, as required by Local Rule 23.3. Defendants responded by opposing class certification and asking the district court to dismiss the claims or grant summary judgment in their favor. No discovery requests were filed by either party; no disclosures were provided; and no discovery occurred. However, Shelton filed a brief opposing summary judgment, and he attached a Rule 56(d) declaration to that brief. *See* Fed.R.Civ.P. 56(d). The declaration stated that counsel needed discovery in order to properly respond to the defendants' motions.

As we noted at the outset, the district court denied Shelton's motion for class certification and granted defendants' motion for summary judgment. The court did so without first addressing Shelton's Rule 56(d) declaration. This appeal followed.

II. JURISDICTION AND STANDARD OF REVIEW

The district court had jurisdiction pursuant to 28 U.S.C. § 1331, and we have jurisdiction to review final decisions of a district court pursuant to 28 U.S.C. p.559 § 1291. We review rulings on class certification for abuse of discretion. A court abuses its discretion "if [its] decision rests upon a clearly erroneous finding of fact, an errant conclusion of law or an improper application of law to fact." *Hayes v. Wal-Mart Stores, Inc.,* 725 F.3d 349, 354 (3d Cir. 2013) (citation and internal quotation marks omitted). Our review of the district court's legal rulings is *de novo. Id.*

To prevail on a motion for summary judgment, the moving party must demonstrate "that there is no genuine dispute as to any material fact and the movant is entitled to judgment as a matter of law." Fed.R.Civ.P. 56(a). In reviewing a grant of summary judgment, we assess the record using the same standard that district courts apply. *Interstate Outdoor Adver., L.P. v. Zoning Bd. of Twp. of Mount Laurel,* 706 F.3d 527, 530 (3d Cir. 2013). We must review the record in the light most favorable to the nonmoving party and draw all reasonable inferences in that party's favor. *Id.*

We review the district court's response to a Rule 56(d) declaration for abuse of discretion. *Murphy v. Millennium Radio Grp. LLC,* 650 F.3d 295, 310 (3d Cir. 2011).

III. CLASS CERTIFICATION

Class actions are an exception to the general rule that litigation must be conducted by individual named parties. *See Comcast Corp. v. Behrend,* ___ U.S. ___, 133 S.Ct. 1426, 1432, 185 L.Ed.2d 515 (2013). Rule 23 of the Federal Rules of Civil Procedure contains the procedural requirements for class action litigation. A party seeking to bring a class action "must affirmatively demonstrate his[or her] compliance" with Rule 23. *Id.* An inquiry under Rule 23 begins with a determination of whether the plaintiff has satisfied the prerequisites of Rule 23(a): numerosity, commonality, typicality, and adequacy of the class representative. Depending on the type of class the movant seeks to certify, s/he must also demonstrate that the class meets certain requirements of Rule 23(b).

Shelton asked the court to certify a class under Rule 23(b)(2), which applies when "the party opposing the class has acted or refused to act on grounds that apply generally to the class, so that final injunctive relief or corresponding declaratory relief is appropriate respecting the class as a whole." Fed.R.Civ.P. 23(b)(2). The district court did not analyze the specific requirements of Rule 23(a) or Rule 23(b)(2). Instead, it denied Shelton's motion for class certification because it found that the proposed class was not "objectively, reasonably ascertainable." *Shelton v. Bledsoe*, No. 3:CV-11-1618, 2012 WL 5250401, at *4 (M.D.Pa. Oct. 24, 2012).

Because we have not yet addressed the issue, this appeal requires us to decide whether ascertainability is a requirement for certification of a Rule 23(b)(2) class that seeks only injunctive and declaratory relief. We must also address the question of whether the district court properly defined the class in analyzing whether class certification was appropriate.

A. Ascertainability

The word "ascertainable" does not appear in the text of Rule 23. However, "[a]lthough not specifically mentioned in the rule, an essential prerequisite of an action under Rule 23 is that there must be a 'class.'" 7A C. Wright, A. Miller, & M. Kane, Fed. Prac. & Proc. Civ. § 1760 (3d ed.2005). Courts have generally articulated this "essential prerequisite" as the implied requirement of "ascertainability"—that the members of a class are identifiable at the moment of certification. Because p.560 the question is intensely fact-specific and the origins of the requirement murky, a precise definition of the judicially-created requirement of ascertainability is elusive. *See Alliance to End Repression v. Rochford*, 565 F.2d 975, 980 n. 6 (7th Cir. 1977) (noting that "[i]t is not clear whether the source of th[e] implied requirement [of ascertainability] is ... Rule 23(a)(2) or more simply something inherent in the very notion of a 'class'"). We recently held, in the context of a Rule 23(b)(3) class action, that certification is only appropriate if the members of the class are "currently and readily ascertainable based on objective criteria." *Marcus v. BMW of N. Am., LLC*, 687 F.3d 583, 593 (3d Cir. 2012).

In *Marcus,* we analyzed the question of ascertainability separately from the question of whether the class was properly defined under Rule 23(c)(1)(B). *See* Fed. R.Civ.P. 23(c)(1)(B) ("An order that certifies a class action must define the class and the class claims, issues, or defenses...."). [1] We have interpreted Rule 23(c)(1)(B) to require a certification order that includes "a readily discernible, clear, and precise statement of the parameters defining the class or classes to be certified." *Wachtel ex rel. Jesse v. Guardian Life Ins. Co. of Am.,* 453 F.3d 179, 187 (3d Cir. 2006). *Marcus* stands for the proposition that ascertainability requires something more than a class capable of clear definition by a court; it requires that the class's members be identifiable. 687 F.3d at 593 ("If class members are impossible to identify without extensive and individualized fact-finding or 'mini-trials,' then a class action is inappropriate."). However, *Marcus* involved a Rule 23(b)(3) class, and it is not clear that the reasons for requiring ascertainability are applicable here, where Shelton attempted to certify a class under Rule 23(b)(2) seeking only injunctive and declaratory relief.

Though classes certified under Rule 23(b)(3) and Rule 23(b)(2) all proceed as "class actions," the two subsections actually create two remarkably different litigation devices. Rule 23(b)(3) requires that "the court finds that the questions of law or fact common to class members predominate over any questions affecting only individual members, and that a class action is superior to other available methods for fairly and efficiently adjudicating the controversy." Fed.R.Civ.P. 23(b)(3). As compared to Rule 23(b)(2), Rule 23(b)(3) "allows class certification in a much wider set of circumstances" including those "in which class-action treatment is not as clearly called for." *Wal-Mart Stores, Inc. v. Dukes,* ___ U.S. ___, 131 S.Ct. 2541, 2558, 180 L.Ed.2d 374 (2011) (citation and internal quotation marks omitted). Because a Rule 23(b)(3) class is such an "adventuresome innovation," *id.,* Congress included additional "procedural safeguards for (b)(3) class members beyond those provided for (b)(1) or (b)(2) class members." *Comcast,* 133 S.Ct. at 1432. In addition to requiring predominance and superiority for such a class, Rule 23 requires that potential class members be given the opportunity to opt-out, and that they receive "best notice that is practicable under the circumstances, including individual notice p.561 to all members who can be identified through reasonable effort." Fed.R.Civ.P. 23(c)(2)(B).

In contrast, "[t]he key to the (b)(2) class is the 'indivisible nature of the injunctive or declaratory remedy warranted—the notion that the conduct is such that it can be enjoined or declared unlawful *only* as to all of the class members or as to none of them.'" *Wal-Mart,* 131 S.Ct. at 2557 (emphasis added) (quoting Richard A. Nagareda, *Class Certification in the Age of Aggregate Proof,* 84 N.Y.U. L.Rev. 97, 132 (2009)). Because there is no right to opt out from such a class, and because significant individual issues in a(b)(2) class might present manageability issues and undermine the value of utilizing the class action mechanism, we have instructed that such classes must be cohesive. *See Barnes v. Am. Tobacco Co.,* 161 F.3d 127, 143 (3d Cir. 1998). However, this requirement comes from Rule 23(b)(2) itself, not from any general requirement of ascertainability. Because the focus in a(b)(2) class is more heavily placed on the nature of the remedy sought, and because a remedy obtained by one member will naturally affect the others, the identities of individual class members are less critical in a(b)(2) action than in a(b)(3) action. *See Wal-Mart,* 131 S.Ct. at 2558 ("When a class seeks an indivisible injunction benefitting all its members at once, there is no reason to undertake a case-specific inquiry into whether class issues predominate or whether class action is a superior method of adjudicating the dispute."); *Barnes,* 161 F.3d at 143 n. 18 ("Injuries remedied through (b)(2) actions are really group, as opposed to individual injuries." (citation omitted)).

Indeed, an Advisory Committee note to Rule 23 notes that "illustrative" examples of a Rule 23(b)(2) class "are various actions in the civil-rights field where a party is charged with discriminating unlawfully against a class, *usually one whose members are incapable of specific enumeration.*" Fed.R.Civ.P. 23 advisory committee's note (1966) (emphasis added). In light of this guidance, a judicially-created implied requirement of ascertainability—that the members of the class be *capable* of specific enumeration—is inappropriate for (b)(2) classes. Moreover, the enforcement of the remedy usually does not require individual identification of class members in (b)(2) class actions: "If relief is granted ... the defendants are legally obligated to comply, and it is usually unnecessary to define with precision the persons entitled to enforce compliance, since presumably at least the representative plaintiffs would be available to seek ... relief if necessary." *Rice v. City of Phila.,* 66 F.R.D. 17, 19 (E.D.Pa.1974).

Thus, it does not follow from our holding in *Marcus* that ascertainability is always a prerequisite to class certification. In the context of a(b)(3) class, the requirement that the class be defined in a manner that allows ready identification of class members serves several important objectives that either do not exist or are not compelling in (b)(2) classes.[2] *See Carrera v. Bayer Corp.*, 727 F.3d 300, 307 (3d Cir. 2013) (noting that ascertainability plays "key roles ... as part of a Rule 23(b)(3) class p.562 action lawsuit"). The ascertainability requirement ensures that the procedural safeguards necessary for litigation as a(b)(3) class are met, but it need not (and should not) perform the same function in (b)(2) litigation. *See Battle v. Pennsylvania*, 629 F.2d 269, 271 n. 1 (3d Cir. 1980) ("Where ... the class action seeks only injunctive or declaratory relief, for which the notice provision of [Rule] 23(c)(2) is not mandatory, the district court has even greater freedom in both the timing and specificity of its class definition.").

Although this issue is a matter of first impression for us, some of our sister courts of appeals have addressed this issue and agree that it is improper to require ascertainability for a(b)(2) class. The Courts of Appeals for the First and Tenth Circuits explicitly rejected an ascertainability requirement for Rule 23(b)(2) classes. The court's analysis in *Shook v. El Paso County* is particularly germane to our inquiry. 386 F.3d 963, 972 (10th Cir. 2004). There, the court explained that "many courts have found Rule 23(b)(2) well suited for cases where the composition of the class is not readily ascertainable; for instance, in a case where the plaintiffs attempt to bring suit on behalf of a shifting prison population." *Id.* at 972. Similarly, the First Circuit explained that a(b)(2) class definition need not be as precise as that of a(b)(3) class. *See Yaffe v. Powers*, 454 F.2d 1362, 1366 (1st Cir. 1972) (holding that, because "notice to the members of a(b)(2) class is not required ... the actual membership of the class need not... be precisely delimited"). Both courts reasoned that the district courts erred in those cases by requiring ascertainability (or "identifiability"), which the courts noted was only applicable to Rule 23(b)(3) classes. *See Shook*, 386 F.3d at 972 (noting that the district court impermissibly "imported additional elements from Rule 23(b)(3) into the (b)(2) analysis [including] identifiability"); *Yaffe*, 454 F.2d at 1366 ("[T]he [district] court applied standards applicable to a subdivision (b)(3) class rather than to a subdivision (b)(2) class.").

The Court of Appeals for the Fifth Circuit has also tied the ascertainability (or "precise class definition") requirement to the procedural protections of Rule 23(b)(3), noting that "[s]ome courts have stated that a precise class definition is not as critical where certification of a class for injunctive or declaratory relief is sought under [R]ule 23(b)(2)." *In re Monumental Life Ins. Co.*, 365 F.3d 408, 413 (5th Cir. 2004). However, the court clarified that, "[w]here notice and opt-out rights are requested [in a(b)(2) class action] ... a precise class definition becomes just as important as in the [R]ule 23(b)(3) context." *Id.* There, plaintiffs sought a mix of injunctive relief and backpay. *Id.* Here, only injunctive and declaratory relief are sought.[3]

Other courts have certified very broadly-defined (b)(2) classes without explicitly discussing ascertainability. For example, the Court of Appeals for the Second Circuit p.563 upheld the certification of a Rule 23(b)(2) class that was probably unascertainable. The class there included children currently in the custody of a city agency, those who would be in custody in the future, and even some children who *should be known* to the city agency. *See Marisol A. v. Giuliani*, 126 F.3d 372, 375 (2d Cir. 1997).[4] In a recent case, a district court for the Southern District of New York explained that "[i]t would be illogical to require precise ascertainability in a suit that seeks no class damages. The general demarcations of the proposed class are clear ... and that definition makes the class sufficiently ascertainable for the purpose of Rule 23(b)(2)." *Floyd v. City of New York*, 283 F.R.D. 153, 172 (S.D.N.Y. 2012). That court also noted that a number of other federal courts have certified unascertainable classes under Rule 23(b)(2). *See id.* at 171-72 nn. 115-17 (collecting cases).[5] Finally, we think it significant that the Supreme Court's analysis of whether a class had been properly certified under Rule 23(b)(2) in *Wal-Mart Stores, Inc. v. Dukes* lacks any inquiry into "ascertainability." 131 S.Ct. at 2557.

The nature of Rule 23(b)(2) actions, the Advisory Committee's note on (b)(2) actions, and the practice of many of other federal courts all lead us to conclude that ascertainability is not a requirement for certification of a(b)(2) class seeking only injunctive and declaratory relief, such as the putative class here. This does not suggest that we are jettisoning the basic requirement that "there must be a 'class'" in a class action. *See* C. Wright, A. Miller, & M. Kane, *supra* § 1760. Rather, we are merely holding that, for certification of a 23(b)(2) class seeking only declaratory or injunctive relief, a properly defined "class" is one that: (1) meets the requirements of Rule 23(a); (2) is sufficiently cohesive under Rule 23(b)(2) and our guidance in *Barnes,* 161 F.3d at 143; and (3) is capable of the type of description by a "readily discernible, clear, and precise statement of the parameters defining the class," as required by Rule 23(c)(1)(B) and our discussion in *Wachtel,* 453 F.3d at 187. No additional requirements need be satisfied.

B. Class Definition

Shelton's proposed class, when properly defined, is easily capable of the type of description demanded by Rule 23(c)(1)(B). As noted above, he seeks certification of a class consisting of

> [a]ll persons who are currently or will be imprisoned in the SMU program at USP Lewisburg. The class period commences from the time of this filing, and continues so long as USP Lewisburg Officials and Corrections Officers persist in the unconstitutional patterns, practices, or policies of (1) placing hostile inmates together in cells or recreation cages, and enforcing this placement through the use of punitive restraints, and (2) failing to take any reasonable measures to protect the inmates from inmate-on-inmate violence by hostile inmates.

A A. 77. The district court noted that Shelton proposed a class of "all persons p.564 who are currently or will be imprisoned in the [SMU]...." *Shelton,* 2012 WL 5250401, at *1. For reasons that are not at all apparent, the district court improperly narrowed the class to inmates "placed with an inmate that prison officials knew, or should have known, posed a threat to that inmate[;]" inmates "housed with a hostile inmate [and] assaulted by the hostile inmate, and prison officials fail[ed] to intervene[;]" and "inmates who, pursuant to a prison practice, are placed in painful punitive restraints for refusing a dangerous cell assignment." *Id.* at 56. The court thereby imposed extra requirements requiring the very individualized, case-by-case determinations that the court then paradoxically ruled were fatal to class certification. Though we have clarified that the type of ascertainability analysis performed by the district court is inappropriate here, it is also important to note that the district court erred by narrowing the definition of the proposed class.

It is difficult to understand why the district court redefined the proposed class in this manner. Courts have discretionary authority to "reshape the boundaries and composition of the class," but when they do so, "that action entails a determination that reformulating the class will better serve the purposes of Rule 23 and the underlying policies of the substantive law than would denying certification altogether." Tobias Barrington Wolff, *Discretion in Class Certification,* 162 U. Pa. L.Rev. 1897, 1925 (2014). Here however, the court appears to have simply misinterpreted or misunderstood the class Shelton was proposing. That resulted in a class definition that undermined, rather than served, the purposes of Rule 23 "and the underlying polices of the substantive law." *See id.* Given the declaratory and injunctive relief that Shelton seeks, the narrowing of the requested class was neither necessary nor appropriate.

Common sense supports the assumption that the Bureau of Prisons ("BOP") knows where inmates in a given institution are housed, and the defendants have offered nothing that would undermine that assumption or support a finding that the BOP would have trouble determining which inmates have been assigned to the SMU at USP-Lewisberg since the complaint was filed. Accordingly, if Shelton has satisfied the other requirements of Rule 23, the district court should have no trouble describing the class as required by Rule 23(c)(1)(B) and, eventually, Rule 23(c)(3)(A). Indeed, in the unlikely event that it becomes necessary to actually identify class members at some point during the litigation, the district court should be able to determine individual members based on the BOP's own records.

The district court also erred in concluding that the class was overly broad because some putative class members have not yet suffered an injury. *See Shelton,* 2012 WL 5250401, at *5. There is no requirement that every class member suffer an injury before a class is certifiable under Rule 23. In fact, we have held to the contrary. In *Hassine v. Jeffes,* we stated:

> Rule 23 does not require that the representative plaintiff have endured precisely the same injuries that have been sustained by the class members, only that the harm complained of be *common* to the class, and that the named plaintiff demonstrate a personal interest or *threat of injury* that is real and immediate, not conjectural or hypothetical.

846 F.2d 169, 177 (3d Cir. 1988) (internal quotation marks and alterations omitted) (second emphasis added).

This is particularly true in the context of a claim under the Eighth Amendment, which protects against the risk—not merely the manifestation—of p.565 harm. As the Supreme Court has explained, "an inmate seeking an injunction to prevent a violation of the Eighth Amendment must show that prison officials are 'knowingly and unreasonably disregarding an objectively intolerable risk of harm, and that they will continue to do so... into the future.'" *Brown v. Plata,* ___ U.S. ___, 131 S.Ct. 1910, 1960, 179 L.Ed.2d 969 (2011) (citing *Farmer v. Brennan,* 511 U.S. 825, 846, 114 S.Ct. 1970, 128 L.Ed.2d 811 (1994)). In *Plata,* prisoners with physical or mental illness challenged a state prison system's medical care system. In deciding the propriety of the remedy that had been granted to the prisoners, who comprised two separate Rule 23 classes, the Court explained that "[p]risoners who are not sick or mentally ill do not yet have a claim that they have been subjected to care that violates the Eighth Amendment, but in no sense are they remote bystanders in [the state's] medical care system. They are that system's next potential victims." *Id.* at 1940. There, as here, the focus was more on the defendants' conduct and policies than on the individual identities or medical issues of each class member. *See id.* (noting that "all prisoners in California are at risk so long as the State continues to provide inadequate care").

We have instructed district courts to consider this aspect of Eighth Amendment claims when deciding whether the requirements of Rule 23 have been met at the class certification stage. *See Hagan v. Rogers,* 570 F.3d 146, 157-58 (3d Cir. 2009) (holding that a class of "inmates ... [who] were either subject to actual skin infections, or were subject to the threat of future injury due to deliberate indifference on the part of prison officials in failing to contain the contagion" should not fail for lack of typicality under Rule 23(a) because all class members were at least "subject to the threat of an injury").

Thus, Shelton's proposed class is not overbroad or improperly defined for purposes of Rule 23. On remand, the district court must consider whether the properly-defined putative class meets the remaining Rule 23 requirements for class certification.

IV. SUMMARY JUDGMENT

Shelton also appeals the district court's entry of summary judgment in favor of defendants on his individual claims under the Federal Tort Claims Act and the Eighth Amendment.[6] We will first discuss the court's failure to consider the declaration Shelton's attorney filed under Fed. R. Civ. P. 56(d) in opposition to summary judgment.

A. Rule 56(d)

As we noted earlier, Shelton's opposition to the defendants' motion for summary judgment included a declaration that his counsel submitted pursuant to Rule 56(d). According to that declaration, Shelton needed discovery in order to properly respond to the defendants' summary judgment motion.

"[I]t is well established that a court 'is obliged to give a party opposing summary judgment an adequate opportunity to obtain discovery.'" *Doe v. Abington Friends Sch.,* 480 F.3d 252, 257 (3d Cir. 2007) (quoting *Dowling v. City of Phila.,* 855 F.2d 136, 139 (3d Cir. 1988)). Rule 56(d) states that "[i]f a nonmovant shows by affidavit or declaration that, for specified reasons, it cannot present facts essential to justify its p.566 opposition, the court may: (1) defer considering the motion or deny it; (2) allow time to obtain affidavits or declarations or to take discovery; or (3) issue any other appropriate order." Fed.R.Civ.P. 56(d).

Defendants rely on the non-precedential decision in *Superior Offshore International, Inc. v. Bristow Group, Inc.,* 490 Fed. Appx. 492, 501 (3d Cir. 2012), to argue that Shelton was required to file a "motion" in order to seek relief under Rule 56(d).

The panel in *Superior Offshore* did state that "[a] Rule 56(d) motion is the proper recourse of a party faced with a motion for summary judgment who believes that additional discovery is necessary before he can adequately respond to that motion." *Id.* (citation and internal quotation marks omitted). We have previously referred to items filed under Rule 56(d) as "motions." *See Murphy*, 650 F.3d at 309-10. More pointedly, the panel in *Doe v. Abington Friends School* explained that, in responding to a motion for summary judgment, "if the non-moving party believes that additional discovery is necessary, the proper course is to file a motion...." 480 F.3d at 257.

However, we do not interpret these statements or our opinions in *Murphy* or *Doe* as actually requiring that an opposition under Rule 56(d) be registered in a *motion* to the court. The unambiguous text of the Rule does not require an opposition on Rule 56(d) grounds to be formally styled as a motion. Indeed, the text of the rule, Advisory Committee's notes, our own precedent, and guidance from other circuit courts all indicate that a formal motion is not required by the Rule.

Rule 56 sets forth the procedure for requesting and opposing summary judgment. It requires only that a party's *request for* summary judgment be styled as a motion. Rule 56(a) provides:

> A party may *move* for summary judgment, identifying each claim or defense... on which summary judgment is sought. The court shall grant summary judgment if the *movant* shows that there is no genuine dispute as to any material fact and the *movant* is entitled to judgment as a matter of law. The court should state on the record the reasons for granting or denying the *motion*.

Id. (emphasis added). The Rule specifically requires a "motion" to be filed, and it refers to the party requesting summary judgment as "the movant." However, no such language is used to refer to the party opposing summary judgment. Rule 56(c) sets out the procedures that must be followed to oppose a motion for summary judgment. It refers to the party opposing a summary judgment not as a "movant," but merely as the "party asserting that a fact ... is genuinely disputed." Fed. R.Civ.P. 56(c)(1). In describing the procedures that must be followed to obtain or oppose summary judgment, Rule 56(c) repeatedly refers to the initial request for summary judgment as a motion, but it requires only affidavits or declarations from the opposing party.[7]

p.567 The current dispute concerns the interpretation and application of Rule 56(d), which by its own terms applies only "When Facts are Unavailable to the Nonmovant." Fed.R.Civ.P. 56(d). The procedure by which the party opposing summary judgment submits an affidavit or declaration under Rule 56(d) supplants the procedure that would otherwise follow under Rule 56(c) if facts were available to the nonmovant. *See* 10B C. Wright, A. Miller, & M. Kane, Fed. Prac. & Proc. § 2740 (3d ed. 2005) ("[W]hen the movant has met the initial burden required for the granting of a summary judgment, the opposing party must either establish a genuine issue for trial ... or explain why he cannot yet do so ...."). As was true with regards to Rule 56(c), it makes little sense to conclude that the drafters would refer to the party presenting such an affidavit or declaration as a "nonmovant" if they intended to require the affidavit or declaration to be presented by motion. Moreover, the text of the Rule does not require that the party who opposes summary judgment by filing an affidavit or declaration must thereafter move for discovery. Rather, the Rule simply allows the court to respond to a Rule 56(d) affidavit or declaration by "allow[ing] time ... to take discovery." Fed.R.Civ.P. 56(d). Thus, no formal discovery motion is contemplated, and we decline to infer any such requirement.

This was readily apparent in the phrasing of the Rule before the 2010 Amendments. *See St. Surin v. V.I. Daily News, Inc.,* 21 F.3d 1309, 1313-14 (3d Cir. 1994) (citing cases that emphasize the requirement of an "affidavit"). The Advisory Committee has explained that the Rules were amended "without substantial change." Fed.R.Civ.P. 56(d), advisory committee's note (2010). Prior to the amendments, Rule 56(f), which became Rule 56(d), was captioned "When Affidavits are Unavailable." The Rule stated: "Should it appear from the affidavits of a party opposing the motion that [s/]he cannot for reasons stated present by affidavit facts essential to justify his [or her] opposition, the court may refuse the application for judgment or may order a continuance to permit affidavits to be obtained or depositions to be taken or discovery to be had or may make such other order as is just." *Costlow v. United States,* 552 F.2d 560, 563 n. 2 (3d Cir. 1977). The old rule thus assumes that the party opposing summary judgment will file an affidavit, not a motion for discovery, in response to a summary judgment motion. Furthermore, the 2010 Amendments to the Federal Rules of Civil Procedure allow for alternatives to a formal affidavit such as "a written unsworn declaration, certificate, verification, or statement subscribed in proper form as true under penalty of perjury." Fed. R.Civ.P. 56, advisory committee's note (2010).

Our holding that a formal motion is not required to request discovery under Rule 56 is consistent with the analysis of other circuit courts of appeals. Although the request for discovery is sometimes—rather casually—characterized as a "motion," courts recognize that the nonmoving party can respond to a motion for summary judgment by filing an affidavit or declaration requesting discovery. For example, before the current amendments to Rule 56 were enacted, the Court of Appeals for the Tenth Circuit stated that it was considering the denial of a Rule 56(f) "motion," but the opposition was actually an affidavit attached to the party's response to the p.568 motion for summary judgment. *Trask v. Franco,* 446 F.3d 1036, 1041-42 (10th Cir. 2006). Other courts have followed similar practices.[8]

Thus, nothing precludes a party from requesting an opportunity for discovery under Rule 56(d) by simply attaching an appropriate affidavit or declaration to that party's response to a motion for summary judgment, and by asserting that summary judgment should not be granted without affording the responding nonmovant an opportunity for discovery. Moreover, we note that district courts usually grant properly filed requests for discovery under Rule 56(d) "as a matter of course," whether the nonmovant's response to a summary judgment motion is characterized as a motion, affidavit, or declaration. *Murphy,* 650 F.3d at 309-10 (quoting *Doe,* 480 F.3d at 257); *cf. Mid-South Grizzlies v. Nat'l Football League,* 720 F.2d 772, 779 (3d Cir. 1983). This is particularly true when there are discovery requests outstanding or where relevant facts are under control of the party moving for summary judgment. *Murphy,* 650 F.3d at 310.

If discovery is incomplete, a district court is rarely justified in granting summary judgment, unless the discovery request pertains to facts that are not material to the moving party's entitlement to judgment as a matter of law. *Doe,* 480 F.3d at 257. Summary judgment may also be granted if the Rule 56(d) declaration is inadequate.

See Koplove v. Ford Motor Co., 795 F.2d 15, 18 (3d Cir. 1986) (finding the affidavit insufficient because it did not specify what discovery was needed or why it had not previously been secured). An adequate affidavit or declaration specifies "what particular information that is sought; how, if disclosed, it would preclude summary judgment; and why it has not been previously obtained." *Dowling,* 855 F.2d at 140 (citing *Hancock Indus. v. Schaeffer,* 811 F.2d 225, 229-30 (3d Cir. 1987)).

Here, the district court granted summary judgment to the defendants without even considering the declaration that Shelton's attorney filed in response to defendants' motion for summary judgment. This was an abuse of discretion. Accordingly, we will reverse the grant of summary judgment and remand so that the district court may consider counsel's declaration regarding the need for discovery.[9]

p.569 B. FTCA Exhaustion

Regardless of whether Shelton's Rule 56(d) declaration justifies discovery in advance of the court's ruling on defendants' motion for summary judgment, it is clear that, because he did not exhaust his administrative remedies, Shelton cannot establish a claim for negligence under the FTCA based on the purported incident in November 2009.

No claim can be brought under the FTCA unless the plaintiff first presents the claim to the appropriate federal agency and the agency renders a final decision on the claim. 28 U.S.C. § 2675(a); *see also McNeil v. United States,* 508 U.S. 106, 112, 113 S.Ct. 1980, 124 L.Ed.2d 21 (1993); *Deutsch v. United States,* 67 F.3d 1080, 1091 (3d Cir. 1995) ("[A] claimant must have first presented the claim, in writing and within two years after its accrual, to the appropriate federal agency, and the claim must have been denied."). This requirement is jurisdictional and cannot be waived. *Rosario v. Am. Export-Isbrandtsen Lines, Inc.,* 531 F.2d 1227, 1231 (3d Cir. 1976).

Here, defendants supported their motion to dismiss and/or for summary judgment on Shelton's FTCA claim with a declaration from Mike Romano, agency counsel for the BOP. Romano stated that, based upon his search of the administrative claims database of the BOP, Shelton had not filed an administrative tort claim regarding any incident on November 26, 2009. Romano did, however, confirm that Shelton had filed seven tort claims regarding other incidents in 2009 and 2011. Shelton's only response to this declaration was his insistence that he needed discovery to prove that he had filed an administrative tort claim. Shelton further argues in a letter to this court that his complaint alleges that he exhausted his remedies as to the November 26, 2009 incident. He claims that allegation is sufficient because he needs discovery to "bolster" his claim that he has appropriately exhausted this claim. However, his argument ignores the fact that the government has already produced the relevant discovery. The government's evidence establishes that Shelton did not exhaust, and Shelton does not explain how any additional discovery could refute the finding that he failed to exhaust any claim arising from a November 26, 2009 incident.

The district court correctly found Shelton's reply inadequate and held that Romano's declaration was sufficient to establish that Shelton had not exhausted any claim arising from the alleged incident on November 26, 2009. Accordingly, the court granted the defendants' motion to dismiss the FTCA claim based on its conclusion that Shelton's failure to exhaust deprived the court of jurisdiction to hear that claim. We agree. Accordingly, we will affirm the district court's finding that it had no jurisdiction to hear Shelton's FTCA claim.

V. CONCLUSION

For the foregoing reasons, we will vacate the order denying Shelton's motion for class certification and the order granting summary judgment to defendants on Shelton's Eighth Amendment claims. We will remand for the district court to consider both issues in a manner consistent with this opinion. We will affirm the district court's dismissal of Shelton's FTCA claim.

[1] We did not analyze ascertainability as an implied requirement of Rule 23(a), as some other courts have done. *See Floyd v. City of New York,* 283 F.R.D. 153, 161 (S.D.N.Y. 2012) ("Some courts have added an 'implied requirement of ascertainability' to the express requirements of Rule 23(a)...." (citing *In re Initial Pub. Offerings Sec. Litig.,* 471 F.3d 24, 30 (2d Cir. 2006))). Instead, in *Marcus* we treated ascertainability as an implied requirement, the analysis of which preceded the Rule 23(a) analysis. *Marcus,* 687 F.3d at 593. This divergence illustrates another ambiguity of the ascertainability standard: the section of Rule 23 from which it is implied.

[2] First, it eliminates serious administrative burdens that are incongruous with the efficiencies expected in a class action by insisting on the easy identification of class members.... Second, it protects absent class members by facilitating the best notice practicable... in a Rule 23(b)(3) action.... Third, it protects defendants by ensuring that those persons who will be bound by the final judgment are clearly identifiable.

Marcus, 687 F.3d at 593 (internal citations and quotation marks omitted); *see also Hayes,* 725 F.3d at 354-55.

[3] The Court of Appeals for the Seventh Circuit has also discussed this issue, though its guidance is less clear. It initially implied a "definiteness" requirement from Rule 23, but it held that "a class that satisfies all of the other requirements of Rule 23 will not be rejected as indefinite when its contours are defined by the defendants' own conduct." *Rochford,* 565 F.2d at 978. Subsequently, it clarified that *Rochford's* "tolerance of a wildly indefinite class definition" is disfavored, *Jamie S. v. Milwaukee Pub. Sch.,* 668 F.3d 481, 496 (7th Cir. 2012), and it suggested an indefinite class may only be certified if its "members could be enumerated eventually." *Rahman v. Chertoff,* 530 F.3d 622, 626 (7th Cir. 2008). However, the classes in each of these more recent cases failed to meet the requirements of Rule 23(a), and certification was inappropriate on that basis. *See Jamie S.,* 668 F.3d at 496-97; *Rahman,* 530 F.3d at 627.

[4] That class was defined as "[a]ll children who are or will be in the custody of the New York City Administration for Children's Services ("ACS"), and those children who, while not in the custody of ACS, are or will be at risk of neglect or abuse and whose status is or should be known to ACS." *Marisol A.,* 126 F.3d at 375.

[5] The district court in *Floyd* describes our decision in *Baby Neal for and by Kanter v. Casey*, 43 F.3d 48 (3d Cir. 1994) as certifying a Rule 23(b)(2) class that was "clearly unascertainable." *Floyd*, 283 F.R.D. at 172 n. 117. It is important to note that we did not specifically address ascertainability in that case.

[6] The district court's order granting summary judgment to the defendants disposed of Shelton's remaining claims and followed its order denying class certification. *See Shelton v. Bledsoe*, No. 3:CV-11-1618, 2012 WL 5267034, at *8-9 (M.D.Pa. Oct. 24, 2012).

[7] Rather than requiring a motion to allege a factual dispute, Rule 56(c)(1) requires that the opposing party "must support the assertion [that a dispute of fact exists] by: (A) citing to particular parts of materials in the record, including depositions, [etc.]" Subdivision (2) provides that "[a] party may object that the material cited to support or dispute a fact cannot be [admitted into evidence.]" Fed. R.Civ.P. 56(c)(2). We do not interpret the reference to "a party" to require that the opponent to a summary judgment motion file an opposing motion. Rather, it is clear from the context that the drafters used the term there for sake of simplicity and clarity. Rule 56(c)(3) only addresses what the reviewing court may consider and is not relevant to our inquiry. Rule 56(c)(4) is entitled "*Affidavits or Declarations*." It provides that affidavits or declarations "used to support or *oppose a motion* must be made on personal knowledge, [and] set out facts that would be admissible in evidence." *Id.* (emphasis added.).

[8] It is clear that many courts' use of the word "motion" to refer to an opposition registered pursuant to Rule 56(d) is imprecise; affidavits and declarations are regularly demanded and accepted. *See Hicks v. Johnson*, 755 F.3d 738, 743 (1st Cir. 2014) (referring to a "rule 56(d) motion" but explaining that "[t]o benefit from the protections of Rule 56(d), a litigant must ordinarily furnish the nisi prius court with a timely statement—if not by affidavit, then in some other authoritative manner" (citation omitted)); *Toben v. Bridgestone Retail Operations, LLC*, 751 F.3d 888, 894-95 (8th Cir. 2014) (considering a properly submitted affidavit under Rule 56(d), but referring to it as a "motion"); *In re World Trade Center Lower Manhattan Disaster Site Litig.*, 758 F.3d 202, 212 n. 3 (2d Cir. 2014) ("[T]o the extent that plaintiffs needed additional time for discovery, they failed to file an affidavit pursuant to [Rule] 56(d)."); *Nguyen v. CNA Corp.*, 44 F.3d 234, 242 (4th Cir. 1995) ("[A] party may not simply assert in its brief that discovery was necessary and thereby overturn summary judgment when it failed to comply with the requirement ... to set out reasons for the need for discovery in an affidavit." (citation omitted)).

[9] To the extent the district court did not address the parties' arguments as to the defendants' motion to seal documents, the district court can consider whether the documents should be sealed on remand. The court's inquiry should take into consideration the amount of time that has passed since the documents were originally filed and whether the institutional concerns that may have initially justified sealing are still sufficient to prevent Shelton from examining those documents.

FOURTH CIRCUIT DECISIONS
Federal Tort Claims Act

845 F.3d 123 (2017)

Laurie L. WOOD, Plaintiff-Appellant,
v.
UNITED STATES of America, Defendant-Appellee.

No. 15-2106.

United States Court of Appeals, Fourth Circuit.

Argued: October 26, 2016.

Decided: January 4, 2017.

Wood v. US, 845 F. 3d 123 (4th Cir. 2017)

p.124 Appeal from the United States District Court for the Eastern District of Virginia, at Norfolk, Raymond A. Jackson, District Judge, (2:14-cv-00469-RAJ-TEM).

ARGUED: Timothy Jon DeMore, Demore Law Firm, Syracuse, New York, for Appellant. Kent Pendleton Porter, Office of the United States Attorney, Norfolk, Virginia, for Appellee. ON BRIEF: Matthew D. Green, Gibson S. Wright, Morris & Morris, P.C., Richmond, Virginia; Brittany E. Aungier, Hiscock & Barclay, LLP, Syracuse, New York, for Appellant. Dana J. Boente, United States Attorney, Office of the United States Attorney, Alexandria, Virginia, for Appellee.

Before WILKINSON, NIEMEYER, and SHEDD, Circuit Judges.

Affirmed by published opinion. Judge Niemeyer wrote the opinion, in which Judge Wilkinson and Judge Shedd joined.

NIEMEYER, Circuit Judge:

Laurie Wood, a City of Norfolk (Virginia) Sheriff's Deputy, was seriously injured during a training session on a Navy base p.125 when she jumped from a training structure onto a set of mats, landing in a gap between them. She commenced this action against the United States under the Federal Tort Claims Act ("FTCA"), alleging that Navy officers negligently allowed the structure, particularly the mats placed adjacent to it, to remain in a dangerous condition and failed to warn her of the dangerous gap between the mats. The district court granted the government's motion to dismiss, concluding that the challenged Navy conduct fell within the FTCA's "discretionary function exception" and therefore that Congress had not waived sovereign immunity for Wood's claim.

On appeal, Wood contends that her complaint alleged a straightforward negligence claim under Virginia law, for which the United States waived sovereign immunity in the FTCA. Specifically, she argues that the Navy's conduct was "not discretionary in nature" so as to be excluded from the waiver of sovereign immunity because it was not the sort of conduct that the discretionary function exception was intended to protect.

Because we conclude that the Navy's decisions regarding the maintenance of its military bases for use by civilian law enforcement involved policy judgments that Congress sought to shield from tort liability under the FTCA, we affirm.

I

Wood was injured while using a piece of training equipment located within the Naval Support Activity Hampton Roads, Northwest Annex ("Northwest Annex"), a restricted access military base of some 3,600 acres in Chesapeake, Virginia. The Northwest Annex, which was owned and operated by the Navy, was managed by two Navy instrumentalities — the Marine Corps Security Force Training Company and the Navy's Center for Security Forces.

By statute, the Department of Defense is authorized to make military facilities such as the Northwest Annex available to state and local civilian law enforcement officers for training purposes, 10 U.S.C. § 372, and to train civilian officers to use those facilities, id. § 373, so long as the civilian training does not "adversely affect the military preparedness of the United States," id. § 376. A Department of Defense directive and several military orders set forth policies regarding the use of military facilities by civilian law enforcement generally, and Standard Operating Procedures set forth procedures governing law enforcement's use of the Northwest Annex specifically.

Before any civilian law enforcement agency may use Northwest Annex facilities for training, one of its officers must qualify under a Marine Corps training program as a Range Safety Officer. During that training, the civilian officer is provided with excerpts of the Standard Operating Procedures, which outline the officer's duties as a Range Safety Officer. The officer is instructed on how to schedule the facilities, coach his fellow officers on the range, respond to accidents, and perform other "basic duties." The officer is also shown a slideshow that admonishes all Range Safety Officers to "REMEMBER! The [Range Safety Officer] is solely responsible for the safety and the proper conduct of the training" at the Navy facility. Once a civilian officer qualifies as a Range Safety Officer, he may schedule use of the Northwest Annex for his law enforcement agency by submitting a request form that specifies the facilities and equipment being requested. This form must then be approved by a Navy or Marine Corps official, depending on which branch is responsible for the requested facility.

p.126 Sergeant Brad Ward of the City of Norfolk Sheriff's Office qualified as a Range Safety Officer in 2011, and in February 2012, he requested use of two facilities at the Northwest Annex — "Munro Village," an outdoor tactical training facility designed to resemble a city block, and the "Simunition House." Sergeant Ward's request form did not include a request for use of the "Ship Mockup," although the form also listed that facility as available. His request was approved by an officer of the Marine Corps, which managed Munro Village.

The "Ship Mockup," which is managed by the Navy and on which Wood was injured, is located near Munro Village and is within the same general area. That equipment, which the Navy referred to as the "Ship in a Box" or the "mock-ship," was a prismatic, three-story structure designed to resemble a foreign merchant ship. The Navy used the equipment to simulate ship-boarding by having soldiers — clad in armor and strapped into safety harnesses — climb a ladder onto the mock-ship's third deck. Several mats were placed beneath the ladder both to recreate the difficulty of beginning a climb from an inflatable boat and to provide additional fall protection if a soldier's harness were to fail.

On April 20, 2012, Wood and other officers, who shared responsibility for training the Sheriff's Office's deputies, arrived at the Northwest Annex in preparation for the training exercises. As Wood and the other Sheriff's Office instructors walked through the Munro Village training facility, they discussed using the mock-ship to create a "bail-out" scenario for trainees to practice exiting a building at an elevated height. They contemplated that the trainees would jump from the mock-ship onto the mats below from the second story, a height of some 20 feet. One instructor, seeking to demonstrate the exercise, climbed up onto the mock-ship's first story and jumped out onto the mats without incident. Wood then climbed onto the second story and jumped off. When she landed, however, two of the mats separated, and she fell through the gap onto the ground. The fall caused a burst fracture of her twelfth thoratic vertebra, rendering her a paraplegic.

After Wood's administrative claim for damages was denied by the Navy, she commenced this action under the FTCA against the United States. She alleged that the United States negligently maintained the mock-ship in a dangerous condition by (1) failing to secure a "top pad" to the mock-ship's mats to prevent them from separating; (2) failing adequately to inspect the condition of the mock-ship and its mats; and (3) failing to warn her, as a lawful invitee, of the dangerous condition created by the possibility of mat separation. The government filed a motion to dismiss Wood's complaint, contending that the Navy's challenged conduct — consisting of safety-related decisions regarding its training facilities when used by civilian law enforcement agencies — fell within the FTCA's discretionary function exception and that therefore the United States could not be sued. The district court agreed and entered an order dismissing Wood's complaint for a lack of subject matter jurisdiction.

After the court entered its order of dismissal, Wood filed a motion to alter or amend the judgment under Federal Rule of Civil Procedure 59(e), claiming that the district court's dismissal of her complaint without allowing for discovery contravened our decision in Kerns v. United States, 585 F.3d 187 (4th Cir. 2009). The district court, however, found that Kerns was inapplicable because "jurisdictional facts" regarding the applicability of the discretionary function p.127 exception were not "'inextricably intertwined' with the merits of Plaintiff's claim." Accordingly, it denied Wood's motion.

From the district court's May 14, 2015 order dismissing her complaint and its August 31, 2015 order denying her motion to alter or amend the judgment, Wood filed this appeal.

II

"[N]o action lies against the United States unless the legislature has authorized it." Dalehite v. United States, 346 U.S. 15, 30, 73 S.Ct. 956, 97 L.Ed. 1427 (1953).

In the FTCA, Congress waived sovereign immunity for claims brought against the United States based on the negligence or wrongful acts or omissions of its employees committed within the scope of employment, accepting liability in the same manner and to the same extent as a private individual would have under like circumstances. 28 U.S.C. §§ 1346(b)(1), 2671-2680. This waiver, however, is circumscribed by numerous exceptions, including an exception for claims "based upon the exercise or performance or the failure to exercise or perform a discretionary function or duty on the part of a federal agency or an employee of the Government, whether or not the discretion involved be abused." Id. § 2680(a) (emphasis added). Because waivers of sovereign immunity must be strictly construed, the plaintiff bears the burden of demonstrating jurisdiction and showing that none of the FTCA's exceptions apply. See Welch v. United States, 409 F.3d 646, 651 (4th Cir. 2005).

In this case, the government challenged the district court's jurisdiction based on the discretionary function exception set forth in § 2680(a), and therefore Wood had the burden of demonstrating that that exception did not apply. To carry her burden, she alleged that the United States' creation and maintenance of an unsafe condition at the mock-ship and its failure to warn her of the condition were "not discretionary in nature and therefore [were] not excepted as discretionary acts from the government's waiver of sovereign immunity."

Acting on the government's motion, the district court dismissed Wood's complaint, concluding that Wood did not carry her burden. In reaching its conclusion, the district court read Wood's complaint to challenge the government's conduct in "the military's maintenance decisions regarding the [mock-ship] as an unauthorized military facility, as opposed to a military facility that has been approved for civilian use." It concluded that

> the government's maintenance of the [mock-ship] when it has not been approved for civilian use falls under the [discretionary function exception] because it implicates financial and staffing considerations. Equipment and facility maintenance considerations, as well as calculations balancing the benefit of increased safety measures and increased costs, objectively fall into the category of decisions that are susceptible to policy analysis.

On appeal, Wood contends that her claim for premises liability is a "garden variety" negligence claim that involves the failure to make premises safe for invitees or to give them warning of a known danger. She asserts that Congress did not intend for these "run of the mill" acts to be shielded by the discretionary function exception. She adds that the government's focus on the training facility's purposes and the Navy's mission in maintaining the premises is "merely a distraction." She also argues that its focus is too broad and general and, moreover, that the district p.128 court's description of her use of the mock-ship as "unauthorized" is not supported by her allegations, which must be accepted at this stage in the proceedings.

The government contends, on the other hand, that Wood's characterization of the conduct at issue is too narrow, collapsing the discretionary function inquiry into the question of negligence on the merits. The government asserts that Wood's complaint actually challenges government decisions regarding the maintenance and inspection of, or the issuance of warnings relating to, military training facilities used by civilian law enforcement. Such decisions, it argues, are within the discretionary function exception for which the government has not waived immunity in the FTCA.

The determination of whether the discretionary function exception applies requires application of a two-step analysis. First, a court must determine whether the conduct in question "involves an element of judgment or choice." Berkovitz ex rel. Berkovitz v. United States, 486 U.S. 531, 536, 108 S.Ct. 1954, 100 L.Ed.2d 531 (1988). When a statute, regulation, or policy prescribes the employee's conduct, the conduct cannot be discretionary and thus is unprotected by the discretionary function exception. Id.; see also United States v. Gaubert, 499 U.S. 315, 322, 111 S.Ct. 1267, 113 L.Ed.2d 335 (1991); Seaside Farm, Inc. v. United States, 842 F.3d 853, 858-59 (4th Cir. 2016). Second, when the challenged conduct is the product of judgment or choice, the court must still determine whether the decision made was "based on considerations of public policy." Berkovitz, 486 U.S. at 537, 108 S.Ct. 1954. This second step of the analysis is designed to prohibit courts from "second guessing" decisions "grounded in social, economic, and political policy through the medium of an action in tort." Gaubert, 499 U.S. at 323, 111 S.Ct. 1267 (quoting United States v. S.A. Empresa de Viacao Aerea Rio Grandense (Varig Airlines), 467 U.S. 797, 814, 104 S.Ct. 2755, 81 L.Ed.2d 660 (1984)). And in this same vein, "when established government policy, as expressed or implied by statute, regulation, or agency guidelines, allows a Government agent to exercise discretion, it must be presumed that the agent's acts are grounded in policy when exercising that discretion." Id. at 324, 111 S.Ct. 1267 (emphasis added). In short, the discretionary function exception is driven by separation of powers concerns, shielding decisions of a government entity made within the scope of any regulatory policy expressed in statute, regulation, or policy guidance, even when made negligently.

The analysis of whether the discretionary function exception applies does not depend on whether the government employee had subjective knowledge of his discretion or subjectively intended to exercise it; the analysis must focus objectively on "the nature of the actions taken and on whether they are susceptible to policy analysis." Gaubert, 499 U.S. at 325, 111 S.Ct. 1267; see also Seaside Farm, 842 F.3d at 858-59; Baum v. United States, 986 F.2d 716, 721 (4th Cir. 1993).

The analysis also does not depend on whether the conduct was that of a high-level agency official making policy or a low-level employee implementing policy. See Dalehite, 346 U.S. at 35-36, 73 S.Ct. 956. Rather, the analysis must focus solely on whether the government conduct involved choice implicating policy. Gaubert, 499 U.S. at 323, 111 S.Ct. 1267. Indeed, relying on a distinction between "day-to-day" actions and "policymaking or planning functions" would be inappropriate in light of the principle that "[d]iscretionary conduct is not confined to policy or planning level. 'It is the nature of the conduct, rather than the status of the actor, that p.129 governs whether the discretionary function exception applies in a given case.'" Id. at 325, 111 S.Ct. 1267 (alteration omitted) (quoting Varig Airlines, 467 U.S. at 813, 104 S.Ct. 2755).

Thus, in Baum v. United States, 986 F.2d 716 (4th Cir. 1993), we ordered dismissal of a suit alleging, in relevant part, that the National Park Service negligently failed to replace a deteriorating guardrail system that broke when the plaintiffs' car struck it. 986 F.2d at 718. We concluded that, just as a statute gave the Park Service discretion to construct the bridge without fear that courts would second-guess its design choices, the FTCA shielded the agency's "decision of how and when to replace a major element of [that] substantial public facility." Id. at 724;

see also Bowman v. United States, 820 F.2d 1393, 1395 (4th Cir. 1987) (holding, on similar facts, that "[w]hether [the] decision grew out of a lack of financial resources, a desire to preserve the natural beauty of the vista, a judgment that the hazard was insufficient to warrant a guardrail, or a combination of all three, ... [it] is obvious that the decision was the result of a policy judgment").

Therefore, taking the facts alleged by Wood in this case as defining the challenged government actions, see Gaubert, 499 U.S. at 325, 111 S.Ct. 1267, and applying the two-step analysis to them, we must determine, on an objective basis, whether the challenged government conduct involved decisions based on considerations of public policy.

Wood alleges, in essence, that pursuant to a request made by the Norfolk Sheriff's Office, the Navy authorized that Office to conduct training exercises on the Navy base in April 2012. She alleges that the Navy was negligent in failing to maintain in a safe configuration the mats on which she was injured, by failing to inspect the mats for the dangerous condition, and by failing to warn invitees, such as Wood, about the dangerous condition. In short, she makes a premises liability claim as an invitee to a Navy military base, and we must decide therefore whether these actions that she challenges are protected by the discretionary function exception.

Applying the two-step analysis to this conduct, we determine first whether the government conduct involved an element of choice, which in turn requires the determination of whether any federal statute, regulation, or policy prescribed the conduct. See Berkovitz, 486 U.S. at 536, 108 S.Ct. 1954. On this aspect of the analysis, the parties apparently agree that there was no mandate contained in any statute, regulation, or policy regarding the maintenance, inspection, and warning with regard to either the mats or the mock-ship. In responding to the government's motion to dismiss, Wood conceded that she was unable to find any such statute, regulation, or military policy, and she does not argue otherwise on appeal. In addition, the government presented affidavits from a Navy captain, a Marine Corps colonel, and the Range Manager at Northwest Annex, stating that there is no policy directly governing such maintenance, inspection, and warning procedures when the facilities are used by a civilian law enforcement agency. Further, the Marine Corps order governing range safety does not require the military to take any specific safety precautions with respect to facilities that are to be used by civilians. Instead, it requires only that civilian agencies, who "may use [military] ranges at the discretion of the installation commander," must "comply with the provisions of this regulation/order." See Range Safety, Army Reg. 385-63, MCO 3570.1C (2012). And the Standard Operating Procedures that apply specifically to the Northwest Annex prescribe no actions p.130 with respect to base safety. As a consequence, the government conduct involving the safety of the mock-ship and the mats required Navy personnel to make choices or exercise judgment.

Even so, for the discretionary function exception to apply, those choices or judgments must also have been "based on considerations of public policy" and thus "of the kind that the discretionary function exception was designed to shield." Berkovitz, 486 U.S. at 537, 108 S.Ct. 1954. In addressing this second step of the analysis, we look to the "objective," "general" nature of the challenged actions and decide whether they inherently involved protected policy judgments. Baum, 986 F.2d at 720-21.

We note first that the statutory scheme governing civilian use of military facilities sets out a basic policy tradeoff between permissive civilian training and constrained military resources. See Gaubert, 499 U.S. at 324, 111 S.Ct. 1267 ("[T]he general aims and policies of the controlling statute will [typically] be evident from its text"). The statutes provide that the Department of Defense may allow civilian law enforcement agencies to use Navy facilities, 10 U.S.C. § 372, and may train civilian officers "in the operation and maintenance of equipment," id. § 373. But they also instruct that civilian use must not interfere with the nation's "military preparedness." Id. § 376. There can be no doubt therefore that the Navy's first-order decision of whether to allow civilian use of its bases at all is shielded by the discretionary function exception.

In allowing civilian use of the Northwest Annex in the particular circumstances of this case, the Navy also had to make several additional decisions — each under the umbrella of its initial decision to allow civilians to use the base at all — and these decisions were necessarily informed by the same policy considerations expressed in the statutes. This is made evident by the Navy's internal policy documents covering civilian use of the facility. See Gaubert, 499 U.S. at 324, 111 S.Ct. 1267 ("[A]n agency may rely on internal guidelines rather than on published regulations"). For example, in deciding whether to authorize use of its base by civilian officers, the Navy has chosen to require that one of those officers qualify as a Range Safety Officer, who is required to be "solely responsible for the safety" of their civilian agency while training on the base. A Navy policy manual also indicates that its officers should provide assistance to local law enforcement "at the lowest cost practicable." Similar documents more generally set forth risk-management frameworks for all Navy decisionmaking. See Chief of Naval Operations Instruction 3500.39C (July 2, 2010). The common thread running through the relevant statutes and policy documents is a recognition that, whenever the Navy exercises its statutory discretion to allow civilian agencies to use its facilities, it must take into account in exercising its judgment military preparedness, the safety of the civilian agencies, and costs. This complicated balance is well illustrated here. Given the designed purpose of the mock-ship and the mats, which were intended only as backup protection for armored soldiers climbing the ship in harnesses, it could be unjustifiably costly to protect against and warn civilian trainees of the dangers arising out of uses for which the facility was not designed. See Baum, 986 F.2d at 722-24 (economic policy considerations underlying bridge construction project encompassed subsequent decisions involving bridge maintenance).

At bottom, the Navy's decision to leave the mats near the mock-ship in a certain condition, its allegedly infrequent inspections of the mock-ship, its decision not to p.131 warn civilian trainees itself about the condition of the ship, and its decision to qualify the user's agent as a Range Safety Officer responsible for safety each fall comfortably within that overarching policy of balancing open civilian use, civilian safety, military preparedness, and costs. And "[w]hen established governmental policy, as expressed or implied by statute, regulation, or agency guidelines, allows a Government agent to exercise discretion," as here, "it must be presumed that the agent's acts are grounded in policy when exercising that discretion." Gaubert, 499 U.S. at 324, 111 S.Ct. 1267 (emphasis added).

Wood argues that if the Navy's maintenance decisions are protected here, it is difficult to see how the United States could ever be liable for injuries on government property. She cites cases from courts in other circuits that have expressed similar concerns in declining to extend the discretionary function exception to particular premises-liability claims. In our view, however, the requirement that shielded conduct be taken pursuant to specific policies expressed in federal law explains some of those courts' reluctance to apply the discretionary function exception in the particular circumstances presented. For example, in Gotha v. United States, 115 F.3d 176, 178 (3d Cir. 1997), a Navy contractor's employee slipped and fell on a military base footpath. In the absence of any statutory, regulatory, or internal policy evidence encompassing the Navy's decisions with respect to employee safety, the Gotha court refused to endorse the government's theory that its conduct inherently involved balancing national security and employee safety. Id. at 181-82.

The reasoning in Gotha, however, has little application here, where the Navy's maintenance decisions with respect to facilities used by civilian law enforcement fall within the overarching policies of a regulatory scheme that gives officers discretion in how to implement that policy. In this case, where Congress by statute and the Navy by internal policy have established a regulatory mission of making military bases available for civilian-law-enforcement training, the Navy's decisions affecting the safety of its bases for civilian trainees should not be subjected to judicial second-guessing. Were we to hold, for example, that Wood could challenge the Navy's decision not to place a warning sign near the mock-ship, it would open the Navy to tort liability for every similar decision made when allowing civilian law enforcement agencies to use its facilities. The threat of tort liability would become a tool to shape Navy policy, which is exactly what the discretionary function exception seeks to avoid.

Wood also contends that the district court incorrectly defined the government's challenged conduct as "maintenance decisions regarding the [mock-ship] as an unauthorized military facility" — a description that assumed, contrary to her claim, that her use of the mock-ship was not authorized and thereby dictated the court's decision. To be sure, while the district court did repeatedly express its assumption that the mock-ship was unauthorized, its ultimate decision did not necessarily rest on that assumption. The district court observed that "the considerations that apply to this decision are magnified when the issue is the military's maintenance of unauthorized facilities." Moreover, its holding was grounded centrally on the fact that the Navy exercised discretion with respect to public policy. As the court stated:

> In this case, the military has declined to adopt any policy to conduct pre-training inspections in order to ensure that requested facilities are safe for civilian use. Instead, the responsibility to conduct p.132 pre-training inspections is with the [Range Safety Officer].... The Court finds that [these matters are susceptible to policy analysis] because these day-to-day operational maintenance decisions regarding the condition in which military facilities are to be left in when they are not in use, implicate economic policy in that they involve considerations such as allocation of military resources.

Thus, while the district court ruled with the assumption that the mock-ship's use was unauthorized, its reasoning applied equally to a situation where use of the mock-ship was authorized.

In any event, whether use of the mock-ship was authorized or not does not implicate whether the district court had jurisdiction under the FTCA. As we have pointed out, the permissive use of the Navy's training facilities by civilian law enforcement is covered by policies announced in statutes, regulations, and orders, and officers' implementation of these policies through decisions with respect to the mock-ship and the mats is therefore protected by the discretionary function exception.

At bottom, we conclude that the government's challenged conduct here falls within the FTCA's discretionary function exception and therefore that the district court correctly concluded that Congress did not, in the FTCA, waive the sovereign immunity of the United States for Wood's negligence claim.

III

Wood also contends that the district court abused its discretion in denying her motion to amend the judgment under Federal Rule of Civil Procedure 59(e) to allow her to engage in jurisdictional discovery, as provided in Kerns, 585 F.3d 187. She argues in particular that the district court should have allowed discovery of whether her use of the mock-ship was unauthorized, which "weighed heavily upon the [District] Court's analysis."

In Kerns, we reversed an order dismissing a plaintiff's complaint under Rule 12(b)(1) because the facts supporting FTCA jurisdiction — bearing on whether the defendant was driving within the scope of her employment — were "inextricably intertwined" with the merits of the plaintiff's tort claim. 585 F.3d at 195. The Kerns decision sought to ensure that plaintiffs facing a motion to dismiss were not unfairly deprived of the additional "procedural safeguards" in Rule 56 (governing summary judgment) when the merits of their claims are bound up with jurisdictional issues. Id. at 195-96.

Kerns, however, does not apply here. As explained above, the application of the discretionary function exception does not turn on whether Wood was authorized to use the mock-ship. That fact would indeed be relevant to the merits of Wood's tort claim. But it is irrelevant to subject matter jurisdiction. See Seaside Farm, 842 F.3d at 858-59. Accordingly, we conclude that the district court did not abuse its discretion in refusing to open discovery to the merits issue in this case.

* * *

For the reasons given, the district court's order dismissing Wood's complaint for lack of subject matter jurisdiction and its order denying her Rule 59(e) motion are
AFFIRMED.

842 F.3d 328 (2016)

John David RAPLEE, Jr., Plaintiff-Appellant,
v.
UNITED STATES of America, Defendant-Appellee.
Maryland Association for Justice, Amicus Supporting Appellant.

No. 14-1217.

United States Court of Appeals, Fourth Circuit.

Argued: October 25, 2016.

Decided: November 22, 2016.

Raplee v. US, 842 F. 3d 328 (4th Cir. 2016)

p.329 Appeal from the United States District Court for the District of Maryland, at Greenbelt, No. 8:13-cv-01318-PWG, Paul W. Grimm, District Judge.

ARGUED: L. Palmer Foret, Ashcraft & Gerel, LLP, Rockville, Maryland, for Appellant. Neil R. White, Office of the United States Attorney, Greenbelt, Maryland, for Appellee. ON BRIEF: Wayne Mansulla, Peter T. Anderson, Ashcraft & Gerel, LLP, Rockville, Maryland, for Appellant.

p.330 Rod J. Rosenstein, United States Attorney, Office of the United States Attorney, Baltimore, Maryland, for Appellee. Michael J. Winkelman, McCarthy & Winkelman LLP, Lanham, Maryland, for Amicus Curiae.

Before NIEMEYER and MOTZ, Circuit Judges, and DAVIS, Senior Circuit Judge.

Affirmed by published opinion. Judge Motz wrote the opinion, in which Judge Niemeyer and Senior Judge Davis joined.

DIANA GRIBBON MOTZ, Circuit Judge:

John Raplee challenges the dismissal of his Federal Tort Claims Act ("FTCA") complaint as untimely. In compliance with state law, Raplee initially filed a medical malpractice claim with Maryland's alternative dispute resolution agency. Although he filed with the state agency within the FTCA's limitations period, he did not file a complaint in federal court until well after that period had passed. Raplee contends that by filing a required state administrative claim, an "action is begun" for the purposes of the FTCA's limitations period. 28 U.S.C. § 2401(b) (2012). Alternatively, he asserts that equitable tolling principles excuse his failure to comply with the limitations period. Because an "action is begun" under the FTCA only by filing a civil action in federal district court, Raplee's claim was untimely. Further, he has not demonstrated any extraordinary circumstances warranting equitable tolling. Accordingly, we affirm the judgment of the district court.

I.

In September 2006, Raplee underwent surgery at the National Institutes of Health, an operating division of the United States Department of Health and Human Services ("HHS"). Raplee alleges that the surgeons "negligently position[ed]" him while he was under anesthesia, resulting in permanent damage to the muscles and nerves in his left foot.

The FTCA renders the United States liable for the torts of its employees, including the surgeons in this case, "in the same manner and to the same extent as a private individual under like circumstances." 28 U.S.C. § 2674. The FTCA requires a plaintiff pursuing a tort claim to follow a multi-step process. First, a plaintiff must file his claim with the appropriate federal agency, which then has the power to settle or deny it. 28 U.S.C. §§ 2401(b), 2675(a). The plaintiff may file a civil action against the United States only if the agency has denied the claim. 28 U.S.C. § 2675(a).

In November 2006, Raplee retained the law firm Ashcraft & Gerel, LLP to represent him in his medical malpractice claim against the United States. On September 16, 2008, Ashcraft & Gerel, through Martin Trpis, filed Raplee's claim with HHS.

Trpis had left Ashcraft & Gerel by May 2010 while Raplee's claim was still under administrative review at HHS. Although lawyers from the firm continued to represent Raplee, no one notified HHS of Trpis's departure, and no other attorney from Ashcraft & Gerel filed an appearance with HHS.

On June 19, 2012, HHS mailed its notice of final denial by certified letter to Trpis at Ashcraft & Gerel. Section 2401(b) of the FTCA bars any tort claim against the United States unless the "action is begun within six months" after the federal agency mails notice of its denial of the claim. 28 U.S.C. § 2401(b). Therefore, Raplee had until December 19, 2012 to begin an action pursuant to the FTCA.

The letter HHS sent to Trpis at Ashcraft & Gerel was returned to HHS as undeliverable. The envelope containing the p.331 letter was stamped "Returned to Sender" with a handwritten note explaining that Trpis was "no longer at this company." HHS confirmed that it had sent the letter to the correct address, but it made no further attempt to send notice of its denial. The record contains no evidence that Raplee, Trpis, or anyone else inquired as to the status of Raplee's claim.

Because the FTCA merely waives sovereign immunity to make the United States amenable to a state tort suit, the substantive law of the state where the tort occurred determines the liability of the United States. 28 U.S.C. § 1346(b)(1); see, e.g., Levin v. United States, ___ U.S. ___, 133 S.Ct. 1224, 1228, 185 L.Ed.2d 343 (2013). Accordingly, as the parties agree, Maryland plaintiffs wishing to bring medical malpractice claims against the United States under the FTCA must comply with Maryland's pre-filing requirements.

On November 8, 2012, Raplee, represented by an Ashcraft & Gerel lawyer (but not Trpis), filed a claim with Maryland's Health Care Alternative Dispute Resolution Office. Under Maryland law, a plaintiff must submit a medical malpractice claim to this state agency before filing the claim in court. Md. Code Ann., Cts. & Jud. Proc. § 3-2A-02(a), -04(a)(1)(i) (West 2016). A plaintiff must then submit an expert report certifying that the claim is meritorious within ninety days. Id. § 3-2A-04(b)(1)(i)(1). Once a claimant has submitted an expert report, he may waive arbitration and proceed to court. Id. § 3-2A-06B(a).

Although Raplee filed his initial claim with the Maryland agency in November 2012 — approximately one month before the FTCA filing deadline in December 2012 — he did not file his expert report until February 2013. And he did not waive arbitration until March 2013. Raplee finally filed a complaint with the federal district court on May 3, 2013 — nearly five months after expiration of his time to begin an action under § 2401(b).

The United States moved to dismiss Raplee's claim for lack of subject matter jurisdiction. The district court granted the motion because, at the time, we considered the FTCA's limitations period to be jurisdictional. See, e.g., Gould v. U.S. Dep't of Health & Human Servs., 905 F.2d 738, 741-42 (4th Cir. 1990) (en banc). On appeal, we held the case in abeyance while the Supreme Court resolved that very issue. In United States v. Kwai Fun Wong, ___ U.S. ___, 135 S.Ct. 1625, 1629, 191 L.Ed.2d 533 (2015), the Court held that the FTCA's limitations period is not a jurisdictional rule but a claims-processing rule that allows for equitable tolling. In light of this decision, we remanded Raplee's case so that the district court could decide whether Raplee was entitled to equitable tolling. The district court concluded that he was not, reasoning that Raplee failed to show that extraordinary circumstances had prevented him from filing in a timely manner.

On appeal, Raplee contends that his claim was timely because, by filing his claim with the state agency, an "action [was] begun" under § 2401(b) of the FTCA. He also contends that, even if his claim was untimely, he is entitled to equitable tolling. We consider these arguments in turn.

II.

In order to determine whether Raplee's claim was timely, we must decide when an "action is begun" under § 2401(b). We review questions of statutory interpretation de novo. Stone v. Instrumentation Lab. Co., 591 F.3d 239, 242-43 (4th Cir. 2009).

p.332 When construing a statute, we start with its text. Lamie v. U.S. Tr., 540 U.S. 526, 534, 124 S.Ct. 1023, 157 L.Ed.2d 1024 (2004). If the meaning of the text is plain — in other words, if it bears only one reasonable interpretation — that meaning controls. Id. "The plainness or ambiguity of statutory language is determined by reference to the language itself, the specific context in which that language is used, and the broader context of the statute as a whole." Robinson v. Shell Oil Co., 519 U.S. 337, 341, 117 S.Ct. 843, 136 L.Ed.2d 808 (1997).

The word "action" in § 2401(b) has only one reasonable meaning: it refers to a federal civil action. The language of the statute and the context in which it occurs confirm this.

"Action" has a settled technical meaning in the law: "action" means a lawsuit. See Black's Law Dictionary 49 (4th ed. 1951) ("The legal and formal demand of one's right ... in a court of justice."). This meaning of "action" has an ancient lineage. See Ex parte Milligan, 71 U.S. (4 Wall.) 2, 112-13, 18 L.Ed. 281 (1866) ("In any legal sense, action, suit, and cause, are convertible terms" and "[i]n law language a suit is the prosecution of some demand in a court of justice." (quoting Cohens v. Virginia, 19 U.S. (6 Wheat.) 264, 407, 5 L.Ed. 257 (1821))).

Moreover, the Supreme Court settled any question about the term's current meaning when the Court promulgated the Federal Rules of Civil Procedure in 1938. The Federal Rules famously abolished distinctions between various types of judicial proceedings — like the distinction between "actions at law" and "suits in equity" —

by announcing that "[t]here shall be one form of action to be known as 'civil action.'" Fed. R. Civ. P. 2 (1938). The Advisory Committee made clear that this innovation in terminology sought to bring uniformity both to federal civil procedure and the United States Code. Id. advisory committee's note to 1937 adoption ("Reference to actions at law or suits in equity in all statutes should now be treated as referring to the civil action prescribed in these rules.").

Congress adopted the language of § 2401(b) against this backdrop, and the statutory context supports the conclusion that all references to "action" in the FTCA refer to a judicial civil lawsuit. For example, § 2401(a) — the text immediately preceding § 2401(b) — provides that "every civil action commenced against the United States shall be barred unless the complaint is filed within six years." 28 U.S.C. § 2401(a) (emphases added). The next sentence provides an exception: "The action of any person under legal disability or beyond the seas at the time the claim accrues may be commenced within three years after the disability ceases." Id. (emphasis added). As another example, § 2402 provides that "any action against the United States under section 1346 shall be tried by the court without a jury." Id. § 2402 (emphases added).

Thus, both the text and statutory context indicate that the word "action" in § 2401(b) refers only to a civil action filed in court. Common sense recommends this understanding all the more strongly when considering a statute of limitations, the very purpose of which is to identify the deadline for filing a lawsuit in court.

The references to § 1346 in the FTCA confirm that the only type of civil action contemplated by § 2401(b) is a federal civil action. See 28 U.S.C. § 1346(b)(1). There can be no doubt that a plaintiff begins an action under the FTCA by bringing "[a] tort claim against the United States." 28 U.S.C. § 2401(b). But the federal district courts have exclusive jurisdiction over p.333 these claims. 28 U.S.C. § 1346(b)(1). Thus, a plaintiff cannot satisfy the FTCA's limitations period by filing an action with a state agency that lacks jurisdiction over such an action.

Raplee seeks to ignore all of this statutory language. He proposes that an "action is begun" under the FTCA as soon as a plaintiff takes some required step toward pursuing a tort claim against the United States. But that would mean Congress enacted a statute of limitations that says nothing specific about what a plaintiff must do to satisfy the limitations period and nothing at all about when a plaintiff's time to file a complaint in federal court elapses. This would make no sense.

In sum, § 2401(b) requires a plaintiff to bring a federal civil action within six months after a federal agency mails its notice of final denial of his claim. Of course, the only way to begin a federal civil action is by filing a complaint with a federal district court. Fed. R. Civ. P. 3. Raplee did not file his complaint with the district court within the six-month limitations period, and therefore his complaint was untimely.

III.

Even so, Raplee contends that the district court erred in refusing to consider his case by tolling the limitations period. In a non-habeas context like this, we generally review denials of equitable tolling for abuse of discretion. Rouse v. Lee, 339 F.3d

238, 247 n.6 (4th Cir. 2003) (en banc). But see Cruz v. Maypa, 773 F.3d 138, 143 (4th Cir. 2014) (noting that in some circumstances review is de novo).

Plaintiffs are entitled to equitable tolling only if they show that they have pursued their rights diligently and extraordinary circumstances prevented them from filing on time. See Holland v. Florida, 560 U.S. 631, 649, 130 S.Ct. 2549, 177 L.Ed.2d 130 (2010). We have explained that equitable tolling is reserved for "those rare instances where — due to circumstances external to the party's own conduct — it would be unconscionable to enforce the limitation period against the party and gross injustice would result." Harris v. Hutchinson, 209 F.3d 325, 330 (4th Cir. 2000). The district court concluded that Raplee failed to demonstrate that extraordinary circumstances prevented him from filing on time. Raplee asserts that the court erred for two reasons.

A.

First, Raplee maintains that HHS wrongfully deprived him of notice that his claim had been denied by failing to send him a second notice. This, he argues, constitutes an extraordinary circumstance.

Wrongful conduct by an opposing party can trigger equitable tolling. Id. However, HHS did nothing wrong in this case. It mailed notice to Raplee's counsel of record at the address counsel had provided — the offices of Ashcraft & Gerel. When the notice was returned undelivered, HHS took the extra step of confirming that it had been sent to the correct address, a step the statute does not require. Raplee does not dispute that HHS sent the notice to the correct address, and the unrebutted record evidence shows that it arrived there. We know of no statute or regulation that requires anything more of HHS, and Raplee has pointed to none.

Furthermore, the failure to receive the notice is largely attributable to action or inaction by past and present lawyers at Ashcraft & Gerel. Those lawyers took no steps to ensure that Raplee's case would be handled seamlessly after Trpis left the firm. They never notified HHS about the departure of one lawyer or the substitution of another. When the certified letter from p.334 HHS arrived at Ashcraft & Gerel's office, the letter was simply rejected without being opened.

Nothing extraordinary occurred here. This is just the type of thing that can happen when busy lawyers inadvertently fail to handle personnel changes and office mail carefully. Such conduct is unfortunately understandable; it hardly qualifies as an extraordinary circumstance. Cf. Irwin v. Dep't of Veterans Affairs, 498 U.S. 89, 96, 111 S.Ct. 453, 112 L.Ed.2d 435 (1990) (holding that equitable tolling did not apply to an untimely action under the Civil Rights Act where the attorney was out of the country when notice arrived at his office); Rouse, 339 F.3d at 251, 253 (holding that equitable tolling did not apply to a death-row inmate's habeas petition where inmate's attorney filed one day late); Harris, 209 F.3d at 331 (holding that an attorney's misinterpretation of AEDPA's limitations period did not warrant tolling).

B.

Raplee also contends that Trpis, his original Ashcraft & Gerel attorney, abandoned him and that this constitutes an extraordinary circumstance under the Supreme Court's decision in Maples v. Thomas, ___ U.S. ___, 132 S.Ct. 912, 181 L.Ed.2d 807 (2012). This argument also fails.

In Maples, a state prisoner on death row procedurally defaulted on his habeas claim because, unbeknownst to him, his attorneys left the firm handling the case and no other attorneys took over for them. The Supreme Court held that the prisoner had demonstrated cause that excused his procedural default because his "attorney abandon[ed] his client without notice, and thereby occasion[ed] the default." Id. at 922.

In a habeas case, like Maples, the injustice of holding a petitioner responsible for his attorneys' abandonment is obvious. There is no redemption for habeas petitioners whose attorneys abandon them in this way. A malpractice suit cannot compensate them for the loss of freedom — or life itself. For that reason, habeas cases are precisely the type of circumstance where abandonment calls for a remedy like equitable tolling.

In contrast, in a civil suit for damages, if a plaintiff misses a deadline because his attorney abandoned him, he can recover those damages from the attorney. For this reason, the Maples rule may not apply in civil actions seeking damages. See Choice Hotels Int'l, Inc. v. Grover, 792 F.3d 753, 755-56 (7th Cir. 2015), cert. denied, ___ U.S. ___, 136 S.Ct. 691, 193 L.Ed.2d 521 (2015) (suggesting as much and declining to apply Maples in a breach of contract case). But see Sneed v. Shinseki, 737 F.3d 719, 728 (Fed. Cir. 2013) (applying Maples, over a dissent, to a veterans' benefits case because of "[t]he special treatment Congress reserved for veterans").

We need not — and do not — here resolve the reach of Maples because, even if Maples applies in civil cases, like the case at hand, it does not help Raplee here. Although the facts of this case bear some similarity to those in Maples, they differ in a crucial respect: abandonment by his attorneys did not cause Raplee to miss the filing deadline. Raplee's original Ashcraft & Gerel attorney left the firm in 2010, but the record offers no evidence that Ashcraft & Gerel lawyers abandoned him. On the contrary, the record clearly establishes other Ashcraft & Gerel attorneys took over Raplee's case almost two years before the Act's deadline passed in December 2012. For example, a lawyer from the firm procured the required expert report as early as January 2011. A lawyer from the p.335 firm continued to represent Raplee before the state agency and the district court, and a lawyer from Ashcraft & Gerel continues to represent Raplee in this appeal. Accordingly, whatever abandonment may have occurred in this case had nothing to do with the untimely filing.

IV.

We recognize that, in some cases, state requirements like Maryland's may place unusually high burdens on FTCA plaintiffs. It takes time and effort to develop a case and secure credible expert testimony. Moreover, there is no guarantee that a state agency will process claims swiftly enough to allow a plaintiff to file within the FTCA's limitations period.

There are, however, procedural devices available to mitigate the burdens of state law filing requirements. A district court has broad power to issue stays to control its docket, and it can use that power to craft a solution to such problems. For example, in a recent case where the plaintiff filed a timely federal FTCA complaint before satisfying Maryland's pre-filing requirements, Chief Judge Catherine Blake stayed the federal proceedings rather than dismiss the case. Anderson v. United States, Civ. No. CCB-08-3, 2008 WL 3307137, at *4 (D. Md. Aug. 8, 2008). This gave the plaintiff an opportunity to satisfy the state requirements without risking an untimely federal filing. (Of course, that solution was unavailable here because Raplee filed an untimely federal complaint.)

We recognize that deciding whether to stay proceedings, as Judge Blake did, "calls for the exercise of judgment, which must weigh competing interests and maintain an even balance." Landis v. N. Am. Co., 299 U.S. 248, 254-55, 57 S.Ct. 163, 81 L.Ed. 153 (1936). But in a typical case, allowing plaintiffs to file their federal complaints under the FTCA before completing state law requirements would seem to promote both the objectives of § 2401(b) and the FTCA's overall purpose of affording private citizens relief for injuries they suffer as a result of the federal government tortfeasors.

This is particularly true given that the FTCA's limitations period is not a jurisdictional rule but a claims-processing one. Kwai Fun Wong, 135 S.Ct. at 1638. Like other claims-processing rules, § 2401(b) "seek[s] to promote the orderly progress of litigation by requiring that the parties take certain procedural steps at certain specified times." Henderson ex rel. Henderson v. Shinseki, 562 U.S. 428, 435, 131 S.Ct. 1197, 179 L.Ed.2d 159 (2011). Plaintiffs cannot avoid this rule absent extraordinary circumstances. However, Congress did not design § 2401(b) as a gauntlet for plaintiffs to run. The statute does not require a plaintiff to complete all state law requirements before filing a complaint with the district court. Rather, a plaintiff fully satisfies the claims-processing objective by filing a complaint with the federal district court within the limitations period while simultaneously working to satisfy state law requirements.

V.

For the foregoing reasons, the judgment of the district court is
AFFIRMED.

814 F.3d 681 (2016)

Jonatan PORNOMO, Administrator of the Estate of Sie Giok Giang, Deceased, Plaintiff-Appellant,

v.

UNITED STATES of America, Defendant-Appellee.

No. 14-2391.

United States Court of Appeals, Fourth Circuit.

Argued: December 8, 2015.

Decided: February 25, 2016.

Pornomo v. US, 814 F. 3d 681 (4th Cir. 2016)

p.683 Appeal from the United States District Court for the Eastern District of Virginia, at Richmond, James R. Spencer, Senior District Judge, (3:14-cv-00307-JRS).

ARGUED: Philip L. Bradfield, the Bradfield Injury Law Firm, PLC, Newport News, Virginia, for Appellant. Megan Barbero, United States Department of Justice, Washington, D.C., for Appellee. ON BRIEF: Benjamin C. Mizer, Principal Deputy Assistant Attorney General, Mark B. Stern, Appellate Staff, Civil Division, United States Department of Justice, Washington, D.C.; Dana J. Boente, United States Attorney, Office of the United States Attorney, Richmond, Virginia; Paul M. Geier, Assistant General Counsel for Litigation, Paula Lee, Trial Attorney, Abel L. Smith, III, Assistant Chief Counsel, FMCSA General Law Division, Sabrina E. Redd, Attorney Advisor, FMCSA General Law Division, Federal Motor Carrier Safety Administration, United States Department of Transportation, Washington, D.C., for Appellee.

Before AGEE and HARRIS, Circuit Judges, and THEODORE D. CHUANG, United States District Judge for the District of Maryland, sitting by designation.

Affirmed by published opinion. Judge CHUANG wrote the opinion, in which Judge AGEE and Judge HARRIS joined.

CHUANG, District Judge:

p.684 On May 31, 2011, Sie Giok Giang, a passenger on a Sky Express interstate bus traveling from North Carolina to New York, was killed when the driver fell asleep at the wheel and ran the bus off the side of a Virginia highway. About seven weeks before the crash, Sky Express had been given an "unsatisfactory" safety rating by the Federal Motor Carrier Safety Administration ("FMCSA"), a rating that ordinarily would require a passenger motor carrier to cease operations after 45 days. The fatal crash occurred after that 45-day period, but during an extension period granted by the FMCSA that allowed Sky Express to remain on the road for an additional 10 days. At issue is whether the discretionary function exception to the Federal Tort Claims Act ("FTCA") bars an FTCA claim against the FMCSA for allowing Sky Express to continue to operate during those 10 days. The district court concluded that, pursuant to that exception, it lacked subject matter jurisdiction and dismissed the case. We affirm.

I.

A.

The present dispute stems from the operation of the federal regulatory scheme for monitoring the safe operation of interstate passenger motor carriers. Congress has charged the Secretary of Transportation ("the Secretary") to "determine whether an owner or operator is fit to operate safely commercial motor vehicles." 49 U.S.C. § 31144(a)(1) (2012). In turn, the Secretary has delegated this authority to the FMCSA. 49 C.F.R. § 1.87(f) (2015). To carry out this mandate, the FMCSA has promulgated regulations that provide for compliance reviews of commercial motor carriers to ensure their safe operation. 49 C.F.R. §§ 385.3, 385.9. Based on a compliance review, a commercial motor carrier is given a safety rating of "satisfactory," "conditional," or "unsatisfactory." *Id.* § 385.3. A "satisfactory" rating means that the motor carrier has adequate safety management controls in place. *Id.* A "conditional" rating means that the motor carrier does not have adequate safety management controls in place and that the lack of those controls "could result" in safety violations. *Id.* An "unsatisfactory" rating means that the motor carrier "does not have adequate safety management controls in place" and that the lack of safety management controls "has resulted" in safety violations. *Id.; see* 49 C.F.R. § 385.5 (delineating salient safety violations).

If a commercial motor carrier receives an "unsatisfactory" rating, it does not have to cease operation immediately. Instead, for passenger carriers, an "unsatisfactory" rating becomes final "beginning on the 46th day after the date of the FMCSA notice of proposed 'unsatisfactory' rating," 49 C.F.R. § 385.13(a)(1), at which point the carrier may not operate until the owner or operator is found to be "fit," 49 U.S.C. § 31144(c)(2). The carrier may seek an upgrade of its rating by submitting to the FMCSA a written description of corrective actions it has taken and documentation of those changes. 49 C.F.R. § 385.17(a)-(c). A request for an upgrade does not toll the 45-day provisional period. However, in 2011, when the events at issue in this case occurred, the regulations provided that "[i]f the motor carrier has submitted evidence that corrective actions have been taken ... and the FMCSA cannot make a final determination within the 45-day period, the period before the proposed safety rating becomes final may be extended for up to 10 days at the discretion of the FMCSA." 49 C.F.R. § 385.17(f)(2011).

In 2012, the FMCSA rescinded this 10-day extension provision to make the regulations "consistent with the policy and the p.685 statutory language" of 49 U.S.C. § 31144(c)(2) and (4). 77 Fed. Reg. 64,759, 64,759 (Oct. 23, 2012). 49 U.S.C. § 31144(c)(2) states that "[w]ith regard to owners or operators of commercial motor vehicles designed or used to transport passengers, an owner or operator who the Secretary determines is not fit may not operate in interstate commerce beginning on the 46th day after the date of such fitness determination and until the Secretary determines such owner or operator is fit." The statute provides the Secretary with discretion to extend operations for some carriers "for an additional 60 days," but expressly excludes passenger carriers from that provision. 49 U.S.C. § 31144(c)(4).

B.

In 2011, Sky Express, Inc., a commercial motor carrier based in Charlotte, North Carolina, operated buses engaged in interstate passenger transportation. On April 7, 2011, the FMCSA conducted a safety compliance review of Sky Express and gave the carrier an "unsatisfactory" rating. On April 12, 2011, the FMCSA sent Sky Express written notice of that rating, explaining that the rating would become final in 45 days, on May 28, 2011, unless Sky Express took "the necessary steps to improve the rating to conditional or satisfactory." J.A. 35. On May 11, 2011, Sky Express submitted a Request for Change to Proposed Safety Rating in which it detailed efforts it had taken to resolve the safety issues identified in the April 7, 2011 compliance review.

After reviewing Sky Express's submission, the FMCSA concluded on May 12, 2011 that Sky Express had failed to provide adequate evidence that it had corrected all of the safety violations and thus decided to conduct a follow-up compliance review. In a May 13, 2011 letter from FMCSA Field Administrator Darrell Ruban to Sky Express, the FMCSA informed Sky Express that it was "denying" Sky Express's request for a change in its rating because the submitted materials did not "provide sufficient evidence that the violations cited in the compliance review have been corrected." J.A. 52. The letter then notified Sky Express that the FMCSA would conduct a follow-up compliance review before June 7, 2011, during which Sky Express would need to provide additional documentation for review by safety investigators. In a second letter sent that same day, the FMCSA informed Sky Express that in order to provide additional time to conduct the follow-up compliance review, the deadline for Sky Express's "unsatisfactory" rating to become final had been extended by 10 days, from May 28, 2011 to June 7, 2011.

During that 10-day extension period, on May 31, 2011 at approximately 4:45 a.m., a Sky Express bus traveling northbound on Interstate 95 crashed in Caroline County, Virginia after the driver fell asleep at the wheel and allowed the bus to go off the road and down an embankment. The bus flipped over and rolled upside down, and Sie Giok Giang, a passenger, suffocated to death when her head became trapped between the collapsed bus roof and the top of her seat.

C.

On April 28, 2014, Appellant Jonatan Pornomo, Giang's adult son and the administrator of Giang's estate, filed a wrongful death action against the United States pursuant to the Federal Tort Claims Act, 28 U.S.C. §§ 1346(b), 2671-2680 (2012), in the United States District Court for the Eastern District of Virginia, Richmond Division. Pornomo alleged that the FMCSA had been negligent in issuing the 10-day extension because the language of 49 U.S.C. § 31144(c) does not permit any extension of the 45-day deadline, such that p.686 the regulation authorizing such an extension, 49 C.F.R. § 385.17(f), was invalid. Pornomo further contended that even if the FMCSA had the authority to issue an extension under 49 C.F.R. § 385.17(f), the criteria for issuance of such an extension had not been met.

The United States filed a Motion to Dismiss for Lack of Subject Matter Jurisdiction, arguing that the district court did not have jurisdiction over Pornomo's claim because the issuance of the 10-day extension was a discretionary act shielded from suit under the discretionary function exception to the FTCA, and because Pornomo's claim that the FMCSA lacked statutory authority to promulgate and apply 49 C.F.R. § 385.17(f) was a challenge to the validity of the regulation that, under 28 U.S.C. § 2342(3)(A), could be raised only in the court of appeals. The Government also argued that subject matter jurisdiction was lacking because the conduct at issue here did not constitute a tort under Virginia law.

The district court granted the Motion, holding that the discretionary function exception applied to the decision to issue the 10-day extension and that the United States therefore had not waived sovereign immunity for this suit. The court found that the plain language of 49 C.F.R. § 385.17(f) afforded the agency discretion to grant an extension. The decision was "still a discretionary decision" even though the regulation provided two preconditions, because those preconditions were "not detailed" or a "safety check list," but instead required the application of FMCSA's "expertise" to determine whether they had been met. J.A. 14-15. The court then concluded that the "FMCSA received a detailed, written corrective action plan from Sky Express but determined, using its judgment, that it needed more information to verify the contents of the plan." *Id.* at 15. It further found that the "FMCSA determined it was unable to make a final determination concerning Sky Express' operating authority registration and therefore granted the extension to provide additional time to conduct a follow-up compliance review." *Id.* The district court thus dismissed the case for lack of subject matter jurisdiction. The district court did not directly address Pornomo's argument that 49 C.F.R. § 385.17(f) was invalid because the enabling statute does not permit any extensions for passenger carriers. It also did not address the Government's argument that the FMCSA's conduct did not constitute a tort under Virginia law.

Pornomo appealed. We have jurisdiction under 28 U.S.C. § 1291.

II.

Pornomo first claims that the district court erred in dismissing the Complaint because the facts related to subject matter jurisdiction are intertwined with the facts central to the merits of his claim. Because Pornomo did not make this argument below, it is waived. *Robinson v. Equifax Information Services, LLC,* 560 F.3d 235, 242 (4th Cir.2009) ("Absent exceptional circumstances... we do not consider issues raised for the first time on appeal.") (quoting *Volvo Const. Equip. N. Am., Inc. v. CLM Equip. Co.,* 386 F.3d 581, 603 (4th Cir.2004)); *Muth v. United States,* 1 F.3d 246, 250 (4th Cir.1993) ("As this court has repeatedly held, issues raised for the first time on appeal generally will not be considered.").

Pornomo also contends that the district court erred in (1) finding that the issuance of the 10-day extension was a discretionary act, such that the court lacked subject matter jurisdiction pursuant to the discretionary function exception to the FTCA; and (2) failing to find that 49 C.F.R. § 385.17(f) (2011) was invalid because its p.687 provision authorizing a 10-day extension exceeded the agency's statutory authority. We address these arguments in turn.

A.

The district court dismissed Pornomo's complaint for lack of subject matter jurisdiction because it found that the United States had not waived sovereign immunity. *See Medina v. United States,* 259 F.3d 220, 223-24 (4th Cir.2001) ("[T]he Government's potential immunity from suit affects our jurisdiction[.]"). We review a district court's dismissal for lack of subject matter jurisdiction de novo. *Suter v. United States,* 441 F.3d 306, 310 (4th Cir. 2006). In determining whether subject matter jurisdiction exists, the reviewing court is not limited to the grounds relied on by the district court, but rather "may affirm on any grounds apparent from the record." *Id.*

B.

"As a sovereign, the United States is immune from all suits against it absent an express waiver of its immunity." *Welch, Jr. v. United States,* 409 F.3d 646, 650 (4th Cir.2005) (citing *United States v. Sherwood,* 312 U.S. 584, 586, 61 S.Ct. 767, 85 L.Ed. 1058 (1941)). Because the default position is that the federal government is immune to suit, any waiver of that immunity "must be 'strictly construed ... in favor of the sovereign.'" *Id.* at 650-51 (quoting *Lane v. Pena,* 518 U.S. 187, 192, 116 S.Ct. 2092, 135 L.Ed.2d 486 (1996)) (ellipses in original).

Pornomo's tort claims are brought under the Federal Tort Claims Act, 28 U.S.C. §§ 1346(b), 2671-2680. The FTCA does not create a new cause of action; rather, it permits the United States to be held liable in tort by providing a limited waiver of sovereign immunity "for injury or loss caused by the negligent or wrongful act of a Government employee acting within the scope of his or her employment." *Medina,* 259 F.3d at 223. The FTCA renders the United States liable for such tort claims "in the same manner and to the same extent as a private individual under like circumstances." 28 U.S.C. § 2674.

The FTCA contains several exceptions to its waiver of immunity. In particular, the FTCA's waiver of sovereign immunity does not extend to any claim "based upon the exercise or performance or the failure to exercise or perform a discretionary function or duty on the part of a federal agency or an employee of the Government, whether or not the discretion involved be abused." 28 U.S.C. § 2680(a).

To determine whether this discretionary function exception applies, courts apply a two-part test. The first step is to decide whether the conduct at issue involves "an element of judgment or choice" by the employee, rather than, for example, "when a federal statute, regulation, or policy specifically prescribes a course of action for an employee to follow." *Berkovitz v. United States,* 486 U.S. 531, 536, 108 S.Ct. 1954, 100 L.Ed.2d 531 (1988). The second step is to determine whether that judgment "is of the kind that the discretionary function exception was designed to shield" in that the judgment relates to a governmental action or decision "based on considerations of public policy." *Id.* at 536-37, 108 S.Ct. 1954; *see Suter,* 441 F.3d at 310-11.

If an action is discretionary within the meaning of the exception, the exception applies "whether or not the discretion involved be abused." 28 U.S.C. § 2680(a);

United States v. Gaubert, 499 U.S. 315, 323, 111 S.Ct. 1267, 113 L.Ed.2d 335 (1991) (noting that discretionary actions are "protected, even if those particular actions were negligent"). It applies "even if the discretion has been exercised erroneously" and is deemed to have frustrated p.688 the relevant policy purpose. *Holbrook v. United States*, 673 F.3d 341, 350 (4th Cir.2012). "The inquiry is thus whether the discretion exists, not whether in later litigation it is alleged to have been abused. Were it otherwise, Congress' intent to shield an agency's discretionary decisions from FTCA lawsuits would be set at naught." *Id.*

III.

"[W]hatever else the discretionary function exception may include, it plainly was intended to encompass the discretionary acts of the Government acting in its role as a regulator of the conduct of private individuals." *United States v. S.A. Empresa de Viacao Aerea Rio Grandense (Varig Airlines)*, 467 U.S. 797, 813-14, 104 S.Ct. 2755, 81 L.Ed.2d 660 (1984). As discussed below, because the FMCSA's decision to grant the 10-day extension pursuant to an existing regulation involved an "element of judgment or choice" and was "based on considerations of public policy," the discretionary function exception applies. *Berkovitz*, 486 U.S. at 536-37, 108 S.Ct. 1954.

Pornomo does not dispute that the matter at issue, government regulators' safety determinations for commercial motor vehicles, involves considerations of public policy. *See United States v. Gaubert*, 499 U.S. 315, 323, 324, 111 S.Ct. 1267, 113 L.Ed.2d 335 (1991) (stating that if a regulation "allows a Government agent to exercise discretion, it must be presumed that the agent's acts are grounded in policy when exercising that discretion"). Thus, the applicability of the discretionary function exception turns on the first prong: whether the conduct at issue involves an element of judgment or choice.

The 10-day extension was issued pursuant to a regulation that states,

> If the motor carrier has submitted evidence that corrective actions have been taken pursuant to this section and the FMCSA cannot make a final determination with the 45-day period, the period before the proposed safety rating becomes final may be extended for up to 10 days *at the discretion* of the FMCSA.

49 C.F.R. § 385.17(f) (2011) (emphasis added). On the face of the regulation, therefore, the act of granting an extension requires an exercise of judgment or choice by the FMCSA. The regulation thus differs markedly from the mandatory provisions at issue in the cases cited by Pornomo in which regulatory action was deemed nondiscretionary. *See Berkovitz*, 486 U.S. at 543-44, 108 S.Ct. 1954 (finding that the discretionary function exception did not bar an FTCA claim against a federal agency for licensing polio vaccine without first receiving mandatory safety data and determining compliance with safety standards); *In re: Sabin Oral Polio Vaccine Prods. Liab. Litig.*, 984 F.2d 124, 127 (4th Cir.1993) (finding that release of a vaccine upon meeting mandatory safety requirements was a nondiscretionary function).

Pornomo nevertheless argues that the discretionary function exception does not bar his claim because § 385.17(f) gives the FMCSA discretion to grant a 10-day extension only if and when two conditions have been met: (1) the motor carrier has submitted evidence that corrective actions have been taken; and (2) the FMCSA cannot make a final determination within the 45-day period. 49 C.F.R. § 385.17 (2011). Pornomo asserts that because the first May 13, 2011 FMCSA letter to Sky Express stated that the company had "failed to demonstrate that adequate corrective actions have been taken to address the acute and/or critical violations" and that the agency was "denying" Sky Express's request to upgrade its safety rating, J.A. 52, the FMCSA had already made a final determination as of that date. Pornomo thus asserts that neither condition p.689 was satisfied, such that the FMCSA was not vested with the discretion referenced in the regulation.

This argument cuts too fine a distinction. "Where there is room for policy judgment and decision there is discretion." *Dalehite v. United States,* 346 U.S. 15, 36, 73 S.Ct. 956, 97 L.Ed. 1427 (1953). In *Holbrook,* this Court held that the discretionary function exception barred an FTCA claim arising from a Federal Aviation Administration ("FAA") issuance of an airworthiness certificate. 673 F.3d at 349. The Court determined that a predicate requirement in the relevant regulation, that an aircraft's application must include a certification from the country of manufacture that the aircraft conformed to its type design and was safe to operate, afforded discretion to the FAA to "make its own findings" whether the submitted documentation satisfied that requirement. *Id.* Likewise, as the district court noted, 49 C.F.R. § 385.17(f) is not a "check list." J.A. at 105. It leaves it to the FMCSA to determine whether a carrier's submission provides evidence that corrective action has been taken, and whether the agency has the resources to reach a final decision within 45 days. Such decisions, which relate to a regulatory agency's "implementation of a mechanism for compliance review" and necessarily require "balancing the objectives sought to be obtained against such practical considerations as staffing and funding," constitute discretionary functions themselves. *Varig Airlines,* 467 U.S. at 819-20, 104 S.Ct. 2755 (holding that the FAA's application of a spot-check system to a particular aircraft was a discretionary function). Discretion thus suffuses 49 C.F.R. § 385.17(f) (2011), rather than, as Pornomo would have it, appearing only after certain mandatory predicates have been satisfied.

The FMCSA, in fact, exercised this discretion. Although Pornomo focuses on the FMCSA's statement in its first May 13, 2011 letter that it was "denying" Sky Express's request, J.A. 52, an FMCSA internal memorandum dated May 12, 2011 indicates that the FMCSA had reviewed Sky Express's submission, found that it had submitted some evidence of corrective actions, but concluded that those actions did not address "all violations" and were "not sufficient to correct the deficiencies discovered during the compliance review." J.A. 44. Rather than close the matter, the FMCSA then determined that it would conduct a follow-up compliance review "prior to June 7, 2011," which would be 10 days after the expiration of the 45-day period. *Id.* at 44. It then informed Sky Express, in the first May 13 letter, of the follow-up compliance review and requested that Sky Express prepare to provide additional documentation "for examination" at that review. *Id.* at 53. Thus, the FMCSA made the judgments that Sky Express had submitted some "evidence that corrective actions have been taken," 49 C.F.R. § 385.17 (2011), and that the FMCSA needed additional time to make a final determination on Sky Express's rating.

Ultimately, it does not matter whether the FMCSA was correct in these judgments. The discretionary function exception applies "whether or not the discretion involved be abused," 28 U.S.C. § 2680(a), and "even if the discretion has been exercised erroneously," *Holbrook,* 673 F.3d at 350 (quoting *Gaubert,* 499 U.S. at 338, 111 S.Ct. 1267 (Scalia, J., concurring in part and concurring in the judgment)) (rejecting the argument that an allegedly erroneous determination by an FAA official that a helicopter conformed to a certificate requirement was not discretionary). "If it were not so, the protection of § 2680(a) would fail at the time it would be needed[.]" *Dalehite,* 346 U.S. at 36, 73 S.Ct. 956. Here, where the FMCSA made judgments on (1) whether Sky Express had p.690 submitted sufficient evidence of corrective action to warrant a follow-up compliance review and (2) whether such a review could reasonably and fairly be conducted without an extension of the 45-day period for establishing fitness, the FMCSA was exercising discretion within the meaning of the FTCA. The FMCSA may have taken certain "calculated risks," but it did so for a governmental purpose pursuant to a governing regulation. *See Varig Airlines,* 467 U.S. at 820, 104 S.Ct. 2755 (holding that the FAA's alleged negligence in failing to check certain specific items in the course of certificating a specific aircraft as part of a spot-check program involved "calculated risks" but fell "squarely within the discretionary function exception"). The district court thus properly concluded that the granting of the 10-day extension was a discretionary decision that could not form the basis of an FTCA claim.

IV.

Pornomo further argues that even if the FMCSA was authorized by 49 C.F.R. § 385.17(f) to exercise its discretion to grant a 10-day extension, that regulation was invalid because the plain and unambiguous language of the underlying statute, 49 U.S.C. § 31144, barred the grant of any such extension. Pornomo's argument is essentially a challenge to the validity of 49 C.F.R. § 385.17(f) (2011). As such, it cannot be the basis of an FTCA claim. As a general matter, "[i]t was not intended that the constitutionality of legislation, the legality of regulations, or the propriety of a discretionary administrative act should be tested through the medium of a damage suit for tort." *Dalehite,* 346 U.S. at 27, 73 S.Ct. 956 (internal quotation mark omitted); *Welch, Jr. v. United States,* 409 F.3d 646, 653 (4th Cir.2005) (stating that the FTCA does "not provide a venue in which to challenge the validity of [a] law"). More specifically, Congress has granted the courts of appeals exclusive jurisdiction to determine the validity of "all rules, regulations, or final orders of the Secretary of Transportation issued pursuant to ... subchapter III of chapter 311... of title 49," which includes 49 U.S.C. § 31144. 28 U.S.C. § 2342(3)(A). Because Pornomo's claim that the grant of a 10-day extension pursuant 49 C.F.R. § 385.17(f) violated 49 U.S.C. § 31144 amounts to a challenge to the validity of that regulation, the district court had no jurisdiction to hear it. *See* 28 U.S.C. § 2342(3)(A).

Even if Pornomo could challenge the validity of 49 C.F.R. § 385.17(f) in the district court, the court would still lack jurisdiction over his FTCA claim because the FMCSA's promulgation of the regulation was itself a discretionary act. "[T]here is no doubt that planning-level decisions establishing programs are protected by the discretionary function exception, as is the promulgation of regulations by which the agencies are to carry out the programs." *Gaubert,* 499 U.S. at 323, 111 S.Ct. 1267. Thus, the FMCSA's decision to promulgate 49 C.F.R. § 385.17(f), even if that decision proved to be an abuse of discretion, would be shielded by the discretionary function exception. *See* 28 U.S.C. § 2680(a).

Pornomo attempts to circumvent this conclusion by asserting that 49 C.F.R. § 385.17(f) is so plainly at odds with the language of 49 U.S.C. § 31144(c)(2) that the promulgation of the regulation could not have been an act of discretion. In support of this argument, he marshals 49 U.S.C. § 31144(c)(2), which requires that passenger carriers stop operating 45 days after they have been deemed unfit, and § 31144(c)(4), which grants the Secretary discretion to "allow an owner or operator who is not fit to continue operating for an additional 60 days" if it is "making a good faith effort to become fit," but expressly p.691 exempts passenger carriers from that provision. The exclusion of passenger carriers from the 60-day extension, Pornomo reasons, must mean that no extension of the 45-day period is permitted. He also notes that in 2012, the FMCSA rescinded the 10-day extension provision in 49 C.F.R. § 385.17(f) to make the regulations "consistent with the policy and the statutory language" of 49 U.S.C. § 31144(c)(2) and (4). 77 Fed. Reg. at 64,759.

Yet Pornomo's conclusion is by no means certain. As drafted, 49 U.S.C. § 31144(c)(2) prohibits owners and operators of commercial passenger carriers from operating under certain conditions. The statute does not expressly proscribe or prescribe a particular course of action for the Secretary of Transportation. Nor does 49 U.S.C. § 31144(c)(4) flatly bar the FMCSA's action, because it exempts passenger carriers only from 60-day extensions, not necessarily ones of more modest duration, such as the one here. *See Berkovitz,* 486 U.S. at 536, 108 S.Ct. 1954 (noting that a government official lacks judgment or choice for the purposes of determining whether the discretionary function exception applies when "a federal statute, regulation, or policy *specifically* prescribes a course of action for an employee to follow") (emphasis added).

While one may conclude, as the FMCSA itself later did, that the better reading of these statutory provisions is that 45 days is a hard deadline for passenger carriers with unsatisfactory ratings, a better reading is not the same as a necessary one. Considering that any waiver of sovereign immunity must be strictly construed, the FMCSA's decision to promulgate a regulation permitting 10-day extensions for passenger carriers was a permissible exercise of judgment subject to the FTCA's discretionary function exception and thus did not waive sovereign immunity. *See Gaubert,* 499 U.S. at 323, 111 S.Ct. 1267. The district court therefore correctly dismissed the case for lack of subject matter jurisdiction.

Having reached this conclusion, we need not address the Government's argument that the FMCSA's conduct does not constitute a tort under Virginia law.

V.

For the foregoing reasons, we affirm the judgment of the district court.
AFFIRMED

811 F.3d 140 (2015)

Joshua RICH, Plaintiff-Appellant,
v.
UNITED STATES of America, Defendant-Appellee.

No. 14-7204.

United States Court of Appeals, Fourth Circuit.

Argued: October 27, 2015.

Decided: December 29, 2015.

Rich v. US, 811 F. 3d 140 (4th Cir. 2015)

Appeal from the United States District Court for the Northern District of West Virginia, at Martinsburg, Gina M. Groh, District Judge, (3:13-cv-00137-GMG-RWT).

ARGUED: Jay Thornton McCamic, McCamic, Sacco & McCoid, PLLC, Wheeling, West Virginia, for Appellant. Alan McGonigal, Office of the United States Attorney, Wheeling, West Virginia, for Appellee. ON BRIEF: William J. Ihlenfeld, II, Assistant United States Attorney, Office of the United States Attorney, Wheeling, West Virginia, for Appellee.

Before KEENAN, WYNN, and DIAZ, Circuit Judges.

Affirmed in part, vacated in part, and remanded by published opinion. Judge KEENAN wrote the opinion, in which Judge WYNN and Judge DIAZ joined.

BARBARA MILANO KEENAN, Circuit Judge:

p.141While serving a fifty-seven year sentence at the United States Penitentiary in Bruceton Mills, West Virginia (USP Hazelton), Joshua Rich was attacked in a recreation area, or "cage," by several other inmates. He was severely beaten and stabbed several times. A nine-inch-long homemade knife was recovered at the scene. Rich suffered serious injuries, including liver laceration, which required numerous invasive surgeries.

p.142 Rich sued the United States under the Federal Tort Claims Act (FTCA), 28 U.S.C. § 1346(b), alleging that prison officials had been negligent in failing to protect him from the attack. The district court granted the government's motion to dismiss for lack of subject matter jurisdiction, concluding that the discretionary function exception to the FTCA applied both to the prison officials' decision not to separate Rich from his attackers, as well as to the manner in which the officials searched other inmates prior to placing them with Rich in the recreation cage.

Upon our review, we affirm the district court's holding that the prison officials' discretionary decision not to separate Rich from his attackers is subject to the discretionary function exception of the FTCA, depriving us of jurisdiction over that claim. However, with regard to Rich's claim that prison officials did not perform the searches properly, we remand for additional discovery because jurisdictional facts are intertwined with the merits of that claim.

I.

In 2008, the United States District Court for the District of Utah sentenced Rich to fifty-seven years' imprisonment for armed bank robbery, in violation of 18 U.S.C. § 2113(a) and (d), and for using and carrying a firearm in relation to a crime of violence, in violation of 18 U.S.C. § 924(c). Rich entered the custody of the Bureau of Prisons (BOP) in September 2008.[1]

According to Rich, he immediately was targeted in prison by a white supremacist group, the "Aryan Brotherhood," for his refusal to follow that group's rules and to participate in the group's criminal schemes. Although transferred frequently to different penitentiaries, Rich contends that he was targeted continually by the Aryan Brotherhood and required separation from the group.[2]

In February 2011, Rich was transferred to USP Hazelton and, on August 5, 2011, five inmates attacked him in a recreation cage within the Special Housing Unit (SHU). The attackers beat Rich and stabbed him repeatedly. A knife measuring about nine inches in length was recovered from the scene.[3] Rich suffered serious injuries and underwent numerous surgeries, including a bronchoscopy for respiratory failure, a laparotomy to repair a laceration to his liver, and open-heart surgery to repair the right atrium of his heart.

Rich sued the United States under the FTCA, alleging one count of negligence asserting that the prison officials had failed to protect him from harm. Rich alleged that the officials should have kept him separated from his attackers, and that the officials failed to screen, "wand," or search the inmates properly prior to placing them in the recreation cage.

p.143 The government moved to dismiss Rich's complaint on the basis that the discretionary function exception to the FTCA, which limits the government's waiver of sovereign immunity for certain kinds of discretionary conduct, applied both to the prison officials' decision whether to separate Rich from his attackers and to the manner in which the prison officials searched the attacking inmates. To support its position, the government included several exhibits with its motion to dismiss. These attachments included portions of Rich's prison file and declarations from the prison officials, who stated that they performed patdowns and searches properly on all inmates before the attack. The attachments also included various "Post Orders" in effect at USP Hazelton on August 5, 2011.[4]

The Post Orders relating to the SHU require that an inmate's hands be restrained behind his body whenever leaving his cell for recreation. Additionally, the Post Orders state that "inmates will be pat searched and screened with the hand-held metal detector before entering and upon exiting the recreation cages." The Post Orders do not otherwise describe how a patdown should be performed. However, the BOP "Program Statement" applicable to all prisons, including USP Hazelton, provides that "[a]ny pat search shall be conducted as outlined in the Correctional Services Manual."[5] Moreover, according to the Post Orders, when an inmate has a prior history of weapons possession, prison officials must perform a "visual search" of the inmate, including a search of the inmate's body cavities, prior to his entry into a recreation cage.

After reviewing these attachments, the district court agreed with the government that the discretionary function exception applied to the prison officials' decisions regarding inmate separation and the manner in which the prison officials performed the patdowns and searches.[6] The court found that the Post Orders "do not mandate a specific course of conduct" for the officers to follow in performing the required searches. The court also concluded that the discretion afforded prison officials is consistent with the public policy of granting prison officials deference in implementing and executing their security measures.

The district court further concluded that Rich was not entitled to any discovery regarding whether additional directives mandated a particular method for performing patdowns and searches. Accordingly, the district court granted the government's motion to dismiss for lack of subject matter jurisdiction. This appeal followed.

II.

On appeal, Rich challenges the district court's conclusion that the discretionary function exception applies to the prison officials' conduct. He argues that the officials had a non-discretionary duty to maintain p.144 and monitor both his prison files and the files of other inmates. Rich contends that if the officials had taken these security measures, they would have known about Rich's history with the Aryan Brotherhood and the need to keep him separated from the group's members. Rich also argues that the Post Orders and other policies imposed mandatory directives that the prison officials search and patdown inmates prior to placing them in the recreation cage, thereby precluding application of the discretionary function exception. Rich contends that, at a minimum, he should have been allowed the opportunity for discovery before the district court determined that the discretionary function exception applied.

In response, the government contends that the officials' decision not to separate Rich from his attackers, as well as the manner in which the searches were performed, are matters within the discretionary function exception. The government asserts that there are no directives governing the separation of prisoners or the proper procedure for performing patdowns and searches. The government argues that, therefore, the prison officials' discretion in these areas implicates public policy considerations that justify application of the discretionary function exception. The government further asserts that the district court did not abuse its discretion when it refused to grant Rich discovery, because no additional information could be uncovered that would establish the district court's jurisdiction.

A.

We review a district court's decision dismissing a case for lack of subject matter jurisdiction *de novo. Taylor v. Kellogg Brown & Root Servs., Inc.,* 658 F.3d 402, 408 (4th Cir.2011). We review a denial of jurisdictional discovery for abuse of discretion. *Durden v. United States,* 736 F.3d 296, 307 (4th Cir.2013).

Although the United States typically is immune from suit, the FTCA provides a waiver of this sovereign immunity when the federal government "would be liable to the claimant in accordance with the law of the place where the act or omission occurred" for certain torts, such as negligence, committed by federal employees acting within the scope of their employment. 28 U.S.C. § 1346(b)(1). However, under the FTCA, the discretionary function exception limits that waiver of immunity in situations involving "the exercise or performance or the failure to exercise or perform a discretionary function or duty... whether or not the discretion involved be abused." 28 U.S.C. § 2680(a).

To determine whether conduct qualifies for the discretionary function exception, courts apply a two-pronged test. First, a court considers whether the challenged governmental conduct involves an element of judgment or choice. *United States v. Gaubert,* 499 U.S. 315, 322, 111 S.Ct. 1267, 113 L.Ed.2d 335 (1991). When a statute, regulation, or policy prescribes a specific course of action, there is no discretion and the exception does not apply. *Id.* Second, if the challenged conduct does involve an element of judgment, the court must then determine whether the judgment was one that the exception was designed to protect, namely, a judgment based on considerations of public policy. *Id.* at 322-23, 111 S.Ct. 1267.

A defendant's assertion that the discretionary function exception applies is an assertion that the court lacks subject matter jurisdiction. *See Indem. Ins. Co. of N. Am. v. United States,* 569 F.3d 175, 180 (4th Cir.2009). In challenging subject matter jurisdiction, a defendant may raise a facial challenge that, even if all the alleged facts are true, the complaint nonetheless p.145 fails to establish jurisdiction. *See Durden,* 736 F.3d at 300.

Alternatively, a defendant may dispute the allegations in a complaint that could establish subject matter jurisdiction. *Kerns v. United States,* 585 F.3d 187, 192 (4th Cir.2009). In that situation, the court may go beyond the allegations in the complaint and "in an evidentiary hearing determine if there are facts to support the jurisdictional allegations." *Id.* Under such circumstances, the complaint's allegations ordinarily are not afforded a presumption of truthfulness. *Id.* If, however, the jurisdictional facts are intertwined with the facts central to the merits of the complaint, "a presumption of truthfulness should attach to the plaintiff's allegations." *Id.* at 193. And, most relevant here, the court "should resolve the relevant factual disputes only after appropriate discovery." *In re KBR, Inc., Burn Pit Litig.,* 744 F.3d 326, 334 (4th Cir.2014) (citation omitted).

B.

We first address whether the discretionary function exception applies to the prison officials' placement of Rich in the recreation cage with his attackers, and whether Rich was entitled to discovery on this claim. To do so, we consider whether the challenged governmental conduct involves an element of judgment or choice and, if so, whether that judgment was based on considerations of public policy. *Gaubert,* 499 U.S. at 322-23, 111 S.Ct. 1267.

The BOP is required to provide for the "protection," "safekeeping," and "care" of "all persons charged with or convicted of offenses against the United States." 18

U.S.C. § 4042(a)(2), (3). Under the statute's broad directives, the BOP retains discretion regarding the implementation of those mandates. *Cohen v. United States*, 151 F.3d 1338, 1342 (11th Cir.1998). This discretion is evident in the regulations regarding the proper handling and review of the Central Inmate Monitoring (CIM) files.

The CIM system is the mechanism by which the Bureau of Prisons monitors and controls the transfer, temporary release, and community activities of certain inmates who present special needs for management, including the need to separate certain inmates from others based on their past behavior. *See* 28 C.F.R. § 524.70-76. Although 28 C.F.R. § 524.72(d) provides that inmates "*may* require separation from a specific disruptive group [such as a prison gang]" (emphasis added), nothing in this regulation requires that any specific action be taken by the various prison officials. Instead, prison officials must consider several factors and exercise independent judgment in determining whether inmates *may* require separation. *See* 28 C.F.R. § 524.72(f). Given this general language in the regulations, we conclude that prison officials exercise broad discretion in this regard and, thus, that the first prong of the discretionary function exception is satisfied.

We turn to consider the second element of the discretionary function exception, namely, whether considerations of public policy are implicated in the discretion given to prison officials in their decisions about the separation of prisoners. *See Gaubert*, 499 U.S. at 322-23, 111 S.Ct. 1267. Although this is an issue of first impression in this Court, other federal appellate courts have held that prisoner placement and the handling of threats posed by inmates against one another are "part and parcel of the inherently policy-laden endeavor of maintaining order and preserving security within our nation's prisons." *Cohen*, 151 F.3d at 1344; *see also Alfrey v. United States*, 276 F.3d 557, 563-65 (9th Cir.2002); *Calderon v. United* p.146 *States*, 123 F.3d 947, 951 (7th Cir.1997). Factors such as available resources, proper classification of inmates, and appropriate security levels are "inherently grounded in social, political, and economic policy." *Dykstra v. U.S. Bureau of Prisons*, 140 F.3d 791, 796 (8th Cir.1998); *cf. Bell v. Wolfish*, 441 U.S. 520, 547-48, 99 S.Ct. 1861, 60 L.Ed.2d 447 (1979) ("Prison administrators... should be accorded wide-ranging deference in the adoption and execution of policies and practices that in their judgment are needed to preserve internal order and discipline and to maintain institutional security.").

We agree with the reasoning of our sister circuits. Prison officials are afforded discretion in determining where to place inmates and whether to keep certain individuals or gangs separated from one another. Because these decisions invoke several policy considerations for prison administrators, they are precisely the kind of determinations that the discretionary function exception is intended to protect. We therefore hold that the discretionary function exception shields the prison officials from liability with respect to whether they should have separated Rich from his attackers.

We also conclude that Rich is not entitled to discovery on this issue. Even accepting all of Rich's allegations regarding his history with the Aryan Brotherhood as true, the discretionary function exception still would apply to the decisions of the officials regarding prisoner placement, ultimately depriving us of jurisdiction. And because no facts that Rich could uncover in discovery would establish jurisdiction, we hold that the district court did not abuse its discretion in refusing Rich discovery regarding the officials' decision to not separate Rich from his attackers. *See Durden,* 736 F.3d at 307-08.

C.

We reach a different conclusion regarding the availability of discovery with respect to Rich's allegations that the prison officials did not search his attackers properly before placing them in the recreation cage. Unlike the allegations underlying Rich's claim regarding the prison officials' duty to separate Rich from his attackers, which failed on their face to establish subject matter jurisdiction, disputed jurisdictional facts are intertwined with the merits of Rich's claim regarding the execution of the patdowns. *See Kerns,* 585 F.3d at 193.

For example, in support of the government's motion to dismiss, the prison officials provided declarations that they did in fact perform patdowns of the inmates involved on the date of the incident. Those declarations stand in direct contrast to Rich's allegation that the officials "failed to properly screen, 'wand,' or search inmates entering the SHU and/or SHU recreation cages." That allegation is relevant not only to whether the discretionary function exception applies and, thus, whether we have subject matter jurisdiction over this claim, but also to the merits of Rich's negligence allegation.

We find no merit in the government's argument that Rich did not allege that the prison officials completely failed to patdown or "wand" his attackers, but alleged only that these searches were not done properly. Rich's complaint can be read fairly to allege both that the officials did not perform the searches properly, and that the officials failed to perform the searches in any manner. Rich maintained this position throughout the litigation. A period of discovery would afford Rich the opportunity to challenge these officials' assertions concerning their performance of the searches.

p.147 Even if we accept the prison officials' uncontested declarations, the fact that they performed patdowns does not resolve the question whether the officials performed those patdowns properly. The BOP's Program Statement provides that "[a]ny pat search shall be conducted as outlined in the Correctional Services Manual," suggesting the existence of more specific directives. Rich should be permitted the opportunity for discovery of that Correctional Services Manual to determine whether more specific directives exist concerning the performance of patdowns.[7]

Additionally, when inmates have a prior history of weapons possession, the Post Orders require a "visual search" of those inmates, involving a search of the body cavity, prior to their entry into a recreation cage. Discovery could uncover whether any of Rich's attackers had a history of weapons possession that would have triggered this visual search requirement. Such an additional mandate would affect any analysis concerning whether the prison officials properly performed searches as required.[8]

Finally, we observe that Rich may be able to establish jurisdiction even if, under typical circumstances, the discretionary function exception applies to the manner in which prison officials perform patdowns. The Second Circuit has acknowledged that discretionary conduct cannot be grounded in a policy decision when that conduct is marked by individual carelessness or laziness. *See Coulthurst v. United States,* 214 F.3d 106 (2d Cir.2000) (concluding that the discretionary function exception would not apply to a prison official's inspection of faulty weight equipment that caused plaintiff's injuries if that inspection was performed in a "carelessly inattentive" manner). The fact that a nine-inch-long knife was recovered at the scene of Rich's attack, in spite of the prison officials' averments that each performed the required searches properly, at least suggests the possibility of careless inattention. In that case, the prison officials would not be shielded by the discretionary function exception because no policy considerations would be implicated.

Discovery provides a procedural safeguard when a jurisdictional inquiry would require the consideration of merits-based evidence. *See Kerns,* 585 F.3d at 193. This safeguard does not disappear simply because the plaintiff is a prisoner. Of course, courts frequently apply the discretionary function exception to prison officials' efforts to ensure the safety of prisoners under difficult circumstances, *e.g., Cohen,* 151 F.3d at 1344; *Alfrey,* 276 F.3d at 564-67; *Calderon,* 123 F.3d at 949-51, and that may be the ultimate outcome here as well. Nevertheless, we conclude p.148 that Rich is entitled to the safeguard of discovery before his complaint is dismissed.

Because the jurisdictional facts regarding the propriety of the prison officials' patdowns are intertwined with the merits of Rich's allegations, the district court "should resolve the relevant factual disputes only after appropriate discovery." *In re KBR, Inc.,* 744 F.3d at 334 (citation omitted). Accordingly, we vacate in part, and remand, to allow Rich to proceed to discovery on the issue whether and how the prison officials performed the patdowns and searches, and whether more specific directives existed regarding the manner of performing the patdowns and searches.

III.

For these reasons, we affirm the district court's decision that the discretionary function exception applies to the prison officials' decision not to separate Rich from his attackers. However, we vacate the district court's judgment with respect to the issue of the prison officials' performance of the patdowns and searches, and remand for additional proceedings consistent with this opinion.

AFFIRMED IN PART, VACATED IN PART, AND REMANDED

[1] Unless otherwise indicated, the facts in Section I are undisputed.

[2] The government disputes Rich's account of his time at the various penitentiaries and the reasons for his separation from other inmates, arguing that Rich's prior Special Housing Unit placements were unrelated to the Aryan Brotherhood. As we explain in Section II.B., this dispute of fact is immaterial to our conclusions.

[3] The government does not dispute the size of the knife recovered from the scene of the attack, though its exact size is nowhere in the record. Although the government refers to the investigative report for Rich's attack as in the record on

page 169 of the joint appendix, we are unable to locate page 169. Nor is the investigative report included in any other part of the record.

[4] "Post Orders" are specific to each institution, based on BOP policy, and state each post's duty hours as well as any special instructions unique to that post. *See* U.S. Dep't of Justice Program Statement No. 5500.14, section 103 (2012), http://www.bop.gov/policy/progstat/5500_014.pdf (describing post orders).

[5] The Correctional Services Manual is not a part of the record before this Court.

[6] The district court noted that Rich only objected to the report and recommendation of the magistrate judge with respect to whether the prison officials performed their searches properly. Accordingly, the court simply adopted the magistrate judge's conclusion regarding separation.

[7] We do not decide whether, even in the absence of more specific mandates, the manner in which a patdown is performed qualifies for the discretionary function exception. We note, however, that the government offers no limiting principle to its rationale as to when the exception should apply. There is always some level of discretion regarding the performance of even the most specific of mandates, which under the government's argument would mean that the discretionary function exception would always apply. Moreover, the government could only suggest reasons of "security" generally as the policy consideration involved in the manner of performing patdowns.

[8] At oral argument, the government contended that providing certain types of information to inmates, such as camera placements and security methods employed by prison officials, would present serious safety risks by allowing inmates to uncover any potential holes in prison safety procedures. We are confident that the district court can implement appropriate measures during the course of discovery to prevent any unnecessary disclosure of critical security information.

736 F.3d 296 (2013)

Maria Nicole DURDEN, Plaintiff-Appellant,
v.
UNITED STATES of America, Defendant-Appellee.

No. 12-2212.

United States Court of Appeals, Fourth Circuit.

Argued: September 19, 2013.

Decided: November 20, 2013.

Durden v. US, 736 F. 3d 296 (4th Cir. 2013)

p.298 ARGUED: Nathan Harrill, Wake Forest University School of Law, Winston-Salem, North Carolina, for Appellant. Joshua Bryan Royster, Office Of The United States Attorney, Raleigh, North Carolina, for Appellee. ON BRIEF: Joseph L. Anderson, Anderson Pangia & Associates, PLLC, Winston-Salem, North Carolina; Douglas P. Desjardins, Transportation Injury Law Group, Washington, D.C., for Appellant. Thomas G. Walker, United States Attorney, Jennifer P. May-Parker, Assistant United States Attorney, Office of The United States Attorney, Raleigh, North Carolina, for Appellee.

Before NIEMEYER, GREGORY, and FLOYD, Circuit Judges.

Affirmed by published opinion. Judge FLOYD wrote the opinion, in which Judge NIEMEYER and Judge GREGORY concurred.

FLOYD, Circuit Judge:

On December 13, 2009, U.S. Army Specialist Aaron Pernell unlawfully entered the home of Maria Durden while inebriated and raped Durden in front of her children. Durden subsequently sued the government pursuant to the Federal Tort Claims Act (FTCA), 28 U.S.C. § 1346(b), alleging that the Army was negligent and therefore is liable for the sexual assault against her. The government moved to dismiss Durden's complaint for lack of subject matter jurisdiction and, alternatively, for failure to state a claim upon which relief can be granted. The district court granted the government's motion with respect to subject matter jurisdiction, and p.299 Durden appealed. For the reasons set forth below, we affirm.

I.

A.

Pernell joined the Army at age eighteen and was deployed to Iraq after he completed his initial training in Georgia and a two-day stay at Fort Bragg, North Carolina. Upon returning to Fort Bragg subsequent to his deployment, Pernell struggled emotionally and began using drugs and abusing alcohol. In March and August of 2009, Pernell told his staff sergeant that he desired to kill himself and eleven current and former members of his unit. After each instance, the sergeant discouraged Pernell from seeking mental-health treatment and cautioned Pernell that receiving such treatment could blemish Pernell's military record. In September 2009, Pernell confided in a fellow soldier that he was unable to sleep due to his drug and alcohol use; the soldier also advised Pernell not to seek mental-health treatment because it could "mess up [Pernell's] career."

On September 10, 2009, Pernell burglarized a home in Fayetteville, North Carolina (which is adjacent to Fort Bragg) and assaulted the home's occupants with a pellet gun. Civilian law enforcement arrested Pernell and charged him with burglary and assault. Pernell was then detained at a civilian jail from September 11 to October 22, 2009, at which time his parents posted bail on his behalf and his platoon leader retrieved him and returned him to Fort Bragg. During the transport back to Fort Bragg, Pernell again expressed a desire to kill himself and eleven members of his unit.

Immediately upon Pernell's return to Fort Bragg, the Army began the process of administratively separating him. According to Durden, Pernell's commanding officer issued orders on October 22, 2009, that Pernell was to have a noncommissioned officer escort at all times—both off and on Fort Bragg—and was to be checked on hourly to ensure that he remained in his barracks. Durden alleges that the orders were given to "prevent harm to innocent base residents." Durden also claims that these orders were not enforced. Specifically, Durden claims that Pernell was permitted to leave his barracks at night to use drugs and consume alcohol and, further, that Pernell's superior officers knew that Pernell violated the orders but did not act to ensure that the orders were followed.

The government paints a somewhat different picture of the restrictions placed on Pernell following his release from civilian jail and the reasons for the restrictions. According to the government, Pernell was not required to have an escort while on Fort Bragg, was not confined to his barracks, and was not required to be checked on hourly; rather, Pernell was required to have an escort only when he left Fort Bragg, which he could not do without first obtaining permission. Through an affidavit, the government asserts that revoking a soldier's leave-and-pass privilege off Fort Bragg is common while the soldier undergoes the process of being administratively separated, or subsequent to being in civilian confinement, "to ensure that the soldier [is] available for administrative proceedings and [does] not go absent without leave." The government also notes that Pernell received event-oriented counseling on October 22, 2009, at which time Pernell's commanding officer first learned of Pernell's desires to harm himself and others. The government claims that Pernell recanted these desires at that time; however, out of an abundance of caution, the Army ordered that Pernell be checked on every two hours during the evening while p.300 in his barracks to ensure that he did not harm himself. Pernell then underwent a scheduled mental-health evaluation on October 30, 2009, after which it was determined that, inter alia, Pernell exhibited a low potential for self-harm and harm to others. As a result of this assessment, Pernell's commanding officer lifted the bihourly evening checks.

Pernell raped Durden on December 13, 2009, at Durden's residence on Fort Bragg. In January 2010, Pernell became a suspect in Durden's rape and consented to giving a DNA sample that was used to identify him as Durden's assailant. Pernell was also identified at that time as being involved in burglaries and sexual assaults that occurred in 2008 and 2009 in Fayetteville. Pernell subsequently requested mental-health treatment, and it was then determined that Pernell posed a medium risk of harm to himself and others. Following this evaluation, the Army—for the first time, according to the government—placed Pernell on barracks restriction and ordered that he be monitored at all times.

On December 8, 2010, a general court-martial convicted Pernell of raping Durden. As a result, Pernell was sentenced to fifty years' imprisonment, had his military rank reduced, and was dishonorably discharged from the Army. On August 11, 2011, Durden sued the government. Durden alleged that the Army was aware that Pernell posed a safety risk to others, had a duty to protect her from Pernell, and breached that duty by failing to execute the October 22, 2009 orders that, according to Durden, required that Pernell be escorted at all times while on Fort Bragg and be checked on hourly when in his barracks.

The government moved to dismiss Durden's complaint for lack of subject matter jurisdiction and, alternatively, for failure to state a claim. Specifically, the government asserted that the Army did not breach any duty owed to Durden under North Carolina law and that Durden's complaint is barred by the FTCA's intentional-tort exception, 28 U.S.C. § 2680(h). The district court granted the government's motion, and Durden appealed. This Court has jurisdiction over Durden's appeal pursuant to 28 U.S.C. § 1291.

B.

This Court reviews de novo a district court's decision on a motion to dismiss for lack of subject matter jurisdiction. *Cooksey v. Futrell,* 721 F.3d 226, 234 (4th Cir.2013). A defendant may contest subject matter jurisdiction in one of two ways: by attacking the veracity of the allegations contained in the complaint or by contending that, even assuming that the allegations are true, the complaint fails to set forth facts upon which jurisdiction is proper. *Kerns v. United States,* 585 F.3d 187, 192 (4th Cir.2009). Here, despite presenting a version of the facts that differs from Durden's version with respect to the restrictions placed on Pernell, the government's challenges to jurisdiction arise under the latter framework. Specifically, the government contends that Durden's allegations, even if true, do not establish that the Army acted negligently. Additionally and alternatively, the government argues that Durden's complaint is barred by the FTCA's intentional-tort exception. Because these are facial—as opposed to factual—challenges to the complaint, Durden "is afforded the same procedural protection as [s]he would receive under a Rule 12(b)(6) consideration," *Kerns,* 585 F.3d at 192 (i.e., we "assume the truthfulness of the facts alleged," *id.* at 193).

On appeal, Durden opposes each of the government's bases for dismissal. We address these bases in turn.

p.301 II.

A.

"As a sovereign, the United States is immune from all suits against it absent an express waiver of its immunity." *Welch v. United States,* 409 F.3d 646, 650 (4th Cir.2005). The FTCA provides for one such waiver, wherein the district courts ... shall have exclusive jurisdiction of civil actions on claims against the United States, for money damages, ... for injury or loss of property, or personal injury or death caused by the negligent or wrongful act or omission of any employee of the Government while acting within the scope of his office or employment, under circumstances where the United States, if a private person, would be liable to the claimant in accordance with the law of the place where the act or omission occurred.

28 U.S.C. § 1346(b)(1).

"An action [for negligence] under the FTCA may only be maintained if the Government would be liable as an individual under the law of the state where the negligent act occurred." *Kerns*, 585 F.3d at 194 (citing 28 U.S.C. § 1346(b)(1)). In North Carolina—where the Army's alleged negligent act or omission occurred—a defendant cannot be held liable for negligence absent a duty owed to the plaintiff and breach of that duty. *Stein v. Asheville City Bd. of Educ.*, 360 N.C. 321, 626 S.E.2d 263, 267 (2006). Accordingly, dismissal of Durden's complaint on the theory that the allegations are insufficient to give rise to a negligence claim requires us to look beyond the four corners of the complaint and to assess whether, under North Carolina law, the Army owed any duty to Durden and, if it did, whether it breached that duty.

This Court considered appeals arising under the same procedural posture as Durden's appeal in *Kerns* and *Rivanna Trawlers Unlimited v. Thompson Trawlers, Inc.*, 840 F.2d 236 (4th Cir.1988), but resolved those cases differently. In *Kerns*, this Court vacated the district court's dismissal for lack of subject matter jurisdiction, stating that where "the jurisdictional facts and the facts central to a tort claim are inextricably intertwined, the trial court should ordinarily assume jurisdiction and proceed to the intertwined merits issues." 585 F.3d at 193. Notably, the government in *Kerns* challenged the truthfulness of the allegations in the plaintiff's complaint—not merely their legal sufficiency, *see id.*—and this Court concluded that discovery "could" reveal information that might assist the plaintiff on the intertwined merits issue, *id.* at 196. By contrast, this Court in *Rivanna*, despite recognizing that the issue at hand was "both a question of subject matter jurisdiction and an element of appellants' asserted claims," treated the district court's dismissal for lack of subject matter jurisdiction as one for failure to state a claim that had been converted into a motion for summary judgment. 840 F.2d at 239.

This case is more akin to *Rivanna* than *Kerns* insofar as the government argued— and the district court held—that, even assuming that Durden's allegations are true, the complaint still fails to establish that the Army breached a duty to her under North Carolina law. *See Durden v. United States*, No. 5:11-CV-442-D, 2012 WL 3834934, at *8 (E.D.N.C. Aug. 31, 2012) ("Durden satisfies the subject matter jurisdiction requirement that the government owed her a duty before the intentional tort was committed.... Durden's alleged facts do not establish that the government breached a duty that it owed to her." (citation omitted)); *id.* at *10 ("Even accepting as true Durden's allegations regarding p.302 the ways that the government restricted Pernell after Pernell returned to Fort Bragg following his September 10, 2009 arrest, Pernell's tendency to commit violent acts did not cause Pernell to be in the government's custody."); *id.* at *13 ("[A]ccepting as true

Durden's allegations regarding the government's efforts to restrain Pernell, these allegations do not establish the existence [of] a duty owed by the government to Durden under North Carolina's version of the Good Samaritan Doctrine."). Moreover, as we explain in greater detail below, Durden's discovery requests, even if granted, would not assist her on the merits of the underlying negligence issue. Thus, despite the district court's "technically incorrect statement" purporting to dismiss Durden's complaint for lack of subject matter jurisdiction, "the court considered the [negligence] issue as though it were the basis of a motion to dismiss for failure to state a claim that had been converted into a motion for summary judgment." *Rivanna*, 840 F.2d at 239 (Powell, J. (Ret.), sitting by designation).

We turn now to whether the district court correctly determined that the government is entitled to judgment as a matter of law. *See* Fed.R.Civ.P. 56(a) (standard for granting summary judgment). In doing so, we examine in turn Durden's three theories of a duty that the Army owed to her under North Carolina law and allegedly breached.

B.

1.

In North Carolina, "a landlord has a duty to exercise reasonable care to protect his tenants from third-party criminal acts that occur on the premises if such acts are foreseeable." *Davenport v. D.M. Rental Props., Inc.*, 718 S.E.2d 188, 189-90 (N.C.Ct.App.2011). Durden's first theory of negligence, then, is that the Army, as landlord of Fort Bragg, breached a duty to protect her from Pernell's reasonably foreseeable attack.

> The most probative evidence on the question of whether a criminal act was foreseeable is evidence of prior criminal activity committed. However, certain considerations restrict [courts] as to which evidence of prior criminal activity is properly considered. General considerations are [1] the location where the prior crimes occurred, [2] the type of prior crimes committed, and [3] the amount of prior criminal activity.

Connelly v. Family Inns of Am., Inc., 141 N.C.App. 583, 540 S.E.2d 38, 41 (2000) (citations omitted). Foreseeability may also be established by a landlord's knowledge of a specific threat against individuals. *See Davenport*, 718 S.E.2d at 191. Durden identifies two incidents that she believes render Pernell's rape of her foreseeable: Pernell's repeated expressed desires to kill himself and members of his unit (viewed collectively) and Pernell's September 10, 2009 burglary and assault in Fayetteville.[1] For the reasons set forth below, however, we hold that these incidents are not sufficient to render Pernell's rape of Durden "foreseeable" under North Carolina law.

As an initial matter, we reject for two reasons Durden's argument that Pernell's
p.303 prior expressed desires to kill himself and members of his unit established foreseeability of the rape. First, even assuming that Pernell's desires tend to show that he had a propensity for violence, Durden has still failed to demonstrate how such desires fall within the purview of "prior *criminal* activity." *See Connelly*, 540

S.E.2d at 41 (emphasis added). To wit, Durden has not alleged what "crime" the mere desire to harm or kill another person, without more, constitutes,[2] and North Carolina courts require more than the mere wishing of harm upon another person to establish criminal liability. *See, e.g., State v. Merrill*, 138 N.C.App. 215, 530 S.E.2d 608, 612-13 (2000) ("evidence [of] defendant's expressions of her desire that the victim be dead," absent assent to the murder plan, insufficient to support a conspiracy-to-murder charge); *see also State v. Miller*, 344 N.C. 658, 477 S.E.2d 915, 921 (1996) (crime of attempt requires an overt act that "must reach far enough towards the accomplishment of the desired result to amount to the commencement of the consummation"). Second, setting aside the criminality (or not) of Pernell's desires, Durden has not demonstrated that the Army should have gleaned from those desires the notion that Pernell would sexually assault any tenant on Fort Bragg, let alone Durden specifically. *See Davenport*, 718 S.E.2d at 191 (citing *Anderson v. 124, Green Street LLC*, No. 09-2626-H, 2011 WL 341709, at *3 (Mass.Super.Ct. Jan. 21, 2011) ("A duty to evict ... may arise where the landlord knows of a specific threat that one tenant poses to another....")).

Turning now to the September 10, 2009 burglary and assault—indeed, a prior criminal activity—we are satisfied that it meets the second of *Connelly*'s three foreseeability criteria insofar as it qualifies as the same "type of prior crime[]" as Pernell's subsequent rape of Durden. *See, e.g., Murrow v. Daniels*, 321 N.C. 494, 364 S.E.2d 392, 397-98 (1988) (prior crimes of armed robbery, kidnapping, assault, vehicle theft, and larceny deemed relevant for determining whether sexual assault against plaintiff was foreseeable). With respect to the first prong—"the location where the prior crimes occurred"—the North Carolina Supreme Court has been clear that "evidence pertaining to the foreseeability of [a] criminal attack *shall not be limited to prior criminal acts occurring on the premises*," and "criminal acts occurring near the premises in question may be relevant to the question of foreseeability." *Id.* at 397 (citation omitted) (internal quotation marks omitted). However, decisions subsequent to *Murrow* have fashioned *Murrow*'s language as an "exception" limited to "criminal activity in the area immediately surrounding [the] defendant['s] premises." *Purvis v. Bryson's Jewelers, Inc.*, 115 N.C.App. 146, 443 S.E.2d 768, 770 (1994) (considering only prior criminal activity that occurred within three blocks of defendant's property); *see Bennett v. Equity Residential*, 692 S.E.2d 489 (N.C.Ct.App.2010) (unpublished table decision) (considering only prior criminal activity that occurred within the defendant's apartment complex where plaintiff resided).

p.304 Here, there is no indication in the record regarding the physical distance between the site of the September 10, 2009 burglary and assault in Fayetteville and the site of Pernell's rape of Durden on Fort Bragg. Although one incident occurred off the military installation and the other on the military installation, North Carolina courts do not appear to be concerned with such formal line-drawing. *See Connelly*, 540 S.E.2d at 42 (considering, for a crime that occurred in North Carolina, prior criminal activity that occurred at the same interstate-highway intersection but on the South Carolina side of the intersection). Nevertheless, it is possible that if the September 10, 2009 burglary and assault was sufficiently far away from Pernell's rape of Durden, then it is "too remote to guide [the] determination" of foreseeability. *Id.* at 41 (excluding from a foreseeability analysis prior crimes that occurred in a neighboring town twenty miles away). Absent additional information about the distance between the locations of the incidents, however, we are unable to determine how relevant—if at all—the September 10, 2009 incident is in a foreseeability calculus with respect to Pernell's rape of Durden.

Regardless, even assuming that Pernell's September 10, 2009 burglary and assault is sufficiently near in proximity to the rape, Durden's argument that the rape was foreseeable fails on *Connelly*'s third criterion—"the amount of prior criminal activity." Durden does not identify any additional criminal activity—other than Pernell's expressed desires to kill himself and others, which we have already excluded categorically—that occurred prior to the rape and that should have alerted the Army that it was foreseeable that she would be attacked. *Cf. Murrow*, 364 S.E.2d at 397-98 ("The plaintiff presented evidence that one hundred incidents of criminal activity at the [relevant] intersection area had been reported to the sheriff's department [during the four and a half years leading up to the crime]."); *Connelly*, 540 S.E.2d at 42 ("The evidence in this case, indicates that in the five years preceding the armed robbery ..., one hundred instances of criminal activity bearing on the issue of foreseeability occurred at the [relevant] intersection."); *Urbano v. Days Inn of Am., Inc.*, 58 N.C.App. 795, 295 S.E.2d 240, 242 (1982) (denying summary judgment on negligence claim where defendant "knew of at least 42 episodes of criminal activity taking place on its motel premises during a period of three years preceding the date of plaintiff's injury," and "[a]t least 12 of the episodes occurred during the three and one half months preceding plaintiff's injury"). Rather, Durden points to a single incident—Pernell's September 10, 2009 burglary and assault— which is not sufficient in hindsight to render a future attack foreseeable for purposes of landlord liability. *See Davenport*, 718 S.E.2d at 191 (citing *Anderson*, 2011 WL 341709, at *3 ("A duty to evict ... may arise, where there is a *history of violence* by one tenant against other tenants." (emphasis added))).

Accordingly, Durden has failed to establish that Pernell's rape of her was foreseeable under North Carolina law, and thus the Army did not breach a duty owed to her as landlord of Fort Bragg.

2.

"In general, there is neither a duty to control the actions of a third party, nor to protect another from a third party." *Scadden v. Holt*, 733 S.E.2d 90, 92 (N.C.Ct.App.2012). However, certain "[s]pecial relationships create a responsibility to take affirmative action for the aid or protection of another, and they arise only in narrow circumstances." *Bridges v. Parrish*, 742 S.E.2d 794, 797 (N.C.2013) (citation omitted) (internal quotation p.305 marks omitted). A "special relationship" can arise between the defendant and the plaintiff, or between the defendant and a third-party tortfeasor. *Scadden*, 733 S.E.2d at 93 n. 2. When the latter type of special relationship exists, "there is a duty upon the actor to control the [tortfeasor's] conduct and to guard other persons against his dangerous propensities." *King v. Durham Cnty. Mental Health Developmental Disabilities & Substance Abuse Auth.*, 113 N.C.App. 341, 439 S.E.2d 771, 774 (1994) (citation omitted) (internal quotation marks omitted). Durden's second theory of negligence, then, is that the Army had a special relationship with Pernell, owed to her a duty to protect her from Pernell pursuant to that relationship, and breached that duty when Pernell raped her.

Durden claims that the Army had a special relationship with Pernell insofar as the Army (1) "[knew] or should [have] know[n] of [Pernell's] violent propensities" and (2) "ha[d] the ability and opportunity to control [Pernell] at the time" that he raped Durden. *Stein*, 626 S.E.2d at 269 (setting forth the two-pronged test for a special relationship). Even assuming, arguendo, that Durden can satisfy both prongs of the special-relationship test and, moreover, that the government was negligent in failing to control Pernell, Durden's claim that the government is liable *pursuant to the FTCA* still fails. That is because "[t]he ability and opportunity to control [a third party] must be more than mere physical ability to control. Rather, it must rise to the level of custody, or legal right to control." *Scadden*, 733 S.E.2d at 93. The FTCA is clear, however, that the government is liable only "under circumstances where the United States, if *a private person*, would be liable to the claimant in accordance with the law of the place where the act or omission occurred." 28 U.S.C. § 1346(b)(1) (emphasis added). Thus, setting aside the Army's ability to control Pernell that attached solely pursuant to his employment status as a soldier, the Army must have had some other legal authority to control him. But Durden cannot demonstrate (nor has she alleged) that the Army had the ability to control Pernell pursuant to some legal authority independent of Pernell's employment status and, accordingly, the Army cannot be said to have a "special relationship" with him for purposes of an FTCA claim. *See Stein*, 626 S.E.2d at 269. Durden's second theory of negligence therefore also fails.

3.

"[U]nder certain circumstances, one who undertakes to render services to another which he should recognize as necessary for the protection of a third person, or his property, is subject to liability to the third person for injuries resulting from his failure to exercise reasonable care in such undertaking." *Quail Hollow E. Condo. Ass'n v. Donald J. Scholz Co.*, 47 N.C.App. 518, 268 S.E.2d 12, 15 (1980). Durden's final theory of negligence, then, is that by undertaking the task of monitoring and controlling Pernell following his release from civilian confinement, the Army voluntarily assumed a duty to protect her from Pernell and breached that duty when Pernell raped her. However, this theory of a duty fails for two reasons.

First, Durden cannot demonstrate that the Army should have recognized that enforcing the October 22, 2009 orders, as Durden alleges, was necessary for the protection of others. On this issue, *Lumsden v. United States*, 555 F.Supp.2d 580 (E.D.N.C.2008), is instructive. In *Lumsden*, Marine corpsmen returned to the tortfeasor (also a corpsman) his vehicle after the vehicle was impounded when it was discovered that he was inhaling ether. p.306 *Id.* at 582. Upon the return of his vehicle, the corpsman became intoxicated on ether that remained in his vehicle and, as a result, he injured the plaintiffs and killed one other person. *Id.* The court denied the government's motion to dismiss the plaintiffs' FTCA claim and allowed the lawsuit to proceed on a general negligence theory. *See id.* at 589-90. Specifically, the court noted that,

If the plaintiffs can show that the Government's agents knew or had reason to know that upon being provided the keys to his car and a canister of ether, [the corpsman] would become intoxicated at his first opportunity and immediately would attempt to drive on a public street while so intoxicated, then the agents' "behavior thus triggers duty [because] the risk is both unreasonable and foreseeable."

Id. at 589 (second alteration in original) (quoting *Mullis v. Monroe Oil Co.*, 349 N.C. 196, 505 S.E.2d 131, 136-37 (1998)).

In contrast to the tortfeasor in *Lumsden*, Pernell had been released from civilian confinement for more than six weeks prior to raping Durden, and there is nothing in the record to indicate that the Army should have known that Pernell was a threat to Durden's safety based solely on the September 10, 2009 incident or his prior expressed desires to kill himself and members of his unit. At the time that Pernell raped Durden, the Army had no reason to suspect that Pernell committed the burglaries and sexual assaults that occurred in 2008 and 2009 in Fayetteville; indeed, it was only after Pernell raped Durden and became a suspect in that rape that authorities also identified him as being involved in the prior incidents. It might be a different case if the Army knew that it was one of its own soldiers, and Pernell specifically, that committed the 2008 and 2009 sexual assaults in Fayetteville. Under those circumstances, the Army may have had reason to know that Pernell was a serial offender and thus owed to Durden a duty to control Pernell upon his release from civilian confinement. *Cf. id.* at 582 ("[T]he Marine Corps, through its agents or officers, were aware that [the tortfeasor] had, *on several occasions*, acquired and inhaled the chemical compound, ether, belonging to the Government." (emphasis added)). Durden does not dispute, however, that the Army did not become aware that Pernell was involved with the 2008 and 2009 crimes until after Pernell raped her.

Second, Durden has not presented any authority suggesting that, "under similar circumstances, a private person in North Carolina would be found to have owed a duty of ordinary care to persons in [Durden's] position." *Id.* at 589-90; *see* 28 U.S.C. § 1346(b)(1) (holding the government liable only "under circumstances where the United States, if a private person, would be liable"). Stated otherwise, Durden has presented no authority suggesting that a private person—even knowing of Pernell's September 10, 2009 burglary and assault, Pernell's expressed desires to kill himself and members of his unit, and Pernell's frequent drug and alcohol abuse—would have been required (or permitted, for that matter) by law to place Pernell under twenty-four-hour surveillance and to confine him to his barracks or a civilian equivalent thereto. To hold otherwise would render every private individual liable for the intentional torts of another person against unknown third parties simply because the individuals knew that the tortfeasor abused alcohol and drugs and committed a violent crime at some point in the past.

Accordingly, Durden's argument that the government breached a voluntarily assumed duty to protect her fails.

p.307 C.

Durden also argues that "[t]he District Court abused its discretion by transforming the [Rule] 12(b)(1) motion into a judgment on the merits without the opportunity for discovery or cross-examination of the witnesses making affidavits, and especially where the jurisdictional question and the merits of the appellant's claim were intertwined." In particular, Durden seeks discovery pertaining primarily to what Pernell's commanding officers knew regarding Pernell's allegedly violent propensities and the extent of the restrictions placed upon him. But Durden has failed to set forth what additional information might be uncovered through discovery beyond the statements in Pernell's affidavit and, moreover, how that information might render the government liable under any of her three theories of negligence. For even if Durden were granted the discovery that she requests, and even if her allegations regarding the orders given by Pernell's commanding officer were confirmed, her theories of negligence would still fall short of the Army being liable for her injuries. Accordingly, the district court did not abuse its discretion by ruling on the government's motion without granting discovery to Durden. *See Carefirst of Md., Inc. v. Carefirst Pregnancy Ctrs., Inc.*, 334 F.3d 390, 402-03 (4th Cir.2003) (standard of review for decisions regarding jurisdictional discovery).

First, with respect to Durden's theory of negligence based on landlord liability, Durden does not seek discovery regarding the Army's knowledge of any and all incidents of "prior criminal activity" on Fort Bragg that might render Pernell's rape of Durden "foreseeable" under North Carolina law, *see Connelly*, 540 S.E.2d at 41; rather, Durden's discovery requests pertain to "the full extent of [the] awareness [of Pernell's commanding officer], or the awareness of others in the chain of command, of the dangerous propensities of Pernell," and any "regulations, procedures, and policies regarding the duties of the [Army] as landlord." But Durden has not shown how information pertaining to Pernell, specifically, and military policy, generally, comes to bear on the foreseeability of a rape on Fort Bragg. *See id.* (foreseeability determined by "prior criminal activity," which is limited to "[1] the location where the prior crimes occurred, [2] the type of prior crimes committed, and [3] the amount of prior criminal activity").

Second, with respect to Durden's theory of negligence based on a "special relationship" between the Army and Pernell, Durden simply has not demonstrated how factfinding would assist her in developing a new legal theory under which the Army had the ability to control Pernell independent from his status as a soldier (i.e., government employee). *See Scadden*, 733 S.E.2d at 93; *see also* 28 U.S.C. § 1346(b)(1).

And third, with respect to Durden's theory of negligence pursuant to a voluntarily assumed duty, Durden has not set forth what additional information the Army might have known about Pernell prior to the rape and that she might learn during discovery that would render the government liable. Presumably, Pernell made known in his affidavit all facts relevant to his criminal history and any propensity for violence or, at a minimum, Durden would have alleged that Pernell had such a criminal history. Discovery, then, would serve the purpose of determining whether the Army knew of Pernell's criminal history; however, discovery is not for the purpose of learning new information about Pernell that the Army would have had no reason to know or undisputedly did not know prior to Pernell's rape of Durden. Pernell's affidavit does not state that he committed p.308 any prior crimes that should have put the Army on notice that he was a serial offender, and Durden does not dispute the government's claim that it was only after Pernell raped Durden and gave a DNA sample that Pernell was linked to the 2008 and 2009 burglaries and sexual assaults in Fayetteville. Thus, although Durden's claim that relevant evidence is "held exclusively within the walls of the defendant" might be true with respect to what the Army knew about Pernell prior to the rape, Durden has not put forth any facts or information about Pernell that she believes that the Army knew in the first instance and that she would know by way of Pernell. Accordingly, discovery would serve no purpose, and it was not error for the district court to reach the merits of Durden's claim at this stage of the litigation.

III.

As an alternative basis for dismissing Durden's complaint, the district court held that the fact that the Army gained knowledge of Pernell's allegedly violent propensity via his government employment was enough to nullify Durden's claims pursuant to the FTCA's intentional-tort exception. The district court overstated the exception's reach, however, and therefore we conclude that the district court erred in dismissing Durden's complaint on this alternative basis.

The FTCA carves out an exception to its own general waiver of immunity that bars recovery for "[a]ny claim arising out of assault[][or] battery." 28 U.S.C. § 2680(h). The Supreme Court defined the scope of the intentional-tort exception in *Sheridan v. United States*, 487 U.S. 392, 108 S.Ct. 2449, 101 L.Ed.2d 352 (1988). In *Sheridan*, three naval corpsmen encountered the tortfeasor, also a naval employee, in a drunken stupor in the hallway of a naval hospital. *Id.* at 394-95, 108 S.Ct. 2449. The corpsmen "attempted to take [the tortfeasor] to the emergency room, but he broke away, grabbing [his] bag and revealing the barrel of the rifle." *Id.* at 395, 108 S.Ct. 2449. The corpsmen then fled from the scene and took no further action to restrain the tortfeasor or to alert authorities that the tortfeasor was intoxicated and in possession of a firearm. *Id.* The tortfeasor later shot and injured one of the plaintiffs and damaged the plaintiffs' vehicle. *Id.* The plaintiffs then sued the government by way of the three corpsmen for negligently allowing the tortfeasor to leave the hospital with a gun while "obviously intoxicated." *Id.* at 393-94, 108 S.Ct. 2449.

The district court in *Sheridan* dismissed the plaintiffs' complaint as barred by the intentional-tort exception, and this Court affirmed, holding that "§ 2680(h) bars actions alleging negligence of the supervising employees when the underlying tort is an assault or battery by a government employee." *Sheridan v. United States*, 823 F.2d 820, 823 (4th Cir.1987). The Supreme Court, however, reversed and allowed the plaintiffs' claim against the government to proceed, reasoning that

the mere fact that [the tortfeasor] happened to be an off-duty federal employee should not provide a basis for protecting the Government from liability that would attach if [he] had been an unemployed civilian patient or visitor in the hospital. Indeed, in a case in which the employment status of the assailant has nothing to do with the basis for imposing liability on the Government, it would seem perverse to exonerate the Government because of the happenstance that [the tortfeasor] was on a federal payroll.

Sheridan, 487 U.S. at 402, 108 S.Ct. 2449.

Here, the district court below held that, unlike in *Sheridan*—where the p.309 drunken tortfeasor's status as a government employee was wholly irrelevant to imposing liability on the government for the corpsmen's negligence—Pernell's status as a government employee was a but—for element of Durden's negligence claim, thus barring the claim. Specifically, the district court held that "even if the government's knowledge of Pernell's tendency to commit criminal acts made Pernell's assaulting Durden foreseeable to the government before December 13, 2009, section 2680(h) still negates the court's subject matter jurisdiction. After all, the government only acquired such knowledge in the course of Pernell's employment." *Durden*, 2012 WL 3834934, at *9; *see id.* ("[B]ecause the government's knowledge of [Pernell's] tendency to commit criminal acts stemmed solely from [his] government employment, the government's breach of any duty owed to [Durden] was not independent of the employment relationship." (citing *Bajkowski v. United States*, 787 F.Supp. 539, 541-42 (E.D.N.C.1991) ("If [the tortfeasor] were not an employee of the Army, the Army would not have had... knowledge of his prior criminal and assaultive behavior...."))). The same could be said, however, about the corpsmen's knowledge of the intoxicated tortfeasor in *Sheridan:* presumably, the corpsmen alleged to have acted negligently would not have been present in the naval hospital that night—and thus would not have gained knowledge of the drunken tortfeasor and put themselves in a position to be negligent in the first instance—were it not for their government employment.

Accordingly, we hold that, although the government's ability (i.e., legal duty) to control a tortfeasor must be independent of the tortfeasor's status as a government employee, knowledge of the tortfeasor's propensity for violence or criminal history gained as a result of such status does not, per se, nullify an FTCA claim. The district court's dismissal on this alternative basis was therefore erroneous.

IV.

For the reasons set forth above, we affirm the district court's grant of summary judgment to the government.

AFFIRMED.

[1] Although Durden does not raise this argument, we note that Pernell's alcohol abuse and drug use, even if criminal acts, do not qualify as "prior criminal activity" for purposes of determining whether Pernell's rape of Durden was foreseeable for at least the reason that they are not the same type of prior crimes. *See Connelly*, 540 S.E.2d at 42 ("instances of public drunkenness, shoplifting, vandalism[,] and disorderly conduct" are not the types of incidents to be considered for purposes of establishing foreseeability of armed robbery).

[2] Durden characterizes Pernell's desires to kill himself and others as "threats." Pernell, however, did not state in his affidavit that he ever intended to act on his desires or that he communicated the desires to those members of his unit whom he wished to harm; rather, Pernell indicated that he expressed the desires to his staff

sergeant and platoon leader in an effort to receive mental-health treatment because, according to Pernell, "[he] knew a report of that kind ought to automatically trigger [his] commitment to a mental health facility."

FIFTH CIRCUIT DECISIONS
Federal Tort Claims Act

MEREDITH MORRIS; JEFFREY MORRIS, Plaintiffs-Appellants,

v.

MICHAEL J. THOMPSON, Defendant-Appellee.

No. 16-50448.

United States Court of Appeals, Fifth Circuit.

Filed March 27, 2017.

Morris v. Thompson, (5th Cir. 2017)

Laura Anne Cavaretta, for Defendant-Appellee.

Erin R. McNiece, for Defendant-Appellee.

Leslie Ernest Katona, Jr., for Defendant-Appellee.

Marie K. Miller, for Defendant-Appellee.

Blakely Ian Mohr, for Plaintiff-Appellant.

Adam Jason Sabrin, for Plaintiff-Appellant.

Caitlin B. Howell, for Plaintiff-Appellant.

Appeals from the United States District Court for the Western District of Texas.

Before: SMITH, CLEMENT, and SOUTHWICK, Circuit Judges.

LESLIE H. SOUTHWICK, Circuit Judge.

Air Force Captain Meredith Morris and her husband Jeffrey sued another Air Force Captain, Michael Thompson, for injuries Captain Morris sustained on Randolph Air Force Base. Thompson filed a motion to dismiss for lack of subject-matter jurisdiction under the *Feres* doctrine, arguing that the injuries occurred incident to military service. The district court granted the motion. We AFFIRM.

FACTUAL AND PROCEDURAL BACKGROUND

The incident at issue occurred on Randolph Air Force Base on May 20, 2011, during "Roll Call." According to Thompson, Roll Call is a squadron-scheduled event, while Morris characterizes it as "unofficial" and "non-compulsory." The parties agree that Roll Call is designed to foster camaraderie and serve team-building purposes by allowing pilots the opportunity to come "together to share their experiences and tell stories." The date and location of the incident are the only facts on which the parties agree.

Meredith Morris ("Morris" denotes Captain Morris and not her husband) claims that she was ordered to physically restrain Thompson during Roll Call when he displayed insubordinate behavior toward superior officers. As a result of this restraint, she claims Thompson grabbed her and "threw her to the ground," which caused her to hit her head on the concrete. During the attack, Thompson "yelled pejorative, insulting, and threatening language" and subsequently choked Morris until she was unable to breathe. Before the attack ended, Morris claims Thompson "pushed her down with such force that her head again hit the concrete floor." Morris alleges Thompson was intoxicated during their altercation, which Thompson denies.

Thompson has a different story. He claims that while he was talking to others, Morris attacked him from behind, while several other servicemembers attacked him from the front. The force of the attack, he says, caused him to fall backward and land on Morris. His assailants then attempted to "duct-tape [him], head and all, to the concrete floor." According to Thompson, he had recently suffered a traumatic brain injury at the time of the incident. During his rehabilitation, he had learned to protect his head because "impacts to his brain during recovery could have [had] catastrophic, if not deadly, consequences." He thus alleges that any violent reaction on his part was defensive in nature.

Morris also claims injuries. She says the attack caused severe damage to her head, neck, and shoulders, which rendered her unable to fly. She also claims medical expenses, lost wages, and lost earning capacity, while her husband claims loss of consortium. Thompson, though, contends that Morris did not sustain any apparent injury at the time of the incident, nor did he observe her receiving medical treatment at that time.

The Morrises filed an administrative claim with the Air Force in May 2013, but it was denied. They then sued the United States in federal court in December 2013. That suit was dismissed in May 2014 due to application of the *Feres* doctrine, which we will later discuss in detail. That dismissal is not before us today.

A few days after they filed the administrative claim, the Morrises sued Thompson in his individual capacity in Texas state court, alleging various tort claims. Thompson did not receive service of process until October 2014. Thompson timely removed the case to the Western District of Texas based on diversity of citizenship. Thompson filed a motion to dismiss for lack of subject-matter jurisdiction under Federal Rule of Civil Procedure 12(b)(1). He argued the case was nonjusticiable under the *Feres* doctrine because it is an action between military service members arising from activities occurring incident to service. The district court agreed and dismissed. The Morrises filed a timely notice of appeal.

DISCUSSION

We review *de novo* the district court's grant of a Rule 12(b)(1) motion to dismiss for lack of subject-matter jurisdiction. *Ramming v. United States,* 281 F.3d 158, 161 (5th Cir. 2001). The party asserting jurisdiction "constantly bears the burden of proof that jurisdiction does in fact exist." *Id.* When ruling on the motion, the district court may rely on the complaint, undisputed facts in the record, and the court's resolution of disputed facts. *Id.* The motion should be granted only if it appears certain the plaintiff cannot prove any set of facts that would entitle her to recovery. *Home Builders Ass'n of Mississippi, Inc. v. City of Madison,* 143 F.3d 1006, 1010 (5th Cir. 1998). The district court's application of the *Feres* doctrine is also a question of law that earns *de novo* review. *Hayes v. United States ex rel. United States Dep't of Army,* 44 F.3d 377, 378 (5th Cir. 1995).

The Morrises present these arguments: (1) the *Feres* doctrine does not bar state-law claims heard in federal court under diversity jurisdiction, and, regardless, the *Feres* doctrine does not apply as between members of the same rank; (2) the *Feres* doctrine is unconstitutional; and (3) at least Jeffrey Morris, a civilian, may sue Thompson for loss of consortium.

(1) Applicability of Feres to Claims Brought Under State Law and by Servicemembers of the Same Rank

The *Feres* doctrine is a narrow exception to tort liability under federal statute: "[T]he Government is not liable under the Federal Tort Claims Act [FTCA] for injuries to servicemen where the injuries arise out of or are in the course of activity incident to service." *Feres v. United States,* 340 U.S. 135, 146 (1950); *see also Meister v. Texas Adjutant Gen.'s Dep't,* 233 F.3d 332, 336 (5th Cir. 2000). The *Feres* Court held the FTCA waived sovereign immunity, "putting the United States government in the same position as any other defendant." *Meister,* 233 F.3d at 336.

After *Feres,* the Supreme Court "authorized a suit for damages against federal officials whose actions violated an individual's constitutional rights. . . ." *Chappell v. Wallace,* 462 U.S. 296, 298 (1983) (citing *Bivens v. Six Unknown Named Agents of Fed. Bureau of Narcotics,* 403 U.S. 388 (1970)). In *Chappell,* though, the Court limited the *Bivens* remedy by holding "that enlisted military personnel may not maintain a suit to recover damages from a superior officer for alleged constitutional violations." *Id.* at 305. The Court later reaffirmed the applicability of the *Feres* incident-to-service test, requiring courts to abstain from interfering in cases arising under such circumstances. *United States v. Stanley,* 483 U.S. 669, 683-84 (1987).

This court has categorized the *Feres* doctrine as one of justiciability. *Filer v. Donley,* 690 F.3d 643, 648-50 (5th Cir. 2012). Although the Supreme Court has only considered this issue in the context of FTCA and *Bivens* claims, we have held that *Feres* bars all lawsuits based on injuries incident to military service. *See Crawford v. Texas Army Nat'l Guard,* 794 F.2d 1034, 1035-36 (5th Cir. 1986). Relevant to this case, claims brought directly under state law are barred by *Feres. Holdiness v. Stroud,* 808 F.2d 417, 426 (5th Cir. 1987).[1] In *Holdiness,* the plaintiff filed suit under 42 U.S.C. §§ 1983, 1985; the FTCA; and Louisiana state law. *Id.* at 420. We followed *Chappell's* command to hesitate before interfering in the relationships between military personnel and the preference for having those disputes adjudicated under the "unique structure of the military establishment." *Id.* at 426. We held that judicial review of a state-law tort claim arising in this context would constitute an "unwarranted intrusion into the military personnel structure" about which the Court has previously warned. *Id.*[2]

The Morrises allege that their case is distinguishable because Thompson removed on the basis of diversity of citizenship. We see no distinction. These are still state-law claims arising in a situation that was incident to service. "[C]ivilian courts may not sit in plenary review over intraservice military disputes." *Crawford,* 794 F.2d at 1035. *Feres* bars state-law claims because adjudication "would undermine military decision-making as surely as federal claims held to be nonjusticiable." *Texas Adjutant Gen.'s Dep't v. Amos,* 54 S.W.3d 74, 78 (Tex. App.-Austin 2001, pet. denied).[3]

The Morrises further argue that the *Feres* doctrine does not apply because Morris and Thompson held the same rank. It is true that the superior-subordinate relationship has at times been relevant in the articulation of the *Feres* doctrine. *Chappell,* 462 U.S. at 300. Nonetheless, the Supreme Court does "not consider the officer-subordinate relationship crucial[.]" *Stanley,* 483 U.S. at 680. In *Stanley,* the Army secretly administered LSD to the plaintiff in order to study its effect on human subjects. *Id.* at 671. The Court "assume[d] that at least some of the defendants were not [his] superior officers. . . ." *Id.* at 680. Accordingly, the key consideration in applying *Feres* in *Stanley* was the incident-to-service test. *Id.* at 683-84. Another circuit held that *Feres* applied even when the parties were of the same rank. *Mattos v. United States,* 412 F.2d 793, 794 (9th Cir. 1969) (per curiam). *Feres* requires that we avoid "judicial intrusion into the area of military performance[.]" *Id.* The relative rank of the plaintiff and defendant are of no moment.

Though neither party disputes that these events occurred incident to military service, we examine the test. We are to consider three factors: (1) the duty status of the service member; (2) the place where the injury occurred; and (3) the activity in which the service member was engaged at the time of the injury. *Walch v. Adjutant Gen.'s Dep't of Texas,* 533 F.3d 289, 297 (5th Cir. 2008). The facts of this case involved actions taken by two active-duty service members on Randolph Air Force Base during a military training function. The Morrises claims are thus incident to service, and *Feres* applies regardless of the rank of the parties or the bringing of state-law claims.

(2) Constitutionality of Feres *and (3) the Consortium Claim*

The Morrises argue that the application of the *Feres* doctrine would interfere with their constitutional rights. They argue that not allowing them to sue military personnel violates their Fifth and Fourteenth Amendment rights, as well as of their right to access courts. These arguments fail. Though the *Feres* doctrine has been subject to criticism, *United States v. Johnson,* 481 U.S. 681, 692-703 (1987) (Scalia, J., dissenting), it is Supreme Court precedent binding on this court.

Finally, the Morrises concede that Jeffrey Morris's loss-of-consortium claim, which is derivative of his wife's claim, will be barred if hers is. *See Schoemer v. United States,* 59 F.3d 29, 30 n.5 (5th Cir. 1995). Because of our holding as to Meredith Morris's claims, Jeffrey Morris's loss-of-consortium claim also fails.

(3) Westfall Act

A new issue was presented for the first time at oral argument. The Morrises' counsel argued that *Feres* does not apply because Thompson did not use the procedures of the Westfall Act[4] to have the factual events on which the state-law claims are based certified as being incident to military service.

Oral argument is far too late a time to be injecting a new issue. Indeed, an issue not properly raised in the district court and timely briefed on appeal is not before us. *Procter & Gamble Co. v. Amway Corp.,* 376 F.3d 496, 499 n.1 (5th Cir. 2004). The Morrises' counsel orally argued that two cases relevant to the argument were in fact cited in their briefing. The Morrises' initial brief, though, cited just one of them and only to support that *Feres* does not apply to state-law claims. *See Day v. Massachusetts Air Nat'l Guard,* 167 F.3d 678 (1st Cir. 1999). That overstates what *Day* held, and, regardless, the brief makes no reference to *Day*'s discussion of the Westfall Act and certification. In the reply brief, the Morrises cited both *Day* and another opinion upon which they wish to rely. *See Lutz v Sec'y of Air Force,* 944 F.2d 1477, 1488 (9th Cir. 1991). That brief cited *Day* and *Lutz* for the proposition that incidents between servicemembers of equal rank and involving activities that were outside of the scope of employment are not subject to *Feres.* Westfall certification again went unmentioned. Even more importantly, questions about Westfall were not presented to the district court.

Despite the lateness of the issue, this court has an independent obligation to confirm that we have jurisdiction regardless of the parties' arguments. *Harold H. Huggins Realty, Inc. v. FNC, Inc.,* 634 F.3d 787, 795 n.2 (5th Cir. 2011). If Thompson's failure to seek certification under the Westfall Act somehow affects our jurisdiction, we must consider the issue.

We thus examine just what the Westfall Act provides. Relevant here, when a federal employee is named in a tort suit, the Attorney General may certify that the employee was "acting within the scope of his office or employment at the time of the incident out of which the claim arose," which will cause the federal employee to be dismissed and the United States substituted as the defendant. 28 U.S.C. § 2679(d)(1). This Act "accords federal employees absolute immunity from common-law tort claims arising out of acts they undertake in the course of their official duties." *Osborn v. Haley,* 549 U.S. 225, 229 (2007) (citing 28 U.S.C. § 2679(b)(1)). For the first time in our courtroom, the Morrises raised that *Feres* cannot bar these claims because the Attorney General never declared anything about Thompson's status as a federal employee at the time of the incident.

We see no jurisdictional defect in having a case proceed against a party who could but did not invoke a statutory procedure to gain immunity. Until immunity is claimed, the individual may be a proper party. Here, the *Feres* doctrine provided its own mechanism for determining the propriety of bringing suit against this airman.

There also was no error in allowing removal. Removal would have been conclusively established had there been a Westfall Act certification. *Osborn,* 549 U.S. at 231. Even without that basis, there was another basis for removal here — complete diversity of the parties. The failure of anyone to seek certification under Westfall does not divest us of the jurisdiction to resolve what is brought to us on this appeal.

AFFIRMED.

[1] In an unpublished opinion, we recently reaffirmed our decision in *Holdiness. Davidson v. United States,* 647 F. App'x 289, 290-91 (5th Cir. 2016). Other circuits have also held that *Feres* applies to state-law claims. *See, e.g., John v. Sec'y of Army,* 484 F. App'x 661, 663-64 (3d Cir. 2012); *Blakey v. U.S.S. Iowa,* 991 F.2d 148, 152 (4th Cir. 1993).

[2] The Morrises characterize the relevant language from *Holdiness* as dicta. Not so. In *Holdiness,* we analyzed each of the plaintiff's claims, devoting an entire section to his state-law tort claim. *See Holdiness,* 808 F.2d at 421-26. There were two grounds on which the claim could have been dismissed, but most of our analysis focused on "the rationale of *Chappell*" and similar cases. *Id.* at 426. The analytical foundation of our holding would have been substantially disrupted had that language been removed. It is binding.

[3] The Morrises attempt to distinguish many Texas cases, but our review convinces us that all support our holding. *See, e.g., Newth v. Adjutant Gen.'s Dep't of Texas,* 883 S.W.2d 356, 360 (Tex. App.-Austin 1994, writ denied).

[4] *See* 28 U.S.C. §§ 2671-2680.

TERESA GONZALEZ, Plaintiff-Appellant,

v.

UNITED STATES OF AMERICA; JOHN DOES A-Z, Defendants-Appellees.

No. 16-60062.

United States Court of Appeals, Fifth Circuit.

Filed: March 22, 2017.

Cynthia Lynn Eldridge, for Defendant-Appellee.

Alben Norris Hopkins, Jr., for Plaintiff-Appellant.

Appeal from the United States District Court for the Southern District of Mississippi.

Before: HIGGINBOTHAM, JONES, and HAYNES, Circuit Judges.

PATRICK E. HIGGINBOTHAM, Circuit Judge.

Teresa Gonzalez was injured while riding her bicycle over a ramp at De Soto National Forest. She sued various United States officials under the Federal Tort Claims Act ("FTCA"), 28 U.S.C. §§ 2671-2680, alleging they failed to inspect and maintain the bicycle trails, and failed to warn her of the hazard. The United States moved to dismiss, arguing that the FTCA's "discretionary function exception" barred Gonzalez's claims. The district court granted the motion. We AFFIRM.

I.

On July 28, 2012, Teresa Gonzalez and Robert Reville, Jr., went to the De Soto National Forest to ride their bicycles at the Bethel Bicycle Trails, which included the Couch Loop Trail. Before they began riding, Gonzalez did not look at the bulletin board at the park's entrance, which contained a sign stating that the Couch Loop Trail was closed. They nevertheless embarked on the Couch Loop Trail. At some point, they took an "alternate route" to the left of the main trail that led to obstacles including a teeter-totter and a ramp. Neither attempted to ride over the teeter-totter, but both decided to ride over the ramp. Gonzalez had never jumped off a ramp before, and when she tried to do so, she fell off and suffered serious injuries.

Gonzalez assumed that the ramp was part of the trail and built by the Forest Service. In fact, the ramp was built illegally by Gulf Coast Bicycle Club members, without the knowledge of the United States Forest Service ("USFS"). The USFS employees were not aware of the ramp's existence before Gonzalez's accident. They were, however, aware of an unauthorized bridge further down the trail, which is why the Couch Loop Trail was closed on the day of Gonzalez's accident.[1]

USFS recreational technician Charles Grice had posted a sign at the trailhead bulletin board that stated the trail was closed, and also flagged the bridge area with boards, signs, and ribbons. The sign at the trailhead bulletin board stated: "Couch Trail CLOSED," and in smaller type, "Bridge Out." The sign was on an 8 ½" by

11" sheet of paper. Gonzalez claims that neither she nor Reville saw any signs, and that she would have obeyed any warning sign she saw.

De Soto National Forest is about 382,000 acres. In 2012, Ronald Smith was the De Soto National Forest District Ranger, the highest ranking officer of a district. Two technicians were responsible for maintaining and inspecting the Bethel Bicycle Trails, full-time technician Charles Grice, and part-time technician, Anthony Bond. Grice testified that inspection and maintenance of the trails included identifying hazards, such as trees, and performing repair work. He spot-checked the trail and checked it when people called. If Grice found an unauthorized structure, he reported it to the ranger. He stated that he and Bond "bush hog the trail pretty much every year," which includes clearing and cleaning the trail. Grice did not know whether he had bush hogged the teeter-totter and ramp area in 2012. The last time Grice remembered inspecting the Couch Loop Trail before Gonzalez's accident was when he was inspecting a trail contractor's work, however he could not remember when that was. Other than checking for unsafe structures or trees and bush hogging, there are no other scheduled inspections of the trail. Since January 2012, Grice was also responsible for posting any warning signs at the trailhead. Grice stated that no one instructed him about the placement of trail closure notices, and that "[w]e just put them on the bulletin board at the trailhead areas." Grice and Bond were not allowed to post warning signs or close a trail without Ranger Smith's authority.

A number of laws, regulations and policies affect the USFS, including the following that Gonzalez highlights in this appeal: (1) The Forest Service Manual — FSM-2300 Recreational, Wilderness, and Related Resource Management ("the Manual"); (2) The Forest Service Handbook — FSH 2309.18 — Trails Management Handbook ("the Handbook"); and (3) the Forest Service-EM7100-15 Sign and Poster Guidelines for the Forest Service ("Sign and Poster Guidelines").

Gonzalez filed a complaint against the United States on February 21, 2014, asserting jurisdiction under 28 U.S.C. § 1346(B)(1). She advanced several negligence theories, essentially alleging that the United States failed to keep its premises safe, failed to perform inspections, and failed to warn of a dangerous condition. The United States moved to dismiss for lack of subject matter jurisdiction, arguing that the discretionary function exception to the FTCA's waiver of sovereign immunity applied. It alternatively moved for summary judgment "because no USFS employee engaged in any negligent act or omission for which the United States may be held liable to the Plaintiff under the FTCA." The district court granted the motion to dismiss based on the FTCA discretionary functions exception, not reaching the government's alternative argument. Gonzalez appealed.

II.

"We review the district court's dismissal for lack of subject-matter jurisdiction over [a plaintiff's] FTCA claim de novo."[2] "Lack of subject-matter jurisdiction may be found in the complaint alone, the complaint supplemented by the undisputed facts as evidenced in the record, or the complaint supplemented by the undisputed facts plus the court's resolution of the disputed facts."[3] The district court here based its conclusion on the complaint and undisputed facts.[4]

III.

The United States enjoys sovereign immunity from suit, meaning it cannot be sued without consent.[5] "The FTCA is recognized as providing a waiver of sovereign immunity and provides the sole basis of recovery for tort claims against the United States."[6] This waiver, however, "is subject to several exceptions."[7] The exception relevant here is the "discretionary function exception,"[8] which "preserves the federal government's immunity . . . when an employee's acts involve the exercise of judgment or choice."[9] The exception is found in 28 U.S.C. § 2680(a):

> Any claim based upon an act or omission of an employee of the Government, exercising due care, in the execution of a statute or regulation, whether or not such statute or regulation be valid, or based upon the exercise or performance or the failure to exercise or perform a discretionary function or duty on the part of a federal agency or an employee of the Government, whether or not the discretion involved be abused.

The Supreme Court has explained, "[t]he exception covers only acts that are discretionary in nature, acts that 'involv[e] an element of judgment or choice,' [] and 'it is the nature of the conduct, rather than the status of the actor' that governs whether the exception applies."[10] "The basis for the discretionary function exception was Congress' desire to 'prevent judicial "second-guessing" of legislative and administrative decisions grounded in social, economic, and political policy through the medium of an action in tort.'"[11]

A two-prong test determines whether the exception applies: (1) "the conduct must be a 'matter of choice for the acting employee[;]'"[12] and (2) the "judgment [must be] of the kind that the discretionary function exception was designed to shield."[13] Both prongs must be met for the exception to apply.[14] With respect to the first prong, "[i]f a statute, regulation, or policy leaves it to a federal agency to determine when and how to take action, the agency is not bound to act in a particular manner and the exercise of its authority is discretionary."[15] On the contrary, "[t]he requirement of judgment or choice is not satisfied if a 'federal statute, regulation, or policy specifically prescribes a course of action for an employee to follow,' because 'the employee has no rightful option but to adhere to the directive.'"[16] Regarding the second prong, the court "consider[s] whether the actions taken are 'susceptible to policy analysis.'"[17] "[T]he proper inquiry . . . is not whether [the official] *in fact* engaged in a policy analysis when reaching his decision but instead whether his decision was 'susceptible to policy analysis.'"[18] In performing the two-prong test, "the question of *whether* the government was negligent is irrelevant."[19]

IV.

The FTCA's discretionary function exception bars Gonzalez's claims. The district court categorized Gonzalez's claims into two groups: (1) the alleged failures to inspect and maintain the trails, and (2) the alleged failures to warn. We adopt the same useful organization.

Gonzalez alleges the government employees failed to meet a number of provisions from the Manual and Handbook. She argues that such provisions prescribe a course of action and contends that "routine property maintenance decisions are not susceptible to the kind of policy analysis shielded by the discretionary function [exception]." Gonzalez compares the government's actions to those of a business operator who makes decisions about premises safety. The Government responds that Ranger Smith and the other USFS officials had discretion in maintaining and inspecting their trails. The Government argues that no specific law or policy proscribed how employees should inspect and maintain the trails, and that the Manual and Handbook offer "general guidance." The Government urges, "[t]he determining factor is whether the challenged actions are 'grounded in the policy of the regulatory regime,'" and concludes that "trail inspection and maintenance are part of the essence of the regulatory regime set forth in the Manual, the Handbook, and the other applicable regulations." The Government asserts that the USFS balanced resources as per USFS policy, and followed the recommendations for maintaining bicycle trails.[20]

In order to determine whether an official's conduct was discretionary, we must first define that conduct.[21] Gonzalez generally suggests that the conduct at issue is some version of "failing to inspect the trails as required." The Government, in turn, describes Gonzalez as arguing "that USFS failed to perform required inspections and maintenance of the Bethel Bicycle Trails" and "further . . . that the National Quality Standards for Trails mandate hazard-free trails." To different extents, each of the above framings assumes that there were clearly prescribed requirements—an inquiry for the first prong of the discretionary function test. Moreover, Gonzalez at times suggests that Grice and Bond failed altogether to inspect the trails—but the record belies this assertion.

The Eleventh Circuit in *Autery v. United States* confronted a similar gateway framing issue. In that case, after a black locust tree in the Great Smokey Mountain National Park fell on a car, the injured passenger and estate of a killed passenger brought an FTCA claim against the United States.[22] In its discretionary function analysis, "[t]he government argue[d] that the conduct to be evaluated [was] 'the Park Service's decision to establish and implement a tree inspection program. Plaintiffs, on the other hand, contend[ed] that 'the conduct at issue [was] the park's failure to carry out the mandates of its then existing policy of identifying and eliminating known hazardous trees.'"[23] The *Autery* court rejected both descriptions.[24] It explained that "[t]he tree inspection program was designed to identify which trees were hazardous. Whether park personnel had discretion in executing that plan is the relevant issue."[25] "[T]he relevant inquiry here," the *Autery* Court concluded, "is whether controlling statutes, regulations and administrative policies mandated that the Park Service inspect for hazardous trees in a specific manner."[26] Similarly, the relevant inquiry in the present case is whether the controlling policies mandated the USFS to inspect and maintain the trails in a specific manner.

We find that they did not. Beginning with the first prong of the discretionary function exception test, the relevant Manual and Handbook provisions contemplate an element of choice as to how USFS employees inspect and maintain the trails. For example, Paragraph 2353.12 in the Manual instructs to "[m]anage each trail to meet the [trail management objectives] identified for that trail, based on applicable land management plan direction, travel management decisions, trail-specific decisions, and other related direction, as well as management priorities and available resources." This language contains the direction to "meet" the identified objectives, but gives room for choice based on the evaluation of various factors. Moreover, although the objectives at 2353.02 list specific goals, they do not prescribe a certain course employees must take to reach those goals. In this way, the "provisions . . . contain generalized, precatory, or aspirational language that is too general to prescribe a specific course of action for an agency or employee to follow."[27]

The Handbook, too, contemplates that employees have some discretion in maintaining the trails. For example, the exhibit in Chapter 10, Paragraph 18, for "trail operation and maintenance considerations" states that the considerations are "*general guidelines* for developing trail prescriptions and managing, operating, and maintaining National Forest System trails."[28] It further states that "[t]he considerations are a *starting point* and likely will need to be adapted to reflect local financial capability and other circumstances."[29] General guidelines for maintaining a trail encompass "acts that are discretionary in nature, acts that 'involv[e] an element of judgment or choice.'"[30] Here, because the "policy leaves it to a federal agency to determine when and how to take action, the agency is not bound to act in a particular manner and the exercise of its authority is discretionary."[31]

Gonzalez emphasizes one of the critical "National Quality Standards for Trails" in the Handbook that states: "hazards do not exist on or along the trail." Gonzalez asserts, "[i]t is inconceivable that a Critical National Quality Standard to inspect the trails to ensure that hazards do not exist and to 'prevent immediate and permanent injury to persons or property' is a duty left up to the choice of low level Forestry Service personnel." In response, the Government points to the footnote associated with the Critical National Quality Standards, which states "[i]f it cannot be met, action must be taken as soon as practicable to correct or mitigate the problem." This language contemplates that the standard may not be met, which cuts against Gonzalez's claim that the standard represents a mandatory prescription. Moreover, even if the standard that "hazards do not exist on or along the trail" is mandatory, the standard does not dictate how officials must meet that standard—which is what the challenged conduct concerns.

Gonzalez contends, "[i]nspecting the bicycle trail does not mean bush hogging some portion of the trail with easy access to a tractor on occasion." But even setting aside Grice's testimony to the contrary, Gonzalez cites to no provision prohibiting this understanding, nor prescribing a different understanding, of how the trails should be inspected. That the policies leave open the question of how to inspect the trails is evidence of choice. Gonzalez also argues that the officials were not familiar with the policies, but in doing so shifts the focus away from the discretionary function test and toward the merits of her negligence claims. Indeed, Grice testified he did not know what the National Quality Standards for trails were, and that he never read the "Trails Management Handbook, Trail Planning" document.[32] Gonzalez emphasizes that Bond could not remember ever inspecting the area of the Couch Loop Trail where the accident occurred, nor did he recall seeing the regulations. Gonzalez also points out that Ranger Smith "had never read the Forestry Service Regulations." Gonzalez asserts, "[t]here is no 'room for choice' if you have no idea what the standards are for performing maintenance and inspections to begin with." While the officials' lack of familiarity with the policies may be strong evidence of a breached duty, such evidence does not affect the inquiry at hand: whether the challenged actions contained an element of judgment. Gonzalez's arguments in this respect better inform the merits of her underlying claims, rather than whether the discretionary function exception applies. Based on the applicable policies, "there was 'room for choice' in making the allegedly negligent decision"[33] to not inspect and maintain the trails in a certain way. At most, the USFS officials abused their discretion, but as the Court in *Katrina Canal Breaches* reminds, such "abuse [is] explicitly immunized by the [discretionary function exception]."[34]

The challenged conduct also meets the second prong of the discretionary function exception test, as the manner in which the USFS officials inspected and maintained the trails was susceptible to policy considerations. Gonzalez asserts that, "[t]here should be little balance when it comes to the safety of the patrons versus the natural environment under the circumstances of this case. Certainly in this instance, removing the hazards and inspecting for additional hazards is reasonable and inexpensive." However, this argument concerns whether the officials best balanced the policy considerations, when the inquiry is whether the challenged actions were susceptible to policy considerations. Indeed, the purpose of the discretionary function exception is "to prevent judicial second-guessing."[35]

In *Gibson v. United States,* this Court held that the discretionary function exception was not met, because the Federal Emergency Management Agency's ("FEMA") conduct in how to provide customers access to their trailers was not susceptible to policy analysis.[36] In *Gibson,* the plaintiff "was at a FEMA storage site . . . inspecting trailers that were to be sold at auction," when he was injured while trying to exit one.[37] Gibson brought suit under the FTCA,[38] alleging a number of claims related to FEMA's policies regarding access to the trailers.[39] The government argued the discretionary function exception applied.[40] Bypassing a determination on the first prong of the test, this Court held "that FEMA's decision about how customers would enter and exit the trailers was not the type of judgment the discretionary function exception was designed to protect."[41] The Court compared FEMA's trailer operation to that of a commercial business,[42] and found that decisions regarding trailer access concerned "'a mundane, administrative, garden-variety, housekeeping problem that is about as far removed from the policies applicable to . . . FEMA's[] mission as it is possible to get.'"[43]

Gonzalez cites extensively to *Gibson,* while the Government attempts to distinguish it by arguing that in *Gibson,* the United States was acting as a commercial business, but in the present case it is operating wilderness. The Government's suggestion that "wilderness cases" are distinct has merit. As the *Gibson* Court pointed out, "[r]ather differently, when the Government acts as landowner of wilderness, certain kinds of maintenance decisions have been found to contain multiple policy considerations."[44] The *Gibson* Court cited to *Theriot v. United States,*[45] which concerned how the United States Army Corps of Engineers "was to notify the public of the existence of a sill," and *Hix v. U.S. Army Corps. of Engineers,*[46] which concerned how the government was to "replace warning signs near jetties in Galveston."[47] Unlike those decisions, which concerned public safety (*Hix*), dangerous objects, vessel traffic, and economics (*Theriot*), among others, in *Gibson*, "the Government operated as a commercial business and welcomed customers to its site as if it were managing a trailer showroom."[48]

Here, the government acts more like the manager of a wilderness area than the operator of a commercial business. Decisions about how to maintain bicycle trails running through 382,000 acres of land with only two recreation technicians seem to invite, if not require, "safety, financial, and other feasibility concerns."[49] Such decisions implicate resource allocation, wilderness considerations, and public safety; in other words, they are "administrative decisions grounded in social, economic, and political policy."[50]

Gaubert teaches that "[f]or a complaint to survive a motion to dismiss, it must allege facts which would support a finding that the challenged actions are not the kind of conduct that can be said to be grounded in the policy of the regulatory regime."[51] The challenged actions here are grounded in USFS policy. Paragraph 2353.03 of the Manual states, for example: "Emphasize long-term cost effectiveness and need when developing or rehabilitating trails," and "Provide a trail system that is environmentally, socially, and financially sustainable." The decisions about how to inspect and maintain the bicycle trails are susceptible to policy considerations so as to satisfy the second prong of the discretionary function exception test.

Gonzalez's failure to warn claims are also barred by the discretionary function exception. Gonzalez argues that the government had a duty to warn her about the ramp, and that, "[t]he Forestry Service Regulation do not give a choice on how to mark a trail." Gonzalez points to a bevy of provisions describing sign standards, and ultimately argues, "the 8 ½ x 11 sheet of copy paper with small black letters posted amongst other cluttered papers was not a discretionary option for those in charge of maintenance and inspection." Gonzalez avers the government's "failure to adequately warn and notify [Gonzalez] of the trail closure involves considerations of safety, not public policy." The Government responds by pointing out that the Couch Loop Trail was closed due to the bridge, not the ramp. The Government insists that Grice's notice on the trailhead followed Guidelines recommendations, and reiterates the district court's conclusion that "the USFS could not possibly warn of a hazard it did not create and of which it had no knowledge." The Government further contends that the decision of how to mark a trail as closed is "grounded in social, economic, and public policy," such as aesthetic and recreation factors, which were similar to the policy considerations in *Katrina Canal Breaches.*

Once again, we must first define the challenged conduct. Gonzalez alleges the USFS "fail[ed] to adequately warn of a known condition and further to warn, based upon the passage of time, of a dangerous condition imputed to the Appellee which caused the Appellant's injuries."[52] The Government characterizes the challenged conduct as "how to mark the trail as closed." Notably, the district court found that "the record reflects that the USFS was unaware of the ramp . . . until after this incident, such that the ramp did not constitute a 'known hazard.'" It further suggested that the USFS did not create the ramp. Because "[f]actual findings are reviewed for clear error,"[53] and because the district court's findings are grounded in the record, this Court accepts the findings that the USFS did not create the ramp, nor know about the ramp.[54] Accordingly, the challenged conduct is the manner in which the trail was marked as closed based on a hazard not known, nor created, by the USFS. Given this, Gonzalez has not pointed to a policy that "specifically prescribes a course of action."[55] Indeed, it is difficult to conceive of a provision mandating the USFS take specific action to warn the public about *unknown* hazards.[56]

But even if we do not accept the district court's findings with respect to the USFS having no knowledge of the bridge,[57] the discretionary function exception would still apply. The USFS's decision to close the Couch Loop Trail in the way it did, i.e., by posting the 8 1/2" x 11" notice at the trailhead, "involve[ed] 'an element of judgment or choice.'"[58] "If a statute, regulation, or policy leaves it to a federal agency or employee to determine when and how to take action, the agency is not bound to act in a particular manner and the exercise of its authority is discretionary."[59] The Sign and Poster Guidelines grant discretion in posting closure signs. For example, Chapter 1.3, "Principles," provides, "[s]igns and posters shall be designed, installed, positioned, and maintained to" "[f]ulfill a legal requirement or an important need," "[c]ommand attention, "[c]onvey a clear, simple meaning," "[c]ommand respect," and "[g]ive adequate time for proper response." Although one could argue these points are mandatory, they do not prescribe how to fulfill them. Moreover, Chapter 5.1, the introduction to the "Trail Signing" chapter, states, "[t]his chapter provides *standards and guidelines* for the use of signs and posters on National Forest System trails."[60]

Still, other provisions in the Sign and Poster Guidelines contain specific instructions. For example, Chapter 1.7.1 indicates designs, colors and "word messages" for signs and posters. It states, "[s]tandard colors have been established for specific purposes and types of signs. It is critical to use the colors specified consistently and only for these purposes to facilitate sign recognition and user response." That being said, Table 5-1 in Chapter 5 blunts the force of Chapter 1.7.1's directive when it gives a "selection guide for materials, colors, and finishes for trail signs, markers, and supports," with several options based on various factors. Reviewing the provisions cumulatively, we detect the requisite element of discretion for the closure sign at issue.[61]

Gonzalez points to Chapter 13.2.4, Sign Placement and Mounting, directing to "[p]ost signs conspicuously. Avoid cluttering signs in one location or where objects may obscure them." But even if this provision can be said to prescribe a specific course of action, Chapter 13.2, discussing "Safety Signs," notes that "[t]hese do not include safety signs designed for roads, recreation sites, [or] *trails*."[62] Although Gonzalez argues "[t]he sign posted by Agent Grice does not meet the standards," she does not explain how. Gonzalez avers, "Agent Grice acknowledged that the sign he posted did not meet the Forestry Standards," but does not provide support. Gonzalez asserts, "[t]he Forestry Service Regulation[s] . . . provide the exact sign, color and instructions for closure of trails and notification of dangerous conditions to patrons on the government's premise." However, Gonzalez fails to specify what provisions regarding sign, color, and instructions the officials had no choice but to follow with respect to creating or posting a closure sign. In short, Gonzalez fails to identify specific provisions that mandate an approach to creating or placing closure signs in these circumstances.

"The next question is whether the government's decision as to the appropriate action for [marking the trail as closed] was based on considerations of public policy."[63] We find it was. For instance, Chapter 5.1 of the Sign and Poster Guidelines states, in relevant part, to select signs to consistently provide: "Route identification," "Guidance and distance [information]," "Safety features, such as snow shelters and resorts," "Route reassurance and confirmation," "User safety: warnings of known hazards," "Notice of restrictions where use control is necessary," and "Protection of resources." These factors—particularly public safety and the protection of resources—are similar to those that this Court has found satisfy the public policy prong of the discretionary function test.[64]

Gonzalez cites to *Cope v. Scott*,[65] for support that a government's failure to place warning signs did not satisfy the policy prong of the discretionary function test. The D.C. Circuit in *Cope* found that "any discretion exercised by the government with respect to where and how to post signs warning of dangerous road conditions did not implicate 'political, social, or economic' policy choices."[66] But *Cope* is inapposite, as it involved signs on a roadway, not in the wilderness.[67] Gonzalez additionally contends "[i]t is inconceivable that the public policy considerations of a pleasant nature experience in an aesthetic atmosphere forego basic patron safety standards." Once again, this argument addresses whether the officials best balanced the policy considerations, when the inquiry is whether the challenged actions were susceptible to policy considerations. Gonzalez further maintains, "[t]he Government offered no evidence to show that its failure to post standard signage as required by regulations for closures was as a result of a policy decision." However, "the proper inquiry . . . is not whether [the official] *in fact* engaged in a policy analysis when reaching his decision but instead whether his decision was 'susceptible to policy analysis.'"[68] Because the USFS's decision about how to post notice of the closed trail was based on "considerations of social, economic, or political public policy"[69] it satisfies the second prong of the discretionary function exception test.

AFFIRMED.

[1] Gonzalez was injured on the ramp before making it to the bridge area.

[2] *Davila v. United States*, 713 F.3d 248, 255 (5th Cir. 2013) (citation omitted).

[3] In re FEMA Trailer Formaldehyde Prod. Liab. Litig. (Mississippi Plaintiffs), 668 F.3d 281, 287 (5th Cir. 2012) (citation omitted) [hereinafter In re FEMA Trailer].

[4] Gonzalez contends that some facts the district court relied upon are disputed. We find the facts pertinent to analyzing the discretionary function exception are undisputed unless noted otherwise. *See In re FEMA Trailer*, 668 F.3d at 287 (court may take into account resolved disputed facts).

[5] *United States v. Navajo Nation*, 537 U.S. 488, 502 (2003) ("It is axiomatic that the United States may not be sued without its consent and that the existence of consent is a prerequisite for jurisdiction." (quotation marks and citation omitted)); *In re FEMA Trailer*, 668 F.3d at 287.

[6] *In re FEMA Trailer,* 668 F.3d at 287 (citing 28 U.S.C. § 1346 and § 2671, et seq.); *In re Supreme Beef Processors, Inc.,* 468 F.3d 248, 252 n. 4. (5th Cir. 2006); *accord Spotts v. United States,* 613 F.3d 559, 566 (5th Cir. 2010).

[7] *Davila,* 713 F.3d at 256.

[8] *United States v. Gaubert,* 499 U.S. 315, 320-22 (1991).

[9] *Tsolmon v. United States,* 841 F.3d, 378, 380 (5th Cir. 2016) (citation omitted).

[10] *Gaubert,* 499 U.S. at 322 (citations omitted).

[11] *Berkovitz by Berkovitz v. United States,* 486 U.S. 531, 536-37 (1988) (citation omitted).

[12] *Spotts,* 613 F.3d at 567 (quoting *Berkovitz by Berkovitz,* 486 U.S at 536).

[13] *Berkovitz by Berkovitz,* 486 U.S. at 536; *accord Tsolmon,* 841 F.3d at 382.

[14] *Davila,* 713 F.3d at 263.

[15] *Spotts,* 613 F.3d at 567 (citation omitted).

[16] *Gaubert,* 499 U.S. at 322 (quoting *Berkovitz,* 486 U.S., at 536)).

[17] *Gibson v. United States,* 809 F.3d, 807, 812 (5th Cir. 2016) (citation omitted).

[18] *Spotts,* 613 F.3d at 572 (quoting *Gaubert,* 499 U.S. at 325); *accord In re FEMA Trailer Formaldehyde Prod. Liab. Litig. (Louisiana Plaintiffs),* 713 F.3d 807, 810 (5th Cir. 2013).

[19] *See Young v. United States,* 769 F.3d 1047, 1054 (9th Cir. 2014) (quotation marks and citation omitted).

[20] *See* The Handbook, Exhibit 01 in Chapter 10, which states for Class 3 developed trails, which include the Bethel Bicycle Trails: "[t]ypically maintenance conducted every 1-3 years or in response to reports of trail or resource damage or significant obstacles to Managed Use and experience level."

[21] *See Young,* 769 F.3d at 1054; *Autery v. United States,* 992 F.2d 1523, 1527 (11th Cir. 1993) ("Before we address whether the government's conduct violated a mandatory regulation or policy, we must determine exactly what conduct is at issue.").

[22] *Autery,* 992 F.2d at 1524.

[23] *Id.* at 1527 (citations omitted).

[24] See id.

[25] *Id.* at 1528.

[26] *Id.*

[27] *Freeman v. United States,* 556 F.3d 326, 338 (5th Cir. 2009).

[28] Emphasis added.

[29] Emphasis added.

[30] *Gaubert,* 499 U.S. at 322 (citations omitted).

[31] *Spotts,* 613 F.3d at 567 (citation omitted).

[32] He also agreed he never read the "forest service handbook."

[33] *Ashford v. United States,* 511 F.3d 501, 505 (5th Cir. 2007) (citation omitted).

[34] *In re Katrina Canal Breaches Litigation,* 696 F.3d 436, 450 (5th Cir. 2012). 28 U.S.C. § 2680(a) states in part: "Any claim . . . based upon the exercise or performance or the failure to exercise or perform a discretionary function or duty

on the part of a federal agency or an employee of the Government, *whether or not the discretion involved be abused."* (emphasis added).

[35] *Berkovitz by Berkovitz,* 486 U.S. at 536-37 (quotation marks and citation omitted).

[36] *See* 809 F.3d, 807, 816-17 (5th Cir. 2016).

[37] *Id.* at 809.

[38] *Id.*

[39] *See id.* at 810 (*e.g.,* "[f]ailing to provide stairs with handrails . . . to inspect mobile homes").

[40] *Id.* at 809.

[41] *Id.* at 813.

[42] *See id.* at 816.

[43] *Id.* at 816-17 (citation omitted).

[44] *Gibson,* 809 F.3d at 815.

[45] 245 F.3d 388 (5th Cir. 1998).

[46] 155 F. App'x. 121 (5th Cir. 2005) (unpublished).

[47] *Gibson,* 809 F.3d at 815 (citations omitted).

[48] *Id.*

[49] *Spotts,* 613 F.3d at 573.

[50] *Berkovitz by Berkovitz,* 486 U.S. at 537 (quotation marks and citation omitted).

[51] *Gaubert,* 499 U.S. at 324-25.

[52] Gonzalez also at times asserts that the USFS failed to adequately warn people about the bridge, but this claim falls short. Gonzalez never made it to the bridge and was not injured on the bridge.

[53] *In re Katrina Canal Breaches Litig.,* 696 F.3d at 444 (citation omitted).

[54] Gonzalez argues that the Mississippi case of *Vu v. Clayton,* 765 So.2d 1253 (Miss. 2000) supports her proposition that the government can be deemed to have constructive knowledge of a hazard based on the passage of time. However, *Vu* concerns a business invitee's premises liability claim based on Mississippi law, not whether constructive knowledge is a viable theory in an FTCA discretionary function exception analysis.

[55] *Berkovitz by Berkovitz,* 486 U.S. at 536.

[56] *Contra Young,* 769 F.3d at 1054 ("In our view, the 'specific allegatio[n] of agency wrongdoing' that we must use in determining whether the discretionary function exception applies in this case is Plaintiffs' allegation that NPS staff failed to warn of a known, latent hazard that the agency itself created.").

[57] The challenged action would then be whether the controlling policies mandated the USFS mark the trail as closed in a specific manner.

[58] *In re Katrina Canal Breaches Litig.,* 696 F.3d at 449 (citations omitted).

[59] *Id.* (quotation marks and citation omitted).

[60] Emphasis added.

[61] *See In re Katrina Canal Breaches Litig.,* 696 F.3d at 452 ("[T]he ostensibly mandatory language, when read in light of the broad goals of the [policies], allowed for the exercise of judgment and choice." (quotation marks and citation omitted)).

[62] Emphasis added.

[63] *Theriot,* 245 F.3d at 399.

[64] *See In re Katrina Canal Breaches Litig.,* 696 F.3d at 452 ("The regulation instructed the Corps to consider several factors, some technical (e.g., shore erosion and accretion) but also many that concern policy (summarized by the catch-all 'needs and welfare of the people'), satisfying prong two as well."); *Theriot,* 245 F.3d at 399-400 (noting policy factors like "the degree of danger an object poses, the vessel traffic type and density, the location of the object in relation to the navigable channel, the history of vessel accidents, and the feasibility and economics, including costs, of erecting and maintaining physical markers in light of the available resources").

[65] 45 F.3d 445 (D.C. Cir. 1995).

[66] *Cope,* 45 F.3d at 446.

[67] *Id.* at 452 ("We agree that in certain circumstances, decisions will be exempt under the FTCA because they involve difficult policy judgments balancing the preservation of the environment against the blight of excess signs. But this is not one of those circumstances. Beach Drive is not the Grand Canyon's Rim Drive, nor Shenandoah's Skyline Drive. Here, the Park Service has chosen to manage the road in a manner more amenable to commuting through nature than communing with it.").

[68] *Spotts,* 613 F.3d at 572 (quoting *Gaubert,* 499 U.S. at 325)).

[69] *Theriot,* 245 F.3d at 397 (citation omitted).

812 F.3d 481 (2016)

TRINITY MARINE PRODUCTS, INC., formerly known as **Trinity Marine Baton Rouge, Inc.**, Plaintiff-Appellant,

v.

UNITED STATES of America, Defendant-Appellee.

No. 14-31130.

United States Court of Appeals, Fifth Circuit.

February 8, 2016.

Trinity Marine Products, Inc. v. US, 812 F. 3d 481 (5th Cir. 2016)

p.484 Appeal from the United States District Court for the Western District of Louisiana.

Frederick W. Addison, III, Esq., Counsel, Nolan Cornelius Knight (argued), Munsch, Hardt, Kopf & Harr, P.C., Dallas, TX, John E. Heinrich, Baton Rouge, LA, for Plaintiff-Appellant.

David Harrison Fulcher (argued), U.S. Attorney's Office, Jackson, MS, for Defendant-Appellee.

Before STEWART, Chief Judge, and BARKSDALE, and PRADO, Circuit Judges.

EDWARD C. PRADO, Circuit Judge:

In 1999, Plaintiff-Appellant Trinity Marine Products, Inc. ("Trinity"), was indicted for illegally storing hazardous waste without a permit. This charge, however, was dismissed in 2003, and it was subsequently revealed several years later that two of the federal agents involved in the investigation and prosecution had used the case as a means to engage in an extramarital affair with one another. It was also disclosed that one of these agents had committed perjury and obstructed justice in attempting to conceal the affair and the true motivation for the prosecution against Trinity. Trinity filed an administrative claim in 2012 and a complaint in federal court in 2013 under the Federal Tort Claims Act ("FTCA") alleging malicious prosecution. Based on the recommendation of a magistrate judge, the district court dismissed Trinity's FTCA claim as time barred. Because we hold that the district court erred by failing to equitably toll the statute of limitations, we affirm in part and reverse in part.

I. FACTUAL AND PROCEDURAL BACKGROUND

In 1996, agents from the Federal Bureau of Investigation ("FBI"), Environmental Protection Agency ("EPA"), United States Marshal Service, Coast Guard, and Louisiana State law enforcement executed a search warrant on a facility owned by the Canal Refining Company ("Canal"). *Vidrine v. United States,* 846 F.Supp.2d 550, 555 (W.D.La.2011). This facility was managed by Hubert P. Vidrine Jr. and used by Trinity to transport oil. *Id.* at 555, 574-75. The warrant was based on the belief that Canal was illegally accepting and receiving hazardous materials without the required permits. *See id.* at 573.

Among the agents involved in executing this warrant were Keith Phillips of the EPA and Ekko Barnhill of the FBI. *Id.* at 574. While they were working on the case, Agents Phillips and Barnhill began having an affair. *Id.* at 585. According to Agent Barnhill, they were only physically intimate while working together on the Canal case, as the investigation offered an opportunity for them to be together without raising the suspicions of Agent Phillips's wife. *See id.* at 624.

In 1999, a federal grand jury indicted Vidrine and Trinity for violating 42 U.S.C. § 6928(d)(2), which makes it illegal to store "hazardous waste ... without a permit." *See Vidrine,* 846 F.Supp.2d at 555, 561. The key to the Government's case was the testimony of Mike Franklin, a hydrocarbons broker who happened to be at the Canal refinery facility when the search warrant was executed. *See id.* at 580, 582. According to Agent Barnhill's notes from a 1998 interview, Franklin "obtained samples of the product TRINITY wanted to sell. These samples were given to [a laboratory] for testing. Results of the test showed one of the sampled products to be over 1000 ppm of chlorinated solvents." *Id.* at 583 (emphasis omitted). p.485 These test results were essential to the Government's case because federal regulations provide that "[i]f the used oil contains greater than or equal to 1,000 ppm total halogens, it is presumed to be a hazardous waste." 40 C.F.R. § 279.53. Chlorinated solvents are a type of halogen. *See Vidrine v. United States,* No. 6:07-CV-1204, 2012 WL 253124, at *35 (W.D.La. Jan. 26, 2012).

No such test results were ever found to exist, however. *Vidrine,* 846 F.Supp.2d at 594. Instead, each of the samples for which test results were available contradicted Franklin's allegations. *Id.* In light of these and other problems with Franklin's story and credibility, the court barred his testimony. *Id.* at 597. With its key witness excluded, the Government moved to voluntarily dismiss the charges. *Id.* at 580 n. 62.

Vidrine filed an administrative claim under the FTCA in 2005 and a complaint in federal court asserting a malicious-prosecution claim in 2007. *Id.* at 556-57. Vidrine's complaint alleged, among other things, that Franklin was not a credible witness and that there was "no tangible, physical evidence to corroborate" Franklin's assertions. It did not contain any allegations regarding Agent Barnhill and Agent Phillips's affair. During the course of litigation in Vidrine's federal case, the district court unsealed the grand jury transcripts from the underlying criminal case. In light of this new evidence, Vidrine filed an amended complaint in 2009 that added the allegation that Agent Phillips provided false testimony to the grand jury. The amended complaint also did not mention the affair or allege that it was the motivation for the investigation or prosecution.

The case proceeded to a bench trial and in September 2011 the court awarded Vidrine $1.677 million in damages for malicious prosecution. In its ruling, the court found that "Agent Phillips deliberately used his investigation and prosecution of Hubert Vidrine to foster, further, facilitate and cloak his extra-marital affair with Agent Barnhill, and perhaps, to exert improper influence over the manner in which she investigated and reported upon this case." *Id.* at 624. The court also found that Agent Phillips took further steps during discovery and the trial "to cover up the affair," including perjuring himself and obstructing justice by repeatedly calling Agent Barnhill to "remind her he had testified that their relationship during the Vidrine investigation was purely professional." *Id.* at 626.

Trinity claims that it did not learn about the extramarital affair and its concealment until 2011 when one of its employees read a blog post which mentioned a Department of Justice press release regarding Agent Phillips. The July 27, 2011 press release stated that Agent Phillips had been indicted for perjury and obstruction of justice for falsely testifying in a deposition "that he did not have an affair with the FBI Special Agent, when, in fact, he did," and "committ[ing] perjury when he testified falsely about the affair." The press release also stated that Agent Phillips obstructed justice by "contact[ing] the FBI Special Agent to influence her not to disclose the existence of the affair." Agent Phillips pleaded guilty and admitted that "[w]hile under oath, [he] testified falsely that he did not have an extramarital affair with FBI Special Agent A, testimony he knew at the time to be false" and that information about the affair "was material to the *Vidrine* civil matter at the time [he] testified falsely."

Trinity filed an administrative FTCA complaint on July 25, 2012 — nine months after Vidrine's FTCA claim was decided and roughly a year after it claims to have p.486 learned about the affair. Trinity then filed a lawsuit for malicious prosecution in federal court on August 23, 2013, invoking the discovery rule and equitable tolling of the statute of limitations. Trinity alleged that it had no reasonable basis to bring its malicious-prosecution claim until it discovered Agent Phillips's deception in July 2011, and, therefore, its claim did not accrue until then. Trinity further alleged that due to Agent Phillips's concealment, it could not have discovered the basis for its claim "until at least March 2011, when an *internal* investigation conducted by the United States, for the first time uncovered evidence" that "an investigative and law enforcement officer *intentionally* had engaged in misconduct to conceal the improper motives for the criminal prosecution of Trinity."

Reasoning that the FTCA's two-year statute of limitations was jurisdictional, a magistrate judge issued a recommendation that the complaint be dismissed for lack of subject-matter jurisdiction. The district judge adopted the magistrate judge's recommendation and entered judgment for the Government. Trinity timely appealed. While briefing was pending in the present appeal, the Supreme Court decided *United States v. Kwai Fun Wong* and held that "the FTCA's time bars are nonjurisdictional and subject to equitable tolling." ___ U.S. ___, 135 S.Ct. 1625, 1638, 191 L.Ed.2d 533 (2015).

II. JURISDICTION AND STANDARD OF REVIEW

The district court had "the jurisdiction to determine its own jurisdiction." *Familia De Boom v. Arosa Mercantil, S.A.*, 629 F.2d 1134, 1137 (5th Cir.1980). To the extent the district court addressed the merits, it had original jurisdiction under 28 U.S.C. § 1346(b)(1). This Court has appellate jurisdiction to review the district court's final decision dismissing the complaint under 28 U.S.C. § 1291.

The district court dismissed Trinity's FTCA claim for lack of subject matter jurisdiction under Federal Rule of Civil Procedure 12(b)(1), concluding that the FTCA's statute of limitations was jurisdictional and had run. In the alternative, the district court concluded that even assuming the FTCA's statute of limitations was not jurisdictional, equitable tolling would not apply in these circumstances.

Because the district court held that the FTCA's statute of limitations was jurisdictional, it concluded that Trinity, as the claimant, bore the burden of showing that the limitations period had not run. However, after the district court made its ruling, the Supreme Court held in *Wong* that this is not the case. *See* 135 S.Ct. at 1638 ("[W]e hold that the FTCA's time bars are nonjurisdictional...."). Accordingly, the district court should have considered the Government's motion to dismiss under Rule 12(b)(6) rather than 12(b)(1), *see* Fed.R.Civ.P. 12(b), and held that the FTCA's statute of limitations is an affirmative defense for which the Government has the burden of proof, *see Sec. Indus. Ins. Co. v. United States,* 702 F.2d 1234, 1251 (5th Cir.1983). That the district court considered this matter under Rule 12(b)(1), however, does not require reversal where "a remand would only require a new Rule 12(b)(6) label for the same Rule 12(b)(1) conclusion." *Morrison v. Nat'l Austl. Bank Ltd.,* 561 U.S. 247, 254, 130 S.Ct. 2869, 177 L.Ed.2d 535 (2010). Nor must we reverse because the district court erred in determining which party bore the burden of proof. Rather, "this court may 'affirm the district court's judgment on any grounds supported by the record.'" *United States ex rel. Farmer v. City of Hous.,* 523 F.3d 333, 338 n. 8 (5th Cir.2008) (quoting *Sobranes Recovery Pool I, LLC v.* p.487 *Todd & Hughes Constr. Corp.,* 509 F.3d 216, 221 (5th Cir.2007)).

The district court also made summary judgment rulings. For instance, it held that even if the FTCA's statute of limitations was not jurisdictional and equitable tolling could apply, Trinity would not be entitled to equitable tolling. This holding was unrelated to the district court's examination of its jurisdiction and necessarily relied on evidence outside the pleadings. Specifically, the district court held that "there is no evidence that Trinity Marine did anything between the date that the indictment was dismissed and the date this suit was filed that might be perceived as diligent pursuit of its legal remedies" and found Trinity's conduct particularly troubling "when its inaction is compared with the actions taken by Mr. Vidrine."

"Although the district court did not explicitly inform the parties that it was converting the motion to dismiss into a summary judgment motion, 'appellate courts may take the district court's consideration of matters outside the pleadings to trigger an implicit conversion.'" *Bellotte v. Edwards,* 388 Fed.Appx. 334, 337 (4th Cir. 2010) (per curiam) (quoting *Bosiger v. U.S. Airways,* 510 F.3d 442, 450 (4th Cir.2007)); *see also, e.g. Exxon Corp. v. Md. Cas. Co.,* 599 F.2d 659, 661 (5th Cir.1979). Under Rule 12(d), a district court may convert a motion to dismiss to a motion for summary judgment so long as it gives the parties a "reasonable opportunity to present all the material that is pertinent to the motion." Fed.R.Civ.P. 12(d).

Here, the parties had ample notice that the district court might consider the extra-pleading material included with the Government's motion to dismiss. Moreover, Trinity filed its own motion for summary judgment that relied on evidence outside the pleadings. Thus, we consider the district court to have implicitly converted the Government's motion to dismiss into a motion for summary judgment. Summary judgment is appropriate where, after "[t]he evidence of the non-movant is ... believed, and all justifiable inferences are to be drawn in his favor," *Anderson v. Liberty Lobby, Inc.,* 477 U.S. 242, 255, 106 S.Ct. 2505, 91 L.Ed.2d 202 (1986), no genuine issue of material fact exists and the moving party is entitled to judgment as a matter of law, Fed.R.Civ.P. 56(a).

III. DISCUSSION

The district court held that Trinity's malicious-prosecution claim accrued on dismissal of the indictment and that because the FTCA's statute of limitations was jurisdictional it could not be equitably tolled. The district court also held that even if it could be tolled, Trinity had not met its burden of establishing that equitable tolling would be appropriate. Finally, the district court rejected Trinity's arguments that the statute of limitations should be tolled under the doctrines of judicial and collateral estoppel. Trinity appeals these rulings.

A. Accrual

Under the FTCA, tort actions are barred "against the federal government unless the claim is first presented to the appropriate federal agency 'within two years after such claim accrues.'" *Johnson v. United States,* 460 F.3d 616, 621 (5th Cir.2006) (quoting *United States v. Kubrick,* 444 U.S. 111, 113, 100 S.Ct. 352, 62 L.Ed.2d 259 (1979)). "The general rule under the FTCA is that a tort action accrues at the time of a plaintiff's injury." *Id.* In *Dubose v. Kansas City Southern Railway Co.,* we explained that the discovery rule governs the accrual of causes of action in federal cases where a plaintiff claims it was not aware of the injury or could not have discovered facts critical to p.488 ascertaining the injury's cause. *See* 729 F.2d 1026, 1030 (5th Cir.1984). Under the discovery rule, "a claim accrues when a plaintiff knows both her injury and its cause." *In re FEMA Trailer Formaldehyde Prods. Liab. Litig.,* 646 F.3d 185, 190 (5th Cir.2011), *abrogated on other grounds by Wong,* 135 S.Ct. 1625. In cases of alleged malicious prosecution, numerous federal courts, including this one, have uniformly concluded that a claim accrues with the termination of the criminal proceeding against the plaintiff. *See, e.g., Brummett v. Camble,* 946 F.2d 1178, 1184 (5th Cir. 1991).

There is no dispute that Trinity was aware of its injury no later than 2003 when the criminal indictment was dismissed. The issue, then, is whether Trinity was aware of the causal connection between its injury and the defendant's actions at this time. The causal-connection element is met if the plaintiff "had knowledge of facts that would lead a reasonable person (a) to conclude that there was a causal connection between the injury and [the defendant's actions] or (b) to seek professional advice, and then, with that advice, to conclude that there was a causal connection." *Adrian v. Selbe,* 364 Fed. Appx. 934, 938 (5th Cir.2010) (per curiam) (alteration omitted) (quoting *Piotrowski v. City of Hous.,* 51 F.3d 512, 516 (5th Cir. 1995)).

In *Ortega v. United States,* 547 Fed. Appx. 384 (5th Cir.2013) (per curiam), this Court rejected a claim similar to the one Trinity makes here. The plaintiffs in *Ortega* argued that their FTCA claims, which alleged that they had been illegally removed, "could not have accrued until May 15, 2009, at the earliest because that is when they learned ... that Mr. Ortega's removal was conducted without a valid removal order." *Id.* at 387. Holding that their claims were nevertheless untimely, we reasoned that the plaintiffs' contention "that they did not discover that there was any injury *at all* until they learned that there had been no removal order against Mr. Ortega" was really an "attempt to define their 'injury' by the *unlawfulness* of Mr.

Ortega's deportation, rather than by the deportation *per se.* However, to define a tortious injury by the unlawfulness of the tortious act causing the injury is circular." *Id.* That the absence of a removal order no doubt strengthened the plaintiffs' claim was irrelevant to accrual of the statute of limitations. Rather, we explained that:

> The Ortegas knew that they had suffered injuries immediately after Mr. Ortega's arrest and deportation on May 28, 2008, and they knew that those injuries were caused by federal agents. These constitute the sort of facts that we consider 'the critical facts of [a plaintiff's] injury and its cause,' which establish accrual.

Id. (alteration in original) (quoting *Dubose,* 729 F.2d at 1030).

This same principle applies with equal force here. Trinity knew that the charges against it were dismissed in 2003 and that any related injury had been caused by agents of the federal government. While information about Agent Phillips and Agent Barnhill's affair certainly strengthens Trinity's claim, it does not alter when the claim accrued. Accordingly, the district court correctly concluded that Trinity's claim accrued before 2009.

B. Equitable Tolling

The fact that Trinity's malicious-prosecution claim accrued as early as 2003, however, is not fatal to its case. In *Wong,* the Supreme Court held that equitable tolling may be applied to claims under the FTCA. 135 S.Ct. at 1638. "The doctrine of equitable tolling preserves a plaintiff's p.489 claims when strict application of the statute of limitations would be inequitable." *Alexander v. Cockrell,* 294 F.3d 626, 629 (5th Cir.2002) (quoting *United States v. Patterson,* 211 F.3d 927, 930 (5th Cir. 2000)). As "[t]he claimant," Trinity "bears the burden of justifying equitable tolling." *Hood v. Sears Roebuck & Co.,* 168 F.3d 231, 232 (5th Cir.1999). This Court has recognized several grounds for equitable tolling, including where a plaintiff is unaware "of the facts giving rise to the claim because of the defendant's intentional concealment of them." *Granger v. Aaron's, Inc.,* 636 F.3d 708, 712 (5th Cir.2011).

The principal issue before this Court is whether Agent Phillips's intentional concealment of his extramarital affair with another investigator should equitably toll the statute of limitations. This Court has previously considered several cases in which a plaintiff asserts that it was prevented from bringing a timely claim due to the defendant's intentional concealment of material facts. In such cases, this Court has held that the limitations period may be tolled "by proving two elements: first, that the defendants concealed the conduct complained of, and second, that the plaintiff failed, despite the exercise of due diligence on his part, to discover the facts that form the basis of his claim." *Texas v. Allan Constr. Co.,* 851 F.2d 1526, 1528 (5th Cir. 1988) (alteration omitted) (quoting *In re Beef Indus. Antitrust Litig.,* 600 F.2d 1148, 1169 (5th Cir.1979)).

The first of these factors is plainly met in this case. Agent Phillips lied under oath and was ultimately charged with, and imprisoned for, perjury and obstruction of justice for his attempts to conceal the affair and material facts relevant to the Trinity prosecution. Trinity argues that the second factor is also met in this case because no amount of diligence would have revealed Agent Phillips's deceptions prior to the release of the government's internal investigation in 2011. The Government objects and contends that equitable tolling should not apply because Trinity failed to take action for eight years following the dismissal of the indictment, during which time its co-defendant, Vidrine, filed suit and succeeded on its malicious-prosecution claim.

While the Government is correct to point out that equitable tolling "is not intended for those who sleep on their rights," *Covey v. Ark. River Co.*, 865 F.2d 660, 662 (5th Cir.1989), this Court held in *Beef Industries* that "[t]he mere filing of a similar lawsuit, without more, does not necessarily give 'good ground' [to support the plaintiff's lawsuit] because that suit might well be frivolous or baseless," *Beef Indus.*, 600 F.2d at 1171. Rather, as we explained in *Allan Construction:* "To justify summary judgment, ... defendants would have had to prove that the plaintiffs had access to information that would independently verify the allegations in the [similar lawsuit's] complaint." 851 F.2d at 1533. Put another way, a defendant can establish that summary judgment is warranted only if it "demonstrate[s] conclusively:" (1) "that the plaintiffs, through the exercise of reasonable diligence, would have discovered adequate ground for filing suit," *id.* (quoting *Beef Indus.*, 600 F.2d at 1171), and (2) either that there is no evidence of reasonable diligence, or, if the plaintiff produces "some evidence of its diligence," that "no reasonable jury could consider [the plaintiff's] attempts reasonably diligent," *id.* at 1534.

A claim for malicious prosecution under the FTCA is dependent on the substantive law of the state where the claim arose, *Cleveland ex rel. Cleveland v. United States*, 457 F.3d 397, 403 (5th Cir. 2006), in this case, Louisiana. Under Louisiana law, a claim of malicious prosecution p.490 requires showing both an "absence of probable cause" and "the presence of malice." *Miller v. E. Baton Rouge Par. Sheriff's Dep't*, 511 So.2d 446, 452 (La.1987). Further, 28 U.S.C. § 2680(h)'s "law enforcement proviso" precludes FTCA malicious-prosecution claims unless the claim is premised on the "acts or omissions of [federal] investigative or law enforcement officers." Thus, the only evidentiary basis for a viable malicious-prosecution FTCA claim "well grounded in fact" within the meaning of *Allan Construction,* would be evidence to support Vidrine's allegations that federal law enforcement officers maliciously instigated the prosecution despite a lack of probable cause.

The Government argues that Trinity would have discovered evidence to independently verify Vidrine's allegations had it exercised reasonable diligence when Agent Phillips's grand jury testimony in the underlying criminal case was unsealed in 2007 and then referenced in Vidrine's amended complaint in 2009. However, neither the unsealed grand jury testimony nor Vidrine's amended complaint *conclusively establish* that Trinity would have discovered evidence to verify Vidrine's allegations that federal law enforcement officials maliciously instigated the case against Vidrine and Trinity despite a lack of probable cause. For instance, the judge who presided over the underlying criminal case, after reviewing the grand jury testimony, concluded that it did not, on its face, contain evidence of impropriety. Even Vidrine's 2009 amended complaint, which referred to the grand jury testimony, stated that the allegation was not based on concrete evidence but rather "upon information and belief" and states: *"If subsequent discovery proves this to be true, then the conduct of such ...* employees of the Government... would constitute [a] ...

conspiracy to maliciously prosecute Mr. Vidrine." Although the grand jury testimony was *later* found to be "replete with misrepresentations, falsehoods, omissions, hyperbole, and inflammatory statements," *Vidrine,* 846 F.Supp.2d at 639, information about the affair as the motive to perpetuate an investigation lacking probable cause was only discovered as a result of the Government's internal investigation, which did not become available until July 2011 — less than two years before Trinity filed its administrative claim. Further, trial testimony in the *Vidrine* civil case provided evidence that Agent Phillips continued to conceal the affair well into 2011. Thus, the Government has not met its burden of conclusively establishing that Trinity would have discovered evidence to support the allegations in Vidrine's complaint through the exercise of reasonable diligence prior to 2011. Accordingly, the district court's holding in this regard must be reversed.

C. Judicial and Collateral Estoppel

Trinity argues that the district court erred in finding that the statute of limitations should not be tolled under the equitable doctrines of judicial and collateral estoppel. The doctrine of judicial estoppel prevents "litigants from asserting contradictory positions for tactical gain." *Republic of Ecuador v. Connor,* 708 F.3d 651, 654 (5th Cir.2013). Judicial estoppel applies only if "the following elements are present: (1) the party against whom judicial estoppel is sought has asserted a legal position which is plainly inconsistent with a prior position; (2) a court accepted the prior position; and (3) the party did not act inadvertently." *Reed v. City of Arlington,* 650 F.3d 571, 574 (5th Cir.2011).

Trinity argues that the Government should be judicially estopped from asserting that Trinity had a factual basis for its malicious-prosecution claim because p.491 the Government vigorously defended itself on the merits in the *Vidrine* litigation. However, asserting that one plaintiff's case is weak in one proceeding is not inconsistent with arguing that a second plaintiff's case is untimely. Further, the court did not accept the Government's prior position in *Vidrine.* Instead, the court in *Vidrine* awarded the plaintiff a nearly $1.7 million judgment. Accordingly, judicial estoppel does not apply because the Government has not taken an inconsistent position that has been adopted by a court.

Under the doctrine of collateral estoppel, "once a court has decided an issue of fact or law necessary to its judgment, that decision is conclusive in a subsequent suit based on a different cause of action involving a party to the prior litigation." *United States v. Mendoza,* 464 U.S. 154, 158, 104 S.Ct. 568, 78 L.Ed.2d 379 (1984). A plaintiff seeking to invoke this doctrine "offensively" must establish four elements:

> (i) The issue under consideration in a subsequent action must be identical to the issue litigated in a prior action; (ii) The issue must have been fully and vigorously litigated in the prior action; (iii) The issue must have been necessary to support the judgment in the prior case; and (iv) There must be no special circumstance that would render [estoppel] inappropriate or unfair.

Kariuki v. Tarango, 709 F.3d 495, 506 (5th Cir.2013) (alteration in original) (quoting *United States v. Shanbaum,* 10 F.3d 305, 311 (5th Cir.1994)).

Here, Trinity fails to establish the first element because the issue in this case is not "identical to the issue litigated in [the] prior action." *Id.* In essence, Trinity argues that the Government should be estopped from arguing that Trinity had a factual basis to investigate a potential malicious-prosecution claim because the court in *Vidrine* found that Agent Phillips went to great lengths to cover up the affair while the *Vidrine* case was ongoing and that Agent Phillips's extramarital affair "was, at least in part (if not in whole), a motivation for Agent Phillips'[s] continued pursuit of Hubert Vidrine [and Trinity], without probable cause." *Vidrine,* 846 F.Supp.2d at 624-25. But this argument overlooks the fact that the Government is not contesting Agent Phillips's fraudulent concealment; instead, they are contesting Trinity's lack of diligence in pursuing its claim. The diligence issue, which pertains to timeliness under the equitable-tolling doctrine, was never at issue in the *Vidrine* litigation. Thus, the equitable-tolling diligence issue is not identical to the issue in the *Vidrine* litigation and collateral estoppel does not apply.

IV. CONCLUSION

For the foregoing reasons, the district court's judgment is AFFIRMED in part and REVERSED in part, and this matter is remanded for further proceedings consistent with this opinion.

841 F.3d 378 (2016)

Amarsaikhan TSOLMON, Plaintiff-Appellant,
v.
UNITED STATES of America, Defendant-Appellee.

No. 15-20609.

United States Court of Appeals, Fifth Circuit.

Filed November 7, 2016.

Tsolmon v. US, 841 F. 3d 378 (5th Cir. 2016)

p.380 Appeal from the United States District Court for the Southern District of Texas.

Gregory Romanovsky, Romanovsky Law Offices, Boston, MA, for Plaintiff-Appellant.

Steve I. Frank, U.S. Department of Justice, Civil Division, Appellate Section, Washington, DC, Fred Turner Hinrichs, U.S. Attorney's Office, Houston, TX, for Defendant-Appellee.

Before KING, SMITH, and COSTA, Circuit Judges.

GREGG COSTA, Circuit Judge:

The Federal Tort Claims Act (FTCA) waives sovereign immunity for many torts committed by federal employees. The statute's "discretionary function" exception preserves the federal government's immunity, however, when an employee's acts involve the exercise of judgment or choice. *United States v. Gaubert,* 499 U.S. 315, 322, 111 S.Ct. 1267, 113 L.Ed.2d 335 (1991). We must decide whether an investigation into someone's immigration status is considered discretionary when that investigation culminates in a detainment mandated by agency policy.

I.

Late one Friday evening, Amarsaikhan Tsolmon was riding on a Greyhound bus to visit his mother in northern Louisiana. The bus was stopped in Lake Charles, Louisiana by Customs and Border Protection (CBP) agents Robert Wilson and Michael Lewandowski, who boarded the bus to perform a routine check of the passengers' immigration status.[1]

When Wilson reached Tsolmon's seat, Tsolmon stated that he was a "Temporary Visitor." This was correct, as Tsolmon is a Mongolian citizen lawfully in the United States on an H-1B temporary worker visa. But Tsolmon did not have a physical copy of his immigration papers, despite a law requiring registered aliens eighteen or over to carry identifying documents. 8 U.S.C. § 1304(e). Instead, he could only produce a Texas identification card.

After being unable to verify Tsolmon's status through CBP's New Orleans dispatch, Wilson escorted him off the bus to continue the investigation. While Wilson contacted CBP to run additional searches, Tsolmon called his roommate in Houston to try to get more identifying information on his immigration status. The roommate provided Wilson information over the p.381 phone and emailed Tsolmon a photo of his I-94 form and Mongolian passport. But for reasons disputed by the parties Wilson was still unable to verify Tsolmon's status. The records check from other CBP offices incorrectly indicated that Tsolmon was an F-2 visa overstay, with no mention of his H-1B temporary worker visa.

With no information validating Tsolmon's legal status, Wilson arrested Tsolmon, took him to the Lake Charles CBP station, and conducted further computer searches to find a record of Tsolmon's visa. Wilson also contacted his Supervisory Patrol Agent Daniel Stanley, who recommended continuing the computer searches and contacting Tsolmon's relatives to see if anyone had identifying numbers or documents on Tsolmon's status. Tsolmon and Wilson spoke on the phone with Tsolmon's mother, but Wilson was still unable to locate records verifying Tsolmon's claimed status. After several hours of searching, Wilson decided to process Tsolmon as a nonimmigrant overstay and issued him a Notice to Appear on the charge that Tsolmon was in violation of his F-2 visa — the only documentation Wilson uncovered through his record search at the time.

Tsolmon was taken to the Southwest Louisiana Correctional Center early Saturday morning, pursuant to CBP policy requiring the detainment of anyone who is issued a Notice to Appear. Tsolmon asserts that at the Correctional Center he was subjected to a medical exam and tuberculosis test, confined in an overcrowded cell without access to clean drinking water, not given access to a phone, and not given paperwork documenting his detainment.

On Sunday, Stanley arrived at the CBP station and conducted a more extensive search for all persons with the last name Tsolmon in a database that Wilson had previously searched. After a few hours, Stanley at last found a record verifying that Tsolmon held a valid H-1B visa. Later that evening, Tsolmon was taken to the Lake Charles CBP station to be released. Soon after, his brother arrived from Houston and drove him home.

Tsolmon filed an administrative claim with CBP alleging that the incident violated his Fourth Amendment rights and constituted false arrest, false imprisonment, intentional infliction of emotional distress, and negligent infliction of emotional distress. After CBP denied his claim, Tsolmon filed the present suit. He originally asserted FTCA claims against the government and *Bivens* claims against the individuals involved in his detention.

His amended complaint asserts only two causes of action against the United States under the FTCA. The first alleges false arrest and false imprisonment under Louisiana tort law based on his "forty-eight hour arrest, detention and imprisonment... [that] was unlawful because it was done without a warrant and without probable cause" in violation of the Fourth Amendment and 8 U.S.C. § 1347(b). The second alleges negligence under Louisiana law, based on allegations that both Wilson and Stanley were "negligent in not verifying Plaintiff's immigration status for almost two days despite having the necessary information to do so." The government moved to dismiss under Rule 12(b)(1) for lack of subject matter jurisdiction.

The district court granted the government's motion, concluding that (1) the alleged conduct falls within the discretionary function exception to the FTCA's waiver of sovereign immunity, 28 U.S.C. § 2680(a), and (2) that the law enforcement proviso, 28 U.S.C. § 2680(h), does not apply.[2] Tsolmon p.382 appeals only the district court's decision that the discretionary function exception applies.

II.

We review *de novo* a dismissal for lack of subject matter jurisdiction. *Ramming v. United States,* 281 F.3d 158, 161 (5th Cir. 2001). In deciding such a motion, courts can consider: "(1) the complaint alone; (2) the complaint supplemented by undisputed facts evidenced in the record; or (3) the complaint supplemented by undisputed facts plus the court's resolution of disputed facts." *Id.* The district court considered the well-pleaded fact from the amended complaint, undisputed facts in the record, and disputed facts viewed in the light most favorable to Tsolmon; it did not resolve disputed facts.

III.

The FTCA is a limited waiver of sovereign immunity that allows plaintiffs to bring state law tort actions against the federal government. 28 U.S.C. § 2674. Courts consider whether the FTCA applies via a Rule 12(b)(1) motion, because whether the government has waived its sovereign immunity goes to the court's subject matter jurisdiction. *Willoughby v. United States ex rel. U.S. Dep't of the Army,* 730 F.3d 476, 479 (5th Cir. 2013); *see also* 28 U.S.C. § 1346(b)(1). Waiver of sovereign immunity is strictly construed, meaning uncertainty is decided in favor of the government. *Willoughby,* 730 F.3d at 480.

The discretionary function exception is one of several limitations on the FTCA's waiver. The exception preserves the government's sovereign immunity when the plaintiff's claim is based on an act by a government employee that falls within that employee's discretionary authority. 28 U.S.C. § 2680(a). Whether an official's actions fall within the exception involves two inquiries: (1) "the conduct must be a 'matter of choice for the acting employee,'" *Spotts v. United States,* 613 F.3d 559, 567 (5th Cir. 2010) (quoting *Berkovitz ex rel. Berkovitz v. United States,* 486 U.S. 531, 536, 108 S.Ct. 1954, 100 L.Ed.2d 531 (1988)); and (2) "the judgment [must be] of the kind that the discretionary function exception was designed to shield,'" *id.* at 568 (quoting *United States v. Gaubert,* 499 U.S. 315, 322-23, 111 S.Ct. 1267, 113 L.Ed.2d 335 (1991)). The plaintiff has the burden of establishing that the discretionary function exception does not apply. *Spotts,* 613 F.3d at 569.

Tsolmon appeals only the district court's determination that the challenged conduct involved judgment or choice. He invokes case law recognizing that if "a federal statute, regulation, or policy specifically prescribes a course of action for an employee to follow," then the government employee does not truly have a choice (or at least a choice that the law will recognize as falling within the discretionary function exception). *Berkovitz,* 486 U.S. at 536, 108 S.Ct. 1954. One example a court has recognized is when a government agent lies or mischaracterizes evidence in a criminal complaint, as the Federal Rules of Criminal Procedure require allegations in a criminal complaint to be sworn as true. *Camacho v. Cannella,* 2012 WL 3719749, at *10 (W.D. Tex. Aug. 27, 2012) (citing FED. R. CRIM. P. 3). Tsolmon argues that his case also involves a mandate that eliminated the officer's discretion, citing the CBP policy requiring officers to detain all aliens issued a Notice to Appear. Although the allegedly negligent actions of the officers led to the issuance of the Notice to Appear, Tsolmon p.383 argues that the decision to detain him after that Notice was issued was nondiscretionary because CBP policy required it.

But the district court determined that the conduct at issue is "the conclusions the CBP agents drew from their investigation of Tsolmon's immigration status and the basis and timing of Agent Wilson's decision to issue [a Notice to Appear] charging Tsolmon with being an alien illegally present in the United States, which [ ] resulted in Tsolmon's arrest and [ ] incarceration." The court based that conclusion largely on the amended complaint, which focuses on the steps the officers took to try to verify Tsolmon's immigration status.

The district court's framing of the relevant conduct is more consistent with Tsolmon's allegations. The amended complaint speaks at length about Wilson's investigation into Tsolmon's immigration status, but never mentions the CBP policy he now asserts is at issue. Nor did Tsolmon raise the CBP policy in his administrative complaint. *See* 28 U.S.C. § 2675 (requiring administrative exhaustion for FTCA claims). Tsolmon's false arrest claim also demonstrates the difficulty of his attempt to separate the policy from the investigative steps. The policy standing alone did not mandate Tsolmon's detention; the preliminary determination to issue a Notice to Appear was a crucial step in the chain of events. We thus evaluate the application of the discretionary function exception with respect to the conduct challenged in Tsolmon's amended complaint, not in the context of a challenge to the CBP policy on which he now focuses.[3]

Having identified the relevant allegations as Wilson's investigation into Tsolmon's immigration statute and decision to issue the Notice to Appear, the remaining analysis is straightforward. "[D]ecisions on when, where, and how to investigate and whether to prosecute" have long been found to be core examples of discretionary conduct for which the United States maintains its immunity. *Sutton v. United States,* 819 F.2d 1289, 1294-95 (5th Cir. 1987). We have applied that not just to officials enforcing the criminal laws, but also to officials enforcing the immigration laws. *Nguyen v. United States,* 2003 WL 1922969, at *1-2 (5th Cir. Mar. 31, 2003). The investigation into Tsolmon's status demonstrates the numerous choices involved in conducting such an inquiry. Wilson had to decide: whether to further investigate Tsolmon after discovering he did not have his immigration papers; which searches to run in the CBP database; with whom to communicate to try to verify Tsolmon's status; and whether to ultimately issue a Notice to Appear when he was unable to verify Tsolmon's status.

Tsolmon relies on a statute to avoid a holding that the agents' conduct falls within the discretionary function exception. This time making an argument that is contained in his pleadings, he contends that the officers exceeded their authority under 8 U.S.C. § 1357(a)(2) when they detained him. That statute provides that to make an arrest without a warrant, an officer p.384 must: (1) have "reason to believe" that a person is in the United States in violation of immigration law or regulation and (2) think that the person "is likely to escape before a warrant can be obtained for his arrest." *Id.* Tsolmon argues that Wilson did not have reason to believe that he was in violation of immigration law or likely to escape before a warrant could be issued.

Tsolmon is correct that the discretionary function exception does not protect officers who break the law or exceed their authority. *Sutton,* 819 F.2d at 1293. As the district court correctly noted, however, the exception fails to protect officers only when the statute governing the action "giv[es] *specific* direction as to any of these functions in a way that would make [the acts] nondiscretionary." *Guile v. United States,* 422 F.3d 221, 231 (5th Cir. 2005). In other words, officers are unprotected only when they use their discretion to act in violation of a statute or policy that specifically directs them to act otherwise. *See, e.g., Collins v. United States,* 783 F.2d 1225, 1230-31 (5th Cir. 1986) (noting that a regulation at issue provided "no room for policy judgment or decision" once certain conditions were met). Section 1357(a)(2), with its judgment-laden "reasonable belief" standard, is not such a statute.[4]

* * *

The judgment of the district court is AFFIRMED.

[1] Given that this case was dismissed at the pleading stage, the recitation of facts is based on Tsolmon's allegations, which must be taken as true at this stage. The recitation is also supplemented with undisputed facts from the government's motion to dismiss.

[2] The law enforcement proviso extends the FTCA's waiver of sovereign immunity to claims against law enforcement officers "arising... out of assault, battery, false imprisonment, false arrest, abuse of process, or malicious prosecution." 28 U.S.C. § 2680(h).

[3] We thus do not decide whether detainment under the policy itself is an act of discretion. To frame that question, however, is to identify the unusual posture of this argument. Indeed, Tsolmon's argument is different from what is typically seen when an FTCA plaintiff invokes a regulation or statute in trying to avoid the discretionary function exception. Those cases involve the allegation that a government employee is *violating* the statute, not that she is *following* it. The difference seems to matter at least at the liability stage. Acting in contravention of a statute not only takes conduct outside the permissible scope of discretion, it also often establishes negligence per se. In contrast, acting pursuant to a statute is not likely to be negligent.

[4] Tsolmon's allegations also do not establish that the agents violated section 1357(a)(2). Wilson was unable to confirm Tsolmon's legal status after multiple attempts to verify it. Tsolmon was arrested at a bus station while travelling between states, which could plausibly give rise to the fear that Tsolmon would not remain in the jurisdiction before a warrant could be obtained.

809 F.3d 807 (2016)

William GIBSON; Rita Gibson, Plaintiffs-Appellants

v.

UNITED STATES of America; Federal Emergency Management Agency, Defendants-Appellees.

No. 14-31303.

United States Court of Appeals, Fifth Circuit.

January 4, 2016.

Gibson v. US, 809 F. 3d 807 (5th Cir. 2016)

Appeal from the United States District Court for the Middle District of Louisiana.

p.809 Michael Carter Palmintier, Esq. (argued), Trial Attorney, deGravelles, Palmintier, Holthaus & Fruge', L.L.P., Reymond bNeal Wilkinson, Baton Rouge, LA, for Plaintiffs-Appellants.

Catherine M. Maraist, Asst. U.S. Atty. (argued), James L. Nelson, Asst. U.S. Atty., Helina S. Dayries, Asst. U.S. Atty., Mary Patricia Jones, Asst. U.S. Atty., U.S. Attorney's Office, Baton Rouge, LA, for Defendant-Appellee.

Before JONES, SMITH, and SOUTHWICK, Circuit Judges.

LESLIE H. SOUTHWICK, Circuit Judge:

William Gibson fell and sustained injuries while exiting a trailer or mobile home owned by the Federal Emergency Management Agency ("FEMA"). Gibson and his wife, Rita Gibson, sued FEMA under the Federal Tort Claims Act ("FTCA"), 28 U.S.C. §§ 2671-2680. The district court granted FEMA's motion for summary judgment on the basis that the claims are barred by the FTCA's discretionary function exception. We REVERSE and REMAND for further proceedings.

FACTUAL AND PROCEDURAL BACKGROUND

Among its many services, FEMA provides trailers or mobile homes to victims of natural disasters. When a trailer is no longer to be used, it is transported to a FEMA storage site. On the day of the accident, November 1, 2010, Gibson was at a FEMA storage site in Baton Rouge, Louisiana, inspecting trailers that were to be sold at auction. In her deposition, FEMA employee Joan Johnson described the Baton Rouge site as "a federal property [with] a fence around it" containing "a hundred and some odd acres," and it typically p.810 "had hundreds ... of trailers." Johnson's job was to accompany customers while they inspected trailers available at auction because members of the public were not allowed to walk around the site unsupervised.

According to the Gibsons, "most of the FEMA trailers were equipped with a set of pull-out steps providing access, [but] the mobile homes were not." The parties on appeal, as well as the district court in its summary judgment opinion, have used the term "trailer" to refer to the relevant mobile home. Because the distinction between trailers and mobile homes is not dispositive in this appeal, we adopt the same terminology. On prior occasions, Gibson would enter the trailers by sitting in the doorway, turning into the trailer, and then standing up. On November 1,

Johnson accompanied Gibson while he inspected four or five trailers without incident. There is some dispute about how Gibson entered these trailers that day — whether he used a small step-stool or a stepladder. Both parties agree, though, that during the final trailer inspection, which had no attached stairs, Gibson used a stepladder to reach the trailer's doorway. The doorway was between two and four feet above the ground. According to Herman Jones, a FEMA employee, this trailer was situated on top of "hard gravel."

Johnson testified that Gibson asked to use her stepladder to enter this final trailer. Gibson, however, contends that he never requested to use Johnson's stepladder; instead, Johnson directed Gibson to use it. During his deposition, Gibson first testified that Johnson set up the stepladder in front of the trailer. Later in that same deposition, though, Gibson testified that he could not remember who set up the stepladder. For her part, Johnson maintains that Gibson set up the stepladder on his own. Gibson conceded that he moved the stepladder around to ensure it was stable before he used it to reach the trailer's entrance.

Gibson successfully used the stepladder to enter the trailer. Before attempting to exit and descend, Gibson contends he tried to get Johnson's attention. Johnson was approximately 40 feet away and talking on her cell phone. After waiting two minutes, Gibson began to descend the stepladder without Johnson's assistance. He remembers holding the trailer and putting both feet securely on the stepladder's rungs. Gibson fell from the stepladder as he attempted to step down, but he does not know what caused his fall. He claims no memory of the fall itself.

In contrast to Gibson's version of events, Johnson maintains she was standing by the door as Gibson exited the trailer. Johnson stated that Gibson had one foot on the ladder when his body started shifting, and he lost his balance as he attempted to put his other foot on the ladder. Johnson instinctively reached for Gibson in an attempt to help but quickly withdrew to prevent herself from being injured. Johnson called for assistance; several FEMA employees arrived to assist Gibson into an ambulance.

The Gibsons allege that the United States is liable under the FTCA for numerous acts of negligence: (1) "[f]ailing to provide stairs with handrails ... to inspect mobile homes"; (2) "[f]ailing to follow [FEMA] safety regulations ... by not providing hand rails for stairs to enter mobile homes"; (3) "[f]ailing to provide a solid surface upon which to place stairs or ladders when entering a mobile home"; (4) "[u]sing an under rated ladder to give to invitees to gain access to [the Government's] mobile homes"; (5) "[f]ailing to follow general safety regulations in the industry"; (6) "[f]ailing to properly train employees on regulations required for invitee p.811 safety"; (7) "[f]ailing to properly supervise employees"; (8) "[s]upplying employees with under rated ladders to give to invitees to inspect mobile homes"; (9) "[f]ailing to train and supervise employees in the proper techniques to spot and hold ladders"; (10) "[f]ailing to require employees to hold ladders firm"; (11) "[f]ailing to properly supervise employees who were constantly using cell phones for personal calls and not properly attending and monitoring invitees"; and (12) "[f]ailing to prevent personal cell phone usage by employees."

The Gibsons sought $9,671,682 in damages "arising out of a significant leg fracture." On cross-motions for summary judgment, the district court entered judgment on behalf of the Government. The Gibsons appeal.

DISCUSSION

Under the doctrine of sovereign immunity, a plaintiff may not sue the United States unless a federal statute explicitly provides the government's consent to be sued. *In re FEMA Trailer Formaldehyde Prods. Liab. Litig. (Miss. Plaintiffs)*, 668 F.3d 281, 287 (5th Cir.2012). The FTCA waives sovereign immunity under certain conditions "and provides the sole basis of recovery for tort claims against the United States." *Id.* (citing 28 U.S.C. §§ 1346, 2671, *et seq.*). Several exceptions, though, limit the waiver of sovereign immunity. Here, the Government contends, and the district court held, that the "discretionary function exception" applies.

The discretionary function exception applies to "[a]ny claim ... based upon the exercise or performance or the failure to exercise or perform a discretionary function or duty on the part of a federal agency or an employee of the Government, whether or not the discretion involved be abused." 28 U.S.C. § 2680(a). The district court granted summary judgment because of this exception, concluding it lacked subject matter jurisdiction.

I. Standard of Review

We review the district court's grant of summary judgment *de novo. Ashford v. United States*, 511 F.3d 501, 504 (5th Cir.2007). "Since the granting of summary judgment is a disposition on the merits of the case, a motion for summary judgment is not the appropriate procedure for raising the defense of lack of subject matter jurisdiction." *Stanley v. Cent. Intelligence Agency*, 639 F.2d 1146, 1157 (5th Cir. Unit B Mar.1981). When there is no jurisdiction, the district court should dismiss the suit without prejudice so that the plaintiffs may pursue a claim in a court that has jurisdiction. *See Ramming v. United States*, 281 F.3d 158, 161 (5th Cir. 2001).

We will review this judgment as a jurisdictional determination despite its label as a summary judgment. We review *de novo* a district court's "construction of immunity" and we review the underlying factual findings for clear error. *See In re Katrina Canal Breaches Litig.*, 696 F.3d 436, 444 (5th Cir.2012).

II. The Discretionary Function Exception

We apply a two-part test to determine whether an agency's conduct qualifies as a discretionary function or duty. *See United States v. Gaubert*, 499 U.S. 315, 322-23, 111 S.Ct. 1267, 113 L.Ed.2d 335 (1991).[1] First, we assess whether the challenged p.812 conduct was "discretionary in nature, [an] act[] that involv[es] an element of judgment or choice." *Id.* at 322, 111 S.Ct. 1267. If we find that the agency's conduct does qualify as discretionary, then we consider whether the actions taken are "susceptible to policy analysis." *Id.* at 325, 111 S.Ct. 1267.

A. Step One: Whether the challenged conduct was an act of discretion.

"If a statute, regulation, or policy leaves it to a federal agency to determine when and how to take action, the agency is not bound to act in a particular manner and the exercise of its authority is discretionary." *Spotts v. United States*, 613 F.3d 559, 567 (5th Cir.2010). In contrast, "the discretionary function exception does not apply if the challenged actions in fact violated a federal statute, regulation, or policy." *Id.* Gibson contends that FEMA had an unwritten "no assistance" policy that barred FEMA employees from helping customers enter and exit trailers, and that Johnson violated that policy by providing him an unsafe ladder.

The district court disagreed. First, the court held that whatever unwritten policy may have existed, the policy failed to prescribe sufficient "specific direction" to establish a nondiscretionary duty. The allegations of FEMA's supposed policy were "too broad and conclusory," the court held, and therefore the alleged FEMA conduct was not "specifically prescribed or prohibited" under the terms of the alleged policy. Second, the district court found that even if FEMA had a sufficient "no assistance" policy, Johnson did not violate that policy.

The district court relied on an unpublished Fifth Circuit case, *Lopez v. U.S. Immigration & Customs Enf't,* 455 Fed. Appx. 427 (5th Cir.2011). In *Lopez,* a federal inmate died of a heart attack allegedly due to deficient prisoner medical care. *Id.* at 429-31. The inmate's estate sued certain federal employees under the FTCA. The district court held the discretionary function exception applied and dismissed all claims for lack of subject matter jurisdiction. *Id.* at 431. On appeal, the plaintiff argued the United States Marshal Service violated the nondiscretionary policies of conducting regular inspections of the prison facility and assuring adequate medical care was provided. *Id.* We affirmed the district court's ruling, in part by noting that when a "policy fails to prescribe 'specific direction' as to what course of action an employee must follow, it generally fails to establish a nondiscretionary duty." *Id.* at 433. While the policy seemed nondiscretionary, it did not define what specific level of compliance was required and what remedial action the Marshal Service should take if it discovered insufficient compliance. *Id.* We held the policy was mere "generalized, precatory, or aspirational language that [was] too general to prescribe a specific course of action for an agency or employee to follow." *Id.* (quoting *Freeman v. United States,* 556 F.3d 326, 338 (5th Cir.2009)).

In the case before us, Herman Jones, a FEMA "logistics management specialist and sales lead," testified in a deposition that FEMA employees "were not supposed to assist the customers in and out of the trailers." Jones also testified that the policy effectively had a corollary, namely, that p.813 FEMA employees were allowed to provide a ladder if the customer requested one. On this record at least, the undisputed evidence is that the policy allowed a FEMA employee to provide a ladder but not assist a customer in using it. Whether the corollary allowed the FEMA employee to place the provided ladder in position at the trailer, which Gibson alleges the employee did, is not clear. The district court's decision that the policy had too little "specific direction" to establish a non-discretionary duty was plausible.

We leave this first step in the analysis unresolved. We find a clearer answer on the applicability of the discretionary function exception by examining whether this conduct was susceptible to policy analysis. We conclude it was not, making the exception inapplicable.

B. Step Two: Whether the challenged conduct is susceptible to policy analysis.

"[E]ven assuming the challenged conduct involves an element of judgment, and does not violate a nondiscretionary duty, we must still decide whether the judgment is of the kind that the discretionary function exception was designed to shield."

Spotts, 613 F.3d at 568 (quotation marks omitted). Specifically, the exception was enacted to "prevent judicial second-guessing of legislative and administrative decisions grounded in social, economic, and political policy through the medium of an action in tort." *Katrina Canal Breaches,* 696 F.3d at 449. "The exception, properly construed, therefore protects only governmental actions and decisions based on considerations of public policy." *Berkovitz by Berkovitz v. United States,* 486 U.S. 531, 537, 108 S.Ct. 1954, 100 L.Ed.2d 531 (1988). The exception only shields those acts that are "based on the purposes that the regulatory regime seeks to accomplish." *Gaubert,* 499 U.S. at 325 n. 7, 111 S.Ct. 1267. Our inquiry is "not whether the decision maker in fact engaged in a policy analysis when reaching his decision but instead whether his decision was susceptible to policy analysis." *In re FEMA Trailer Formaldehyde Prods. Liab. Litig. (La. Plaintiffs),* 713 F.3d 807, 810 (5th Cir.2013).

The district court determined that decisions about how FEMA would provide access were related to FEMA's purpose in offering the trailers for sale: "[P]racticality and costs are certainly policy considerations touching on these decisions," the court noted, and "the cost of rebuilding steps for all of the trailers would have seriously cut into the net price FEMA obtained from the sale of these units." Further, FEMA's "no assistance" approach reduced costs and risks that a customer's fall could harm a FEMA employee. For the reasons that follow, we hold that FEMA's decision about how customers would enter and exit the trailers was not the type of judgment the discretionary function exception was designed to protect.

The Government's decisions about routine property maintenance, decisions with which any private landowner would be concerned, are not susceptible to the kind of policy analysis shielded by the discretionary function exception. *See Gotha v. United States,* 115 F.3d 176, 181-82 (3d Cir.1997). Moreover, budgetary constraints on their own are often an insufficient policy goal to trigger the exception's protections. *See O'Toole v. United States,* 295 F.3d 1029, 1035-37 (9th Cir.2002). These limits to the exception are particularly potent where the Government's actions are those of the operator of a business who is making the same decisions a private landowner would make. *See generally* 2 LESTER S. JAYSON & HON. ROBERT C. p.814 LONGSTRETH, HANDLING FEDERAL TORT CLAIMS § 9.10[4] (2015) (collecting cases).

The Third Circuit held that the discretionary function exception did not apply where an independent contractor sued the United States Navy after she fell on Navy property. *Gotha,* 115 F.3d at 178. The plaintiff Gotha was working at a Navy base that had two facilities separated by a steep incline. *Id.* While it was dark, Gotha was walking from the upper facility to the lower when she fell and suffered an ankle injury. *Id.* Gotha sued the United States under the FTCA, alleging negligence for the Government's failure to provide a stairway with handrails between the two facilities and failure to provide sufficient lighting. *Id.* The district court held the discretionary function exception barred Gotha's suit and dismissed the case. *Id.* In doing so, the district court relied on an affidavit submitted by the Government, claiming "[i]n evaluating a decision whether to install an outdoor staircase and artificial lighting there are military, social and economic considerations involved." *Id.* at 181.

The Third Circuit reversed, explaining the "case [was] not about a national security concern, but rather a mundane, administrative, garden-variety, housekeeping problem that is about as far removed from the policies applicable to the Navy's mission as it is possible to get." *Id.* Further, the court noted "[i]t is difficult to conceive of a case more likely to have been within the contemplation of Congress when it abrogated sovereign immunity than the one before us." *Id.* at 182. More recently, the Third Circuit has revised its holding in *Gotha,* concluding the discretionary function exception does not apply "where the Government is aware of a specific risk of harm, and eliminating the danger would not implicate policy but would involve only garden-variety remedial measures." *S.R.P. ex rel. Abunabba v. United States,* 676 F.3d 329, 340 (3d Cir.2012).

Similarly, the Ninth Circuit held the discretionary function exception did not apply where ranch owners alleged the Bureau of Indian Affairs ("BIA") negligently maintained an irrigation system on government-owned property, damaging the ranch owners' land. *See O'Toole,* 295 F.3d 1029. The Government claimed "its failure to repair and maintain the ... irrigation system was the result of a policy decision involving allocation of scarce BIA resources," and thus the discretionary function exception barred suit. *Id.* at 1032.

On appeal, the Ninth Circuit recognized a spectrum on which to assess the policy prong of the discretionary function exception. On one end, negligent driving by a government official does not implicate the kinds of policy considerations protected by the exception. *Id.* at 1035 (referencing a hypothetical first described in *Gaubert,* 499 U.S. at 325 n. 7, 111 S.Ct. 1267). On the other end of the spectrum are cases "where the government employee's exercise of judgment is directly related to effectuating agency policy goals.... such as the regulation and oversight of [savings and loan associations] by the Federal Home Loan Bank Board, *see Gaubert,* 499 U.S. at 332-34, 111 S.Ct. 1267; the release of vaccine lots by the Bureau of Biologics of the Food and Drug Administration, *see Berkovitz,* 486 U.S. at 545-48, 108 S.Ct. 1954; and the enforcement and implementation of airline safety standards by the [FAA], *see Varig,* 467 U.S. at 814-20, 104 S.Ct. 2755." *Id.* Turning to the facts of its own case, the *O'Toole* court held "that an agency's decision to forgo, for fiscal reasons, the routine maintenance of its property — maintenance that would be expected of any other landowner — is not the kind of policy decision that the discretionary function exception protects." *Id.* at 1036. In p.815 so holding, the court cautioned that "[t]he danger of the discretionary function exception... swallow[ing] the FTCA is especially great where the governments takes on the role of a private landowner." *Id.* at 1037.

The discretionary function exception is particularly inapt where the Government acts as the operator of a business. In many such cases, FTCA actions proceed without any stated consideration of the discretionary function exception at all. *See generally* JAYSON & LONGSTRETH, *supra,* § 9.10[4] (collecting cases). If the district court in this case reaches the merits, it will apply Louisiana law to determine whether the Government is liable. *See* 28 U.S.C. § 1346(b)(1). Louisiana law provides that an "owner or person having custody of immovable property has a duty to keep the property in a reasonably safe condition and must discover any unreasonably dangerous condition on the premises and either correct that condition or warn potential victims of its existence." *Daigle v. City of Shreveport,* 78 So.3d 753, 765 (La. Ct.App.2011) (interpreting LA. CIV.CODE ANN. art. 2315).

In one of our decisions applying Louisiana law, a plaintiff slipped and fell on a United States Post Office's icy steps; she sued the Government under the FTCA. *Salim v. United States,* 382 F.2d 240, 241-42 (5th Cir.1967). We recognized the Government was "causally negligent in failing to supply its employees with" a chemical capable of melting ice. *Id.* at 242-43. We considered an analogous case recently, in an unpublished decision. *Gourgeot v. United States,* 372 Fed.Appx. 489 (5th Cir. 2010). There, again applying Louisiana law, we assessed an FTCA suit for a slip-and-fall that occurred outside a Post Office. *Id.* at 490. In both *Salim* and *Gourgeot,* FTCA claims were considered on their merits without any discussion of the discretionary function exception.

Rather differently, when the Government acts as landowner of wilderness, certain kinds of maintenance decisions have been found to contain multiple policy considerations. FEMA relies on several of these inapposite wilderness cases in an attempt to support its contention that sufficient policy considerations were present in this case. It refers us to a decision in which we considered how the United States Army Corps of Engineers was to notify the public of the existence of a sill (an underwater dam formed naturally from sediment) in the Mississippi River. *Theriot v. United States,* 245 F.3d 388 (5th Cir.1998). We determined the Corps of Engineers' decision was subject to policy considerations. *Id.* at 399-400. Those considerations include "the degree of danger an object poses, the vessel traffic type and density, the location of the object in relation to the navigable channel, the history of vessel accidents, and the feasibility and economics, including costs, of erecting and maintaining physical markers in light of the available resources." *Id.* Likewise, in a recent unpublished decision, we held the Government's decision about how to replace warning signs near jetties in Galveston was a choice subject to policy considerations. *Hix v. U.S. Army Corps. of Eng'rs,* 155 Fed.Appx. 121, 127 (5th Cir. 2005). There, we noted the policy considerations underlying the Government's decision to replace warning signs, "ensuring public safety in the [surrounding] area ... without encouraging public use of the jetties." *Id.* at 127. Unlike in *Theriot* and *Hix,* here, the Government operated as a commercial business and welcomed customers to its site as if it were managing a trailer showroom.

Also distinguishable is a case in which a vessel allided with a wharf in New p.816 Orleans, allegedly due to inadequate dredging of the river. *MS Tabea Schiffahrtsgesellschaft MBH & Co. KG v. Bd. of Comm'rs of Port of New Orleans,* 636 F.3d 161, 163 (5th Cir.2011). The ship's owner sued, alleging that the Government had neglected its "statutory duty to dredge and maintain the Mississippi River as a navigable waterway." *Id.* On appeal, we analyzed the two-part test for application of the discretionary function exception. *Id.* at 165-66. For the second part of the test, we discussed the requirement that the relevant governmental decision must be "grounded in social, economic, or public policy." *Id.* at 166 (citing *Gaubert,* 499 U.S. at 322-23, 111 S.Ct. 1267). If the Government is given discretion, "it must be presumed that the agent's acts are grounded in policy when exercising that discretion." *Id.* (quoting *Gaubert,* 499 U.S. at 324, 111 S.Ct. 1267). Overcoming the presumption requires a plaintiff to "allege facts which would support a finding that the challenged actions are not the kind of conduct that can be said to be grounded in the policy of the regulatory regime." *Id.* (quoting *Gaubert,* 499 U.S. at 324-25, 111 S.Ct. 1267). We held that by statute, the Corps of Engineers was required to consider whether dredging projects were "economically justified or environmentally acceptable." *Id.* at 167. Maintaining the navigability of the Mississippi River involve "quintessentially discretionary" judgments that were "susceptible to policy analysis." *Id.* at 168.

We find little in common between the judgments of maintaining thousands of miles of waterways and deciding how to allow customers access to trailers being offered for sale. In *MS Tabea,* the Government conducted a complex policy analysis, balancing costs with environmental concerns. Here, the Government has only suggested FEMA would have more money for future projects by requiring customers to find their own way into the trailers.

In a helpful contrasting situation also involving FEMA, we recently dealt with FEMA's provision of emergency housing units that emitted formaldehyde. *See FEMA Trailer Formaldehyde (La. Plaintiffs),* 713 F.3d 807. We noted FEMA's decisions to provide this housing were susceptible to policy analysis because the agency had to consider "what would provide the safest, most feasible, convenient, and readily available housing assistance." *Id.* at 810.

In contrast, FEMA's decision here to allow customers to fend for themselves in entering and exiting trailers did not require the kind of policy analysis relevant to the exception. FEMA operated this site in Baton Rouge like a commercial business. "The mere association of a decision with regulatory concerns is not enough; exempt decisions are those fraught with ... public policy considerations." *Cope v. Scott,* 45 F.3d 445, 449 (D.C.Cir.1995) (quotation marks omitted). The Government at times is to be treated as if it were a private landowner in assessing its exposure to common tort liability. *See Salim,* 382 F.2d at 241-42. This is one of those times.

We conclude the plaintiffs have overcome the presumption that this was a sufficiently policy-laden decision by alleging facts that show the conduct — how to provide customers invited onto the premises with reasonably safe access to the trailers — was not "grounded in the policy of the regulatory regime." *Gaubert,* 499 U.S. at 325, 111 S.Ct. 1267. Instead, to use a sister circuit's descriptive list, the decision concerned "a mundane, administrative, garden-variety, housekeeping problem that is about as far removed from the policies applicable to the Navy's [or here, FEMA's] p.817 mission as it is possible to get." *See Gotha,* 115 F.3d at 181.

The judgment is REVERSED and the cause is REMANDED for further proceedings.

[1] At the pleading stage, the plaintiff has the burden to "invoke the court's jurisdiction by alleging a claim that is facially outside of the discretionary function exception." *Freeman v. United States,* 556 F.3d 326, 334 (5th Cir. 2009). Nonetheless, we previously noted it is unclear whether the plaintiff or the government bears the ultimate burden of proving the discretionary function exception applies. *See St. Tammany Par. ex rel. Davis v. Fed. Emergency Mgmt. Agency,* 556 F.3d 307, 315 n. 3 (5th Cir.2009). Our sister circuits are split on this question. *See id.* (collecting cases). This issue was not addressed by the district court or raised by the parties on appeal, and thus we leave it for another day.

810 F.3d 330 (2016)

Thomas R. TUBESING, Plaintiff-Appellant
v.
UNITED STATES of America, Defendant-Appellee.

No. 15-30347.

United States Court of Appeals, Fifth Circuit.

January 6, 2016.

Tubesing v. US, 810 F. 3d 330 (5th Cir. 2016)

Appeal from the United States District Court for the Middle District of Louisiana.

p.331 Scott Damon Wilson, Baton Rouge, LA, for Plaintiff-Appellant.

Catherine M. Maraist, Helina S. Dayries, Mary Patricia Jones, Assistant U.S. Attorneys, U.S. Attorney's Office, Baton Rouge, LA, for Defendant-Appellee.

Before PRADO, SOUTHWICK, and GRAVES, Circuit Judges.

JAMES E. GRAVES, Circuit Judge:

Thomas Tubesing ("Tubesing") appeals the district court's dismissal of his claims p.332 under the Federal Tort Claims Act ("FTCA"), 28 U.S.C. §§ 1346(b) and 2671 *et seq.* The district court found that it lacked subject-matter jurisdiction based upon its conclusion that Tubesing's FTCA claims were precluded by the Civil Service Reform Act of 1978 ("CSRA"), Pub.L. No. 95-454, 92 Stat. 1111 (codified as amended at 5 U.S.C. § 1101 *et seq.*). We AFFIRM.

I.

In October 2003, Tubesing began employment with the United States as a contract employee in the Division of the Strategic National Stockpile, a subset of the Centers for Disease Control and Prevention ("CDC"). Within a year, Tubesing was transferred to the Division's Program Preparedness Branch and assigned to work as a Public Health Advisor in Louisiana.

On December 10, 2006, Tubesing was hired as a full-time federal employee, and later received a promotion on April 15, 2007. With the promotion, Tubesing agreed to move from Atlanta to Baton Rouge to work exclusively on Louisiana's bio-terrorism preparedness program. Shortly after arriving in Baton Rouge, Tubesing allegedly discovered and subsequently reported what he considered "substantial and specific dangers" to public health. Tubesing was terminated on December 7, 2007.

After his termination, Tubesing appealed to the Merit Systems Protection Board ("MSPB") with claims that his firing was in retaliation for reporting the perceived public health threats. On November 25, 2008, an administrative law judge found in Tubesing's favor and ordered he be restored to his *status quo ante* position, retroactive to December 7, 2007, by January 19, 2009. Tubesing was placed back on the CDC payroll by January 9, 2009, but alleges that other issues — including administrative leave removal, job restoration, back pay, contributions, and health insurance — remained. Aggrieved that he had not been adequately restored to his status quo position, Tubesing filed a petition for enforcement with the MSPB on

January 21, 2009. An administrative law judge again found for Tubesing, and the MSPB affirmed the judge's ruling.

Tubesing asserts that in relation to his reports of public health threats, his termination, and his appeals and petitions, the CDC never fully restored him to his position and took various other adverse actions against him.

On October 9, 2014, Tubesing filed suit against the United States under the Federal Tort Claims Act ("FTCA"), 28 U.S.C. §§ 1346(b) and 2671 *et seq.*, alleging that his employers' actions constituted numerous torts, including fraud and intentional infliction of emotional distress. In response, the United States moved to dismiss Tubesing's claims pursuant to Fed. R.Civ.P. 12(b)(1) on December 30, 2014. On March 24, 2015, the district court granted the United States' motion and dismissed Tubesing's claims. This appeal followed.

II.

The question before us is whether Tubesing can proceed under the FTCA to seek redress for his employment-related claims; or, as the district court determined, Tubesing's FTCA claims are precluded by the CSRA because they fall within the statute's intended reach. Tubesing argues that the CSRA applies only to "personnel decisions" that are specifically listed in the statute, such as "a promotion" or "a reinstatement." Our review of the statute and applicable law, however, leads us to conclude that Tubesing's claims are covered under the CSRA.

p.333 III.

The CSRA includes an elaborate framework for evaluating adverse personnel action against federal employees. *Rollins v. Marsh,* 937 F.2d 134, 137 (5th Cir. 1991) (citing *United States v. Fausto,* 484 U.S. 439, 108 S.Ct. 668, 98 L.Ed.2d 830 (1988)). This framework aims to provide "an integrated scheme of administrative and judicial review, designed to balance the legitimate interests of the various categories of federal employees with the needs of sound and efficient administration." *Id.* Additionally, Chapter 23 of the CSRA — the portion of the CSRA most relevant to this case — prohibits certain personnel practices and establishes merit-system principles that govern civil-service employment. *Id.* The merit-system principles include treating employees fairly and equitably and "with proper regard for their privacy and constitutional rights." *Id.* "Prohibited personnel practices include the taking of any 'personnel action' that violates merit-system principles." *Id.* The CSRA further provides federal employees with remedies against prohibited personnel practices, remedies that include staying or correcting the practice and seeking disciplinary action against the offenders. *Id.*

This court, in *Rollins v. Marsh,* considered whether two federal employees' claims against the United States for constitutional and privacy violations were precluded by statutory remedies provided by the CSRA. *Id.* at 134. The *Rollins* plaintiffs sought relief under the FTCA, stemming from their claim of improper suspension from federal employment after submitting nude photographs for publication. *Id.* at 135. Recognizing that "the CSRA remedies [are] the comprehensive and exclusive procedures for settling work-related controversies between federal civil-service employees and the federal government," we affirmed the district court's dismissal of the Rollins' claims because their available remedies under the CSRA precluded recovery under the FTCA. *Id.* at 139-40 (citing *Bush v. Lucas,* 462 U.S. 367, 103 S.Ct. 2404, 76 L.Ed.2d 648 (1983) and *Fausto,* 484 U.S. at 439, 108 S.Ct. 668). In consideration of the CSRA's purpose, we refused "to permit FTCA claims to supplant the CSRA's remedial scheme [or] to defeat [the statute's] purpose." *Id.* at 139 (citing *Rivera v. United States,* 924 F.2d 948, 951 (9th Cir.1991)).

The Ninth Circuit has also held, in certain instances, that actions brought by federal employees under the FTCA are precluded by the CSRA. Those decisions — which turned on a critical examination as to whether the respective plaintiffs' claims fit within the prohibited personnel practices and employment-related issues covered by the CSRA — are particularly illustrative in this matter.

In *Lehman v. Morrissey,* 779 F.2d 526 (9th Cir.1985), Joan Lehman brought several employment-related claims, including a claim for intentional infliction of emotional distress, against her former supervisors in the United States Forest Service and the United States. Upon review of the kinds of activities complained of by Lehman, the Ninth Circuit determined that the FTCA claims were preempted by the CSRA; thus, Lehman's remedies were covered by the statute. *Id.* at 526-27. That court further noted that Lehman's claims involving lack of effective training, obstruction of her ability to compete, and interference with the merit system were specifically prohibited by the CSRA. *Id.* at 527. Thus, the Ninth Circuit affirmed the judgment of dismissal, as "[the CSRA] provided Lehman's sole recourse." *Id.* at 528.

p.334 Four years later, the Ninth Circuit held that a plaintiff's claims — including rape and sustained physical sexual abuse — could go forth under the FTCA because they were not preempted by the CSRA. *Brock v. United States,* 64 F.3d 1421 (9th Cir.1995). In allowing the plaintiff to pursue her claims under the FTCA, the Ninth Circuit recognized the CSRA's broad purpose and preemptive effect, but determined that "[the defendant's] rape and continued physical sexual abuse of [the plaintiff] fit[] no category of personnel actions listed in § 2302(a)(2)." *Id.* at 1424. In distinguishing *Lehman,* the *Brock* court cautioned that its ruling resulted from the specifics of that case. *Id.* at 1425. Thus, "because the alleged rape and physical abuse d[id] not involve personnel actions and was not perpetrated with respect to the supervisor's authority, the CSRA d[id] not preempt Brock's FTCA claim." *Id.*

IV.

The CSRA clearly and categorically includes the specific activities and claims of which Tubesing complains. Here, Tubesing, a federal employee, lists a multitude of perceived agency infractions in furtherance of his FTCA claims. Tubesing, for example, alleges:

> Agency officials conspired to and did sabotage [his] ability to accomplish his job duties and objectives, and schemed to impede the performance of his duties, by requiring him to perform work out-side his job description, implementing onerous reporting requirements, intimidating other employees who cooperated with him, shifting blame to him for shortcomings and problems caused by

others, interfering with his ability to discover pre-existing problems and shortcomings within the state agency, making materially false and fraudulent statements and representations, falsifying documents, testifying falsely in the administrative proceeding following his termination, depriving Louisiana citizens of the benefits of good and efficient decision making, and committing other negligent and wrongful acts that caused [him] to suffer harm, financial losses, and severe emotional distress.

It is clear that all of Tubesing's claims stem from his employment relationship with the CDC. It is even more clear that each of Tubesing's claims — which directly relate to the relevant § 2302(a) and (b) subsections describing personnel practices and prohibitions — finds a home within the larger CSRA framework.

Section 2302's prohibited personnel practices broadly cover a number of violations in an effort to provide examples of the type of claims that may be subject to employee action. Tubesing's litany of complaints — including that his employer sabotaged his ability to accomplish his job duties and objectives, required him to perform work outside his job description, and blamed him for mistakes by others — all fall squarely within the CSRA's sphere. The CSRA's reach further extends to Tubesing's claims involving training, reassignment and transfer, and changes in working conditions. Hence, because Tubesing is a federal employee, and due to the nature of his employment-related claims, the CSRA provides Tubesing's sole remedy against his employer.

V.

In an effort to overcome the preclusive effect of the CSRA, Tubesing points this court to several actions that are not specifically listed as prohibited personnel practices. According to Tubesing, these actions fall outside the CSRA's scope. We disagree. Congress never intended that the CSRA would cover *only* those prohibitions expressed therein. Tubesing's allegations, p.335 which involve claims that the CSRA is expected to cover, however, clearly fall within the statute's confines.

For the foregoing reasons, the judgment of the district court is AFFIRMED.

764 F.3d 445 (2014)

Denise PLEASANT, Administratrix; Lavardis Whitman; Chassiti Williams, Plaintiffs-Appellants

v.

UNITED STATES of America, on behalf of OVERTON BROOKS VETERANS ADMINISTRATION HOSPITAL; Insurance Company A; Insurance Company B; Insurance Company C, Defendants-Appellees.

No. 12-31268.

United States Court of Appeals, Fifth Circuit.

August 19, 2014.

Pleasant v. Overton Brooks VA Hospital, 764 F. 3d 445 (5th Cir. 2014)

p.446 Winnifred Hollingsworth Jackson, Esq., Attorney, Shreveport, LA, for Plaintiffs-Appellants.

John A. Broadwell, Assistant U.S. Attorney, U.S. Attorney's Office, Shreveport, LA, for Defendants-Appellees.

Before DAVIS, GARZA, and DENNIS, Circuit Judges.

PER CURIAM:

In this Federal Tort Claims Act ("FTCA") case, Plaintiffs-Appellants Denise Pleasant, Larvardis Whitman, and Chassiti Williams appeal the dismissal of their complaint against the Veterans Administration ("VA"). In their complaint, the plaintiffs assert wrongful-death and survival causes of action available under Louisiana law. The decedent, Nathan Chaney, died on May 13, 2006, in the emergency room of Overton Brooks VA Medical Center in Shreveport, Louisiana. Whitman and Williams are Chaney's children, and Pleasant is Chaney's sister and court-appointed estate administratrix. Pleasant filed a claim on behalf of Chaney's estate as administratrix and putatively on behalf of Whitman and Williams, who were both minors at the time. Pleasant was not the children's tutor or guardian.[1] After the VA denied the claim, all three plaintiffs filed suit pursuant to the FTCA. The district court dismissed the case for lack of subject-matter jurisdiction, finding that the plaintiffs did not timely exhaust their administrative remedies before filing suit against the VA because, the district court concluded, under Louisiana law, only the children's tutors, and not Pleasant as administratrix, had legal capacity p.447 to file a valid administrative claim. Thus, the district court concluded, Whitman and Williams did not timely exhaust their administrative remedies as required by the FTCA because no one with legal authority filed a claim with the VA on behalf of the two children before the two-year statute of limitations expired. We conclude that the administrative notice of claim filed by Pleasant was sufficient to give the agency written notice of the children's claims sufficient to enable the agency to investigate and to place a value on the claims, and was therefore sufficient to preserve the claims. Accordingly, we REVERSE and REMAND for further proceedings.

I.

On May 13, 2006, Nathan Chaney suffered a seizure and died in the emergency room of Overton Brooks VA Medical Center in Shreveport, Louisiana, allegedly due to the VA's negligence. Chaney was survived by his sister, Denise Pleasant; his mother, Muriel Lee Chaney Thomas; and his two then—minor children, Chassiti B. Williams and Lavardis R. Whitman, and their respective mothers. In 2007, Pleasant was appointed by a Louisiana court as administratrix of Chaney's estate. The only asset of Chaney's estate was the malpractice claim against the VA hospital.

On May 8, 2008, within the two-year statute of limitations, *see* 28 U.S.C. § 2401(b), Pleasant filed an administrative claim as administratrix and on behalf of herself, Williams, and Whitman, against the VA Medical Center and various physicians and staff members, with the Office of Veterans Affairs. At the time Pleasant filed the notice of claim, both Whitman and Williams were minors, but they both became adults later in 2008.

Pleasant used "Standard Form 95" ("SF-95") to file the FTCA claim. The form identified the claimant as "Denise Pleasant, administratrix," identified the nature of the claim as "wrongful death," and identified the loss amount as $500,000. Pleasant appended a document similar to a complaint in a lawsuit to the SF-95 she filed with the Office of Veterans Affairs. That document stated that Nathan Chaney had died and was "survived by his sister, Denise Pleasant, mother, Muriel Lee Chaney Thomas, and minor children, Chassiti B. Williams and Lavardis R. Whitman." The remainder of the document set forth allegations regarding Chaney's medical care and death. The final paragraph was in the nature of a prayer for relief and stated that petitioner Denise Pleasant prayed that a claim for death be reviewed and that an award be made based on the allegedly substandard medical care that caused the death of Nathan Chaney.

Counsel for Pleasant and the VA commenced settlement negotiations. The VA concedes that it was aware that Pleasant was bringing a claim on her own behalf and on behalf of Whitman and Williams, and that it had sufficient notice of the nature of the claims and the identity of the claimants. In June of 2010, during settlement negotiations, counsel for the VA for the first time called into question Pleasant's authority under Louisiana law to file the administrative claim on behalf of Whitman and Williams. Pleasant denied that it was necessary for the children's tutors, rather than the administratrix of their father's estate, to file the notice of claim with the VA, but in an abundance of caution she also attached new SF-95s signed and dated by Whitman and Williams, each dated July 14, 2010, after they had become adults. The VA issued a final denial of all administrative claims filed by Pleasant, Williams, and Whitman.

Pleasant, Whitman, and Williams filed this FTCA suit in the U.S. District Court p.448 for the Western District of Louisiana on March 9, 2011.[2] The Government moved to dismiss, arguing that Whitman and Williams were the only proper beneficiaries and that they did not timely present their claims to the VA. The matter was referred to a magistrate judge, who recommended that the district court deny the motion because the VA had notice of the claim and because the claim, which named all of the potential beneficiaries, had been timely filed, regardless of the capacity in which Pleasant had filed the claim. The district court disagreed and granted the motion to dismiss for lack of subject-matter jurisdiction. The district court found that the children did not timely present their administrative claim to the VA before filing suit because, the district court concluded, under Louisiana law only the children's tutors, and not an administratrix, had legal capacity to file the administrative claim. Thus, district court concluded, Whitman and Williams did not timely present their notice of claim as required by the FTCA because no one with legal authority filed a claim with the VA on behalf of the two children before the two-year statute of limitations expired. This appeal followed.[3]

II.

The FTCA grants a limited waiver of sovereign immunity for tort suits brought against the United States or its agencies. 28 U.S.C. §§ 2674, 2679(a). Plaintiffs may recover against the United States and its agencies under the FTCA "in the same manner and to the same extent as a private individual under like circumstances" under substantive state law. *Id.* § 2674. Before a plaintiff may bring a lawsuit under the FTCA, the claim must be presented to the appropriate federal agency and be finally denied by the agency in writing. *Id.* § 2675(a). A plaintiff must provide the agency with her notice of claim within two years after her claim accrues. *Id.* §§ 2401(b), 2675(a). "A claim is properly presented within the meaning of § 2675(a) when the agency is given sufficient written notice to commence investigation and the claimant places a value on the claim." *Transco Leasing Corp. v. United States,* 896 F.2d 1435, 1442, *amended on other grounds on reh'g,* 905 F.2d 61 (5th Cir.1990) (citing *Adams v. United States,* 615 F.2d 284, 289, *decision clarified on denial of reh'g,* 622 F.2d 197 (5th Cir.1980)).

The parties do not dispute that under Louisiana law, Pleasant, because she was not the tutor or guardian of Whitman or Williams during the events giving rise to this suit, could not file or maintain a lawsuit on behalf of her niece and nephew before they became adults.[4] The question presented is whether Whitman and Williams' claim against the VA arising from the death of their father was preserved for purposes of the FTCA when Pleasant filed the administrative notice of claim with the VA for them, even though p.449 Pleasant lacked the legal authority under Louisiana law to represent the children's rights.[5] This is a question of law that we review *de novo. See Willoughby v. United States ex rel. U.S. Dep't of the Army,* 730 F.3d 476, 479 (5th Cir.2013) (per curiam), *cert. denied,* ___ U.S. ___, 134 S.Ct. 1307, 188 L.Ed.2d 303 (2014). For the reasons that follow, we hold that the notice of claim filed by Pleasant, because it gave written notice to the VA of the nature and value of the FTCA claims arising from Chaney's death, was sufficient to preserve the children's claims. *Transco Leasing,* 896 F.2d at 1444; *Adams,* 615 F.2d at 289.

The purpose of the FTCA's administrative-presentment requirement is to allow the federal agency promptly to investigate and, if appropriate, settle claims without having to resort to federal courts. *See, e.g., McNeil v. United States,* 508 U.S. 106, 111-12 & n. 7, 113 S.Ct. 1980, 124 L.Ed.2d 21 (1993) (explaining that the purpose of the notice-of-claim requirement is to facilitate the agency's prompt investigation and settlement of claims); *Rise v. United States,* 630 F.2d 1068, 1071 (5th Cir.1980) ("The statutory purpose of requiring an administrative claim is 'to ease court congestion and avoid unnecessary litigation, while making it possible for the

Government to expedite the fair settlement of tort claims asserted against the United States.'" (citation omitted)); *accord Transco Leasing,* 896 F.2d at 1442; *Adams,* 615 F.2d at 288-89. We have explained that the purpose of the FTCA's notice-of-claim requirement "will be served as long as a claim brings to the Government's attention facts sufficient to enable it thoroughly to investigate its potential liability and to conduct settlement negotiations with the claimant." *Rise,* 630 F.2d at 1071. Accordingly, we have held, a notice of claim requirement is satisfied "if the claimant (1) gives the agency written notice of his or her claim sufficient to enable the agency to investigate and (2) places a value on his or her claim." *Adams,* 615 F.2d at 289; *accord Transco Leasing,* 896 F.2d at 1442.

The district court erred in imposing additional requirements on the children beyond their obligation to provide the agency with (1) written notice of the claim sufficient to enable investigation and (2) a value of the claim. *See Transco Leasing,* 896 F.2d at 1442; *Adams,* 615 F.2d at 289. Our opinion in *Transco Leasing* is instructive on this point. *See* 896 F.2d 1435. In *Transco Leasing,* after an airplane pilot died in a mid-air collision, his executor, a bank, sought to recover damages on behalf of the decedent's widow and daughter. *Id.* at 1439-40. The district court dismissed the wrongful death claims of the widow and daughter, concluding that they did not satisfy the notice requirements of the FTCA because the bank, rather than the claimants themselves, had filed the notice of claim, and because the bank failed to comply with § 14.3(e) of the regulations, which requires that a claim presented by a legal representative "shall be presented in the name of the claimant." *Id.* at 1440-41, 1443. We reversed, holding that it was enough that the Bank, as executor, preserved the claims on behalf of the family members and that "the administrative claim form submitted by the Bank, on behalf of the ... widow and daughter, satisfied the jurisdictional notice requirements identified in *Adams:* (1) the agency p.450 was given sufficient written notice to commence investigation; and (2) a value was placed on the claim." *Id.* at 1444; *see Adams,* 615 F.2d at 289.

While in *Transco Leasing* we observed that the bank was a legal representative authorized by state law to pursue wrongful death claims on behalf of statutory beneficiaries, we did not imply that an individual or entity filing a notice of claim on behalf of beneficiaries must have the legal authority under state law to pursue the beneficiaries' legal rights in court. *See* 896 F.2d at 1444. To the contrary, we cited with approval the view that "the administrative claims requirements of the FTCA are 'meant to benefit claimants and in no way are designed to preclude them from their day in court.' The requirements are 'intended to lessen the court case load through fair settlement, not procedural default.'" *Id.* (quoting *Van Fossen v. United States,* 430 F.Supp. 1017, 1017, 1022 (N.D.Cal.1977)). In support, we relied upon several cases holding that a notice of claim was properly presented notwithstanding the plaintiff's lack of authority under state law to bring a claim on behalf of other beneficiaries. *See id.* at 1443-44 (citing *Champagne v. United States,* 573 F.Supp. 488, 493-94 (E.D.La.1983) (holding that a notice of claim filed by the widow of a decedent on behalf of her adult daughter, on whose behalf the mother had no authority to file a lawsuit under Louisiana law, was sufficient under the FTCA because the claim form listed the daughter by name and put a value on the claim), and *Van Fossen,* 430 F.Supp. at 1020-22 (holding notice of claim was properly presented even though under Virginia law it was filed by the incorrect party)); *see also, e.g., Downs v. United States,* 382 F.Supp. 713, 728-29 (M.D.Tenn.1974) (holding notice of claim was properly presented notwithstanding plaintiff's lack of "capacity" under Florida law to bring claim on behalf of other beneficiaries), *rev'd on other grounds,* 522 F.2d 990 (6th Cir.1975).

As our opinion in *Transco Leasing* demonstrates, for a notice of claim to be sufficient, a person or entity filing a notice of claim on behalf of other beneficiaries need not have the legal authority to pursue those claims in state court. Indeed, the regulations implementing the FTCA clearly contemplate that notice of claims will be presented by estate administrators and other legal representatives. *See* 28 C.F.R. § 14.3. Section 14.3(c) provides that "[a] claim based on death may be presented by the executor or administrator of the [decedent's] estate, or by any other person legally entitled to assert such a claim in accordance with applicable State law."[6] This section contemplates that an estate's representative to file a notice of claim— regardless of whether, under state law, that executor or administrator has the legal right or capacity to represent the decedent's beneficiaries in a lawsuit.[7]

p.451 Considering the foregoing principles and authorities, we conclude that an FTCA notice of claim need not be filed by a party with the legal authority or capacity under state law to represent the beneficiaries' interests in state court. State-law authority or capacity to represent beneficiaries is not required simply to put the government on notice of the nature and value of a claim.

In coming to a contrary decision, the district court relied on this Court's unpublished summary calendar opinion in *Johnson v. United States,* 287 Fed.Appx. 328 (5th Cir.2008) (per curiam), which held that the plaintiff, who was under Texas law the heir of the decedent, could not maintain the FTCA suit because she had not established a state-law prerequisite to recovery. *Id.* at 329. Texas law required heirs to "allege and prove that there is no administration pending and none is necessary" before they have "capacity" to bring a survival action. *Id.* at 330 (quotation marks, alteration, and emphasis omitted). Because the plaintiff had failed to do this, we concluded that she was not a proper beneficiary under state law, and that therefore the United States could not be held liable. *Id.* at 329-30. Although in *Johnson* we used the state-law term "capacity" to refer to the Texas requirement that heirs allege and prove that no estate administration is pending, we employed that term to refer to the *substantive* scope of the agency's liability: because a private individual would not be subject to suit under Texas law if the plaintiff did not make the requisite showing that no estate administration was pending, the United States would not be subject to suit under those circumstances, either. *See id.*[8] In *Johnson,* we did not purport to address the sufficiency of the plaintiff's presentment of her notice of claim. Accordingly, *Johnson* is inapposite.

We conclude that the plaintiffs' notice of claim was timely presented in this case. The government acknowledges that it had actual, written notice of the claim sufficient to enable the VA to investigate and to place a value on the claim.[9] The basic "notice" function of the administrative exhaustion requirement was therefore satisfied. *See Transco Leasing,* 896 F.2d at 1444; *Adams,* 615 F.2d at 289.[10]

III.

For the foregoing reasons, we REVERSE the district court's order dismissing
p.452 this case for lack of subject-matter jurisdiction and REMAND for further
proceedings.

EMILIO M. GARZA, Circuit Judge, dissenting:

The majority concludes that "an FTCA notice of claim need not be filed by a
party with the legal authority or capacity under state law to represent the
beneficiaries' interests in state court." *Ante* at 451. Under this errant view of the law,
any person, regardless of his or her connection to the actual claimant or the claim,
could satisfy the jurisdictional notice-of-claim prerequisite in 28 U.S.C. § 2675(a).
The majority's conclusion shows little regard for the United States' limited waiver
of its sovereign immunity for personal injury or death claims under "circumstances
where the United States, if a private person, would be liable to the claimant *in
accordance with the law of the place where the act or omission occurred,*" 28 U.S.C. § 1346(b)(1)
(emphasis added), and fails to give meaningful weight to the term "claimant" as
understood in our controlling precedents and the text of 28 U.S.C. § 2675(a). As
our precedents and the statute make clear, the party filing a notice-of-claim must
have the legal authority to press the claim asserted. In this appeal there is no
dispute that Denise Pleasant, as administratrix of her deceased brother's estate, did
not have the legal authority to bring claims on behalf of his children. *Ante* at 448.
Therefore, the children's claims were not properly presented to the Veteran's
Administration ("VA") for agency consideration within the meaning of § 2675(a).

Distilled, the question presented in this appeal is whether a party filing a notice-
of-claim on behalf of other beneficiaries must have the legal authority to represent
those beneficiaries. That is, whether a party lacking legal authority to assert claims
on behalf of others may nonetheless act to preserve their claims for later
adjudication in the federal courts. The answer begins with the text of 28 U.S.C. §
2675(a), which provides that "an action shall not be instituted upon a claim against
the United States ... unless the *claimant* shall have first presented the claim to the
appropriate Federal agency and *his claim* shall have been finally denied by the agency
in writing...." *Id.* (emphasis added). On its face, this language indicates that the
person presenting the claim for agency review must be a person with control over
the claim. The meaning of the word "claimant" is clarified by the inclusion of the
phrase *"his claim."* This result is additionally supported by the principle that
"[s]tatutes waiving [the] sovereign immunity of the United States are to be
'construed strictly in favor of the sovereign.'" *Jeanmarie v. United States,* 242 F.3d 600,
604 (5th Cir.2001) (quoting *McMahon v. United States,* 342 U.S. 25, 27, 72 S.Ct. 17, 96
L.Ed. 26 (1951)).

Here, neither of the children timely presented to the VA notice of the claims
arising out of their father's death. While Pleasant filed a claim form that alerted the
VA to existence of the claims, she had no legal authority to act on the children's
behalf. Significantly, Pleasant does not dispute this. Under Louisiana law,
unemancipated minors lack "the procedural capacity to sue", LA.CODE CIV. P.
art. 683(A), and must be represented by a tutor, *id.* art. 683(B) ("[T]he tutor is the

proper plaintiff to sue to enforce a right of an unemancipated minor...."). "Upon the death of either parent, the tutorship of minor children belongs of right to the other," unless a court appoints a substitute tutor. LA. CIV.CODE art. 250. Pleasant was not the children's tutor, and her role as the administratrix of her brother's estate did not bestow the legal right to "enforce a right of an unemancipated minor" p.453 under Louisiana law. Thus, the "claimants" did not present their claim to the agency, and therefore did not satisfy the notice-of-claim prerequisite for federal jurisdiction. *See* 28 U.S.C. § 2675(a).

In reaching the opposite conclusion, the majority fails to address the meaning of the term "claimant" as used in the statute. Rather, today's opinion exclusively relies on our precedents establishing only what is sufficient for "presenting" a claim under § 2675(a). In *Transco Leasing Corp. v. United States,* 896 F.2d 1435, 1442, *amended on other grounds on reh'g,* 905 F.2d 61 (5th Cir.1990), a bank was appointed executor of a pilot's estate. The bank, as executor, filed a notice-of-claim for wrongful death claims on behalf of the pilot's wife and daughter, who, in turn, did not file notices individually. The *Transco* court held that the bank's notice-of-claim was sufficient to preserve the wife's and daughter's wrongful death claims. The *Transco* court held that "[a] claim is properly presented within the meaning of § 2675(a) when the agency is given sufficient written notice to commence investigation and the claimant places a value on the claim." We have found these elements acceptable for "presentation" purposes because they are sufficient to "bring[] to the Government's attention facts sufficient to enable it thoroughly to investigate its potential liability and to conduct settlement negotiations with the claimant." *Rise v. United States,* 630 F.2d 1068, 1071 (5th Cir.1980). While *Transco* undoubtedly establishes that these are the only two requirements for properly *presenting* a claim, that case does not govern the issue before us—that is, the scope of the term "claimant."

Although *Transco* addresses a distinct legal question from the case at bar, its analysis supports the position that a person filing notice of a claim under § 2675(a) must have actual legal authority to file that claim.

First, in holding that the Bank could validly file the notice-of-claim on behalf of the wife and daughter, the *Transco* court was directly guided by state law, finding that the Texas Wrongful Death Act "confers upon the executor of an estate the authority to pursue a wrongful death action [in place of the individuals entitled to bring such an action]." *Transco,* 896 F.2d at 1443. In other words, the bank's notice of claim was sufficient to preserve the wife's and daughter's claims only because the bank possessed the legal authority to press those claims under state law. In concluding on this point, the court explicitly stated that "the Bank, as independent executor of [the Pilot's] estate, is a legal representative *authorized by state law* to pursue claims for wrongful death on behalf of the statutory beneficiaries." *Id.* at 1444. (emphasis added). Second, the *Transco* court found that "[t]he 'claimants' within the meaning of § 2675(a) are [the pilot's] widow and daughter." *Id.* at 1443. Later, the court wrote that the wife and daughter were the "actual claimants." *Id.* Both of these references are couched directly within a discussion of the rights arising out of the Texas Wrongful Death Act. Accordingly, the majority's conclusion that *Transco* "does not imply that an individual or entity filing a notice of claim on behalf of beneficiaries must have the legal authority under state law to pursue the beneficiaries' legal rights in court," *ante* at 450, is incorrect.

The requirement that a claimant under § 2675(a) have legal authority to file a notice-of-claim is further supported by the Eighth Circuit's *en banc* decision in *Mader v. United States,* 654 F.3d 794 (8th Cir. 2011) (en banc). *Mader* holds that "a properly 'presented' claim under § 2675(a) must include evidence of a representative's authority to act on behalf of the claim p.454 beneficiaries under state law." *Id.* at 803. Such authority is required because federal agencies are only authorized to settle claims under the FTCA in "circumstances where the United States, if a private person, would be liable to the claimant *in accordance with applicable state law.*" 28 U.S.C. § 1346(b)(1); *Mader,* 654 F.3d at 801 (emphasis added). The *Mader* court found that "under Nebraska law [which governed the wrongful death claim asserted by a widow for her husband's death], a private tortfeasor cannot be legally liable to a non-personal representative for the wrongful death of a decedent," *id.* at 801 (internal citations omitted), and therefore determined that evidence of the representative's legal status under state law was essential to allow the government agency to decide whether to settle, and to legally effect any such settlement eventually reached. Significantly, the *Mader* court found that a representative's actual authority to act on behalf of a claim's beneficiaries under state law is "fundamental to the meaningful administrative consideration and settlement process contained in [§ 2675(a)]." *Id.* at 803. For example, without proof of authority to press the claim, "any agreements with [the purported representative] on behalf of the claim's beneficiaries, including a release of claims [for settlement], would have been ineffective." *Id.* at 802. Therefore, actual authority to present a claim is not only implicit in the text of § 2675(a), but it is also essential to the scheme envisioned by Congress: The requirement allows federal agencies to reach final settlement for a limited class of tort claims before they can be brought in the judicial system. *Id.* at 803-804 ("[Proof of authority] is not a pointless administrative hurdle—it is fundamental to the meaningful administrative consideration and settlement process contemplated [in the FTCA]."). This purpose is frustrated if the filing party does not have the legal capacity to settle the claim.[1]

For the foregoing reasons, I would affirm the district court's dismissal for lack of subject matter jurisdiction. Respectfully, I dissent.

[1] Tutorship in Louisiana is similar to guardianship in common-law jurisdictions. *See generally* FRANK L. MARAIST, 1A LA. CIV. L. TREATISE § 6.1 (2014).

[2] Chaney's mother is not a named plaintiff in this action.

[3] The district court had jurisdiction over this suit under the FTCA. 28 U.S.C. §§ 1346(b), 2674. We have jurisdiction to review timely appeals from the final decisions of district courts. 28 U.S.C. § 1291; *see* FED. R.APP. P. 4(a)(1)(B).

[4] *See* LA.CODE CIV. P. art. 683(B); LA. CIV.CODE art. 250 ("Upon the death of either parent, the tutorship of minor children belongs of right to the other."); LA.CODE CIV. P. art. 4061.1 (providing that natural tutor of minor child may file action for damages on behalf of child based on a delictual obligation). On appeal, the Government does not contend that Whitman and Williams would be ineligible under Louisiana substantive law to recover for the VA's medical malpractice causing Chaney's death.

[5] Of course, Whitman and Williams are now adults, and as such may maintain suit on their own; their prior incapacity is not a bar to their ability to maintain this suit now as adults. *See, e.g., Lewis v. Ascension Parish Sch. Bd.*, 662 F.3d 343, 347 (5th Cir.2011) (per curiam) (stating, in context of minor's capacity to sue under Louisiana law, that "capacity to sue can be cured").

[6] Nothing in the applicable regulations indicate that the category of claims "based on death" cover only a decedent's own wrongful-death claims, to the exclusion of other personal-injury claims "based on death," such as survivor claims for personal injury. *Cf.* 28 C.F.R. §§ 14.3(b) & (c).

[7] While § 14.3(c) includes the phrase "in accordance with applicable state law," we read that phrase to modify only the phrase immediately preceding it—*viz.*, the phrase "any other person legally entitled to assert such a claim[.]" *See Barnhart v. Thomas,* 540 U.S. 20, 26, 124 S.Ct. 376, 157 L.Ed.2d 333 (2003) (explaining that "the grammatical 'rule of the last antecedent'" provides that "a limiting clause or phrase ... should ordinarily be read as modifying only the noun or phrase that it immediately follows"); *accord, e.g., Paroline v. United States,* ___ U.S. ___ 134 S.Ct. 1710, 1721, 188 L.Ed.2d 714 (2014). Thus, section 14.3(c) provides that an FTCA claim "based on death" may be presented by (1) the executor or administrator of the decedent's estate, or (2) by any other person who, in accordance with applicable state law, is legally entitled to assert such a claim.

[8] *See also* 28 U.S.C. § 2674 ("The United States shall be liable, respecting the provisions of this title relating to tort claims, in the same manner and to the same extent as a private individual *under like circumstances.*" (emphasis added)).

[9] Contrary to the suggestion of the dissent and the district court, for the reasons just given, Louisiana procedural law does not govern whether a claim is presented under the FTCA. Furthermore, even if we were to look to state law, under Louisiana law, a party's lack of capacity does not defeat the claim; it "merely retards the progress of the action," it does not "defeat the action," LA.CODE CIV. PROC. art. 923, meaning that the claim would be dismissed without prejudice, the prescriptive period would be interrupted, and the claim could be refiled, *see Jackson v. Hous. Auth. of New Orleans,* 478 So.2d 911 (La.Ct. App. 4th Cir.1985) (filing of claim on behalf of minor child by child's relative without legal authority to do so did not defeat child's claim because action could be refiled by party with proper authority); HON. MAX TOBIAS, JR., *et al.,* LA. PRAC. CIV. PRETRIAL § 9:65 (2013-2014 ed.).

[10] Because on appeal the parties did not brief whether Pleasant may be a proper beneficiary in her own right under Louisiana law, that argument is waived and accordingly we do not consider or reach this question.

[1] In an attempt to bolster today's holding, the majority asserts that "Louisiana procedural law does not govern whether a claim is presented under the FTCA." *Ante* at 451 n. 9. This demonstrates the majority's continued misapprehension of the issue before the court. Without question, the procedural law governing claim presentation under the FTCA *is the FTCA itself*—the Act requires agency notice, sets the deadline for effecting such notice, and mandates that claims be presented as a precedent to federal jurisdiction. State law is relevant insofar as it gives substantive meaning to the term "claimant" as used in § 2675(a). This is the only

function ascribed to Louisiana law by the statute. The majority's approach does not give any meaning to the term "claimant," allowing *any* person to file a claim—sufficient to create federal jurisdiction—on behalf of an injured party.

For this same reason, the majority's observation that, under Louisiana procedural law, "a party's lack of capacity ... 'merely retards the progress of the action,'" *ante* at 451 n. 9, is entirely beside the point. A plaintiff's ability, as in *Jackson v. Hous. Auth. Of New Orleans*, 478 So.2d 911 (La.Ct.App. 4th Cir. 1985), to later refile a previously dismissed complaint, now identifying the proper claimant (the tutor), while simultaneously benefiting from a toll of the prescription period, is not remotely germane to the FTCA's notice-of-claim provisions. Under § 2675(a), state law merely establishes who is properly considered a "claimant," it does not usurp the FTCA's procedural requirements. Here, Louisiana law makes plain that minors may assert claims only through a legal tutor. Denise Pleasant was not the children's tutor, and therefore lacked capacity to assert their claims. Accordingly, the children—the actual "claimants"—never presented their claims to the VA.

765 F.3d 521 (2014)

Clarence LEE, Sr., Individually and as Next Friend of C.L., a Minor; Angelia Lee, Individually and as Next Friend of C.L., a Minor, Plaintiffs-Appellees,
v.
UNITED STATES of America, Defendant-Appellant.

No. 13-50905.

United States Court of Appeals, Fifth Circuit.

August 28, 2014.

Lee v. US, 765 F. 3d 521 (5th Cir. 2014)

p.522 Jamal K. Alsaffar, Tom Jacob (argued), Archuleta Law Firm, Austin, TX, Rudy A. Garza, Hornberger, Sheehan, Fuller, Belter, Wittenber & Garza, San Antonio, TX, Kirk Louis Pittard, Esq., Kelly, Durham & Pittard, L.L.P., Dallas, TX, for Plaintiffs-Appellees.

James Francis Gilligan, Jr., Esq., Assistant U.S. Attorney, U.S. Attorney's Office, San Antonio, TX, Mark William Pennak (argued), Matthew Miles Collette, U.S. Department of Justice, Washington, DC, for Defendant-Appellant.

Before STEWART, Chief Judge, and WIENER and COSTA, Circuit Judges.

CARL E. STEWART, Chief Judge:

The government appeals the district court's award of damages in a medical malpractice suit under the Federal Tort Claims Act (FTCA). The government does not challenge the district court's finding that it was liable; rather, it contends that the district court should have applied the Texas periodic payment statutory scheme, Texas Civil Practice & Remedies Code §§ 74.501-507, and that the district court erred in its order of post-judgment interest. For the following reasons, we VACATE the district court's judgment insofar as it failed to fashion a damages award similar to that contemplated by the Texas periodic payment statutory scheme and awarded post-judgment interest not in compliance with 31 U.S.C. § 1304(b)(1)(A). We REMAND to the district court for further proceedings in accordance with this opinion.

I.

A.

Angelia Lee took her son, C.L., to the pediatric clinic at Randolph Air Force Base (clinic) for his "well-baby" appointments. During these appointments, C.L. should have received his required immunizations and vaccinations. However, the clinic failed to give C.L. the required doses of the Prevnar vaccine, which is designed to prevent invasive pneumonia. C.L. only received two of the required four doses for the Prevnar vaccine.

On December 14, 2004, Angelia took C.L. to the Brooke Army Medical Center emergency clinic (emergency clinic); he had breathing problems, a fever, and other cold symptoms. The emergency clinic diagnosed C.L. with an upper respiratory infection but then proceeded to send him home. Two days later, Angelia took C.L.

p.523 to the clinic because, in addition to his previous symptoms, he was not eating or sleeping properly. An x-ray was done, which showed that C.L. had pneumonia; nonetheless, the nurse practitioner treating C.L. sent him home. On December 17, 2004, Angelia again took C.L. to the clinic. C.L. now had an increased heart rate and had lost weight. The nurse practitioner again sent C.L. home and instructed Angelia to bring him back in three days. The next day Angelia called the clinic because C.L. had greenish yellow eyes. The nurse practitioner assured Angelia that C.L.'s eye color was merely a side effect of the medication and that there was no need to bring C.L. to the clinic before his appointment. Angelia disregarded this advice and took C.L. to the emergency room. After waiting three hours to be seen, C.L. was given antibiotics. C.L. was transferred the next day to Christus Santa Rosa Children's Hospital and was diagnosed with bilateral pneumonia. C.L. was placed into a coma and had to begin dialysis treatment. Ultimately, C.L. had to receive a kidney transplant from his father.

B.

The Lees filed suit against the government under the FTCA, alleging medical malpractice. The Lees moved for partial summary judgment, which the district court granted. The district court found that the government breached the applicable standard of care in its treatment of C.L. A bench trial was held on the remaining issues, and the district court ruled in favor of the Lees. The district court awarded $4,863,523 for "future medical and healthcare needs" and $250,000 for "past and future physical pain and suffering, past and future mental anguish, past and future physical impairment, and past and future physical disfigurement." The government timely appealed. Thereafter, the government filed a motion for an indicative ruling with the district court, raising the issues now presented on appeal. The district court denied the motion, reasoning that the issues raised by the government "are now before the Fifth Circuit for consideration."

II.

A.

We will first address the government's contention that the district court erred by failing to apply the periodic payment scheme. Before we reach the merits of that issue, however, we must determine whether the government waived this argument. Lastly, we will examine the district court's post-judgment interest award.

B.

In FTCA suits, state substantive law applies; however, the Federal Rules of Civil Procedure (FRCP) govern "the manner and time in which defenses are raised and when waiver occurs." *Simon v. United States,* 891 F.2d 1154, 1156 (5th Cir. 1990) (citation and internal quotation marks omitted). Whether the Texas periodic payment scheme constitutes an affirmative defense under FRCP 8(c) "is determined by looking to the substantive law of Texas." *Lucas v. United States,* 807 F.2d 414, 417 (5th Cir.1986). FRCP 8(c)(1) mandates that parties "affirmatively state any avoidance or affirmative defense" in their responsive pleadings. An avoidance "is an allegation or statement of new matter, in opposition to a former pleading, which, admitting the facts alleged in such former pleading, shows cause why they should not have their ordinary legal effect." *Simon,* 891 F.2d at 1157 (citation and internal quotation marks omitted).

Generally, failure to comply with FRCP 8(c) results in waiver of the avoidance p.524 or affirmative defense. *Simon,* 891 F.2d at 1157. However, if "a defendant raises the issue at a pragmatically sufficient time, and if the plaintiff is not prejudiced in its ability to respond, there is no waiver of the defense." *Vanhoy v. United States,* 514 F.3d 447, 450 (5th Cir.2008) (citation and internal quotation marks omitted).

Vanhoy involved a situation similar to the case *sub judice.* In *Vanhoy,* the plaintiffs sued the government under the FTCA, alleging medical malpractice. *Id.* at 449. On appeal, the government argued that the district court erred by refusing to adjust the judgment so that it resembled § 40:1299.43 of the Louisiana Medical Malpractice Act (MMA). *Id.* at 449–50. The plaintiffs claimed that the government's argument was an affirmative defense that the government waived because it failed to produce supporting evidence at trial. *Id.* at 450. We assumed without deciding that the government's argument was an affirmative defense. *Id.* However, we concluded that the defense was not waived. *Id.* at 451. First, we reasoned that the defense raised a legal question that did not need any factual development. *Id.* at 450. Second, although the defense was not raised in the government's answer, the government argued the defense in multiple motions and its pretrial order. *Id.* at 450–51. Therefore, there was no waiver because it was "raised at a pragmatically sufficient time" and the plaintiffs "were not prejudiced in their ability to respond." *Id.* at 451; *see also Lucas,* 807 F.2d at 418 (holding that the government did not waive a defense it did not plead under similar circumstances). Conversely, we have held that the government waived a defense it did not plead when the defense entailed more than a legal issue. *Simon,* 891 F.2d at 1159. For example, in *Simon,* the government failed to plead a defense which would have dictated the parties' trial strategy. *Id.*

C.

The government argues that it did not waive the application of the Texas periodic payment statutory scheme because it is not an affirmative defense. However, even assuming that the statutory scheme is an affirmative defense, the government contends that the argument is not waived because it raised the issue at a pragmatically sufficient time and Appellees were not prejudiced in responding to the request. The government also claims that this request cannot be waived because it implicates sovereign immunity. We refrain from deciding whether a request to apply the periodic payment statutory scheme is an affirmative defense because, even assuming that it is, we hold that the government did not waive the argument.

Before we delve into our analysis, we briefly detail the Texas periodic payment statutory scheme. Under Texas Civil Practice & Remedies Code § 74.503(a), "[a]t the request of a defendant physician or health care provider or claimant, the court shall order that" medical damages "be paid in whole or in part in periodic payments rather than by a lump-sum payment." For future non-medical damages, however, the district court "may order" periodic payments. *Id.* § 74.503(b). The district court is required to "make a specific finding" of the amount necessary to "compensate the claimant for the future damages" and specify the payment recipient, payment amount, payment intervals, and the "number of payments or the period of time over which payments must be made." *Id.* § 74.503(c), (d). Upon the death of the payment recipient, periodic payments terminate for all damages "other than future loss of earnings" and "any p.525 security given reverts to the defendant." *Id.* § 74.506(b), (d).

Unlike the situation in *Vanhoy,* the government failed to properly raise this issue until after the trial concluded.[1] Nonetheless, the government requested that the periodic payment scheme be applied "at a pragmatically sufficient time and the [Appellees] were not prejudiced in their ability to respond." *See Vanhoy,* 514 F.3d at 451. As we stated in *Rogers v. McDorman,* "the prejudice inquiry considers whether the plaintiff had sufficient notice to prepare for and contest the defense." 521 F.3d 381, 387 (5th Cir.2008). In *Lucas,* the government did not waive its affirmative defense, in spite of its failure to plead it, because it was a purely legal issue that was raised at trial. 807 F.2d at 418. The government's defense did "not affect the plaintiffs' proof of damages, but simply limit[ed] the dollar amount of recovery on the damages the plaintiff *is* able to prove." *Id.* By comparison, in *Ingraham v. United States,* the government's affirmative defense was waived when it failed to raise the affirmative defense before the conclusion of the trial. 808 F.2d 1075, 1079-80 (5th Cir. 1987). We noted that the plaintiffs would have altered their trial strategy had they known of the government's intent to raise the defense. *Id.* at 1079.

It was not until after the conclusion of the trial that the government specifically mentioned the periodic payment scheme in its trial brief and proposed findings of fact and conclusions of law. However, similar to the statute in *Vanhoy,*[2] the applicability of the periodic payment scheme is a legal issue "without the need for factual proof." *Vanhoy,* 514 F.3d at 450. It is not until the district court actually applies the statutory scheme that it would need to engage in any factual determination. *See, e.g.,* Tex. Civ. Prac. & Rem.Code § 74.503(c), (d) (stating that courts must "make a specific finding of the dollar amount of periodic payments that will compensate the claimant for the future damages"). The government therefore did not have to present evidence regarding the applicability of the periodic payment scheme. Additionally, Appellees were not prejudiced by the government's failure to raise this issue. To the contrary, Appellees will have the opportunity to present evidence on many of the issues they raise in later proceedings.[3] In fact, Appellees had the right to request the application of the periodic payment scheme after trial as the government did.

Appellees argue that the application of the periodic payment scheme does not implicate sovereign immunity because the amount of the government's liability is unchanged. However, that argument fails to p.526 fully appreciate the sovereign immunity waiver in the FTCA. The waiver is effective only to the same extent as a private individual in a similar circumstance. *See* 28 U.S.C. § 2674 ("The United States shall be liable ... in the same manner and to the same extent as a private individual under like circumstances...."). Thus, even if the government is not subjected to additional liability, the government is entitled to request the application of the same statutory mechanisms available to private individuals.

In addition, Appellees claim that the government is precluded from requesting periodic payments because it presented evidence regarding lump sum awards and failed to produce evidence supporting the imposition of a reversionary trust. However, we fail to see how the evidence presented at trial has any impact on the district court's duty to apply a mandatory statute.[4] *See* Tex. Civ. Prac. & Rem.Code § 74.503(a) (stating that once requested, a "court *shall order* that medical [damages]... be paid in whole or in part in periodic payments" (emphasis added)). Because we hold that the government did not waive this argument, we proceed to consider whether the district court erred by not applying the Texas periodic payment statutory scheme.

III.

A.

The district court's decision not to apply the Texas periodic payment statutory scheme is reviewed de novo. *Vanhoy,* 514 F.3d at 451. "The question ... is a legal one requiring interpretation of both [Texas] and federal statutes." *Id.*

B.

The Texas periodic payment scheme has not been applied by many courts; however, the courts to apply the statute have treated § 74.503(a) as mandatory when the enumerated conditions are satisfied. For instance, in *St. Joseph Regional Health Center v. Hopkins,* the Texas court of appeals stated that once requested, "the trial court shall order periodic payments, rather than a lump sum, for future damages ... awarded in a health care liability claim." 393 S.W.3d 885, 886 (Tex.App.-Waco 2012, pet. denied) (internal quotation marks omitted). Likewise, in *Prabhakar v. Fritzgerald,* the Texas court of appeals held that the trial court erred by failing to order periodic payments once the defendant complied with the statutory requirements. No. 05-10-00126-CV, ___ S.W.3d ___, ___, 2012 WL 3667400, at *11 (Tex. App.-Dallas Aug. 24, 2012); *see also Christus Health v. Dorriety,* 345 S.W.3d 104, 117 (Tex.App.-Houston [14th Dist.] 2011, pet. denied).

Conversely, in *McLeod v. United States,* the district court held that, even if the periodic payment scheme was not waived, it was not required to apply it. No. 5:06-civ-00017-WRF, at *11 (W.D.Tex. April 8, 2010). A portion of the damages awarded fell within the permissive section of the statutory scheme, § 74.503(b). *Id.* at *12. The district court first noted that it would not order periodic payments under § 74.503(b). *Id.* As for those damages that fell under the mandatory portion of § 74.503(a), the court relied on *Vanhoy* in holding that the application of the statute would impose too onerous of a burden on the court to determine, among other things, the terms of the trust, and to appoint p.527 a trustee. *Id.* at *13-14.

Moreover, the court declined to order periodic payments on a record which it found to be "devoid of any factual evidence and devoid of any argument or explanation for the grounds supporting periodic payments and how to structure them." *Id.* at *14. Even assuming that § 74.503(a) is mandatory, the court stated that the defendant presented insufficient evidence to permit the application of the statute. *Id.* at *15.

When presented with statutes similar to the Texas periodic payment scheme, other circuits have held that district courts erred when they failed to order periodic payments. For instance, in *Dutra v. United States,* the Ninth Circuit held that the district court erred by failing to apply the applicable periodic payment statute, § 4.56.260 of the Washington Revised Code. 478 F.3d 1090, 1091 (9th Cir.2007). Under § 4.56.260, if requested by a party, courts are required to order that future economic damages be paid in periodic payments. *Id.* The Ninth Circuit reasoned that "[t]he FTCA authorizes courts to craft remedies that approximate the results contemplated by state statutes, and nothing in the FTCA prevents district courts from ordering the United States to provide periodic payments in the form of a reversionary trust." *Id.* at 1092.

The Tenth Circuit reached a similar result in *Hill v. United States,* 81 F.3d 118 (10th Cir.1996). In *Hill,* the government argued that the district court should have placed the plaintiff's future damages in a reversionary trust. *Id.* at 120. Under Colorado law, a health care provider could pay an adverse judgment periodically. *Id.* Moreover, payments ceased for all damages, except for future earnings, upon the recipient's death. *Id.* The Tenth Circuit held that the government "may not be ordered to make periodic payments in the manner in which the [statute] provides." *Id.* However, the court held that the government was entitled to a reversionary trust for the future medical expenses similar to that envisioned under the statute. *Id.* at 121. As the Fourth Circuit described it, "the FTCA permits courts to craft remedies that approximate state periodic payment statutes, including reversionary trusts." *Cibula v. United States,* 664 F.3d 428, 433 (4th Cir.2012) (internal quotation marks omitted).

C.

Appellees urge us to follow our decision in *Vanhoy* and not impose a reversionary trust for the future damages. Appellees argue that a reversionary trust is not warranted because the statutory scheme does not provide for such a remedy. Rather, a reversionary trust is only permitted, Appellees contend, when it serves the best interest of the child. Moreover, Appellees state that an implicit understanding existed between the parties that the damages award would be a lump sum. Appellees also argue that imposing a reversionary trust would burden the district court with additional administrative obligations. Appellees' arguments are unavailing. We hold that the district court erred by not applying the Texas statutory scheme. Although the district court could not impose a continuing obligation on the government, it should have structured the damage award in a manner resembling the periodic payment scheme.

Section 74.503(a) states that, if requested, "the court *shall order* that medical, health care, or custodial services awarded in a health care liability claim be paid in whole or in part in periodic payments." (emphasis added). A court has the discretion to decline ordering periodic payments only in regard to other future damages not encompassed in the subsection (a) or when the defendant "is not adequately insured." p.528 Tex. Civ. Prac. & Rem.Code § 74.503(b), § 74.505(a). The district court awarded $4,863,523 for "future medical and healthcare needs" and $250,000 for "past and future physical pain and suffering, past and future mental anguish, past and future physical impairment, and past and future physical disfigurement." The district court was therefore obligated to apply the statute once the government submitted its request. *See St. Joseph Reg'l Health Ctr.*, 393 S.W.3d at 886; *Prabhakar,* ___ S.W.3d at ___, 2012 WL 3667400, at *11; *see also Christus Health*, 345 S.W.3d at 117. Because a private individual would be entitled to the application of the statutory scheme, the government should also be permitted to have its damage award structured in the manner envisioned by the statute. *See* 28 U.S.C. § 2674 ("The United States shall be liable ... in the same manner and to the same extent as a private individual under like circumstances...."); *see also Dutra,* 478 F.3d at 1092 (reaching an identical conclusion with a similar statute); *Hill,* 81 F.3d at 121.

Although, at first glance, *Vanhoy* appears to foreclose the government's request, the Texas periodic payment scheme is distinguishable from the statute at issue in *Vanhoy.* In *Vanhoy,* the government sought to have the district court impose "a reversionary trust from which [the plaintiff's] future medical care damages may be *distributed as needed.*" 514 F.3d at 451 (emphasis added). Distinguishing *Owen v. United States,* 935 F.2d 734 (5th Cir. 1991), we held that the reversionary trust implicated different concerns.[5] *Id.* at 452-53. Because the FTCA does not permit continuing obligations against the government, the government could not be required "to make periodic payments of future medical care damages ... on an asincurred basis the way that" the statute envisions. *Id.* at 452. Whereas the statute in *Owen* required only a single action, we reasoned that the MMA imposed an obligation throughout the victim's lifetime. *Id.* at 452-53.

As for the government's request for a reversionary trust in *Vanhoy,* we held that Louisiana law did not permit private individuals to request reversionary trusts and, thus, the government was not entitled to request one. *Id.* at 453. Moreover, the plaintiffs objected to a reversionary trust and the government was unable to proffer how the trust would best serve the plaintiff's interests. *Id.* We distinguished *Hill, Hull,* and *Dutra. Id.* at 453-54. *Hill, Hull,* and *Dutra* involved "guardian ad litem situations." *Id.* at 453. Furthermore, we observe that the Tenth Circuit stated in *Hill* and *Hull* that it could create the reversionary trust only when it would be in the child's best interest. *Id.* In *Dutra,* the statute at issue required courts to impose the payment method that would best provide for the claimant's future needs. *Id.* Additionally, the statutes in *Hill* and *Dutra* were distinguishable from the Louisiana statutes. *Id.* at 453-54. Because there was no authority mandating that the damages award be structured as the government requested, we held that, similar to *Frankel* and *Reilly,* the government's request for periodic payments and a reversionary trust must be denied. *Id.* at 454-55. We expressed concern for the administrative burden the imposition of a reversionary trust would require. *Id.* at 455. However, we stated that the case would be different had there been a statute mandating the damages award requested by the government. *Id.*

p.529 The Texas periodic payment scheme differs greatly from the statute presented in *Vanhoy. See Wood v. United States,* No. SA-1-CV-941, 2011 WL 1790832, at *2 (W.D.Tex. May 10, 2011) (noting differences between the two statutes); *McLeod,* No. 5:06-cv-00017-WRF, at *13 (same). The Texas scheme does not mandate that the government make payments on an asincurred basis for the lifetime of the plaintiff; to the contrary, § 74.503(c) requires the district court to "make a specific finding of the dollar amount of periodic payments" to satisfy the judgment and subsection (d) mandates that courts note in their judgment the "number of payments or the period of time over which payments must be made." The onerous administrative burden that we feared in *Vanhoy* is therefore not present with the application of the Texas scheme. Furthermore, there is statutory authority for the damages award requested by the government in the case *sub judice. See* Tex. Civ. Prac. & Rem.Code § 74.503.

We have stated that awards constituting continuing obligations on the United States are not appropriate under the FTCA. *Vanhoy,* 514 F.3d at 452 ("[N]owhere does the FTCA authorize damage awards that require the United States to perform continuing obligations."). However, unlike the situation in *Vanhoy,* the district court can craft the damages award to mirror that of the Texas periodic payment scheme. As we noted in *Owen,* "[t]he 'like circumstances' inquiry is not overly stringent." 935 F.2d at 737. Here, the district court could order "periodic payments in the form of a reversionary trust" thereby avoiding any semblance of imposing an ongoing obligation on the government. *See Dutra,* 478 F.3d at 1092. Structuring the damages award in this manner would sufficiently mirror the Texas periodic payment scheme to comply with the FTCA. *See Cibula,* 664 F.3d at 433-34; *Hill,* 81 F.3d at 121; *Dutra,* 478 F.3d at 1092. Appellees are correct that the Texas scheme does not explicitly mention a reversionary trust. *See* Tex. Civ. Prac. & Rem.Code §§ 74.505-506. However, the statutory scheme does state that upon the termination of the payments under the statute, "any security given reverts to the defendant." *Id.* § 74.506(d). Moreover, "the FTCA permits courts to craft remedies that 'approximate' state periodic payment statutes." *Cibula,* 664 F.3d at 433. Appellees' argument that Congress must expressly provide for this payment structure is unavailing. Private individuals are entitled to have the Texas scheme applied and the FTCA mandates treatment of the government in the same manner as a private individual in similar circumstances. *See* 28 U.S.C. § 2674.

Appellees' reliance on *McLeod* is not persuasive. In *McLeod,* the court declined to apply the Texas periodic payment scheme because the record was "devoid of any factual evidence and devoid of any argument or explanation for the grounds supporting periodic payments and how to structure them." *McLeod,* No. 5:06-cv-00017-WRF, at *14-15. However, the court does not have discretion as to whether it must order periodic payments for at least a portion of the damages for medical care. Tex. Civ. Prac. & Rem.Code § 74.503. Moreover, a lack of evidence is not a reason to decline to award periodic payments; rather, as we noted previously, a court has discretion to decline to impose periodic payments for "future damages other than medical, health care, or custodial services" and if the defendant "is not adequately insured." *Id.* § 74.503(b), § 74.505(a).

IV.

A.

The government also argues that the district court's post-judgment interest p.530 award does not comply with 31 U.S.C. § 1304, an error that Appellees do not contest. The government acknowledges that it failed to raise this issue until its motion for an indicative ruling but contends that this argument is not waived because it is jurisdictional. Appellees urge us to simply modify the district court's judgment to comply with § 1304.

B.

In *Dickerson ex rel. Dickerson v. United States,* the government did not challenge the district court's award of post-judgment interest until its reply brief. 280 F.3d 470, 478 (5th Cir.2002). Nonetheless, we addressed the government's argument because recovery under the FTCA is limited to the government's waiver of sovereign immunity and "the government's sovereign immunity, being a jurisdictional prerequisite, may be asserted at any stage of the proceedings." *Id.*

C.

The United States is required to pay interest "only when specifically provided for by statute because only by statute can the United States waive its sovereign immunity." *Id.* (citation and internal quotation marks omitted). Under 28 U.S.C. § 1961(a), "[i]nterest shall be allowed on any money judgment in a civil case recovered in a district court." 31 U.S.C. § 1304(b)(1)(A) provides that "[i]nterest may be paid ... on a judgment of a district court, only when the judgment becomes final after review on appeal ... and then only from the date of filing of the transcript of the judgment with the Secretary of the Treasury through the day before the date of the mandate of affirmance."

D.

Because this issue has jurisdictional implications, it is properly before us. *Dickerson,* 280 F.3d at 478. We hold that the district court erred when it ordered post-judgment interest to accrue from the date of judgment. As both parties acknowledge, the district court should have ordered post-judgment interest to begin accruing "from the date of filing of the transcript of the judgment with the Secretary of the Treasury through the day before the date of the mandate of affirmance." 31 U.S.C. § 1304(b)(1)(A); *Dickerson,* 280 F.3d at 478-79 ("Section 1304 applies to post-judgment interest in FTCA cases because § 1304 lists 28 U.S.C. § 2414 as one of the statutes covered thereby and [28 U.S.C.] § 2414 is the statutory authority for payment of judgments against the United States.").

V.

For the foregoing reasons, we VACATE the district court's judgment insofar as it failed to fashion a damages award similar to the Texas Periodic Payment statutory scheme and awarded post-judgment interest not in compliance with 31 U.S.C. § 1304(b)(1)(A). We therefore REMAND to the district court for further proceedings in accordance with this opinion.

[1] In its answer, the government merely referenced "Texas Civil Practice & Remedies Code, Chapter 74." We need not decide, however, whether the government adequately raised the Texas periodic payment scheme in its answer because we hold that the government sufficiently raised the issue after the trial.

[2] In *Vanhoy*, the statute at issue provided "that private malpractice awards for future medical care expenses" would be paid from a fund set up by state health care providers and would be paid as the "charges accrue[d], with payment ceasing on the death of the victim." *Vanhoy*, 514 F.3d at 449.

[3] As for Appellees' argument that ordering periodic payments will permit the government "to double dip in reductions" to the award, Appellees misunderstand the periodic payment scheme. The district court must "make a specific finding of the dollar amount of periodic payments that will compensate the claimant for the future damages." Tex. Civ. Prac. & Rem.Code § 74.503(c). So, when applied properly, claimants are adequately compensated. The statutory scheme does not ensure that the government will pay fewer damages to Appellees.

[4] Appellees also argue that the government waived its argument that the district court should have ordered periodic payments for the future pain and suffering damages. However, this appeal only concerns the future medical care damages.

[5] In *Owen*, we stated that the government was entitled to the state damages cap in a FTCA suit. 935 F.2d at 737-38.

730 F.3d 476 (2013)

John E. WILLOUGHBY; Wendy Willoughby, Plaintiffs-Appellants
v.
UNITED STATES of America, on behalf of the UNITED STATES DEPARTMENT OF THE ARMY, Defendant-Appellee.

No. 12-40915.

United States Court of Appeals, Fifth Circuit.

September 17, 2013.

Willoughby v. US Dept. of the Army, 730 F. 3d 476 (5th Cir. 2013)

p.477 Mark Clyde Burgess, Esq., Attorney, Jonathan Ross Prazak, Boyd, Poff & Burgess, L.L.P., Texarkana, TX, for Plaintiff-Appellant.

Robert Austin Wells, Esq., Assistant U.S. Attorney, U.S. Attorney's Office, Tyler, TX, for Defendant-Appellee.

p.478 Before DeMOSS, DENNIS, and PRADO, Circuit Judges.

PER CURIAM:

Plaintiffs-Appellants John and Wendy Willoughby (together, "the plaintiffs" or "Willoughby") appeal from dismissal of their Federal Tort Claims Act claim against the United States Army. John Willoughby, an employee of a private Army contractor, was injured on the job when he tripped and fell. Willoughby received workers' compensation benefits through his employer's policy. The employer's contract with the Army required the employer to provide workers' compensation benefits for employees, which were then treated as an expense that the Army would reimburse. Because Willoughby found the benefits he received to be insufficient to cover his needs, he sued the Government for negligence and premises liability.

The Government moved to dismiss, invoking Texas' workers' compensation exclusive-remedy rule. Under Texas law, general contractors who require subcontractors to provide workers' compensation insurance to their employees and who pay for that coverage are "statutory employers" protected by the exclusive-remedy provision. The plaintiffs argued that the Government was unlike a "statutory employer" because the Government did not follow certain Texas regulations governing statutory employers. The district court granted the motion to dismiss, and Willoughby appealed. Finding no error, we affirm.

I.

The plaintiffs allege that on June 8, 2007, John Willoughby was injured while working at the federal Red River Army Depot ("RRAD") when he tripped over a bundle of cables and fell onto the floor of the Depot, requiring significant medical treatment.[1] At the time of the accident, Willoughby was employed by a government contractor, Lear Siegler Services, Inc. ("LSI"), as a mechanic at RRAD. LSI had contracted with the U.S. Army to provide additional workforce to support the Army's mission at RRAD. Willoughby received workers' compensation benefits for his injury through LSI's workers' compensation insurance plan, which the Government required LSI to provide to its employees working at RRAD. However, because Willoughby found the benefits he received to be insufficient to cover his needs, he sued the Government for negligence and premises liability.

Willoughby filed suit against the Government in the United States District Court for the Eastern District of Texas. The Government moved to dismiss under Federal Rules of Civil Procedure 12(b)(1) and 12(b)(6), arguing that it was entitled to assert the state-law defense that recovery against it was precluded by Texas' Workers' Compensation Act's exclusive remedy rule because the Government, through LSI, had already paid Willoughby the workers' compensation benefits he was due.[2] After a hearing, the district court concluded that the Government was entitled to raise the exclusive-remedy defense as a Texas "statutory employer,"[3] and p.479 granted the motion to dismiss. The plaintiffs appealed.

II.

The district court had jurisdiction over this suit under the Federal Tort Claims Act ("FTCA"). 28 U.S.C. §§ 1346(b), 2674. Willoughby timely exhausted his administrative remedies by submitting a claim for personal injury with the Department of the Army, which the Army denied. The question of whether the United States has waived sovereign immunity pursuant to the FTCA goes to the court's subject-matter jurisdiction, *see, e.g., In re FEMA Trailer Formaldehyde Prods. Liab. Litig. (Miss. Plaintiffs)*, 668 F.3d 281, 289 (5th Cir.2012); *Spotts v. United States*, 613 F.3d 559, 566-67, 573 (5th Cir.2010), and may therefore be resolved on a Rule 12(b)(1) motion to dismiss, *see, e.g., Ramming v. United States*, 281 F.3d 158, 161 (5th Cir.2001).

This Court has jurisdiction to review the final decisions of district courts. 28 U.S.C. § 1291. The district court entered final judgment in favor of the defendant on July 19, 2012, and the plaintiffs filed their notice of appeal on August 13, 2012, making the appeal timely. *See* FED. R.APP. P. 4(a)(1)(A).

III.

We conduct a de novo review of orders granting the Government's motion to dismiss an FTCA complaint under Rules 12(b)(1) and 12(b)(6). *E.g., Ramming*, 281 F.3d at 161. The plaintiffs, as the parties asserting federal subject-matter jurisdiction, bear the burden of proving that its requirements are met. *See id.* "When a Rule 12(b)(1) motion is filed in conjunction with other Rule 12 motions, the court should consider the Rule 12(b)(1) jurisdictional attack before addressing any attack on the merits." *Id.* (citation omitted).

"In applying Rule 12(b)(1), the district court has the power to dismiss for lack of subject matter jurisdiction on any one of three separate bases: (1) the complaint alone; (2) the complaint supplemented by undisputed facts evidenced in the record; or (3) the complaint supplemented by undisputed facts plus the court's resolution of disputed facts. Here, the district court did not resolve any disputed facts, so we ... consider the allegations in the plaintiff's complaint as true. Our review is limited to determining whether the district court's application of the law is correct and, to the extent its decision was based on undisputed facts, whether those facts are indeed undisputed. We then ask if dismissal was appropriate." *Spotts,* 613 F.3d at 565-66 (quotation marks, citations, alterations, and footnote omitted).

IV.

A.

The Federal Tort Claims Act ("FTCA") is the exclusive remedy for suits against the United States or its agencies sounding in tort. 28 U.S.C. § 2679(a). The FTCA grants a limited waiver of sovereign immunity and allows tort claims against the United States "in the same manner and to the same extent as a private individual under like circumstances." *Id.* § 2674. "[T]he words 'like circumstances' do not restrict a court's inquiry to the *same circumstances,* but require it to look further afield." *United States v. Olson,* 546 U.S. 43, 46-47, 126 S.Ct. 510, 163 L.Ed.2d 306 (2005) (citing *Indian Towing Co. v. United States,* 350 U.S. 61, 64, 76 S.Ct. 122, 100 L.Ed. 48 (1955); S.Rep. No. 1400, 79th Cong., 2d Sess., 32 (1946) (stating that purpose of FTCA was to make the tort liability of the United States "the same as that of a private person under like circumstance, in accordance with the local p.480 law")). All that is required is "a similar analogy" because the plain text of § 2679 uses the modifier "like" rather than "the same," and that language reflects a deliberate choice on the part of Congress to delimit the scope of the FTCA's limited waiver of sovereign immunity. *See id.; Indian Towing,* 350 U.S. at 64, 76 S.Ct. 122; *see also, e.g., United States v. Nordic Vill., Inc.,* 503 U.S. 30, 33-34, 112 S.Ct. 1011, 117 L.Ed.2d 181 (1992) ("[T]he Government's consent to be sued must be construed strictly in favor of the sovereign[.]") (citation and quotation marks omitted).

"Whether a private person in 'like circumstances' would be subject to liability is a question of sovereign immunity and, thus, is ultimately a question of federal law. Because the federal government could never be exactly like a private actor, a court's job in applying the standard is to find the most reasonable analogy. Inherent differences between the government and a private person cannot be allowed to disrupt this analysis. The Fifth Circuit has consistently held that the Government is entitled to raise any and all defenses that would potentially be available to a private citizen or entity under state law. Therefore, if a private person under 'like circumstances' would be shielded from liability pursuant to a state statute, lower courts must decline to exercise subject-matter jurisdiction." *In re FEMA Trailer Formaldehyde Prods. Liab. Litig.,* 668 F.3d at 288-89 (citing *Olson,* 546 U.S. at 44, 126 S.Ct. 510) (other citations omitted).

The government is authorized by Congress to provide workers' compensation insurance for federal employees;[4] however, Congress has not granted permission for the government to provide coverage to contractors.[5] Accordingly, the United States cannot directly pay workers' compensation benefits to non-federal employees or employees of independent contractors.[6] Instead, the Army provided in its contract with LSI that LSI must provide workers' compensation coverage for its employees in compliance with Texas law, but the Army agreed to pay the cost of the premiums directly to LSI as an "allowable cost."[7] The government argues that under the Texas Workers' Compensation Act, p.481 it is entitled to raise the exclusive remedy defense because Willoughby received workers' compensation benefits that the government contractually required LSI to provide.

The Texas Workers' Compensation Act ("TWCA") provides that workers' compensation benefits are the exclusive remedy for employees against employers for work-related injuries and deaths.[8] In some situations general contractors may be liable for the injuries sustained by the employees of their subcontractors if the subcontractor is under-or uninsured. Texas, however, extends its exclusive-remedy protection to general subcontractors who, by written agreement, require their subcontractors to obtain workers' compensation insurance. TEX. LAB.CODE § 406.123(a). Section 406.123(a) of the TWCA provides:

> A general contractor and a subcontractor may enter into a written agreement under which the general contractor provides workers' compensation insurance coverage to the subcontractor and the employees of the subcontractor.

Id. A premises owner is considered a "general contractor" within the meaning of section 406.123 if the owner "provides" workers' compensation to a contractor who performs work for the owner. *Entergy Gulf States, Inc. v. Summers,* 282 S.W.3d 433, 438-39 (Tex.2009).

If the general contractor or premises owner "provides" workers' compensation insurance in this manner, it becomes a statutory employer of the subcontractor's employees for the purposes of the TWCA:

> An agreement under this section makes the general contractor the employer of the subcontractor and the subcontractor's employees only for purposes of the workers' compensation laws of this state.

TEX. LAB.CODE § 406.123(e). If a general contractor or premises owner adheres to the requirements of section 406.123, then as a "statutory employer" it is effectively immune from the claims brought by a subcontractor because the employee's workers' compensation benefits are his or her exclusive remedy. *See id.* § 408.001(a). To become a statutory employer under Texas law, a premises owner or general contractor need not personally obtain or directly pay for the insurance or benefits. *HCBeck, Ltd. v. Rice,* 284 S.W.3d 349, 353 (Tex.2009) (citing TEX. LAB.CODE § 406.123(a)). Rather, "[t]he Act only requires that there be a written agreement to provide workers' compensation insurance coverage." *Id.*

However, the TWCA and the Texas Administrative Code set out additional procedural requirements that statutory employers must follow, for instance:

> (f) A general contractor shall file a copy of an agreement entered into under [section 406.123] with the general contractor's workers' compensation insurance carrier not later than the 10th day after the date on which the contract is executed ...

> (g) A general contractor who enters into an agreement with a subcontractor under [section 406.123] commits an administrative violation if the contractor fails to file a copy of the agreement as required by Subsection (f).

TEX. LAB.CODE § 406.123(f)-(g). The Administrative Code sets out similar requirements:

> p.482 An agreement between a general contractor and a subcontractor made in accordance with the Texas Labor Code, § 406.123(a),(d),(e) or (*f*) shall:

(1) be in writing;

(2) state that the subcontractor and the subcontractor's employees are employees of the general contractor for the sole purpose of workers' compensation coverage;

(3) indicate whether the general contractor will make a deduction for the premiums;

(4) specify whether this is a blanket agreement or if it applies to a specific job location and, if so, list the location;

(5) contain the signatures of both parties;

(6) indicate the date the agreement was made, the term the agreement will be effective, and estimated number of workers affected by the agreement.

28 TEX. ADMIN. CODE § 112.101(a). In a similar vein, section 406.005 of the TWCA requires employers to notify each employee of whether the employee is covered by workers' compensation insurance at a "conspicuous location" at the employer's principal place of business in language adopted by the Labor Commissioner, or else be held in administrative violation. TEX. LAB.CODE § 406.005. Essentially, these additional procedures ensure that the employees receive sufficient notice of their rights and the terms of the workers' compensation insurance benefits available to them.

B.

The parties agree that in this case the Government has taken the basic steps it needs to take to avail itself of the exclusive-remedy rule as a statutory employer, *viz.,* by requiring, in writing, that LSI provide its employees with workers' compensation benefits. *See HCBeck,* 284 S.W.3d at 353 ("The Act only requires that there be a written agreement to provide workers' compensation insurance coverage."); *Entergy,* 282 S.W.3d at 438-39 (holding a premises owner is a "general contractor" for purposes of the statutory employer provision). What the parties dispute is the significance of the Government's failure to adhere to the letter of the filing and notice requirements in the above code and regulatory provisions. Willoughby argues that if the Government is not *required* to give notice that its independent contractors' employees are covered by the TWCA, as Texas law requires of other employers in the State, the employees will not be assured of receiving the required notice such that they can make an informed election regarding their coverage.

This Court has held that the government does not waive its sovereign immunity under the FTCA in situations involving minor procedural differences between the government and private actors. In *Owen v. United States,* 935 F.2d 734 (5th Cir. 1991), this Court held that the United States could take advantage of Louisiana's cap on medical-malpractice damages applicable by statute to state-licensed medical providers who provide proof of financial responsibility and participate in a patients' compensation fund, despite the fact that the United States had not contributed to the fund as is required of state providers. *Id.* at 737. We reasoned that because the tort victim would be subject to the damages cap if the tortfeasor had been an in-state provider, and because the solvency of the Government could not reasonably be questioned, the Government was "like" employers who participated in the scheme. *See id.* at 737-38. Similarly, in *Roelofs v. United States,* 501 F.2d 87 (5th Cir.1974), this Court held that the Army was entitled to assert Louisiana's statutory employer p.483 defense to an FTCA claim because the Army required its contractor to maintain workers' compensation insurance for its employees; the court rejected the plaintiffs' argument that because the Government cannot be forced by a state to purchase workers' compensation insurance, it is inherently on unequal footing with state private actors. *Id.* at 90-92.

While the facts of *Roelofs* are similar to this case, there the plaintiffs did not allege that the Government failed to follow substantive filing and notice regulations, as Willoughby argues here.[9] However, the filing and notice regulations here are akin to the damages cap at issue in *Owen.* Here, as in *Owen,* the government's failure to adhere to the procedural requirements did not make a meaningful difference in the outcome of the litigation from the plaintiff's perspective.[10] Willoughby has not claimed that he did not know that he was covered by workers' compensation insurance, or that he would have done anything differently, such as opted out of LSI's workers' compensation insurance, had the government given him the notice required by Texas law that he was covered by the TWCA.

Of course, the notice requirement is important because it allows employees to make an informed choice about their workers' compensation insurance coverage options. Employees are permitted to opt out of workers' compensation coverage and to retain their common-law rights of action to recover damages for personal injuries against the employer, albeit on a fault basis. *See* TEX. LAB.CODE § 406.034. Section 406.034 allows employees to opt out of the workers' compensation system, including the applicability of the exclusive-remedy bar. *See id.; see also Tex. Workers' Comp. Comm'n v. Garcia,* 893 S.W.2d 504, 532 (Tex.1995).[11] Thus, the notice requirement serves a critical function in ensuring that the employee is able to make an informed election concerning his or her rights.[12]

p.484 However, Willoughby has not alleged or implied that he lacked notice of his right to opt out of his workers' compensation insurance coverage or that he would have opted out if the government had given him the required notice. Instead, he argues that the government may never assert this state-law defense because Texas cannot force the government to adhere to the filing and notice regulations or to pay the administrative fines for failing to do so. We rejected that argument in *Roelofs* and held that, notwithstanding the fact that the Government cannot be forced to purchase workers' compensation insurance or else be fined, the government may nevertheless be under "like circumstances" as a private employer. *See* 501 F.2d at 90-02. This theoretical difference simply is not enough under the "like circumstances" test. Because Willoughby does not allege a lack of notice or prejudice from any lack of notice, the federal government is in "like circumstances" as a Texas statutory employer. Accordingly, Willoughby's workers' compensation benefits are his exclusive remedy, and his claims against the Government were properly dismissed.

V.

For the foregoing reasons, we AFFIRM the judgment of the district court.

[1] Wendy Willoughby alleges that she suffered a loss of companionship as a result of her husband's injuries. The parties do not dispute that Wendy Willoughby's claims are derivative of her husband's claims against the United States. For simplicity's sake, both Willoughbys' claims are discussed as if they were unitary.

[2] *See* TEX. LAB.CODE § 408.001(a) (exclusive-remedy provision).

[3] *See id.* §§ 406.123(a), (e), 408.001(a).

[4] *See, e.g.,* Federal Employees' Compensation Act (FECA), 5 U.S.C. §§ 8101 *et seq.*

[5] *Cf.* 42 U.S.C. § 1651(a) (providing that the Government must provide workers' compensation coverage to employees on certain military bases); 48 C.F.R. § 28.309(a) (requiring the Government to provide such coverage to certain contractors by contract pursuant to § 1651(a)); *id.* § 52.228-3 (setting out required language for contract provision required by § 28.309(a)).

[6] *See McWhinnie v. United States,* No. 08-6071, 2009 WL 8764296, at *3 (6th Cir. Nov. 25, 2009) (unpublished).

[7] The master contract provided, in relevant part: "[T]he contractor shall pay their employees at least the wages and fringe benefits found by the Department of Labor to prevail in the locality (Clause I-24 'Service Contract Act, as amended'). This is a requirement of all subcontracts under this contract. The prime contractor is responsible [*sic*] to make sure all subcontractors comply with this requirement." Contract ¶ A-2 (citing 48 C.F.R. § 22.10). Section 22.1002-1 (a subsection of § 22.10) of the Code of Federal Regulations provides, in relevant part, that "General Service contracts over $2,500 shall contain mandatory provisions regarding minimum wages and fringe benefits, safe and sanitary working conditions, notification to employees of the minimum allowable compensation, and equivalent Federal employee classifications and wage rates." 48 C.F.R. § 22.1002-1. The master contract lists, as a fringe benefit, "Workers' Compensation Insurance (Defense Base Act)," incorporating by reference 48 C.F.R. § 52.228-3. Contract at ¶ I-38. The Task Order for LSI also incorporated § 52.228-3. Task Order at ¶ IF0395.

[8] TEX. LAB.CODE § 408.001(a) ("Recovery of workers' compensation benefits is the exclusive remedy of an employee covered by workers' compensation insurance coverage or a legal beneficiary against the employer of an agent or employee of the employer for the death of or a work-related injury sustained by the employee.").

[9] For the same reason, this case is distinguishable from a district court case, *Doss v. United States,* 793 F.Supp.2d 859 (E.D.Tex. 2011), with facts similar to those in this case.

[10] As another court has explained, in *Owen,* "the effect of the statutory scheme placed the tort victim in exactly the same position that would have resulted had the victim been injured by any other similarly-situated private party." *Hill v. United States,* 81 F.3d 118, 121 (10th Cir.1996).

[11] Section 406.034 provides, in relevant part:

(a) Except as otherwise provided by law, unless the employee gives notice as provided by Subsection (b), an employee of an employer waives the employee's right of action at common law or under a statute of this state to recover damages for personal injuries or death sustained in the course and scope of the employment.

(b) An employee who desires to retain the common-law right of action to recover damages for personal injuries or death shall notify the employer in writing that the employee waives coverage under this subtitle and retains all rights of action under common law....

(d) An employee who elects to retain the right of action or a legal beneficiary of that employee may bring a cause of action for damages for injuries sustained in the course and scope of the employment under common law or under a statute of this state....

TEX. LAB.CODE § 406.034(a), (b), (d).

[12] *Ferguson v. Hosp. Corp. Int'l, Ltd.,* 769 F.2d 268, 271 (5th Cir.1985) ("Because the workers' compensation scheme remains voluntary in Texas, an employer's notice ... is critical[.]"), *superseded on other grounds as stated in, e.g., Warnke v. Nabors Drilling U.SA, L.P.,* 358 S.W.3d 338, 344 n. 5 (Tex.App. 2011); *cf., e.g., Esquivel v. Mapelli Meat Packing Co.,* 932 S.W.2d 612, 616 (Tex.App. 1996) ("[C]overage, and, hence the exclusivity bar of the workers' compensation statute[,] does not hinge on whether notice has been provided to the employee.").

SIXTH CIRCUIT DECISIONS
Federal Tort Claims Act

751 F.3d 712 (2014)

Bobby G. JACKSON, Plaintiff-Appellant,

v.

UNITED STATES of America, Defendant-Appellee.

No. 13-1243.

United States Court of Appeals, Sixth Circuit.

Argued: December 3, 2013.

Decided and Filed: May 12, 2014.

Rehearing Denied July 2, 2014.

Jackson v. US, 751 F. 3d 712 (6th Cir. 2014)

p.713 ARGUED: Phillip S. Serafini, Serafini, Michalowski, Derkacz & Associates, P.C., Sterling Heights, Michigan, for Appellant. Andrew J. Lievense, United States Attorney's Office, Detroit, Michigan, for Appellee. ON BRIEF: Phillip S. Serafini, Serafini, Michalowski, Derkacz & Associates, P.C., Sterling Heights, Michigan, for Appellant. Andrew J. Lievense, United States Attorney's Office, Detroit, Michigan, for Appellee.

p.714 Before: SILER, McKEAGUE, and WHITE, Circuit Judges.

McKEAGUE, J., delivered the opinion of the court, in which SILER, J., concurred. WHITE, J. (pp. 721-24), delivered a separate dissenting opinion.

OPINION

McKEAGUE, Circuit Judge.

This case involves the Federal Tort Claims Act, namely, whether plaintiff Bobby Jackson timely brought her suit against the United States. The district court found that she did not, and granted the United States' motion to dismiss. The district court further declined to apply equitable tolling to Jackson's claim. We affirm.

I.

On January 13, 2009, Bobby Jackson was involved in a car accident with Michele Battistelli, an Assistant Special Agent in Charge who worked at the Detroit Field Office of the U.S. Immigration and Customs Enforcement Agency, a component of the U.S. Department of Homeland Security. According to Jackson, Battistelli's negligent driving resulted in a head-on collision while Jackson was stopped at an intersection. Jackson suffered multiple injuries, including damage to her head and spinal cord.

After the accident, Jackson retained the services of Michael Shaffer, an attorney with the law firm Gursten, Koltonow, Gursten, Christensen and Raitt, P.C., known also as Michigan Autolaw. On March 5, 2009, Shaffer submitted Jackson's administrative claim for Damage, Injury, or Death. Shaffer, however, erroneously mailed Jackson's claim to the Department of Homeland Security, which then forwarded Jackson's claim to the Immigration and Customs Enforcement Agency. On June 17, 2009, the Immigration and Customs Enforcement Agency received

Jackson's claim. The cover letter included with Jackson's claim listed Shaffer's mailing address as being located on Evergreen Road in Southfield, Michigan. The claim form itself included Jackson's name and mailing address.

On July 7, 2009, the Immigration and Customs Enforcement Agency confirmed receipt of Jackson's claim in correspondence to Shaffer. This receipt letter was sent to the Evergreen Road address provided by Shaffer on the cover letter. Shaffer received the receipt letter. The receipt letter stated that the agency would process Jackson's claim pursuant to the Federal Tort Claims Act ("FTCA"), which allows an agency "up to six months to adjudicate a damage claim, beginning from the date the agency receives the claim." The letter advised, "[o]nce we complete our adjudication, we will send you a letter informing you of our findings. If the agency fails to adjudicate your claim within six months of the date of receipt, or if it denies the claim, you can file a lawsuit in the appropriate United States District Court."

On March 8, 2011, the Immigration and Customs Agency via certified mail sent a "final determination" denying Jackson's administrative claim. This denial letter noted that if Jackson was dissatisfied with the agency's decision, she could file suit in the appropriate district court "no later than six months after the date of mailing of this notice of final denial." The agency sent the denial letter to the Evergreen Road address Shaffer provided on the cover letter, the same address to which it sent the receipt letter. On March 23, 2011, the U.S. Postal Service returned the denial letter to the Immigration and Customs Agency, marking the denial letter as "Not Deliverable as Addressed. Unable to Forward." p.715 Apparently, Shaffer's firm had changed locations in May of 2010.

The parties disagree whether a forwarding order was in place. Jackson contends that Michigan Autolaw put in place a one-year forwarding order for its mail when it moved, and that for eight months after the forwarding order expired it regularly sent a runner to collect the mail. In response, the government notes that a one-year forwarding order would have been in effect when the denial letter was mailed, yet that certified letter was marked unable to be forwarded, and tracking information for the letter stated that Michigan Autolaw had moved and left no forwarding address.[1] The parties also disagree whether the information about changing locations was conveyed to the Immigration and Customs Agency. According to the government, Shaffer never informed the Immigration and Customs Agency of the new address. Regardless, the denial letter never reached Jackson or Jackson's attorney. Despite receiving the undelivered mail, the agency took no further action.

Further complicating the situation is the fact that Jackson may have switched attorneys, or at least relied on the services of multiple counsel. Jackson contends that at some point Shaffer transferred her case to Phillip Serafini, an attorney at the law firm Serafini, Michalowski, Derkacz & Associates. She argues that the agency was aware of this change due to an alleged February 2, 2011 phone conversation between Serafini and Toya Azian, a paralegal specialist with the Immigrations and Customs Enforcement Agency. According to Jackson, Azian called Serafini and asked him to submit a demand letter. In support, Jackson submits an affidavit from Serafini as well as Serafini's handwritten notes regarding the phone call. The Government counters that the "agency's claim file contains no record of that phone call or that any such information regarding a new lawyer was provided to the agency in writing or otherwise, and [Azian] no longer works for the agency." Def.

Br. at 18. The parties do not dispute that Serafini did not send formal notice to the agency that he was counsel of record in the case or submit the requested demand letter.

On January 11, 2012, Jackson filed suit in the U.S. District Court for the Eastern District of Michigan under the FTCA. Jackson also filed a tort case against Battistelli in state court that Battistelli removed to federal court, which was then consolidated with Jackson's federal court claim after Battistelli was dismissed as a party to the case. The government moved to dismiss Jackson's suit for lack of subject matter jurisdiction on the grounds that her filing was untimely. The government argued that the agency's mailing of the March 8, 2011 denial letter triggered a six-month window in which Jackson had to file her suit, meaning her last opportunity to file suit was on September 8, 2011. As a result, according to the government, Jackson's filing of her claim on January 11, 2012 — four months after the six-month limitation period — was barred by the FTCA. Jackson argued that the six-month limitation period was not triggered because neither she nor her attorney received the denial letter. In the alternative, Jackson argued that the limitation period should be equitably tolled to allow her to file her suit.

On January 30, 2013, the district court granted the United States' motion to dismiss for lack of subject matter jurisdiction. p.716 The district court ruled that the plain language of the FTCA indicated that the mailing of the denial letter triggered the six-month limitation period, thus rendering Jackson's filing of her suit on January 11, 2013 untimely and barred by the FTCA. The district court further did not equitably toll the limitation period on the grounds that Jackson was not diligent or reasonable in not filing suit, reasoning that the July 7, 2009 receipt letter received by Shaffer communicated that Jackson "could have filed suit as early as December 2009 [and] yet [she] did not do so." R. 16, Dist. Ct. Opn. at 9, PageID #111 ("As such, [Jackson] had nearly two years to file suit."). The district court also noted that Jackson could not "claim a lack of notice or constructive knowledge of the filing requirement" given her knowledge of the FTCA's requirements and her having filed her claim within the two-year accrual period. Finally, the district court observed that applying equitable tolling to Jackson's claim would prejudice the United States. This appeal followed.

II.

The first issue concerns the district court's dismissal of Jackson's complaint for lack of subject matter jurisdiction. The district court did so on the grounds that Jackson filed her claim against the United States outside of the time period permitted by the FTCA. "We review de novo a district court's judgment dismissing a complaint for the lack of subject matter jurisdiction." *Davis v. United States,* 499 F.3d 590, 593 (6th Cir.2007) (citing *Sutton v. St. Jude Med. S.C., Inc.,* 419 F.3d 568, 570 (6th Cir.2005)).

The doctrine of sovereign immunity shields the United States from lawsuits. *See Dep't of the Army v. Blue Fox, Inc.,* 525 U.S. 255, 260, 119 S.Ct. 687, 142 L.Ed.2d 718 (1999). Suits brought against the United States are therefore dismissed unless a claimant can point to an express waiver of sovereign immunity. *See id.* (citing *FDIC v. Meyer,* 510 U.S. 471, 475, 114 S.Ct. 996, 127 L.Ed.2d 308 (1994)); *see also Lane v.*

Pena, 518 U.S. 187, 192, 116 S.Ct. 2092, 135 L.Ed.2d 486 (1996) ("A waiver of the Federal Government's sovereign immunity must be unequivocally expressed in statutory text, and will not be implied." (internal citations omitted)). As noted by the district court, "when Congress enacts a statute that waives federal sovereign immunity ... a court may not enlarge the waiver beyond what the language requires." R. 16, Dist. Ct. Opn. at 4, PageID #106 (internal quotation marks and citations omitted).

The waiver at issue in this case is the one provided under the FTCA. The FTCA allows a claimant to bring a cause of action "against the United States, for money damages ... for injury or loss of property, or personal injury or death caused by the negligent or wrongful act or omission of any employee of the Government while acting within the scope of his office or employment[.]" 28 U.S.C.A. § 1346(b)(1). This waiver of sovereign immunity requires a claimant to abide by the terms of § 2401(b):

A tort claim against the United States shall be forever barred unless it is presented in writing to the appropriate Federal agency within two years after such claim accrues or unless action is begun within six months after the date of mailing, by certified or registered mail, of the notice of final denial of the claim by the agency to which it was presented.

28 U.S.C. § 2401(b) (emphasis added). With respect to situations in which the agency's delay precludes the claimant from bringing a claim — for example, when an agency has not yet issued a notice of denial p.717 — a claimant may sue the United States according to the terms of § 2675(a):

An action shall not be instituted upon a claim against the United States ... unless the claimant shall have first presented the claim to the appropriate Federal agency and his claim shall have been finally denied by the agency in writing and sent by certified or registered mail. *The failure of an agency to make final disposition of a claim within six months after it is filed shall, at the option of the claimant any time thereafter, be deemed a final denial of the claim for purposes of this section.*

28 U.S.C. § 2675(a) (emphasis added). Therefore, a claimant may sue the United States pursuant to the FTCA six months after presenting a claim to an agency. *See id.* A claimant may no longer sue the United States six months after the time that an agency mails a denial letter. 28 U.S.C. § 2401(b).

Applying that standard here, on January 13, 2009 (the date of the car accident), Jackson's claim accrued. On June 17, 2009, her claim was presented to the agency. On December 17, 2009, Jackson could have brought suit against the United States. Nearly one and a half years passed, during which time Jackson did not bring suit. On March 8, 2011, the agency sent its denial letter by certified mail (which Jackson did not receive). On September 8, 2011, the six-month limitation period during which Jackson was required to bring suit closed. On January 11, 2012 — four months after the window closed — Jackson filed her suit. The plain language of the FTCA foreclosed Jackson's ability to file suit at that time, meaning that her filing was untimely and must be dismissed. *See* 28 U.S.C. § 2401(b).

Jackson argues that an "undelivered notice of denial" does not trigger the six-month limitation window outlined in the FTCA. Pl. Br. at 12. This is incorrect. The FTCA unambiguously states that the six-month limitation window runs "from the date of mailing." 28 U.S.C. § 2401(b). As our sister circuits have noted, the FTCA does not require that the claimant receive the denial letter in order to commence the six-month limitation period. *See Berti v. V.A. Hosp.*, 860 F.2d 338, 340 (9th Cir.1988) (declining to read a receipt requirement into the FTCA); *Carr v. Veterans Admin.*, 522 F.2d 1355, 1357 (5th Cir.1975) (same). The FTCA requires only that the agency mail the denial by certified mail. This the agency did. An added receipt requirement would constitute a burden on the agency to guarantee delivery, and would in fact be construing the FTCA in favor of plaintiffs suing the United States, when the Supreme Court has instructed courts to do the opposite. *See Lane*, 518 U.S. at 192, 116 S.Ct. 2092 ("Moreover, a waiver of the Government's sovereign immunity will be strictly construed, in terms of its scope, in favor of the sovereign." (internal citations omitted)).

Another factor leading to the same conclusion is 28 C.F.R. § 14.9(a), the Department of Justice regulation construing the FTCA's six-month limitation provision. *See Chevron, U.S.A., Inc. v. Natural Res. Def. Council, Inc.*, 467 U.S. 837, 843-44, 104 S.Ct. 2778, 81 L.Ed.2d 694 (1984); *see also* 28 U.S.C. § 2672 (granting the Attorney General authority to promulgate regulations). Section 14.9(a) states:

> Final denial of an administrative claim shall be in writing and *sent to the claimant, his attorney, or legal representative by certified or registered mail.* The notification of final denial may include a statement of the reasons for the denial and shall include a statement that, if the claimant is dissatisfied with the agency action, he may file suit in an appropriate U.S. District Court not later than 6 p.718 months after the date of mailing of the notification.

28 C.F.R. § 14.9(a) (emphasis added). Jackson argues that, in light of the returned denial letter, the agency was required to mail the denial letter to both her *and* her counsel even though the regulation clearly states that an agency's sending the denial to the claimant *or* her legal representative is sufficient to trigger the six-month limitation window.[2] *See id.* While the agency's mailing the returned denial letter to Jackson herself may have been the preferred course of action, it was not the required course of action. Again, reading an additional requirement into this regulation — that the agency must send the denial to multiple parties — runs counter to a court's duty to construe waivers of sovereign immunity in favor of the government.[3] *See Lane*, 518 U.S. at 192, 116 S.Ct. 2092.

In sum, the plain language of the FTCA indicates that the Immigration and Customs Enforcement Agency's mailing the denial letter triggered the six-month limitation period. Furthermore, the Department of Justice Regulation clarifies that the agency was required only to send the denial letter to either Jackson *or* her attorney, not Jackson *and* her attorney. Because Jackson filed her suit after the six-month limitation period ran, her claim was untimely. Therefore, we agree with the district court that the government's motion to dismiss for lack of subject matter jurisdiction should be granted.

III.

The next issue concerns the district court's decision not to equitably toll Jackson's claim, which, given that the parties dispute certain facts, is reviewed under an abuse of discretion standard. *See Dunlap v. United States,* 250 F.3d 1001, 1007 n. 2 (6th Cir.2001) (noting that the abuse of discretion standard applies to a district court's refusal to apply the doctrine of equitable tolling when facts are in dispute); *Truitt v. Cnty. of Wayne,* 148 F.3d 644, 648 (6th Cir.1998) ("We review a district court's decision regarding equitable tolling for an abuse of discretion."). Equitable tolling allows a federal court "to toll a statute of limitations when a litigant's failure to meet a legally-mandated deadline unavoidably arose from circumstances beyond that litigant's control." *Robertson v. Simpson,* 624 F.3d 781, 783 (6th Cir.2010) (internal quotation marks and citation omitted). While "equitable tolling may be applied in suits against the government, courts will only do so sparingly, and not when there has only been a garden variety claim of excusable neglect." *Chomic v. United States,* 377 F.3d 607, 615 (6th Cir.2004) (internal quotation marks and citation omitted). Jackson carries the burden of establishing her entitlement to p.719 equitable tolling. *See Robertson,* 624 F.3d at 784.

The issue of equitable tolling raises two questions. First is the question of whether equitable tolling applies to the FTCA's limitations period, which depends on whether the time limitations in the FTCA are jurisdictional in nature. This question has prompted some variance within this circuit. *See, e.g., Bazzo v. United States,* 494 Fed.Appx. 545, 546 (6th Cir.2012) ("The question whether § 2401(b)'s exhaustion provisions constitute jurisdictional requirements divides circuit courts and even prompts inconsistent rulings within this circuit.").[4] Moreover, the government argues that equitable tolling is not available in light of recent Supreme Court precedent. *See generally John R. Sand & Gravel Co. v. United States,* 552 U.S. 130, 128 S.Ct. 750, 169 L.Ed.2d 591 (2008) (ruling that 28 U.S.C. § 2501 was jurisdictional and thus not subject to equitable tolling). If equitable tolling does not apply, Jackson cannot recover. If equitable tolling does apply, this raises the second question as to whether the district court abused its discretion in not equitably tolling Jackson's claim. The district court did not address the first question, finding that "even if equitable tolling applies, [Jackson] has not shown her entitlement to such relief." R. 16, Dist. Ct. Opn. at 9, PageID #111.

We agree with the district court that we need not decide the issue of whether the time limitations in the FTCA are jurisdictional in nature because, even assuming that equitable tolling is available, we find that the district court did not abuse its discretion in not equitably tolling Jackson's claim. *See generally Bazzo,* 494 Fed.Appx. at 547 ("We need not resolve this circuit split today. Assuming the availability of equitable tolling, Bazzo has not shown that the district court abused its discretion in denying relief"). To determine whether equitable tolling is available to a plaintiff, a court considers five factors: (1) the plaintiff's lack of notice of the filing requirement; (2) the plaintiff's lack of constructive knowledge of the filing requirement; (3) the plaintiff's diligence in pursuing her rights; (4) an absence of prejudice to the defendant; and (5) the plaintiff's reasonableness in remaining ignorant of the particular legal requirement. *Truitt,* 148 F.3d at 648. We find that the district court's weighing of these factors and denial of equitable tolling to be well within its discretion.

As to the first and second factors, notice and constructive knowledge, the district court noted that Jackson could not claim a lack of notice or constructive knowledge of the filing requirement given her knowledge of the FTCA's filing requirements and her having filed her claim within the two-year accrual period. The district court could reasonably ascertain from this information that Jackson and her counsel were aware of the relevant provisions in the FTCA governing when a claim could be filed. While it is true that the district court did not focus on the six-month deadline triggered by the agency's denial letter, p.720 the district court was not required to emphasize the six-month limitation period over the two-year accrual period in evaluating the notice and constructive knowledge factors.

The district court's analysis of the final three factors also did not amount to an abuse of discretion. As to the third factor, diligence, and the fifth factor, reasonableness, the district court's observation that the July 7, 2009 receipt letter received by Shaffer communicated that Jackson "could have filed suit as early as December 2009" as well as its reliance on the fact that Jackson did not file her suit despite having had nearly two years to do so was sound and did not amount to an abuse of discretion. R. 16, Dist. Ct. Opn. at 9, PageID #111. Moreover, the district court's attention to the fact that a full four months — rather than mere days or a week — had passed between the six-month statutory deadline and the filing of Jackson's claim was similarly reasonable and not an abuse of discretion. Finally, the district court did not abuse its discretion in considering the fourth factor, prejudice, as it noted the difficulty the government would have in litigating a matter that was filed four months beyond the limitations period.

Although Jackson argues that a situation in which a denial letter was never delivered mandates application of equitable tolling, she cites to no authority supporting her claim. We note that the denial letter presumably would have been properly delivered had either Shaffer or Serafini updated the agency with the correct mailing address. However we also take note of cases in which courts ruled that equitable tolling did not apply despite the fact that actions taken by the claimant's counsel played a role in the untimely filing. In *Bazzo,* a claimant sought to file a negligence suit against the physician who delivered her daughter, a physician who, the claimant later learned — after the two-year accrual limitation period expired — was an employee at a federally-funded medical facility. 494 Fed.Appx. at 546-47. The district court labeled her counsel's work as a "below-the-radar investigation" but still did not equitably toll the limitations period. *Id.* at 547. This court affirmed the district court's decision, despite the fact that the claimant's counsel offered "no explanation for these oversights." *Id.; see also Ramos v. U.S. Dep't of Health & Human Servs.,* 429 Fed.Appx. 947, 951 (11th Cir.2011) (declining to apply equitable tolling where claimant's "counsel conceded that there was a government website listing federally funded clinics, that [the alleged tortfeasor] was listed on the site, and that he had been unaware of and had not checked the website"). A similar analysis applies to Jackson's claim. Contrary to Jackson's assertion, it was within the district court's discretion not to apply equitable tolling to the limitations period. We thus find no abuse of discretion in the district court's decision.

IV.

The final issue concerns Jackson's state-law tort claim against Battistelli. Jackson argues that her state-law tort claim against Battistelli should have survived dismissal of her FTCA claim. This is incorrect.

When a tort claim is brought against a federal employee, the Federal Employees Liability Reform and Tort Compensation Act of 1988, commonly known as the Westfall Act, applies. *See* Pub.L. No. 100-694, §§ 5-6, 102 Stat. 4563 (1988). The Westfall Act "empowers the Attorney General to certify that the employee was acting within the scope of his office or employment at the time of the incident ..." giving rise to the claim. *Gutierrez de Martinez* p.721 *v. Lamagno,* 515 U.S. 417, 420, 115 S.Ct. 2227, 132 L.Ed.2d 375 (1995) (quoting 28 U.S.C. § 2679(d)(1)). Upon certification, the United States is substituted for the employee as a defendant, and the claim is litigated under the FTCA and is subject to dismissal on any basis applicable to FTCA claims. *See* 28 U.S.C. § 2679(d)(4) (providing that the claims "shall be subject to the limitations and exceptions applicable to those [FTCA] actions"); *Dolan v. United States,* 514 F.3d 587, 593 (6th Cir.2008) ("[I]f the defendant federal employee was acting in the scope of his or her employment, substitution of the United States as defendant is appropriate and the district court must assess the plaintiff's claims pursuant to the [FTCA] ... the case must be dismissed for lack of jurisdiction."); *see also United States v. Smith,* 499 U.S. 160, 166, 111 S.Ct. 1180, 113 L.Ed.2d 134 (1991) ("[T]he FTCA [is] the exclusive mode of recovery for the tort of a Government employee even when the FTCA itself precludes Government liability."). Any suit against the employee "arising out of or related to the same subject matter" is precluded. 28 U.S.C. § 2679(b)(1). Because the government certified that Battistelli was acting within the scope of his employment when the accident occurred, Jackson's claim against Battistelli must be dismissed.

V.

For the reasons discussed above, the district court's grant of the government's motion to dismiss for lack of subject matter jurisdiction, its decision not to equitably toll Jackson's claim, and the dismissal of Jackson's state-law tort claim against Battistelli are AFFIRMED.

HELENE N. WHITE, Circuit Judge, dissenting.

The majority affirms the district court's decision not to apply equitable tolling to the limitations period of Jackson's FTCA suit. I find tolling warranted and therefore dissent.

I.

As the majority notes, the issue of equitable tolling raises two questions: (1) whether the FTCA's limitations provision, 28 U.S.C. § 2401(b), is jurisdictional and not subject to tolling, and (2) whether equitable tolling is available to Jackson on the merits.

A.

Our decision in *Glarner v. United States Department of Veterans Administration*, 30 F.3d 697 (1994), resolves the first question. In *Glarner*, we looked to the Supreme Court's decision in *Irwin v. Dept. of Veterans Affairs*, 498 U.S. 89, 111 S.Ct. 453, 112 L.Ed.2d 435 (1990), which created a rebuttable presumption that equitable tolling applies to suits against the United States. *Irwin*, 498 U.S. at 95-96, 111 S.Ct. 453 ("We therefore hold that the same rebuttable presumption of equitable tolling applicable to suits against private defendants should also apply to suits against the United States. Congress, of course, may provide otherwise if it wishes to do so."). Observing that nothing indicated that Congress had "provided otherwise" with respect to § 2401(b), we concluded that *Irwin*'s rebuttable presumption was fully applicable and, therefore, § 2401(b) was a nonjurisdictional statute of limitations that was subject to tolling. *See Glarner*, 30 F.3d at 701 ("[T]he VA first argues that the doctrine of equitable tolling cannot apply to § 2401(b) because the latter is a jurisdictional statute of limitations that cannot be equitably tolled. This assertion is incorrect.").

p.722 Somewhat confusingly, we have never cited *Glarner* for this proposition, and since *Glarner*, the court has referred to § 2401(b) as jurisdictional without reference to *Glarner*. *See, e.g., Humphrey v. United States Attorney Gen.'s Office*, 279 Fed.Appx. 328, 332 (6th Cir.2008) ("The requirement that a claim pursuant to the FTCA be commenced within six months of an administrative denial is a jurisdictional prerequisite to suit and a failure to comply warrants dismissal"); *Sullivan ex rel. Lampkins v. Am. Cmty. Mut. Ins. Co.*, 208 F.3d 215 (6th Cir.2000) (table) (describing the two-year deadline for filing administrative claims as jurisdictional); *see also Bazzo v. United States*, 494 Fed.Appx. 545, 546 (6th Cir.2012) (comparing *Glarner* with *Humphrey* and *Sullivan* and observing, "[t]he question whether § 2401(b)'s exhaustion provisions constitute jurisdictional requirements divides circuit courts and even prompts inconsistent rulings within this circuit."). Nonetheless, as Judge Stranch recognized in her dissent in *Bazzo, Glarner* has not been overruled and is the law of the circuit. *Bazzo*, 494 Fed. Appx. at 548 (Stranch, J. dissenting) ("Until the Supreme Court or our Court sitting *en banc* holds that the exhaustion provisions of 28 U.S.C. § 2401(b) are jurisdictional requirements, I would affirm the district court's decision that the statute is not jurisdictional and that equitable tolling may be applied based on our prior decision in *Glarner*.").

The government contends that the Supreme Court's decision in *John R. Sand & Gravel Co. v. United States*, 552 U.S. 130, 128 S.Ct. 750, 169 L.Ed.2d 591 (2008), implicitly overruled *Glarner*, but it did not. In *John R.*, the Court held that the statute of limitations for filing actions in the United States Court of Federal Claims, 28 U.S.C. § 2501, is a jurisdictional limitations period not subject to waiver. The government points to language in the decision distinguishing statutes of limitations that "seek primarily to protect defendants against stale or unduly delayed claims" which may be treated as an affirmative defense, from those that seek "to achieve a broader system-related goal, such as ... limiting the scope of a governmental waiver of sovereign immunity" which are "more absolute" and which "the Court has sometimes referred to ... as 'jurisdictional.'" *John R.,* 552 U.S. at 133-34, 128 S.Ct. 750. The government argues that § 2401(b) falls in the latter category and accordingly, under *John R.* is jurisdictional and cannot be tolled. But *John R.* did not employ that distinction to categorize § 2501 and then find tolling inapplicable. Rather, consistent with *Irwin,* the Court held that congressional silence in the face of the Court's *long-held precedent* finding § 2501 jurisdictional was sufficient to rebut *Irwin*'s presumption that equitable tolling applied. *Id.* at 137-38, 128 S.Ct. 750 ("Specific statutory language ... could rebut [*Irwin*'s] presumption by demonstrating Congress' intent to the contrary. And if so, a definitive earlier interpretation of the statute, finding a similar congressional intent, should offer a similarly sufficient rebuttal."). Because no such Supreme Court precedent exists with respect to § 2401(b), Congressional silence does not rebut *Irwin*'s presumption that equitable tolling is available. Accordingly, *John R.* does not undermine this court's decision in *Glarner. See Arteaga v. United States,* 711 F.3d 828, 833 (7th Cir.2013) (Posner, J.) (finding the FTCA limitations provision non-jurisdictional and subject to tolling, and noting "[t]he opinion in *John R. Sand & Gravel* actually reaffirms the presumption that equitable tolling applies to statutes of limitations in suits against the government, while emphasizing that the presumption is rebuttable") (citation omitted); *see also Santos ex rel. Beato v.* p.723 *United States,* 559 F.3d 189, 197 (3d Cir. 2009) (stating, when concluding that *John R.* did not invalidate its prior determination that the FTCA limitations provision is non-jurisdictional and subject to tolling, "the Court in *John R.* applied but did not overrule *Irwin*"). Because *Glarner* remains good law, the FTCA's limitations provision is subject to equitable tolling.

B.

As to the whether the filing deadline should have been tolled in this case, I would answer in the affirmative. As noted, to determine whether equitable tolling applies in a given case, the court considers five factors: (1) the plaintiff's lack of notice of the filing requirement; (2) the plaintiff's lack of constructive knowledge of the filing requirement; (3) the plaintiff's diligence in pursuing her rights; (4) an absence of prejudice to the defendant; and (5) the plaintiff's reasonableness in remaining ignorant of the particular legal requirement. *Truitt v. Wayne Cnty.,* 148 F.3d 644, 648 (6th Cir.1998). We review a district court's decision to deny equitable tolling for an abuse of discretion, i.e., we reverse if the district court relies on clearly erroneous findings of fact, or improperly applies the law or uses an erroneous legal standard. *Romstadt v. Allstate Ins. Co.,* 59 F.3d 608, 615 (6th Cir.1995).

Here, the district's court's factual determination that Jackson had actual notice of the filing deadline was clearly erroneous. Jackson's attorneys were surely aware of the FTCA's general filing requirements, but it is undisputed that neither Jackson nor her attorneys were aware that the agency had mailed the denial letter, triggering the six-month deadline. In other words, Jackson had no notice of the actual deadline for filing suit: September 8, 2011. Further, the district court erred as a matter of law when it stated, as a basis for its prejudice finding, that Congress did not intend to waive sovereign immunity for late-filed claims. *See* R. 16, Dist. Ct. Opn. at 10 (finding that tolling would prejudice the government because it "would be required to litigate a matter that unquestionably was filed beyond the limitations period and over which Congress did not intend to waive sovereign immunity"). The statement was akin to finding that Congress did not intend for equitable tolling to apply to FTCA claims, which — pursuant to *Irwin* and *Glarner* — is plainly incorrect. In addition, the district court's determination that Jackson was not diligent because she *could have* filed suit as early as December 2009 — six months after the agency received her claim — is, at least, questionable. The FTCA permits, but does not require, claimants to deem a claim denied and file suit at any time after the agency fails to adjudicate the claim within six months of receiving it. *See* 28 U.S.C. § 2675(a) ("The failure of an agency to make final disposition of a claim within six months after it is filed shall, *at the option of the claimant any time thereafter,* be deemed a final denial of the claim for purposes of this section.") (emphasis added); *Conn v. United States,* 867 F.2d 916, 920 (6th Cir. 1989) (rejecting a requirement that the claimant exercise the option within a "reasonable" time, observing, "the language of the statute places the option in the claimant's hands"). Jackson cannot be fairly deemed to have lacked diligence because she exercised the discretion squarely granted her under the statute.

Further, the equities weigh in Jackson's favor where the agency *knew* that the six-month filing deadline was triggered by its denial of Jackson's claim, and also *knew* — because its letter was returned undelivered — that Jackson was not aware that her claim had been denied. It did not even follow up using information readily available p.724 in Jackson's file by re-mailing the denial to Jackson at her personal address provided on her claim form. There was also evidence that the agency was aware that Serafini had replaced Shaffer as Jackson's attorney, and had his phone number. I would find that the district court abused its discretion in denying equitable tolling, and would allow Jackson's suit to proceed.

[1] Jackson herself admits that computer tracking information provided by the U.S. Postal Service indicated that the denial letter could not be delivered because Michigan Autolaw had "Moved, left no address."

[2] To support her argument, Jackson points only to *Matos v. United States,* 380 F.Supp.2d 36, 40 (D.P.R.2005), a case in which a district court determined that the six-month limitations window was not triggered because the agency had "available the necessary information to ensure that delivery by certified mail be achieved" in light of the fact that the agency had two addresses for the claimant's counsel. This reasoning runs contrary to that relied on by other courts. *See generally Berti,* 860 F.2d at 340 ("[T]he running of the statutory period [begins] from the date of mailing of a certified or registered letter."); *Carr,* 522 F.2d at 1357 ("[T]he plain words of the statute... specify that an action be begun within six months after the 'date of mailing.'"). Furthermore, this case is not controlling authority in this circuit.

[3] Moreover, as the government notes, the agency might have been reprimanded for directly communicating with an individual who was represented by counsel. *See* Def. Br. at 22 n.1.

[4] *Compare Glarner v. U.S. Dep't of Veterans Admin.,* 30 F.3d 697, 701 (6th Cir.1994) ("[T]he VA first argues that the doctrine of equitable tolling cannot apply to § 2401(b) because the latter is a jurisdictional statute of limitations that cannot be equitably tolled. This assertion is incorrect."), *with Rogers v. United States,* 675 F.2d 123, 124 (6th Cir. 1982) ("There is no equitable exception to the jurisdictional prerequisites of the Federal Tort Claims Act in this Circuit and we decline to create one."), *and Humphrey v. U.S. Att'y Gen.'s Office,* 279 Fed.Appx. 328, 332 (6th Cir.2008) ("The requirement that a claim pursuant to the FTCA be commenced within six months of an administrative denial is a jurisdictional prerequisite to suit and a failure to comply warrants dismissal on the merits.").

766 F.3d 576 (2014)

Walter J. HIMMELREICH, Plaintiff-Appellant,
v.
FEDERAL BUREAU OF PRISONS, et al., Defendants,
J. Fitzgerald, et al., Defendants-Appellees.

No. 13-4212.

United States Court of Appeals, Sixth Circuit.

Decided and Filed: September 9, 2014.

ON BRIEF: Lisa Hammond Johnson, United States Attorney's Office, Cleveland, Ohio, for Appellee. Walter Himmelreich, Danbury, Connecticut, pro se.

Before: COLE, Chief Judge; MOORE and GIBBONS, Circuit Judges.

OPINION

PER CURIAM.

In 2010, Walter J. Himmelreich—a federal prisoner—filed a complaint against numerous defendants, alleging several p.577 causes of action. The district court dismissed the complaint for failure to state a claim. On appeal, in Case No. 11-3474, we affirmed the dismissal of the majority of the claims and defendants, but we vacated and remanded two claims for further proceedings: a claim of retaliation in violation of the First Amendment based on Himmelreich's placement in administrative detention for sixty days in 2009, allegedly in retaliation for his filing of a claim under the Federal Tort Claims Act ("FTCA"); and a claim of failure to protect in violation of the Eighth Amendment based on an assault on Himmelreich by another inmate in 2008. On remand, the remaining defendants moved for summary judgment, arguing that Himmelreich had failed to exhaust his administrative remedies on the two claims at issue and that his Eighth Amendment claim was barred because he had elected to file a claim under the FTCA regarding the assault incident. The district court found the defendants' arguments to be valid and granted their motion for summary judgment. Himmelreich now appeals pro se, and we unanimously agree that oral argument is not needed. Fed. R.App. P. 34(a). For the reasons stated below, we conclude that Himmelreich's failure to exhaust his administrative remedies should have been excused and that the FTCA's judgment bar does not apply to this case. Consequently, we once again VACATE the district court's judgment and REMAND the case for further proceedings consistent with this opinion.

I.

The Prison Litigation Reform Act ("PLRA"), 110 Stat. 1321-71, 42 U.S.C. § 1997e(a), prevents a prisoner from filing suit "with respect to prison conditions ... until such administrative remedies as are available are exhausted." In *Woodford v. Ngo,* 548 U.S. 81, 126 S.Ct. 2378, 165 L.Ed.2d 368 (2006), the Supreme Court interpreted this language as requiring "proper exhaustion," meaning that a prisoner must "make full use of the prison grievance process" and "compl[y] with the system's critical procedural rules." *Id.* at 93-95, 126 S.Ct. 2378. There are few exceptions to this strict rule, but we have excused a prisoner's lack of complete compliance when the improper actions of prison officials render the administrative remedies functionally unavailable. *See generally Brock v. Kenton Cnty.,* 93 Fed. Appx. 793, 798 (6th Cir.2004) (collecting cases).

Himmelreich admits that he did not complete all of the steps in the prison grievance process, but he claims to have been "intimidated by Captain Fitzgerald... into not filing any more Administrative Remedies" with regard to his Eighth Amendment claim against the B-Unit Disciplinary Team. R. 47 at 10 (Pl.'s Resp. to Mot. for Summ. J.) (Page ID # 278). In determining whether Himmelreich fits within this exception, we must ask whether Captain Fitzgerald's threats and actions would "deter a person of ordinary firmness from [continuing with the grievance process]." *See Thaddeus-X v. Blatter,* 175 F.3d 378, 396 (6th Cir.1999) (en banc) (internal quotation marks omitted); *Bell v. Johnson,* 308 F.3d 594, 603 (6th Cir.2002).

Himmelreich alleges that Captain Fitzgerald told him that if Himmelreich continued with his grievances regarding the attack, "[she would] personally see that [Himmelreich was] transferred to a penitentiary and [he would] more than likely be attacked and not just beat up." R. 47 at 7 (Pl.'s Resp. to Mot. for Summ. J.) (Page ID # 275). When Himmelreich filed his FTCA lawsuit, he claimed that Captain Fitzgerald followed through with her threats and placed him in the Special Housing Unit ("SHU"). *Id.* at 11 (Page p.578 ID # 279). Once Himmelreich was put in the SHU, Captain Fitzgerald allegedly yelled, "'You want to know why you're in here? You're in here because of the fuckin' Tort Claim you filed! That's why you're in here!'" R. 1 at 15 (Compl. at ¶ 66) (Page ID # 15).

Unlike the vague and conclusory allegations at issue in *Boyd v. Corrections Corp. of America,* 380 F.3d 989, 997 (6th Cir.2004), Himmelreich's claims of intimidation are specific. If Himmelreich's allegations are true, which we must assume at this stage in the litigation, *Risher v. Lappin,* 639 F.3d 236, 240 (6th Cir.2011), a reasonable jury could conclude that Captain Fitzgerald's actions and statements would deter a person of ordinary firmness from continuing with the grievance process. Accordingly, we conclude that Himmelreich has demonstrated that a genuine issue of material fact exists as to whether Captain Fitzgerald improperly prevented Himmelreich from exhausting his administrative remedies.

In reaching this conclusion, we reject the government's argument that Himmelreich's filing of other administrative complaints and the FTCA lawsuit near the time that he claims to have been threatened prevents a finding of intimidation. We do not believe that minor complaints related to "requests to watch [the] *Passion of the Christ* movie," R. 45-4 at 2 (Grievance Record) (Page ID # 251), and to requests "to make a [weekly] call to [his] parents while in [the] SHU," *id.* at 11 (Page ID # 260), are relevant when Captain Fitzgerald purportedly told Himmelreich "that if he didn't stop [with his complaints about the assault] she would ship him to an ADX [higher-security prison], or better yet, to a [penitentiary] where she knows he will get shanked and probably killed," R. 1 at 14 (Compl. at ¶ 59) (Page ID # 14). Complaints and grievances related to petty requests and those related to prison-official misconduct are wholly different, particularly when there are specific allegations in the record that Captain Fitzgerald actually retaliated against Himmelreich for filing grievances and lawsuits related to a specific assault. In our view, this retaliation and intimidation—if proven true—would render the grievance process functionally unavailable for a person of ordinary firmness. Thus, we VACATE the district court's grant of summary judgment on the basis of a failure to exhaust.

II.

The district court also found that the FTCA's judgment bar, 28 U.S.C. § 2676, applied in this case and, for this alternative reason, granted the government summary judgment with respect to Himmelreich's Eighth Amendment claim. Section 2676 states in full: "The judgment in an action under section 1346(b) of this title shall constitute a complete bar to any action by the claimant, by reason of the same subject matter, against the employee of the government whose act or omission gave rise to the claim." According to the district court, "[t]he plain language of section 2676 requires that the bar apply to all actions by the Plaintiff, not just judgments on the merits." R. 53 at 6-7 (D. Ct. Op.) (Page ID #436-37) (citing *Manning v. United States,* 546 F.3d 430, 437-38 (7th Cir.2008)). We disagree.

A careful reading of the record shows that the district court dismissed Himmelreich's FTCA action for a lack of subject-matter jurisdiction. R. 34 at 2-5 (D. Ct. Rule 12(b)(1) Op.) (Page ID #171-74) (Case Number 4:10-cv-307); *see also* R. 31 at 1 (Gov't Rule 12(b)(1) Mot.) (Page ID # 136) (Case Number 4:10-cv-307). Specifically, the district court found that the discretionary-function exception applied, which deprived the district court of subject-matter p.579 jurisdiction. Therefore, the district court granted the government's Rule 12(b)(1) motion and dismissed the action for a lack of jurisdiction. R. 34 at 2-5 (D. Ct. Rule 12(b)(1) Op.) (Page ID # 171-74) (Case Number 4:10-cv-307).

A dismissal for lack of subject-matter jurisdiction does not trigger the § 2676 judgment bar. Put bluntly, in the absence of jurisdiction, the court lacks the power to enter judgment. *See* 10A Charles Alan Wright, Arthur Miller, & Mary Kay Kane, *Federal Practice & Procedure* § 3713 (3d ed.1998) ("If the court has no jurisdiction, it has no power to enter a judgment on the merits and must dismiss the action."). Because we hold that district courts lack subject-matter jurisdiction over an FTCA claim when the discretionary-function exception applies, as it did here, *see Kohl v. United States,* 699 F.3d 935, 939-40 (6th Cir.2012), we do not view the district court's dismissal of Himmelreich's previous action as implicating the FTCA's judgment bar. Accordingly, we conclude that the district court erred in citing the judgment bar as an independent basis for granting summary judgment on Himmelreich's Eighth Amendment claim. *See* R. 53 at 6-7 (D. Ct. Op.) (Page ID # 436-37).

In reaching its conclusion, the district court relied upon *Harris v. United States,* 422 F.3d 322 (6th Cir.2005), and *Manning,* 546 F.3d 430, but it misreads both of these cases. In *Harris,* the plaintiff simultaneously filed *Bivens* and FTCA claims against the United States and government officials. 422 F.3d at 324. The district court "entered a 'judgment' on the merits of [the] FTCA claims," and we concluded that this judgment barred consideration of the plaintiff's *Bivens* claim. *Id.* at 334.

Specifically, we held that § 2676 "fails to draw a distinction between a decision for or against the government" and that § 2676 bars a *Bivens* action regardless of which party prevailed on the merits of the FTCA claim. *Id.* at 334-35. Holding that a judgment on the merits, irrespective of who won, triggers the judgment bar is a far cry from holding that any disposition of an FTCA action prevents other suits, a distinction that the *Harris* panel explicitly recognized by citing *Hallock v. Bonner*, 387 F.3d 147, 155 (2d Cir.2004), *reversed on other grounds sub nom. Will v. Hallock*, 546 U.S. 345, 126 S.Ct. 952, 163 L.Ed.2d 836 (2006). *See Harris*, 422 F.3d at 335. In *Hallock*, the Second Circuit stated that "an action brought under the FTCA and dismissed for lack of subject matter jurisdiction because it falls within an exception to the restricted waiver of sovereign immunity provided by the FTCA does not result in a 'judgment in an action under section 1346(b) [the Federal Tort Claims Act].'" 387 F.3d at 155 (quoting 28 U.S.C. § 2676).[1] *Harris* described this precise holding in a parenthetical and cited the case approvingly. 422 F.3d at 335.

Manning does not hold to the contrary or support the district court's statement that "[t]he plain language of section 2676 requires that the bar apply to all actions by the Plaintiff, not just judgments on the merits." R. 53 at 6-7 (D. Ct. Op.) (Page ID # 436-37) (citing *Manning*, 546 F.3d at 437-38). In *Manning*, the plaintiff "concede[d] that the district court entered a 'judgment' on the merits of his FTCA claim" (a fact that we believe renders *Manning* completely irrelevant to this case). 546 F.3d at 433. Nonetheless, in that case, the plaintiff argued that the p.580 judgment bar could not be "appl[ied] retroactively to nullify a *previous Bivens* judgment." *Id.* The Seventh Circuit disagreed and applied the § 2676 judgment bar retroactively. *Id.* at 438. Nowhere did the Seventh Circuit hold in *Manning* that a dismissal of an FTCA claim for a lack of subject-matter jurisdiction qualifies as a judgment under § 2676. In *Williams v. Fleming*, 597 F.3d 820 (7th Cir.2010), the Seventh Circuit expressly punted on that question, the one before us now, stating: "[w]e need not address [the] contention [that any dismissal, whether or not on the merits, suffices for application of § 2676] today...." *Id.* at 822 n. 2.

Moreover, the Seventh Circuit's disposition of this question, in particular, is unhelpful. The Seventh Circuit treats the dismissal of an FTCA action due to the application of the discretionary-function exception as a decision on the merits. *See Collins v. United States*, 564 F.3d 833, 837-38 (7th Cir.2009). We have repeatedly taken the opposite view, which is that we lack subject-matter jurisdiction over an FTCA claim if the discretionary-function exception applies in a given case. *See, e.g., Kohl*, 699 F.3d at 939-40; *Milligan v. United States*, 670 F.3d 686, 695 (6th Cir. 2012) ("[I]t is evident that the discretionary function exception bars subject matter jurisdiction for the [plaintiffs'] claims."). In other cases, a dismissal for a lack of subject-matter jurisdiction carries no preclusive effect. *See, e.g., Marrese v. Am. Academy of Orthopaedic Surgeons*, 470 U.S. 373, 382, 105 S.Ct. 1327, 84 L.Ed.2d 274 (1985); *Wilkins v. Jakeway*, 183 F.3d 528, 533 n. 6 (6th Cir.1999); Restatement (Second) of Judgments § 26(1)(c) (1982). We see no reason to depart from that general rule in this situation.

In *Harris*, we also noted that the purpose of a judgment bar is to prevent the possibility of double recoveries and the cost of defending multiple suits regarding the same conduct for the government. 422 F.3d at 335-36. It is not punitive in nature. Holding that a plaintiff's filing of an FTCA action, when that statute does not permit recovery, prevents the plaintiff from alleging the correct cause of action furthers neither of these interests. Seeing no compelling reason in the text or purpose of § 2676 to conclude that a dismissal for a lack of jurisdiction triggers the judgment bar, we hold that the district court erred in applying the judgment bar here and VACATE its decision accordingly.

III.

For the forgoing reasons, we VACATE the district court's grant of summary judgment and REMAND for proceedings consistent with this opinion.

[1] *See also Pellegrino v. U.S. Transp. Sec. Admin.*, No. 09-5505, 2014 WL 1489939, at *8-9 (E.D.Pa. April 16, 2014); *Saleh v. Wiley,* No. 09-cv-02563-PAB-KLM, 2012 WL 4356224, at *3-4 (D.Colo. June 12, 2012); *Kyei v. Beebe,* No. CV 01-1266-PA, 2005 WL 3050442, at *2 n. 3 (D.Or. Nov. 13, 2005).

775 F.3d 768 (2014)

LEFT FORK MINING COMPANY, INC.; Bennett Resources, LLC; Cumberland River Energies, LLC; Blackstar Land & Mining Company, Ltd.; Manalapan Land Company, Ltd., Plaintiffs-Appellants,

v.

Irving T. HOOKER, et al., Defendants-Appellees.

No. 14-5450.

United States Court of Appeals, Sixth Circuit.

Argued: November 18, 2014.

Decided and Filed: December 31, 2014.

Left Fork Min. Co., Inc. v. Hooker, 775 F. 3d 768 (6th Cir. 2014)

p.770 ARGUED: John M. Williams, Rajkovich, Williams, Kilpatrick & True, PLLC, Lexington, Kentucky, for Appellant. Cheryl D. Morgan, United States Attorney's Office, Lexington, Kentucky, for Appellees. ON BRIEF: John M. Williams, Todd C. Myers, Rajkovich, Williams, Kilpatrick & True, PLLC, Lexington, Kentucky, for Appellant. Cheryl D. Morgan, Charles P. Wisdom, Jr., United States Attorney's Office, Lexington, Kentucky, for Appellees.

Before: MERRITT, WHITE, and DONALD, Circuit Judges.

OPINION

BERNICE BOUIE DONALD, Circuit Judge.

This is an appeal from the district court's dismissal of a claim for money damages brought under *Bivens v. Six Unknown Named Agents of Federal Bureau of Narcotics,* 403 U.S. 388, 91 S.Ct. 1999, 29 L.Ed.2d 619 (1971). The district court found that the existence of an alternate remedial scheme created by statute precluded a judicially-created damages remedy in this case. For the reasons stated herein, we AFFIRM.

I.

Plaintiffs-Appellants are the owners, operators, and other parties[1] with a financial interest in the Straight Creek underground coal mine in Bell County, Kentucky, and include the Left Fork Mining Company ("Left Fork"), which leases and operates the mine.[2] Straight Creek is an underground slope mine containing two separate seams of coal: the upper seam is the Rim Seam and the lower seam is the Straight Creek Seam. Until its flooding, Left Creek mined in three sections of the Rim Seam, while working to rehabilitate the Straight Creek Seam. Mines like Straight Creek are subject to regular safety inspections pursuant to the Federal Mine Health and Safety Act of 1977 ("Mine Act") (30 U.S.C. § 801 *et seq.*). The Mine Act authorizes the Secretary of Labor to promulgate mandatory health and safety regulations for all mines (30 C.F.R. § 75.370 *et seq.*). The Federal Mine Safety and Health Administration ("MSHA"), a division of the Department of Labor ("DOL"), acts on behalf of the Secretary of Labor and enforces the Mine Act. The Mine Act generally requires at least four annual inspections and, in some instances, more frequent, "spot," inspections, p.771 such as in the event of excessive methane liberation. 30 U.S.C. § 813(i). Defendants-Appellees Irvin Hooker,[3] Clayton "Eddie" Sparks, Dannie Lewis, Dennis Cotton, Charles Maggard, and Sam Creasy are mine inspectors or supervisors employed by the MSHA (collectively, "MSHA employees"). The Mine Act mandates that an inspector *must* issue a citation to a mine operator for any conditions the inspector observes that are in violation of the Mine Act or its attendant regulations. 30 U.S.C. § 814(a).

During a routine inspection on March 22, 2011, MSHA inspector Tom Middleton noted elevated methane gas readings from behind a seal meant to confine methane and other dangerous gases and prevent entry to the Straight Creek mine's ventilation system. Given the high likelihood of a significant and substantial safety threat, Middleton issued an order ("Imminent Danger Order") under section 107(a) of the Mine Act, 30 U.S.C. § 817(a) and a citation under section 104(a) of the Mine Act, 30 U.S.C. § 814(a). In the event of an accident, which includes an unplanned inundation of a mine by a gas, section 103(k) of the Mine Act, 30 U.S.C. § 817(a), authorizes MSHA agents to issue orders they deem appropriate to ensure safety of any persons in the mine. Acting pursuant to this authorization, Middleton issued a second order ("No Access Order" or "K Order") proscribing Left Fork's access to the mine. The No Access Order closed the mine for all activity, but was modified by Middleton multiple times that day to allow for ventilation, conducting of required examinations, re-energizing of power, monitoring of the seals, and de-watering of the mine. Middleton also issued a second citation pursuant to section 104(a) of the Mine Act, 30 U.S.C. § 814(a) for maintenance issues related to a crack above mine seals that was allegedly leaking.[4]

Left Fork advised Middleton that the elevated methane readings were likely the result of a faulty ventilation curtain and proposed investigating the situation. But because the No Access Order was already in place, Middleton did not permit access to the mine and Left Fork was required to submit an abatement plan to repair the seals.

The next day, Left Fork complied and submitted an abatement plan seeking approval to repair the crack in the strata above the seal. MSHA did not respond in writing to the submitted abatement plan. Instead, a few days later, on March 29, 2011, Middleton issued an order pursuant to section 104(b) of the Mine Act, 30 U.S.C. § 814(b) ("Abatement Order" or "Original B Order") alleging that Left Fork failed to submit a plan to repair affected seals in accordance with the second p.772 citation issued on March 22, 2011.[5] Left Fork counters that it could not abate the condition because the MSHA would not allow Left Fork access to the mine. On April 8, 2011, Left Fork submitted a second plan for abatement which was denied in writing on April 11, 2011.

Between May 2011 and January 2012, the No Access Order was modified to remove electrical power and stop all work at the mine. This period was also characterized by a series of back-and-forth negotiations between the parties. Left Fork would submit a plan, the MSHA would request changes, Left Fork would comply, and the MSHA would request more changes. On January 11, 2012, MSHA employee Dannie Lewis inspected the mine and noted numerous hazards. The same day, Lewis modified the Abatement Order ("Modified Abatement Order" or "Modified B Order") to require that Left Fork de-energize all power and withdraw all miners. When the mine was de-energized, underground electric water pumps shut down and the mine began to flood.[6]

On January 17, 2012, Left Fork filed a Notice of Contest before the Federal Mine Safety and Health Review Commission ("Commission") challenging the issuance of the Modified Abatement Order pursuant to section 100.6 of the Mine Act.[7] The Commission, which bears singular responsibility for adjudicating disputes under the Mine Act (such as challenges to orders issued by the MSHA), is an independent adjudicative agency created by Congress to provide impartial review of legal disputes arising under the Mine Act. *See* 30 U.S.C. §§ 823(a) and (d). The Commission's Administrative Law Judges ("ALJs") decide cases at the trial level and the five-member Commission provides appellate review. *Id.* Further appeals of the Commission's decisions are to the appropriate United States court of appeals. 30 U.S.C.A. § 816(a)(1). The Commission is authorized to grant hearings, including on an expedited basis, and to grant temporary relief as requested by mine operators. *Id.*

Left Fork requested an expedited hearing, which was held on January 30-31, 2012, almost three weeks after the mine began to flood. Notably, Left Fork did not request temporary relief in the interim. On April 3, 2012, an ALJ invalidated the Abatement Order and Modified Abatement Order against Left Fork and held that (1) although the excessive methane levels "did meet the criteria for the application of the safety standard for excessive methane," the MSHA erred in modifying the Abatement Order (which was erroneously issued in the first place), and (2) the MSHA should have either issued a new citation or modified the Imminent Danger Order to achieve the same result of shutting off power and withdrawing miners, concluding "Simply put, the [MSHA] Inspector and his Supervisor chose the wrong method to close down the Straight Creek [] Mine." PageID 30. Neither party appealed from the ALJ's decision.

p.773 Despite the ALJ's favorable ruling, Left Fork experienced significant flood damage in the interim.[8] Left Fork filed the instant action against the MSHA employees, seeking "[r]easonable compensation for the denial of [Left Fork's] rights and the unlawful destruction of [Left Fork's] Property and Equipment in an amount to be determined at trial." PageID 18.

In its complaint, Left Fork alleged that the MSHA employees violated Left Fork's Fifth Amendment rights to due process of law when they ordered the de-energizing of Straight Creek mine. Left Fork also claimed that when MSHA employees ordered the de-energizing of Straight Creek mine, they did so maliciously and with the knowledge that the mine would flood and cause Left Fork property damage. Left Fork asserts that the MSHA employees were motivated by the desire to retaliate or punish Left Fork over the dispute regarding how to fix the mine seals. Left Fork also alleged a series of state common-law tort claims, including trespass, intentional interference with contract, abuse of process, and civil conspiracy.

In response, the MSHA employees filed a motion to dismiss indicating, inter alia, that Left Fork's state common-law tort claims should be dismissed on absolute immunity grounds and that the Mine Act's statutory scheme precludes a cause of action under *Bivens*. Alternatively, the MSHA employees argued that Left Fork's allegations did not amount to a constitutional violation and, even if they did, the MSHA employees were entitled to qualified immunity. The district court found that

Left Fork did not satisfy the requirements of the Federal Torts Claims Act ("FTCA") for bringing various state common-law tort claims against the MSHA employees and that Left Fork was precluded by the Mine Act from seeking a remedy under *Bivens.* Having found that Left Fork had no cause of action under *Bivens,* the district court declined to address the alternate arguments made by the MSHA employees and dismissed Left Fork's case with prejudice.

On appeal, Left Fork does not challenge the district court's dismissal of the state common-law tort claims. Therefore we consider only the dismissal of Left Fork's constitutional claim pursuant to *Bivens.*

II.

We review de novo the district court's dismissal of a case pursuant to Rule 12(b)(6) of the Federal Rules of Civil Procedure. *See Bright v. Gallia Cnty.,* 753 F.3d 639, 648 (6th Cir.2014); *Bassett v. NCAA,* 528 F.3d 426, 430 (6th Cir.2008). In so doing, we accept all material allegations contained in the complaint as true, and construe them in the light most favorable to the non-moving party. *Top Flight Entm't, Ltd. v. Schuette,* 729 F.3d 623, 630 (6th Cir.2013). To the extent that any of the factual assertions are in conflict, we accept the facts as stated by Left Fork in its complaint and consider whether those facts constitute constitutional violations that warrant relief under *Bivens.* To find that Left Fork's complaint survives a motion to dismiss, we must find that it contains some viable legal theory under which the claimants may seek relief. *See Mezibov v. Allen,* 411 F.3d 712, 716 (6th Cir. 2005); *Ashcroft v. Iqbal,* 556 U.S. 662, 679, 129 S.Ct. 1937, 173 L.Ed.2d 868 (2009) (citing *Bell Atl. Corp. v. Twombly,* 550 U.S. 544, 556, 127 S.Ct. 1955, 167 L.Ed.2d p.774 929 (2007)) ("[O]nly a complaint that states a plausible claim for relief survives a motion to dismiss."). In other words, even if Left Fork has a "cause of action, [the] complaint might nevertheless be dismissed under Rule 12(b)(6) unless it can be determined that judicial relief is available." *Davis v. Passman,* 442 U.S. 228, 244, 99 S.Ct. 2264, 60 L.Ed.2d 846 (1979) (considering whether a judicially-created damages-remedy is an appropriate form of relief).

III.

In *Bivens,* in the absence of a federal statute that provides for damages against a federal employee for allegedly violating the Constitution, the Supreme Court recognized a limited, implied cause of action against federal employees for particularly egregious violations of the Fourth Amendment in an unlawful search and seizure case brought by a private citizen. *See Wheeldin v. Wheeler,* 373 U.S. 647, 649-52, 83 S.Ct. 1441, 10 L.Ed.2d 605 (1963) (citing *Bivens,* 403 U.S. at 390, 91 S.Ct. 1999). The Supreme Court awarded a judicially-created damages remedy, finding that Bivens would otherwise be without *any* remedy for an unconstitutional invasion of his rights by federal agents. *Bivens,* 403 U.S. at 390, 91 S.Ct. 1999 (emphasis added). Since then, the Supreme Court has extended the *Bivens* rationale to allow direct claims arising under the Fifth Amendment. *See Thomas v. Shipka,* 818 F.2d 496, 500 (6th Cir.1987).

Under *Bivens,* a plaintiff must initially demonstrate (1) a challenged action attributable to a person acting under color of federal law, and (2) conduct that deprives the party of a constitutionally protected interest. *Schweiker v. Chilicky,* 487 U.S. 412, 418-21, 108 S.Ct. 2460, 101 L.Ed.2d 370 (1988). If those elements are satisfied, the Court then proceeds to a two-step inquiry to ascertain whether a *Bivens* damages remedy should be inferred. *Wilkie v. Robbins,* 551 U.S. 537, 550, 127 S.Ct. 2588, 168 L.Ed.2d 389 (2007) (citing *Bush v. Lucas,* 462 U.S. 367, 378, 103 S.Ct. 2404, 76 L.Ed.2d 648 (1983)). A *Bivens* remedy is available only if (1) there are no "alternative, existing process[es]" for protecting a constitutional interest and, (2) even in the absence of an alternative, there are no "special factors counselling hesitation before authorizing a new kind of federal litigation." *Id.* Left Fork has demonstrated that the challenged action here (the de-energizing of the Straight Creek mine) was attributable to individuals employed by a federal agency (the MSHA) who were acting under color of federal law (the Mine Act). Left Fork has also demonstrated that the de-energizing of the mine resulted in damage to property, ostensibly in violation of the Fifth Amendment, which protects individuals from being "deprived of life, liberty, or property without due process of law." U.S. Const., Amend. V. Accordingly, Left Fork has met the two threshold considerations for a *Bivens* claim. We therefore proceed to the two-step inquiry outlined in *Wilkie.*

A.

The district court's careful discussion of the Supreme Court's analysis in *Wilkie* is persuasive. Because the motion to dismiss was predicated only on the first step of the *Wilkie* analysis, which is a prerequisite for the second step, the district court appropriately limited its discussion to the first step. The district court properly concluded that the statutory scheme set forth by Congress pursuant to the Mine Act provides an alternative existing process for protecting Left Fork's constitutional interest and therefore precludes Left Fork from invoking a cause of action under *Bivens.*

p.775 The Mine Act's extensive and comprehensive review process is precisely the kind of remedial structure that precludes a judicially-created remedy. Although the Supreme Court has not ruled on the applicability of a *Bivens* remedy in Mine Act cases, the Court has held that the Act "establishes a detailed structure for reviewing violations of 'any mandatory health or safety standard, rule, order, or regulation promulgated' under the Act." *Thunder Basin Coal Co. v. Reich,* 510 U.S. 200, 207, 114 S.Ct. 771, 127 L.Ed.2d 29 (1994) (quoting § 30 U.S.C. 814(a)). Under the Mine Act, mine operators may contest citations or orders issued under sections 104 and 107 within thirty days. *See* 30 U.S.C. §§ 815(a), (d). Such challenges are first heard by an ALJ, and may also be heard by the Commission at its discretion. 30 U.S.C. § 823(d)(2). In addition to the procedure for contesting an order, the Mine Act authorizes the Commission to grant temporary relief from any order (including those issued under sections 103(k) and 104) or modification thereof. 30 U.S.C. § 815(b)(2);[9] *see also Performance Coal Co. v. Fed. Mine Safety & Health Review Comm'n,* 642 F.3d 234, 239 (D.C.Cir.2011). The Mine Act also prescribes specific circumstances under which judicial review of the administrative proceedings is permitted. Under section 106(a)(1), "[a]ny person adversely affected or aggrieved by an order of the Commission issued under this chapter may obtain review of such order in any United States court of appeals for the circuit in which the violation is alleged to have occurred or in the United States Court of Appeals for the District of Columbia Circuit." 30 U.S.C. § 816(a)(1).

Left Fork argues that the Mine Act's remedial structure is insufficient to prevent losses to its property or to subsequently make it whole. Even if Left Fork is correct, it does not mean that an alternative, existing process for protecting its constitutional interest is absent. The opportunity for administrative review under the Mine Act exists precisely so that mine operators and miners can protect their constitutional interests. Indeed, Left Fork utilized this very opportunity in filing a Notice of Contest with the Commission which resulted in the ALJ invalidating the contested orders. After availing itself of this remedy, Left Fork now seeks money damages on account of property loss which occurred during the interim. To the extent that the Mine Act does not permit such relief, Left Fork is correct that there is no "alternative, existing process" for receiving financial compensation. Left Fork is also correct that the ALJ's vacatur of the Abatement Order as issued and modified by the MSHA employees did not prevent the Straight Creek mine from flooding. And while it is true that the Mine Act does not provide a damages remedy when an MSHA employee's order is subsequently deemed invalid, the adequate alternative remedy contemplated by *Bivens* p.776 does not necessitate financial compensation either.

As the district court noted, the Supreme Court has made it clear that the lack of money damages for constitutional torts is insufficient to give rise to a new *Bivens* remedy when an alternative remedial scheme exists, and even in the absence of an alternative, "a *Bivens* remedy is a subject of judgment." *Wilkie,* 551 U.S. at 550, 127 S.Ct. 2588, *see also Bush,* 462 U.S. at 378, 103 S.Ct. 2404. Therefore, the lack of money damages under the Mine Act does not automatically entitle Left Fork to a judicially created remedy under *Bivens.*

B.

Assuming arguendo that Left Fork's complaint survives the first step of the *Bivens* test for relief, we next consider whether there are special factors that counsel hesitation before we authorize a new kind of federal litigation for coal mine operators who are regulated by the Mine Act. Given that the motion to dismiss Left Fork's complaint was predicated on the failure to satisfy the first step of the *Bivens* test for relief, the district court's inquiry did not extend into an explicit analysis of the second step. However, the court indirectly noted that (1) the congressional intent behind the Mine Act (i.e. to provide comprehensive and non-judicial remedies for aggrieved mine operators), and (2) the existence of statutory mechanisms giving meaningful, if not complete, relief, were both special factors that counseled hesitation in authorizing *Bivens* relief in this case. We agree that special factors counseling hesitation are present in this case.

The first special factor counseling hesitation in this case is that the Mine Act established a comprehensive remedial structure, as explained in detail above. The lack of money damages and judicial review available under the Mine Act should not be presumed to be "inadvertent." *Jones v. Tenn. Valley Auth.*, 948 F.2d 258, 263-64 (6th Cir.1991). ("[C]ourts must give appropriate deference to indications that congressional inaction has *not been inadvertent* and should not create *Bivens* remedies when the design of a government program *suggests* that Congress has provided what it considers to be adequate remedies for constitutional violations.") (emphasis added). Congressional intent based on the legislative history of the Mine Act also supports this presumption. *Id.* That the plaintiffs cannot seek relief in the form of damages does not compel us to second-guess the remedial scheme devised by Congress by creating a new freestanding claim for damages. *Id.*

Moreover, the Mine Act expressly authorizes direct judicial review in only two provisions: actions enjoining habitual operator violations of health and safety standards and actions to collect payment of civil penalties. 30 U.S.C. §§ 818(a) and 820(j). Both of these provisions empower the Secretary of Labor to seek district court review but do not afford the same right to mine operators. *Thunder Basin,* 510 U.S. at 209 & n. 11, 114 S.Ct. 771. Instead, mine operators "are to complain to the Commission and then to the court of appeals." *Id.* Such a limitation implies that Congress intended challenges by mine operators under the Mine Act to be limited to a single review process. Allowing a *Bivens* claim to proceed here would be tantamount to a multi-review process.

Further, the Supreme Court has held that "Such 'special factors' include the existence of statutory mechanisms giving meaningful remedies against the United States, even though those remedies do not provide 'complete relief' to the claimant." *Schweiker,* 487 U.S. at 423, 108 S.Ct. 2460. p.777 *Schweiker* suggests that "meaningful" should be understood based on Congressional intent and not a plaintiff's perspective alone. In *Schweiker,* employees of the Social Security Administration allegedly violated the plaintiff's due process rights in denying disability claims. However, because the Social Security Act provided a mechanism for redress, including the reinstatement of benefits when denial was erroneous, the Supreme Court found special factors counseling hesitation. *Id.* The Supreme Court was not persuaded by the fact that the Social Security Act did not provide any monetary remedy for a constitutional violation claimed, or for the emotional distress and delay that a denial of benefits might occasion. *Id.* This is because Congress is presumed to have balanced governmental efficacy with individual rights in designing the statute. *Id.* Left Fork argues that the alternate existing remedies in *Schweiker* and *Bush* were more effective in making the plaintiffs whole than Left Fork's remedies under the Mine Act. We cannot consider the efficacy of the remedy without also asking whether Congress intended the existing remedies to be supplemented by judicial action. In this case we think that it did not. Supreme Court jurisprudence holding that "effective" relief is not always "complete" relief, and the Mine Act's clear limitations on judicial remedies, counsel us against recognizing *Bivens* relief in this case.

Left Fork argues on appeal that a remedy *must* be "equally effective" in order to preclude a *Bivens* claim. *Carlson v. Green,* 446 U.S. 14, 18-19, 100 S.Ct. 1468, 64 L.Ed.2d 15 (1980)(granting a federal prisoner a *Bivens* remedy for violations of his constitutional rights even though the allegations could also support a suit against the United States under the FTCA). This argument is unpersuasive. If Congress explicitly declares a statutory scheme to be "equally effective" as a constitutional remedy, the availability of a constitutional remedy is eliminated. However, even if Congress does *not* do so, a constitutional remedy is not automatically available. We must nevertheless consider whether special factors, such as Congressional intent to preclude a judicially-created constitutional remedy, exist. In *Carlson,* the FTCA would have provided relief to the plaintiff but the Supreme Court allowed a *Bivens* claim against federal prison officials for Eighth Amendment violations because Congress had not "explicitly declared" that the FTCA was "to be a substitute for recovery directly under the Constitution and viewed as equally effective." *Carlson,* 446 U.S. at 18-19, 100 S.Ct. 1468. Indeed, unlike the Mine Act, it is clear that "Congress views FTCA and *Bivens* as parallel, complementary causes of action ... this provision should be viewed as a *counterpart* to the *Bivens* case and its progeny [*sic*]." *Id.* at 20, 100 S.Ct. 1468 (citing S.Rep.No.93-588, p. 3 (1973) (legislative history to the 1973 amendment to the FTCA)). Here, Congress has explicitly limited judicial review through the Mine Act.

In addition to *Carlson,* the Supreme Court has extended *Bivens* relief in only one other case. *See Davis,* 442 U.S. at 244, 99 S.Ct. 2264. Like *Carlson, Davis* diverges significantly from the instant case. *Davis* involved a secretary to a Congressman who claimed that her Fifth Amendment rights were violated when her employment was terminated on the basis of gender. *Davis,* 442 U.S. at 244, 99 S.Ct. 2264. For seeking redress, she claimed that she had no effective means of relief other than under *Bivens. Id.* Despite the existence of a remedy under Title VII, the Supreme Court allowed Davis' discrimination claim because there was no evidence that Congress intended to preclude a judicially created remedy. *Davis,* 442 U.S. at p.778 236, 99 S.Ct. 2264. ("[J]udicial review of congressional employment decisions is constitutionally limited only by the reach of the Speech or Debate Clause of the Constitution," therefore, judicial review was warranted in the case to the extent that the Congressman was not shielded by the Clause.) Unlike in *Davis,* the Mine Act explicitly circumscribes judicial review in this case.

Special circumstances notwithstanding, Left Fork claims damages under *Bivens* because the alleged constitutional violations by the MSHA employees involved improper motive and illegality. *See e.g., Hartman v. Moore,* 547 U.S. 250, 126 S.Ct. 1695, 164 L.Ed.2d 441 (2006) (holding that individuals do not have the right to be free from retaliatory criminal prosecutions unless they were brought without probable cause). Citing to the Mine Act's provisions for imposing criminal penalties against mine operators, 30 U.S.C. § 820(d), Left Fork likens the MSHA employees' actions to those of federal agents in bringing unlawful criminal prosecutions. Left Fork's analogy is inconsonant because the MSHA employees' issuance and modification of the Abatement Order, the action which underlies this lawsuit, only served to de-energize the Straight Creek Mine and withdraw miners; no penalties, civil or criminal, were imposed on Left Creek through the challenged orders. Therefore the element of probable cause that is integral to examining the validity of a criminal prosecution is entirely absent in this case.

Even if a finding of improper motive were to somehow dispense with our consideration of "special circumstances" in this case, Left Fork has done little to show how the MSHA employees' actions stemmed from improper motive, aside from stating that they were. *Top Flight,* 729 F.3d at 630 (holding that the bald assertion of legal conclusions is not enough to constitute a claim for relief.)

Moreover, the record contains no evidence of improper motive. Therefore, we find that Left Fork has not sufficiently pled improper motive in its complaint to withstand a motion to dismiss. "[U]nadorned, the-defendant-unlawfully-harmed-me accusation" is insufficient to support an action. *Iqbal*, 556 U.S. at 678, 129 S.Ct. 1937 (citing *Twombly*, 550 U.S. at 555, 127 S.Ct. 1955; Fed.R.Civ.P. 12(b)(6)).

IV.

Given the Mine Act's comprehensive process for protecting constitutional interests, which expressly incorporates judicial review, we decline to create a judicial remedy in this case. Left Fork is precluded from obtaining relief under *Bivens* and the district court properly dismissed its complaint for failure to state a claim upon which relief can be granted. For the foregoing reasons, we AFFIRM the district court's decision.

[1] Left Fork operates Straight Creek under a lease agreement with Manalapan Land Company, Ltd. and Black Star Mining Company, Ltd. Under the agreement, Left Fork pays Manalapan and Black Star royalties for the coal mined on their property. Left Fork then supplies the coal to Cumberland River Energies, LLC, which sells the coal to various third-party purchasers. Bennett Resources LLC leases mining equipment to Left Fork. Collectively, these companies make up the appellants in this case.

[2] On November 11, 2013, Left Fork, Bennett Resources, LLC, and Cumberland River Energies, LLC filed for bankruptcy under Chapter 7. Although the pending lawsuit was listed in the respective bankruptcy schedules, none of the parties attempted to substitute the appointed bankruptcy trustees in the pending district court action. On March 17, 2014 the district court dismissed the complaint and the Plaintiffs-Appellants filed a notice of appeal on April 14, 2014. The appointed trustees hold the exclusive right to assert the instant appeal on behalf of Left Fork, Bennett Resources, LLC, and Cumberland River Energies, LLC. Therefore, those parties must file a motion for substitution in accordance with Fed. R.App. P. 43(a) and (b).

[3] The death of Irving Hooker, a public officer sued in his official capacity, during the pendency of this appeal does not necessitate substitution. See Fed. R.App. P. 43(c)(2) ("When a public officer who is a party to an appeal or other proceeding in an official capacity dies, resigns, or otherwise ceases to hold office, the action does not abate. The public officer's successor is automatically substituted as a party. Proceedings following the substitution are to be in the name of the substituted party, but any misnomer that does not affect the substantial rights of the parties may be disregarded. An order of substitution may be entered at any time, but failure to enter an order does not affect the substitution.")

[4] Mine operators may contest orders issued under section 103, 107 (and any modification therein) within 30 days of issuance. 29 C.F.R. § 2700.22. The Administrative Law Judge's decision in this case suggests that Left Fork contested the No Access Order, Imminent Danger Order, and accompanying citations. Those cases were assigned to a different Administrative Law Judge, however, and the record does not indicate the outcomes.

[5] It is unclear from the record whether Left Fork contested the Abatement Order when it was first issued.

[6] Left Fork states that the MSHA approved Left Fork's plans for abatement on January 13, 2012, but only on the condition that Left Fork would begin construction within three days. Despite approving Left Fork's plan, MSHA employees refused to allow Left Fork to stop the flooding or retrieve any equipment that could be salvaged.

[7] The Mine Act's Procedural Rules provide that an operator may contest a citation or an order issued under section 104 of the Act, 30 U.S.C. 814, or a modification of a citation or an order issued under section 104 of the Act. *See* 29 C.F.R. § 2700.20.

[8] Recognizing that a favorable decision may come too late to prevent flood damage to Left Fork's property, at the conclusion of the hearing, the ALJ urged the parties to "meet and work out a plan to prevent destruction of a mine," and then contact his office. PageID 34. However, no such contact occurred.

[9] "An applicant may file with the Commission a written request that the Commission grant temporary relief from any modification or termination of any order or from any order issued under section 814 of this title together with a detailed statement giving the reasons for granting such relief. The Commission may grant such relief under such conditions as it may prescribe, if—(A) a hearing has been held in which all parties were given an opportunity to be heard; (B) the applicant shows that there is substantial likelihood that the findings of the Commission will be favorable to the applicant; and(C) such relief will not adversely affect the health and safety of miners. No temporary relief shall be granted in the case of a citation issued under subsection (a) or (f) of section 814 of this title. The Commission shall provide a procedure for expedited consideration of applications for temporary relief under this paragraph." 30 U.S.C. § 815(b)(2).

SEVENTH CIRCUIT DECISIONS
Federal Tort Claims Act

JOHNNIE WATKINS, as Guardian of the Estate of Johnnice Ford, a disabled person, Plaintiff-Appellant,

v.

UNITED STATES OF AMERICA, Defendant-Appellee.

No. 16-2109.

United States Court of Appeals, Seventh Circuit.

Argued January 6, 2017.

Decided April 27, 2017.

Harry Charles Lee, for Plaintiff-Appellant.

Sarah J. North, for Defendant-Appellee.

Patrick J. Condron, for Plaintiff-Appellant.

Appeal from the United States District Court for the Northern District of Illinois, Eastern Division, No. 1:15-cv-08350—Ronald A. Guzmán, *Judge.*

Before WOOD, *Chief Judge,* and BAUER and ROVNER, *Circuit Judges.*

ROVNER, Circuit Judge.

This appeal is from the district court's dismissal, on statute of limitations grounds, of a medical malpractice claim. The plaintiff, Johnnie Watkins, filed the action on behalf of her adult daughter Johnnice Ford, who is a disabled person. The complaint alleged that Ford sought treatment at the emergency room of Ingalls Memorial Hospital, where she was treated by Dr. Bari Parks-Ballard, an employee of Family Christian Health Center. She asserts that Parks-Ballard failed to properly diagnose and treat Ford, who was eventually diagnosed with Wernicke's encephalopathy and who sustained neurological injuries including permanent disability. Because Family Christian Health Center operated pursuant to grant money from the Public Health Services, an agency of the United States government, the action was brought pursuant to the Federal Tort Claims Act (FTCA) and the United States is the defendant. The district court dismissed the action as filed beyond the relevant statute of limitations, and the plaintiff appeals that determination. On appeal, the plaintiff argues that the court erred in taking judicial notice of Ford's prior lawsuit and dismissing the case based on the statute of limitations without allowing her to establish that Ford suffered from a mental disability. We agree with the reasoning of the district court and affirm.

As the district court recognized, the FTCA constitutes a limited waiver of the United States' sovereign immunity, which allows individuals to pursue actions against the federal government for "personal injury or death caused by the negligent or wrongful act or omission of any employee of the Government while acting within the scope of his office or employment." 28 U.S.C. § 2675(a); *Warram v. United States,* 427 F.3d 1048, 1049 (7th Cir. 2005). The applicable FTCA statute of limitations bars any such claim not presented in writing to the appropriate agency within two years of the claim's accrual. Under the savings clause, that time period can be extended as long as the plaintiff filed a civil suit concerning the underlying tort claim within two years of its accrual and presented that case to the appropriate federal agency within 60 days of the civil suit's dismissal.

In assessing the timeliness of the 2015 action, we must first identify when the claim accrued, because the limitations period begins to run at that time. In *United States v. Kubrick,* 444 U.S. 111, 118 (1979), the Supreme Court held that a cause of action for purposes of the limitations period accrues when the claimant knows, or would reasonably be expected to know, of the existence of her injury and who caused it, whether or not the claimant is aware that there was negligence or a wrongful act involved. See also *Blanche v. United States,* 811 F.3d 953, 958 (7th Cir. 2016). In *Barnhart v. United States,* 884 F.2d 298, 299 (7th Cir. 1989), we addressed a claim that the injury itself impaired the ability of the plaintiff to understand and pursue her claim, and we considered that such incapacity could toll the accrual date; we held that the proper focus in determining when the claim accrued under the discovery rule in such cases remains on the claimant's awareness or ability to discover and comprehend the cause of her injuries. In *Blanche* we further noted that the plaintiff need not know that her injury was caused by a doctor; "the accrual date is when the plaintiff has enough information to suspect, or a reasonable person would suspect, that the injury 'had a doctor-related cause.'" 811 F.3d at 958, quoting *Arroyo v. United States,* 656 F.3d 663, 672-73 (7th Cir. 2011).

In determining that the claim accrued as of August 2010, the district court took judicial notice of a state court medical malpractice claim filed in August 2010 by Ford against Ingalls Memorial Hospital, Dr. Parks-Ballard, and Family Christian Health Center. See *Ennenga v. Starns,* 677 F.3d 766, 773 (7th Cir. 2012) (noting that in considering a motion to dismiss, courts may take judicial notice of facts readily ascertainable from the public court record such as the dates on which certain actions were taken). The district court noted that the August 2010 complaint contained virtually the same allegations as those in this case regarding the failure to timely diagnose and treat her encephalopathy. Ford voluntarily dismissed that complaint within a month after its filing, but its relevance is in its reflection of Ford's awareness that those defendants caused her injuries.

Because the complaint reflects an awareness that her injuries were caused by the defendant (through its agents), at a minimum the claim accrued as of August 2010. Pursuant to the limitations provision applicable to FTCA claims, Ford could proceed with her claim against the United States only if she (1) presented her claim to the appropriate agency within two years of the date of the claim's accrual; or (2) filed a civil suit within 2 years from that date of accrual and presented that case to the appropriate federal agency within 60 days of the civil suit's dismissal. See 28 U.S.C. § 2679(d)(5); *Blanche,* 811 F.3d at 957-58. The plaintiff failed to satisfy either of those alternate avenues. The claim was not presented to the administrative agency until January 19, 2015, which was approximately 4-1/2 years after the date the claim accrued. Nor was the claim presented to the appropriate agency within 60 days from the dismissal of a civil suit that was filed within 2 years from the date of accrual. No claim was submitted to the agency within 60 days of the dismissal of the August 2010 action, and no other civil suit was filed within 2 years of the claim's accrual, which was August 2010 at the latest. On that basis, the district court granted the defendant's motion to dismiss the complaint.

Watkins raises a number of challenges to that reasoning. First, Watkins argues that the district court improperly failed to credit her allegations that Ford suffered from a mental disability since September 2008. Watkins alleged in the complaint that Ford "has been disabled since September 10, 2008, when she was diagnosed with Wernicke's encephalopathy," and that Ford "has been unable to manage her person, and estate and unable to recognize the cause of her action due to her diagnosis of Wernicke's encephalopathy." Plaintiff's First Amended Complaint § 6. The complaint further provided that Watkins brought the cause of action as Ford's legal guardian "due to Johnnice Ford's inability to make medical, legal, and financial decisions for herself." *Id.* at § 7. Watkins asserts that the district court failed to consider those allegations as true, as required in addressing a Rule 12(b)(6) motion, and that if it had done so, it would have necessarily concluded that Ford's mental disability prevented her from recognizing the "doctor-related cause of her injuries."

But the district court properly took judicial notice of the state court complaint filed by Ford's counsel in August 2010, which contained the same essential allegations as the present suit. We need not speculate as to whether the alleged mental disability impacted Ford's ability to recognize the cause of her injuries, because the 2010 lawsuit establishes that Ford was *actually* aware of the cause of her injuries. Watkins argues, however, that the court erred in taking judicial notice of that 2010 complaint, alleging that the filing of the complaint establishes only two facts—that Ford's name appears in the caption and that the complaint was filed on a certain date. She asserts that the record is devoid of evidence that Ford had any awareness of its filing. That bare allegation, without more, is insufficient to render the 2010 complaint irrelevant to these proceedings. Watkins provides nothing more than mere speculation that the complaint was filed without Ford's awareness. She includes no argument as to how the attorney who filed the complaint would be aware of the injuries to Ford and the circumstances which caused those injuries without Ford's participation and awareness. Moreover, she never alleges that she has, or could provide, evidence calling into question the legitimacy of the complaint, such as affidavit evidence from the attorney who filed it indicating that he or she communicated with someone other than Ford, or evidence that the attorney engaged in such unethical behavior in other such cases by purporting to bring a cause of action on behalf of a person without that person's knowledge or consent. Although the appeal is here on a motion to dismiss, the complaint and the public court record establish that Ford was aware of the injury and its cause, and in fact was pursuing legal action on such claims, as of August 2010. To survive dismissal, Watkins must allege some non-speculative basis to dispute that conclusion. Absent a claim that there is a plausible, good-faith basis to challenge the legitimacy of the August 2010 complaint, the court is entitled to take judicial notice that the complaint was filed by Ford in 2010 which contained the same essential allegations as the complaint before us now.

Moreover, although the complaint alleges that Ford has been disabled since September 10, 2008, when she was diagnosed with Wernicke's encephalopathy, and has been unable to manage her person and estate and to recognize the cause of her action due to that diagnosis, there is no allegation that any guardian was appointed for Ford until Watkins was named her guardian on January 14, 2015. Accordingly, the 2010 complaint with Ford as plaintiff cannot be attacked on the basis that Ford legally could act only through a guardian.

Watkins questions whether the district court considered the statements of Ford's physicians and case workers regarding her brain damage, such as a statement in

2008 by her physician that she was unable to attend to her financial affairs since she was unresponsive for unknown reasons and that he could not predict when she would be able to attend to her personal affairs. Although in November 2008, a case manager issued a report indicating that due to Watkins' cognitive limitations and physical impairments, she was unable to care for her children, and Watkins was appointed as guardian for those children, no guardian was appointed for Ford and nothing indicated a total inability to understand her own circumstances or to appreciate the cause of her injuries. As we concluded earlier, however, we need not assess whether the allegations of Ford's disability would have been sufficient to permit an inference that Ford was unable to recognize the cause of her injuries, because the allegations in the complaint filed in 2010 establish that at least as of that date she in fact possessed such knowledge. Contrary to Watkins' argument to this court, the court in taking judicial notice of that 2010 complaint did not take notice of the validity of the substance of the allegations within it, but rather took notice only of the existence and timing of those allegations. Whether the allegations are valid or not, the court can take notice of their presence in the complaint, and that presence demonstrates Ford's awareness of those potential allegations at that time. Because the cause of action accrued at least as of that date, the complaint in this case was not filed within the limitations period. As we uphold the dismissal on that ground, we need not consider the defendant's alternative argument that dismissal would also be proper under Illinois' statute of repose. See *Augutis v. United States,* 732 F.3d 749 (7th Cir. 2013).

Accordingly, the decision of the district court is AFFIRMED.

761 F.3d 779 (2014)

The SMOKE SHOP, LLC, Plaintiff-Appellant,
v.
UNITED STATES of America, Defendant-Appellee.

No. 13-3921.

United States Court of Appeals, Seventh Circuit.

Argued June 2, 2014.

Decided August 4, 2014.

Smoke Shop, LLC v. US, 761 F. 3d 779 (7th Cir. 2014)

p.780 John J.E. Markham, II, Attorney, Markham & Read, Boston, MA, for Plaintiff-Appellant.

Matthew Dean Krueger, Attorney, Office of the United States Attorney, Milwaukee, WI, for Defendant-Appellee.

Before FLAUM and WILLIAMS, Circuit Judges, and DOW, District Judge.[*]

FLAUM, Circuit Judge.

In 2012, the Drug Enforcement Administration seized over $110,000 worth of smokable "incense products" from a Delavan, Wisconsin retailer called The Smoke Shop. At the time of seizure, the DEA believed that the incense products, which contained synthetic cannabinoids, were controlled substance analogues and therefore illegal under federal drug laws. Smoke Shop contested this assertion and moved for the return of its inventory in federal district court. Later, the substances in the incense products were scheduled by the Attorney General, rendering them contraband. This eliminated Smoke Shop's hopes of recovering its goods, so it brought a conversion action against the federal government for damages under the Federal Tort Claims Act.

The district court dismissed Smoke Shop's FTCA suit on two alternative grounds. It found, first, that the government enjoyed sovereign immunity from Smoke Shop's suit under the detained-goods exception to the FTCA. Second, the court found that Smoke Shop failed to exhaust its administrative remedies because it did not submit a claim for damages to either the DEA or the Department of Justice before filing suit. We affirm on both grounds.

I. Background

This case is before us on a motion to dismiss, so we rely on the allegations in the plaintiff's complaint, without vouching for their truth. *Golden v. State Farm Mut. Auto. Ins. Co.,* 745 F.3d 252, 255 (7th Cir.2014).

The Smoke Shop is a small retail store in downtown Delavan that sells assorted novelties, tobacco products, smoking accessories, and what Smoke Shop describes as "incense products." As the government's testing later revealed, the incense products in question contained two marijuana-mimicking synthetic cannabinoids, XLR-11 and p.781 UR-144. *See generally* Eliza Gray, *The Rise of Fake Pot,* TIME, Apr. 21, 2014, at 26. Despite these intoxicating properties, Smoke Shop's complaint avows that the incense products are marked "NOT FOR HUMAN

CONSUMPTION," and have "numerous legitimate and legal uses ... ranging from religious ceremonies to the removal of pet odors."

On September 13, 2012, two DEA agents and three local police officers came into the store and seized 8,000 packages containing several different brands of the incense products. The agents told Smoke Shop's owner, David Yarmo, that they were taking the seized inventory to the local police station for testing, and that Smoke Shop would get back whatever was not found to be illegal. Believing that the products contained no controlled substances, Yarmo consented to their seizure.

Several days later, Yarmo went to the local police station to inquire about his inventory. He was told that the DEA had shipped the products to a federal testing facility, so Yarmo next turned to the DEA. Those agents told Yarmo there was "no way" that the DEA would ever return the incense products and that if Yarmo wanted to get the products back he would have to "sue them."

Smoke Shop then filed a motion for the return of property in federal district court. *See* Fed.R.Crim.P. 41(g) ("A person aggrieved by an unlawful search and seizure of property or by the deprivation of property may move for the property's return... in the district where the property was seized."). In response, the government filed a letter informing the district court that half of the seized products had tested positive for XLR-11 and UR-144, which the DEA considered to be controlled substances under the Controlled Substances Analogue Act, *see* 21 U.S.C. §§ 802(32), 813, 841(a)(1). Because the tested incense products were considered contraband, the government explained, the DEA could not return them. The letter also indicated that the remaining products were due to be tested.

The district court held a hearing on the Rule 41(g) motion in which Smoke Shop's and the government's experts debated whether XLR-11 and UR-144 constituted controlled substance analogues, and the parties continued to brief the issue. While this dispute was ongoing, however, the Attorney General exercised his power under the Controlled Substances Act to schedule XLR-11 and UR-144 as schedule I controlled substances on a temporary basis "to avoid an imminent hazard to the public safety." 21 U.S.C. § 811(h).

As a result of the Attorney General's action, the district court dismissed Smoke Shop's Rule 41(g) motion. The court opined that the Attorney General's "decision to schedule UR-144 and XLR-11 suggests that they were not analogues in the first instance, and now, Mr. Yarmo must recoup his losses through further litigation against the government." *The Smoke Shop, LLC v. United States,* 949 F.Supp.2d 877, 879 (E.D.Wis.2013). Accordingly, the court suggested that Smoke Shop amend its pleadings to effect this "further litigation."

Smoke Shop took the court up on its suggestion and filed an amended complaint against the United States for unlawful conversion under the Federal Tort Claims Act, seeking compensatory damages. Smoke Shop alleged that the government took its incense products — collectively worth about $110,000 — with no legal grounds to do so, and that the government only later declared the substances in the products illegal.

The district court dismissed Smoke Shop's complaint under Federal Rule of p.782 Civil Procedure 12(b)(6) on two independent grounds. First, the court found that Smoke Shop's action was barred by sovereign immunity. Though the FTCA waives the federal government's immunity for the torts of its employees, 28 U.S.C. § 1346(b)(1), claims arising from the detention of goods by law enforcement officers are excepted from that waiver, *id.* § 2680(c). To make matters more complicated, the Civil Asset Forfeiture Reform Act amended § 2680(c) to "re-waive" the government's immunity in detention-of-goods cases where the goods were "seized for the purpose of forfeiture" and certain other requirements are met. *See id.* § 2680(c)(1)-(4). However, the district court found that CAFRA's re-waiver did not apply to Smoke Shop's claim because the DEA did not, in fact, seize the incense products for the purpose of forfeiture — it seized them in connection with a criminal investigation.

The district court also concluded that Smoke Shop failed to exhaust its administrative remedies. Before a plaintiff can bring an FTCA action in court, she must present an FTCA "claim" to the appropriate federal agency within two years after the claim accrues. *See id.* §§ 2401(b), 2675(a). The district court found that Smoke Shop's Rule 41(g) motion did not qualify as a claim for money damages under § 2675(a), and that its FTCA action was therefore barred.[1]

II. Discussion

We review the district court's grant of a motion to dismiss de novo. *Augutis v. United States,* 732 F.3d 749, 752 (7th Cir. 2013).

A. The FTCA's detained-goods exception and CAFRA's rewaiver provision

The detained-goods exception to the FTCA preserves the federal government's immunity from suits arising from "the detention of any goods, merchandise, or other property by any officer of customs or excise or any other law enforcement officer." 28 U.S.C. § 2680(c); *see also Ali v. Fed. Bureau of Prisons,* 552 U.S. 214, 128 S.Ct. 831, 169 L.Ed.2d 680 (2008) (holding that § 2680(c) covers law enforcement officers of any kind). But in 2000, Congress, "reacting to public outcry over the government's too-zealous pursuit of civil and criminal forfeiture," passed the Civil Asset Forfeiture Reform Act. *United States v. Khan,* 497 F.3d 204, 208 (2d Cir.2007). Among other reforms, CAFRA "rewaived" the government's immunity — that is, once more opened the government up to suit under the FTCA — for tort actions stemming from law-enforcement detentions of property. But CAFRA's exception-to-the-exception only applies if four conditions are met:

> (1) the property was seized for the purpose of forfeiture under any provision of Federal law providing for the forfeiture p.783 of property other than as a sentence imposed upon conviction of a criminal offense;
>
> (2) the interest of the claimant was not forfeited;
>
> (3) the interest of the claimant was not remitted or mitigated (if the property was subject to forfeiture); and
>
> (4) the claimant was not convicted of a crime for which the interest of the claimant in the property was subject to forfeiture under a Federal criminal forfeiture law.

28 U.S.C. § 2680(c).

We must decide whether the DEA's seizure and detention of Smoke Shop's incense products qualifies for CAFRA's re-waiver. The first condition is the one the parties contest: whether the products were "seized for the purpose of forfeiture," a phrase to which our court has yet to give a definitive construction.

Adopting the reasoning of *Foster v. United States,* 522 F.3d 1071 (9th Cir. 2008), the district court found that CAFRA's re-waiver did not apply to these facts. *Foster* interpreted the requirement that the property have been "seized for the purpose of forfeiture" to mean that the property must have been seized *solely* for the purpose of forfeiture. *Id.* at 1075. The Ninth Circuit thus held that "the fact that the government may have had the possibility of a forfeiture in mind when it seized Plaintiff's property" was insufficient to bring the detention within the scope of CAFRA's re-waiver "when criminal investigation was [also] a legitimate purpose of the initial seizure." *Id.* In other words, the Ninth Circuit interpreted § 2680(c)(1) to preserve the government's immunity whenever a federal officer seized the plaintiff's property pursuant to a criminal investigation *at least in part* — even if the officer may have envisioned that the goods would be forfeited down the line.

The Ninth Circuit reasoned that its interpretation gave effect to the congressional purposes behind the FTCA's detained-goods exception, including "ensuring that certain governmental activities not be disrupted by the threat of damage suits." *Kosak v. United States,* 465 U.S. 848, 858, 104 S.Ct. 1519, 79 L.Ed.2d 860 (1984) (internal quotation marks omitted); *see also Foster,* 522 F.3d at 1078. Reading CAFRA's re-waiver as extending to any law enforcement investigation in which the officers might contemplate forfeiture would undermine that objective. For instance, "[a]ny waiver of sovereign immunity for damage to [property seized during an investigation] could hamper law enforcement officers' effectiveness in carrying out the important purposes underlying the seizure and redirect their attention from the possibility of danger in executing the search warrant to the possibility of civil damages." *Foster,* 522 F.3d at 1078.

The Ninth Circuit also grounded its reading in § 2680(c)(1)'s text. The court explained that "the statute's use of the definite phrase 'the purpose of forfeiture,' as opposed to an indefinite phrase 'a purpose of forfeiture,' suggests that the property be seized *only* for the purpose of forfeiture. Had Congress drafted the text to provide for re-waiver 'if the property was *seized and forfeited,*' then it would apply when both purposes underlie a single seizure. Congress, however, did not do so." *Id.* at 1077-78.

Our court has not adopted *Foster's* "sole-purpose test" in applying CAFRA's re-waiver provision. However, we employed *Foster* in an unpublished decision (as have two other circuits). *Pearson v. United States,* 373 Fed.Appx. 622, 624 (7th Cir.2010); *Shigemura v. United States,* 504 Fed.Appx. 678, 680 (10th Cir.2012); *Bowens v. U.S. Dep't of Justice,* 415 Fed. p.784 Appx. 340, 343 (3d Cir.2011). And in another case, we more or less applied *Foster's* logic: we found that because the government demonstrated that a detention occurred "for a criminal investigation and not for purposes of forfeiture," CAFRA's rewaiver did not apply. *On-Site Screening, Inc. v. United States,* 687 F.3d 896, 898 (7th Cir.2012).

We now formally adopt *Foster's* sole-purpose test. We agree that an alternative reading of § 2680(c)(1) — one that would waive the government's immunity whenever an officer envisioned the possibility of the seized goods' forfeiture —

would eviscerate the FTCA's detained-goods exception in the context of criminal investigations. When the government seizes property for law enforcement purposes, "in practice, forfeiture often follows eventually. Thus, in every criminal seizure the government necessarily must anticipate at least the possibility of a future forfeiture, a dual motivation that would be nearly impossible to disprove in any particular case." *Foster*, 522 F.3d at 1079.

We would be wary of the *Foster* interpretation if it marginalized CAFRA's re-waiver. After all, Congress meant to carve out some category of detained-goods suits and render the government liable on those claims. But the legislative history of CAFRA suggests that the seizure of property pursuant to *a criminal investigation* was not the problem Congress was seeking to address. Instead, CAFRA's reforms targeted the abuse of *forfeiture actions,* which — like criminal investigations — are often carried out by law enforcement pursuant to seizure warrants. *See* 18 U.S.C. § 981(b)(2) ("Seizures pursuant to this section shall be made pursuant to a warrant obtained in the same manner as provided for a search warrant under the Federal Rules of Criminal Procedure...."). A House Judiciary Committee report shows that Congress was predominantly concerned with making property owners whole where the government unsuccessfully brings a forfeiture action and damages or loses the seized property while the action is pending. *See* H.R.Rep. No. 106-192, at 18 (1999) ("Seized property awaiting forfeiture can be quickly damaged.... It cannot be categorized as victory when a boat owner gets back, for instance, a rusted and stripped hulk of a vessel."). In an earlier report, the House Judiciary Committee described CAFRA's proposed changes to the FTCA as allowing "property owners who prevail in forfeiture actions [to] sue the government for any negligent destruction or damage to the property." H.R.Rep. No. 105-358, at 49 (1997). Our adoption of *Foster* thus leaves CAFRA's exception intact in the areas where it was intended to be employed.

Indeed, Smoke Shop frames its argument in *Foster*'s terms. That is, Smoke Shop argues that the incense products *were* seized for the sole purpose of forfeiture — which, if plausibly alleged in the complaint, would permit Smoke Shop to take advantage of CAFRA's re-waiver. In support of its claim that the DEA was not pursuing a criminal investigation when it seized the products, Smoke Shop points out that the DEA did not have a search warrant to search the store, and that no federal criminal charges were ever filed against the business or Yarmo. Smoke Shop also stresses that a DEA agent told Yarmo that he would never get his products back and that he would have to file suit. Smoke Shop acknowledges that the government never initiated a forfeiture action with respect to the seized goods. But it argues that a formal action was unnecessary, because under 21 U.S.C. § 881(f), controlled substances are summarily forfeited. *See id.* § 881(f)(1) ("All controlled substances in schedule I or II that are possessed, transferred, sold, or offered for p.785 sale ... shall be deemed contraband and seized and summarily forfeited to the United States."). Because the government viewed these incense products as contraband all along, Smoke Shop argues, it must have envisioned the products' forfeiture under 21 U.S.C. § 881 from the moment it seized them.

But Smoke Shop's theory is unpersuasive. First, though it invokes 21 U.S.C. § 881 to support its argument that the seizure was "for the purpose of forfeiture" under 28 U.S.C. § 2680(c)(1), Smoke Shop does not realize that § 881 would seem to wholly undermine its case that it meets the condition set out in § 2680(c)(2): that "the interest of the claimant was not forfeited." Putting aside the parties' disagreement over whether the incense products constituted controlled substance analogues at the time of their initial seizure, there is now no dispute that these products are schedule I controlled substances as a result of the Attorney General's scheduling them. As such, by operation of § 881(f)(1), Smoke Shop's interest in the products *was* forfeited. And this result makes sense: we imagine that Congress did not intend for plaintiffs to obtain damages for lost items that were eventually deemed contraband (even if the plaintiff tried to fight that designation initially, as Smoke Shop did here). That said, the government never raised this argument about the interaction between 21 U.S.C. § 881(f)(1) and 28 U.S.C. § 2680(c)(2).

In any event, Smoke Shop's complaint fails to make out a plausible case that its situation qualifies for § 2680(c)(1). Though we accept the facts alleged in the complaint as true, Smoke Shop's assertion that "[t]he defendants seized the property for the purpose of forfeiture" is the type of legal conclusion not entitled to this presumption of truth. *Ashcroft v. Iqbal,* 556 U.S. 662, 678, 129 S.Ct. 1937, 173 L.Ed.2d 868 (2009). Putting statements like these aside, we must determine whether the remaining factual allegations "plausibly suggest an entitlement to relief." *Id.* at 681, 129 S.Ct. 1937. "If the allegations give rise to an obvious alternative explanation, then the complaint may stop short of the line between possibility and plausibility of entitlement to relief." *McCauley v. City of Chicago,* 671 F.3d 611, 616 (7th Cir. 2011) (alterations, citations, and quotation marks omitted).

When examined in context, the facts alleged in Smoke Shop's complaint give rise to an obvious alternative explanation: that the DEA seized Smoke Shop's inventory in connection with its investigation of a possible drug crime. DEA agents raided the store with local law enforcement officers in tow. The agents did not have a search warrant, but they didn't need one, as Yarmo consented to the search and seizure of his inventory. All along, the DEA maintained that it was testing the products to see if they contained an illegal substance under federal drug laws. And sure enough, tests revealed that the products did contain substances that the government considered illegal under the Controlled Substances Analogue Act.

True, the government never charged Smoke Shop with a crime. But just because the government had not yet indicted does not mean that we must assume — contrary to the circumstances of the seizure and testing — that one was not contemplated. And in fact, Smoke Shop tells us in its brief on appeal that six months after the seizure, Yarmo was served with a grand jury subpoena seeking financial documents and other information from Smoke Shop. We may "consider new factual allegations raised for the first time on appeal provided they are consistent with the complaint," *Chavez v. Ill. State Police,* 251 F.3d 612, 650 (7th Cir.2001), p.786 and this allegation further confirms our commonsense intuition that the DEA was conducting a criminal investigation. *Cf. McCauley,* 671 F.3d at 616 ("Making the plausibility determination is 'a context-specific task that requires the reviewing court to draw on its judicial experience and common sense.'" (quoting *Iqbal,* 556 U.S. at 679, 129 S.Ct. 1937)). Thus, Smoke Shop has not plausibly alleged that the DEA seized the incense products solely for the purpose of forfeiture. This situation therefore falls outside the scope of CAFRA's re-waiver provision — and within the scope of the detained-goods exception — and the district court was right to dismiss Smoke Shop's FTCA suit on this ground.

B. Presentation of a claim under 28 U.S.C. § 2675(a)

We also affirm the district court on its alternative holding: Smoke Shop's failure to exhaust its administrative remedies before filing its FTCA action.

28 U.S.C. § 2675(a) states that "[a]n action shall not be instituted upon a claim against the United States for money damages for ... loss of property ... unless the claimant shall have first presented the claim to the appropriate Federal agency and his claim shall have been finally denied by the agency in writing." In other words, the FTCA bars would-be tort plaintiffs from bringing suit against the government unless the claimant has previously submitted a claim for damages to the offending agency, because Congress wants agencies to have an opportunity to settle disputes before defending against litigation in court. *See McNeil v. United States*, 508 U.S. 106, 112 & n. 7, 113 S.Ct. 1980, 124 L.Ed.2d 21 (1993).

The term "claim" is undefined in the statute. But a corresponding regulation instructs that a proper administrative claim under the FTCA contains four elements: (1) notification of the incident; (2) a demand for money damages in a sum certain; (3) the title or legal capacity of the person signing; and (4) evidence of the person's authority to represent the claimant. 28 C.F.R. § 14.2(a); *see also Kanar v. United States*, 118 F.3d 527, 528 (7th Cir.1997).

Several courts consider 28 U.S.C. § 2675(a)'s exhaustion requirement to go to the court's subject-matter jurisdiction over the FTCA action, *see, e.g., Valadez-Lopez v. Chertoff*, 656 F.3d 851, 855 (9th Cir.2011); *Estate of Trentadue ex rel. Aguilar v. United States*, 397 F.3d 840, 852 (10th Cir.2005), and one of our early decisions confronting the meaning of the FTCA's administrative claim requirement, *Best Bearings Co. v. United States*, 463 F.2d 1177, 1179 (7th Cir.1972), operated under this same assumption. For many of those courts (though not *Best Bearings*), it followed that the definition in 28 C.F.R. § 14.2(a) was not authoritative, because the Attorney General lacked the delegated power from Congress to determine the extent of Article III jurisdiction. *See, e.g., GAF Corp. v. United States*, 818 F.2d 901, 920 & n. 110 (D.C.Cir.1987).

However, our court no longer treats § 2675(a) as a jurisdictional prerequisite. *See Glade ex rel. Lundskow v. United States*, 692 F.3d 718, 723 (7th Cir.2012). And for good reason: For the federal courts to adjudicate a case, there must be a case or controversy within the meaning of Article III (a requirement not at issue here), and a statutory grant of authority (here, the provision of the FTCA, 28 U.S.C. § 1346(b)(1), granting federal courts the authority to adjudicate actions for the torts of government employees). Section 2675(a)'s exhaustion requirement is neither of these; it is better characterized as a "condition precedent to the plaintiff's ability to prevail." *Kanar*, 118 F.3d p.787 at 530. Read this way, the word "claim" in § 2675(a) is simply a term in need of definition — i.e., a statutory gap for the Attorney General to fill pursuant to congressional delegation. *Id.* And our reading of § 2675(a) better aligns with the Supreme Court's guidance that the label "jurisdictional" should be used "not for claim-processing rules, but only for prescriptions delineating the classes of cases ... falling within a court's adjudicatory authority." *Kontrick v. Ryan*, 540 U.S. 443, 455, 124 S.Ct. 906, 157 L.Ed.2d 867 (2004); *accord Gonzalez v. Thaler*, ___ U.S. ___, 132 S.Ct. 641, 648-49, 181 L.Ed.2d 619 (2012).

In any event, as a result of our decision in *Kanar*, there is not much of a practical difference between our circuit's position — which considers 28 C.F.R. § 14.2(a) to be definitional — and the circuits that consider § 2675(a) as limiting the federal courts' power to adjudicate FTCA actions. The courts in the latter category require a claimant to file "(1) a written statement sufficiently describing the injury to enable the agency to begin its own investigation, and (2) a sum certain damages claim." *Blair v. IRS*, 304 F.3d 861, 864 (9th Cir. 2002); *accord GAF Corp.*, 818 F.2d at 919 n. 106 (collecting cases). By its terms, the regulation demands slightly more. *See* 28 C.F.R. § 14.2(a) (including the additional requirement that the person signing establish her title and authority to pursue the claim). But in *Kanar*, we reasoned that § 2675(a) does not require would-be FTCA plaintiffs to comply with "every jot and tittle" of the regulation. 118 F.3d at 530. So long as the proper agency had the opportunity to settle the claim for money damages before the point of suit, we said, technical deficiencies in the administrative claim could well be a case of "[n]o harm, no foul." *Id.* at 531. Thus, the underlying purpose of our approach to § 2675(a)'s requirement — like the courts that eschew the regulation — is to ensure that the claimant "does not hinder the settlement process that a claim is supposed to initiate." *Id.*

Smoke Shop admits that it did not file a formal administrative claim with the DEA or the U.S. Attorney's office before filing its FTCA action. But Smoke Shop maintains that its motion to the district court under Federal Rule of Criminal Procedure 41(g) gave the government constructive notice of its claim — so, no harm, no foul. The district court disagreed, concluding that asking for the return of seized property is not the equivalent of presenting a proper administrative claim under the FTCA.

Smoke Shop's Rule 41(g) motion certainly satisfied the first, third, and fourth requirements of 28 C.F.R. § 14.2(a). But the government maintains that the Rule 41(g) motion lacked the second requirement: a demand for money damages in a sum certain. Smoke Shop merely asked for the incense products back — it made no claim to money damages should the property not be returned.

Smoke Shop's omission of the money-damages element is only fatal if it can be said to have "hinder[ed]" or "thwarted" the settlement process "that Congress created as a prelude to litigation." *Kanar*, 118 F.3d at 531. Unfortunately for Smoke Shop, we have never held that a request for the return of property — unaccompanied by a statement that the claimant would seek money damages if the property was not returned — satisfies § 2675(a). In fact, in *Best Bearings*, we said just the opposite. 463 F.2d at 1179 ("The request for return of the [seized] bearings was not presentation of plaintiff's claim to the government agency as required by § 2675(a)...."). True, *Best Bearings* assumed that § 2675(a) was a jurisdictional requirement, a position we have now abandoned. *See Glade*, 692 F.3d at 723. Yet p.788 this conceptual shift does not undermine the logical underpinnings of *Best Bearings'* holding that a request for the return of seized property is not the equivalent of a demand for money damages. Yarmo did submit a declaration that itemized the seized inventory, including each product's respective value. But it was by no means clear that Smoke Shop was asking the government for money damages in those amounts in lieu of the property's return — it seems that Yarmo merely wanted to convey to the court the importance of the loss to his business. Thus, Smoke Shop simply did not tell the government that it intended to bring a tort suit against it.

Smoke Shop argues that it put the government on constructive notice that it intended to fight this matter. It was foreseeable to the government, Smoke Shop argues, that if the attempt to get the products back using Rule 41(g) didn't work, Smoke Shop would likely seek money damages next. But Smoke Shop loses sight of the fact that the FTCA is an exception to the immunity the federal government ordinarily enjoys from tort actions. As such, Congress can make "[m]en ... turn square corners" before haling the government into court — "[i]f [the government] attaches even purely formal conditions to its consent to be sued those conditions must be complied with." *Rock Island, A. & L.R. Co. v. United States,* 254 U.S. 141, 143, 41 S.Ct. 55, 65 L.Ed. 188 (1920) (Holmes, J.); *cf. McNeil,* 508 U.S. at 111-13, 113 S.Ct. 1980 (submitting a claim after initiating FTCA litigation does not fulfill § 2675(a), even if the litigation has not advanced substantially). Congress decided that it wanted agencies to have a chance to settle damages claims before facing litigation. And without being presented with an actual claim for money damages, the DEA and the U.S. Attorney's office were ill-equipped to make a fully informed assessment of Smoke Shop's claim.

As in our past cases, Smoke Shop's oversight hindered or thwarted the settlement process envisioned by the FTCA. *See Kanar,* 118 F.3d at 531 (attorney's failure to comply with the agency's request that he provide proof of his capacity to represent the claimant hindered the settlement process and barred the claimant's FTCA suit); *Best Bearings,* 463 F.2d at 1179 (business's request to the FBI and the U.S. Attorney's office for the return of seized property did not satisfy § 2675(a)); *Antonelli v. Sherrow,* 246 Fed.Appx. 381, 385 (7th Cir. 2007) (prisoner's letters to ATF agents demanding the return of a seized computer did not qualify as FTCA claims because the letters did not request money damages). In all of those cases, the agency had the same "constructive notice" of the claimant's position that Smoke Shop alleges the DEA had here. But constructive notice that an individual has a grievance with the agency does not facilitate settlement negotiation of the individual's claim for money damages — or at least, not as directly as the FTCA demands.

Nothing prevented Smoke Shop from submitting an administrative claim to the government at the time of the seizure. In fact, Smoke Shop's failure to do so — and its decision to file a criminal procedure motion with the district court instead — may have led the government to believe that Smoke Shop was forgoing the civil-litigation route, or at least that Smoke Shop was not contemplating it at that time. Thus, Smoke Shop's failure to exhaust is a second ground for us to affirm the district court.[2]

p.789 III. Conclusion

Smoke Shop's action is barred by the detained-goods exception to the FTCA. Smoke Shop also failed to exhaust its administrative remedies by submitting a proper claim for money damages before filing its FTCA suit. We thus AFFIRM the district court's dismissal of Smoke Shop's suit.

[*] Of the Northern District of Illinois, sitting by designation.

[1] The government moved to dismiss the complaint under both Rule 12(b)(1) (lack of subject-matter jurisdiction) and Rule 12(b)(6) (failure to state a claim). The district court correctly dismissed the complaint pursuant to Rule 12(b)(6). We have held that "the statutory exceptions enumerated in [28 U.S.C.] § 2680(a)-(n) ... limit the breadth of the Government's waiver of sovereign immunity [under the FTCA], but they do not accomplish this task by withdrawing subject-matter jurisdiction from the federal courts." *Parrott v. United States,* 536 F.3d 629, 634 (7th Cir. 2008). Similarly, the FTCA's administrative exhaustion requirement is better thought of as a "condition precedent to the plaintiff's ability to prevail," not a jurisdictional rule (as we will discuss in part II.B). *Kanar v. United States,* 118 F.3d 527, 530 (7th Cir.1997); *accord Glade ex rel. Lundskow v. United States,* 692 F.3d 718, 723 (7th Cir.2012).

[2] In its brief on appeal, Smoke Shop also argues that "[c]onstruing the statutes as the district court did ignores the promise of the due process clause of the Fifth Amendment that property will not be taken absent due process." Smoke Shop's argument on this front is waived, as it did not pursue a due process theory in the district court, and we find that its constitutional argument — comprised of ipse dixit and little else — is undeveloped on appeal. *Puffer v. Allstate Ins. Co.,* 675 F.3d 709, 718 (7th Cir.2012).

771 F.3d 1021 (2014)

Charles D. KELLER, Plaintiff-Appellant,
v.
UNITED STATES of America, Defendant-Appellee.

No. 13-3113.

United States Court of Appeals, Seventh Circuit.

Submitted May 23, 2014.[*]

Decided November 17, 2014.

Charles D. Keller, United States Penitentiary I, Coleman, FL, for Plaintiff-Appellant.

p.1022 Jeffrey L. Hunter, Attorney, Office of the United States Attorney, Indianapolis, IN, for Defendant-Appellee.

Before WILLIAMS, TINDER, and HAMILTON, Circuit Judges.

HAMILTON, Circuit Judge.

Plaintiff Charles D. Keller, a federal prisoner, has sued the federal government to recover damages for an assault by another prisoner that he suffered in the United States Penitentiary in Terre Haute, Indiana. Keller appeals from a grant of summary judgment in the government's favor, so we must consider the evidence in the light most favorable to him and draw all reasonable inferences in his favor. *Parrott v. United States,* 536 F.3d 629, 630-31 (7th Cir.2008). Accordingly, we must assume the facts are as stated in this opinion, but without vouching for their objective truth.

When Keller was admitted to the Terre Haute facility, he told the intake psychologist, Dr. Joseph Bleier, that he suffered from mental illness that affected his ability to function and feared that he would be attacked if he were placed in the general prison population. Dr. Bleier nevertheless placed Keller in the general population. While on his way to lunch on October 25, 2007, Keller was attacked by another inmate without provocation. The attack lasted several minutes without intervention by guards. Keller was beaten brutally and left lying unconscious in the prison yard. The attack occurred at the base of prison watchtower 7, which stands at the boundary between Units 1 and 2 of the prison yard. No prison guard saw the attack. Keller was eventually spotted lying face-down and unconscious on the ground. Examinations by the prison medical staff and a nearby hospital emergency room revealed extensive injuries to his face and head.

Keller filed suit against the United States under the Federal Tort Claims Act, see 28 U.S.C. § 2674, alleging that the attack resulted from the prison's negligence. He argues that several prison employees violated mandatory regulations and orders governing their conduct, thus allowing the attack to occur and continue. According to Keller, Dr. Bleier did not examine all of his available medical documents before deciding to release him into the general prison population, as required by applicable regulations. Keller also contends that the prison guards assigned to Tower 7, Unit 1, and Unit 2 failed to monitor their assigned areas of the yard because they were lazy or inattentive in violation of their post orders. The district court granted the government's motion for summary judgment based on the discretionary function exception to liability under the Act. See 28 U.S.C. § 2680(a). This appeal followed.

The Federal Tort Claims Act (FTCA) gives district courts exclusive jurisdiction over claims "for injury or loss of property, or personal injury or death caused by the negligent or wrongful act or omission of any employee of the government while acting within the scope of his office or employment, under circumstances where the United States, if a private person, would be liable to the claimant in accordance with the law of the place where the act or omission occurred." 28 U.S.C. § 1346(b)(1); see also 28 U.S.C. § 2674. Prisoners can sue under the FTCA "to recover damages from the United States Government for personal injuries sustained during confinement in a federal prison, by reason of the negligence of a government employee." *United States v. Muniz,* 374 U.S. 150, 150, 83 S.Ct. 1850, 10 L.Ed.2d 805 (1963); see also, e.g., *Coulthurst v. United States,* 214 F.3d 106 (2d Cir.2000) (allowing prisoner to pursue p.1023 FTCA claim); *Bultema v. United States,* 359 F.3d 379 (6th Cir.2004) (same); *Gil v. Reed,* 381 F.3d 649, 659 (7th Cir.2004) (same); *Mackovich v. United States,* 630 F.3d 1134 (8th Cir.2011) (same).

This waiver of the United States' sovereign immunity is limited by several exceptions, including the discretionary function exception codified in 28 U.S.C. § 2680(a). The exception is in the second half of a provision that states in full: "The provisions of this chapter and section 1346(b) of this title shall not apply to—(a) Any claim based upon an act or omission of an employee of the Government, exercising due care, in the execution of a statute or regulation, whether or not such statute or regulation be valid, or based upon the exercise or performance or the failure to exercise or perform a discretionary function or duty on the part of a federal agency or an employee of the Government, whether or not the discretion involved be abused."

Case law elaborates the scope of this discretionary function exception. Two requirements must be met. First, the act involved must be discretionary in the sense that it "involves an element of judgment or choice." *Palay v. United States,* 349 F.3d 418, 427 (7th Cir.2003), quoting *United States v. Gaubert,* 499 U.S. 315, 322, 111 S.Ct. 1267, 113 L.Ed.2d 335 (1991) (internal formatting omitted). This means that where an employee deviates from a course of action prescribed by federal statute, regulation or policy, the employee's acts are not immune from suit. *Gaubert,* 499 U.S. at 322, 111 S.Ct. 1267; *Berkovitz v. United States,* 486 U.S. 531, 536, 108 S.Ct. 1954, 100 L.Ed.2d 531 (1988); *Palay,* 349 F.3d at 427. Second, "the exception protects only governmental actions and decisions based on considerations of public policy." *Gaubert,* 499 U.S. at 322, 111 S.Ct. 1267; *Palay,* 349 F.3d at 427-28; *Calderon v. United States,* 123 F.3d 947, 949 (7th Cir.1997).

The discretionary function exception is an affirmative defense to liability under the FTCA that the government must plead and prove. *Parrott v. United States,* 536 F.3d 629, 634-35 (7th Cir.2008); *Reynolds v. United States,* 549 F.3d 1108, 1112 (7th Cir.2008); *Stewart v. United States,* 199 F.2d 517, 520 (7th Cir.1952); *S.R.P. ex rel. Abunabba v. United States,* 676 F.3d 329, 333 n. 2 (3d Cir.2012) (collecting cases from other circuits). To support summary judgment under the exception, the government must offer evidence that shows beyond reasonable dispute that its conduct was shielded by the exception. The district court, however, placed the burden on Keller to prove that the exception did not apply. This was a legal error that requires reversal unless the error was harmless.

The government argued in its summary judgment briefs that the discretionary function exception always shields the government from liability for inmate violence, citing our decision in *Calderon v. United States*, 123 F.3d 947 (7th Cir.1997). That argument substantially overstates our holding in *Calderon* and overlooks other cases on point. See, e.g., *Parrott*, 536 F.3d at 638 (reversing summary judgment based on discretionary function exception where prisoner alleged guards failed to comply with order separating him from another prisoner); *Palay*, 349 F.3d at 432 (reversing dismissal on pleadings based on discretionary function exception where prisoner alleged guards' negligence allowed other prisoners to beat him). "Unstated but implicit in *Calderon* is the assumption that prison officials in that case had taken note of the threats against the plaintiff in that case and weighed the relevant considerations in deciding how best to act (or not) in response to those threats." *Palay*, 349 F.3d at 432.

p.1024 By contrast, if prison officials behaved negligently without making a discretionary judgment of the type shielded by the exception, the discretionary function exception would not apply to their conduct. *Id.* Prison guards who "left the unit unattended in order to enjoy a cigarette or a snack," for example, would not be covered by the exception, because they would not have made the kind of discretionary judgment that the exception is designed to protect. *Id.* In other words, if prison personnel violate a mandatory regulation, the exception does not apply because "there is no room for choice and the action will be contrary to policy." *Gaubert*, 499 U.S. at 324, 111 S.Ct. 1267; see also *Parrott*, 536 F.3d at 638.

Here, Keller has alleged that both the intake psychologist and the prison guards assigned to monitor the relevant sections of the yard violated mandatory regulations that governed their conduct. Unlike the guards in *Calderon*, Keller argues, the guards and intake psychologist in this case did not exercise discretion allowed to them under applicable regulations, but rather failed to comply with mandatory regulations and orders. If that is the case, then their alleged negligence would not fall within the scope of the discretionary function exception. See *Gaubert*, 499 U.S. at 324, 111 S.Ct. 1267; *Parrott*, 536 F.3d at 638; *Palay*, 349 F.3d at 432.

At this stage, the record in this case presents a situation similar to *Parrott v. United States*, 536 F.3d 629 (7th Cir.2008). Parrott, also a federal prisoner at the Terre Haute facility, alleged that prison guards violated a mandatory separation order so that another inmate was able to attack him. We reversed summary judgment for the government because the discretionary function exception would not protect the government from liability under those circumstances. *Parrott*, 536 F.3d at 638. We see no reason to take a different approach in this case. We reject the government's argument that all prisoner attacks fall within the discretionary function exception.

We therefore turn to the record to determine whether the discretionary function exception applied in this case. We cannot conclude, based on the evidence in the record, that the exception necessarily shields the government from liability for the attack on Keller. Keller contends that both the intake psychologist who screened him upon arrival at the Terre Haute facility and the prison guards assigned to Units 1 and 2 violated mandatory orders before the attack. According to Keller, the intake psychologist did not examine all of his available medical documents, as required by applicable regulations, before deciding to release him into the general prison population. Keller also argues that the prison guards assigned to Unit 1 and Unit 2 failed to monitor their assigned areas of the yard because they were lazy or inattentive, violating their post orders.[1]

The scant record available to both the district court and this panel makes it difficult to determine what procedures and regulations applied to the intake psychologist and prison guards at the Terre Haute facility. The government objected to nearly all of Keller's discovery requests on the ground that releasing the information requested to a prisoner would create safety concerns. A magistrate judge reviewed the disputed documents *in camera,* concluded that many were not relevant to Keller's case, and allowed the government to release the rest in heavily redacted p.1025 form. The district court did not have the unredacted documents before it when it ruled on the government's summary judgment motion, which was based on the court's determination that the documents contained no mandatory procedures or directives violated by the prison guards stationed at Units 1 and 2.

These extensive redactions make it impossible for this court to ascertain exactly what regulations and procedures governed the conduct of the intake psychologist and the prison guards. The information we do have, however, suggests that both the intake psychologist and the prison guards were subject to specific regulations and orders governing their conduct. For example, we know from the record that Program Statement 5324.07 requires psychology services to "develop local procedures to clear inmates with a PSY ALERT assignment," which suggests that the Terre Haute facility had mandatory local procedures that needed to be followed when clearing inmates. Dr. Bleier's affidavit similarly refers to procedures used to clear inmates like Keller who had a "PSY ALERT." Those procedures are not in the record, and in their absence, we cannot conclude as a matter of law that they did not constrain Dr. Bleier's discretion to place Keller in the general population.[2]

The government has also failed to establish that the actions of the prison guards assigned to Units 1 and 2 are protected by the discretionary function exception. The government relies on the declaration of a prison administrator that guards assigned to different areas of the compound are interchangeable and that guards do not need to be in any particular area at any given time. However, the heavily redacted documents in the record suggest that prison guards are assigned to specific areas of the yard and are required to monitor their areas and to respond to emergency situations within them. In other words, guards cannot choose, at least without a good reason, to stop monitoring their assigned areas without violating their explicit responsibilities under the post orders. Keller alleges that the guards stopped monitoring their assigned areas as required by the post orders because they were lazy and inattentive. There is no evidence to the contrary in the record. Based on the summary judgment record, then, we cannot conclude as a matter of law that the guards' behavior is shielded by the discretionary function exception.

If as the government suggests in its brief the guards made a "policy" choice that caused them to neglect an area of the yard because they were pursuing other policy objectives within their discretion (such as walking the perimeter or supervising trash collection), then perhaps that would be shielded by the discretionary function exception. But there is no evidence to that effect in the record, and the government's say-so in its briefs is not enough to support summary judgment. The government points to no evidence in the record to contradict Keller's claims that the guards were simply lazy or inattentive. "That type of carelessness would not be covered by the discretionary function exception, as it involves no element of choice or judgment grounded in public policy considerations." *Palay,* 349 F.3d at 432.

p.1026 Accordingly, we conclude that the government did not sustain its burden to prove as a matter of law that the discretionary function exception shielded it from liability for the brutal attack that seriously injured Keller. Summary judgment was improperly granted for the government on that basis, and the district court's error was not harmless.

We do not reach Keller's claims that the district court abused its discretion in denying his motion to compel discovery or his motion for appointment of counsel. Keller is free to pursue further discovery on remand, and can of course renew his motion for appointment of counsel as well. We note in closing, however, that the district court may wish to revisit its determination on both matters in light of this opinion. See *Parrott,* 536 F.3d at 638-39 (finding that district court had abused its discretion in handling injured prisoner's discovery requests). The district court's resolution of the discovery disputes in this case resulted in a record so limited that it could not support summary judgment for the government. A better-developed record would have allowed the district court and this court to assess better the merits of the government's motion for summary judgment.

We REVERSE the district court's grant of summary judgment and REMAND the case for further proceedings consistent with this opinion.

[*] After an examination of the briefs and the record, we concluded that oral argument was unnecessary. Thus, the appeal was submitted on the briefs and the record. See Fed. R.App. P. 34(a)(2).

[1] Keller concedes that there is a blind spot at the base of Tower 7, so the guards stationed in Tower 7 cannot see the area where Keller was attacked. Accordingly, Keller cannot base his claim upon alleged negligence by the Tower 7 guards.

[2] Both Dr. Bleier and the chief psychologist at the Terre Haute facility stated in their affidavits that no mandatory procedures were violated in Keller's screening. Neither affidavit, however, discusses what those procedures were or whether they constrained Dr. Bleier's discretion. On the other hand, the affidavits suggest that mandatory procedures governed intake screening at the Terre Haute facility, reinforcing our conclusion that remand is necessary to determine the nature of those procedures and whether Dr. Bleier complied with or violated them.

746 F.3d 753 (2014)

Joseph W. BUECHEL, Plaintiff-Appellant,
v.
UNITED STATES of America, Defendant-Appellee.

No. 13-2278.

United States Court of Appeals, Seventh Circuit.

Argued November 13, 2013.

Decided March 7, 2014.

Buechel v. US, 746 F. 3d 753 (7th Cir. 2014)

p.755 Nicole A. Allen, Attorney, Kevin McCall, Attorney, Jenner & Block LLP, Chicago, IL, for Plaintiff-Appellant.

Jennifer Hudson, Attorney, Office of the United States Attorney, Fairview Heights, IL, for Defendant-Appellee.

Before MANION, KANNE, and HAMILTON, Circuit Judges.

HAMILTON, Circuit Judge.

In July 2006, Joseph Buechel was incarcerated at FCI-Greenville, a federal correctional institution in Greenville, Illinois. Buechel contracted Methicillin-Resistant *Staphylococcus aureus,* known as MRSA, which is a type of staph infection resistant to certain antibiotics. Buechel's MRSA infection was so severe that it nearly killed him. He survived, but he had to be hospitalized for more than forty days and was left with serious and permanent damage to his heart and lungs. He brought suit against the United States under the Federal Tort Claims Act, 28 U.S.C. § 1346(b), alleging that his MRSA infection and resulting injuries were caused by FCI-Greenville's negligence.

Though Buechel's administrative claim and complaint described his allegations of negligence in broader terms, the district court issued a pretrial order that limited Buechel's negligence claim to a theory that he contracted MRSA from contact with one fellow inmate, Joseph Hansen, in the prison laundry in mid-July 2006, or more generally as a result of sloppy procedures in handling infected laundry in the prison. Viewing Buechel's claim and the admissible evidence through this narrow lens, the court found after a bench trial that Buechel had not proved by a preponderance of the evidence that he had contracted MRSA from either Hansen or the laundry procedures. p.756 Accordingly, the district court entered judgment in favor of the government.

Buechel appeals. We find no error in the district court's finding that Buechel failed to prove that he contracted MRSA from Hansen and/or as a result of inadequate laundry procedures. However, the district court erred when it limited Buechel's negligence claim, without his consent, to just those two theories. Buechel's administrative claim and complaint presented a broader theory that FCI-Greenville was negligent more generally in its failure to adhere to its MRSA-containment policies in 2006, causing his MRSA infection. We affirm in part but vacate the judgment in favor of the government and remand for further proceedings on that broader theory.

I. *Negligence Claims Presented at Trial*

The district court found that Buechel failed to prove his MRSA infection was caused by negligence in either permitting Hansen to work with him in the prison laundry in mid-July 2006 or failing to use proper laundry procedures to prevent the spread of MRSA. We review these findings of fact only for clear error. Fed. R.Civ.P. 52(a)(6); *Gaffney v. Riverboat Servs. of Ind., Inc.,* 451 F.3d 424, 447 (7th Cir.2006) (The district court's findings of fact "are entitled to great deference and shall not be set aside unless they are clearly erroneous."). Under this standard, we will not reverse unless, after reviewing all the evidence, we are left with "'the definite and firm conviction that a mistake has been committed.'" *Anderson v. City of Bessemer City,* 470 U.S. 564, 573, 105 S.Ct. 1504, 84 L.Ed.2d 518 (1985), quoting *United States v. United States Gypsum Co.,* 333 U.S. 364, 395, 68 S.Ct. 525, 92 L.Ed. 746 (1948). As long as the district court's conclusions are "plausible in light of the record viewed in its entirety," we will not disturb them. *Fyrnetics (Hong Kong) Ltd. v. Quantum Grp., Inc.,* 293 F.3d 1023, 1028 (7th Cir.2002), quoting *Anderson,* 470 U.S. at 573-74, 105 S.Ct. 1504. On the merits of Buechel's negligence theories that were within the scope of the court's pretrial order and were presented at trial, we affirm the district court.

When Buechel first arrived in FCI-Greenville in June 2006, he was healthy and had no symptoms of a MRSA or non-MRSA staph infection. In mid-July 2006, Buechel and Hansen worked together in the prison laundry to fix a washing machine and dryer as part of their prison maintenance jobs. Then, on July 20, 2006, Buechel was diagnosed with MRSA. Buechel testified that during their work assignment, Hansen had an open wound on his face that was oozing infected pus. Buechel's expert, Dr. Robert Greifinger, testified that "the most likely source" of Buechel's MRSA infection "was discharge from [the] persistent infection of Mr. Hansen" as they passed tools back and forth while working together in the prison laundry. Dr. Greifinger believed that the fact that Buechel and Hansen had hand-to-hand contact while Hansen had a draining wound and the timing of their respective diagnoses of infection were consistent with the conclusion that Buechel had become infected with MRSA as a result of working with Hansen. The district court rejected this theory. It found that Buechel was not credible, that Dr. Greifinger was not persuasive, and that the evidence did not show either that Hansen had MRSA in mid-July 2006 or that he had a seeping wound on his face during the work assignment with Buechel.

Hansen had tested positive for a non-MRSA staph infection in March 2006, again in May 2006, and again nearly a year later, in April 2007. In each of these p.757 laboratory tests, the staph bacteria infecting Hansen were found to be resistant to a different set of antibiotics. None of the lab tests showed Hansen to be MRSA-positive. Hansen's infections also had profiles of antibiotic resistance different from the profile of Buechel's MRSA infection. For example, Hansen's May 2006 infection was resistant to Bactrim, while Buechel's infection was susceptible to Bactrim. Dr. Greifinger conceded in his written report that there was no laboratory evidence that Buechel's infecting organism was the same as Hansen's infecting organism. He testified at trial that it was theoretically possible for Hansen's staph infection to have metamorphosed into MRSA between May and July 2006, and then to have metamorphosed back into non-MRSA staph by April 2007, but the district court understandably found this theoretical possibility to be speculative.

The district court's findings that Hansen did not have MRSA in mid-July 2006 and that Buechel was not infected with the same organism as Hansen find reasonable support in the record and are not clearly erroneous.

The district court also rejected Buechel's assertion that Hansen had a seeping wound on his face when they worked together in the prison laundry that would have enabled transmission of an infection between them. The court explained why it did not find Buechel's testimony about Hansen's wound credible. "[I]n light of his demeanor while testifying, his interest in giving testimony favorable to himself, and his testimony's inconsistency with Hansen's medical records documenting no draining wounds and Hansen's daily supervisor's testimony that he never saw any drainage from Hansen's face, Buechel's testimony on this matter was incredible." Hansen's medical records reflect that on June 21 and 22, 2006, he had a wound on his forehead above his right eyebrow with "very scanty exudate," and prison staff restricted him from working during that time. Hansen and Buechel did not work together until a month later, in mid-July. The only contemporaneous medical record, dated July 18, 2006, states that Hansen had multiple lesions on his back, arm, and legs, but none on his face and none that were draining. In other words, Hansen's medical records do not support Buechel's testimony that Hansen had a draining wound on his face in mid-July 2006. Here, too, we have no grounds to disturb the district court's finding of fact based on conflicting evidence.

We also find no clear error in the district court's conclusion that the evidence did not prove that Buechel contracted MRSA from FCI-Greenville's laundry procedures. In 2006, the Bureau of Prisons and FCI-Greenville had MRSA Guidelines in place stating that MRSA-infected inmates whose wound drainage could not be contained with dressing should have their laundry "treat[ed] ... as potentially infectious" and "bagged" and washed at least every other day. Biohazard laundry was supposed to be washed separately from other inmate laundry. Buechel presented evidence that FCI-Greenville Health Services did not give biohazard laundry bags to inmates infected with either MRSA or non-MRSA staph. Additionally, Buechel testified that Health Services did not instruct infected inmates to wash their clothes separately and did not instruct MRSA-infected inmates on how to wash their clothes if they had draining wounds.

The district court, however, was not persuaded that Buechel contracted MRSA as a result of FCI-Greenville's laundry procedures. The court found that Buechel did not offer evidence that the prison's laundry temperature or laundry disinfecting procedures were inadequate to prevent the transmission of MRSA. Dkt. 161 at 7; see also Tr. 211 (Dr. Greifinger did not know if p.758 housing unit laundry machines heated water to a high enough temperature to kill MRSA bacteria, or if clothes were laundered with or without bleach). Without such evidence, the court found, there was nothing to tether FCI-Greenville's failure to provide biohazard bags and instructions on proper laundry procedures to Buechel's infection. The district court did not clearly err in rejecting this theory that Buechel contracted MRSA as a result of inadequate laundry procedures. Accordingly, we affirm on the merits of the negligence theories that were presented and heard at trial.

II. *Scope of Buechel's Negligence Claim*

As noted, however, the theories that Buechel presented at trial were limited over his objection. The district court ruled in a September 13, 2012 pretrial order that Buechel's negligence claim would be "limited to the conditions leading to the possible transmission of a staphylococcus infection in the laundry facility but not necessarily limited to contamination from Joseph [Hansen]." This ruling was based on the district court's interpretation of the scope of Buechel's *pro se* administrative tort claim and *pro se* complaint. Buechel argues on appeal that the district court erred by unduly limiting his claims. He contends that his *pro se* documents also asserted a broader theory that FCI-Greenville was negligent by failing to follow its own 2006 MRSA-containment policies, resulting in his infection. We conclude that the district court's reading of Buechel's claim was too restrictive and ran contrary to the imperative that courts construe *pro se* claims generously. In a new trial after remand, Buechel should be permitted to present evidence on his broader theory that the prison's failure to follow its own policies in 2006 amounted to negligence that caused his MRSA infection and resulting injuries.

A. *The Federal Tort Claims Act and Its Exhaustion Requirement*

The Federal Tort Claims Act permits a person to bring suit in federal court against the United States:

> for injury or loss of property, or personal injury or death caused by the negligent or wrongful act or omission of any employee of the Government while acting within the scope of his office or employment, under circumstances where the United States, if a private person, would be liable to the claimant in accordance with the law of the place where the act or omission occurred.

28 U.S.C. § 1346(b)(1). Pursuant to this provision, federal inmates may bring suit for injuries they sustain in custody as a consequence of the negligence of prison officials. *United States v. Muniz*, 374 U.S. 150, 150, 83 S.Ct. 1850, 10 L.Ed.2d 805 (1963). Like any other federal tort claimant, however, an inmate may not bring such a suit unless he has first presented his claim to the appropriate federal agency and that agency has denied the claim. See 28 U.S.C. § 2675(a); 28 C.F.R. § 14.2(a) (requiring claimant to execute a "Standard Form 95 or other written notification of an incident, accompanied by a claim for money damages in a sum certain for ... personal injury ... alleged to have occurred by reason of the incident...."). Once the agency denies or fails to take action on an inmate's claim, he has six months to file a suit. 28 U.S.C. § 2401(b).

B. *Administrative and District Court Proceedings*

To comply with the administrative claim requirement, Buechel completed a complaint form and submitted it to FCI-Greenville for review on October 12, 2006. In support of his claim, and without outside legal assistance, he wrote:

> p.759 Lack of Medical Treatment / Refuse to treat a highly contagious disease i.e.,: Staff infection with this lack of treatment has indangered the lifes of myself

and other inmates *and also the inmate that I caught this highly contagious disease to continue to interact in general population.*

Dkt. 139, Ex. 1 (emphasis added). When his claim was not resolved to his satisfaction, he filled out a Form 95, describing his claim as follows:

Caught Staph Infestion from an INMATE JOE HANSON who works in [maintenance services], wherein *the institution failed to quarantine Hanson to prevent transmittal of disease.*

Dkt. 139, Ex. 4 (emphasis added).

Buechel next filed suit, setting forth his claim yet again, and still without the assistance of counsel. His claim narrative continues for more than two pages but begins:

Defendant's medical and Executive Departmental employees are intentionally disregarding basic manditory medical biohazard containment quarantine and decontamination procedures of infectious diseases ... when Mr. "Joe Hanson" an inmate at federal correctional institution in Greenville, Illinois, was *allowed to return to his job assignment in ("CMS") after being diagnosed with the "staph infection virus"* that ended up being transmitted to plaintiff during a machanical operation on a laundry unit which ["Hanson"] and the plaintiff were passing tools between each other....

Dkt. 1 at 4 (emphasis added). It bears repeating that Buechel was acting without the assistance of a lawyer both at the administrative complaint stage and when he drafted and filed his complaint in court.

Buechel's complaint passed screening under 28 U.S.C. § 1915A and the district court appointed counsel to represent him.[1] After surviving two motions to dismiss, Buechel's negligence claim proceeded to discovery and the government then moved for summary judgment.[2] In its motion the government argued that Buechel had failed to exhaust his administrative remedies and that his negligence claim should be treated as a medical malpractice claim (and thus subject to the district court's prior dismissal of that claim). The district court rejected both of these arguments, though it put off a definitive ruling on the government's failure-to-exhaust argument until trial. Regarding the scope of Buechel's administrative complaint, however, the court wrote:

Despite the fact that this paragraph was not included in the section of the administrative complaint form designated for describing the "basis of claim," this paragraph was sufficient to alert a legally sophisticated reader that Buechel was complaining about the inadequacy of measures to prevent Hansen from transmitting staph to him. A legally sophisticated reader would have known that such a claim encompassed the practice of allowing sick inmates like Hansen to come into contact with Buechel — which is explicit in the administrative claim form in the allegation of "failed to quara[n]tine" — as well as the failure to p.760 ensure those sick inmates do not transmit their diseases to those with whom they come in contact — which is implicit in the allegation of failure to "prevent tran[s]mittal." Because Buechel's administrative claim form sets forth enough facts to alert a legally sophisticated reader to the presence of both aspects of his claim, it satisfies the presentment requirement. Thus, the United States is not entitled to summary judgment on the grounds that Buechel failed to exhaust his administrative remedies. The Court notes, however, that Buechel's remaining claim in this case is limited to negligence that allowed Hansen to transmit pathogens to him and does not include a general claim about prison hygiene practices unconnected to Hansen.

Buechel v. United States, 2012 WL 948368, at *5 (S.D.Ill. March 20, 2012) (emphasis added). We agree with the first portion of this passage, which recognized that Buechel had alleged a failure to ensure that MRSA-infected inmates did not spread their infections. But the last sentence seems to conflict with that appropriately generous reading of the *pro se* documents. While acknowledging that Buechel had claimed that the prison had "failed to quara[n]tine" inmates "like Hansen" in the operative documents, the court then, and without reference to those documents, also restricted that claim to contact with Hansen.

Given this internal contradiction in the order, the issue arose again at the pretrial conference. Aided by counsel, Buechel argued that his administrative complaint forms and *pro se* complaint presented a claim that his MRSA infection was caused by FCI-Greenville's negligent and more general failure to segregate MRSA-positive inmates, including but not limited to Hansen, from the general inmate population. The government's position was that Buechel's claim should be construed as limited to infection only by Hansen. The court's ruling was terse:

> In light of the language in plaintiff's complaint and the scope of his administrative tort claim, the Court finds that the issues in this case are limited to the conditions leading to the possible transmission of a staphylococcus infection in the laundry facility but not necessarily limited to contamination from Joseph Hansen.

Buechel argues this ruling was an error.

C. *Analysis*

At each stage of the federal tort claim process, *pro se* administrative complaint forms are "entitled to a generous construction." *Palay v. United States,* 349 F.3d 418, 425-26 (7th Cir.2003) ("[I]f the claim would have been apparent to a 'legally sophisticated' reader of the form, then [the Court] will charge the agency with notice of that claim and deem it to have been exhausted."), quoting *Murrey v. United States,* 73 F.3d 1448, 1452-53 (7th Cir.1996) ("Clearly, the entire [Standard Form 95] was intended to be read, and if it was read the [plaintiff's] claim would leap out at the legally sophisticated reader."). Though an inmate is required to plead sufficient facts to put the agency on notice of the claim so that it may investigate, an inmate is not required to plead legal theories. *Palay,* 349 F.3d at 425-26. Any claim "implicit in the facts" should be deemed to have been presented to the agency. *Id.* at 426, quoting *Murrey,* 73 F.3d at 1452; see also *Haines v. Kerner,* 404 U.S. 519, 520-21, 92 S.Ct. 594, 30 L.Ed.2d 652 (1972) (*pro se* complaint entitled to generous construction). We review *de novo* the district court's reading of Buechel's administrative claim, giving Buechel the benefit of every reasonable inference that may be drawn from his allegations. p.761 *Palay,* 349 F.3d at 425 (using Rule 12(b)(6) standard to decide whether *pro se* complainant had exhausted administrative remedies).

Here, though Buechel was clearly complaining about his medical treatment — *i.e.* "Lack of Medical Treatment / Refuse to treat a highly contagious disease" — he was also complaining of the prison's failure to quarantine infected inmates properly, including Hansen but not necessarily limited to him. ("[A]lso the inmate that I caught this highly contagious disease to continue to interact in general population;" "the institution failed to quarantine [Hansen] to prevent transmittal of disease;" "medical and executive departmental employees are intentionally disregarding basic mandatory medical biohazard containment quarantine and decontamination procedures of infectious diseases;" "[Hansen] was allowed to return to his job assignment ... after being diagnosed with [a staph infection].")

Buechel's claim set forth his observations and his lay beliefs concerning how he contracted MRSA. As a *pro se* claimant without legal or medical training, he was not required to do more than that. It was up to the prison administration to fill in the gaps, to the extent possible. Buechel provided enough information from which a legally sophisticated reader could recognize that when he claimed he had contracted MRSA after coming into contact with Hansen and that the prison was disregarding biohazard and quarantine procedures, he was making a more general claim that FCI-Greenville was not adhering to sound MRSA-containment policies.

As noted above, the district court's summary judgment ruling had seemed to recognize this. *Buechel,* 2012 WL 948368, at *5 (noting that Buechel had explicitly alleged the government "failed to quara[n]tine" and "prevent tran[s]mittal," based also on allegation that a sick inmate "like Hansen" had come into contact with Buechel). But the summary judgment ruling and the September 13, 2012 pretrial order then imposed a hurdle for Buechel's negligence claim that would be unreasonably difficult for any complainant to meet at the stage of the administrative claim or complaint, never mind that Buechel had been acting without outside legal or medical advice. By limiting Buechel's *pro se* claim to contact with Hansen, *Buechel,* 2012 WL 948368, at *5, and/or the prison laundry, Dkt. 141, the court effectively required Buechel to pinpoint when and how he had contracted MRSA in order to state a viable negligence claim. This imposed too heavy a burden for any claimant and plaintiff, but especially for a prisoner acting *pro se.*

To see why, set aside the challenges posed for prison inmates for a moment, and consider a different person trying to figure out how he contracted MRSA, perhaps after a routine visit to a doctor's office.[3] The patient was called back into the exam room, put on a gown, and sat on an exam table. A nurse entered and took vital signs. Then the doctor entered and performed a routine physical examination. Perhaps some blood was drawn for lab work. Even in that simple scenario, how could a lay person possibly figure out how he contracted MRSA? Did the doctor or nurse not wash her hands? Was the exam table not decontaminated between patients? p.762 What about the thermometer? Perhaps the syringe was unclean? MRSA is exceptionally contagious and is easily transmitted by casual contact. It would be difficult for any person, no matter his education or background, to figure out exactly how he contracted it. How was Buechel supposed to do it? Instead, he did what he could, and put forth the facts that he had, including his suspicions about Hansen. But the "legally sophisticated reader" we attribute to the government agency is expected to look more closely and to see that he was also complaining more generally about the prison's failure to follow appropriate MRSA-containment guidelines, including taking reasonable measures to keep healthy prisoners separated from the contagion.

The government argues that the district court's pretrial ruling limiting Buechel's negligence claim did not limit Buechel's claims but expanded them. It also argues that Buechel could have amended his complaint after counsel was appointed, but he failed to so. We reject both of these quasi-waiver arguments. First, the court's ruling was not an expansion of Buechel's claims, and it was not a "grant" of Buechel's request. Buechel asked the district court to recognize that the negligence claim presented in his *pro se* administrative claim and complaint encompassed the theory "that the United States was negligent because FCI-Greenville employees failed to adequately segregate MRSA-positive inmates, *including but not limited to inmate James Joseph Hansen,* from the general inmate population, and that this caused Plaintiff's MRSA infection and seriously injured him." Buechel did not "request" that his claims be *limited* to contact and conditions within and relating to the prison laundry. The government's insistence that Buechel "prevailed" is groundless.

The government's contention that Buechel had the opportunity to amend his complaint but failed to do so, even after counsel was appointed, also is not a ground to hold him to the court's pretrial ruling. As discovery proceeded, but before the summary judgment and pretrial rulings were issued, Buechel questioned whether amending the complaint was necessary to clarify that his claim was not limited to the Hansen theory. Dkt. 70 at 5 (responding to government's argument that discovery relating to other inmates besides Hansen was irrelevant) ("To the extent this Court believes it is necessary for Plaintiff to amend his complaint on the sole issue of other inmates who may have caused Plaintiff's MRSA infection, Plaintiff requests the Court grant him leave to do so."); Dkt. 74 at 4 ("Causation is an element of negligence that Buechel must prove, and there is ample authority that supports either allowing Buechel to amend his complaint on the sole issue of causation, or to read the complaint so that it is not limited to Hansen.").

Each of these motions was before the magistrate judge, who did not explicitly respond to Buechel's assertion that he should be allowed to replead if necessary to expand his claim beyond Hansen. Implicitly, however, the magistrate judge's ruling seemed to confirm that Buechel's *pro se* documents were sufficient for a broader negligence claim to go forward. See Dkt. 75 at 1-2 ("[C]ounsel was appointed to ensure that this action was properly litigated because plaintiff was found incapable of adequately representing himself; therefore, plaintiff's appointed counsel will not now be strictly constrained by the original pleadings."); Dkt. 76 at 2 ("[C]ounsel was appointed to ensure that this action was properly litigated because plaintiff was found incapable of adequately representing himself; therefore, plaintiff's appointed counsel will not now be strictly p.763 constrained by the original pleadings. With that said, the fact that information may be discoverable does not necessarily mean that it will ultimately be admissible, or that the scope of the complaint is being broadened.").

Buechel raised the issue again in the brief he submitted to the district court judge on the scope of the claim. Dkt. 139 at 8-9 (The "evidence warrants either a finding that Plaintiff's complaint has been constructively amended to include the possibility that inmates other than Hansen caused his MRSA infection, or warrants allowing Plaintiff to formally amend the complaint prior to trial."). Buechel raised the issue but did not receive a clear answer from the court until just before trial, when it was too late to cure the problem. A district court is not obliged to give legal advice to a party, with counsel or *pro se,* but this was an issue that needed to be resolved when there was time to fix it.

More to the point, however, Buechel correctly believed that he had properly pled a negligence claim that encompassed the prison's failure to adhere to BOP and internal policies regarding MRSA, including its failure to quarantine infected inmates, and that amendment was unnecessary. Buechel did not need to replead a claim that was properly pled. Accordingly, we reject the government's contention that he should, on appeal, be bound to the district court's ruling.

In sum, a prison administrator or other legally sophisticated reader interpreting Buechel's claim should not have understood it as limited to contact with Hansen but should have recognized the more general assertion that inmates with MRSA were not being segregated from uninfected inmates, contrary to the prison's policies. Buechel was alleging that the prison was negligent in failing to quarantine infected inmates, including but not limited to Hansen, and certainly not limited to the confines of the prison laundry or laundry procedures. The district court's ruling otherwise was an undue restriction on Buechel's claim and on the evidence it considered at trial. Accordingly, we must vacate the judgment in favor of the United States.

III. *Merits of the Expanded Negligence Claim*

Because the district court construed Buechel's claim too narrowly, the court did not consider evidence related to Buechel's theory that in 2006, FCI-Greenville had policies in place to control infections such as MRSA, that it failed to follow those policies, and that its failures proximately caused him to contract MRSA. Buechel argues that this evidence, properly considered, proves causation and that the district court's judgment should be reversed.

Ordinarily we review factual findings claims for clear error. See Fed.R.Civ.P. 52(a)(6). Here, however, neither side has had a full opportunity to present its evidence on this theory and the district court has not had the opportunity to address it. We therefore remand to the district court to consider this evidence in the first instance. See *FMS, Inc. v. Volvo Constr. Equipment N.A.,* 557 F.3d 758, 763 (7th Cir.2009) ("When the parties brief an issue that has not been addressed by the district court, it is not unusual for this court to remand so that the district court may consider the issue in the first instance.").

Illinois law governs Buechel's broader claim. See 28 U.S.C. § 1346(b)(1) (predicating FTCA liability "in accordance with the law of the place where the act or omission occurred"). To establish a claim for negligence under Illinois law, a plaintiff must prove the existence of a duty of care p.764 owed by the defendant to the plaintiff, a breach of that duty, and an injury proximately caused by that breach. *Thompson v. Gordon,* 241 Ill.2d 428, 349 Ill.Dec. 936, 948 N.E.2d 39, 45 (2011). Under Illinois law, that means Buechel must show that FCI-Greenville breached a duty to him and that its breach was both a "cause in fact" and a "legal cause" of his MRSA infection. *Simmons v. Garces,* 198 Ill.2d 541, 261 Ill.Dec. 471, 763 N.E.2d 720, 732 (2002). "A defendant's conduct is a 'cause in fact' of the plaintiff's injuries only if that conduct is a material element and a substantial factor in bringing about the injury." *Abrams v. City of Chicago,* 211 Ill.2d 251, 285 Ill.Dec. 183, 811 N.E.2d 670, 675 (2004). A defendant's conduct is a material element and a substantial factor in bringing about injury if, absent that conduct, the injury would not have occurred. *First Springfield Bank & Trust v. Galman,* 188 Ill.2d 252, 242 Ill.Dec. 113, 720 N.E.2d 1068, 1072 (1999). On the other hand, legal cause is largely a question of foreseeability. *Abrams,* 285 Ill.Dec. 183, 811 N.E.2d at 675. The relevant inquiry is whether the injury is of a type that a reasonable person would see as a likely result of his or her conduct. *Galman,* 242 Ill.Dec. 113, 720 N.E.2d at 1072, citing *Lee v. Chicago Transit Auth.,* 152 Ill.2d 432, 178 Ill.Dec. 699, 605 N.E.2d 493, 503 (1992).

Buechel contends that FCI-Greenville had three primary infection control policies in place in 2006: (1) the Bureau of Prisons MRSA Guidelines; (2) a memorandum issued by FCI-Greenville Warden Sara Revell on May 1, 2006; and (3) the BOP program statement on Infectious Disease Management. Pl. Exs. 9, 10, 11. Among other things, these policies required that infected inmates whose wound drainage could not be controlled with dressings be housed in single cells, that inmates with MRSA and non-MRSA staph infections be placed in special housing if drainage from their wounds could not be controlled with dressings, and that inmates with MRSA and non-MRSA staph infections be evaluated by medical staff to determine whether it was appropriate for them to work in the prison. Buechel argues that he has proved that FCI-Greenville breached its policies that required MRSA-positive inmates with uncontrolled draining wounds to be segregated from the general inmate population, and thus has proved that Buechel's MRSA infection was caused by this failure.

Buechel is incorrect. First, the district court never found that FCI-Greenville breached the policies at issue. Even if the district court finds on remand that Buechel has satisfied that burden, for FCI-Greenville to be liable, he must also prove that FCI-Greenville's breach of these policies *caused* his infection. In other words, if FCI-Greenville failed to adhere to its MRSA-containment policies in 2006, then Buechel must show by a preponderance of the evidence that its failure was a material element and a substantial factor in his infection and that his infection was a foreseeable result.

Buechel's reliance on *Duvall v. Dallas County,* 631 F.3d 203, 208-09 (5th Cir. 2011) and *DeGidio v. Pung,* 920 F.2d 525, 529-31 (8th Cir.1990), is not persuasive at this stage of the case for the simple reason that in each case, the court of appeals was evaluating the sufficiency of the evidence supporting a verdict for the plaintiff. Here, we have no findings of fact on Buechel's expanded negligence claim, much less findings in his favor. In *Duvall,* the Fifth Circuit found that the evidence was sufficient to uphold a jury's verdict in favor of an inmate who had contracted an infection in a county jail. The jury in that case heard evidence that the MRSA infection rate in the jail was close to twenty p.765 percent, while other jails had infection rates of one or two percent. The jury also heard evidence that it was possible to contain MRSA but that jail officials were not willing to take the necessary steps to control the outbreak. *Duvall,* 631 F.3d at 208. But even the evidence in *Duvall* did not result in a directed verdict for the plaintiff — which is essentially the result Buechel requests on appeal without the theory having even been tried. Instead, the evidence in *Duvall* went to the jury, and the jury found causation. We remand for just such an evaluation of the evidence in Buechel's case.

Likewise, in *DeGidio,* the district court held a bench trial on whether the procedures for tuberculosis prevention and control at the prison where the plaintiff was incarcerated violated the Eighth Amendment. 920 F.2d at 527-31 (reciting district court's findings regarding defendants' failures to respond quickly and effectively to tuberculosis outbreak, exacerbating outbreak). Based on a series of factual findings, the appellate court upheld the district court's verdict that the defendants' reckless behavior amounted to deliberate indifference to the serious needs of inmates. *Id.* at 533. Again, here we have no such factual findings or legal conclusions in Buechel's favor on his broader claim. Buechel must prove to the district court in the first instance that FCI-Greenville breached the MRSA-containment policies that were in effect in the prison in 2006, and that any such breaches caused his MRSA infection.

The government protests that Buechel's theory that FCI-Greenville was negligent in failing to follow its own policies, possibly causing Buechel's MRSA infection, amounts to a never-before-argued theory of *res ipsa loquitur.* We disagree. For the doctrine of *res ipsa loquitur* to apply, a plaintiff must prove that he or she was injured (1) in an occurrence that ordinarily does not happen in the absence of negligence, (2) by an agency or instrumentality within the defendant's exclusive control. See *Heastie v. Roberts,* 226 Ill.2d 515, 315 Ill.Dec. 735, 877 N.E.2d 1064, 1076 (2007), citing *Gatlin v. Ruder,* 137 Ill.2d 284, 148 Ill.Dec. 188, 560 N.E.2d 586, 590 (1990); *Metz v. Central Illinois Electric & Gas Co.,* 32 Ill.2d 446, 207 N.E.2d 305, 307 (1965). Buechel does not rely on *res ipsa loquitur* to fill a causation gap in his negligence claim, however. He intends to offer evidence at trial concerning the prison's policies, its deviations from those policies, and whether those deviations caused his MRSA infection. In all likelihood that evidence will be largely circumstantial, but circumstantial evidence of causation is still evidence.

The doctrine of *res ipsa loquitur* could not have applied to Buechel's claim in any case. Perhaps someday medicine will eradicate staph infections like MRSA, but in the present day, MRSA is prevalent enough that infections can and do occur in spite of adherence to best practices and by inadvertent means that cannot be attributed to institutional or individual negligence. See Centers for Disease Control and Prevention, Methicillin-resistant Staphylococcus aureus (MRSA) Infections, General Information about MRSA in the Community, http://www.cdc.gov/mrsa/community/index.html (last visited March 6, 2014) ("Studies show that about one in three people carry staph in their nose, usually without any illness. Two in 100 people carry MRSA."). Also, though preventive measures can and should be put in place where possible, no measure is fail-safe even in the absence of negligence.

Res ipsa loquitur is meant to bridge an evidentiary gap when an injury could not have happened but for the defendant's negligence. That framework simply does p.766 not apply in a case like this one. MRSA infections can and do happen in the absence of institutional negligence. *E.g.,* Centers for Disease Control and Prevention, Methicillin-resistant Staphylococcus aureus (MRSA) Infections, General Information about MRSA in Healthcare Settings, http://www.cdc.gov/mrsa/healthcare/ (last visited March 6, 2014) ("MRSA is usually spread by direct contact with an infected wound or from contaminated hands, usually those of healthcare providers. *Also, people who carry MRSA but do not have signs of infection can spread the bacteria to others and potentially cause an infection.*")

(emphasis added). Here, however, Buechel has circumstantial evidence of causation. It remains to be seen on remand whether that evidence will be sufficient to prove causation and find that FCI-Greenville was negligent.

Conclusion

We affirm the district court's verdict at trial. However, we find that the district court erred when it limited Buechel's negligence claim to the Hansen/laundry theory. Accordingly, we VACATE the judgment in favor of the United States and REMAND for further proceedings consistent with this opinion. In a new trial upon remand, the district court should allow Buechel to present evidence that FCI-Greenville negligently failed to adhere to MRSA-containment procedures that were in place in the prison in 2006, and that such failure(s) caused Buechel's MRSA infection.

[1] The district court appointed J. Kevin McCall of Jenner & Block, LLP, to represent Buechel. Mr. McCall and the firm continued to represent Buechel on appeal, and we are grateful to them and to Nicole A. Allen, Brij B. Patnaik, and Chelsea L. Warren for their able assistance.

[2] The district court construed Buechel's filings as including a medical malpractice claim. This claim ultimately was dismissed with prejudice, and Buechel does not appeal that ruling.

[3] Although it has evolved to include persons exposed to other communities, including inmate populations, MRSA is most often associated with health care environments. See Federal Bureau of Prisons Clinical Practice Guidelines, *Management of Methicillin-Resistant Staphylococcus aureus (MRSA) Infections,* 1 (April 2012), http://www.bop.gov/ resources/pdfs/mrsa.pdf (last visited March 6, 2014).

758 F.3d 861 (2014)

E.Y., A Minor, by his Mother and Next Friend Tenille WALLACE, et al., Plaintiffs-Appellants,

v.

UNITED STATES of America, Defendant-Appellee.

No. 13-2854.

United States Court of Appeals, Seventh Circuit.

Argued May 20, 2014.

Decided July 10, 2014.

p.862 Keith A. Hebeisen, Attorney, Clifford Law Offices, P.C., Chicago, IL, for Plaintiffs-Appellants.

Kurt Lindland, Attorney, Office of the United States Attorney, Chicago, IL, for Defendant-Appellee.

Before KANNE, TINDER, and HAMILTON, Circuit Judges.

HAMILTON, Circuit Judge.

Tenille Wallace brings this suit on behalf of herself and her young son, E.Y., who has been diagnosed with diplegic cerebral palsy. She alleges that E.Y.'s illness resulted from medical malpractice by two separate healthcare providers: the federally-funded p.863 Friend Family Health Center, where she received her prenatal care, and the private University of Chicago Hospital, where she gave birth. The present appeal involves the timeliness of her suit based on the actions of the Friend Center.

The Friend Center and its doctors are federally funded, and as explained below, federal law makes Ms. Wallace's suit against the Center a suit against the United States under the Federal Tort Claims Act (FTCA). She needed to file suit against the Friend Center within the FTCA's two-year statute of limitations. See 28 U.S.C. § 2401(b). The district court denied the government's motion to dismiss because Ms. Wallace's claim could have accrued less than two years before she filed suit. Eventually, though, the district court granted summary judgment for the government, finding that Ms. Wallace's suit against the Friend Center and thus the United States was filed about two weeks too late.

Ms. Wallace appeals, arguing that although she was aware she might have a claim against the University Hospital more than two years before filing this suit, she remained unaware that the Friend Center might be involved until she received a partial set of medical records from the Center on December 14, 2006, making her suit timely. Although Ms. Wallace's claims against the University Hospital and other non-federal-remain pending in the district court, the district court properly entered a separate final judgment under Federal Rule of Civil Procedure 54(b) on the claims against the United States, so we have jurisdiction over the appeal.

We reverse. Reading the evidence in Ms. Wallace's favor as we must at summary judgment, a reasonable trier of fact could find that Ms. Wallace was unaware and had no reason to be aware of the Friend Center's potential involvement in her son's injuries until less than two years before she filed her suit. Although Ms. Wallace soon suspected that the University Hospital might have caused her son's injuries during delivery, the evidence does not show beyond reasonable dispute that she similarly suspected or should have suspected that the Friend Center's prenatal care had contributed to her son's injuries until she and her lawyers received incomplete records from the Center suggesting that something was amiss. That did not occur until December 14, 2006. She filed suit less than two years later, on December 10, 2008, so her suit should not have been dismissed on summary judgment as untimely. In essence, we think the district court was correct at the motion to dismiss stage when it denied the government's motion to dismiss on statute of limitations grounds using the same reasoning we adopt here.

I. *Factual and Procedural Background*

Ms. Wallace appeals from the district court's grant of summary judgment for the government, so we construe all evidence and draw all reasonable inferences from that evidence in her favor. *Gil v. Reed*, 535 F.3d 551, 556 (7th Cir.2008); *Del Raso v. United States*, 244 F.3d 567, 570 (7th Cir.2001).

In 2004, Tenille Wallace became pregnant with her first child, E.Y. She received her prenatal care at the federally-funded Friend Family Health Center. Her last prenatal appointment took place on March 29, 2005. A week later, on April 4, 2005, Ms. Wallace went to the University of Chicago Hospital for delivery. Things did not go smoothly. Her son, E.Y., was eventually delivered by caesarean section. E.Y. was born limp and purple. Ms. Wallace was not allowed to hold him. Soon thereafter (we are not told exactly when), a doctor at the University of Chicago Hospital told Ms. Wallace that E.Y. might p.864 have suffered oxygen deprivation during delivery.

E.Y. remained at the hospital for many weeks before Ms. Wallace could take him home. He developed slowly. In May 2006, a doctor at La Rabida Children's Hospital diagnosed E.Y. with diplegic cerebral palsy and explained the diagnosis to Ms. Wallace. There is no indication in the record that the doctor told Ms. Wallace that E.Y.'s injuries could have been caused by prenatal complications. That same month, Ms. Wallace discussed what she had learned with her uncle, a Chicago attorney. Based on the information Ms. Wallace shared with him, her uncle told her that she might have a case and recommended that she consult an attorney.

In mid-November 2006, Ms. Wallace met with attorneys at Clifford Law Offices and signed a retainer agreement. On November 28, 2006, her attorneys requested her medical records from both the University Hospital and the Friend Center. On December 14, 2006, the Center provided a partial set of Ms. Wallace's prenatal records to her attorneys. The Center did not provide Ms. Wallace's attorneys with all of her prenatal records until October 2007.

Ms. Wallace filed this suit on December 10, 2008. She alleges that the University Hospital, a Hospital doctor, the Friend Center, and a Center doctor had all committed medical malpractice that caused E.Y.'s injuries. After the case was removed to federal court and the United States was substituted as defendant for the Center and its doctor, the district court dismissed the case against the United States because Ms. Wallace had failed to exhaust available administrative remedies. She then presented her claim to the Department of Health and Human Services, exhausted all available remedies, and re-filed her case in November 2010. (Despite the dismissal, Ms. Wallace's case is still considered to have been filed on December 10, 2008 because she filed her claim with the Department within 60 days of the dismissal. See 28 U.S.C. § 2679(d).)

The government then moved to dismiss Ms. Wallace's refiled suit on statute of limitations grounds. It argued that Ms. Wallace's claim against the Friend Center had accrued at the latest in November 2006 when her lawyers requested her medical records from both the University Hospital and the Friend Center. That would make Ms. Wallace's December 10, 2008 suit untimely by about two weeks beyond the FTCA's two-year statute of limitations. The district court denied the motion to dismiss, reasoning that requesting medical records from the Center did not necessarily mean that Ms. Wallace suspected that the Center had contributed to E.Y.'s injuries: "it makes sense to obtain all records with respect to a pregnancy and childbirth in pursuing a cause of action." The court concluded that the pleadings did not show that Ms. Wallace's claim accrued before she received the partial set of medical records from the Center on December 14, 2006, making her December 10, 2008 lawsuit timely under the FTCA.

At the close of discovery, the government moved for summary judgment on statute of limitations grounds. The motion repeated many of the same arguments it had made in its motion to dismiss. This time, the court agreed with the government, concluding that Ms. Wallace's claim against the Center accrued by November 2006 when she requested records from both the Center and the Hospital. According to the court, requesting records from the Center "indicated that she understood that the actions of Center doctors could be related to E.Y.'s injuries," so her claim against the Center had accrued by that time. Since Ms. Wallace had not filed her suit until December 10, 2008, her suit was untimely under the FTCA. The court p.865 accordingly granted summary judgment in favor of the United States. This appeal followed.

II. *Analysis*

The Friend Family Health Center is a federally-funded public health center. Federal law treats Ms. Wallace's suit against the Center and one of its doctors as a tort action against the United States. See 42 U.S.C. § 233(g) (federally-funded health centers and their doctors are considered federal employees for purposes of tort claims). The Federal Tort Claims Act (FTCA) and its two-year statute of limitations thus apply to Ms. Wallace's suit against the Center. See 28 U.S.C. § 2401(b). Ms. Wallace filed her lawsuit on December 10, 2008, so her claim must have accrued on or after December 10, 2006 for her suit to be timely. Federal law governs when a claim accrues under the FTCA. *McCall v. United States,* 310 F.3d 984, 987 (7th Cir.2002).

Our circuit's case law regarding when a medical malpractice claim under the FTCA accrues has been evolving over the past several decades. Beginning with *Stoleson v. United States,* 629 F.2d 1265, 1268 (7th Cir.1980), we have said repeatedly that a claim accrues when the plaintiff discovers, or a reasonable person in the plaintiff's position would have discovered, that she has in fact been injured by an act or omission attributable to the government. E.g., *Arroyo v. United States,* 656 F.3d 663, 668 (7th Cir.2011); *Jastremski v. United States,* 737 F.2d 666, 669 (7th Cir.

1984). That standard has two alternative tests: a subjective one focused on the plaintiff's actual knowledge, and an objective one based on the knowledge of a reasonable person in the plaintiff's position. *Arroyo,* 656 F.3d at 669. Either form of knowledge is sufficient to start the clock on the statute of limitations. To determine when a claim accrued, we must consider both when the plaintiff knew her injury's cause and when a reasonable person in the plaintiff's position would have figured it out. *Id.*

Under this standard, accrual depends on when the plaintiff (or a reasonable person in the plaintiff's position) would have actually discovered that the government is responsible for her injuries. Starting with *Nemmers v. United States,* however, we have also said that the statute of limitations starts to run "when the plaintiff has the information *necessary to discover* both his injury and its cause." 795 F.2d 628, 629 (7th Cir.1986) (emphasis added); see also *Arteaga v. United States,* 711 F.3d 828, 831 (7th Cir.2013); *Arroyo,* 656 F.3d at 669. In other words, a plaintiff's claim accrues when "an individual acquires information that would prompt a reasonable person to make 'a deeper inquiry into a potential [government-related] cause.'" *Arroyo,* 656 F.3d at 669, quoting *Nemmers,* 795 F.2d at 632; see also *Arteaga,* 711 F.3d at 831.

Under this different rule, the issue is not when a reasonable person would have actually discovered the government's involvement. Instead, the issue is when a reasonable person would have been prompted to *inquire further* as to the government's potential involvement in her injuries. *Id.* Under this test, accrual no longer waits for discovery of actual causation but is triggered instead by information sufficient to prompt a reasonable person to inquire.

Neither *Arteaga* nor *Arroyo* explicitly rejected the earlier actual knowledge rule, and our previous cases also have not addressed the tension between the actual knowledge rule and the emerging rule based on inquiry notice. See *Arteaga,* 711 F.3d at 831 (citing the old standard and then, "equivalently," the new one); *Arroyo,* 656 F.3d at 669 (citing both standards without comment). In our view, p.866 however, these cases show a common-law evolution that spans thirty years of case law and has produced a new standard for claim accrual under the FTCA.[1]

Under these circumstances, we see no reason to avoid recognizing that new standard. We hold, therefore, that a plaintiff's medical malpractice claim against the federal government accrues when either (1) the individual becomes subjectively aware of the government's involvement in the injury, or (2) the individual acquires information that would prompt a reasonable person to inquire further into a potential government-related cause of the injury, whichever happens first. *Arteaga,* 711 F.3d at 831; *Arroyo,* 656 F.3d at 669.[2]

This case presents a new twist on this problem. Our prior cases involving accrual of medical malpractice claims under the FTCA have presented questions about when a plaintiff should have realized that an injury was caused by medical malpractice rather than having been a result of natural illnesses or processes. In those cases, the government was the only potential tortfeasor. See, e.g., *Arteaga,* 711 F.3d at 830; *Arroyo,* 656 F.3d at 671; *Drazan v. United States,* 762 F.2d 56, 58-59 (7th Cir.1985). In that situation, when a patient is injured, suspecting any doctor-related cause is equivalent to suspecting a governmental cause because the government is the only institution that treated the patient. See, e.g., *Arroyo,* 656 F.3d at 670-71 (using "government-related cause" and "doctor-related cause" interchangeably).

This case presents a different problem. Ms. Wallace received care from two different institutions, one governmental and one private. E.Y.'s injuries could have been the result of malpractice by either institution or both or neither. This case therefore requires us to determine when a medical malpractice claim under the FTCA accrues when there are multiple potential tortfeasors, some governmental and some private.

The government argues for a simple rule: suspecting *any* doctor-related cause for an injury should trigger the statute of limitations as to *all* doctor-related causes p.867 for that injury, whether private or governmental. We do not think this is a sound rule, nor is it consistent with the reasoning of our prior case law. In both *Arroyo* and *Drazan,* the plaintiff's injuries could have been caused by two things: nature and/or the government. We held in both cases that knowledge of one potential cause did not start the statute of limitations running as to all potential causes. *Arroyo,* 656 F.3d at 671; *Drazan,* 762 F.2d at 59. Rather, "the knowledge that is required to set the statute of limitations running is knowledge of the government cause, not just of the other cause." *Drazan,* 762 F.2d at 59. This same logic applies in a situation where the plaintiff's injuries could have been caused by several different non-natural causes, some governmental and some private. In such a situation, the plaintiff (or a reasonable person in her position) may not suspect that the government caused or contributed to her injuries even when she comes to suspect a private actor was negligent.

In applying the FTCA statute of limitations to claims of medical malpractice, we have long avoided requiring would-be plaintiffs to engage in paranoid investigations of everyone who has ever provided them with medical care. *Drazan,* 762 F.2d at 59 (rejecting rule that would have the "rather ghoulish consequence" of requiring such investigations); *Arroyo,* 656 F.3d at 671-72; *Nemmers v. United States,* 795 F.2d 628, 631-32 (7th Cir.1986). The relationship between doctor and patient is built on trust. Doctors have the obligation to care for their patients and the specialized knowledge to make good medical choices and to deliver effective care. Patients typically lack specialized medical knowledge and are unable to assess and treat their own maladies. They put their trust in doctors to provide competent medical care. And all should recognize that even the best medical care cannot guarantee a good outcome. A negative outcome of medical care is not proof of negligence. Given the complexities of the human body, its injuries and illnesses, and medical treatment, and the special relationship between doctor and patient, the law should not encourage patients to assume their doctors are responsible for negative outcomes, let alone penalize patients who do not turn on their doctors at the first sign of trouble. The government's proposed rule would encourage just this sort of behavior. We decline to adopt it.

We agree with the government, however, that adopting a rule that unduly narrows the scope of related claims and causes would also have troubling consequences. Statutes of limitations serve important purposes, including protecting "defendants and the courts from having to deal with cases in which the search for truth may be seriously impaired by the loss of evidence, whether by death or disappearance of witnesses, fading memories, disappearance of documents, or otherwise." *United*

States v. Kubrick, 444 U.S. 111, 117, 100 S.Ct. 352, 62 L.Ed.2d 259 (1979). These considerations are even more important in the context of the FTCA, which waives the United States' sovereign immunity. The statute of limitations is a condition of that waiver and thus should not be extended by judicial interpretation. *Id.* at 117-18, 100 S.Ct. 352. Adopting too narrow a view of which doctor-related causes are sufficiently connected to a suspected cause would have the effect of eroding the FTCA's statute of limitations, a result we have many reasons to avoid.

Goodhand v. United States, 40 F.3d 209 (7th Cir.1994), offers some guidance in approaching the question of claim accrual when there is more than one potential tortfeasor. In *Goodhand,* the plaintiff had suffered an injury as a result of two different medical procedures carried out by the p.868 same doctor in close succession: birth of her baby and a later surgical repair of a perineal tear. She sued, alleging that the doctor had committed medical malpractice during both procedures. One question in the case was whether the plaintiff's suspicion that the first medical procedure (the delivery method) had caused her injury would trigger the statute of limitations as to the second medical procedure (the surgical repair). We held that it did not. Although the same doctor had carried out both procedures, "we cannot think of a reason why the case should be decided differently than if two different doctors had been responsible for the two mistakes, the two injuries. Then certainly the running of the statute of limitations against one for his act would not bar a suit against the other based on the other's act." 40 F.3d at 215.

Goodhand suggests a straightforward approach to our present problem. When a person suspects, or a reasonable person would suspect, that her injury was caused by negligent medical care, claims regarding other doctor-related causes of that injury that share a time and place with the injury's suspected cause also accrue. All claims arising from the same surgery, for example, against surgeon, anesthetist, and nurse, would arise together. However, claims that are distinct in time, or distinct in place, or that relate to a different injury do not accrue solely on that basis. This test is consistent with Goodhand and our other prior FTCA cases and maintains limits on claim accrual without undermining the FTCA's statute of limitations. To stay consistent with *Goodhand,* though, the differences in time and place may be quite small, as in the time between the *Goodhand* baby's birth and the surgical repair of the perineal tear.

We now examine whether Ms. Wallace's suit is timely under this approach. The prenatal care Ms. Wallace received at the Friend Center and the care she received at the University Hospital during delivery differed in both time and place. A reasonable person would not necessarily have suspected that the Center's care was negligent merely because she suspected that the Hospital's care was negligent. Viewing the evidence through the summary judgment lens, and giving Ms. Wallace the benefit of conflicts in the evidence and reasonable inferences favorable to her case, the earliest time she possessed enough information to make a reasonable person inquire further about the Center's possible negligence was December 14, 2006, when she and her lawyers received her partial records from the Center. Only at that time was there a solid indication that something might have been amiss with her prenatal care, making that the first time that a reasonable person necessarily would have inquired further. See *Arroyo,* 656 F.3d at 669. Unless Ms. Wallace subjectively had solid grounds for suspecting that the Center had committed medical malpractice before she and her lawyers received the partial records from the Center, her suit is timely. *Id.*

The government argues that the requests for records from both the University Hospital and the Friend Center show that Ms. Wallace suspected that the Center had caused or contributed to E.Y.'s injuries. That is one plausible inference, but it is not the only one. One could also reasonably infer, as the district court did at the motion to dismiss stage, that Ms. Wallace's attorneys requested records from the Center to ensure that they had a complete picture of her course of treatment and to establish a baseline measure of Ms. Wallace's and E.Y.'s health and care prior to delivery. It would be reasonable for diligent lawyers to anticipate that other health care providers like the University Hospital and its staff might defend claims against them by at least investigating p.869 whether Ms. Wallace's prenatal care was up to proper standards of care. Looking into that evidence as part of a prudent investigation does not necessarily imply serious suspicion of negligence.

Both inferences are reasonable, and which one the trier of fact makes is crucial to Ms. Wallace's case. If we make the first inference, as the district court did in granting summary judgment, Ms. Wallace's suit is untimely; if we make the second, as the district court did in denying the government's motion to dismiss, it is not. And while it is not unusual for a district court to deny a motion to dismiss because pleadings are sufficient but to grant summary judgment because evidence is lacking, this case does not fit that model. At both procedural stages, the question was the significance of the records request to the Friend Center, and at least two inferences were and are reasonable. The district court erred in granting summary judgment for the government on the ground that Ms. Wallace's suit was untimely. See *Drazan,* 762 F.2d at 59-60 (court cannot infer claim accrual from mere fact of requesting records from treatment provider; the issue is why the records were requested).

We therefore REVERSE the district court's grant of summary judgment and REMAND for further proceedings consistent with this opinion.

[1] Other circuits have also moved toward an inquiry notice rule for accrual of medical malpractice claims under the FTCA. See, e.g., *Kronisch v. United States,* 150 F.3d 112, 121 (2d Cir.1998) (a claim accrues when the plaintiff has "knowledge of, or knowledge that could lead to, the basic facts of the injury, i.e., knowledge of the injury's existence and knowledge of its cause or of the person or entity that inflicted it") (internal citation and quotation omitted); *Hughes v. United States,* 263 F.3d 272, 275 (3d Cir.2001) ("the statute of limitations is tolled until the putative plaintiff possesses facts which would enable a reasonable person to discover the alleged malpractice") (internal quotation and citation omitted); *Johnson v. United States,* 460 F.3d 616, 621 (5th Cir.2006) ("the limitations period begins to run when the plaintiff has knowledge of facts that would lead a reasonable person (a) to conclude that there was a causal connection between the treatment and injury *or* (b) *to seek professional advice,* and then with that advice, to conclude that there was a causal connection between the treatment and injury") (internal quotations and citations omitted, emphasis in original).

[2] This rule is consistent with *United States v. Kubrick,* 444 U.S. 111, 123, 100 S.Ct. 352, 62 L.Ed.2d 259 (1979), which held that claim accrual under the FTCA is not delayed until a potential plaintiff knows that his injury was caused by malpractice. *Kubrick* was focused on accrual based on a plaintiff's subjective knowledge rather

than what a reasonable person in the plaintiff's position would suspect. It also did not address when a potential plaintiff has sufficient knowledge about her injury's cause to start the statute of limitations running. In any case, under both *Kubrick* and the claim accrual standard we adopt here, a plaintiff's FTCA claim has accrued by the time she is subjectively aware of both her injury and its cause. See *id.*

732 F.3d 749 (2013)

Jerome AUGUTIS, Plaintiff-Appellant,
v.
UNITED STATES of America, Defendant-Appellee.

No. 12-3536.

United States Court of Appeals, Seventh Circuit.

Argued September 13, 2013.

Decided October 9, 2013.

Augutis v. US, 732 F. 3d 749 (7th Cir. 2013)

p.751 Carl P. Clavelli, Attorney, Chicago, IL, for Plaintiff-Appellant.

Jeffrey M. Hansen, Attorney, Office of the United States Attorney, Chicago, IL, for Defendant-Appellee.

Before BAUER, FLAUM, and ROVNER, Circuit Judges.

FLAUM, Circuit Judge.

After doctors at a Veterans Affairs hospital amputated his right leg below the knee, Jerome Augutis filed an administrative claim for medical malpractice under the Federal Tort Claims Act (FTCA). When his claim was denied, he requested reconsideration; when that too was denied, he filed suit in federal court. By this time, however, over five years had elapsed since the amputation. The district court dismissed the case because under the FTCA the United States is liable only to the extent a private would be under state law, and in Illinois plaintiffs must bring medical malpractice claims within four years of the allegedly negligent act or omission. Augutis now appeals. He contends that the FTCA does not incorporate Illinois's fouryear limit, that the limit is preempted by the FTCA's own statute of limitations, and that it does not bar his suit in any case. We affirm the decision of the district court.

I. Background

On July 14, 2006, Jerome Augutis underwent reconstructive surgery on his right foot at the Edward Hines, Jr. VA Hospital in Hines, Illinois. Complications led doctors to amputate his leg below the knee on September 22. Augutis alleges that his amputation was the result of negligent treatment, and on July 11, 2008 he timely filed an administrative complaint with the Department of Veterans Affairs. The Department denied the claim on September 27, 2010 and instructed Augutis that he had six months to request reconsideration or file suit.

Augutis timely filed a request for reconsideration on March 21, 2011. On October 3, 2011, the Department wrote to inform him that "our office has not completed our reconsideration," but that, "[b]ecause the six-month period [during which no lawsuit may be filed] has passed, suit can now be filed in Federal district court, or, additional time can be permitted to allow the agency to reach a decision." The letter also noted that "FTCA claims are governed by a combination of Federal and state laws" and that "[s]ome state laws may limit or bar a claim or law suit." Three days later, on October 6, the Department formally denied Augutis's request for reconsideration. The denial letter explained that "a tort claim that is administratively denied may be presented to a Federal district court for judicial consideration ... within 6 months," although it again noted that "[s]ome state laws may limit or bar a claim or law suit."

Augutis filed suit in federal court on April 3, 2012, over five years after the alleged malpractice occurred, but within six months of the Department's final dismissal. p.752 The United States filed a motion to dismiss, pointing to Illinois's statute of repose, 735 ILCS 5/13-212(a), which requires a medical malpractice claim to be brought within four years of the date the alleged malpractice occurred. The district court granted the motion, observing that the FTCA makes the United States liable for personal injuries caused by its negligence "only to the extent it would be liable as a private person under Illinois law." Because Augutis could not sue a private party in 2012 for malpractice that occurred in 2006, it reasoned, he could not sue the United States under the FTCA, either.

II. Discussion

We review the district court's grant of a motion to dismiss de novo. *Reger Dev., LLC v. Nat'l City Bank,* 592 F.3d 759, 763 (7th Cir.2010).

In order to take advantage of the FTCA's "limited waiver" of sovereign immunity, *Luna v. United States,* 454 F.3d 631, 634 (7th Cir.2006), a claimant must present his claims to the appropriate agency within two years of the date that the claims accrue. 28 U.S.C. § 2401(b). If the agency fails to make a final disposition within six months, the claim is deemed denied and the claimant may file in federal court. 28 U.S.C. § 2675(a). Alternatively, the claimant can give the agency more time to resolve the claim; if the claim is eventually denied, the claimant has another six months to file a lawsuit. 28 U.S.C. § 2401(b).

A claimant who clears these procedural hurdles is not automatically free to recover under the FTCA, however. That is because the FTCA's jurisdictional grant only covers "circumstances where the United States, if a private person, would be liable to the claimant in accordance with the law of the place where the act or omission occurred." *Morisch v. United States,* 653 F.3d 522, 530 (7th Cir.2011) (quoting 28 U.S.C. § 1346(b)(1)); *see also* 28 U.S.C. § 2674 ("The United States shall be liable ... in the same manner and to the same extent as a private individual under like circumstances...."). Put another way, the FTCA "incorporates the substantive law of the state where the tortious act or omission occurred." *Midwest Knitting Mills, Inc. v. United States,* 950 F.2d 1295, 1297 (7th Cir.1991).

The government contends that the Illinois statute of repose for medical malpractice claims, 735 ILCS 5/13-212, is substantive law, and thus bars Augutis's suit even though he complied with the FTCA's own procedural requirements. We agree.

A. Illinois's statute of repose is part of the substantive law of the state where the tortious act or omission occurred

Section 13-212 of the Illinois Code of Civil Procedure states that "[e]xcept as provided in Section 13-215 of this Act, no action for damages for injury or death against any physician or hospital ... shall be brought more than 2 years after the date on which the claimant knew ... of the existence of the injury ... *but in no event shall such action be brought more than 4 years after the date on which occurred the act or omission or occurrence alleged in such action to have been the cause of such injury or death.*" 735 ILCS 5/13-212(a) (emphasis added).

Illinois courts have described section 13-212 as a "bifurcated" provision that "provid[es] both a statute of limitations and a statute of repose." *Kanne v. Bulkley,* 306 Ill.App.3d 1036, 240 Ill.Dec. 97, 715 N.E.2d 784, 787 (1999). Statutes of limitations and statutes of repose are close cousins, but they serve different goals and operate in slightly different ways. "[A] statute of limitations is a procedural device ... [whose] running simply p.753 bars suit. A statute of repose by contrast is substantive. It extinguishes any right to bring any type of cause of action against a party, regardless of whether such action has accrued." *Boggs v. Adams,* 45 F.3d 1056, 1060 (7th Cir.1995) (citation and internal quotation marks omitted). Statutes of repose "give[] effect to a policy different from that advanced by a period of limitations," namely, "terminat[ing] the possibility of liability after a defined period of time, *regardless* of a potential plaintiff's lack of knowledge." *Mega v. Holy Cross Hosp.,* 111 Ill.2d 416, 95 Ill.Dec. 812, 490 N.E.2d 665, 668 (1986) (emphasis added).

In keeping with these labels, Illinois courts have consistently construed the four-year limit in section 13-212 as a substantive limit on liability, not a procedural bar to suit. *See, e.g., Orlak v. Loyola Univ. Health Sys.,* 228 Ill.2d 1, 319 Ill.Dec. 319, 885 N.E.2d 999, 1003 (2007); *Cunningham v. Huffman,* 154 Ill.2d 398, 182 Ill.Dec. 18, 609 N.E.2d 321, 325 (1993); *Ferrara v. Wall,* 323 Ill.App.3d 751, 257 Ill.Dec. 553, 753 N.E.2d 1179, 1181-82 (2001). Indeed, in *Hinkle v. Henderson,* 85 F.3d 298 (7th Cir.1996), we described the section as "an excellent example of how statutes of limitations and statutes of repose operate." *Id.* at 301. The first part, we said, "is a statute of limitations, because its running is contingent on accrual —plaintiff must have 'discovered' his injury." *Id.* The second part, by contrast, "is a statute of repose, because it begins to run regardless of 'discovery' and sets an outer limit within which a cause of action must be brought." *Id.*

Augutis argues that 735 ILCS 5/13-212 is not actually substantive law because statutes of repose ordinarily begin to run regardless of discovery, while Illinois allows the fouryear limit to be tolled by the doctrine of fraudulent concealment. *See DeLuna v. Burciaga,* 223 Ill.2d 49, 306 Ill.Dec. 136, 857 N.E.2d 229, 243-44 (2006). It is true that Illinois courts have recognized that applying a fraudulent concealment exception to section 13-212 creates an "arguable logical inconsistency." *Id.,* 223 Ill.2d 49, 857 N.E.2d at 242. But even so, they have continued to treat the section as a statute of repose that serves substantive, not procedural, goals. *See, e.g., Orlak,* 319 Ill.Dec. 319, 885 N.E.2d at 1003. Similarly, in *Hinkle,* we recognized that section 13-212 was "substantive, extinguishing the *right* to bring a cause of action," 85 F.3d at 301, even though we later noted that Illinois has "expressly except[ed]... fraudulent concealment from the operation of the statute of repose." *Id.* at 304. We continue to take the Illinois courts at their word when they describe section 13-212 as a substantive limitation on the cause of action for medical malpractice.[1]

Augutis also argues that even if section 13-212 is a statute of repose, it is preempted by the FTCA's own procedural scheme. Although we presume that Congress does not intend to supplant state law, we recognize that "state law may be preempted by federal legislation either by express provision, by implication, or by a conflict between federal and state law." *Frank Bros., Inc. v. Wis. Dept. of Trans.,* p.754 409 F.3d 880, 885 (7th Cir.2005) (internal quotation marks omitted). None of those circumstances is present here, however. The FTCA does not expressly preempt state statutes of repose, nor does it impliedly preempt state substantive law; to the contrary, it expressly incorporates it. *See* 28 U.S.C. § 1346(b); *Molzof v. United States,* 502 U.S. 301, 305, 112 S.Ct. 711, 116 L.Ed.2d 731 (1992) ("[T]he extent of the United States' liability under the FTCA is generally determined by reference to state law."). And here there is no conflict between state and federal law because it was possible for Augutis to have satisfied the requirements of both regimes.

Augutis filed his administrative claim within two years of the date that his cause of action accrued. Although he did not receive a response for twenty-six months, by which time the statute of repose had run, after six months he was free to bring an action in federal court under 28 U.S.C. § 2675(a) (the "deemed denied" provision). In other words, Augutis had approximately eighteen months to file suit while complying with both the FTCA procedures and the Illinois statute of repose. By choosing instead to continue pursuing his administrative claim, Augutis allowed the statute of repose's fouryear clock to expire, extinguishing his nascent federal claim. That result was unfortunate—and Augutis may understandably feel frustrated with the pace of the administrative claims process —but that cannot cause us to expand the FTCA's limited waiver of sovereign immunity.

We therefore conclude that, as a substantive limitation on the tort of medical malpractice, the Illinois statute of repose is part of "the substantive law of the state where the tortious act or omission occurred." *Midwest Knitting Mills,* 950 F.2d at 1297. In so doing, we join two of our sister circuits, which have also determined that "an FTCA claim does not lie against the United States where a statute of repose would bar the action if brought against a private person in state court." *Anderson v. United States,* 669 F.3d 161, 165 (4th Cir.2011); *Smith v. United States,* 430 Fed.Appx. 246, 246-47 (5th Cir.2011) (per curiam); *cf. Huddleston v. United States,* 485 Fed.Appx. 744, 745-46 (6th Cir. 2012) (dismissing an FTCA suit where the plaintiff did not file his administrative claim until after the state statute of repose had run).

B. Augutis's FTCA claim is barred by the Illinois statute of repose for medical negligence claims

Augutis filed his FTCA action in federal court six months after the Department of Veterans Affairs denied his request for reconsideration, but over five years after the allegedly negligent act or omission occurred. The Illinois statute of repose states that "in no event shall [a medical malpractice action] be brought more than 4 years after the date on which occurred the act ... alleged in such action to have been the cause of such injury or death." 735 ILCS 5/13-212(a).

Augutis briefly suggests that his administrative claim was an "action" within the meaning of section 13-212, but that is not what the word means in this context. An action must be filed in a court, not with a federal agency. *See* 735 ILCS 5/2-201(a) ("Every action, unless otherwise expressly provided by statute, shall be commenced by the filing of a complaint."). In passing, he also argues that he was under a "legal disability" during the pendency of his administrative claim. Like fraudulent concealment, legal disability can toll the statute of repose. *See* 735 ILCS 5/13-212(c). However, the purpose of section 13-212(c) is "to protect the rights of those who are not *competent* to do so themselves." *DeLuna,* 306 Ill. p.755 Dec. 136, 857 N.E.2d at 239 (emphasis added). As Augutis alleges nothing that would call into question his competency to file a federal action—one that, as discussed above, he was free to bring six months after he filed his administrative claim pursuant to 28 U.S.C. § 2675(a)—that provision is inapposite here.

Finally, Augutis argues that the United States ought to be equitably estopped from invoking the statute of repose because the letters he received from the Department of Veterans Affairs caused him to believe he could delay filing suit in district court. As a general matter, equitable estoppel does not apply to statutes of repose. *See McCann v. Hy-Vee, Inc.,* 663 F.3d 926, 930 (7th Cir.2011). Yet even if Illinois were to recognize an estoppel exception, and even if equitable estoppel were available against the federal government (an open question, *see Solis-Chavez v. Holder,* 662 F.3d 462, 471 (7th Cir. 2011)), that doctrine cannot help Augutis. As the government points out, the Department's first letter to Augutis was sent on September 27, 2010-i.e., shortly *after* the four-year repose period had elapsed. Equitable estoppel requires that there be some detriment to the party that reasonably relies on another party's misrepresentation. *See LaBonte v. United States,* 233 F.3d 1049, 1053 (7th Cir.2000). But by the time Augutis received anything to rely on, his claim had already been extinguished.[2]

In short, this is not a case "where the United States, if a private person, would be liable to the claimant in accordance with the law of the place where the act or omission occurred." 28 U.S.C. § 1346(b)(1). Accordingly, Augutis's FTCA claim is barred.

III. Conclusion

For the foregoing reasons, we AFFIRM the district court's dismissal of Augutis's case.

[1] Several of our sister circuits have also treated statutes of repose as substantive provisions despite a fraudulent concealment exception. *See Huddleston v. United States,* 485 Fed. Appx. 744, 745-46 (6th Cir.2012); *Sanford v. Shea,* 103 Fed.Appx. 878, 881 (6th Cir.2004); *Appletree Square I, Ltd. P'ship v. W.R. Grace & Co.,* 29 F.3d 1283, 1285 (8th Cir.1994); *cf. First United Methodist Church of Hyattsville v. U.S. Gypsum Co.,* 882 F.2d 862, 866 (4th Cir.1989) (noting that Maryland expressly applied its fraudulent concealment statute to the medical malpractice statute of repose, but not to its statute of repose for improvements to realty).

[2] We do not mean to imply that the Department's September 27, 2010 letter was in fact misleading. Although there is no need to decide that question, we note that the language at issue is required by 28 C.F.R. § 14.9(a).

EIGHTH CIRCUIT DECISIONS
Federal Tort Claims Act

829 F.3d 600 (2016)

COMPART'S BOAR STORE, INC., Plaintiff-Appellant

v.

UNITED STATES of America, Defendant-Appellee.

No. 15-3147.

United States Court of Appeals, Eighth Circuit.

Submitted: June 14, 2016.

Filed: July 13, 2016.

p.602 Appeal from United States District Court for the District of Minnesota — Minneapolis.

p.603 Counsel who presented argument on behalf of the appellant was Gary W. Koch, of New Ulm, MN. The following attorney appeared on the appellant brief; Matthew C. Berger, of New Ulm, MN.

Counsel who presented argument on behalf of the appellee was Friedrich A. P. Siekert, AUSA, of Minneapolis, MN.

Before MURPHY and SHEPHERD, Circuit Judges, and PERRY,[1] District Judge.

MURPHY, Circuit Judge.

In 2011 Compart's Boar Store (Compart), a producer of breeding swine, intended to export over three hundred pigs to China. China suspended all imports from Compart, however, after it was notified by the United States government that the test results from a small set of the blood samples were "inconclusive" for Porcine Reproductive and Respiratory Syndrome virus (PRRSv). Compart subsequently brought a negligence suit against the United States under the Federal Tort Claims Act (FTCA). The district court[2] dismissed Compart's action for lack of jurisdiction after concluding that it fell within the FTCA's discretionary function exemption. Compart appeals and we affirm.

I.

The export of pigs to China is governed by the Quarantine and Health Requirements of the People's Republic of China for Swine Exported from the United States (China Protocol). Under the China Protocol the National Veterinary Services Laboratories (NVSL) must test pigs prior to their export to China for PRRSv, a viral disease which can cause pigs to have spontaneous abortions, pneumonia, lethargy, and lack of appetite. NVSL is overseen by the Animal and Plant Health Inspection Service which is an agency of the USDA.

NVSL tests pigs for PRRSv using two immonufluorescent antibody (IFA) tests and a virus isolation test. If the pigs pass the first IFA test they are isolated in a quarantine facility for 30 days and tested again using another IFA test. Ten percent of the quarantined pigs are also tested for PRRSv using a virus isolation test. NVSL's procedure for virus isolation tests is set out in a document entitled

Isolation of Porcine Reproductive and Respiratory Syndrome Virus (PRRSV) from Porcine Specimens (hereinafter VISOP).

This VISOP requires testing blood samples on two cell lines, known as SAM and MARC cells. The cultures are then examined for cell damage over approximately seven days. If no cell damage is observed, the cultures are frozen and thawed and the process is repeated. If no cell damage is observed for a second time, the cultures are stained and examined for fluorescence. The presence of fluorescence ordinarily indicates the presence of PRRSv. The VISOP provides the following guidance for interpreting the stained cultures:

> If fluorescence is observed in any cultures inoculated with submitted specimens, and is comparable to fluorescence observed in the positive slides, and no fluorescence is observed in the negative controls, the specimen is reported as positive for PRRS virus isolation. If no fluorescence is observed in any but the positive control slides, the specimens are considered negative for PRRS virus isolation.

p.604 The VISOP provides no guidance, however, on what action to take when the cultures do not appear positive or negative.

In 2011 Ag World International Corporation secured a contract to export pigs to China. After Chinese buyers selected over three hundred of Compart's pigs to be included in the shipment, the pigs underwent PRRSv testing. During the first IFA test, all of Compart's pigs tested negative for PRRSv. They were then placed in a quarantine facility where they passed a second IFA test. During the virus isolation test, NVSL did not observe any cell damage in either the MARC or SAM cells. Nevertheless, a NVSL lab technician observed fluorescence in some of the stained MARC cells. The fluorescence was unusual because it was not as bright as typical positive slides and not as dark as typical negative slides. NVSL personnel then conducted additional testing that yielded similar results. NVSL then issued a final report stating that all PRRSv tests were negative with the exception of a few samples whose results were "inconclusive." China subsequently suspended all swine imports from Compart.

Compart filed suit against the United States, alleging that NVSL was negligent in testing its pigs for PRRSv and in reporting the results to China. The district court granted the government's motion to dismiss for lack of jurisdiction under Rule 12(b)(1). The court concluded that the discretionary function exemption to the Federal Tort Claims Act (FTCA) barred Compart's claims. Compart appeals.

II.

We review de novo motions to dismiss for lack of jurisdiction under Rule 12(b)(1). Herden v. United States, 726 F.3d 1042, 1046 (8th Cir. 2013). The plaintiff has the burden of proving subject matter jurisdiction. Id. To determine our court's jurisdiction, we may look outside the pleadings. Id. We review for clear error the district court's "determination of disputed factual issues." Osborn v. United States, 918 F.2d 724, 730 (8th Cir. 1990).

Sovereign immunity shields the United States and its agencies from suit absent a waiver. FDIC v. Meyer, 510 U.S. 471, 475, 114 S.Ct. 996, 127 L.Ed.2d 308 (1994).

Under the FTCA the United States has consented to be sued in tort "in the same manner and to the same extent as a private individual under like circumstances." 28 U.S.C. § 2674. The FTCA contains numerous exceptions to this waiver of sovereign immunity, however. E.g., id. § 2680. If an exception applies, "the bar of sovereign immunity remains." Dolan v. U.S. Postal Serv., 546 U.S. 481, 485, 126 S.Ct. 1252, 163 L.Ed.2d 1079 (2006).

One exception is the discretionary function exemption, which deprives courts of jurisdiction over any claim "based upon the exercise or performance or the failure to exercise or perform a discretionary function or duty on the part of a federal agency or an employee of the Government, whether or not the discretion involved be abused." 28 U.S.C. § 2680(a). The purpose of the exception is to "prevent judicial second-guessing of legislative and administrative decisions grounded in social, economic, and political policy through the medium of an action in tort." United States v. Gaubert, 499 U.S. 315, 323, 111 S.Ct. 1267, 113 L.Ed.2d 335 (1991) (internal quotations omitted).

The discretionary function exemption applies if two requirements are met. See Gaubert, 499 U.S. at 322-23, 111 S.Ct. 1267 (1991). First, we must consider whether the suit concerns "acts that are discretionary in nature, [that is] acts that involve an element of judgment or choice." Id. at 322, 111 S.Ct. 1267 (internal quotations p.605 omitted). Government employees act with discretion unless they are following a regulation or policy that is "mandatory and... clearly and specifically define[s] what the employees are supposed to do." C.R.S. ex rel. D.B.S. v. United States, 11 F.3d 791, 799 (8th Cir. 1993). Second, we must determine whether the government acted or based its decision "on considerations of public policy." Gaubert, 499 U.S. at 323, 111 S.Ct. 1267 (internal quotations omitted). When the first step is satisfied, we presume that the governmental action involved considerations of public policy. Id. at 324, 111 S.Ct. 1267. It is the plaintiff's burden to rebut that presumption. Herden, 726 F.3d at 1048.

The district court correctly concluded that the challenged governmental action here was discretionary. Governmental action is discretionary when a governmental policy "predominately uses permissive rather than mandatory language." Herden, 726 F.3d at 1047. Even when some provisions of a policy are mandatory, governmental action remains discretionary if all of the challenged decisions involved "an element of judgment or choice." Hart v. United States, 630 F.3d 1085, 1086 (8th Cir. 2011) (internal quotations omitted). In this case, the VISOP predominantly uses permissive rather than mandatory language. For example, the VISOP offers NVSL scientists ranges for the amount of blood to be used in the tests, the time for initial incubation, and the length of thaw times for the frozen samples. Moreover, the VISOP does not provide any guidance on how to interpret stained slides for fluorescence or what to do if these slides appear inconclusive for PRRSv — the challenged decisions here.

Compart argues that our decision in McMichael v. United States, 751 F.2d 303 (8th Cir. 1985) compels the opposite conclusion. In that case, the plaintiffs claimed that government inspectors failed to regularly perform a 51 step safety compliance check. Id. at 307. We concluded that the safety compliance check was mandatory, not discretionary, as it listed "a number of precise inspections to perform." Id. at 307. A rote 51 step inspection list is not analogous to the VISOP which consisted of mainly permissive guidelines that allowed NVSL personnel to use their judgment for most testing and reporting decisions.

The district court also correctly determined that Compart did not rebut the presumption that NVSL PRRSv testing and reporting decisions was susceptible to policy analysis. One of the hallmarks "of a decision susceptible to policy analysis is one in which a federal employee must weigh or balance competing interests." Herden, 726 F.3d at 1050. The agency's decision here involved weighing several competing interests when testing and reporting for the virus. Incorrectly reporting the results as negative could have undermined China's confidence in the government's PRRSv testing procedures. Yet incorrectly reporting the results as positive could have resulted in harsh consequences for Compart and undermined United States pork producers' confidence in NVSL. As the district court concluded, determining "what to do in this sensitive situation plainly involved ... considerations of public policy."

Compart argues that the testing and reporting merely involved professional scientific discretion, rather than considerations of public policy. It claims that this case is similar to Lather v. Beadle County, 879 F.2d 365 (8th Cir. 1989), where the plaintiff alleged that a government psychologist negligently evaluated him. In that case we concluded that the psychologist's conduct did not involve considerations of public policy because the treatment was "professional [and] nongovernmental." p.606 Id. at 368. Compart's reliance on Lather is misplaced. There, the psychologist had a "singular goal, i.e., providing appropriate medical care to a patient" and was not faced with weighing competing interests like NVSL was required to do here. See Herden, 726 F.3d at 1051 (distinguishing Lather).

Since NVSL's testing and reporting of Compart's swine was governed by discretionary governmental procedures and susceptible to policy analysis, the discretionary function exemption precludes jurisdiction over Compart's negligence claims.

III.

For these reasons we affirm the district court's dismissal of this action.

[1] The Honorable Catherine D. Perry, United States District Judge for the Eastern District of Missouri, sitting by designation.

[2] The Honorable Patrick J. Schiltz, United States District Judge for the District of Minnesota.

788 F.3d 758 (2015)

Norma SORACE, Administratix of the Estate of Melanie Sorace, deceased; Jahneva Cannaday, deceased; Guardian for Dominique Harris and Tamara Sorace, Plaintiff-Appellant

v.

UNITED STATES of America, Defendant-Appellee.

No. 14-2683.

United States Court of Appeals, Eighth Circuit.

Submitted: March 12, 2015.

Filed: May 27, 2015.

Sorace v. US, 788 F. 3d 758 (8th Cir. 2015)

p.761 Terry L. Pechota, Pechota Law Office, Rapid City, SD, argued, for appellant.

Kevin Koliner, Asst. U.S. Atty., Sioux Falls, SD, argued (Brendan V. Johnson, U.S. Atty., Sioux Falls, SD, Cheryl Schrempp DuPris, Asst. U.S. Atty., Pierre, SD, on the brief), for appellee.

Before WOLLMAN and COLLOTON, Circuit Judges, and WHITE,[1] District Judge.

WHITE, District Judge.

p.762Norma Sorace ("Sorace"), Administratix of the Estates of Melanie Sorace and Jahneva Cannaday, a minor, filed suit against the United States of America alleging a claim under the Federal Tort Claims Act ("FTCA") based upon a drunk-driving accident on the Rosebud Sioux Indian Reservation in South Dakota. Melanie Sorace and Jahneva Cannaday were killed when an intoxicated Shad Dillon ("Dillon") crashed his pickup into a vehicle driven by Melanie Sorace. Sorace alleges that the Rosebud Sioux Tribe's Police Department ("RST PD") was negligent in failing to locate and arrest Dillon prior to the accident. The United States of America ("United States") filed a motion to dismiss, which the district court[2] granted. Sorace appeals, and we affirm.

I.

On June 30, 2011, Dillon was driving on a highway running through Antelope, South Dakota. Dillon was intoxicated and speeding. Dillon's pick up truck struck Melanie Sorace's car as she proceeded through an intersection with the highway. Melanie Sorace and her daughter, Jahneva Cannaday, were killed, and two of Melanie Sorace's other children were injured. Dillon pleaded guilty to Involuntary Manslaughter in violation of 18 U.S.C. §§ 1153 and 1112 and was sentenced to 40 months in prison.

Sorace, as Administratix of Melanie Sorace and Jahneva Cannaday's estates and guardian of the injured children, filed a negligence claim under the FTCA against the United States. Sorace alleged that the RST PD was operating pursuant to a contract entered into under 25 U.S.C. § 450f, *et seq.*

Pursuant to Federal Rules of Civil Procedure 12(b)(1) and (b)(6), the United States filed a motion to dismiss Sorace's complaint. First, the United States argued that, under South Dakota law, no legally actionable duty of care was owed to Melanie Sorace and her children to control the misconduct of Dillon. The United States further argued that even if South Dakota's "special duty" exception to the public duty doctrine applied, Sorace failed to allege sufficient facts to state a claim upon which relief could be granted. In response, Sorace filed a memorandum with factual affidavits, but did not file a motion to amend the complaint or to convert the motion to one for summary judgment. The district court, assuming that the RST PD had actual knowledge of Dillon's dangerous driving, held that Sorace failed to allege sufficient facts suggesting a special relationship between the parties and dismissed Sorace's complaint for failure to state a claim.

II.

We review *de novo* the district court's dismissal of an action for failure to state a claim under Federal Rule of Civil Procedure 12(b)(6). *O'Neil v. Simplicity, Inc.,* 574 F.3d 501, 503 (8th Cir.2009) (citing *Briehl v. General Motors Corp.,* 172 F.3d 623, 627 (8th Cir.1999)). We accept the factual allegations of the complaint as true, but the allegations must supply sufficient "facts to state a claim to relief that is plausible on its face." *Bell Atlantic Corp. v. Twombly,* 550 U.S. 544, 570, 127 S.Ct. 1955, 167 L.Ed.2d 929 (2007); *see also Ashcroft v. Iqbal,* 556 U.S. 662, 129 S.Ct. 1937, 173 L.Ed.2d 868 (2009).

p.763 The FTCA waives the government's immunity in certain tort suits by providing that the "United States shall be liable [for torts] ... in the same manner and to the same extent as a private individual under like circumstances[.]" 28 U.S.C. § 2674. This provision is sometimes called the "private analogue" requirement. *Barnes v. United States,* 448 F.3d 1065, 1066 (8th Cir.2006). The determination of whether a private analogue exists is made in accordance with the law of the place where the relevant act or omission occurred. *Id.* (citing 28 U.S.C. § 1346(b)(1)). Section 1346(b)'s reference to "law of the place" means the law of the State, not any tribal reservation, provides the source of substantive liability under the FTCA. *LaFromboise v. Leavitt,* 439 F.3d 792, 795 (8th Cir.2006). Therefore, we hold that the district court correctly determined Sorace had to demonstrate the existence of an actionable claim under South Dakota law to state a claim under the FTCA.

The district court outlined two choices under South Dakota law for the private analogue under the FTCA.[3] The district court noted that where the alleged negligent act involves conduct peculiar to law enforcement, identifying the appropriate private analogue can be difficult. Under either the negligence standard for a private citizen or the public duty rule, Sorace failed to allege facts sufficient to state a claim for which relief should be granted.

For a private citizen, the analogue for an FTCA claim under South Dakota state law is a negligence claim, which requires proof of duty, breach of that duty, proximate and factual causation, and actual injury. *Hewitt v. Felderman,* 2013 S.D. 91, ¶ 16, 841 N.W.2d 258, 263. The existence of a duty in a negligence claim is a question of law. *Kirlin v. Halverson,* 2008 S.D. 107, ¶ 28, 758 N.W.2d 436, 448 (quoting *State Auto Ins. v. B.N.C.,* 2005 S.D. 89, ¶ 20, 702 N.W.2d 379, 386).

Generally, South Dakota law imposes no affirmative duty to prevent the misconduct of third parties. *Kirlin,* 2008 S.D. 107, ¶ 30, 758 N.W.2d at 448; *Walther v. KPKA Meadowlands Ltd. P'ship,* 1998 S.D. 78, ¶ 17, 581 N.W.2d 527, 531. South p.764 Dakota, however, may find that a duty exists to prevent the misconduct of a third party, if the plaintiff shows (1) the existence of a special relationship between the parties, and (2) the third party's injurious act was foreseeable. *Kirlin,* 2008 S.D. 107, ¶ 31, 758 N.W.2d at 448-49. In the complaint, Sorace alleged that the RST PD was negligent for failing to stop Dillon's vehicle. Sorace failed to allege a special relationship as required for a negligence claim under South Dakota law. The district court properly dismissed Sorace's complaint for failure to state a claim for negligence.

Even if the Court does not apply the negligence standard for a private citizen, Sorace's complaint also failed to state a claim under the public duty rule. Under South Dakota law, the public duty rule "provides that the police owe a duty to the public at large and not to an individual or smaller class of individuals." *Walther,* 1998 S.D. 78, ¶ 17, 581 N.W.2d at 531. South Dakota also has a "special duty" exception to the public-duty rule, which "recognizes that there may be some situations where it is found a duty is owed to a particular class of persons separate from that owed to the general public." *Walther,* 1998 S.D. 78, ¶ 18, 581 N.W.2d at 532. The South Dakota Supreme Court adopted the following four-part test to determine whether a special duty exists: (1) actual knowledge of the dangerous condition; (2) reasonable reliance by persons on the state's representations and conduct; (3) an ordinance or statute that sets forth mandatory acts clearly for the protection of a particular class of persons rather than the public as a whole; and (4) failure by the state to use due care to avoid increasing the risk of harm. *Tipton v. Town of Tabor (Tipton I),* 538 N.W.2d 783, 787 (S.D.1995) (applying the test from *Cracraft v. City of St. Louis Park,* 279 N.W.2d 801, 806-07 (Minn.1979)). Actual knowledge of a dangerous situation alone is insufficient to establish a special duty. *Tipton v. Town of Tabor (Tipton II),* 1997 S.D. 96, ¶ 28, 567 N.W.2d 351, 364.

The district court applied the four part test from *Tipton I* to determine whether the RST PD owed a "special duty" to Melanie Sorace and her children. The district court assumed for purposes of the motion to dismiss that the RST PD had actual knowledge of Dillon's drunk driving, but held that none of the other *Tipton* factors were present. We agree with the district court that Sorace did not allege and cannot allege any of the other *Tipton* factors.

First, Sorace has not alleged any reasonable reliance by Melanie Sorace. For reasonable reliance to have occurred, Sorace must have alleged that Melanie Sorace "depended on specific actions or representations" which caused her to "forgo other alternatives of protecting" herself. *Tipton II,* 1997 S.D. 96, ¶ 31, 567 N.W.2d at 364-65 (citations omitted). The complaint contains no allegation that Melanie Sorace relied on any statement from the RST PD, knew that Dillon was driving while intoxicated, or contacted the police prior to the accident. Instead, Sorace relies on allegations that third parties contacted the RST PD to report Dillon's behavior. Sorace maintains that the statements made to third parties constitutes reasonable reliance when the victims were damaged by the danger that was promised to be remedied. However, Sorace's reliance on statements made to third parties is misplaced. All of the assurances in the cited cases were made to the persons injured or to the minor victims' parents, not to third persons. *See Champagne v. Spokane Humane Society,* 47 Wash.App. 887, 737 P.2d 1279, 1284 (1987) (on the day before the attack, the Society assured the parent of the child later injured that the area would p.765 be patrolled); *De Long v. Erie Cnty.,* 60 N.Y.2d 296, 469 N.Y.S.2d 611, 457 N.E.2d 717, 721 (1983) (emergency dispatcher told victim reporting burglary that police would come "right away"); *Sorichetti by Sorichetti v. City of New York,* 65 N.Y.2d 461, 492 N.Y.S.2d 591, 482 N.E.2d 70, 76 (1985) (police department created the "clear impression" that "some action would be taken" to enforce the order of protection).

In an attempt to demonstrate reasonable reliance, Sorace refers to the affidavit of Elizabeth Bordeaux, Dillon's ex-girlfriend. Bordeaux attested that she contacted the RST PD on the day of the accident to report that Dillon was driving intoxicated, and the dispatcher told her that "action would be taken." While this information may assist in a finding that the RST PD had actual knowledge of the dangerous condition, it does not provide any evidence of reasonable reliance on the part of Melanie Sorace. Under South Dakota law, promises to third parties are insufficient to demonstrate reasonable reliance. *Tipton II,* 1997 S.D. 96, ¶ 32, 567 N.W.2d at 365 ("Reliance must be based on personal assurances."); *Walther,* 1998 S.D. 78, ¶ 28, 581 N.W.2d at 533 ("no personal assurances" to a domestic violence victim from the police that she would be protected); *Pray v. City of Flandreau,* 2011 S.D. 43, ¶ 13, 801 N.W.2d 451, 455 (woman who fell when a dog broke loose from its owner provided "no evidence that she relied on specific actions or representations of the city, which caused her to forego other alternatives of protecting herself"). Likewise, a general belief by others that a proposed danger would be remedied is also not sufficient. *Tipton II,* 1997 S.D. 96, ¶ 33, 567 N.W.2d at 365 ("Trusting upon some feeling they would be safe wherever they went in Tabor is perhaps comprehensible; however, it does not rise to the level of reliance causing them to forgo self-precaution."); *Walther,* 1998 S.D. 78, ¶ 28, 581 N.W.2d at 533 (victim's "general statement that she somehow relied on the system is not enough"). Bordeaux's alleged contact with the RST PD is not enough to show reasonable reliance by Melanie Sorace.

The third factor of South Dakota's special-duty test "'permits recovery against a government entity for negligent failure to enforce its laws only when there is language in a statute or ordinance which shows an intent to protect a particular and circumscribed class of persons.'" *Tipton II,* 1997 S.D. 96, ¶ 35, 567 N.W.2d at 365-66 (quoting *Tipton I,* 538 N.W.2d at 786). The district court held that the Code of Federal Regulations, the Bureau of Indian Affairs (BIA) Manual, the BIA Law Enforcement Handbook, Rosebud Sioux Tribal Code sections 6-1, 6-2, 6-3, a Rosebud Sioux Tribe Rule of Criminal Procedure, and South Dakota Codified Laws §§ 23A-32, 32-23-1, 32-23-1.1, and 32-23-1.3 did not demonstrate an intent to protect a particular class of persons, as required under the third *Tipton* factor.

Sorace claims that the district court erred in finding that federal and tribal regulations, handbooks, and laws were not applicable because they were not the substantive laws of South Dakota. However, we find that only the law of the State is relevant under our analysis of FTCA claims. *See Klett v. Pim,* 965 F.2d 587, 589 (8th Cir.1992) (quoting *Gelley,* 610 F.2d at 562) ("'[F]ederally imposed obligations, whether general or specific, are irrelevant to our inquiry under the FTCA, unless state law imposes a similar obligation upon private persons.'"). Moreover, even if we considered all of the manuals, laws and regulations cited by Sorace, they fail to create a private cause of action under the FTCA.

p.766 First, Sorace's citation to the code of federal regulations is misplaced. 25 C.F.R. §§ 12.12, 12.13 and 12.14 provide the standards and potential penalties for the law enforcement programs managed by the BIA, as set forth in the BIA Manual and the BIA Law Enforcement Handbook. 25 C.F.R. § 11.301(b)(3) gives law enforcement the right to arrest a person if the officer has probable cause to believe that the person committed an offense. None of these provisions identifies a particular class protected and cannot be the basis of a special duty.

Similarly, the handbooks and tribal codes cited by Sorace do not enure to the benefit of a specific group. The BIA Law Enforcement Handbook sections cited by Sorace simply indicate that law enforcement has authority to arrest drivers where there is probable cause to believe the driver is impaired or under the influence of alcohol or drugs. The Rosebud Sioux Tribal Code sections cited by Sorace criminalize driving under the influence of alcohol and reckless driving, provide that an officer may arrest a person for a crime without the crime being committed in the presence of the officer, and allow for damages when a person has suffered a detriment from the unlawful act or omission of another. These citations provide no indication that they are intended to protect any particular class.

Furthermore, the South Dakota statutes cited do not create a private duty to any specific group. South Dakota Codified Laws §§ 32-23-1, 32-23-1.1, and 32-23-1.3 allow law enforcement to arrest, without a warrant, and later criminally charge a driver for suspicion of driving under the influence of alcohol. These are general laws and a circumscribed class of people to be protected is not identified. Likewise, South Dakota Codified Laws § 21-10-1 simply creates a cause of action for nuisance. The South Dakota Supreme Court has already held that the nuisance statute does not "create a special class or mandatory duty, either." *Tipton II,* 1997 S.D. 96, ¶ 36, 567 N.W.2d at 366.

In sum, Sorace's complaint failed to allege a specific South Dakota statute or regulation that imposes a mandatory duty on the police to protect a particular person or class of persons. Therefore, Sorace's complaint also failed to establish this prong of the special duty test. *See Pray,* 2011 S.D. 43, ¶ 9, 801 N.W.2d 451, 454 ("she must show some duty owed to her as an individual or as a member of a class, rather than to the public as a whole").

Finally, we find that the RST PD did not increase the risk of harm to Melanie Sorace and her children by failing to arrest Dillon. *See Tipton II,* 1997 S.D. 96, ¶ 38, 567 N.W.2d 351, 366 ("Under this factor official action must either cause harm itself or expose plaintiffs to new or greater risks, leaving them in a worse position than they were before official action."); *Pray,* 2011 S.D. 43, ¶ 14, 801 N.W.2d at 456 ("The city's actions must either cause the harm itself or have exposed Pray to new or greater risks, leaving Pray in a worse position than she would have been before the city's actions."). In her complaint, Sorace alleges that the RST PD did not arrest Dillon after receiving complaints that he was driving erratically. She does not allege that the police increased Dillon's threat or exposed Melanie Sorace to additional harm that was not otherwise present. As a result, Sorace failed to allege that

Melanie Sorace and her children were in a worse position than before Dillon's erratic driving was reported to the RST PD because of an official action.

We conclude that the district court properly granted the United States' motion to dismiss.

p.767 III.

Sorace also argues that the motion to dismiss should have been converted into a motion for summary judgment because the United States relied on an affidavit[4] in support of its motion.

"If, on a motion under Rule 12(b)(6) ..., matters outside the pleadings are presented to and not excluded by the court, the motion must be treated as one for summary judgment under Rule 56." Fed.R.Civ.P. 12(d). "'Rule 12(b)(6) motions are not automatically converted into motions for summary judgment simply because one party submits additional matters in support of or [in] opposition to the motion.'" *Casazza v. Kiser*, 313 F.3d 414, 417 (8th Cir.2002) (alteration in original) (quoting *Missouri ex rel. Nixon v. Coeur D'Alene Tribe*, 164 F.3d 1102, 1107 (8th Cir.1999)). "A district court does not convert a motion to dismiss into a motion for summary judgment when, for example, it does not rely upon matters outside the pleadings in granting the motion." *Gorog v. Best Buy Co.*, 760 F.3d 787, 791 (8th Cir.2014) (citing *BJC Health Sys. v. Columbia Cas. Co.*, 348 F.3d 685, 688 (8th Cir.2003)).

The district court clearly stated that it was dismissing Sorace's complaint under Fed.R.Civ.P. 12(b)(6) and that it was "in no position to delve into the competing affidavits" regarding whether the police received reports about Dillon. The district court instead stated that it accepted the facts alleged in Sorace's complaint as true, including that the RST PD received multiple reports that a pickup truck was driving erratically through Mission, South Dakota and, therefore, that the RST PD had actual knowledge of Dillon's dangerous driving. Nothing in the record indicates that the district court considered any of the affidavits that were provided by the parties.

We hold the district court did not err as a matter of law in not converting the motion to dismiss into a motion for summary judgment.

IV.

Finally, Sorace appeals from the district court's dismissal of her complaint because she contends that the district court should have granted her request for leave to file an amended complaint rather than dismissing her action. We review for abuse of discretion the district court's decision to deny leave to amend a complaint. *O'Neil*, 574 F.3d at 505; *United States v. Fairview Health Sys.*, 413 F.3d 748, 749 (8th Cir.2005). "Although leave to amend shall be freely given when justice so requires, *see* Fed.R.Civ.P. 15(a), plaintiffs do not have an absolute or automatic right to amend." *Fairview Health Sys.*, 413 F.3d at 749 (citing *Meehan v. United Consumers Club Franchising Corp.*, 312 F.3d 909, 913 (8th Cir.2002)) (internal quotations omitted).

Sorace argues that the district court abused its discretion by not allowing her leave to amend her complaint to allege that the *Tipton* factors were satisfied. Sorace did not submit a proposed amended pleading to the district court, however. Instead, she noted in her response to the United States' motion to dismiss that "if the court grants the motion, plaintiff requests leave to amend the complaint to cure any defect." The District of South p.768 Dakota's Local Rule 15.1 requires a plaintiff to submit a proposed amended pleading with a motion to amend the complaint. A district court does not abuse its discretion in denying leave to amend where a plaintiff has not followed applicable procedural rules. *O'Neil*, 574 F.3d at 505 (citing *Drobnak v. Andersen Corp.*, 561 F.3d 778, 787 (8th Cir.2009)); *see also Meehan*, 312 F.3d at 914 ("[T]he district court was not required to engage in a guessing game.").

Further, the district court did not abuse its discretion because amendment of Sorace's complaint would have been futile. "Futility is a valid basis for denying leave to amend." *Fairview Health Sys.*, 413 F.3d at 749 (citing *Moses.com Sec., Inc. v. Comprehensive Software Sys., Inc.*, 406 F.3d 1052, 1065 (8th Cir.2005)). Although Sorace maintains she could have easily alleged that the *Tipton* factors were satisfied, the record does not support that proposition. In response to United States' motion to dismiss, Sorace offered the affidavits of Elizabeth Bordeaux and Luke Black Bear stating that the RST PD received reports about Dillon prior to his motor vehicle accident with Melanie Sorace. The district court already assumed for purposes of the motion to dismiss that Sorace could have satisfied the first prong of the *Tipton* test such that those affidavits added nothing to the district court's analysis. Sorace's counsel also provided copies of the BIA Manual, the BIA Law Enforcement Handbook, and the Rosebud Sioux Trial Code. We previously held that these tribal handbooks and laws do not protect a particular class of people and do not satisfy the third factor of the *Tipton* test. It is apparent to us that Sorace attempted to satisfy the *Tipton* factors before the district court through these submissions but was unable to do so. Thus, we have before us no evidence that Sorace would have been able to satisfy the *Tipton* factors if she were given an additional opportunity.

Accordingly, we find the district court did not abuse its discretion in refusing to grant Sorace leave to amend her complaint.

The Judgment is affirmed.

[1] The Honorable Ronnie L. White, United States District Judge for the Eastern District of Missouri, sitting by designation.

[2] The Honorable Roberto A. Lange, United States District Judge for the District of South Dakota.

[3] Several courts of appeals have applied a state's public-duty rule when considering claims under the FTCA. *See Stratmeyer v. United States*, 67 F.3d 1340, 1347-48 (7th Cir.1995) (USDA veterinarian did not owe special duty to cattle lessees to quarantine all of the cattle at supplier's farm because there was no evidence of any relationship between them); *Crider v. United States*, 885 F.2d 294, 298 (5th Cir.1989) (United States Park Service rangers owed no duty to arrest a drunk driver who later injured plaintiff in a car accident); *Gelley v. Astra Pharm. Products, Inc.*, 610 F.2d 558, 561 (8th Cir.1979) (no special duty created when the

government allowed a company to market an allegedly misbranded drug). In *United States v. Olson,* the Supreme Court reaffirmed that a court must "look to the state-law liability of private entities, not to that of public entities, when assessing the Government's liability under the FTCA 'in the performance of activities which private persons do not perform.'" 546 U.S. 43, 46, 126 S.Ct. 510, 163 L.Ed.2d 306 (2005) (quoting *Indian Towing Co. v. United States,* 350 U.S. 61, 64, 76 S.Ct. 122, 100 L.Ed. 48 (1955)). Since *Olson,* at least one district court has held that "[t]he 'public duty' doctrine has no application to an FTCA action, however. Whether or not state or local law enforcement officers would be liable under state law on the same or analogous facts is irrelevant under the [FTCA]." *Lumsden v. United States,* 555 F.Supp.2d 580, 595 (E.D.N.C.2008); *see also Durden v. United States,* 736 F.3d 296, 301 (4th Cir.2013) (Army did not breach its duty as landlord to protect resident from rape by Army servicemen). We need not determine whether the public duty rule applies to a FTCA claim, however, because Sorace's complaint fails to allege sufficient facts under either the negligence standard for a private citizen or the public duty rule.

[4] Specifically, Sorace claims that the district court improperly relied on the affidavit of Edwin Young, the acting Chief of Police of the Rosebud Sioux Tribe Law Enforcement Services. Young attested that the Rosebud Sioux Tribe Law Enforcement Services did not receive any telephone calls regarding Dillon's erratic driving prior to Dillon's motor vehicle accident with Melanie Sorace.

785 F.3d 1227 (2015)

Mary Ann METTER, as Personal Representative of the Estate of Edward O. Metter, Deceased, Plaintiff-Appellant

v.

UNITED STATES of America, Defendant-Appellee.

Justin Erickson and Jennifer Erickson, Husband and Wife, Plaintiffs-Appellants

v.

United States of America, Defendant-Appellee.

Nos. 14-2001, 14-2002.

United States Court of Appeals, Eighth Circuit.

Submitted: February 13, 2015.

Filed: May 11, 2015.

Metter v. US, 785 F. 3d 1227 (8th Cir. 2015)

p.1229 Andrew D. Sibbernsen, Sibbernsen, Strigenz & Sibbernsen, P.C., Omaha, NE, argued, for appellants.

Thomas Pulham, Civ. Div., U.S. Dept. of Justice, Washington, DC, argued (Stuart P. Delery, Asst. Atty. Gen., Mark B. Stern, Civ. Div., U.S. Dept of Justice, Washington, DC, Deborah R. Gilg, U.S. Atty., Omaha, NE, on the brief), for appellee.

Before RILEY, Chief Judge, LOKEN and SMITH, Circuit Judges.

RILEY, Chief Judge.

On October 9, 2011, while fishing with his son-in-law and grandson near Gavins Point Dam on the Missouri River in Cedar County, Nebraska, Edward Metter was tragically struck and killed when a parked pickup truck came out of gear and rolled down an unprotected river bank. Mary Ann Metter, Metter's widow and personal representative of his estate, brought survival and wrongful death actions under the Federal Tort Claims Act (FTCA), 28 U.S.C. §§ 1346, 2671-2680, against the U.S. Army Corps of Engineers (Corps), asserting the Corps negligently maintained the site. The grandson, Justin Erickson, and his wife, Jennifer Erickson, brought a separate suit against the Corps raising the same theories of liability for the mental and physical harms to Justin caused by witnessing his grandfather's death and any losses suffered by Jennifer. The Corps filed a motion to dismiss, or in the alternative, for summary judgment. The district court[1] granted the Corps' motion to dismiss the claims under Federal Rules of Civil Procedure 12(b)(1) for lack of subject matter jurisdiction, finding (1) the claims were barred by the FTCA's discretionary function exception, and (2) the United States did not waive sovereign immunity.[2] Mary Ann and the Ericksons (collectively, appellants) appeal. We affirm.

I. BACKGROUND

A popular spot for fishing, Gavins Point Dam, lake, and associated facilities are operated and managed by the Omaha District of the Corps. Guardrails line most of the parking areas along Training Dike Road where Metter was killed. Due to p.1230 historic flooding beginning in May 2011, the Corps removed two sections of guardrail in June 2011 to allow heavy equipment access to the river shoreline and to facilitate ongoing flood-related repairs, closing these areas for public use. David Becker, the Corps' Operations Project Manager, inspected the remaining wooden guardrail posts and determined they needed to be replaced. On August 30, 2011, the Corps hired C.B.M.C., a Tennessee contractor, to install new guardrail posts by September 30, 2011.

On September 19, C.B.M.C. assured the Corps it would complete the project the following week. In an attempt to reduce contract costs and meet the planned September 30 deadline, Corps personnel removed the remaining guardrails and posts on September 28. Becker testified the Corps reopened the area along the river to the public, but did not post parking restrictions or public advisories because he believed removal of the guardrails did not endanger the public. Despite the Corps' repeated attempts to contact C.B.M.C. between September 26 and October 7, C.B.M.C. did not perform as promised. The fatal accident occurred on October 9, before the Corps terminated C.B.M.C.'s contract and re-awarded the project to another contractor. The new contractor replaced the guardrails before November 30.

The appellants brought suit against the Corps under the FTCA, alleging the accident occurred as a result of the Corps' negligence in failing to (1) "timely replace the guardrail and posts along the parking area on Training Dike Road," (2) "make a reasonable inspection of the parking area," (3) "maintain a reasonably safe parking area," and (4) "warn[] the public of the hazardous condition that existed on the parking area." The Corps moved to dismiss the case on jurisdictional grounds, arguing its decisions relating to the removal and re-installation of the guardrails were protected by the discretionary function exception to the FTCA. The district court agreed and granted the motion, and appellants appeal.

II. DISCUSSION

"It is well settled that the United States may not be sued without its consent," *Hinsley v. Standing Rock Child Protective Servs.*, 516 F.3d 668, 671 (8th Cir.2008), but under the FTCA, an injured party can hold the United States liable in tort

> for injury or loss of property, or personal injury or death caused by the negligent or wrongful act or omission of any employee of the Government while acting within the scope of his office or employment, under circumstances where the United States, if a private person, would be liable to the claimant in accordance with the law of the place where the act or omission occurred.

28 U.S.C. § 1346(b)(1). However, 28 U.S.C. § 2680(a)—commonly referred to as the discretionary function exception to the FTCA—prohibits "[a]ny claim ... based upon the exercise or performance or the failure to exercise or perform a discretionary function or duty on the part of a federal agency or an employee of the Government, whether or not the discretion involved be abused."

A two-part test determines when the discretionary function exception applies. First, the agency action must "'involv[e] an element of judgment or choice.'" *United States v. Gaubert*, 499 U.S. 315, 322, 111 S.Ct. 1267, 113 L.Ed.2d 335 (1991) (alteration in original) (quoting *Berkovitz v. United States,* 486 U.S. 531, 536, 108 S.Ct. 1954, 100 L.Ed.2d 531 (1988)). Second, we must "decide[ ] 'whether that judgment is of the kind that the discretionary p.1231 function exception was designed to shield.'" *Id.* at 322-23, 111 S.Ct. 1267 (quoting *Berkovitz,* 486 U.S. at 536, 108 S.Ct. 1954). "'[I]t is the nature of the conduct'" and whether the conduct is "susceptible to policy analysis" "'rather than the status of the actor that governs whether the exception applies.'" *Id.* at 325, 111 S.Ct. 1267 (alteration in original) (quoting *Varig Airlines v. United States,* 467 U.S. 797, 813, 104 S.Ct. 2755, 81 L.Ed.2d 660 (1984)). "[T]he exception 'protects only governmental actions and decisions based on considerations of public policy,'" and there is a rebuttable presumption that the government "agent's acts are grounded in policy" "[w]hen established governmental policy ... allows [the] agent to exercise discretion." *Id.* at 323-24, 111 S.Ct. 1267 (quoting *Berkovitz,* 486 U.S. at 537, 108 S.Ct. 1954); *see also Audio Odyssey, Ltd. v. United States,* 255 F.3d 512, 519 (8th Cir.2001); *Dykstra v. U.S. Bureau of Prisons,* 140 F.3d 791, 795-96 (8th Cir.1998).

"We review de novo a district court's grant of a motion to dismiss under the discretionary function exception to the FTCA." *Dykstra,* 140 F.3d at 795.

Appellants "concede that there was an 'element of choice' in the [Corps'] actions," but propose that after the Corps decided to replace the guardrails, "it [was] no longer exercising a discretionary policy-making function" that was "'susceptible to policy analysis'" and should be required to follow through "in a non-negligent manner." (Quoting *Gaubert,* 499 U.S. at 322, 325, 111 S.Ct. 1267). We must decide whether the Corps' decision—to remove the guardrails and not post warning signs—is "susceptible to policy analysis." We conclude it is.

A. Corps' Actions Were Discretionary

Becker testified two regulations in chapter 3 of the Corps' Engineering Manual XXXX-X-XXX (Manual) were "relevant to the siting of parking areas ... and the necessity of guardrails or other railings at or near parking areas." The first provision, paragraph 3-3(a)(1), provides, in relevant part:

> Overlooks and their support facilities should be sited on gently sloping terrain. The area where the entrance, exit and parking facilities will be located should not exceed 7 percent grades and the section of roadway passing the potential site should not exceed 5 percent grade.

The second provision, paragraph 3-3(a)(2), provides, in relevant part:

> Precipitous drop offs should be made safe by the provision of appropriate railing.

We agree with the district court that nothing in the Manual prescribes "a specific, mandatory duty upon the Corps to install or maintain (or to not remove) guardrails, to provide warnings, or to restrict parking" applicable to Training Dike Road. We also agree that "[t]he use of permissive language, rather than mandatory terms, such as 'must' or 'shall,' shows that these [Manual] provisions are merely guidelines." Becker described the slope of the embankment from the road to the river as "not precipitous" at the site of the accident. The decision to replace the guardrails was made in the context of the operation of a much larger project—the Corps' duty to maintain the associated recreation areas and facilities—and the Corps had authority to decide how to best effectuate those duties.

B. Susceptible to Policy Analysis

In deciding whether the nature of the Corps' actions is "susceptible to policy analysis," "[t]he focus of the inquiry is not on the agent's subjective intent." *Gaubert*, 499 U.S. at 325, 111 S.Ct. 1267. Rather, we look to whether the decision p.1232 being challenged is "grounded in social, economic, or political policy." *Id.* at 323, 111 S.Ct. 1267.

Looking first at appellants' contention that the Corps' failure to warn was not a public policy decision, we find guidance in *Layton v. United States*, 984 F.2d 1496 (8th Cir.1993). In *Layton*, we concluded the United States Forest Service's "decision whether or not to issue warnings [was] susceptible to policy analysis [because] it involve[d] balancing safety against cost: the more effort the Forest Service expended to discover dangers and warn contractors of them, the greater the safety benefit but also the greater the cost to the government." *Id.* at 1504-05; *accord Hinsley*, 516 F.3d at 673 ("[T]he decision to warn is, at its core, a policy decision."); *Demery v. U.S. Dep't of Interior*, 357 F.3d 830, 834 (8th Cir.2004) (concluding the "decision ... whether to warn ... is susceptible to a policy analysis" because it requires balancing interests like "increased safety ... with ... the cost of erecting warnings").

Appellants urge us to follow *Cope v. Scott*, 45 F.3d 445 (D.C.Cir.1995), which held the discretionary function exception did not apply to the National Park Service's failure to warn adequately about the nature of a road surface because the Park Service could not "articulate how the placement of additional or different signs on Beach Drive implicates ... economic, social, or political concerns." *Id.* at 452. The Park Service posted "no less than twenty-three traffic control, warning, and informational signs" on the section of road where an accident occurred, and there was no evidence that "engineering and aesthetic concerns" prevented the posting of additional warning signs. *Id.* at 451-52 (internal marks omitted). In *Cope*, the court found the Park Service had already made a specific policy decision to favor safety over aesthetics and this involved "engineering judgment" based on objective scientific principles not susceptible to policy analysis. *Id.* at 452. Our facts are different, and *Cope* is not binding. Appellants have not alleged or presented evidence to show the Corps had either adopted a safety policy or established priorities to guide the Corps' decisions in maintaining Training Dike Road and the facilities at Gavins Point Dam, and appellants have failed to rebut the presumption that the Corps' decision not to post warning signs was grounded in policy. *See Gaubert*, 499 U.S. at 323-24, 111 S.Ct. 1267.

We next turn to appellants' proposition that the Corps' failure to replace the guardrails by a specific date was not itself a policy decision, but instead was a negligent failure to follow through on an earlier policy determination that the guardrails should be replaced. Appellants rely on *Aslakson v. United States*, 790 F.2d 688, 693 (8th Cir.1986), for the proposition that "[w]here the challenged governmental activity involves safety considerations under an established policy rather than the balancing of competing public policy considerations, the rationale for the [discretionary function] exception falls away." Appellants claim there is evidence of an "established policy" of protecting the area where the accident occurred because "guardrails ha[d] been in place for at least thirty years." Appellants argue the "policy was reaffirmed when Mr. Becker determined that the deteriorating guardrails should be replaced" by September 30.

Unlike the government agency in *Aslakson*, whose "policy clearly required it to elevate its power lines if safety considerations compelled such action," *id.*, there was no clear policy that bound the Corps to prioritize safety considerations or maintain guardrails. As the district court observed, p.1233 "[t]he Corps could have decided to issue a binding policy," but chose not to.

We recognize a distinction between the Corps (1) exercising discretion and deciding to replace the guardrails, and (2) deciding to issue a regulation or forming a policy requiring the installation or maintenance of guardrails. Because the Corps had the discretion to decide if, how, and when to replace the guardrails, it had the discretion to alter its initial decision to replace the guardrails by September 30 when the first contractor failed to perform. *See, e.g., Gaubert*, 499 U.S. at 331, 111 S.Ct. 1267 (deciding conduct of bank regulators did not "fall outside the discretionary function exception" when the conduct "involved the mere application of technical skills and business expertise ... at the operational level" rather than at a policy-making level, because "the challenged actions involved the exercise of choice and judgment"); *Shansky v. United States*, 164 F.3d 688, 695 (1st Cir.1999) (determining "[a]n agency that has discretion to make policy choices" can adjust the "balance of relevant concerns" over time, and when the "overall policy decision [is] protected by the discretionary function exception," the protection extends to "component" decisions).

More importantly, the Corps need not have made a "conscious decision regarding policy factors," so long as the decision to remove the guardrails was susceptible to a "balancing of public policy objectives." *Kiehn v. United States*, 984 F.2d 1100, 1105 (10th Cir.1993) (internal marks omitted). Here, as the district court observed, the Corps had to "balance the overall purpose of Training Dike Road with the recreational uses of the area, the allocation of funds," the timing of repairs and maintenance work, "and the safety of drivers," anglers, and other users. The Corps removed the guardrails and posts itself to save money and to expedite the project— both reasons reflect the discretionary exercise of choice and judgment. When the first contractor, C.B.M.C., failed to perform in accordance with the September 30 schedule, the Corps exercised choice and judgment to retain a new contractor with a revised schedule, yet no guardrails were at the site on October 9, 2011. We conclude the Corps' discretionary actions were "susceptible to policy analysis" within the meaning of *Gaubert*.

III. CONCLUSION

We affirm the well-reasoned decision of the district court.

[1] The Honorable John M. Gerrard, United States District Judge for the District of Nebraska.

[2] The district court also granted the Corps' motion to substitute the United States as defendant. *See Duncan v. Dep't of Labor*, 313 F.3d 445, 447 (8th Cir.2002) (per curiam).

781 F.3d 408 (2015)

TRI-NATIONAL, INC., Plaintiff-Appellee

v.

Larry D. YELDER; Yelder-N-Son Trucking, Inc., Defendants.
Canal Insurance Company, Defendant-Appellant.

No. 14-1595.

United States Court of Appeals, Eighth Circuit.

Submitted: January 13, 2015.

Filed: March 20, 2015.

p.410 Daniel Thomas Rabbitt, Jr., argued, Saint Louis, MO, (Allan S. Jones and Kristi Anne Driskill, Vestavia Hills, AL, on the brief), for Plaintiff-Appellee.

Shanna Keel Surratt, argued, Cape Girardeau, MO, (Susan P. Layton, Stephen Ray Southard, and Wade Schuster, Cape Girardeau, MO, on the brief) for Defendant-Appellant.

Before RILEY, Chief Judge, COLLOTON and KELLY, Circuit Judges.

RILEY, Chief Judge.

This insurance dispute presents an issue of first impression in our circuit: whether the federally mandated Motor Carrier Act (MCA) of 1980 MCS-90[1] endorsement for motor carriers requires a tortfeasor's insurer to compensate an injured party when the injured party has already been compensated by its own insurer. The district court[2] decided the MCS-90 endorsement requires such compensation, and we agree. Having appellate jurisdiction under 28 U.S.C. § 1291, we affirm the district court's summary judgment.

I. BACKGROUND

On June 14, 2007, while operating a semi tractor and trailer, Larry D. Yelder Sr., an employee of Yelder-N-Son Trucking, Inc. p.411 (collectively, Yelder defendants), collided with a Tri-National, Inc. truck, causing extensive property damage. Tri-National filed a claim with its insurer, Harco Insurance Company, which paid Tri-National $91,100 and retained a subrogation interest in the claim.

At the time of the accident, the Yelder defendants were insured by Canal Insurance Company under policy number 488142 (Canal policy), which included an MCS-90 endorsement. In 2010, in the District Court for the Middle District of Alabama, Canal sought a declaratory judgment against the Yelder defendants and Harco, among others, declaring (1) Canal had no duty to defend or indemnify the Yelder defendants under the Canal policy, and (2) the MCS-90 endorsement did not require Canal to satisfy Harco's subrogation claim. The Alabama court entered default judgment against the Yelder defendants only, stating Canal had no duty to defend or indemnify the Yelder defendants under the Canal policy, but the Alabama court made no declaration about the MCS-90 endorsement.

In June 2010, Harco filed a motion to dismiss for failure to join an indispensable party, Tri-National. At a pretrial conference, Harco represented to the Alabama court that it was "not [Harco's] intention to ever make a claim against [Canal]," and that it "would be Tri-National who would go after Canal, not Harco." Canal responded that "[i]f it's on the record that [Harco] won't go after Canal, then we're okay with that." The Alabama district court then dismissed Harco without prejudice "[b]y agreement of the parties made during a pretrial conference."

Tri-National sued the Yelder defendants in Missouri state court and in July 2012 obtained a $91,100 default judgment. In November 2012, Tri-National filed a petition for equitable garnishment in Missouri state court against Canal in an effort to collect on the Missouri state court's default judgment. According to Tri-National, the decision to file the petition was Harco's, Tri-National had no input in the decision, and any proceeds from the garnishment action are "supposed to go directly to Harco."

Claiming diversity jurisdiction under 28 U.S.C. § 1332(a)(1), Canal removed the action to the federal district court for the Eastern District of Missouri. On opposing motions for summary judgment, the district court granted Tri-National's motion and denied Canal's. Canal appeals, claiming the district court erred by finding (1) Tri-National was the real party in interest, rather than its insurer, Harco; (2) the Alabama dismissal did not bar Tri-National's suit for equitable garnishment in Missouri; and (3) the MCS-90 endorsement required Canal to satisfy Tri-National's default judgment against the Yelder defendants.

II. DISCUSSION

A district court must "grant summary judgment if the movant shows that there is no genuine dispute as to any material fact and the movant is entitled to judgment as a matter of law." Fed.R.Civ.P. 56(a). We review the district court's grant of summary judgment de novo. *See, e.g., Allstate Indem. Co. v. Rice,* 755 F.3d 621, 623 (8th Cir.2014).

A. Real Party in Interest

Canal contends the district court erred by finding Tri-National, not Harco, is the real party in interest in this case. *See* Fed.R.Civ.P. 17(a)(1) ("An action must be prosecuted in the name of the real party in interest."). When removing the action to federal court, Canal asserted diversity jurisdiction, and we consult Missouri substantive law to determine whether p.412 Harco, as the subrogee, is the real party in interest. *See Cascades Dev. of Minn., LLC v. Nat'l Specialty Ins.,* 675 F.3d 1095, 1098 (8th Cir.2012) ("A 'real party in interest is the person who, under governing substantive law, is entitled to enforce the right asserted.'" (quoting *Iowa Pub. Serv. Co. v. Med. Bow Coal Co.,* 556 F.2d 400, 404 (8th Cir.1977))); *cf. Dubuque Stone Prods. Co. v. Fred L. Gray Co.,* 356 F.2d 718, 723 (8th Cir.1966) ("In diversity cases, state substantive law is consulted to determine whether an assignee qualifies as a real party in interest under Rule 17(a).").

Although Tri-National received $91,100 in payment for its loss from Harco, Tri-National, not Harco, holds the default judgment from the Missouri state court against the Yelder defendants. In Missouri, Tri-National, as "the judgment creditor[,] may proceed in equity against" the Yelder defendants and Canal "to reach and apply the insurance money to the satisfaction of the judgment," Mo.Rev.Stat. § 379.200, and Harco may not. "Unlike some states, which provide that legal title to a property damage claim passes to the injured party's insurer once the insurer pays the injured party's claim, Missouri provides that the legal title to the cause of action remains in the insured, and that the insurer's only interest is an equitable right to subrogation." *Hagar v. Wright Tire & Appliance, Inc.,* 33 S.W.3d 605, 610 (Mo. Ct.App.2000). "The *exclusive right* to pursue the tortfeasor remains with the insured, which holds the proceeds for the [subrogee] insurer." *Keisker v. Farmer,* 90 S.W.3d 71, 74 (Mo.2002) (en banc) (emphasis added). "In a subrogation situation, since the insured still holds the legal right to the claim, the insurer cannot sue the tortfeasor directly but must wait and assert its subrogation interest against any recovery the insured makes against the tortfeasor." *Hagar,* 33 S.W.3d at 610.

"The only relevant exception to this rule is when the insured assigns his or her property damage claim against the tortfeasor to the insurer.... An assignment... gives the insurer full legal title to the claim and permits the insurer to pursue it against the tortfeasor." *Id.* With no evidence of an assignment in the record before us, Tri-National, not Harco, is the only appropriate plaintiff to bring this equitable garnishment action under Missouri substantive law.

Canal cites *United States v. Aetna Casualty & Surety Co.,* 338 U.S. 366, 70 S.Ct. 207, 94 L.Ed. 171 (1949), where the Supreme Court decided an "important question under the Federal Tort Claims Act" (FTCA)—whether "an insurance company [may] bring suit in its own name against the United States upon a claim to which it has become subrogated by payment to an insured who would have been able to bring such an action." *Id.* at 367-68, 70 S.Ct. 207. In *Aetna Casualty,* the Court affirmed three courts of appeals who had allowed the insurers' suits to proceed. *See id.* at 368-69, 383, 70 S.Ct. 207. The Court analyzed the question in consideration of a statute that forbade assignment of claims against the United States, at least partly "to prevent possible multiple payment of claims." *Id.* at 368, 373, 70 S.Ct. 207. The Court concluded "it was the understanding of Congress that subrogation claims were not within the bar of [the FTCA anti-assignment statute] when it passed the [FTCA]." *Id.* at 376, 70 S.Ct. 207. The Supreme Court then stated,

> If then, [the anti-assignment statute] is inapplicable, the [United States] Government must defend suits by subrogees as if it were a private person. Rule 17(a) of the Federal Rules of Civil Procedure, 28 U.S.C., which were specifically made applicable to Tort Claims litigation, provides that "Every action shall p.413 be prosecuted in the name of the real party in interest," and of course an insurer-subrogee, who has substantive equitable rights, qualifies as such. If the subrogee has paid an entire loss suffered by the insured, it is the only real party in interest and must sue in its own name.

Id. at 380-81, 70 S.Ct. 207.

Canal argues we should apply this last statement from *Aetna Casualty* in this case—a suit based on diversity of citizenship, not the FTCA—and find Harco, the subrogee, is the real party in interest. We question whether this extension of *Aetna Casualty*—a case whose reasoning is firmly grounded on the fact that the United States was a defendant in the FTCA suit—is proper. *See, e.g., St. Paul Fire & Marine Ins. Co. v. Universal Builders Supply,* 409 F.3d 73, 81 (2d Cir.2005) (opining that in

Aetna Casualty, "the Supreme Court[] discuss[ed] the requirements of Rule 17(a) in the context of subrogation" and making no reference to the FTCA); *Krueger v. Cartwright,* 996 F.2d 928, 931-32 (7th Cir.1993) ("The general rule in federal court is that if an insurer has paid the entire claim of its insured, the insurer is the real party in interest under Federal Rule of Civil Procedure 17(a) and must sue in its own name." (citing *Aetna Casualty,* 338 U.S. at 380-81, 70 S.Ct. 207)); *Dudley v. Smith,* 504 F.2d 979, 983 (5th Cir.1974). We do agree with the *Dudley* court's observation that "where the suit is by the insured ... for the full amount of the loss,... [a]ny multiplicity of suit risk can be obviated by final judgment of the district court." *Id.* We conclude Canal is at no risk of being subjected to more than one suit here, and a reading of *Aetna Casualty* does not change our conclusion to apply Missouri substantive law establishing Tri-National as the real party in interest.

B. Alabama Litigation

Canal claims the Alabama court's judgment precludes the Missouri federal district court from considering this case under the doctrines of res judicata (claim preclusion) and collateral estoppel (issue preclusion), which bar a rehearing of the issue here.

"'The law of the forum that rendered the first judgment controls the res judicata analysis.'" *C.H. Robinson Worldwide, Inc. v. Lobrano,* 695 F.3d 758, 764 (8th Cir.2012) (quoting *Laase v. Cnty. of Isanti,* 638 F.3d 853, 856 (8th Cir.2011)). Because the first judgment here was by the United States District Court for the Middle District of Alabama, sitting in diversity, "we must give that federal diversity judgment the same claim-preclusive effect that [Alabama] state courts would give to a state court judgment." *Id.* (citing *Semtek Int'l., Inc. v. Lockheed Martin Corp.,* 531 U.S. 497, 508, 121 S.Ct. 1021, 149 L.Ed.2d 32 (2001)). In Alabama, in order for either res judicata or collateral estoppel to bar a second claim, a final judgment on the merits of the prior claim is required. *See, e.g., Equity Res. Mgmt., Inc. v. Vinson,* 723 So.2d 634, 636 (Ala. 1998) (res judicata); *Shelby Cnty. Planning Comm'n v. Seale,* 564 So.2d 900, 901-02 (Ala.1990) (collateral estoppel).

The Alabama court here entered two judgments. In the first, it granted a default judgment in favor of Canal as to the Yelder defendants only, stating Canal had no duty to defend or indemnify the Yelder defendants under the Canal policy and making no determination on the merits as to Canal's obligations under the MCS-90 endorsement to Tri-National (who was not a party to the suit) or even to Harco (who was a party). In the second judgment, the Alabama court dismissed Harco without prejudice "[b]y agreement of the parties," with the expressed understanding p.414 that "Tri-National is not a party so they can still sue [Canal]." We conclude the Alabama court did not render a prior final judgment on the merits as to Tri-National's present claim on the MCS-90 endorsement issue and therefore Tri-National's claim is not barred.[3] *See Ex parte Sealy, LLC,* 904 So.2d 1230, 1236 (Ala.2004) ("'The effect of a voluntary dismissal without prejudice is to render the proceedings a nullity and leave the parties as if the action had never been brought.'" (quoting *In re Piper Aircraft Distrib. Sys. Antitrust Litig.,* 551 F.2d 213, 219 (8th Cir.1977))).

C. MCS-90 Endorsement[4]

Canal argues the district court erred by finding the MCS-90 endorsement obligated Canal to reimburse Tri-National for its losses.

"Congress enacted the MCA, in part, to address abuses that had arisen in the interstate trucking industry which threatened public safety," where motor carriers attempted "to avoid financial responsibility for accidents that occurred while goods were being transported in interstate commerce." *Canal Ins. Co. v. Distrib. Servs., Inc.,* 320 F.3d 488, 489 (4th Cir.2003). "[T]he Secretary of Transportation issued a regulation mandating that every liability insurance policy covering a 'motor carrier' contain the MCS-90 endorsement." *Id.; see* 49 C.F.R. § 387.15, illus. I. "The MCS-90 provides a broad guaranty that the insurer will pay certain judgments incurred by the insured regardless of whether the motor vehicle involved is specifically described in the policy or whether the loss was otherwise excluded by the terms of the policy." *Century Indem. Co. v. Carlson,* 133 F.3d 591, 594 (8th Cir.1998). "[T]he primary purpose of the MCS-90 is to assure that injured members of the public are able to obtain judgment from negligent authorized interstate carriers." *John Deere Ins. Co. v. Nueva,* 229 F.3d 853, 857 (9th Cir.2000). "The operation and effect of the MCS-90 endorsement is a matter of federal law." *Canal Ins.,* 320 F.3d at 492.

The MCS-90 endorsement states,

> In consideration of the premium stated in the policy to which this endorsement is attached, the insurer (the company) agrees to pay, within the limits of liability described herein, any final judgment recovered against the insured for public liability resulting from negligence in the operation, maintenance or use of motor vehicles subject to the financial responsibility requirements of Sections 29 and 30 of the Motor Carrier Act of 1980 regardless of whether or not each motor vehicle is specifically described in the policy and whether or not such negligence occurs on any route or in any territory authorized to be served by the insured or elsewhere....
>
> It is further understood and agreed that, upon failure of the company to pay any final judgment recovered against the insured as provided herein, the judgment creditor may maintain an action in any court of competent jurisdiction against the company to compel such payment.

p.415 49 C.F.R. § 387.15, illus. I. "MCS-90 endorsements are not treated as coverage where *other insurance policies are available* to provide full coverage for the victim's injuries." *Nat'l Indem. Co. v. Ozark Mountain Sightseeing, Inc.,* 46 Fed.Appx. 864, 865 (8th Cir.2002) (unpublished per curiam) (emphasis added); *see also Carolina Cas. Ins. Co. v. Yeates,* 584 F.3d 868, 871 (10th Cir.2009) (en banc) (holding "the MCS-90 endorsement only applies where: (1) the underlying insurance policy to which the endorsement is attached does not provide coverage for the motor carrier's accident, *and* (2) the motor carrier's insurance coverage is either not sufficient to satisfy the federally-prescribed minimum levels of financial responsibility or is nonexistent").

Canal urges us to deny coverage to Tri-National under the Yelder defendants' MCS-90 endorsement because *Tri-National's* insurance policy, through Harco, provided full compensation for Tri-National's injuries, and Tri-National has already been made whole for its losses by Harco. Canal proposes the injured party's own insurance be considered as other available insurance that would preclude coverage under the MCS-90 endorsement. *See, e.g., Nat'l Indem.*, 46 Fed.Appx. at 865. As the district court set out in detail, Canal tries to bolster its argument by citing cases that do not allow coverage under the MCS-90 endorsement as a resolution of the dispute among various insurers of the tortfeasor motor carrier. But those cases do not address the situation here, where the benefit of the judgment is not for the tortfeasor's insurer and ultimately will go to Harco, the injured party's insurer, as subrogee.

We find Canal's proposal—that Tri-National must wait to receive payment on its claim with Harco until Tri-National receives payment on its default judgment against the Yelder defendants, likely years after the negligent act—untenable. Canal would have us remove the MCA's protection against negligent tortfeasors for members of the public who prudently carry their own insurance, shifting the burden of protection and the financial burden from the tortfeasor's insurer to the injured party's insurer. We find Canal's proposition "would defeat the purpose of the regulations adopted to implement the [MCA], which is to 'assure that injured members of the public would be able to obtain judgments collectible against negligent authorized carriers.'" *Global Hawk Ins. Co. v. Century-Nat'l Ins. Co.,* 203 Cal.App.4th 1458, 138 Cal.Rptr.3d 363, 369 (2012) (quoting *T.H.E. Ins. Co. v. Larsen Intermodal Servs., Inc.,* 242 F.3d 667, 672 (5th Cir.2001)[5]).

Previously, in a controversy among tortfeasors' insurers, one of whom purchased an assignment of the injured party's judgment against the tortfeasor and then sought contribution from the other tortfeasors' insurers, we stated that a policy "ensuring speedy satisfaction of judgments attributed to negligent truckers[ ] is best served by a rule that allows ultimate financial burdens to be allocated *after* injured members of the public are compensated." *Redland Ins. Co. v. Shelter Mut. Ins. Co.,* 193 F.3d 1021, 1022 (8th Cir.1999). Here too, we do not want to "encourage insurers" like Harco "to engage in wrangling over such allocations *before* the public is compensated," *id.* at 1022-23, rather than p.416 satisfy Tri-National's claim from the out-set, as Harco did in this case.

We also note that under the MCS-90 endorsement, Canal has the right—and Harco does not—to demand reimbursement from the Yelder defendants. *See* 49 C.F.R. § 387.15, illus. I ("The insured agrees to reimburse the company for any payment made by the company on account of any accident, claim, or suit involving a breach of the terms of the policy, and for any payment that the company would not have been obligated to make under the provisions of the policy except for the agreement contained in this endorsement.").

We conclude that the fact Harco satisfied Tri-National's claim does not preclude Tri-National from asserting its rights as a member of the general public under the MCS-90 endorsement.

III. CONCLUSION

We agree with the district court that the circumstance of Tri-National carrying its own insurance with Harco does not absolve Canal of its obligations under the MCS-90 endorsement. We affirm.

[1] Pub.L. No. 96-296, 94 Stat. 793.

[2] The Honorable Stephen N. Limbaugh, Jr., United States District Judge for the Eastern District of Missouri.

[3] Canal also asserts Tri-National is judicially estopped from bringing this claim because Harco stated in the Alabama litigation that it did "not [intend] to ever make a claim against [Canal]." Like the district court, we find no inconsistency and note Harco stated "[it] would be Tri-National who would go after Canal, not Harco," which is exactly what has happened here.

[4] An MCS-90 Endorsement is an "Endorsement for Motor Carrier Policies of Insurance for Public Liability Under Sections 29 and 30 of the [MCA]." 49 C.F.R. § 387.15, illus. I.

[5] The Fifth Circuit approved the reasoning of the First Circuit in *Canal Insurance Co. v. Carolina Casualty Insurance Co.,* 59 F.3d 281, 283 (1st Cir.1995), describing the MCS-90 obligation "as one of suretyship" and decided "the insurer's obligations under MCS-90 are triggered when the policy to which it is attached provides no coverage to the insured." *T.H.E.,* 242 F.3d at 672.

S.H., a minor, by her guardian ad litem, Chantal Holt; WILLIAM KENNETH HOLT; CHANTAL HOLT, Plaintiffs-Appellees,

v.

UNITED STATES OF AMERICA, Defendant-Appellant.

No. 15-15000.

United States Court of Appeals, Ninth Circuit.

Argued and Submitted December 15, 2016 — San Francisco, California.

Filed April 10, 2017.

Appeal from the United States District Court for the Eastern District of California; D.C. No. 2:11-cv-01963-MCE-DAD, Morrison C. England, Jr, District Judge, Presiding.

John Samuel Koppel (argued) and Mark B. Stern, Attorneys, Appellate Staff; Benjamin B. Wagner, United States Attorney; Benjamin C. Mizer, Principal Deputy Assistant Attorney General; Civil Division, United States Department of Justice, Washington, D.C.; for Defendant-Appellant.

Steven B. Stevens (argued), Steven B. Stevens APC, Los Angeles, California; Martin M. Berman, Law Offices of Martin M. Berman, Palm Springs, California; for Plaintiffs-Appellees.

Before: Carlos F. Lucero,[*] Susan P. Graber, and Andrew D. Hurwitz, Circuit Judges.

Opinion by Judge Lucero, Concurrence by Judge Graber.

SUMMARY[**]

Federal Tort Claims Act

The panel vacated the district court's judgment in favor of plaintiffs who brought a Federal Tort Claims Act ("FTCA") action against the United States; held that the plaintiffs' claims arose in Spain and therefore were barred by the FTCA's foreign country exception; and remanded with instructions to dismiss for lack of subject matter jurisdiction.

Plaintiff S.H. was born prematurely while her family was stationed at a United States Air Force base in Spain, and as a consequence of her premature birth, S.H. suffered a permanent brain injury that led to a diagnosis of cerebral palsy after she returned to the United States.

The FTCA generally waives the United States' sovereign immunity from suits in torts, but the waiver is subject to certain exceptions. Under the foreign country exception, the FTCA's waiver of immunity does not apply to any claim arising in a foreign country.

The panel held that an injury is suffered where the harm first impinges upon the body, even if it is later diagnosed elsewhere. The panel concluded that the brain injury S.H. suffered at or near the time of her birth impinged upon her body in

Spain; thus, that was where the plaintiffs' claims arose. The panel further held that S.H.'s cerebral palsy was derivative of the harm she sustained at birth.

Judge Graber concurred in the result. She wrote separately because, in her view, the timing and content of the administrative claim filed by plaintiffs, while they were still in Spain, foreclosed their claims under the FTCA.

OPINION

LUCERO, Circuit Judge.

In *Sosa v. Alvarez-Machain*, 542 U.S. 692 (2004), the Supreme Court held that the foreign country exception to the Federal Tort Claims Act ("FTCA") "bars all claims based on any injury suffered in a foreign country." *Id.* at 712. The Court left unanswered, however, the issue currently before us: How to determine where an injury is "suffered." We hold that an injury is suffered where the harm first "impinge[s]" upon the body, even if it is later diagnosed elsewhere. *See* Restatement (First) Conflict of Laws § 377, n.1 (1934).

Applying that test to the facts of this case, we conclude that the foreign country exception bars plaintiffs' claims. S.H., the daughter of William and Chantal Holt, was born prematurely while the family was stationed at a United States Air Force ("USAF") base in Spain. As a consequence of her premature birth, S.H. sustained a permanent injury to the white matter of her brain; she was diagnosed as suffering from cerebral palsy after the family returned to the United States. The Holts filed suit against the United States, contending that officials at a USAF base in California negligently approved the family's request for commandsponsored travel to a base in Spain ill-equipped to deal with Mrs. Holt's medical needs. They further argue that S.H.'s injury—the cerebral palsy diagnosis—first occurred upon their return to the United States. At trial, the district court agreed that the injury occurred in South Carolina and awarded damages of $10,409,700. Although we are sympathetic to the plaintiffs' situation, we agree with the United States that the injury at issue was suffered in Spain. We exercise jurisdiction under 28 U.S.C. § 1291 and reverse.

I

A

Mr. Holt is a Master Sergeant in the USAF. He and his wife have four children. In 2004, when the family was stationed at Edwards Air Force Base in California, Mr. Holt was informed that he was being transferred to the USAF Air Base at Rota Naval Station in Spain. Shortly thereafter, a pregnancy test at the Edwards Air Force Base medical clinic confirmed that Mrs. Holt was pregnant with their third child.

After learning he was to be transferred overseas, Mr. Holt requested command-sponsored travel for his family. To obtain approval for this program, family members must be screened to ensure that the overseas base is capable of addressing their medical needs. Dr. Richard Stahlman, chief of the medical staff at Edwards Air Force Base, approved the Holt family's command-sponsored travel to

Spain. The district court found that Dr. Stahlman knew Mrs. Holt was pregnant and had experienced two prior preterm deliveries and a miscarriage at the time he cleared her for overseas travel.

In March 2005, when Mrs. Holt was approximately twenty weeks pregnant, the family relocated to Spain. There, Mrs. Holt was treated by Dr. Dennis Szurkus, a specialist in obstetrics and gynecology at Naval Hospital Rota. During an ultrasound appointment on May 11, 2005, Dr. Szurkus determined that Mrs. Holt was exhibiting signs of preterm labor and had her transferred by ambulance to an off-base hospital—Puerto Real Hospital—where she underwent an emergency cesarean section. S.H. was born on May 12, at approximately 31 weeks gestation. She had difficulty eating and breathing and was kept in the neonatal intensive care unit for seventeen days.

In the months following S.H.'s birth, the Holts saw several doctors in Spain regarding her medical issues and expressed concern that S.H. was not developing like her two older siblings, both of whom were also born preterm. Doctors told the Holts that S.H. had strabismus, poor head control, low tone in her abdominal muscles, and significant motor and developmental delays. S.H. also experienced seizure-like symptoms, for which she was prescribed phenobarbital. When she was approximately five months old, S.H. underwent an MRI, which showed periventricular leukomalacia, an injury to the white matter of her brain.

At around nine months of age, S.H. was evaluated by a neurologist, Dr. Lisa Smith, who found that S.H. had abnormally brisk reflexes and a mild increase in dynamic tone in her lower extremities. Dr. Smith did not rule out cerebral palsy at that time but declined to render a diagnosis. Two other doctors in Spain did conclude that S.H. had cerebral palsy.[1]

The family returned to the United States in mid-2006. Late that year, S.H. was diagnosed with tetraplegia of all four extremities. At the age of two, while living in South Carolina, S.H. was definitively diagnosed with cerebral palsy. It is undisputed that S.H.'s premature birth was the cause of her cerebral palsy.

B

In June 2006, while the Holts were still in Spain, they filed an administrative claim seeking damages from the government for S.H.'s "catastrophic neurological injuries, seizures, learning deficits, physical limitations," and "cerebral palsy." They alleged that these injuries resulted from the negligent approval of Mrs. Holt's command-sponsored travel overseas. The administrative claim was denied.

Having exhausted administrative remedies, the Holts filed the instant action in district court. The government unsuccessfully moved for summary judgment, contending that the FTCA's foreign country exception barred the Holts' medical malpractice claims. Following a bench trial, the court awarded the Holts $10,409,700 in damages. The government filed a motion to alter or amend the judgment under Fed. R. Civ. P. 59(e). The court granted the motion in part but ultimately declined to alter the damages award. The government timely appealed the amended judgment and all related interlocutory orders.

II

We review a district court's findings of fact following a bench trial for clear error. *Kohler v. Presidio Int'l, Inc.*, 782 F.3d 1064, 1068 (9th Cir. 2015). However, "[w]hether the United States is immune from liability in a FTCA action is a question of federal law subject to de novo review." *Montes v. United States*, 37 F.3d 1347, 1351 (9th Cir. 1994) (italics omitted).

The FTCA generally waives the United States' sovereign immunity from suits in tort, "render[ing] the Government liable in tort as a private individual would be under like circumstances." *Richards v. United States*, 369 U.S. 1, 6 (1962); *see also* 28 U.S.C. § 2674. But that waiver is subject to certain exceptions. *See generally* 28 U.S.C. § 2680. Under the foreign country exception, the FTCA's waiver of immunity does not apply to "[a]ny claim arising in a foreign country." *Id.* § 2680(k).

In *Sosa*, the Supreme Court held that the foreign country exception "bars all claims based on any injury suffered in a foreign country, regardless of where the tortious act or omission occurred." 542 U.S. at 712. The Court noted that the foreign country exception codified Congress' "unwilling[ness] to subject the United States to liabilities depending upon the laws of a foreign power." *Id.* at 707 (alteration in original) (quoting *United States v. Spelar*, 338 U.S. 217, 221 (1949)). At the time the FTCA was passed, "the dominant principle in choice-of-law analysis for tort cases was *lex loci delicti:* courts generally applied the law of the place where the injury occurred." *Id.* at 705. Accordingly, the Court concluded that Congress likely intended the phrase "arising in" to have the same meaning in § 2680(k) as it did in state choice-of-law statutes: that is, to "express the position that a claim arises where the harm occurs." *Id.* at 711.[2]

The question at the center of this appeal is where S.H.'s injury was "suffered" for the purposes of the foreign country exception. *Id.* at 712. The *Sosa* opinion offers various formulations of *lex loci delicti,* but provides little guidance on this specific issue. *See, e.g., id.* at 705 (claim arises "where the last act necessary to establish liability occurred; *i.e.,* the jurisdiction in which injury was received" (quoting John W. Ester, *Borrowing Statutes of Limitation & Conflict of Laws,* 15 U. Fla. L. Rev. 33, 47 (1962))); *id.* at 706 ("the place where the harmful force takes effect upon the body" (quoting Restatement (First) of Conflict of Laws § 377, n.1 (1934) (emphasis omitted))). In the ordinary case, an injury will be experienced in the same place it is inflicted, thereby obviating the need for further analysis. *See, e.g., id.* at 698 (seeking damages for false arrest in Mexico). However, the inquiry becomes more complicated when, as in this case, plaintiffs allege injuries manifesting after the initial infliction of harm.

The district court concluded that state accrual law should determine where an injury is suffered. Relying on California law, it held that S.H.'s cerebral palsy occurred in the United States because it was not until the Holts arrived in South Carolina that doctors could identify S.H.'s symptoms as cerebral palsy. But as we have previously noted, "[q]uestions of interpretation under the [FTCA's] exclusion provisions are controlled by federal law." *Ramirez v. United States*, 567 F.2d 854, 856 (9th Cir. 1977); *accord United States v. Neustadt*, 366 U.S. 696, 706 (1961) ("[W]hether [a] claim is outside the intended scope of the Federal Tort Claims Act . . . depends solely upon what Congress meant by the language it used. . . ."). The district court acknowledged this principle as a general matter but concluded that because California law governed the United States' liability under 28 U.S.C. § 1346(b)(1), it also determined where the Holts' claims arose. However, § 2680(k) states that § 1346(b) "shall not apply to" any claim falling within the foreign country exception.

The district court also failed to recognize that the question of when a claim accrues for statute of limitations purposes is analytically distinct from the question of where a claim arises under the foreign country exception. *See Manemann v. United States*, 381 F.2d 704, 705 (10th Cir. 1967) ("[I]n the case at bar we are not concerned with either the time or place of an accrued cause of action for the purpose of applying a statute of limitations or a principle of conflict of law. We are concerned only as to whether appellant's claim arose in a foreign country within the contemplation of section 2680(k). . . ."); *In re Joint E. & S. Dist. Asbestos Litig.*, 721 F. Supp. 433, 435 (E.D.N.Y. & S.D.N.Y. 1988) (stating that the "last event" required to establish liability "is not necessarily plaintiff's discovery of his illness; so to hold would be to confuse the beginning of plaintiff's cause of action with the beginning of its end, i.e., with the starting of the statute of limitations" (internal quotation marks omitted)). There may be some overlap in the standards applied to these questions. *See United States v. Kubrick*, 444 U.S. 111, 120 (1979) (recognizing that "the general rule under the [FTCA] has been that a tort claim accrues at the time of the plaintiff's injury"). But the statute of limitations inquiry is concerned with a plaintiff's knowledge, *see id.* at 118-24, to ensure that a limitations period does not lapse before a reasonably diligent plaintiff is aware of her injury, *see In re Joint E. & S. Dist. Asbestos Litig.*, 721 F. Supp. at 435 (equating "plaintiff's discovery of his illness" with the "starting of the statute of limitations"). In deciding where a claim arises under the foreign country exception, however, we are not concerned with the possibility of a blameless plaintiff losing a claim through delay. Thus, we ask only where "the last act necessary to establish liability occurred," *Sosa*, 542 U.S. at 705 (internal quotation marks omitted), without taking into account what the plaintiff knew or did not know.[3]

To determine where the Holts' claims arose for the purposes of the foreign country exception, we must therefore look to governing choice-of-law principles at the time Congress enacted the FTCA. And, as the Supreme Court held in *Sosa*, we must apply *lex loci delicti. Id.* The Restatement (First) of Conflict of Laws, upon which the Supreme Court relied in *Sosa*, provides that "[t]he place of wrong is . . . where the last event necessary to make an actor liable for an alleged tort takes place." § 377. The Restatement illustrates application of this rule when an individual "sustains bodily harm" as follows:

> Such a force is first set in motion by some human being. It is quite immaterial in what state he set the force in motion. It must alone or in cooperation with other forces harm the body of another. The person harmed may thereafter go into another state and die from the injury or suffer other loss therefrom. The place where this last event happens is also immaterial. The question is only where did the force impinge upon his body.

Id. § 377, n.1. Thus, an injury "occurs" where it is first suffered, even if a negligent act later results in further or more serious harm. *Accord Williams v. Gyrus ACMI, Inc.*, 790 F. Supp. 2d 410, 415 (D. Md. 2011) (holding that plaintiff's injury occurred for purposes of *lex loci delicti* at the time shim was left in her body, "even if she did not begin to experience pain or other symptoms from the shim's presence until she relocated" to another state).

It is undisputed that S.H.'s cerebral palsy resulted from the brain injury she sustained in Spain as a consequence of her premature birth. The district court held that the Holts' claims arose in the United States because that is where S.H.'s cerebral palsy definitively manifested itself. In reaching that determination, the court distinguished between S.H.'s brain injury and her cerebral palsy diagnosis, reasoning that because plaintiffs were suing to recover for the latter harm, and cerebral palsy is not a disease but rather a collection of symptoms, plaintiffs' claims could not have arisen prior to those symptoms being present and diagnosable. But S.H.'s premature birth caused appreciable injury while the Holts were in Spain, even if cerebral palsy was not definitively diagnosed in that country. Under *lex loci delicti,* as it was interpreted at the time of the FTCA's passage, the fact that a plaintiff suffers some "other loss" in a different jurisdiction is "immaterial." Restatement (First) Conflict of Laws § 377, n.1. "The question is only where did the force impinge upon [her] body." *Id.* The undisputed facts of this case indicate that the force—the brain injury S.H. suffered at or near the time of her birth—impinged upon her body in Spain; thus, that is where the Holts' claims arose. *See Sosa,* 542 U.S. at 705-06.[4]

Our conclusion is consistent with the application of the foreign country exception by other federal courts. In *Thompson v. Peace Corps,* 159 F. Supp. 3d 56 (D.D.C. 2016), the court held that the foreign country exception barred the plaintiff's FTCA claims, which were based on injuries she sustained as a result of taking an anti-malarial drug in Burkina Faso. *Id.* at 61. The court reasoned that although the plaintiff "complain[ed] of continuing side effects after her return home," as well as "a permanent brain injury," the court lacked jurisdiction because the "claims based on those injuries arose out of the administration of mefloquine in BurkinaFaso." *Id.* at 58, 61. Similarly, the District of Columbia Circuit has twice held that a district court lacked jurisdiction over a plaintiff's claims for emotional or economic injuries occurring in the United States because those injuries were derivative of harm suffered abroad by the plaintiffs' spouses. *See Gross v. United States,* 771 F.3d 10, 13 (D.C. Cir. 2014) (holding that foreign country exception applied because wife's economic injuries in the United States were derivative of injuries husband suffered as a result of imprisonment in Cuba); *Harbury v. Hayden,* 522 F.3d 413, 423 (D.C. Cir. 2008) (holding that foreign country exception applied to claims for emotional injuries that wife suffered in United States but that resulted from physical abuse and death of husband in Guatemala). In both cases, the court expressed concern that plaintiffs would be able to "plead around the FTCA's foreign-country exception simply by claiming injuries . . . that are derivative of the foreign-country injuries at the root of the complaint." *Harbury,* 522 F.3d at 423.

Like the injuries alleged in these cases, S.H.'s cerebral palsy is derivative of the harm she sustained at birth. As the Holts recognize, cerebral palsy is not itself a disease, but rather a group of non-progressive motor conditions. It is therefore a description of symptoms manifesting from S.H.'s brain injury, rather than a separate, compensable harm. Moreover, to hold that the Holts' claims did not arise until cerebral palsy could be definitively diagnosed would enable plaintiffs in similar circumstances to avoid application of the foreign country exception, either by pleading their injuries in a particular way or by relocating to the United States before obtaining a diagnosis. *Cf. Sosa,* 542 U.S. at 702-03 (rejecting idea that "allegations of negligent medical care . . . can . . . be repackaged as headquarters claims based on . . . the offering of bad advice" in the United States, even though harm is suffered overseas, because the practice would "swallow the foreign country exception whole" (citations omitted)); *Harbury,* 522 F.3d at 423 (prohibiting plaintiffs from "plead[ing] around" the foreign country exception by claiming domestic injuries "that are derivative of the foreigncountry injuries at the root of the complaint"). Jurisdiction under the FTCA cannot turn on whether the Holts framed their suit as seeking damages for S.H.'s cerebral palsy or the brain injury she sustained at birth.

III

Because the Holts' claims against the United States arose in Spain, the FTCA's foreign country exception bars their suit. Accordingly, the district court's order is VACATED, and we REMAND the case with instructions to dismiss for lack of subject matter jurisdiction.[5] The parties shall bear their own costs on appeal.

GRABER, Circuit Judge, concurring in the result:

I concur in the result reached by the majority opinion. I write separately because, in my view, the timing and content of the administrative claim filed by Plaintiffs, while they were still in Spain, forecloses their claims under the Federal Tort Claims Act ("FTCA").

The FTCA requires that a plaintiff exhaust administrative remedies:

An action shall not be instituted upon a claim against the United States for money damages for injury or loss of property or personal injury or death caused by the negligent or wrongful act or omission of any employee of the Government while acting within the scope of his office or employment, unless the claimant shall have first presented the claim to the appropriate Federal agency and his claim shall have been finally denied by the agency. . . .

28 U.S.C. § 2675(a). The administrative claim need not be detailed; rather, "a skeletal claim form, containing only the bare elements of notice of accident and injury and a sum certain representing damages, suffices." *Avery v. United States,* 680 F.2d 608, 610 (9th Cir. 1982).

Although an administrative claim need not be detailed to satisfy § 2675(a), such a claim serves to exhaust only those basic theories encompassed in its scope. Of course, an FTCA plaintiff may seek a greater amount of damages than the sum certain contained in the administrative claim if "the increased amount is based upon newly discovered evidence not reasonably discoverable at the time of presenting the claim to the federal agency, or upon allegation and proof of intervening facts, relating to the amount of the claim." 28 U.S.C. § 2675(b). For instance, an FTCA plaintiff who files an administrative claim and later suffers additional harm flowing from the incidents described in that claim may be able to recover for the additional harm. *Richardson v. United States,* 841 F.2d 993, 998-99 (9th Cir.), *amended,* 860 F.2d 357 (9th Cir. 1988). But the plaintiff cannot come into court seeking redress on an entirely different claim.

The majority opinion correctly holds that Plaintiffs exhausted their FTCA claims. That is because those claims are encompassed by the administrative claim—that is, they relate to the same core set of facts. *See Nagrampa v. MailCoups, Inc.,* 469 F.3d 1257, 1264 n.2 (9th Cir. 2006) (en banc) ("Under the federal system, the word 'claim' denotes the allegations that give rise to an enforceable right to relief." (internal quotation marks and brackets omitted)); *see also Khan v. United States,* 808 F.3d 1169, 1172-73 (7th Cir. 2015) ("All that must be specified [under 28 U.S.C. § 2675(a)], therefore, is facts plus a demand for money; if those two things are specified, the claim encompasses any cause of action fairly implicit in the facts." (internal quotation marks omitted)). Although it is true that some facts—such as the definitive diagnosis of cerebral palsy—occurred after the filing of the administrative claim, it is undisputed that S.H.'s cerebral palsy resulted from the brain injury that she suffered at birth, and that her brain injury was the focus of Plaintiffs' administrative claim.

S.H. was born in Spain, where the family continued to reside for more than an additional year before returning to the United States. While still in Spain, Plaintiffs filed an administrative claim seeking damages for, among other things, "catastrophic neurological injuries, seizures, learning deficits, [and] physical limitations" already suffered by S.H. as a result of her premature and difficult birth. The claim form also asserted, among other things, that "negligence on the part of medical healthcare providers, penultimately in Rota, Spain at USNaval Hospital, resulted in negligent failure to promptly recognize and treat [the mother's] abruptio placenta, causing catastrophic injuries," and that care "at USNH Rota Spain failed to conform to the standard of medical and surgical care in the community." It is clear that, in bringing suit under the FTCA, Plaintiffs pressed the same "claim" that they had presented to the government.[1]

What this means is that Plaintiffs' claims necessarily "arose" in Spain, because a claim cannot be "presented" to the appropriate agency under 28 U.S.C. § 2675(a) until *after* it has arisen. In other words, by filing an administrative claim while still in Spain, containing allegations of a premature birth that caused brain injuries to S.H., Plaintiffs necessarily admitted[2] that *some* claims based on those facts already had arisen; because the claims in this action are the same as those presented to the government in the administrative process, those claims arose in Spain.

This would be a tragic case in any event, but the fact that it is the foreign-country exception that ultimately bars relief makes it especially tragic, as it was the alleged negligence of the United States that led to Plaintiffs' being in a foreign country in the first place. But only Congress is in a position to provide relief to Plaintiffs and those in similar situations. We are bound by *Sosa v. Alvarez-Machain,* 542 U.S. 692 (2004), and, therefore, are compelled to reverse the district court's judgment.

[*] The Honorable Carlos F. Lucero, United States Circuit Judge for the U.S. Court of Appeals for the Tenth Circuit, sitting by designation.

[**] This summary constitutes no part of the opinion of the court. It has been prepared by court staff for the convenience of the reader.

[1] Those doctors were Dr. Paul Shales, a developmental pediatrician at the Educational, Developmental and Intervention Services Clinic at Rota, and Dr.

Anthony Delgado, a general pediatrician at the Rota pediatric clinic. The district court found Dr. Shales' diagnosis unreliable.

[2] *Sosa* recognized that Congress' intent in enacting the foreign country exception was to prevent the United States from being subjected to liability under the laws of a foreign power. *See* 542 U.S. at 707. However, the Court also acknowledged that under its interpretation of the statute, the foreign country exception would apply even "when a State's choice-of-law approach would not apply the foreign law of place of injury." *Id.* at 711. In rejecting a more selective approach, the Court noted that Congress did not write the statutory language to bar claims only "when foreign law would be applied" but rather to bar all claims "arising in" a foreign country. *Id.* The Court further reasoned that even if such a meaning could be inferred from the language of the statute, it would result in "a scheme of federal jurisdiction that would vary from State to State, benefiting or penalizing plaintiffs accordingly." *Id.* Thus, a consequence of the Court's decision in *Sosa* is that the foreign country exception will sometimes bar suits that would not have triggered the application of foreign law.

[3] It is for this same reason that we reject any suggestion that the Holts' administrative claim, which lists "cerebral palsy" as an injury caused by the USAF's negligence, establishes that S.H. had cerebral palsy in Spain. Where an injury is suffered for the purposes of the foreign country exception is an objective inquiry, one that does not depend on what the Holts knew at a particular time.

[4] We recognize that courts have sometimes interpreted *lex loci delicti* to different effect in the context of long-latency diseases. *See, e.g., Pounders v. Enserch E&C, Inc.,* 306 P.3d 9, 13 (Ariz. 2013) (noting that "[f]or long-latency diseases, the 'last event' takes place when the disease is discoverable because, until then, a legally compensable injury does not exist"); *Trahan v. E.R. Squibb & Sons, Inc.,* 567 F. Supp. 505, 507-08 (M.D. Tenn. 1983) (rejecting argument that "last event" occurred when plaintiff's mother ingested DES, absent any evidence that "improper development of the plaintiff's cervix occurred immediately upon her mother's ingestion of the drug"). But in those cases, there was no evidence that the plaintiffs' exposure to a toxic substance resulted in any immediate harm beyond the cellular level. By comparison, S.H.'s brain injury, resulting from her premature birth, had appreciable effects while the Holts were living in Spain. *See In re "Agent Orange" Prod. Liab. Litig.,* 580 F. Supp. 690, 707 (E.D.N.Y. 1984) (explaining, for purposes of *lex loci delicti,* that "harmful force" of Agent Orange affected military service members immediately, even though "many of the more serious symptoms did not manifest themselves until years later").

[5] The United States raises a number of other issues on appeal; however, our conclusion that the district court lacked jurisdiction obviates the need to address those arguments.

[1] Indeed, had Plaintiffs pressed a *different* claim, that claim would not have been exhausted.

[2] I do not necessarily mean "admitted" in the sense of a binding judicial admission. *See SEC v. Caserta,* 75 F. Supp. 2d 79, 95 n.9 (E.D.N.Y. 1999) (discussing split in authority over the circumstances in which admissions made in an administrative proceeding function as judicial admissions). Rather, the timing

and content of the administrative claim limit the scope of the subsequent lawsuit. So although the majority opinion is quite right that Plaintiffs' listing of "cerebral palsy" as an injury on the administrative claim does not establish that S.H. actually had cerebral palsy while still in Spain, the fact that the administrative claim is generally about brain injuries suffered at birth means that a claim related to injuries of that sort had arisen by the time the administrative claim was filed.

848 F.3d 880 (2017)

Sundus Shaker SALEH, on behalf of herself and those similarly situated, Plaintiff-Appellant,

v.

George W. BUSH; Richard B. Cheney; Donald Rumsfeld; Condoleezza Rice; Colin Powell; Paul Wolfowitz; Does 1-10, inclusive; and the United States of America, Defendants-Appellees.

No. 15-15098.

United States Court of Appeals, Ninth Circuit.

Argued and Submitted December 12, 2016 San Francisco, California.

Filed February 10, 2017.

Saleh v. Bush, 848 F. 3d 880 (9th Cir. 2017)

p.884 Appeal from the United States District Court for the Northern District of California; D.C. No. 3:13-cv-01124-JST, Jon S. Tigar, District Judge, Presiding.

Dave Inder Comar (argued), Comar Law, San Francisco, California, for Plaintiff-Appellant.

Patrick G. Nemeroff (argued) and Matthew M. Collette, Attorneys, Appellate Staff; Melinda Haag, United States Attorney; Benjamin C. Mizer, Principal Deputy Assistant Attorney General; Civil Division, United States Department of Justice, Washington, D.C.; for Defendants-Appellees.

Jerome Paul Wallingford, San Diego, California, for Amicus Curiae Lawyers for International Law.

Rajeev E. Ananda, New York, New York, for Amicus Curiae Planethood Foundation.

Before: Susan P. Graber and Andrew D. Hurwitz, Circuit Judges, and Richard F. Boulware,[**] District Judge.

OPINION

GRABER, Circuit Judge:

Plaintiff Sundus Shaker Saleh sues several individuals who served as high-ranking officials in the administration of President George W. Bush. Plaintiff claims that the former officials conspired to engage in, and did engage in, a war of aggression against Iraq and that, in doing so, they violated the "law of nations" within the meaning of the Alien Tort Statute ("ATS"), 28 U.S.C. § 1350. The district court substituted the United States for the officials as the sole defendant pursuant to the Westfall Act, 28 U.S.C. § 2679(d)(1), and then dismissed the case because Plaintiff had not exhausted her administrative remedies as required by the Federal Tort Claims Act ("FTCA"). Plaintiff argues that substitution of the United States was improper because the former officials are not entitled to official immunity. Because we conclude that the individual defendants are entitled to official immunity under the Westfall Act and that the United States properly was substituted as the sole defendant, we affirm.

FACTUAL AND PROCEDURAL HISTORY[1]

In 2003, Kurdish Army troops forced Plaintiff and her family to leave their home in Jalawla, Iraq, and flee to Baghdad. The troops, who were aligned with the United States, were taking part in what has become known as the Iraq War, a military action that officially began on March 19, 2003, but that, Plaintiff claims, Defendants[2] had been planning for years. Plaintiff p.885 endured many hardships in Baghdad. Eventually she was forced to leave Iraq and move to Jordan. In this case, she seeks to represent "a class of persons consisting of all innocent Iraqi civilians who, through no fault of their own, suffered damage" from the Iraq War.

Plaintiff claims that Defendants Cheney, Rumsfeld, and Wolfowitz began advocating for an invasion of Iraq and for the removal of Iraqi President Saddam Hussein from power as early as 1997. In January 1998, Rumsfeld and Wolfowitz sent President Clinton a letter urging him to "implement a '*strategy for removing Saddam's regime from power*,' which included a 'willingness to *undertake military action* as diplomacy is clearly failing.'" (Emphasis in complaint.) They sent a similar letter to Speaker of the House Newt Gingrich and Senate Majority Leader Trent Lott later that year.

Defendant Bush became President in January 2001, and appointed the other Defendants to high-ranking positions within his administration. According to Plaintiff, Defendants almost immediately began to discuss a possible invasion and occupation of Iraq, with Defendant Rumsfeld stating at an early National Security Council meeting that "what we really want to think about is going after Saddam." As then-Treasury Secretary Paul O'Neill later put it:

> From the start, we were building the case against Hussein and looking at how we could take him out and change Iraq into a new country. And, if we did that, it would solve everything. It was all about finding *a way to do it*. That was the tone of it. The President saying, "Fine. Go find me a way to do this."

(Emphasis in complaint.)

According to Plaintiff, the September 11, 2001 attacks provided Defendants with a pretext to launch an invasion of Iraq. Defendants Wolfowitz and Rumsfeld "openly pushed for war against Iraq" on the day of the attacks, despite the lack of evidence tying Iraq to the attacks. Defendant Bush was less eager to take action without evidence of a link between Iraq and the September 11 attackers. He asked various officials to "go back over everything" to try to find evidence that Saddam Hussein had been involved with Al Qaeda. Over the course of the next year or so, Defendants began planning for the invasion of Iraq, even as they struggled to find such a link.

Beginning around August 2002, Defendants allegedly mounted a coordinated campaign to convince "the public, the Congress and the allies of the need to confront the threat from Saddam Hussein." As part of that campaign, Defendants and others "continually used fabricated intelligence from unreliable sources in order to prep the public for an invasion of Iraq." For instance, Defendant Bush claimed in his 2003 State of the Union address that Iraq had tried to "obtain large quantities of uranium from Africa," despite the fact that this claim was "unconfirmed and highly unlikely." During that time period, Defendants also continued to plan for an invasion of Iraq. According to Plaintiff, Defendants were committed to the invasion whether or not the United Nations approved of the action and whether or not United Nations inspectors uncovered evidence that Iraq was developing nuclear weapons.

On March 7, 2003, International Atomic Energy Agency Director General Mohamed ElBaradei "reported to the UN Security Council that there was no indication 'of resumed nuclear activities,' 'that Iraq has attempted to import uranium,' [or] 'that Iraq has attempted to import aluminum tubes for use in centrifuge enrichment.'" Nonetheless, less than two weeks later, the United States invaded p.886 Iraq. Congress authorized the use of military force to "defend the national security of the United States against the continuing threat posed by Iraq." Authorization for Use of Military Force Against Iraq Resolution of 2002, Pub. L. No. 107-243, 116 Stat. 1498 ("Authorization for Use of Military Force"), but Defendants did not secure United Nations authorization for the war.

Plaintiff brought this action in 2013. She alleges that Defendants' conduct in planning and executing the Iraq War amounted to the "crime of aggression" and a conspiracy to commit the crime of aggression,[3] which she claims was a violation of the "law of nations" within the meaning of the ATS. After she filed an amended complaint in September 2013, the United States filed a certification that Defendants had been "acting within the scope of their federal office or employment at the time of the incidents [at issue] in this matter." Under 28 U.S.C. § 2679(d)(1), the United States was then substituted as the sole defendant. Thereafter, the amended complaint was dismissed because Plaintiff had failed to exhaust her administrative remedies as required by the FTCA, 28 U.S.C. § 2675(a). Plaintiff filed a second amended complaint. The United States again filed a "scope certification," and the district court again substituted the United States and dismissed the action, this time with prejudice. The district court also denied Plaintiff's motion for an evidentiary hearing to challenge the scope certification. Plaintiff timely appeals both the dismissal of the action and the denial of her motion for an evidentiary hearing.

STANDARDS OF REVIEW

"We review the dismissal [for lack of subject matter jurisdiction] and the denial of the challenge to certification de novo.... We review the decision whether to conduct an evidentiary hearing for abuse of discretion." *McLachlan v. Bell*, 261 F.3d 908, 910 (9th Cir. 2001) (footnote omitted).

DISCUSSION

The Alien Tort Statute grants "district courts ... original jurisdiction of any civil action by an alien for a tort only, committed in violation of the law of nations or a treaty of the United States," 28 U.S.C. § 1350. Not every violation of the law of nations gives rise to a claim that can be brought under the ATS. Rather, "any claim based on the present-day law of nations [must] rest on a norm of international character accepted by the civilized world and defined with a specificity comparable to the features of the 18th-century paradigms" that the drafters of the ATS had in mind — "violation of safe conducts, infringement of the rights of ambassadors, and piracy." *Sosa v. Alvarez-Machain,* 542 U.S. 692, 724-25, 124 S.Ct. 2739, 159 L.Ed.2d 718 (2004). The set of "ATS torts" — violations of norms of international law giving rise to claims cognizable under [p.887] the ATS — is, therefore, not frozen in time, but the Supreme Court has instructed us to be wary of adding to that set. *See id.* at 729, 124 S.Ct. 2739 ("[T]he door to further independent judicial recognition of actionable international norms ... is still ajar subject to vigilant doorkeeping, and thus open to a narrow class of international norms today."). Perhaps not surprisingly, only a few new ATS torts have been recognized by federal appellate courts since *Sosa* was decided. *See, e.g., Doe I v. Nestle USA, Inc.,* 766 F.3d 1013, 1022 (9th Cir. 2014) (holding that a violation of the "prohibition against slavery" gives rise to a claim under the ATS); *Abdullahi v. Pfizer, Inc.,* 562 F.3d 163, 169 (2d Cir. 2009) (concluding that a violation of the "prohibition... against nonconsensual human medical experimentation" is an ATS tort).

Plaintiff asks us to recognize a violation of the norm against aggression as an ATS tort. We need not decide that issue. Assuming, without deciding, that engaging in aggression constitutes an ATS tort,[4] Plaintiff's claims against Defendants nonetheless fail, because Congress has granted Defendants official immunity from those claims. The only proper defendant in this case is therefore the United States, and Plaintiff's claims against the United States are barred because Plaintiff failed to exhaust administrative remedies as required by the FTCA.

We first address the question whether Defendants are entitled to immunity under the terms of the Westfall Act. We then address Plaintiff's argument that, even if the Westfall Act purports to confer immunity on Defendants, immunity cannot attach because Plaintiff has alleged that Defendants violated a *jus cogens* norm of international law.[5]

A. *Defendants' Official Immunity Under the Westfall Act*

"The concept of the immunity of government officers from personal liability springs from the same root considerations that generated the doctrine of sovereign immunity. While the latter doctrine — that the 'King can do no wrong' — did not protect all government officers from personal liability, the common law soon recognized the necessity of permitting officials to perform their official functions free from the threat of suits for personal liability." *Scheuer v. Rhodes,* 416 U.S. 232, 239, 94 S.Ct. 1683, 40 L.Ed.2d 90 (1974), *abrogated on other grounds by Harlow v. Fitzgerald,* 457 U.S. 800, 102 S.Ct. 2727, 73 L.Ed.2d 396 (1982). "[T]he scope of absolute official immunity afforded federal employees is a matter of federal law, to be formulated by [p.888] the courts in the absence of legislative action by Congress." *Westfall v. Erwin,* 484 U.S. 292, 295, 108 S.Ct. 580, 98 L.Ed.2d 619 (1988) (internal quotation marks omitted), *superseded on other grounds by* Pub. L. No. 100-694, 102 Stat. 4563 (1988), codified at 28 U.S.C. § 2679(d). "The purpose of such official immunity is not to protect an erring official, but to insulate the decisionmaking process from the harassment of prospective litigation." *Id.*

The Westfall Act,[6] which was enacted in response to the Supreme Court's decision in *Westfall,* "accords federal employees absolute immunity from common-law tort claims arising out of acts they undertake in the course of their official duties." *Osborn v. Haley,* 549 U.S. 225, 229, 127 S.Ct. 881, 166 L.Ed.2d 819 (2007). The immunity extends to both "negligent" and "wrongful" "act[s] or omission[s] of any employee ... acting within the scope of his office or employment." 28 U.S.C. § 2679(b)(1). The Act does not set out a test to determine whether an employee was "acting within the scope of his office or employment"; rather, Congress intended that courts would apply "the principles of *respondeat superior* of the state in which the alleged tort occurred" in analyzing the scope-of-employment issue. *Pelletier v. Fed. Home Loan Bank of S.F.,* 968 F.2d 865, 876 (9th Cir. 1992). The same analysis was employed before passage of the Westfall Act to determine whether the United States could be liable for an employee's torts under the FTCA. *Id.* at 875-76.

The Westfall Act provides a procedure by which the federal government determines whether an employee is entitled to immunity. When a current or former federal employee is sued and the employee believes that he is entitled to official immunity, he is instructed to "deliver ... all process served upon him ... to his immediate supervisor" or other designated official, who then "furnish[es] copies of the pleadings and process therein to the United States attorney for the district embracing the place wherein the proceeding is brought, to the Attorney General, and to the head of his employing Federal agency." 28 U.S.C. § 2679(c). The Attorney General then determines whether, the defendant employee was acting within the scope of his office or employment at the time of the incident out of which the claim arose." *Id.* § 2679(d)(1). If so, the Attorney General issues a "scope certification," which "transforms an action against an individual federal employee into one against the United States." *Hui v. Castaneda,* 559 U.S. 799, 810, 130 S.Ct. 1845, 176 L.Ed.2d 703 (2010). The "United States shall be substituted as the party defendant," 28 U.S.C. § 2679(d)(1), and the employee is released from any liability: "The remedy against the United States... is exclusive of any other civil action or proceeding for money damages by reason of the same subject matter against the employee whose act or omission gave rise to the claim or against the estate of such employee. Any other civil action or proceeding for money damages arising out of or relating to the same subject matter against the employee or the employee's estate is precluded without regard to when the act or omission occurred." *Id.* § 2679(b)(1).

The Westfall Act does not provide immunity to an official from a suit "brought for a violation of the Constitution of the [p.889] United States." *Id.* § 2679(b)(2)(A). That preserves claims against federal officers under *Bivens v. Six Unknown Named Agents of Federal Bureau of Narcotics,* 403 U.S. 388, 91 S.Ct. 1999, 29 L.Ed.2d 619 (1971). *Hui,* 559 U.S. at 807, 130 S.Ct. 1845. The Act also does not provide immunity from a suit "brought for a violation of a statute of the United States under which such action against an individual is otherwise authorized." 28 U.S.C. § 2679(b)(2)(B). Neither exception applies here.

But Plaintiff argues that Defendants' actions were not taken within the scope of their employment and that, therefore, they are not entitled to immunity under the Westfall Act in the first place. Plaintiff's argument embraces two distinct theories. The first theory is that Defendants in this case acted outside the scope of their employment because they (1) started planning the attack on Iraq before they ever took office, (2) attacked Iraq out of personal motives, and (3) were not employed to instigate an unlawful war. The second theory is that the scope-of-employment inquiry under the Westfall Act must be conducted with an eye toward the United

States' treaty obligations. That is, the statute should not be construed to allow an act to be deemed "official" when the United States has entered into treaties condemning that same act. We will address those two theories in turn, and we will then address Plaintiff's challenge to the district court's denial of her request for an evidentiary hearing concerning the scope certification.

1. *The Scope-of-Employment Test*

"The Attorney General's decision regarding scope of employment certification [under the Westfall Act] is conclusive unless challenged. Accordingly, the party seeking review bears the burden of presenting evidence and disproving the Attorney General's decision to grant or deny scope of employment certification by a preponderance of the evidence." *Green v. Hall,* 8 F.3d 695, 698 (9th Cir. 1993) (per curiam) (citation and footnote omitted). "To rebut the [scope] certification ..., a plaintiff must 'allege sufficient facts that, taken as true, would establish that the defendant's actions exceeded the scope of his employment.'" *Wuterich v. Murtha,* 562 F.3d 375, 381 (D.C. Cir. 2009) (brackets omitted) (quoting *Stokes v. Cross,* 327 F.3d 1210, 1215 (D.C. Cir. 2003)). "[W]here a plaintiff fails to allege sufficient facts to rebut the certification, the United States must be substituted as the defendant...." *Id.*

As noted above, when determining whether a federal officer's actions fall within "the scope of his office or employment" for purposes of the Westfall Act, we apply "the principles of *respondeat superior* of the state in which the alleged tort occurred." *Pelletier,* 968 F.2d at 876. We agree with the parties that the *respondeat superior* law of the District of Columbia applies in this case.

District of Columbia courts routinely "look[] to the Restatement (Second) of Agency" in determining whether an employee's actions fall within the scope of employment. *Rasul v. Myers,* 512 F.3d 644, 655 (D.C. Cir. 2008) (internal quotation marks omitted), *vacated,* 555 U.S. 1083, 129 S.Ct. 763, 172 L.Ed.2d 753 (2008), *reinstated in relevant part,* 563 F.3d 527, 528-29 (D.C. Cir. 2009) (per curiam). "The Restatement provides [that]: '(1) Conduct of a servant is within the scope of employment if, but only if: (a) it is of the kind he is employed to perform; (b) it occurs substantially within the authorized time and space limits; (c) it is actuated, at least in part, by a purpose to serve the master[;] and (d) if force is intentionally [p.890] used by the servant against another, the use of force is not unexpectable by the master. (2) Conduct of a servant is not within the scope of employment if it is different in kind from that authorized, far beyond the authorized time or space limits, or too little actuated by a purpose to serve the master.'" *Council on Am. Islamic Relations v. Ballenger,* 444 F.3d 659, 663 (D.C. Cir. 2006) (per curiam) (quoting Restatement (Second) of Agency § 228 (1958)). "District of Columbia law liberally construes the doctrine of respondeat superior, at least with respect to the first prong of the Restatement." *Kashin v. Kent,* 457 F.3d 1033, 1039 (9th Cir. 2006) (ellipses omitted) (quoting *Stokes,* 327 F.3d at 1216). "The test for scope of employment is an objective one, based on all the facts and circumstances." *Ballenger,* 444 F.3d at 663 (brackets omitted) (quoting *Weinberg v. Johnson,* 518 A.2d 985, 991 (D.C. Cir. 1986)).

Plaintiff claims that Defendants (particularly Wolfowitz and Rumsfeld) were not acting within the scope of their employment in carrying out the Iraq War because they started planning the war before taking office. There are at least two problems with this argument. First, the alleged tortious acts of aggression — the invasion of Iraq — took place after Defendants occupied public office, and what took place in the late 1990s was not planning, but only advocacy. During most of that time, neither Wolfowitz nor Rumsfeld could have known that he would soon be in a position to help implement his policy preferences. Second, pre-employment statements of intent or belief do not take the later acts of public officials outside the scope of their employment. Under Plaintiff's theory, every time a politician honors a campaign promise, she could be considered to be acting outside the scope of her employment. Or, if a passionate advocate for voting rights were appointed to head the Civil Rights Division of the Department of Justice, his or her bringing a lawsuit to enforce voting rights would be viewed as outside the scope of his or her employment.

Plaintiff makes a similar argument with respect to Defendants' motives, which bear on the third prong of the Restatement test — whether an employee's actions were "actuated, at least in part, by a purpose to serve the master." Plaintiff asserts that she has "alleged that Defendants were solely motivated by personal, selfish purposes," but that assertion is not borne out by the factual allegations in the second amended complaint. Plaintiff conflates a policy preference or worldview — which is "personal" in the sense that it may be deeply felt or tied to one's sense of morality or identity — that motivates one to advocate for certain positions, with a desire to serve one's individual interests. A federal official would act out of "personal" motives and not be "actuated ... by a purpose to serve the master" if, for instance, he used the leverage of his office to benefit a spouse's business, paying no heed to the resulting damage to the public welfare. But that is not what Plaintiff has alleged. Rather, she has alleged that Defendants were committed to certain foreign policy objectives in which they believed. Even if those alleged objectives or beliefs were misguided or in contravention of international norms, the motives were not "personal" in the scope-of-employment sense; Defendants' conduct was "actuated, at least in part, by a purpose to serve the master," the United States. *Ballenger,* 444 F.3d at 663.

Finally, Plaintiff argues that Defendants "were not employed to execute a pre-existing war." But Defendants, as members of the executive branch, were charged broadly with guiding the United States' foreign [p.891] policy and with ensuring national security. *Dep't of Navy v. Egan,* 484 U.S. 518, 529-30, 108 S.Ct. 818, 98 L.Ed.2d 918 (1988). And Congress authorized Defendant Bush "to use the Armed Forces of the United States as he determine[d] to be necessary and appropriate in order to ... defend the national security of the United States against the continuing threat posed by Iraq." Authorization for Use of Military Force § 3(a). The actions that Defendants took in connection with the Iraq War were part of their official duties, even if some Defendants had hoped to be able to take those actions years before taking office.

In summary, reading the Westfall Act in a straightforward manner and applying District of Columbia *respondeat superior* law to the facts alleged in the operative complaint, we hold that Defendants' alleged actions fell within the scope of their employment.

2. *Construing the Westfall Act With an Eye Toward Treaty Obligations*

Plaintiff next argues that the Westfall Act should not be interpreted so as to regard as "official" an act condemned by treaty. Plaintiff cites as support for this proposition the United Kingdom case of *Regina v. Bartle & the Commissioner of Police for the Metropolis & Others ex parte Pinochet* (No. 3), [2000] 1 A.C. 147 (H.L.) (appeal taken from Q.B. Div'l Ct.) (U.K.), *reprinted in* 38 I.L.M. 581 (1999), in which the House of Lords ruled that former Chilean leader Augusto Pinochet was not entitled to official immunity for the role that he played in ordering acts of torture and other violations of international law. Many of the Law Lords reasoned that Pinochet's acts could not be considered official because the Convention Against Torture[7] forbade such acts, and Chile was a party to that treaty. 38 I.L.M. at 595 (opinion of Lord Browne-Wilkinson); *id.* at 626-27 (opinion of Lord Hope); *id.* at 638-39 (opinion of Lord Hutton); *id.* at 642-43 (opinion of Lord Saville). The United States has signed several treaties and other international agreements condemning aggressive war,[8] and Plaintiff argues that interpreting the Westfall Act to allow for immunity in this case would conflict with those agreements.

This argument suffers from at least two fatal flaws. First, the equivalent of the "scope of employment" test in the *Pinochet* case was a creature of *international* law, not a test set out by a *domestic* statute. The Law Lords were tasked with determining whether Pinochet's actions could be considered "official" as a matter of international law. The effect of a treaty on that international-law analysis has little bearing on that same treaty's effect on the scope-of-employment analysis under domestic law.

Second, although we have suggested that ambiguous statutes should be interpreted to avoid conflicts even with non-self-executing treaties,[9] *Kim Ho Ma v.* p.892 *Ashcroft,* 257 F.3d 1095, 1114 (9th Cir. 2001), the Westfall Act is not, in any relevant way, ambiguous. With the Westfall Act — which was enacted after the passage of each of the treaties and agreements to which Plaintiff cites — Congress clearly intended to grant federal officers immunity to the same extent that the United States would have been liable for those employees' tortious acts under the FTCA (subject to exceptions that are not relevant to today's analysis). *Pelletier,* 968 F.2d at 876. When the Westfall Act was passed, it was clear that this immunity covered even heinous acts. *See, e.g., Hoston v. Silbert,* 681 F.2d 876, 877-80 (D.C. Cir. 1982) (per curiam) (holding that United States Marshals were acting in the scope of their employment when they allegedly beat an unarmed, shackled prisoner and left him to die in a holding cell).

In short, the treaties and charters cited by Plaintiff do not alter our conclusion that the Westfall Act, by its plain terms, immunizes Defendants from suit.

3. *Denial of an Evidentiary Hearing*

Plaintiff next argues that she should have been afforded an opportunity to challenge the scope certification at an evidentiary hearing. But because the allegations in the operative complaint, taken as true, do not establish that Defendants acted outside the scope of their employment, an evidentiary hearing would be a futile exercise.[10] *See McLachlan,* 261 F.3d at 910-11 (finding no abuse of discretion in district court's denial of hearing to challenge scope certification "because[,] even viewing the evidence in the light most favorable to [the plaintiff] and accepting his version of events, dismissal was appropriate"); *see also Wuterich,* 562 F.3d at 381 (holding that a plaintiff "may, if necessary, attain 'limited discovery' to resolve any factual disputes over" the scope-of-employment issue, but *only if* he or she "alleg[es] sufficient facts that, taken as true, would establish that the defendant's actions exceeded the scope of [his or her] employment" (brackets omitted) (quoting *Stokes,* 327 F.3d at 1214-15)). Accordingly, the district court did not abuse its discretion in denying Plaintiff an evidentiary hearing to challenge the scope certification.[11]

B. *Jus Cogens Violations and Domestic Official Immunity*

Finally, Plaintiff argues that Defendants cannot be immune under the Westfall Act because she alleges violations of a *jus cogens* norm of international law. "[A] *jus cogens* norm, also known as a 'peremptory norm' of international law, 'is a norm accepted and recognized by the international community of states as a whole as a norm from which no derogation is permitted and which can be modified p.893 only by a subsequent norm of general international law having the same character.'" *Siderman de Blake v. Argentina,* 965 F.2d 699, 714 (9th Cir. 1992) (quoting Vienna Convention on the Law of Treaties art. 53, May 23, 1969, 1155 U.N.T.S. 332). "Whereas customary international law derives solely from the consent of states, the fundamental and universal norms constituting *jus cogens* transcend such consent." *Id.* at 715. "Because *jus cogens* norms do not depend solely on the consent of states for their binding force, they enjoy the highest status within international law." *Id.* (internal quotation marks omitted). "International law does not recognize an act that violates *jus cogens* as a sovereign act." *Id.* at 718.

Plaintiff contends that Congress simply cannot immunize a federal official from liability for a *jus cogens* violation. In effect, Plaintiff argues that (1) there is a *jus cogens* norm prohibiting the provision of immunity to officials alleged to have committed *jus cogens* violations[12] and, (2) insofar as the Westfall Act violates that norm, it is invalid. The argument is premised on the idea that "[i]nternational law does not recognize an act that violates *jus cogens* as a sovereign act," so that an official who is alleged to have engaged in such an act cannot cloak himself in the immunity of the sovereign. *Siderman de Blake,* 965 F.2d at 718.

We assume, without deciding, that the prohibition against aggression is a *jus cogens* norm.[13] But even assuming that the prohibition against aggression is a *jus cogens* norm, Plaintiff's argument that Congress cannot provide immunity to federal officers in courts of the United States for violations of that norm is in serious tension with our caselaw. In *Siderman de Blake,* we held that Congress could grant a foreign government immunity from suit for alleged violations of the *jus cogens* norm against torture. *Id.* at 718-19. After recognizing that immunity might not be available as a matter of customary international law, we noted that we were dealing "not only with customary international law, but with an affirmative Act of Congress" — in that case, the Foreign Sovereign Immunities Act. *Id.* at 718.

Siderman de Blake dealt with foreign sovereign immunity, whereas this case concerns the official immunity of domestic officers. But, if anything, that difference cuts against Plaintiff. The immunity of foreign officials in our courts flows from different considerations than does the immunity of domestic officials. *Sanchez-Espinoza v. Reagan*, 770 F.2d 202, 207 n.5 (D.C. Cir. 1985); *accord Universal Consol. Cos. v. Bank of China*, 35 F.3d 243, 245 (6th Cir. 1994) ("[D]omestic sovereign immunity and foreign sovereign immunity are two separate concepts, the first based in constitutional law and the second in customary international law."). Given those different origins, it should be easier for the violation of a *jus cogens* norm to override foreign sovereign immunity than domestic official immunity. Therefore, our holding in *Siderman de Blake* — that Congress can provide immunity to a foreign government for its *jus cogens* violations, even when such immunity is inconsistent with principles of international law — compels the conclusion that Congress also can provide immunity p.894 for federal officers for *jus cogens* violations.[14]

CONCLUSION

Defendants are entitled to immunity under the Westfall Act. Accordingly, the United States was properly substituted as the sole defendant. Because Plaintiff did not exhaust her administrative remedies against the United States, the district court properly dismissed the case for lack of subject matter jurisdiction.

AFFIRMED.

[**] The Honorable Richard F. Boulware, United States District Judge for the District of Nevada, sitting by designation.

[1] We recount the facts as alleged in Plaintiff's second amended complaint. *See McLachlan v. Bell*, 261 F.3d 908, 909 (9th Cir. 2001) (holding that, when reviewing a dismissal in the absence of an evidentiary hearing, "we accept as true the factual allegations in the complaint").

[2] The defendants are former President George W. Bush, former Vice President Richard B. Cheney, former Secretary of Defense Donald Rumsfeld, former National Security Advisor and Secretary of State Condoleezza Rice, former Secretary of State Colin Powell, former Deputy Secretary of Defense Paul Wolfowitz, 10 other former high-ranking officials in the Bush Administration, and the United States. In this opinion, we use "Defendants" to refer only to the individual defendants, who were the named defendants below. We refer to the United States, which was substituted as the sole defendant, as the United States.

[3] Like Plaintiff, we use the shorthand term "aggression" to refer to both aggression itself and conspiracy to commit aggression, both of which Defendants are alleged to have engaged in. For purposes of this case, we define aggression as the waging of unprovoked war. *See, e.g.*, Depositary Notification, Amendments to the Rome Statute of the International Criminal Court on the Crime of Aggression, Reference C.N.651.2010 (Nov. 29, 2010) (defining aggression in a similar, though more complex, way). A slightly different definition of aggression is "the use of military force as an instrument of advancing national policy." Grant M. Dawson, *Defining Substantive Crimes Within the Subject Matter Jurisdiction of the International Criminal Court: What is the Crime of Aggression?*, 19 N.Y.L. Sch. J. Int'l & Comp. L. 413, 432 (2000). Our analysis does not depend on the precise definition of aggression.

[4] Because we resolve this case on the ground that Plaintiff failed to exhaust administrative remedies as required by the FTCA — a jurisdictional requirement under our caselaw, *Brady v. United States,* 211 F.3d 499, 502 (9th Cir. 2000) — we do not address any other threshold issues. *See Ruhrgas AG v. Marathon Oil Co.,* 526 U.S. 574, 578, 119 S.Ct. 1563, 143 L.Ed.2d 760 (1999) (holding that "there is no unyielding jurisdictional hierarchy").

[5] Plaintiff also contends that judicial estoppel should bar the United States and Defendants from arguing that Defendants are entitled to immunity, because the United States took a different position during the Nuremberg Trials following World War II. We are not persuaded. The immunity claimed by Defendants and the United States comes from the Westfall Act, which did not exist at the time of the Nuremberg Trials. Thus, even assuming that the current position of the United States were clearly inconsistent with the position taken at the Nuremberg Trials, the new position rests on an intervening change in law and therefore is not subject to judicial estoppel. *See Longaberger Co. v. Kolt,* 586 F.3d 459, 470 (6th Cir. 2009) (collecting cases), *abrogated on other grounds by Montanile v. Bd. of Trs. of Nat'l Elevator Indus. Health Benefit Plan,* ___ U.S. ___, 136 S.Ct. 651, 193 L.Ed.2d 556 (2016).

[6] The Act is officially called the Federal Employees Liability Reform and Tort Compensation Act of 1988, but it is "commonly known as the Westfall Act." *Gutierrez de Martinez v. Lamagno,* 515 U.S. 417, 419-20, 115 S.Ct. 2227, 132 L.Ed.2d 375 (1995).

[7] United Nations Convention Against Torture and Other Forms of Cruel, Inhuman or Degrading Treatment or Punishment, Dec. 10, 1984, 1465 U.N.T.S. 85.

[8] Plaintiff cites the following treaties and agreements: the United Nations Charter, June 26, 1945, 59 Stat. 1031, T.S. No. 993; the Agreement for the Prosecution and Punishment of the Major War Criminals of the European Axis and Charter of the International Military Tribunal, Aug. 8, 1945, 59 Stat. 1544, 82 U.N.T.S. 279 [London Charter]; the Charter of the International Military Tribunal for the Far East, Jan. 19, 1946, T.I.A.S. No. 1589; and the Kellogg-Briand Peace Pact, Aug. 27, 1998, 46 Stat. 2343, 94 L.N.T.S. 57.

[9] The proposition that statutes should be construed to avoid conflicts with non-self-executing treaties has been the subject of some debate by both courts and commentators. *See Fund for Animals, Inc. v. Kempthorne,* 472 F.3d 872, 879 (D.C. Cir. 2006) (Kavanaugh, J., concurring) (opining that "the canon against construing an ambiguous statute to abrogate a treaty ... should not apply in cases involving non-self-executing treaties"); *see also* Rebecca Crootof, Note, *Judicious Influence: Non-Self-Executing Treaties and the Charming Betsy Canon,* 120 Yale L.J. 1784, 1790-91 (2011) (arguing that ambiguous statutes should be read to avoid conflicts with non-self-executing treaties). By contrast, there is no doubt that when a *self-executing* treaty and a statute "relate to the same subject, the courts will always endeavor to construe them so as to give effect to both, if that can be done without violating the language of either." *Whitney v. Robertson,* 124 U.S. 190, 194, 8 S.Ct. 456, 31 L.Ed. 386 (1888).

[10] Plaintiff did not seek leave to amend the complaint for a third time.

[11] Plaintiff also argues that she was entitled to a jury determination of the correctness of the scope certification. But a judge, not a jury, is the "appropriate trier of any facts essential to certification." *Osborn,* 549 U.S. at 252, 127 S.Ct. 881.

[12] Or, alternatively, Plaintiff contends that there is a prohibition on defining an official's scope of employment under domestic law to include actions that violate *jus cogens* norms.

[13] *See, e.g.,* Evan J. Criddle & Evan Fox-Decent, *A Fiduciary Theory of Jus Cogens,* 34 Yale J. Int'l L. 331, 333 (2009) (describing the prohibition on aggression as a "recognized peremptory norm[]").

[14] *Siderman de Blake* also forecloses the alternative formulation of Plaintiff's argument — that an official's scope of employment under domestic law cannot include actions that violate *jus cogens* norms. We held in *Siderman de Blake* that actions violating *jus cogens* norms, although not recognized as sovereign acts under international law, could constitute sovereign acts for purposes of the Foreign Sovereign Immunities Act. 965 F.2d at 718-19. Similarly, Defendants' alleged violations of a *jus cogens* norm can be considered to be within the scope of their employment as a matter of domestic law.

755 F.3d 860 (2014)

Maritza GALLARDO, Plaintiff-Appellant,

v.

UNITED STATES of America, Defendant-Appellee.

No. 12-55255.

United States Court of Appeals, Ninth Circuit.

Argued and Submitted January 8, 2014.

Filed April 15, 2014.

Amended June 3, 2014.

Gallardo v. US, 755 F. 3d 860 (9th Cir. 2014)

p.861 Randall Jonathan Paulson (argued), Law Offices of Randall J. Paulson, Santa Ana, CA, for Plaintiff-Appellant.

Adam C. Jed (argued) and Mark B. Stern, United States Department of Justice, Washington, D.C.; Donald W. Yoo, Office of the United States Attorney, Los Angeles, CA, for Defendant-Appellee.

Before: WILLIAM A. FLETCHER, MILAN D. SMITH, JR. and PAUL J. WATFORD, Circuit Judges.

ORDER AND AMENDED OPINION

ORDER

The court's opinion, filed April 15, 2014, and published at *Gallardo v. United States,* 2014 WL 1424469 (9th Cir. Apr. 15, 2014), is hereby amended as follows:

The first two paragraphs of Part III.B previously read:

In the alternative, Gallardo argues that the statute of limitations should be equitably tolled. When the district court dismissed Gallardo's claim, equitable tolling was not available under the FTCA. *See Marley,* 567 F.3d at 1038. In 2013, however, we overruled *Marley,* holding in *Wong v. Beebe* that equitable tolling of the statute of limitations is available in FTCA actions. 732 F.3d at 1033.

The government makes two arguments against equitable tolling. First, the government argues that Gallardo did not raise equitable tolling in the district court and has therefore waived this argument. But at the time the district court ruled on the motion to dismiss, equitable tolling was foreclosed by *Marley.* The argument became available only later, while this case was on appeal, when we decided *Wong.* We therefore hold that Gallardo's equitable tolling argument is not waived. *See, e.g., Romain v. Shear,* 799 F.2d 1416, 1419 (9th Cir. 1986) (an exception to waiver exists "when a new issue arises while appeal is pending because of a change in law").

Gallardo v. United States, No. 12-55255, slip op. 9 (9th Cir. Apr. 15, 2014). The opinion is amended so that these two paragraphs now read:

> In the alternative, Gallardo argues that the statute of limitations should be equitably tolled. The government makes two arguments against equitable tolling.
>
> First, it argues in a supplemental brief that Gallardo did not argue equitable tolling in the district court and has therefore waived this argument. In its answering brief, the government had argued on the merits that equitable tolling was not available under the FTCA. It contended that we had "overruled" *Alvarez-Machain v. United States,* 107 F.3d 696, 701 (9th Cir.1996) (holding that equitable tolling is available under the FTCA), in our 2009 decision in *Marley,* in which we held that equitable tolling is not available in FTCA actions. After the government's answering brief was filed, we overruled *Marley,* holding in *Wong* that equitable tolling is available. The government then argued, for the first time, that Gallardo had waived her equitable tolling argument by not raising it in the district court. Because the government failed to argue waiver in its answering brief, its waiver argument is itself waived. *See Clem v. Lomeli,* 566 F.3d 1177, 1182 (9th Cir.2009). p.862 Even if the government had not "waived the waiver," however, we would be inclined to hold that Gallardo has not waived her equitable tolling argument. *See Romain v. Shear,* 799 F.2d 1416, 1419 (9th Cir.1986) (an exception to waiver exists "when a new issue arises while appeal is pending because of a change in law"). At the time of the district court's decision, *Marley* was still on the books. It clearly held that our prior holding in *Alvarez-Machain* was no longer good law. *See Marley,* 567 F.3d at 1037-38 (explaining that the holding in *Alvarez-Machain* "has no precedential value"). Only after our en banc decision in *Wong* did it become clear that *Marley* was not good law.

Future petitions for rehearing will not be entertained.

OPINION

W. FLETCHER, Circuit Judge:

Plaintiff Maritza Gallardo appeals from the district court's dismissal of her Federal Tort Claims Act ("FTCA") action against the United States as time-barred. Gallardo's claim arose out of an alleged sexual assault committed by a sergeant in the U.S. Marine Corps ("the Corps") while he was on a recruitment detail at her middle school. Gallardo did not file an administrative claim for negligence against the Corps until four years after the assault. The FTCA's statute of limitations is two years unless tolled. 28 U.S.C. § 2401(b).

While this appeal was pending, we decided *Wong v. Beebe,* 732 F.3d 1030 (9th Cir.2013) (en banc), holding that equitable tolling of the statute of limitations is available in FTCA actions. *See id.* at 1033. We overruled *Marley v. United States,* 567 F.3d 1030, 1038 (9th Cir.2009), which held that equitable tolling is unavailable. In light of this change in the law, we vacate the district court's dismissal of Gallardo's FTCA claim and remand for that court to determine whether equitable tolling is appropriate in the circumstances of this case.

I. Background

A. Alleged Sexual Assault

The following narrative is based on allegations by Gallardo in her complaint and on statements by her mother, Maria Gallardo, in a declaration submitted to the district court in connection with its jurisdictional ruling under Federal Rule of Civil Procedure 12(b)(1). For present purposes, we assume the truth of these allegations and statements. *See Brown v. Elec. Arts, Inc.,* 724 F.3d 1235, 1247 (9th Cir.2013).

In March 2006, middle-school student Maritza Gallardo met U.S. Marine Corps Sergeant Ross Curtis at a civilian youth disciplinary "boot camp." While Gallardo was at the camp, Curtis asked her for her Myspace address. After Gallardo left the camp, Curtis sent messages to her Myspace address between March and May, suggesting that they "hang out" together. Gallardo "resisted" Curtis's overtures.

In May 2006, Curtis represented the Corps, in his "Dress Blues" uniform, at Gallardo's middle school career day. During the career day, they acknowledged each other but did not speak. Gallardo left the school grounds at the end of the day. Curtis saw her leave and called her, asking her to return to the school. Gallardo returned, and she and several other students accepted Curtis's offer to give them a ride home. After Curtis had dropped off everyone except Gallardo, he "drove around for some time and parked in a nearby neighborhood." After he and Gallardo "talked for a while," Curtis "began driving ... and eventually parked" again. Curtis "began ... kissing her, fondling her breasts, asking her to tou[c]h his p.863 erect penis and eventually attempting sexual penetration." Gallardo began to cry. Curtis stopped, told her not to tell anyone what had happened, and drove her home.

B. Curtis's Criminal Prosecution

In August 2008, law enforcement officials arrested Curtis, now a civilian, for a sexual assault on another minor. While searching Curtis's computer, officials found pictures and Myspace messages that he had sent to Gallardo. Detectives interviewed Gallardo at her home in the fall of 2008.

The following year, Gallardo and her mother were subpoenaed for Curtis's criminal trial. During the trial, Gallardo's mother learned from a female member of the Corps that Curtis had assaulted her, but that her military superiors had taken no disciplinary action against him after she reported the assault. Gallardo later learned that in March 2006, two months before Curtis sexually assaulted her on career day, he had been court-martialed for sexually assaulting three female members of the Corps. The result of Curtis's court-martial was that "the Corps retained his enlistment, assigned him to recruitment detail, and he was scheduled to be discharged in June 2006."

C. Proceedings Below

In May 2010, after learning of Curtis's history of sexually assaulting women, and of the Corps' knowledge of those assaults at the time it assigned him to the recruitment detail at her middle school, Gallardo filed an administrative claim with the Corps and the Department of Defense. The gravamen of Gallardo's claim was that the assault occurred because of the Corps' negligence in assigning a known sex offender to work with middle-school students. Gallardo's administrative claim was denied in December 2010.

Gallardo then filed suit in federal district court based on the same allegations as those in her administrative claim. Defendants moved to dismiss Gallardo's claim as untimely under the FTCA's two-year statute of limitations. In response, Gallardo argued that "her claim did not accrue until the facts of [Curtis's] military record became known at the time of his criminal trial" in 2009.

The district court agreed with defendants, holding under *United States v. Kubrick,* 444 U.S. 111, 100 S.Ct. 352, 62 L.Ed.2d 259 (1979), that Gallardo's claim accrued at the time of Curtis's assault. Gallardo timely appealed.

II. Standard of Review

"We review de novo a district court's interpretation of the statute of limitations under the FTCA, and its decision as to whether a statute of limitations bars a claim." *Hensley v. United States,* 531 F.3d 1052, 1056 (9th Cir.2008) (citations omitted).

III. Discussion

On appeal, Gallardo makes two arguments. First, she argues that the district court erred in concluding that her claim accrued at the time of Curtis's assault. Second, she argues that the statute of limitations should be equitably tolled. We disagree with her first argument. However, her second argument may have merit. In light of our intervening precedent in *Wong v. Beebe* holding that equitable tolling is available in FTCA actions, we remand to the district court to consider Gallardo's equitable tolling argument in the first instance.

A. Accrual of Gallardo's Claim

A plaintiff bringing an FTCA claim against the United States must first file an
p.864 administrative claim with the appropriate agency "within two years after such claim accrues." 28 U.S.C. § 2401(b). Otherwise, it is "forever barred." *Id.*

Gallardo argues that her claim did not accrue until 2009, when she learned of the Corps' negligence. We disagree. Gallardo's argument is foreclosed by *Kubrick.* The Supreme Court held in *Kubrick* that once a plaintiff becomes aware of her injury and its immediate cause, her claim accrues. 444 U.S. at 122, 100 S.Ct. 352. In so deciding, the Supreme Court declined to "hold that Congress intended that 'accrual' of a claim must await awareness by the plaintiff that [her] injury was negligently inflicted." *Id.* at 123, 100 S.Ct. 352.

Our post-*Kubrick* precedents are consistent with the conclusion that Gallardo's claim accrued at the time of Curtis's assault. For example, in *Hensley v. United States,* 531 F.3d 1052 (9th Cir.2008), we held that the plaintiffs' claim against the United States resulting from an accident involving a vehicle driven by a naval officer "accrued at the time of the collision and not later when the Attorney General certified that the [officer] was acting within the scope of his federal employment at the time of the collision." *Id.* at 1054. "[A]s a general rule, ignorance of the involvement of government employees is irrelevant to accrual of a federal tort claim." *Id.* at 1056. We wrote that *Kubrick* does not allow for "delay[ing] accrual of a federal tort claim until plaintiff knows or has reason to know of the culpability of federal agents." *Id.* (quoting *Gibson v. United States,* 781 F.2d 1334, 1344 (9th Cir.1986)). We explained:

> At the moment Eich [the naval officer] struck Mrs. Hensley's car with his own, the Hensleys knew both the fact of the injury and its immediate physical cause. The fact that Mrs. Hensley suffered an injury was immediately apparent; the cause (a collision) was immediately apparent; and even the identity of the person who inflicted the injury (Eich) was immediately apparent. Therefore, the Hensleys' claim accrued at the time of the accident.

Hensley, 531 F.3d at 1057 (citation omitted).

Gallardo cannot distinguish her case from *Hensley.* She emphasizes on appeal that "she could not have known or had reason to suspect" that the Corps was "complicit" in her injury "because the cause known at the time was [Curtis's] assault." But, as we held in *Hensley,* "ignorance of the involvement of United States employees is irrelevant." *Id.* at 1057 (quoting *Dyniewicz v. United States,* 742 F.2d 484, 487 (9th Cir.1984)). Here, Gallardo "knew both the fact of the injury and its immediate physical cause," *id.,* in May 2006. Because Gallardo did not file her administrative claim until four years later, the FTCA's two-year statute of limitations, absent tolling, had run.

B. Equitable Tolling

In the alternative, Gallardo argues that the statute of limitations should be equitably tolled. The government makes two arguments against equitable tolling.

First, it argues in a supplemental brief that Gallardo did not argue equitable tolling in the district court and has therefore waived this argument. In its answering brief, the government had argued on the merits that equitable tolling was not available under the FTCA. It contended that we had "overruled" *Alvarez-Machain v. United States,* 107 F.3d 696, 701 (9th Cir.1996) (holding that equitable tolling is available under the FTCA), in our 2009 decision in *Marley,* in which we held that equitable tolling is not available in FTCA actions. After the government's answering p.865 brief was filed, we overruled *Marley,* holding in *Wong* that equitable tolling is available. The government then argued, for the first time, that Gallardo had waived her equitable tolling argument by not raising it in the district court.

Because the government failed to argue waiver in its answering brief, its waiver argument is itself waived. *See Clem v. Lomeli,* 566 F.3d 1177, 1182 (9th Cir.2009). Even if the government had not "waived the waiver," however, we would be inclined to hold that Gallardo has not waived her equitable tolling argument. *See Romain v. Shear,* 799 F.2d 1416, 1419 (9th Cir.1986) (an exception to waiver exists "when a new issue arises while appeal is pending because of a change in law"). At the time of the district court's decision, *Marley* was still on the books. It clearly held that our prior holding in *Alvarez-Machain* was no longer good law. *See Marley,* 567 F.3d at 1037-38 (explaining that the holding in *Alvarez-Machain* "has no precedential value"). Only after our en banc decision in *Wong* did it become clear that *Marley* was not good law.

Second, the government argues that *Wong* does not control because that case involved a different provision of the FTCA's statute of limitations. The statute imposes two deadlines:

> A tort claim against the United States shall be forever barred unless it is presented in writing to the appropriate Federal agency within *two years* after such claim accrues or unless action is begun within *six months* after the date of mailing ... of notice of final denial of the claim by the agency to which it was presented.

28 U.S.C. § 2401(b) (emphasis added). The provision at issue in *Wong* was the six-month time limit for filing suit after agency denial of a claim. *See* 732 F.3d at 1033-34. The applicable provision here is the two-year time limit for filing a claim with the agency. Although these two provisions are part of the same statutory subsection, the government contends that our holding in *Wong* applies only to the six-month provision.

Our language and reasoning in *Wong* foreclose the government's argument. We repeatedly stated in *Wong* that § 2401(b) is nonjurisdictional and subject to equitable tolling, without distinguishing between the six-month and two-year provisions. *See, e.g., id.* at 1033 ("We hold that § 2401(b) is not 'jurisdictional,' and that equitable tolling is available under the circumstances presented in this case."); *id.* at 1038 ("Several factors underlie our conclusion that § 2401(b) is nonjurisdictional."); *id.* at 1049 ("[N]othing in § 2401(b) suggests that it is inconsistent with equitable tolling. To the contrary, the FTCA goes out of its way in its efforts to treat the United States the same as private tort defendants.").

Conclusion

We hold that *Wong*'s conclusion that 28 U.S.C. § 2401(b) is nonjurisdictional and subject to equitable tolling applies to the entirety of that subsection. We therefore vacate the district court's decision holding that Gallardo's FTCA claim is time-barred. We remand to the district court to consider Gallardo's equitable tolling argument in the first instance. We otherwise affirm. Each side shall bear its own costs.

AFFIRMED in part, VACATED in part, and REMANDED.

769 F.3d 1047 (2014)

Donna YOUNG; Gerald Young, husband and wife, and as guardians for minor child
J.Y., Plaintiffs-Appellants,

v.

UNITED STATES of America, Defendant-Appellee.

No. 13-35287.

United States Court of Appeals, Ninth Circuit.

Argued and Submitted July 11, 2014.

Filed October 17, 2014.

Young v. US, 769 F. 3d 1047 (9th Cir. 2014)

p.1050 Wayne Mitchell, Anderson & Mitchell PLLC, Seattle, WA, for Plaintiffs-
Appellants.

Priscilla To-Yin Chan (argued), Assistant United States Attorney; Jenny A.
Durkan, United States Attorney, Seattle, WA, for Defendant-Appellee.

Before: ARTHUR L. ALARCÓN, A. WALLACE TASHIMA, and MARY H.
MURGUIA, Circuit Judges.

OPINION

MURGUIA, Circuit Judge:

Plaintiffs Donna and Gerald Young and their minor daughter J.Y. appeal the
district court's order dismissing their complaint against the United States for
negligently failing to warn visitors at Mount Rainier National Park of a hazard that
the National Park Service both knew of and created. Donna sustained severe
injuries when she fell into a twelve-footdeep hole that had formed underneath the
snow in an area near the Park's main visitor center. The Youngs sued the United
States for damages relating to Donna's injuries, but the district court dismissed their
complaint for lack of subject matter jurisdiction, finding the action barred by the
discretionary function exception to the Federal Tort Claims Act. *See* 28 U.S.C. §
2680(a). On appeal, the United States maintains that the Park Service's decision not
to warn of the hazard was policy-driven—that is, guided by policies relating to
access, historic and natural resource preservation, and conservation —and is
therefore protected under the discretionary function exception. We conclude that
the Park Service's decision not to warn of the known hazard was not susceptible to
those policy considerations and therefore is not protected under the exception.
Accordingly, we reverse the district court's judgment and remand this case for
further proceedings.

I. Facts and Procedural History

Mount Rainier National Park ("the Park") was established in 1899 as the fifth
national park in the United States. Over 97 percent of the Park's 235,000 acres is
dedicated wilderness area, while the remaining three percent includes developed

areas such as roadways and visitor centers. In 1997, the entire park was designated as a National Historic Landmark District.

Each year, the Park receives about 1.5 to 2 million visitors, many of whom have little or no experience with alpine environments. Most of those visitors stop at the p.1051 Jackson Visitor Center (JVC), the Park's most popular visitor area, at some point during their stay. The JVC is located in an area of the Park known as "Paradise," which is situated on the southern slope of Mount Rainier and receives an average annual snowfall of 641 inches. In recent years, Paradise has been called "one of the snowiest places on the planet."

When the JVC was constructed in 2008, the National Park Service (NPS or "the Park Service") installed a transformer nearby to power the visitor center building. The NPS installed the transformer approximately 150 feet away from the visitor center building in a snowfield across a two-lane road that services the area. According to NPS staff, the area in which the transformer is located is "accessible but it's not attractive,"; "[i]t's not one of the areas that [the NPS] develop[s] and maintain[s] to get people out of the parking lot and onto the snow." The transformer operates year-round, releasing heat as it transfers electricity from nearby power lines to the JVC building.

The snowfield in which the transformer is located often accumulates more snow than other areas of the Park, because the NPS's road-plowing operations deposit snow there during in the winter. As a result, the field generally is covered in snow between November and mid-July. At one point, the area surrounding the transformer was marked with stakes so that the Park's snowplow operator would know where the transformer was located; the Park's staff was afraid that "the weight of the [snowplow], which is considerable, could collapse onto the transformer" underneath the snow. At the time of the incident giving rise to this appeal, there were no warning signs at or near the transformer's location.

Plaintiffs Donna and Gerald Young and their minor daughter J.Y. live in Santa Clara, California. In June 2010, they decided to "explore the Northwest" and travel to Washington. While in Washington they visited Mount Rainier National Park, where they hoped to "look around a little bit" and get their National Park Passport Books stamped at the JVC. They arrived at the Park in the early evening, just before the JVC was scheduled to close.

After the Youngs had parked their car, Donna and J.Y. went into the visitor center, looked around, got their passport books stamped, and then left the JVC to look for Gerald outside. They found Gerald standing in the snowfield across the road, where he was taking pictures of the mountain views. J.Y. walked away from her parents to explore snowfield. While she was exploring, she found a small hole, about two or three inches in diameter, in the snow. She asked Donna to come look at it.

When Donna approached the hole, the snow beneath her collapsed, and she fell approximately twelve feet, landing on a concrete pad on the ground underneath the transformer. According to the NPS Case Incident Record documenting Donna's fall, the transformer's heat had caused the snow above it to "mel[t] out," creating a large cavity beneath a "snow ceiling [that] was thin directly overtop of the transformer." Donna suffered severe injuries as a result of the fall.

Plaintiffs sued the United States under the Federal Tort Claims Act (FTCA), which permits individuals to sue the government for money damages to compensate for injuries arising out of the negligent acts of government employees. *See* 28 U.S.C. § 1346(b)(1). In their complaint, Plaintiffs alleged that the NPS negligently failed to warn Plaintiffs of a known, latent hazard (the transformer) the agency had created in the area of the JVC. Plaintiffs sought damages for physical injuries, p.1052 medical costs, economic losses, pain and suffering, and loss of consortium.

The government moved to dismiss Plaintiffs' complaint for lack of subject matter jurisdiction, *see* Fed.R.Civ.P. 12(b)(1), arguing that Plaintiffs' claim was barred by the discretionary function exception to the FTCA, *see* 28 U.S.C. § 2680(a) (excepting from the FTCA's waiver of immunity "[a]ny claim based upon ... the exercise or performance or the failure to exercise or perform a discretionary function or duty on the part of a federal agency or an employee of the Government, whether or not the discretion involved be abused"). According to the government, the NPS's decision not to place warning signs in the area of the transformer was a discretionary, policy-driven decision involving consideration of "NPS's policies and practices with respect to the discovery, warning and elimination of hazards."

The district court, applying the two-step test established in *Berkovitz v. United States,* 486 U.S. 531, 536-37, 108 S.Ct. 1954, 100 L.Ed.2d 531 (1988), for determining whether the discretionary function exception protected the agency's actions, granted the government's motion to dismiss. The court concluded that the NPS's decisions regarding "maintenance of the Park, decisions to identify and warn visitors from hazards, and the protection of visitors from hazards" were policy-driven decisions protected under the exception. Plaintiffs timely appealed the district court's order.

II. Standard of Review

We review de novo the district court's order dismissing Plaintiffs' complaint for lack of subject matter jurisdiction. *Terbush v. United States,* 516 F.3d 1125, 1128 (9th Cir.2008). In doing so, we generally accept as true the factual allegations of Plaintiffs' complaint and ask "whether the allegations state a claim sufficient to survive a motion to dismiss." *United States v. Gaubert,* 499 U.S. 315, 327, 111 S.Ct. 1267, 113 L.Ed.2d 335 (1991) (citing *Berkovitz,* 486 U.S. at 540, 108 S.Ct. 1954). Allegations of jurisdictional facts, however, are not afforded presumptive truthfulness; on a motion to dismiss for lack of subject matter jurisdiction, the court may hear evidence of those facts and "resolv[e] factual disputes where necessary." *Robinson v. United States,* 586 F.3d 683, 685 (9th Cir.2009) (internal quotation marks omitted) (alteration in original); *see also Augustine v. United States,* 704 F.2d 1074, 1077 (9th Cir.1983). We ordinarily review those factual findings for clear error. *Robinson,* 586 F.3d at 685.

When the jurisdictional motion "involv[es] factual issues which also go to the merits," a court should employ the standard applicable to a motion for summary judgment because "resolution of [those] jurisdictional facts is akin to a decision on the merits." *Augustine v. United States,* 704 F.2d 1074, 1077 (9th Cir. 1983). In that posture, the moving party "should prevail only if the material jurisdictional facts are not in dispute and the moving party is entitled to prevail as a matter of law." *Id.* Although Plaintiffs bear the initial burden to establish subject matter jurisdiction under the FTCA, it is the government's burden to establish that the discretionary function exception applies. *Oberson v. U.S. Dep't of Agric.,* 514 F.3d 989, 997 (9th Cir.2008).

In this case, the question whether the Park Service knew or should have known of the hazard created by the transformer is a disputed issue of jurisdictional fact that is "so intertwined" with the substantive dispute that resolution of the former depends, at least in part, on resolution of the latter. *See Augustine,* 704 F.2d at 1077 ("[W]here the jurisdictional issue and p.1053 the substantive issue are so intertwined that the question of jurisdiction is dependent on factual issues going to the merits, the jurisdictional determination should await a determination of the relevant facts on either a motion going to the merits or at trial."). Thus, if the fact of the Park Service's knowledge of the hazard changes our analysis as to whether the discretionary function exception applies, then Plaintiffs' complaint should not have been dismissed at this stage, and the question of jurisdiction instead should have awaited a determination on the merits.

III. Analysis

FTCA waives the government's immunity from suits arising out of certain negligent acts of federal employees. *See* 28 U.S.C. § 1346(b)(1).[1] The government's immunity is restored, however, under what is known as the "discretionary function exception," with respect to claims arising out of certain discretionary duties of federal agencies and employees. *See* 28 U.S.C. § 2680(a). The exception excludes from the FTCA's waiver of immunity

> [a]ny claim based upon ... the exercise or performance or the failure to exercise or perform a discretionary function or duty on the part of a federal agency or an employee of the Government, whether or not the discretion involved be abused.

Id.

To determine whether a particular claim is barred by the FTCA's discretionary function exception, we must conduct a two-step inquiry. *See Berkovitz,* 486 U.S. at 536-37, 108 S.Ct. 1954. At the first step, we must consider whether the agency's allegedly negligent conduct is discretionary —that is, "whether the action is a matter of choice for the acting employee." *Id.* at 536, 108 S.Ct. 1954. Conduct is not discretionary unless it "involves an element of judgment or choice." *Id.* Thus, the exception will not apply "when a federal statute, regulation, or policy specifically prescribes a course of action for an employee to follow" but the employee fails to follow it. *Id.* At the second step, we must determine whether the particular exercise of discretion was "of the kind that the discretionary function exception was designed to shield." *Id.* The decision must be one that is "grounded in social, economic, and political policy." *Id.*

"Whether a challenged action falls within the discretionary function exception requires a particularized analysis of the specific agency action challenged." *GATX/Airlog Co. v. United States,* 286 F.3d 1168, 1174 (9th Cir.2002). Thus, before turning to *Berkovitz*'s two-step inquiry, we must first identify Plaintiffs' "specific allegations of agency wrongdoing." 486 U.S. at 540, 108 S.Ct. 1954. To identify the particular agency conduct with which Plaintiffs take issue, we look to the allegations of Plaintiffs' complaint. *See Whisnant v. United States*, 400 F.3d 1177, 1184-85 (9th Cir.2005).

In their complaint, Plaintiffs alleged that the Park Service employees were negligent "when they failed to protect Donna Young from falling into the sinkhole caused by the transformer, failed to warn p.1054 Donna Young of the presence of the latent, dangerous sinkhole, and failed to make the area safe for visitors." Plaintiffs further alleged that Park Service employees knew or should have known that the transformer would emit heat, that it would thereby create a large cavern in the snow, and that park visitors would walk on the snow in the area of the hazard. In other words, Plaintiffs alleged that the Park Service was negligent in failing to warn of a hazard that it both knew of and created.

The district court framed Plaintiffs' allegations more broadly, however. It concluded that "the conduct at issue is the NPS's maintenance of the Park, decisions to identify and warn visitors from hazards, and the protection of visitors from hazards." Framed in that way, the district court assessed whether NPS's decisions about whether to warn the public of "hazards of a general nature within the park, whether known or unknown" and however created, were policy driven. Plaintiffs take issue with that characterization, contending that it fails to account for their allegations that the agency knew of the hazard and created it. We agree.

Our cases make clear that when determining whether the discretionary function exception applies in a particular case, "the question of how the government is alleged to have been negligent is critical." *Whisnant*, 400 F.3d at 1185. Had Plaintiffs actually alleged, for example, that the NPS was negligent in failing to warn of any danger, whether known or unknown and however created, their claim would likely be barred, just as the district court concluded. *See, e.g., Terbush*, 516 F.3d at 1137; *Blackburn v. United States*, 100 F.3d 1426, 1434 (9th Cir.1996); *Valdez v. United States*, 56 F.3d 1177, 1178 (9th Cir.1995); *Childers v. United States*, 40 F.3d 973, 975 (9th Cir.1994). But that is not what Plaintiffs alleged. Instead, they alleged that the government was negligent in failing to warn of a particular danger that it knew of and created—allegations that, in our view, are meaningfully different because they encompass conduct that may not be shielded by the Park Service's broad discretion. The distinction is therefore important, and the district court erred in mischaracterizing Plaintiffs' allegations.

Nonetheless, the government urges us to adopt the district court's broad characterization, lest the analysis "impermissibly collaps[e] the discretionary-function inquiry into a question of whether the government was negligent." But the government misses the point. We recognize, as we have before, that "the question of *whether* the government was negligent is irrelevant to the applicability of the discretionary function exception." *Whisnant*, 400 F.3d at 1185. By contrast, the question of *how* the government was negligent remains "critical" to the discretionary function exception inquiry—indeed, determining the precise action the government took or failed to take (that is, how it is alleged to have been negligent) is a necessary predicate to determining whether the government had discretion to take that action. *See generally id.*

In our view, the "specific allegatio[n] of agency wrongdoing" that we must use in determining whether the discretionary function exception applies in this case is Plaintiffs' allegation that NPS staff failed to warn of a known, latent hazard that the agency itself created. With that allegation of wrongdoing in mind, we turn to the *Berkovitz* two-step inquiry.

A.

In this case, the analysis at *Berkovitz*'s first step—whether the decision at issue "involve[d] an element of judgment or choice"—is relatively straightforward. The parties agree that the Park's decision p.1055 not to place warnings signs at or near the transformer was a discretionary decision. Neither party identifies any statute, regulation, or policy prescribing any specific course of conduct for warning against hazards the agency created. The conduct was therefore a matter of choice for the Park Service staff and was discretionary under *Berkovitz*.

B.

The parties' dispute lies in the analysis at *Berkovitz*'s second step— whether the decision was policy-driven. *See* 486 U.S. at 536-37, 108 S.Ct. 1954. The discretionary function exception protects against "judicial 'second-guessing' of legislative and administrative decisions" only in certain circumstances. *Id.* (quoting *United States v. Varig Airlines*, 467 U.S. 797, 814, 104 S.Ct. 2755, 81 L.Ed.2d 660 (1984)). Such instances generally involve decisions that are "based on considerations of public policy"-specifically, "social, economic, and political policy." *Id.* at 537, 108 S.Ct. 1954.

Our court has acknowledged the "weaving lines of precedent regarding what decisions are susceptible to social, economic, or political policy analysis," particularly in cases in which the allegation of agency wrongdoing involves a failure to warn. *Whisnant*, 400 F.3d at 1181. We have noted that "Government actions can be classified along a spectrum, ranging from those 'totally divorced from the sphere of policy analysis,' such as driving a car, to those 'fully grounded in regulatory policy,' such as the regulation and oversight of a bank." *Id.* (quoting *O'Toole v. United States*, 295 F.3d 1029, 1035 (9th Cir.2002)).

We begin by reviewing the specific policies that the government contends formed the basis of the agency's decision. The government first points to the Organic Act, 16 U.S.C. §§ 1-4, the statute through which the National Park Service was created. The Organic Act provides,

> The service thus established shall promote and regulate the use of the Federal areas known as national parks, monuments, and reservations hereinafter specified, ... by such means and measures as conform to the fundamental purpose of the said parks, monuments, and reservations, which purpose is to conserve the scenery and the natural and historic objects and the wild life therein and to provide for the enjoyment of the same in such manner and by such means as will leave them unimpaired for the enjoyment of future generations.

16 U.S.C. § 1. We have recognized that the Organic Act "sets forth the broad policy considerations that govern NPS's management of national parks" and that, under the Organic Act, "[m]uch of the NPS's work is 'grounded' in [a] broad mandate to balance conservation and access." *Terbush,* 516 F.3d at 1130.

The government also relies on more specific policies, all of which were established pursuant to the NPS's authority under the Organic Act, to justify its decision not to warn of the hazard created by the transformer. Specifically, it points to the NPS's 2006 Management Policies and the NPS's Director's Order # 50C as additional bases for its conduct.

The NPS's 2006 Management Policies apply nationwide and, like the Organic Act, also require the NPS, in providing for visitor safety, to balance its safety measures against considerations of conservation and access:

> The saving of human life will take precedence over all other management actions as the Park Service strives to protect human life and provide for injury-free visits. The Service will do this within the constraints of the 1916 Organic Act. p.1056 The primary—and very substantial— constraint imposed by the Organic Act is that discretionary management activities may be undertaken only to the extent that they will not impair park resources and values.

The policies go on to state that, at the park-specific level, "[t]he means by which public safety concerns are to be addressed is left to the discretion of superintendents and other decision-makers ... who must work within the limits of funding and staffing." "Examples include decisions about whether to install warnings signs...." Similarly, under Director's Order # 50C, park superintendents must "use their discretion to determine the level of program resources and the types of programs needed to manage visitor risk within their park." "Superintendents should strive to minimize the frequency and severity of visitor incidents by developing a range of appropriate prevention strategies ... includ[ing]... where appropriate, feasible, and consistent with the park mission, providing warnings about dangerous conditions (e.g., weather, construction areas) that may cause risk to visitors." Director's Order # 50C specifies that superintendents should exercise that discretion in light of "NPS policies relating to public safety, health, and the environment."

Against the backdrop of those and other related agency policies, our cases have identified important distinctions between protected and unprotected agency actions. The NPS's decisions with respect to the design and construction of roadways and trails, for example, are discretionary decisions that are "clear[ly] link[ed]" to social and political policies relating to access and resource preservation. *ARA Leisure Servs. v. United States,* 831 F.2d 193, 195 (9th Cir.1987); *see also Terbush,* 516 F.3d at 1137 (holding that the NPS's decision not to warn of a rockfall hazard involved a "process of identifying and responding to hazards in the wild" and "implicate[d] the NPS's broader policy mandates to balance access with conservation and safety"); *Childers,* 40 F.3d at 975 (concluding that the NPS's decision not to warn of unmaintained trails was "inextricably linked to central policy questions" relating to access and preservation). Such decisions are therefore protected under the discretionary function exception.

NPS decisions not to provide warnings at other natural features within the national parks, even where the NPS has provided access to those features, may likewise be protected. In *Valdez v. United States,* the plaintiffs sued the United States alleging a failure to erect barriers at the top of certain waterfalls in Kings Canyon National Park and a failure to warn of the dangers the waterfalls posed to the public. 56 F.3d at 1178. Relying on *Childers,* we held that the NPS's decision not to warn of natural, obvious risks "clearly implicates a choice between the competing policy considerations of maximizing access to and preservation of natural resources versus the need to minimize potential safety hazards." *Id.* at 1180. A year later, we held that the NPS's decision not to warn of the dangers of diving off Stoneman Bridge at Yosemite National Park was protected by the discretionary function exception because the decision was "based on considerations of visitor enjoyment, preservation of the historical features of the bridge, the need to avoid a proliferation of man-made intrusions, and protection of wildlife and the general riparian environment." *Blackburn,* 100 F.3d at 1434.

Those cases suggest that, when the NPS decides whether to warn of dangers that exist naturally in its national parks, those decisions generally are guided by considerations of policy. The NPS must balance, for example, its purpose to provide visitor p.1057 access to park resources against its need to protect the public from harm. It must also consider its obligation to preserve the natural environment "for the enjoyment of future generations." *See* 16 U.S.C. § 1. And, at times, it must consider how best to protect wildlife and park ecosystems and to preserve historical features of the lands it maintains.

But those policies, while crucial to the NPS's operations, cannot shield every decision the Park Service makes. For that reason, we have declined to "quickly accept that every minute aspect of the NPS's work is touched by the policy concerns of the Organic Act." *Terbush,* 516 F.3d at 1130. Because "[i]t is not sufficient for the government merely to [wave] the flag of policy as a cover for anything and everything it does that is discretionary," we have demanded "some support in the record" that the particular decision the NPS made was actually susceptible to analysis under the policies the government identified. *Id.* at 1134. Cases in which the government cannot provide such support delimit the scope of the discretionary function exception's reach.

Summers v. United States was such a case. In *Summers,* the plaintiffs alleged that the government had failed to warn visitors at Rodeo Beach of the hazards of stepping on hot coals at the beach's fire pits. 905 F.2d 1212, 1214 (9th Cir.1990). The government, in response, offered "no evidence ... that NPS's failure to post warnings of the sort that would have prevented [the plaintiff's] injury was the result of a decision reflecting the competing considerations of the Service's sign policy." *Id.* at 1215. Finding "nothing in the record to indicate that the failure to provide signs resulted from a decision grounded in economic, social, or political policy," we concluded that the government's failure to warn was not protected by the discretionary function exception. *Id.* at 1215-16. We reached a similar conclusion in *Oberson v. United States Department of Agriculture,* 514 F.3d at 997-98, noting that the government offered "no evidence to show that its failure to post a warning [at the location of a known hazard] was the result of a policy decision."

Our decision in *Sutton v. Earles*, 26 F.3d 903, 910 (9th Cir.1994), also dealt with a circumstance in which the agency's decision was not susceptible to policy analysis. In *Sutton*, we held that the Navy's failure to post speed limit signs after it placed buoys in navigable waterways was not protected by the discretionary function exception. Faced with a circumstance where, as here, the hazard at issue was both known to and created by the agency, we concluded that the agency's decision not to warn of that hazard was not policy-based. Specifically, we held that "[a] decision not to warn of a specific, known hazard for which the acting agency is responsible is not the kind of broader social, economic or political policy decision that the discretionary function exception is intended to protect." *Id.*

* * * * * *

Relying on those cases to guide our analysis, we must decide where this case falls along the spectrum of government conduct we have described. We conclude that the NPS's decision not to warn of the latent dangers associated with the transformer near the JVC was a decision "totally divorced" from the policies that the government has identified as the basis for its decision. *See Whisnant*, 400 F.3d at 1181. In so doing, we reject the government's argument that its decision required it to "balance safety, access, and preservation" in making judgments about (1) managing snow, (2) prioritizing inspections, (3) prioritizing and responding to hazards once identified, and (4) deciding "what signs, poles, fences or other barriers would p.1058 best educate, deter and prevent the public from accessing places where hazards may be found."

We have little doubt that NPS staff members make discretionary decisions every day about managing snow, prioritizing inspections, and responding to hazards. But those decisions are not at issue in this case, so we reject the government's efforts to make this case about them. Relying, as we must, on the facts alleged in Plaintiffs' complaint, this case is about the NPS's decision not to place a warning sign at the location of the buried transformer, even though the NPS knew that the transformer emitted heat, knew that it was buried under twelve feet of snow, and knew that it was located right across the road from the Park's most popular visitor area. The NPS's decision in that respect is not susceptible to considerations of any social, economic, or political policy that the government has identified.

As noted, the government argues that its decision was driven by policy considerations relating to access, historic and natural resource preservation, and conservation. It contends that this case is just like *Childers, Blackburn*, and *Valdez*— cases in which the agency had failed to warn in circumstances that we found to implicate considerations of access, resource preservation, and conservation. *See Childers*, 40 F.3d at 975-76 (unmaintained trails relate to access and resource preservation); *Blackburn*, 100 F.3d at 1434 (historic bridge relates to access, preservation, and the environment); *Valdez*, 56 F.3d at 1180 (barriers atop waterfalls relate to access and resource preservation). But here, those considerations are irrelevant.

The snowfield in which the transformer is located is approximately 150 feet from the visitor center building. While the snowfield is accessible—and, indeed, often accessed—NPS staff members claim that it is "not attractive." While the NPS was aware that visitors can access the area, the area is "not one of the areas that [the NPS] develop[s] and maintain[s] to get people out of the parking lot onto the snow." In other words, although visitors access the area of the transformer, the NPS does not *seek* to provide access to it. Thus, this is not a case in which the government is faced with policy considerations related to providing access to visitors in the face of known dangers.

This is also not a decision susceptible to policy matters such as historic or natural resource preservation. NPS staff members suggest that their decisions about where to place warning signs throughout the Park are often affected by their responsibility to protect the "look and feel of [the] historic district" and the "natural environment [and] the ecosystem." They note that "[t]he superintendent has the discretion to act upon hazards that would help prevent serious injury or fatality based on a number of things, and that includes the mission of what our legal mandate is, which is to protect—protect the park resources and the values that are in the park, and to ensure that they're going to be there for future generations." But their decision not to warn about the dangers associated with the transformer— infrastructure that itself takes away from the "look and feel of the historic district"— cannot reasonably be "linked" to those policies. Where, as here, the hazard is not located "in the wild," *see Terbush,* 516 F.3d at 1137, has no connection to visitor enjoyment or "protection of wildlife and the general alpine environment," *see Blackburn,* 100 F.3d at 1434, and was created by the agency itself, the Park Service's decision not to warn can only be considered "totally divorced" from the policies on which it purports to rely, *see O'Toole,* 295 F.3d at 1035.

p.1059 IV. Conclusion

The Organic Act and the regulations promulgated pursuant to its directive afford the National Park Service substantial discretion in making decisions related to the operation of our national parks. In making those decisions, NPS staff must consider policies concerning access; visitor enjoyment; historical, wildlife, and natural resource preservation; and conservation. 16 U.S.C. § 1. Above all, however, the Park Service must "striv[e] to protect human life and provide for injury-free visits." Where, as here, warning against a hazard known to and created by the NPS would not implicate concerns for access, visitor enjoyment, or environmental preservation, the *only* policy the NPS must consider is one it appears to have ignored: visitor safety.

In a similar case, we stated that

> a failure to warn involves considerations of safety, not public policy. It would be wrong to apply the discretionary function exception in a case where a low-level government employee made a judgment not to post a warning sign, or to erect a guardrail, or to make a safer path. Such a judgment would be no different than a judgment made by a private individual not to take certain measures to ensure the safety of visitors. To interpret such a judgment as discretionary would be too expansive an interpretation of [Congress's] intent in creating the discretionary function exception.

Faber v. United States, 56 F.3d 1122, 1125 (9th Cir.1995). Here, there is no apparent connection between the agency's decision and the policies it identifies as the basis for that decision. The only rationale for protecting the decision therefore "falls away." *See ARA Leisure Servs.,* 831 F.2d at 195. For that reason, we conclude that the NPS's decision not to warn of a hazard that it knew of and created—and that it placed near a visitor center serving 1 million visitors annually—cannot be shielded by the FTCA's discretionary function exception.[2] Because that is so, the district court erred in determining, at least at this stage, that it lacked jurisdiction over this case. We therefore reverse the district court's judgment and remand the case for further proceedings.

REVERSED AND REMANDED.

[1] Specifically, the FTCA waives the government's immunity with respect to claims for money damages for

injury or loss of property, or personal injury or death caused by the negligent or wrongful act or omission of any employee of the Government while acting within the scope of his office or employment, under circumstances where the United States, if a private person, would be liable to the claimant in accordance with the law of the place where the act or omission occurred.

28 U.S.C. § 1346(b)(1).

[2] Construing the facts in the light most favorable to the Plaintiffs, as we are required to do under *Augustine,* 704 F.2d at 1077, we assume that the Park Service knew of the hazard created by the transformer.

732 F.3d 1030 (2013)

KWAI FUN WONG; Wu-Wei Tien Tao Association, Plaintiffs-Appellants,

v.

David V. BEEBE, a former Immigration and Naturalization Service (nka Department of Homeland Security) Official; United States of America, Defendants-Appellees.

No. 10-36136.

United States Court of Appeals, Ninth Circuit.

Argued and Submitted En Banc March 20, 2013.

Filed October 9, 2013.

Kwai Fun Wong v. Beebe, 732 F. 3d 1030 (9th Cir. 2013)

p.1032 Thomas Martin Steenson (argued), Tom Steenson, Portland, OR; Beth Creighton, Creighton & Rose, Portland, OR, for Plaintiffs-Appellants.

Anne Murphy (argued), James George Bartolotto, and Barbara L. Herwig, Attorneys, United States Department of Justice, Civil Division, Washington, D.C.; R. Joseph Sher, Assistant United States Attorney, Alexandria, VA, for Defendants-Appellees.

Before: ALEX KOZINSKI, Chief Judge, and HARRY PREGERSON, A. WALLACE TASHIMA, M. MARGARET McKEOWN, WILLIAM A. FLETCHER, MARSHA S. BERZON, RICHARD R. CLIFTON, JAY S. BYBEE, CARLOS T. BEA, MILAN D. SMITH, JR., and MARY H. MURGUIA, Circuit Judges.

p.1033 Opinion by Judge BERZON; Concurrence by Chief Judge KOZINSKI; Dissent by Judge TASHIMA; Dissent by Judge BEA.

OPINION

BERZON, Circuit Judge:

We agreed to hear this case en banc to clarify whether the statute of limitations in 28 U.S.C. § 2401(b) of the Federal Tort Claims Act ("FTCA") may be equitably tolled. We hold that § 2401(b) is not "jurisdictional," and that equitable tolling is available under the circumstances presented in this case.

I. BACKGROUND

A. Statutory Background

The FTCA contains three timing rules that govern when a plaintiff may file a claim against the United States in the district court: First, 28 U.S.C. § 2675(a) establishes an administrative exhaustion requirement, which states that "[a]n action shall not be instituted upon a claim against the United States ... unless the claimant shall have first presented the claim to the appropriate Federal agency and his claim shall have been finally denied by the agency." Section 2675 further provides that "[t]he failure of an agency to make final disposition of a claim within six months after it is filed shall, at the option of the claimant any time thereafter, be deemed a final denial of the claim." *Id.*

Second, one statute of limitations in § 2401(b) sets a two-year deadline within which a claimant must present his claim "to the appropriate Federal agency ... after such claim accrues." *Id.* § 2401(b); *see United States v. Kubrick*, 444 U.S. 111, 119-21, 100 S.Ct. 352, 62 L.Ed.2d 259 (1979).

Finally, § 2401(b) also establishes a second limitations period—that "[a] tort claim against the United States shall be forever barred ... unless action is begun within six months after the ... final denial of the claim by the agency to which it was presented." 28 U.S.C. § 2401(b).

With this statutory framework in mind, we turn to the procedural history of this case, the material facts of which are not in dispute.

B. Facts

More than a decade ago, Kwai Fun Wong ("Wong") and Wu Wei Tien Tao Association ("the Association"), a religious organization, sued the United States and several Immigration and Naturalization Service ("INS") officials for claims arising out of Wong's detention. *See Wong v. INS (Wong I)*, 373 F.3d 952 (9th Cir.2004); *Wong v. Beebe (Wong II)*, 381 Fed.Appx. 715 (9th Cir.2010) (per curiam). The only remaining claim is one under the FTCA, alleging negligence against the United States based on the conditions of her confinement.

Wong and the Association filed their original complaint in the district court on May 18, 2001. That same day, Wong filed her negligence claim with the INS pursuant to the FTCA's administrative exhaustion requirement, 28 U.S.C. § 2675(a). Under § 2675(a), Wong was required to wait six months—until November 19, 2001—or until the INS denied the claim, before filing her negligence claim in the district court. *See* 28 U.S.C. §§ 1346(b)(1), 2675(a).

On November 14, 2001, Wong filed a motion in the district court seeking leave to file a Second Amended Complaint adding the negligence claim "on or after November 20, 2001"—*i.e.,* after the six-month waiting period required under § 2675(a) had expired. The INS issued a written decision denying Wong's administrative claim on December 3, 2001.

p.1034 At that point, Wong had until June 3, 2002, to file her negligence claim in the district court. Here is why: Pursuant to § 2675(a), Wong was prohibited from filing her claim in the district court until after she presented it to the INS and the INS "finally decided [the claim] ... in writing and sent [it] by certified or registered mail." 28 U.S.C. § 2675(a). Alternatively, § 2675(a) gave Wong the option to treat the INS's "failure ... to make final disposition of [her] claim within six months after it [was] filed" as the "final denial of the claim." *Id.* Wong attempted to exercise that option when she filed her motion in the district court seeking leave to file her amended complaint "on or after November 20, 2001"—six months after she filed her claim with the INS. Had her motion been granted, then, pursuant to § 2401(b), Wong would have had six months—until May 20, 2002—to file her amended complaint with the added FTCA claim in the district court. *See id.* § 2401(b). As noted, however, the INS denied Wong's claim on December 3, 2001, thereby starting anew the clock on the six-months limitations period in § 2401(b). Thus, the relevant deadline for filing Wong's claim in the district court was June 3, 2002. *See Lehman v. United States,* 154 F.3d 1010, 1015 (9th Cir.1998).

On April 5, 2002, more than five months after Wong filed her motion seeking leave to amend, the magistrate judge issued Findings and Recommendations ("F & R") recommending that Wong be permitted to file an amended complaint adding her FTCA claim. The district court did not issue an order adopting the F & R until June 25, 2002, three weeks after the six-month filing deadline had expired.

Wong did file an amended complaint on August 13, 2002, which included the FTCA claim. The district court, relying on *Marley v. United States,* 567 F.3d 1030, 1038 (9th Cir.2009), held that § 2401(b) was "jurisdictional," and that equitable tolling was therefore not available to excuse Wong's untimely filing of her claim. The district court dismissed Wong's FTCA claim for lack of jurisdiction. This appeal followed.

II. DISCUSSION

A. Applicability of Equitable Tolling to FTCA Claims

1. General Background

Irwin v. Department of Veterans Affairs, 498 U.S. 89, 111 S.Ct. 453, 112 L.Ed.2d 435 (1990), sets forth the "general rule ... govern[ing] the applicability of equitable tolling in suits against the Government." *Id.* at 95, 111 S.Ct. 453. That case considered whether the "rule of equitable tolling" applied to an untimely Title VII claim brought against the government. *Id.* at 94-95, 111 S.Ct. 453. Noting that "[t]ime requirements in lawsuits between private litigants are customarily subject to equitable tolling," *Irwin* held that "the same rebuttable presumption of equitable tolling applicable to suits against private defendants should also apply to suits against the United States." *Id.* at 95-96, 111 S.Ct. 453 (internal quotation marks omitted).

Irwin's "general rule" is not without exception. Some statutes of limitation are "more absolute," and do not permit "court[s] to consider whether certain equitable considerations warrant extending a limitations period." *John R. Sand & Gravel Co. v. United States,* 552 U.S. 130, 133-34, 128 S.Ct. 750, 169 L.Ed.2d 591 (2008). "As convenient shorthand, the Court has sometimes referred to the time limits in such statutes as 'jurisdictional.'" *Id.* at 134, 128 S.Ct. 750 (citing *Bowles v. Russell,* 551 U.S. 205, 210, 127 S.Ct. 2360, 168 L.Ed.2d 96 (2007)).

The "jurisdiction" terminology used in the government-defendant equitable
p.1035 tolling context can, however, be misleading. In a series of recent cases, the Supreme Court has "pressed a stricter distinction between *truly* jurisdictional rules, which govern 'a court's adjudicatory authority,' and nonjurisdictional 'claim-processing rules,' which do not." *Gonzalez v. Thaler,* ___ U.S. ___, 132 S.Ct. 641, 648, 181 L.Ed.2d 619 (2012) (quoting *Kontrick v. Ryan,* 540 U.S. 443, 454-55, 124 S.Ct. 906, 157 L.Ed.2d 867 (2004) (emphasis added)). This distinction is critical for present purposes, because, while courts "[have] no authority to create equitable

exceptions to jurisdictional requirements," *Bowles,* 551 U.S. at 214, 127 S.Ct. 2360, nonjurisdictional claim-processing requirements remain "subject to [*Irwin's*] rebuttable presumption in *favor* of equitable tolling." *Holland v. Florida,* 560 U.S. 631, 130 S.Ct. 2549, 2560, 177 L.Ed.2d 130 (2010) (internal quotation marks omitted).

Applying these principles to the particular statute of limitations here, our case law has come to contradictory results. *Alvarez-Machain v. United States (Alvarez-Machain I),* 107 F.3d 696, 701 (9th Cir. 1996), held that "[e]quitable tolling is available for FTCA claims in the appropriate circumstances." Twelve years later, *Marley* held precisely the opposite, stating "that the statute of limitations in 28 U.S.C. § 2401(b) is jurisdictional and, consequently, equitable doctrines that otherwise could excuse a claimant's untimely filing do not apply."[1] 567 F.3d at 1032; *see also Adams v. United States,* 658 F.3d 928, 933 (9th Cir.2011) (applying *Marley*).

We agreed to hear this case to resolve the conflict between *Alvarez-Machain I* and *Marley. See Atonio v. Wards Cove Packing Co.,* 810 F.2d 1477, 1478-79 (9th Cir.1987) (en banc). Doing so, we join with several other circuits in concluding that § 2401(b) is subject to equitable tolling. *See Arteaga v. United States,* 711 F.3d 828, 832-33 (7th Cir.2013); *Santos ex rel. Beato v. United States,* 559 F.3d 189, 194-98 (3d Cir.2009); *Perez v. United States,* 167 F.3d 913, 916-17 (5th Cir.1999).

2. Jurisdictional vs. Nonjurisdictional Claim-Processing Rules

As a threshold matter, we must decide whether § 2401(b) is a "jurisdictional" rule, to which equitable doctrines cannot apply, or a nonjurisdictional "claim-processing rule" subject to *Irwin's* presumption in favor of equitable tolling. Both *Alvarez-Machain I* and *Marley* were decided without the benefit of the Supreme Court's most recent decisions clarifying the difference between these two categories. Accordingly, before turning to § 2401(b) itself, we discuss the Court's efforts in recent years to "bring some discipline" to the "jurisdictional" label. *See Henderson ex rel. Henderson v. Shinseki,* ___ U.S. ___, 131 S.Ct. 1197, 1202-03, 179 L.Ed.2d 159 (2011); *see also Gonzalez,* 132 S.Ct. at 648.

The consequences of labeling a particular statutory requirement "jurisdictional" are "drastic." *Gonzalez,* 132 S.Ct. at 648. A court's "[s]ubject-matter jurisdiction can never be waived or forfeited," p.1036 "objections [to the court's jurisdiction] may be resurrected at any point in the litigation," and courts are obligated to consider *sua sponte* requirements that "go[] to subject-matter jurisdiction." *Id.; see also Henderson,* 131 S.Ct. at 1202; *Proctor v. Vishay Intertechnology Inc.,* 584 F.3d 1208, 1219 (9th Cir.2009).

The Court has clarified in recent years that the term "'[j]urisdiction[al]' refers to a court's adjudicatory authority ... [and] properly applies *only* to prescriptions delineating the classes of cases (subject-matter jurisdiction) and the persons (personal jurisdiction) implicating that authority." *Reed Elsevier, Inc. v. Muchnick,* 559 U.S. 154, 160-61, 130 S.Ct. 1237, 176 L.Ed.2d 18 (2010) (emphasis added) (internal quotation marks and citation omitted). Under this narrow interpretation, the term "jurisdictional" "refers [only] to a tribunal's power to hear a case." *Union Pac. R.R. Co. v. Bhd. of Locomotive Eng'rs & Trainmen Gen. Comm. of Adjustment, Cent. Region,* 558 U.S. 67, 81, 130 S.Ct. 584, 175 L.Ed.2d 428 (2009) (internal quotation marks omitted). So-called "claim-processing rules," by contrast, "are rules that seek to promote the orderly progress of litigation by requiring that the parties take certain procedural steps at certain specified times." *Henderson,* 131 S.Ct. at 1203.

"To ward off profligate use of the term 'jurisdiction,' [the Court has] adopted a 'readily administrable bright line' for determining whether to classify a statutory limitation as jurisdictional." *Sebelius v. Auburn Reg'l Med. Ctr.,* ___ U.S. ___, 133 S.Ct. 817, 824, 184 L.Ed.2d 627 (2013) (quoting *Arbaugh v. Y & H Corp.,* 546 U.S. 500, 516, 126 S.Ct. 1235, 163 L.Ed.2d 1097 (2006)). Specifically, courts must now ask "whether Congress has 'clearly state[d]' that the rule is jurisdictional; absent such a clear statement ... 'courts should treat the restriction as nonjurisdictional in character.'" *Id.* (quoting *Arbaugh,* 546 U.S. at 515-16, 126 S.Ct. 1235). Congress need not "incant magic words in order to speak clearly." *Id.* Rather, courts are to review a statute's language, "context, and relevant historical treatment" to determine whether Congress clearly intended a statutory restriction to be jurisdictional. *Reed Elsevier, Inc.,* 559 U.S. at 166, 130 S.Ct. 1237.

Applying this bright-line rule in a spate of recent cases, the Court has held nonjurisdictional various statutory limitations on the substantive coverage of statutes or the procedures for enforcing them. *See, e.g., Union Pac. R.R.,* 558 U.S. at 81-82, 130 S.Ct. 584 (holding not jurisdictional a Railway Labor Act procedural rule requiring proof of a prearbitration settlement conference); *Reed Elsevier,* 559 U.S. at 164-66, 130 S.Ct. 1237 (holding not jurisdictional the Copyright Act registration requirement); *Gonzalez,* 132 S.Ct. at 648-52 (holding not jurisdictional certain provisions of the Antiterrorism and Effective Death Penalty Act of 1996 ("AEDPA") requiring issuance of a certificate of appealability indicating which specific issues sufficiently implicate the denial of a constitutional right); *but see Bowles,* 551 U.S. at 209-10, 127 S.Ct. 2360 (holding jurisdictional a time limit for filing a notice of appeal in a civil case under 28 U.S.C. § 2107(c)).

As the issue here pertains to a statute of limitations, the Court's recent decisions applying the "clear statement" rule to statutory time limits are particularly instructive. *Henderson* held that "a veteran's failure to file a notice of appeal within the 120-day period" required under 38 U.S.C. § 7266(a) "should [not] be regarded as having 'jurisdictional' consequences." 131 S.Ct. at 1200. Canvassing the Court's recent case law discussing jurisdictional versus nonjurisdictional rules, *Henderson* explained that "[f]iling deadlines ... are p.1037 *quintessential* claim-processing rules." *Id.* at 1203 (emphasis added). "[E]ven if important and mandatory," such rules, "should not be given the jurisdictional brand." *Id.*

Turning to the text of § 7266, *Henderson* emphasized that the relevant provision "'does not speak in jurisdictional terms or refer in any way to the jurisdiction of the [Veterans Court].'" *Id.* at 1204 (quoting *Zipes v. Trans World Airlines, Inc.,* 455 U.S. 385, 394, 102 S.Ct. 1127, 71 L.Ed.2d 234 (1982) (alteration in original)). Although "§ 7266 is cast in mandatory language"—providing that a claimant "*shall* file a notice of appeal ... within 120 days"—*Henderson* "rejected the notion that 'all mandatory prescriptions, *however emphatic,* are ... properly typed jurisdictional.'" *Id.* at 1204-05 (quoting *Union Pac. R.R.,* 558 U.S. at 81, 130 S.Ct. 584) (emphasis added). Indeed, as *Henderson* noted, Congress placed § 7266 "in a subchapter entitled 'Procedure,'" and not in the "Organization and Jurisdiction" subchapter of the statute, which "suggests Congress regarded the 120-day limit as a claim-processing rule." *Id. Henderson* therefore found no clear statement indicating that § 7266 was "jurisdictional." *Id.; see also Holland,* 130 S.Ct. at 2560 (holding not jurisdictional AEDPA's statute of limitations in 28 U.S.C. § 2244(d)).

More recently, *Auburn Regional Medical Center* considered whether the Medicare Act's 180-day statutory deadline for filing an administrative appeal challenging Medicare reimbursements is jurisdictional. 133 S.Ct. at 821. The Court held that it is not. "Key to our decision," the Court explained, is that "filing deadlines ordinarily are not jurisdictional; indeed, we have described them as 'quintessential claim-processing rules.'" *Id.* at 825 (quoting *Henderson,* 131 S.Ct. at 1203).

Auburn Regional Medical Center went on to reject the notion that the 180-day limit was "jurisdictional simply because it is placed in a section of a statute that also contains jurisdictional provisions." *Id.* at 825. Nor was it significant in *Auburn Regional Medical Center* that Congress "expressly made ... *other* time limits in the Medicare Act" nonjurisdictional. *Id.* (emphasis added). Structural considerations such as these did not provide a "clear statement" that Congress intended the 180-day limit to be jurisdictional. The limitations provision was therefore "most sensibly characterized as a nonjurisdictional prescription." *Id.* at 826.

Finally, we applied a similar analysis in a recent en banc case addressing whether the exhaustion-of-remedies requirement of the Individuals with Disabilities Education Act ("IDEA"), 20 U.S.C. § 1415(*l*), is jurisdictional. *See Payne v. Peninsula Sch. Dist.,* 653 F.3d 863 (2011) (en banc). Based on the Supreme Court's recent line of cases "clarifying the difference between provisions limiting our subject matter jurisdiction, which cannot be waived ..., and 'claims processing provisions,'" we concluded that § 1415(*l*) is not jurisdictional for three reasons. *Id.* at 867-69 (citing cases).

First, "we observe[d] that nothing in § 1415 mentions the jurisdiction of the federal courts." *Id.* at 869. "Second, nothing in the relevant jurisdictional statutes requires exhaustion under the IDEA." *Id.* at 870. "Without clearer instruction from Congress," we declined to "infer" a jurisdictional exhaustion-of-remedies requirement. *Id.* "Finally, we [could] find no reason why § 1415(*l*) should be read to make exhaustion a prerequisite to the exercise of federal subject matter jurisdiction." *Id.* To the contrary, we suggested that there were "many good reasons why" § 1415(*l*) should not qualify as jurisdictional. Most notably, determining whether a plaintiff had exhausted her remedies p.1038 is an "inexact science," subject to various "fact-specific" questions such as whether exhaustion would be futile. *Id.* Thus, we summarized, § 1415(*l*) is not jurisdictional, as it "is not clearly labeled jurisdictional, is not located in a jurisdiction-granting provision, and admits of congressionally authorized exceptions." *Id.* at 870-71 (quoting *Reed Elsevier,* 559 U.S. at 166, 130 S.Ct. 1237); *see also Leeson v. Transamerica Disability Income Plan,* 671 F.3d 969, 979 (9th Cir.2012) (holding that an employee's status as a plan "participant" is an element of his ERISA claim, not a jurisdictional limitation).

3. § 2401(b) Is Not Jurisdictional

Marley stated that "[r]esolution of the present case ... [first] depends on how to categorize the six-month filing deadline of § 2401(b)"—as a "jurisdictional" requirement or as a nonjurisdictional "claim-processing rule." 567 F.3d at 1035. That is true, but only in the asymmetrical sense that if the deadline is jurisdictional, it cannot be tolled; as will appear, even if it is not jurisdictional, tolling may still be precluded by a sufficiently clear congressional expression of that restriction. We hold that § 2401(b) falls squarely in the claim-processing category, and so overrule *Marley's* contrary conclusion.

Several factors underlie our conclusion that § 2401(b) is nonjurisdictional.

a. *Language*

First, by its terms, § 2401(b) provides only that "[a] tort claim against the United States shall be forever barred unless ... action is begun within six months" of mailing of notice of the final agency denial. 28 U.S.C. § 2401(b). That statement "does not speak in jurisdictional terms or refer in any way to the jurisdiction of the [federal courts]." *Henderson,* 131 S.Ct. at 1204; *see also Payne,* 653 F.3d at 869-70. Rather, § 2401(b) merely states what is ordinarily true of statutory filing deadlines: once the limitations period ends, whether extended by the application of tolling principles or not, a plaintiff is "forever barred" from presenting his claim to the relevant adjudicatory body. *See Kubrick,* 444 U.S. at 117, 100 S.Ct. 352.

Notably, although the exact language differs, § 2401(b) is the same in its lack of a reference to jurisdiction as the general, non-tort statute of limitations contained in § 2401(a), which establishes a six-year filing deadline for "every civil action commenced against the United States." 28 U.S.C. § 2401(a). And *Cedars-Sinai Medical Center v. Shalala,* 125 F.3d 765, 770 (9th Cir.1997), held subsection (a) nonjurisdictional, emphasizing that it "does not speak of jurisdiction, but erects only a procedural bar."[2]

Contrary to the government's assertion, § 2401(b) does not contain such unusually emphatic language that we may infer congressional intent to limit the adjudicatory authority of the federal courts from that language. We have held on prior occasions that statutes of limitations containing the phrase "forever barred" are subject to equitable tolling. For example, the 1955 Clayton Act Amendments provided that any action to enforce a right under §§ 15, 15a, and 15c of the Act "shall be *forever barred* unless commenced within four years after the cause of action accrued." 15 U.S.C. § 15b (emphasis added); *see also* Pub.L. No. 137, 69 Stat. 283 (1955). *Mt.* p.1039 *Hood Stages, Inc. v. Greyhound Corp.,* 616 F.2d 394, 396-407 (9th Cir.1980), determined that § 15b could be equitably tolled. *See also Hexcel Corp. v. Ineos Polymers, Inc.,* 681 F.3d 1055, 1060-61 (9th Cir.2012) (discussing tolling under § 15b); *cf. Rotella v. Wood,* 528 U.S. 549, 561, 120 S.Ct. 1075, 145 L.Ed.2d 1047 (2000) (indicating that equitable tolling may be available for civil claims brought under the Racketeer Influenced and Corrupt Organizations Act ("RICO"), which applies the same four-year statute of limitations in 15 U.S.C. § 15b).

Likewise, the 1947 amendments to the Fair Labor Standards Act ("FLSA")— which were enacted on the heels of the FTCA—provided that every action under the FLSA "shall be *forever barred* unless commenced within two years after the cause of action accrued" 29 U.S.C. § 255(a) (emphasis added); *see also* Pub.L. No. 40, § 6(b), 61 Stat. 84, 88 (1947). *Partlow v. Jewish Orphans' Home of Southern California,* 645

F.2d 757, 760-61 (9th Cir.1981), *abrogated on other grounds by Hoffmann-La Roche, Inc. v. Sperling,* 493 U.S. 165, 110 S.Ct. 482, 107 L.Ed.2d 480 (1989), held that this statute of limitations could be equitably tolled.

In various other statutes enacted in the mid-twentieth century, Congress included limitations provisions "forever barr[ing]" untimely claims. *See, e.g.,* Automobile Dealer Franchise Act of 1956, 84 Pub.L. No. 1026, § 3, 70 Stat. 1125 (1956), *codified at* 15 U.S.C. § 1223 ("Any action brought pursuant to this Act shall be *forever barred* unless commenced within three years after the cause of action shall have accrued.") (emphasis added); National Traffic and Motor Vehicle Safety Act of 1966, Pub.L. No. 89-563, § 111(b), 80 Stat. 718, 725 (1966), *as amended by* Pub.L. No. 103-272, 108 Stat. 745 (1994) ("Any action brought pursuant to this section shall be *forever barred* unless commenced within three years after the cause of action shall have accrued.") (emphasis added); Agricultural Fair Practices Act of 1967, Pub.L. No. 90-288, § 6(a), 82 Stat. 93, 95 (1967), *codified at* 7 U.S.C. § 2305(c) (same); National Mobile Home Construction and Safety Standards Act of 1974, Pub.L. No. 93-383, § 613, 88 Stat. 633, 707 (1974), *codified at* 42 U.S.C. § 5412(b) (same). Viewed against this backdrop, § 2401(b)'s "forever barred" language appears to be more a vestige of mid-twentieth-century congressional drafting conventions than a "clear statement" of Congress's intent to include a jurisdictional filing deadline in the FTCA.

Moreover, even if one does read the "forever barred" language in § 2401(b) as an especially emphatic limitation on FTCA claims, the Supreme Court's recent line of cases clarifying the jurisdictional/nonjurisdictional distinction make plain that not all "'mandatory prescriptions, *however emphatic,* are ... properly typed jurisdictional.'" *Henderson,* 131 S.Ct. at 1205 (quoting *Union Pac. R.R.,* 558 U.S. at 81, 130 S.Ct. 584) (emphasis added); *see also Gonzalez,* 132 S.Ct. at 651; *Kontrick,* 540 U.S. at 454, 124 S.Ct. 906. And nothing in the text of § 2401(b) suggests that it is anything other than a straightforward filing deadline—a "quintessential claim-processing rule[]." *Henderson,* 131 S.Ct. at 1203.

Undeterred by the statute's silence as to whether the limitations period is jurisdictional (and by its placement in a section not directed at jurisdiction), Judge Bea offers a grand theory as to why § 2401(b) nonetheless clearly states a jurisdictional rule, positing that there are two types of statutes of limitations: "Plain Statutes of Limitations" and "Consequence Statutes of Limitations." Bea Dissent at 1063, 1065. The latter purportedly "provide mandatory consequences for failures to act according to their prescriptions," *id.* at 1066, and so p.1040 "require the courts to respond in a certain way to a party's failure to timely act." *Id.* Judge Bea's dissent goes on to maintain that *whenever* a limitations provision states that a claim "shall be ... barred," or "forever barred," "Congress has spoken in jurisdictional terms" and the courts lack authority to adjudicate the claim—even if there is no mention of jurisdiction or placement in a jurisdiction provision. *Id.* at 1066-67.

Judge Bea's consequential language approach is not one that the Supreme Court has ever articulated or relied upon in determining whether a particular limitations provision is jurisdictional. Indeed, the Court criticized this approach in *Irwin,* noting that, "[a]n argument can undoubtedly be made that the ... language is more stringent ..., but we are not persuaded that the difference ... is enough to manifest a different congressional intent with respect to the availability of equitable tolling."

498 U.S. at 95, 111 S.Ct. 453. While the Court has held jurisdictional certain limitations provisions containing the phrase "shall be ... barred," it has never relied on the notion of "consequential" language to do so.[3] Instead, the Court has repeatedly eschewed a "magic words" approach to determining whether procedural requirements are jurisdictional, repeatedly taking a multifactor approach to the inquiry. *See Reed Elsevier,* 559 U.S. at 165, 130 S.Ct. 1237; *Auburn Reg'l Med. Ctr.,* 133 S.Ct. at 824.

Beyond that observation, we shall bypass ruling on whether Judge Bea's "consequential" language theory is a helpful construct in some circumstances. As with most attempts to create rigid dichotomous categories, the trick is not in devising the categories but in placing various circumstances into one or the other category. Although, according to Judge Bea, a limitations provision containing "shall ... be barred" language "'set[s] forth an inflexible rule requiring dismissal,'" Bea Dissent at 1068 (quoting *Holland,* 130 S.Ct. at 2560), the words relied upon simply do not have that import.

First, as to the word "shall," the Court consistently has rejected arguments "seiz[ing] on the word 'shall'" to suggest that "'all mandatory prescriptions, however emphatic, are ... properly typed jurisdictional.'" *Gonzalez,* 132 S.Ct. at 651 (quoting *Henderson,* 131 S.Ct. at 1205); *see also Dolan v. United States,* 560 U.S. 605, 130 S.Ct. 2533, 2539, 177 L.Ed.2d 108 (2010) (holding that a statute's use of the word "shall" alone does not render statutory deadline jurisdictional).

Second, § 2401(b) does not in terms order *courts* to do anything, including dismiss any untimely claim. Like the exhaustion-of-remedies requirement at issue in *Payne,* "neither the word 'courts' nor the word 'jurisdiction' appears in [§ 2401(b)]." *Payne,* 653 F.3d at 869. Instead, the phrase "shall be ... barred" is couched in the passive tense, and so could as well be directed to the plaintiff, barring him from filing the suit, as to the court, directing it to bar the filing. The "shall be ... barred" language of the six-month filing deadline therefore does not express "an inflexible rule requiring dismissal whenever p.1041 its clock has run." *Holland,* 130 S.Ct. at 2560 (internal quotation marks omitted).

Third, the word "forever" in § 2401(b) cannot supply the missing link with regard to declaration of an inflexible rule. *See* Bea Dissent at 1068-69. The word "forever" is most commonly understood as one focusing on *time,* not on scope or degree of flexibility in a static time frame. *See* Webster's New International Dictionary of the English Language 990 (2d ed.1940) (defining "forever" to mean "[f]or a limitless time or endless ages; everlastingly; eternally," and "[a]t all times; always; incessantly"); Oxford English Dictionary (2013) (defining "forever" to mean "[a]lways, at all times; in all cases ... [t]hroughout all time, eternally; throughout all past or all future time; perpetually"). As such, the term "forever" is most naturally read to emphasize that an untimely FTCA claim, once barred, is precluded permanently, not temporarily or until some later event occurs. A claimant therefore cannot refile the claim, nor may the time bar be lifted once it is imposed. So understood, the term "forever" does have a function in the statute, just not the one Judge Bea posits.[4] Thus, as the Fifth Circuit observed, "the use of the words 'forever barred' [in § 2401(b)] is irrelevant to equitable tolling, which properly conceived does not resuscitate stale claims, but rather prevents them from becoming stale in the first place."[5] *Perez,* 167 F.3d at 916.

In sum, nothing in the language of § 2401(b)—including the term "shall ... be barred," and the word "forever"—supplies a "clear statement" that Congress intended the six-month filing deadline to be jurisdictional.[6]

p.1042 b. Placement

The "context" surrounding § 2401(b) likewise does not "clearly" indicate Congress's intent to "rank" this provision as jurisdictional. *Auburn Reg'l Med. Ctr.,* 133 S.Ct. at 824.

The jurisdiction-granting provision of the FTCA is located at 28 U.S.C. § 1346(b)(1) and provides that "[s]ubject to the provisions of chapter 171 of this title, the district courts ... shall have exclusive jurisdiction of civil actions on claims against the United States ... under circumstances where the United States, if a private person, would be liable to the claimant." Section 1346(b)(1) makes no mention of the six-month filing deadline in § 2401(b). Furthermore, while § 1346(b)(1) does cross-reference "the provisions of chapter 171," it does *not* cross-reference § 2401(b), which is located in chapter 161, not chapter 171. Thus, the FTCA's statute of limitations "is located in a provision separate from [the provision] granting federal courts subject-matter jurisdiction over [FTCA] claims." *Reed Elsevier,* 559 U.S. at 164, 130 S.Ct. 1237 (internal quotation marks omitted); *see also Henderson,* 131 S.Ct. at 1205.

Further, even if § 1326(b) did mention the six-month filing deadline in § 2401(b), the Court's recent guidance on this subject indicates that an otherwise nonjurisdictional rule's location within a statutory scheme does not automatically transform the rule into a jurisdictional prerequisite. Thus, a rule "does not become jurisdictional simply because it is placed in a section of a statute that also contains jurisdictional provisions." *Auburn Reg'l Med. Ctr.,* 133 S.Ct. at 825; *see also Gonzalez,* 132 S.Ct. at 651.

Not satisfied with the plain language of § 1346(b), the government looks elsewhere for a "clear statement" of § 2401(b)'s jurisdictional import: the legislative history of the FTCA. According to the government, "[t]he FTCA's limitations provision is found outside of chapter 171 only as a happenstance of recodification." In his dissent, Judge Tashima likewise relies on the earlier version of the FTCA to conclude that "Congress provided a clear statement [that the FTCA's limitations provision was jurisdictional] when enacting the provision in 1946," and that statement remains clear today. Tashima Dissent at 1059.

In the first place, and dispositively, it is improper to consider legislative history in this instance. "[T]he authoritative statement is the statutory text, not the legislative history or any other extrinsic material." *Exxon Mobil Corp. v. Allapattah Servs., Inc.,* 545 U.S. 546, 568, 125 S.Ct. 2611, 162 L.Ed.2d 502 (2005). Consequently, "when the statute's language is plain, the sole function of the courts—at least where the disposition required by the text is not absurd—is to enforce it according to its terms." *Hartford Underwriters Ins. Co. v. Union Planters Bank, N.A.,* 530 U.S. 1, 6, 120 S.Ct. 1942, 147 L.Ed.2d 1 (2000) (quoting *United States v. Ron Pair Enters., Inc.,* 489 U.S. 235, 241, 109 S.Ct. 1026, 103 L.Ed.2d 290 (1989)) (internal quotation marks omitted). The current statutory language of § 1326(b), the FTCA jurisdictional provision, cross-references other provisions of the FTCA but not the chapter containing the limitations provision, p.1043 § 2401(b). There is no ambiguity whatever in this regard; chapter 171 is not, and does not include, chapter 161, period.[7]

Secondly, even if we were to consider the FTCA's legislative history, we could find no "clear statement" as to jurisdiction. *See Exxon Mobil,* 545 U.S. at 568-69, 125 S.Ct. 2611. Congress first enacted the FTCA in 1946 as Title IV of the Legislative Reorganization Act ("1946 Act"). *See* Pub.L. No. 79-601, tit. IV, 60 Stat. 812, 842-47 (1946). The provisions of the FTCA were codified in chapter 20 of Title 28 of the United States Code. *See* 28 U.S.C. §§ 921-46 (1946).[8] As originally codified, the FTCA's grant of jurisdiction read:

> Subject to the provisions of this chapter, the United States district court for the district court wherein the plaintiff is resident or wherein the act or omission complained of occurred ... shall have exclusive jurisdiction to hear, determine, and render judgment on any claim against the United States, for money only ... on account of personal injury or death caused by the negligent or wrongful act or omission of any employee of the Government while acting within the scope of his office or employment, under circumstances where the United States, if a private person, would be liable to the claimant for such damage, loss, injury, or death in accordance with the law of the place where the act or omission occurred.

28 U.S.C. § 931(a) (1946). Congress recodified and reorganized all of Title 28 in 1948, and, in the course of doing so, placed the FTCA's limitations provision in its current location in chapter 161, while placing most of the other FTCA provisions formerly located in chapter 20 in chapter 171. Pub.L. No. 80-773 ("1948 Act"), 62 Stat. 869, 970-74 (1948); *id.* 62 Stat. 869, 982-85. The jurisdiction-granting provision was relocated to chapter 85 and codified at 28 U.S.C. § 1346(b). *Id.* at 933. Because § 1346(b) was no longer located in the same chapter as the other FTCA provisions, the "subject to" phrase was changed to refer to "the provisions of chapter 173 of this title." *Id.*

As Judge Tashima points out, the reference in the 1948 version of § 1346(b) to chapter 173 was a scrivener's error, as there was no chapter 173 of Title 28. Tashima p.1044 Dissent at 1056. A year later, Congress corrected the error, changing the language of § 1346(b) to read: "[s]ubject to the provisions of chapter 171." *See* Pub.L. No. 81-55, 63 Stat. 62 (1949). But that correction did nothing to erase the fact that the only cross-reference in the jurisdictional provision, § 1346(b), is to a chapter, chapter 171, which *does not* contain the FTCA limitations provisions.

Nor does the directive of the 1948 Act that we are not to "infer ... a legislative construction from the chapter in which a provision appears" override the plain terms of § 1346(b) as revised. No *inference* is required to conclude that the FTCA jurisdictional provision is no longer "subject to" the limitations section. Instead, one need only read § 1346(b) to determine that that is so; again, chapter 161 is not chapter 171, period. Thus, although the Court "does not presume that the 1948 revision worked a change in the underlying substantive law unless an intent to make such a change is clearly expressed," *John R. Sand & Gravel Co.,* 552 U.S. at 136, 128 S.Ct. 750 (internal quotation marks omitted), that intent *was* clearly expressed when the cross-reference to § 1346(b) was revised to include many provisions of the FTCA but not the applicable limitations period.

Under Judge Tashima's "inference" approach to the clear statutory language, it would not have mattered what Congress wrote into the FTCA's jurisdictional grant in 1948 (and later corrected in 1949). Congress could have revised the statute to read "Subject to the provisions of chapter 171" (as it eventually did); "Subject to the provisions of chapter 171 and 161"; or "Subject to the provisions of chapter 161," and Judge Tashima's interpretation would still be the same—"subject to any provision of the original FTCA as codified in 1946."[9]

We hold, instead, that § 1346(b) means what it says: that the district courts "shall have exclusive jurisdiction of civil actions on claims against the United States[] for money damages," "[s]ubject to the provisions of chapter 171." 28 U.S.C. § 1346(b). The FTCA's legislative history cannot supply a "clear statement" to the contrary. Accordingly, there is no contextual reason to think that the limitations period provisions are jurisdictional.[10]

p.1045 c. *Exceptions*

In holding § 2401(b) "jurisdictional," *Marley* found it significant that Congress "explicitly included some exceptions to the deadlines in § 2401(a), but included no such exceptions in § 2401(b)." 567 F.3d at 1037. Section 2401(a) provides, in relevant part, that an "action of any person under legal disability or beyond the seas at the time the claim accrues may be commenced within three years after the disability ceases." 28 U.S.C. § 2401(a). *Marley* reasoned that "[b]ecause Congress chose to extend the time limit in § 2401(a) under certain circumstances, but did not include any exceptions to the limitations period of § 2401(b), we must conclude that Congress intended the deadlines of § 2401(b) to be adhered to strictly." 567 F.3d at 1037 (emphasis omitted).

That conclusion cannot be squared with *Auburn Regional Medical Center,* which rejected the argument that a statutory time limit "should be viewed as jurisdictional because Congress could have expressly made the provision nonjurisdictional, and indeed did so for other time limits in the [statute]." 133 S.Ct. at 825. Although "Congress's use of certain language in one part of the statute and different language in another can indicate that different meanings were intended," that interpretive principle cannot, without more, provide the "clear statement" required to classify § 2401(b) as "jurisdictional." *Id.* at 825-26 (internal quotation marks omitted); *see also Santos,* 559 F.3d at 195-96.

d. *Earlier Cases*

Finally, unlike in *Bowles,* 551 U.S. at 210-13, 127 S.Ct. 2360, and *John R. Sand & Gravel,* 552 U.S. at 137-39, 128 S.Ct. 750, there has not been a venerable, consistent line of cases treating the FTCA limitations period as jurisdictional counseling against switching gears now. Although we have held that § 2401(b) is jurisdictional, *see Marley,* 567 F.3d at 1035-36 (citing *Berti v. V.A. Hosp.,* 860 F.2d 338, 340 (9th Cir.1988); *Augustine v. United States,* 704 F.2d 1074, 1077 (9th Cir.1983); *Blain v. United States,* 552 F.2d 289, 291 (9th Cir.1977) (per curiam); *Mann v. United States,* 399 F.2d 672, 673 (9th Cir.1968)), unlike in *Bowles* and *John R. Sand & Gravel,* there is no Supreme Court precedent on the question. *See Reed Elsevier,* 559 U.S. at 173-74, 130 S.Ct. 1237 (Ginsburg, J. concurring) (rejecting citation to non-Supreme Court precedent because *Bowles* and *John R. Sand & Gravel* "relied on longstanding decisions of *this* Court typing the relevant prescriptions 'jurisdictional'") (emphasis in original). And we have also held otherwise in *Alvarez-Machain I,* 107 F.3d 696.

Further, the pre-*Alvarez-Machain I* cases cited in *Marley* preceded both *Irwin* and the Supreme Court's more recent decisions clarifying the distinction between jurisdictional and nonjurisdictional rules. Indeed, our pre-*Alvarez-Machain I* decisions are emblematic of the "drive-by jurisdictional rulings" to which the Supreme Court has cautioned against giving "precedential effect" in its more recent cases. *See Arbaugh,* 546 U.S. at 511, 126 S.Ct. 1235. For example, *Berti,* a three-page opinion, labels § 2401(b) "jurisdictional," but provides no analysis as to the meaning or significance of that term.[11] *See Berti,* 860 F.2d at 340. Accordingly, this is certainly not the "exceptional [case] in which p.1046 a 'century's worth of precedent and practice in American courts' rank [the] time limit as jurisdictional." *Auburn Reg'l Med. Ctr.,* 133 S.Ct. at 825 (quoting *Bowles,* 551 U.S. at 209 n. 2, 127 S.Ct. 2360).

e. *Purpose*

Finally, with regard to the particular role of the FTCA's six-month limitations period for filing suit we "find no reason why [§ 2401(b)] should be read ... [as] a prerequisite to the exercise of federal subject matter jurisdiction." *Payne,* 653 F.3d at 870.

First, the consideration that the FTCA authorizes suits against the federal government does not, standing alone, supply such a reason. In so concluding, "[w]e ... have in mind that the [FTCA] waives the immunity of the United States and that in construing the statute of limitations, which is a condition of that waiver, we should not take it upon ourselves to extend the waiver beyond that which Congress intended." *Kubrick,* 444 U.S. at 117-18, 100 S.Ct. 352; *see also Block v. North Dakota ex rel. Bd. of Univ. and Sch. Lands,* 461 U.S. 273, 287, 103 S.Ct. 1811, 75 L.Ed.2d 840 (1983). But the fact that the FTCA is predicated on a sovereign immunity waiver does not make the six-month filing deadline a jurisdictional prerequisite, not subject to equitable tolling. Although waivers must be "strictly construed," *Irwin* explained that "[o]nce Congress has made such a waiver,... making the rule of equitable tolling applicable to suits against the Government, in the same way that is applicable to private suits, amounts to little, if any, broadening of the congressional waiver." *Irwin,* 498 U.S. at 94-95, 111 S.Ct. 453.

John R. Sand & Gravel, 552 U.S. 130, 128 S.Ct. 750, is not to the contrary. That case did note that "[t]he Court has often read the time limits of these [sovereign immunity waiver] statutes as more absolute," *id.* at 133-34, 128 S.Ct. 750, and "has sometimes referred to the time limits in such statutes as 'jurisdictional.'"[12] *Id.* at 133-34, 128 S.Ct. 750 (citing *Bowles,* 551 U.S. at 210, 127 S.Ct. 2360). But *John R. Sand & Gravel* did not turn on any bright-line distinction between statutes of limitation that "protect a defendant's case-specific interest in timeliness," and those "limiting the scope of a governmental waiver of sovereign immunity." 552 U.S. at 133-34, 128 S.Ct. 750. Instead, *John R. Sand & Gravel* reiterated and applied *Irwin's* presumption that equitable tolling applies to statutes of limitations in suits against the government, distinguishing *Irwin* on the grounds that "*Irwin* dealt with a different limitations statute [that] ..., while similar to [§ 2501] in language, is unlike [§ 2501] in the key respect that the Court had not previously provided a definitive interpretation." *Id.* at 137, 128 S.Ct. 750.

Second, there is no reason to think § 2401(b) more concerned with "achiev[ing] a broader system-related goal" than simply with protecting the government's "case-specific interest in timeliness." *Id.* at 133, 128 S.Ct. 750. *Holland* is instructive in this regard. As noted above, *Holland* held that AEDPA's statute of limitations in 28 U.S.C. § 2244(d) is not jurisdictional, and therefore is "subject to a 'rebuttable presumption' in favor 'of equitable p.1047 tolling.'" 130 S.Ct. at 2560 (quoting *Irwin*, 498 U.S. at 95-96, 111 S.Ct. 453). Doing so, *Holland* rejected the argument "that equitable tolling undermines AEDPA's basic purposes." *Id.* at 2562. While acknowledging AEDPA's systemic goal of "eliminat[ing] delays in the federal habeas review process," *Holland* emphasized that AEDPA "[does] not seek to end every possible delay at all costs." *Id. Holland* therefore declined to read § 2244(d) as indicating "congressional intent to close courthouse doors that a strong equitable claim would ordinarily keep open." *Id.*

Section 2401(b) likewise does not evince congressional intent to foreclose the application of equitable principles for the sake of "broader system-related goals." As *Kubrick* explained, § 2401(b)'s "obvious purpose[]... is to encourage the prompt presentation of claims." 444 U.S. at 117, 100 S.Ct. 352. That is consistent "with the general purpose of statutes of limitations: 'to protect defendants against stale or unduly delayed claims.'" *Credit Suisse Sec. (USA) LLC v. Simmonds*, ___ U.S. ___, 132 S.Ct. 1414, 1420, 182 L.Ed.2d 446 (2012) (quoting *John R. Sand & Gravel*, 552 U.S. at 133, 128 S.Ct. 750).

McNeil v. United States, 508 U.S. 106, 113 S.Ct. 1980, 124 L.Ed.2d 21 (1993), does not detract from our conclusion. *McNeil* strictly construed the administrative exhaustion requirement in 28 U.S.C. § 2675(a), holding that an FTCA action filed before exhaustion had been completed could not proceed in the district court even where the litigation had not substantially progressed. 508 U.S. at 111-13, 113 S.Ct. 1980. The exhaustion requirement, unlike the § 2401(b) limitations period, *is* tied by explicit statutory language to jurisdiction, and was deemed "jurisdictional" in *Brady v. U.S.*, 211 F.3d 499, 502 (9th Cir.2000). The "straightforward statutory command" in § 2675(a), *McNeil* explained, served "[t]he interest in orderly administration of this body of litigation." *Id.* at 112, 113 S.Ct. 1980.

Judge Bea maintains that *McNeil's* concern about the "orderly administration of [FTCA] litigation" with respect to the exhaustion-of-remedies requirement in § 2675(a) compels us also to treat § 2401(b)'s six-month filing deadline as jurisdictional. We disagree. Strict enforcement of an exhaustion requirement serves to assure a particular administrative interest—namely, the interest in assuring that agency officials have a full opportunity to investigate and consult internally with regard to claims for compensation due to negligence by agency employees. Further, that purpose recognized by the Supreme Court in *McNeil*—reducing court congestion by keeping claims out of court until an administrative agency has had a chance to settle them—is not implicated by § 2401(b)'s sixth-month post-exhaustion limitations period. *See id.* at 111-12, 112 n. 8, 113 S.Ct. 1980. Where agency exhaustion is required, there is notice of the claim and of the need for information collection, as well as an opportunity to settle the claim, well before suit is filed in court.

In short, nothing in the text, context, or purpose of § 2401(b) clearly indicates that the FTCA's six-month limitations period implicates the district courts' adjudicatory authority. We therefore hold that § 2401(b) is a nonjurisdictional claim-processing rule subject to the presumption in favor of equitable tolling, and so overrule *Marley's* contrary holding.

4. The *Irwin* Presumption in Favor of Equitable Tolling

Having concluded that § 2401(b) is a nonjurisdictional statute of limitations subject to *Irwin's* presumption in favor of equitable tolling, we must next determine whether that presumption has been overcome in this case. *See Holland,* 130 S.Ct. p.1048 at 2560; *Albillo-De Leon v. Gonzales,* 410 F.3d 1090, 1098 (9th Cir.2005). "It is hornbook law that limitations periods are customarily subject to equitable tolling, unless tolling would be inconsistent with the text of the relevant statute. Congress must be presumed to draft limitations periods in light of this background principle." *Young v. United States,* 535 U.S. 43, 49-50, 122 S.Ct. 1036, 152 L.Ed.2d 79 (2002) (internal quotation marks and citations omitted). We must therefore ask whether "there [is] good reason to believe that Congress did *not* want the equitable tolling doctrine to apply" to § 2401(b). *United States v. Brockamp,* 519 U.S. 347, 350, 117 S.Ct. 849, 136 L.Ed.2d 818 (1997). There is no such reason.

As an initial matter, we note that the *Irwin* presumption regarding the tolling of limitations periods in suits against the federal government is particularly strong in FTCA cases. Various provisions of the FTCA confirm that suits against the government are to be treated no differently than suits against private defendants.

For example, § 2674, governing the "Liability of [the] United States," states that "[t]he United States shall be liable, respecting the provisions of this title relating to tort claims, *in the same manner and to the same extent as a private individual under like circumstances.*" 28 U.S.C. § 2674 (emphasis added); *see Arteaga,* 711 F.3d at 833. Likewise, § 1346(b)(1) grants the district courts exclusive jurisdiction over civil actions against the government "under circumstances where the United States, *if a private person,* would be liable." *Id.* § 1346(b)(1) (emphasis added). Thus, as a general matter, the FTCA places suits against the United States on equal footing with suits against private individuals.

The *Irwin* presumption is further strengthened by the "discovery" rule applicable to § 2401(b): A plaintiff is required to file her claim with the relevant federal agency "within two years after such claim accrues," *id.* § 2401(b). Applying the common law discovery rule—which does not appear in the statute—courts view a claim as "'accru[ing]' within the meaning of [§ 2401(b)] when the plaintiff knows both the existence and the cause of his injury." *See Kubrick,* 444 U.S. at 119-21 and n. 7, 100 S.Ct. 352. As a practical matter, this common law rule "extends the statute of limitations by delaying the date on which it begins to run." *Arteaga,* 711 F.3d at 833. Application of a common law discovery rule not enunciated in the statute to aspects of § 2401(b) reinforces the notion that the FTCA's statutes of limitations admit of common law exceptions.

Without the discovery rule, the deadlines contained in § 2401(b) would closely resemble a "statute of repose": "a fixed, statutory cutoff date, usually independent of any variable, such as claimant's awareness of a violation." *Munoz v. Ashcroft,* 339 F.3d 950, 957 (9th Cir.2003). "[L]ike a jurisdictional prerequisite," a statute of repose is not subject to equitable tolling. *Albillo-De Leon,* 410 F.3d at 1097 n. 5; *see also Lampf, Pleva, Lipkind, Prupis & Petigrow v. Gilbertson,* 501 U.S. 350, 363, 111 S.Ct. 2773, 115 L.Ed.2d 321 (1991); *Albano v. Shea Homes Ltd. P'ship,* 634 F.3d 524, 534-36 (9th Cir.2011). While a nonjurisdictional statute of limitations "bars plaintiff[s] from bringing an already accrued claim after a specified period of time," a statute of repose "terminates a right of action after a specific time, even if the injury has not yet occurred." *Fields v. Legacy Health Sys.,* 413 F.3d 943, 952 n. 7 (9th Cir.2005).[13]

p.1049 Far from setting a fixed cutoff date, § 2401(b) "is in the traditional form of a statute of limitations." *Johnson v. Aljian,* 490 F.3d 778, 781 n. 12 (9th Cir.2007). As such, just as it is subject to the common law discovery rule, so the presumption favoring equitable tolling applies.

That § 2401(b) acts as a condition on the FTCA's waiver of sovereign immunity does not alter our conclusion, essentially for the same reasons discussed earlier with regard to the jurisdictional question. With or without a waiver of sovereign immunity, the key inquiry, following *Irwin,* remains whether equitable tolling "is inconsistent with the text of the relevant statute."[14] *United States v. Beggerly,* 524 U.S. 38, 48, 118 S.Ct. 1862, 141 L.Ed.2d 32 (1998); *see also John R. Sand & Gravel,* 552 U.S. at 139, 128 S.Ct. 750. For the reasons already discussed, nothing in § 2401(b) suggests that it is inconsistent with equitable tolling. To the contrary, the FTCA goes out of its way in its efforts to treat the United States the same as private tort defendants.

Neither *Brockamp,* 519 U.S. 347, 117 S.Ct. 849, nor *Beggerly,* 524 U.S. 38, 118 S.Ct. 1862, two cases in which the Supreme Court held the *Irwin* presumption rebutted, indicates that the same conclusion is appropriate here. *Brockamp* held that a statute of limitations for filing tax refund claims foreclosed application of equitable tolling, citing as evidence of Congress's intent the statute's "highly detailed," "technical," and "unusually emphatic form." 519 U.S. at 350, 117 S.Ct. 849. *Brockamp* further emphasized that "tax law," the subject matter of the statute of limitations in that case, "is not normally characterized by case-specific exceptions reflecting individual equities," given the more than "200 million tax returns" and "more than 90 million refunds" processed each year. *Id.* at 352, 117 S.Ct. 849. *Beggerly,* in turn, determined that an "unusually generous" twelve-year statute of limitations was "incompatible" with equitable tolling, in large part because the underlying subject matter concerned "ownership of land," p.1050 and equitable tolling would "throw a cloud of uncertainty over [property] rights." 524 U.S. at 48-49, 118 S.Ct. 1862.

For reasons similar to those relied upon in the Supreme Court's more recent *Holland* decision, the statute of limitations here "differs significantly from the statutes at issue in [*Brockamp*] and [*Beggerly*]." *Holland,* 130 S.Ct. at 2561. *Holland* held AEDPA's one-year statute of limitations in 28 U.S.C. § 2244(d) nonjurisdictional and "subject to a 'rebuttable presumption' in favor 'of equitable tolling.'" *Id.* at 2560 (quoting *Irwin,* 498 U.S. at 95-96, 111 S.Ct. 453) (emphasis omitted). Applying that presumption, *Holland* explained that, unlike the statute of limitations at issue in *Brockamp*, § 2244(d) "does not contain language that is 'unusually emphatic,' nor does it 're-iterat[e]' its time limitation." *Id.* at 2561. Moreover, "unlike the subject matters at issue in both *Brockamp* and *Beggerly*—tax collection and land claims—AEDPA's subject matter, habeas corpus, pertains to an area of the law where equity finds a comfortable home." *Id.* Accordingly, "neither AEDPA's textual characteristics nor the statute's basic purposes 'rebut' the basic presumption set forth in *Irwin.*" *Id.* at 2562.

The same conclusion applies to § 2401(b). As discussed above, the FTCA's limitations provision is not cast in particularly emphatic language given its provenance; nor is it unusually generous. *See* Part II.A.3. And, unlike the limitations provision in *Brockamp*, § 2401(b) does not "reiterate[] its limitations several times in several different ways." *Brockamp*, 519 U.S. at 351, 117 S.Ct. 849. Instead, § 2401(b) "reads like an ordinary, run-of-the-mill statute of limitations," reflecting its period of enactment. *Holland*, 130 S.Ct. at 2561.

Furthermore, like the statute of limitations at issue in *Holland*, § 2401(b) "pertains to an area of the law where equity finds a comfortable home." *Id.* As *Irwin* noted, "[t]ime requirements in lawsuits between private litigants are customarily subject to 'equitable tolling.'" 498 U.S. at 95, 111 S.Ct. 453. And, as discussed above, the FTCA places tort suits against the United States on equal footing with tort suits against private individuals, exposing the government to liability "in the same manner and to the same extent as a private individual under like circumstances." 28 U.S.C. § 2674. That Congress saw fit to include a time limit on such claims without any specific limitations on tolling indicates, if anything, that it intended to allow the operation of normal equitable tolling principles that would be applicable in ordinary tort suits against private individuals, not that it harbored an intention otherwise.

Rouse v. United States Department of State, 567 F.3d 408 (9th Cir.2009) (analyzing the Privacy Act's two-year statute of limitations, 5 U.S.C. § 552a(g)(5)), reached a similar result to the one we reach here. In that case, a U.S. citizen sued the "U.S. Department of State under the Privacy Act for damages arising from his imprisonment in a foreign country." 567 F.3d at 412. *Rouse* held, first, that the citizen's claims were "sufficiently similar to traditional tort actions such as misrepresentation and false light to warrant the application of *Irwin's* rebuttable presumption." *Id.* at 416. Next, *Rouse* distinguished § 552a(g)(5) from the limitations provisions at issue in *Brockamp* and *Beggerly*, noting that § 552a(g)(5) lacked "detail[ed],... technical language" and did not concern an "area[] of law where the running of a defined statute of limitations is of special importance.'" *Id.* at 417 (first alteration in original) (internal quotation marks omitted). *Rouse* therefore concluded that the *Irwin* presumption had not been rebutted in that case.

p.1051 Finally, for the reasons similar to those we surveyed in declining to infer § 2401(b)'s "jurisdictional" status from other FTCA provisions and subsection (a) of § 2401, *see supra* Part II.A.3, Congress's decision to include explicit exceptions in other FTCA limitations provisions does not rebut the *Irwin* presumption.[15] As *Holland* explained, the fact that a statute "is silent as to equitable tolling while containing one provision that expressly refers to a different kind of tolling" does not foreclose the application of equitable tolling. 130 S.Ct. at 2561-62; *see also Young*, 535 U.S. at 53, 122 S.Ct. 1036 (rejecting the argument that an "express tolling provision, appearing in the same subsection as the [limitations] period, demonstrates a statutory intent *not* to toll the [limitations] period").

In short, the *Irwin* presumption is not overcome. Nothing in § 2401(b)'s text or context indicates that Congress intended to preclude courts from *ever* applying equitable tolling to claims filed outside of the six-month limitations period.

B. Wong Is Entitled to Equitable Tolling

Concluding, as we do, that equitable adjustment of the limitations period in § 2401(b) is not prohibited, does not decide under what circumstances equitable tolling may be appropriate. Whether a particular untimely claim may be excused for a particular reason varies with the reason. We decide only that under the circumstances presented here, the usual principles governing equitable tolling apply and we can find no "good reason to believe that Congress did *not* want the equitable tolling doctrine to apply." *Brockamp,* 519 U.S. at 350, 117 S.Ct. 849.

We assume for present purposes, without deciding, that Wong's FTCA claim was filed in the district court too late. In doing so, we pause to note that whether this is so depends on: (1) whether the claim could be considered filed in the district court at a point earlier than the amendment actually adding the FTCA claim was filed; and (2) whether, if so, the relevant filing date was (a) November 14, 2001, the date Wong's formal motion to file the amended complaint was filed; (b) November 20, 2001, the date as of which the motion to file the amended complaint requested that the complaint be amended; or (c) December 10, 2001, the date Wong's Reply Memorandum on the motion to amend, which reiterated the request to amend, was filed. Adopting the first of these possible dates would create its own timeliness problem—whether the court claim was filed too early—under *McNeil,* 508 U.S. at 111-13, 113 S.Ct. 1980; adopting the second might also raise a *McNeil* problem.[16]

Although there may be a defensible road through this thicket yielding the result that the FTCA claim was timely filed, at least constructively, *cf.* Fed.R.Civ.P. 15(c), reaching that result would entail one or more novel rulings concerning when FTCA claims added by amendment are considered p.1052 filed. Moreover, and notably, any such ruling would in all likelihood itself rest on an equitable adjustment of the usual application of limitations periods, because some form of constructive filing date, different from the date the amended complaint was actually filed in the district court, would be required. In the end, then, there is little difference in the underlying justification between applying traditional equitable tolling principles and devising a novel equitable solution to the filing date problem in this case. We therefore proceed along the established, traditional route.

In applying equitable tolling, courts "follow[] a tradition in which courts of equity have sought to 'relieve hardships which, from time to time, arise from a hard and fast adherence' to more absolute legal rules, which, if strictly applied, threaten the 'evils of archaic rigidity.'" *Holland,* 130 S.Ct. at 2563 (quoting *Hazel—Atlas Glass Co. v. Hartford—Empire Co.,* 322 U.S. 238, 248, 64 S.Ct. 997, 88 L.Ed. 1250 (1944)). Thus, the equitable tolling doctrine "enables courts to meet new situations [that] demand equitable intervention, and to accord all the relief necessary to correct ... particular injustices." *Id.* (internal quotation marks omitted) (alterations in original).

"[L]ong-settled equitable-tolling principles" instruct that "'[g]enerally, a litigant seeking equitable tolling bears the burden of establishing two elements: (1) that he has been pursuing his rights diligently, and (2) that some extraordinary circumstances stood in his way.'" *Credit Suisse*, 132 S.Ct. at 1419 (quoting *Pace v. DiGuglielmo*, 544 U.S. 408, 418, 125 S.Ct. 1807, 161 L.Ed.2d 669 (2005) (emphasis omitted)); *see also Ramirez v. Yates*, 571 F.3d 993, 997 (9th Cir.2009). As to the first element, "[t]he standard for reasonable diligence does not require an overzealous or extreme pursuit of any and every avenue of relief. It requires the effort that a reasonable person might be expected to deliver under his or her particular circumstances." *Doe v. Busby*, 661 F.3d 1001, 1015 (9th Cir.2011). Central to the analysis is whether the plaintiff was "without any fault" in pursuing his claim. *Fed. Election Comm'n v. Williams*, 104 F.3d 237, 240 (9th Cir.1996).

With regard to the second showing, "a garden variety claim of excusable neglect, such as a simple miscalculation that leads a lawyer to miss a filing deadline, does not warrant equitable tolling." *Holland*, 130 S.Ct. at 2564 (internal quotation marks and citations omitted). Instead, a litigant must show that "extraordinary circumstances were the cause of his untimeliness and ... ma[de] it impossible to file [the document] on time." *Ramirez*, 571 F.3d at 997 (internal quotation marks and citations omitted) (second alteration in original). Accordingly, "[e]quitable tolling is typically granted when litigants are unable to file timely [documents] as a result of external circumstances beyond their direct control." *Harris v. Carter*, 515 F.3d 1051, 1055 (9th Cir.2008).

Applying these longstanding principles in this case, we conclude that whatever may be the case regarding other bases for tolling, Wong's circumstances easily justify equitable tolling. As noted, Wong's claim was untimely because it was not filed within the six-month window running from December 3, 2001—the date on which the INS denied Wong's administrative claim— to June 3, 2002. That result was not the consequence of any fault or lack of due diligence on Wong's part. If anything, Wong took special care in exercising due diligence: Wong first sought leave to file her amended complaint "on or after November 20, 2001," which was, at the time that request was filed, the first day following p.1053 exhaustion of her administrative remedies on which Wong would have been permitted to file her claim in the district court. And, even after the INS denied her claim, thereby starting anew the six-month deadline under § 2401(b), *see Lehman*, 154 F.3d at 1014-15, Wong filed a Reply Memorandum reiterating her request to file an amended complaint including the FTCA claim. As the Magistrate Judge noted, it was "due solely to the delay inherent in the Magistrate Judge system" that no action was taken with respect to those requests until the six-month limitations period had already run. Moreover, by informing the parties and the court of her desire to file an FTCA claim well before the filing deadline and requesting leave to do so, Wong fulfilled the notice concern that partially underlies limitations statutes. *See Crown, Cork & Seal Co., Inc. v. Parker*, 462 U.S. 345, 352, 103 S.Ct. 2392, 76 L.Ed.2d 628 (1983); *Am. Pipe & Constr. Co. v. Utah*, 414 U.S. 538, 554, 94 S.Ct. 756, 38 L.Ed.2d 713 (1974).

We are not persuaded by the government's assertion that Wong was dilatory in seeking to file her claim because she did not expressly request a timely ruling from the district court. Nor are we persuaded that Wong should have filed an entirely new complaint alleging the FTCA claim rather than waiting for a ruling on the motion to amend. Wong was entitled to expect a timely ruling on her request to amend, which was made with a great deal of time to spare. And filing a new suit on the same facts as one pending would have been inefficient for all concerned— which is why amendments alleging new causes of action on the same factual allegations are permitted. *See* Fed.R.Civ.P. 15. Thus, Wong put forth the "effort that a reasonable person might be expected to deliver under ... her particular circumstances." *Busby,* 661 F.3d at 1015.

In short, Wong's claim was rendered untimely because of external circumstances beyond her control. In light of these circumstances, we conclude that equitable tolling properly applies to excuse Wong's late-filed amended complaint, and that her FTCA claim against the United States therefore may proceed.

REVERSED and REMANDED.

Chief Judge KOZINSKI, concurring in the judgment:

I agree with Judges Tashima and Bea that 28 U.S.C. § 2401(b) is jurisdictional, but can't dissent because a plaintiff like Wong who begins her FTCA action too early can cure the defect by filing a motion to amend the premature complaint. *See Valadez-Lopez v. Chertoff,* 656 F.3d 851, 855-58 (9th Cir.2011). Wong filed such a motion before she had finally exhausted her administrative remedies, which was too soon. *See* 28 U.S.C. § 2675(a); *McNeil v. United States,* 508 U.S. 106, 112-13, 113 S.Ct. 1980, 124 L.Ed.2d 21 (1993). But, on December 10, 2001, after the INS denied her claim and before the six-month section 2401(b) window slammed shut, Wong filed a reply memorandum reiterating her request for leave to file a second amended complaint.

While we don't typically treat a reply as a motion, there's nothing to preclude us from doing so. In this case, Wong's request had all the physical attributes of a motion: It was made in writing, filed with the court, served on the other side, prayed for relief and "state[d] with particularity" why she was entitled to it. *See* Fed. R.Civ.P. 7(b). She pointed out that "the court currently has jurisdiction over plaintiffs' FTCA claims and plaintiffs should be allowed to amend the complaint to add those claims." In her conclusion, she again prayed for this relief: "[P]laintiffs p.1054 should be granted leave to file their Second Amended Complaint."

The government concedes that if Wong moved for leave to amend her complaint during the six months following the INS's denial of her claim, she's entitled to maintain her lawsuit. *Cf. McNeil,* 508 U.S. at 107-10 & n. 5, 113 S.Ct. 1980; *Valadez-Lopez,* 656 F.3d at 855-58. Wong *did* file such a motion, albeit within a document captioned "Reply Memorandum."

The majority claims that construing Wong's reply as a motion would be "novel," maj. op. 1051, but we regularly treat non-motion filings as motions when equity calls for it. *See, e.g., United States v. Rewald,* 835 F.2d 215, 216 (9th Cir.1987) (construing notice of appeal as motion for remand); *United States v. Aguirre-Pineda,* 349 Fed.Appx. 212, 2009 WL 3368445, at *1 (9th Cir.2009) (construing letter as motion for appointment of counsel); *Rapanan v. Nikkei Manor/Mikkei Concerns,* 42 Fed.Appx. 976, 2002 WL 1891677 (9th Cir. 2002) (construing letter as motion for extension of time to request oral argument). And there's certainly nothing novel about finding a motion nested within a document that serves another purpose. *See,* *e.g., United States v. Harvey,* 55 Fed.Appx. 445, 446 (9th Cir.2003) (construing opening brief as motion to withdraw as counsel of record). Sometimes, we're even required to do so. *See, e.g.,* Ninth Circuit Rule 22-1(e) ("Uncertified issues raised and designated in [an appellant's opening brief] will be construed as a motion to expand the COA...."). But even if it were novel, so what? Novelty is not an enemy of justice; we're judges, not plumbers.

We owe Wong the benefit of our compassion and creativity. After all, had the district court acted on her motion within the section 2401(b) six-month period, she wouldn't be in this fix. But federal district courts are chronically overworked, facing volumes of motions and briefing every day. It thus took the court more than seven months to act on this routine motion—a delay Wong didn't cause and couldn't have foreseen. The government suggests that, instead of waiting for the district court to act on her motion, Wong should have refiled it. Yeah, right. How many litigants have the nerve to vex a federal judge with a clone motion while the original is still pending? Bad things can happen to those who twist the tiger's tail. *See, e.g., Nugget Hydroelectric, L.P. v. Pac. Gas & Elec. Co.,* 981 F.2d 429, 439 (9th Cir.1992) (affirming imposition of sanctions for filing duplicative motions). Instead, Wong used her reply sensibly: She reiterated her request to amend, advanced new arguments in support of that request and pointed out that the court had acquired jurisdiction to grant it. To treat Wong's document as a legal nullity because she called it a reply rather than a motion is inequitable and nonsensical. I thought we had abandoned such pedantry in 1938. *See* 5 Charles Alan Wright & Arthur R. Miller, *Federal Practice and Procedure* § 1196 (3d ed.2004) ("Fortunately, under federal practice the technical name attached to a motion or pleading is not as important as its substance."); *see also* Jack B. Weinstein, *The Ghost of Process Past: The Fiftieth Anniversary of the Federal Rules of Civil Procedure and Erie,* 54 Brook. L.Rev. 1, 2-3 (1988) ("When the Rules were first adopted, they were optimistically intended to clear the procedural clouds so that the sunlight of substance might shine through.").

The majority claims that construing Wong's reply as satisfying section 2401(b) would itself be "an equitable adjustment of the usual application of limitations periods." Maj. op. 1052. If we're willing to do that, my colleagues argue, we should avoid this procedural "thicket" and just equitably toll the statute of limitations. *Id.* "In the end," the majority concludes, "there is little difference in the underlying justification between" its approach and mine. *Id.* But the FTCA's text, context and relevant p.1055 historical treatment prohibit equitable tolling of the statutory deadline, not equitable construction of court filings. The majority and I may emerge on the same side—but I take the road our law provides. And that makes all the difference.

McNeil v. United States, 508 U.S. 106, 113 S.Ct. 1980, 124 L.Ed.2d 21 (1993), confirms this. *McNeil* dealt with section 2675(a), a different timing provision of the FTCA, which bars instituting an action in federal court before the administrative claim is "finally denied by the agency." 508 U.S. at 111, 113 S.Ct. 1980 (quoting 28 U.S.C. § 2675(a)). The Court held in no uncertain terms that this exhaustion requirement is jurisdictional. *McNeil,* 508 U.S. at 113, 113 S.Ct. 1980; *see also* Bea Dissent at 1075. But it also left open the possibility that a plaintiff who had filed a complaint prematurely might, after agency denial, file something else that "constitute[d] the commencement of a new action." *McNeil,* 508 U.S. at 110-11, 113

S.Ct. 1980. The Court explained: "As the case comes to us, we assume that the Court of Appeals correctly held that nothing done by petitioner after the denial of his administrative claim on July 21, 1989, constituted the commencement of a new action." *Id.* at 110, 113 S.Ct. 1980. The Court reiterated this later in the opinion: "Again, the question whether the Court of Appeals should have liberally construed petitioner's letter [requesting counsel] as instituting a new action is not before us." *Id.* at 113 n. 9, 113 S.Ct. 1980. Thus, while finding a similar FTCA timing requirement to be jurisdictional, the Court made clear that the statute didn't impair our traditional power to liberally construe court filings—even mere letters—when equity calls for us to do so. If a letter asking for counsel can be "liberally construed ... as instituting a new action," why not a reply? The Court saw no contradiction between construing the statute strictly and construing a pleading liberally. That's plenty good enough for me.

The delays inherent in the federal judiciary caused Wong's problem, and in good conscience we should use such powers as we have to make it up to her. Had she filed nothing within the relevant time-frame, there would be nothing for us to construe and she'd be barred by the statute. *See* Bea Dissent; Tashima Dissent. But Wong *did* file, and that document contains a crystal clear motion to amend the complaint. We owe it to Wong to recognize this. I therefore concur in the judgment of the majority but in the reasoning of the dissents (as far as they go).

TASHIMA, Circuit Judge, joined by BEA, Circuit Judge, dissenting:

I join Judge Bea's dissenting opinion in full. I write separately to clarify the Federal Tort Claims Act's ("FTCA's") legislative history. This history, once understood in full context, dispels any doubt that the FTCA's limitations provision was intended to be jurisdictional.

I.

Two provisions of the FTCA are central for present purposes—the limitations provision, currently codified at 28 U.S.C. § 2401(b), and the jurisdiction-granting provision, currently codified at 28 U.S.C. § 1346(b). I begin with a brief history of these two provisions.

The FTCA was originally enacted in 1946 as Title IV of the Legislative Reorganization Act. *See* Pub.L. No. 79-601 ("1946 Act"), tit. IV, 60 Stat. 812, 842-47 (1946). Pursuant to the 1946 Act, the provisions of the FTCA were codified in Chapter 20 of Title 28. *See* 28 U.S.C. §§ 921-946 (1946). Among these provisions was the jurisdiction-granting provision, which read, in pertinent part:

> p.1056 *Subject to the provisions of this chapter,* the United States district court for the district wherein the plaintiff is resident or wherein the act or omission complained of occurred, including the United States district courts for the Territories and possessions of the United States, sitting without a jury, shall have exclusive jurisdiction to hear, determine, and render judgment on any claim against the United States, for money only, accruing on and after January 1, 1945, on account of damage to or loss of property or on account of personal injury or death caused by the negligent or wrongful act or omission of any employee of the Government while acting within the scope of his office or

employment, under circumstances where the United States, if a private person, would be liable to the claimant for such damage, loss, injury, or death in accordance with the law of the place where the act or omission occurred.

Id. § 931(a) (emphasis added). The FTCA thus conferred exclusive federal jurisdiction over tort actions against the United States, but "[s]ubject to the provisions of Chapter 20. Included within Chapter 20 was the FTCA's limitations provision, then-codified at 28 U.S.C. § 942. *See id.* § 942. Accordingly, as originally enacted in the 1946 Act, the FTCA's grant of jurisdiction was "[s]ubject to" the limitations provision.

Congress recodified and reorganized Title 28 in 1948. *See* Pub.L. 80-773 ("1948 Act"), § 1, 62 Stat. 869 (1948). As part of the recodification, most of the provisions formerly grouped under Chapter 20 were regrouped under Chapter 171. *See id.* at 982-85. The limitations provision, however, was removed from this grouping and placed in its current location in Chapter 161, at 28 U.S.C. § 2401(b). *See id.* at 970-71. There, it was situated alongside 28 U.S.C. § 2401(a), which provides for a six-year statute of limitations in other types of civil actions against the United States. *See id.* at 971.

Also removed from the former Chapter 20 grouping was the jurisdiction-granting provision, which was recodified in Chapter 85, at 28 U.S.C. § 1346(b). *See id.* at 930, 933. Similarly to the limitations provision, this move consolidated the jurisdiction-granting provision with the other provisions of Title 28 granting jurisdiction in civil actions against the United States. *See id.* at 933. Because the reference to "this chapter" in the opening clause of § 1346(b) was now stale—given that § 1346(b) was no longer in the same chapter as the other FTCA provisions—the clause was changed to read, "Subject to the provisions of chapter 173 of this title." *Id.*

However, there was no Chapter 173 of Title 28. Rather, this was a scrivener's error that should have read Chapter 171. Throughout the drafting history of the 1948 Act, the chapter that would become Chapter 171—titled "Tort Claims Procedure"—had been designated Chapter 173, with the cross-reference in § 1346(b) corresponding to this designation. *See, e.g.,* H.R. 2055, 80th Cong., chs. 85, 173 (1947). When the chapter was renumbered to 171 via a late Senate amendment, *see* S.Rep. No. 80-1559, at 8 (1948), the drafters simply failed to update the cross-reference in § 1346(b). It is thus evident that, as of the 1948 Act, the opening clause of § 1346(b) should have read, "Subject to the provisions of chapter 171 of this title." Indeed, a year later, Congress amended § 1346(b) to correct this error and change the cross-reference to Chapter 171. *See* Pub.L. 81-55, 63 Stat. 62 (1949); *see also* S.Rep. No. 81-135, at 1-2 (1949).

II.

The history of the limitations and jurisdiction-granting provisions, as recounted p.1057 above, taken in conjunction with the considerations discussed below, offer "a clear indication that Congress wanted the [limitations] rule to be jurisdictional." *Henderson ex. rel. Henderson v. Shinseki,* ___ U.S. ___, 131 S.Ct. 1197, 1203, 179 L.Ed.2d 159 (2011) (internal quotation marks omitted). First, and most importantly, it is plain that the limitations provision was jurisdictional as of the original 1946 Act, for the grant of jurisdiction was expressly "[s]ubject to"—that is, "contingent or conditional upon"—compliance with that provision. *See* Webster's New World Dictionary 1333 (3d Coll. ed.1994); *see also* Webster's New International Dictionary 2509 (2d ed.1940) (defining "subject to" as "[b]eing under the contingency of; dependent upon or exposed to (some contingent action)"). It is difficult to imagine a more "clear statement" as to Congress' intent.[1] *See Sebelius v. Auburn Reg'l Med. Ctr.,* ___ U.S. ___, 133 S.Ct. 817, 824, 184 L.Ed.2d 627 (2013).

If one accepts this proposition—which the majority only obliquely disputes[2]— then, in order to find § 2401(b) non-jurisdictional, one must conclude that Congress intended to strip the limitations provision of its jurisdictional status only two years later, through the 1948 Act. Under long-established Supreme Court precedent, however, we are not to "presume that the 1948 revision worked a change in the underlying substantive law unless an intent to make such a change is clearly expressed." *John R. Sand & Gravel Co. v. United States,* 552 U.S. 130, 136, 128 S.Ct. 750, 169 L.Ed.2d 591 (2008) (internal quotation marks omitted); *see also Keene Corp. v. United States,* 508 U.S. 200, 209, 113 S.Ct. 2035, 124 L.Ed.2d 118 (1993) (citing cases applying this rule). Here, not only is such "clearly expressed" intent lacking, but there is an abundance of evidence to the contrary—that Congress had no desire to alter the jurisdictional status of the limitations provision.

In the Reviser's Notes to the 1948 Act,[3] Congress explained that § 2401 "consolidates" the FTCA's limitations provision with the six-year limitations period of 28 U.S.C. § 2401(a), which, like § 2401(b), had formerly been codified elsewhere in Title 28. *See* H.R. Rep. 80-308, at A185 (1947); *see also* 28 U.S.C. § 41(20) (1946) (former section of six-year limitations period). This purely organizational function— p.1058 to consolidate the provisions of Title 28 setting forth limitations periods in actions against the government—is the obvious reason that Congress separated § 2401(b) from the other FTCA provisions and placed it in chapter 161.[4] If there were any doubt as to whether a substantive purpose was intended, the Reviser's Notes then added, "Subsection (b) of the revised section [2401] simplifies and restates [former 28 U.S.C. § 942], *without change of substance.*" H.R. Rep. 80-308, at A185 (emphasis added).

Congress provided equally definitive guidance in the actual text of the 1948 Act. In an uncodified provision, Congress instructed, "*No inference of a legislative construction is to be drawn by reason of the chapter in Title 28 ... in which any [] section is placed.*" 1948 Act, § 33, 62 Stat. at 991 (emphasis added). Of course, precisely such an inference is required to find § 2401(b) non-jurisdictional, because one must assume that Congress intended to alter the jurisdictional status of the limitations provision by removing it from the FTCA Chapter and placing it in Chapter 161.

In short, there is no indication—let alone a "clearly expressed" indication— that Congress intended to alter the jurisdictional status of the limitations provision through the 1948 Act.

III.

The majority offers several responses to this historical evidence, none of which is persuasive. First, the majority contends that "it is improper to consider legislative history" because the statutory text is "plain." Maj. Op. at 1042. It is a curious statute that is unambiguous but manages to produce an intracircuit split, several en banc dissents, and dozens of pages of analysis by the majority to justify its conclusion. These considerations aside, the fact is that the goal of the jurisdictional inquiry is "to ascertain Congress' intent." *Henderson,* 131 S.Ct. at 1204. The majority recognizes that we must look to factors such as "context" and "relevant historical treatment" to discern this intent, Maj. Op. at 1036 (quoting *Reed Elsevier, Inc. v. Muchnick,* 559 U.S. 154, 130 S.Ct. 1237, 1246, 176 L.Ed.2d 18 (2010)), but it provides no reason why legislative history may not similarly be considered.[5] The majority, in effect, invokes the requirement that there be evidence of clear congressional intent, and it then seeks to shut the door on the very evidence that could support this showing.

Perhaps recognizing that its "plain text" argument sits on shaky ground, next, the majority implicitly acknowledges that the limitations provision was jurisdictional under the original 1946 Act, but it contends that the 1948 revision undid this status. Maj. Op. at 1043-44. In this regard, the majority does at least make a passing reference to the rule that we are not to presume the 1948 Act effected substantive change unless "clearly expressed." Maj. Op. at 1044. According to the majority, though, such clear expression can be found in Congress' amending the cross-reference p.1059 in § 1346(b) to Chapter 171, which did not include the limitations provision. Maj. Op. at 1044.

This argument quickly falls apart upon considering the history of the two key provisions. As explained, the removal of the limitations provision from the FTCA Chapter was solely for organizational purposes, to consolidate the provisions of Title 28 setting forth limitations periods in actions against the government. Likewise, the redesignation of the cross-reference in § 1346(b), to Chapter 171, was merely an artifact of reorganization. The jurisdiction granting provision previously referenced "this chapter"—referring to the FTCA Chapter of Title 28—but this reference became outdated once the jurisdiction-granting provision was stripped out of the FTCA Chapter. Congress simply updated the cross-reference, inserting the new number of the FTCA Chapter, Chapter 171. In the end, therefore, the majority's argument is entirely circular. The majority relies on the reorganization, and nothing else, as a clear expression that the reorganization effected substantive change.[6]

Finally, the majority falls back on the notion that the FTCA's "drafting history" cannot supply a clear statement of Congress' intent. Maj. Op. at 1044. The 1946 Act, however, does not reflect "drafting history." It is the statutory scheme as enacted by Congress. And it is the scheme put into place only two years prior to the revisions that produced the current statutory language, revisions that we are to presume did not effect any substantive change. Under these circumstances, it is entirely reasonable to rely on the 1946 Act as providing a "clear indication" of Congress' intent. *Henderson,* 131 S.Ct. at 1205.

IV.

Given the legislative history recited above, I have little difficulty concluding that the FTCA's limitations provision was intended to be jurisdictional. Congress provided a clear statement to this effect when enacting the provision in 1946. When reorganizing Title 28 only two years later, Congress did not "clearly express[]," or provide any indication at all, that it intended to disturb this status. For these reasons, as well as the reasons outlined in Judge Bea's dissenting opinion, I respectfully dissent.

BEA, Circuit Judge, with whom TASHIMA, Circuit Judge, joins, dissenting:

The majority opinion permits courts, for equitable reasons, to extend the time in which a tort action can be begun against the Government, after the obligatory administrative claim has been filed and denied. Because I believe Congress clearly expressed its intent that 28 U.S.C. § 2401(b) would limit the jurisdiction of federal courts by providing that tort claims "shall be forever barred" unless action is begun within the six-month period following denial of the administrative claim by p.1060 the concerned agency, with no exceptions, I respectfully dissent.

I. The "Jurisdictional" vs. "Claim-Processing" Distinction and Our Inquiry

The majority is correct, of course, in noting that the Supreme Court has created a rebuttable presumption that equitable tolling applies to suits against the United States. *See Irwin v. Dep't of Veterans Affairs,* 498 U.S. 89, 95-96, 111 S.Ct. 453, 112 L.Ed.2d 435 (1990).[1] But that presumption is not universally applicable. As the majority admits, it has no application to certain kinds of "more absolute" statutes of limitations. *See John R. Sand & Gravel Co. v. United States,* 552 U.S. 130, 133-34, 128 S.Ct. 750, 169 L.Ed.2d 591 (2008).[2] These "more absolute" statutes "seek not so much to protect a defendant's case-specific interest in timeliness as to achieve a broader system-related goal, such as facilitating the administration of claims, limiting the scope of a governmental waiver of sovereign immunity, or promoting judicial efficiency." *Id.* at 133, 128 S.Ct. 750. The Court has described the time limits in such statutes of limitations as "jurisdictional." *See id.* at 134, 128 S.Ct. 750.

The majority believes the distinction between these "more absolute" or "jurisdictional" statutes, to which courts cannot create exceptions based on equitable considerations, and mere "claim-processing rules," to which *Irwin*'s rebuttable presumption p.1061 applies, is "critical for present purposes." *See* Op. at 1034-35. The majority calls § 2401(b) a "quintessential claim-processing rule," *see* Op. at 1039, but calling something a name does not change its nature.[3] And the critical question is not whether *we* characterize § 2401(b) as a "quintessential claim-processing rule," *see* Op. at 1039, but whether *Congress* mandated that its prescribed time limit be jurisdictional, *see Henderson v. Shinseki,* ___ U.S. ___, 131 S.Ct. 1197, 1203, 179 L.Ed.2d 159 (2011) (noting that "Congress is free to attach the conditions that go with the jurisdictional label to a rule that [courts] would prefer to call a claim-processing rule.").[4] To make this determination, the court must "look to see if there is any clear indication that Congress wanted the rule to be jurisdictional." *Id.* (internal quotation marks and citation omitted). And, to find such a "clear indication," we must examine the statute's "text, context and relevant historical treatment." *Reed Elsevier, Inc. v. Muchnick,* 559 U.S. 154, 166, 130 S.Ct. 1237, 176 L.Ed.2d 18 (2010).[5]

II. The Statute's Text

Section 2401(b) provides, in relevant part, that "[a] tort claim against the United States shall be forever barred unless... action is begun within six months after the date of mailing, by certified or registered mail, of notice of final denial of the claim by the agency to which it was presented." 28 U.S.C. § 2401(b).

A. Reading § 2401(b) with § 2675.

Perhaps where the majority goes wrong is in considering § 2401(b) as a stand-alone statute of limitations, rather than considering it in conjunction with the complementary administrative exhaustion requirement of 28 U.S.C. § 2675. The Court has instructed against such a restrictive view p.1062 of statutory conditions for bringing suit. *See United States v. Dalm*, 494 U.S. 596, 601, 110 S.Ct. 1361, 108 L.Ed.2d 548 (1990).[6] Instead, courts should read together "provisions which qualify an [individual]'s right to bring ... suit upon compliance with certain conditions." *Id.*[7] Here, two statutory provisions qualify an individual's right to file suit for tort against the United States. *See* 28 U.S.C. § 2675(a); 28 U.S.C. § 2401(b). First, § 2675 provides that "[a]n action shall not be instituted upon a claim against the United States for money damages ..., unless the claimant shall have first presented the claim to the appropriate Federal agency and his claim shall have been finally denied by the agency in writing and sent by certified or registered mail." 28 U.S.C. § 2675(a). This section requires that an administrative claim be made to the responsible agency, and it disallows suit until the denial of such claim is final. *See id.* No such administrative claims filing is needed to commence an action against a private person under applicable state law. *Irwin*, 498 U.S. at 96, 111 S.Ct. 453 (reasoning that principles "applicable to suits against private defendants should also apply to suits against the United States").

Section 2401(b) is § 2675(a)'s logical complement. It provides that:

> [a] tort claim against the United States shall be forever barred unless it is presented in writing to the appropriate Federal agency within two years after p.1063 such claim accrues or unless action is begun within six months after the date of mailing, by certified or registered mail, of notice of final denial of the claim by the agency to which it was presented.

28 U.S.C. § 2401(b). This provision establishes the time limits applicable to presenting an administrative claim and beginning a civil action. As in *Dalm*, the import of these two sections is clear when they are read together: Unless an administrative claim is presented to the responsible agency before action is begun, and unless both the claim and the action are begun within the time limits imposed by § 2401(b), the tort claim against the United States "shall be forever barred."

B. Section 2401(b) Refers to Courts' Jurisdiction.

The majority holds, in a rather conclusory fashion, that § 2401(b) "does not speak in jurisdictional terms or refer in any way to the jurisdiction of the federal courts." Op. at 1038 (internal quotations and citations omitted). I disagree. While it is true that § 2401(b) does not mention the term "jurisdiction," the same is true of several statutes of limitations the Court has found to be jurisdictional. *See John R. Sand & Gravel,* 552 U.S. at 134, 128 S.Ct. 750 (holding 28 U.S.C. § 2501 jurisdictional, despite the absence of the term "jurisdiction"); *Bowles v. Russell,* 551 U.S. 205, 213, 127 S.Ct. 2360, 168 L.Ed.2d 96 (2007) (same with respect to 28 U.S.C. § 2107(a) and (c))[8]; *Dalm,* 494 U.S. at 609, 110 S.Ct. 1361 (same with respect to 26 U.S.C. § 7422(a) and 26 U.S.C. § 6511(a)).[9] The majority fails to appreciate a crucial difference between the statutes of limitations the Court has deemed jurisdictional and those to which the Court has applied equitable tolling: whether the statute expressly mandates a consequence for the failure timely to file.

1. Plain Statutes of Limitations: No Consequences Mandated for Failure Timely to File

Some statutes of limitations require that certain actions be performed within a specified period of time without specifying consequences to be applied where the actions are not performed as prescribed. *See, e.g.,* 17 U.S.C. § 411(a) ("[Subject to certain exceptions], no civil action for infringement of the copyright in any United States work shall be instituted until preregistration or registration of the copyright claim has been made in accordance with this title."); 28 U.S.C. § 2244(d)(1) ("A 1-year period of limitation shall apply to an application for a writ of habeas corpus by a person in p.1064 custody pursuant to the judgment of a State court."); 38 U.S.C. § 7266(a) ("In order to obtain review by the Court of Appeals for Veterans Claims of a final decision of the Board of Veterans' Appeals, a person adversely affected by such decision shall file a notice of appeal with the Court within 120 days after the date on which notice of the decision is mailed...."); F.R. Bankr.P. 4004(a) ("[A] complaint ... objecting to the debtor's discharge shall be filed no later than 60 days after the first date set for the meeting of creditors under § 341(a)."). These statutes, as evidenced by the quotations above, are often written in mandatory terms. Significantly, while they make *parties'* actions mandatory, they do not contain mandatory *consequences* for noncompliance.

The Court has instructed that "if a statute does not specify a consequence for noncompliance with statutory timing provisions, the federal courts will not in the ordinary course impose their own coercive sanction." *Barnhart v. Peabody Coal Co.,* 537 U.S. 149, 159, 123 S.Ct. 748, 154 L.Ed.2d 653 (2003).[10] It makes good sense, then, that the Court has regularly held that statutes of limitations lacking provisions specifying consequences do not speak in jurisdictional terms or refer to the courts' jurisdiction. *See, e.g., Henderson,* 131 S.Ct. at 1204 (holding that the terms of 38 U.S.C. § 7266(a) "do not suggest, let alone provide clear evidence, that the provision was meant to carry jurisdictional consequences"); *Holland v. Florida,* 560 U.S. 631, 130 S.Ct. 2549, 2560, 177 L.Ed.2d 130 (2010) (holding that 28 U.S.C. § 2244(d)(1) "does not set forth an inflexible rule requiring dismissal whenever its clock has run" (internal quotation marks and citations omitted))[11]; *Reed Elsevier,* p.1065 559 U.S. at 165, 130 S.Ct. 1237 (holding that 17 U.S.C. § 411(a) "does not speak in jurisdictional terms or refer in any way to the jurisdiction of the district courts" (citation omitted)); *Kontrick v. Ryan,* 540 U.S. 443, 454, 124 S.Ct. 906, 157 L.Ed.2d 867 (2004) (holding that "the filing deadline[] prescribed in Bankruptcy Rule[]

4004 ... do[es] not delineate what cases bankruptcy courts are competent to adjudicate").[12] These cases stand for the general proposition identified above: If the statutory text does not mandate dismissal as the consequence for noncompliance, the courts should not read the statute as having jurisdictional consequences (i.e. mandatory dismissal without exception). Instead, per *Irwin's* instruction, the courts should presume equitable tolling may be applied to the statute in question, and then proceed to determine whether that presumption has been rebutted and, if not, whether the running of the timing provision should be tolled for equitable reasons. *See Irwin,* 498 U.S. at 95-97, 111 S.Ct. 453.[13]

2. Consequence Statutes of Limitations: Mandatory Consequences for a Failure Timely to File

In contrast, however, are statutes of limitations that specify the consequences of a party's failure to adhere to a prescribed time limit. *See, e.g.,* 26 U.S.C. § 7422(a) ("No suit or proceeding shall be maintained in any court for the recovery of any internal revenue tax ... until a claim for refund or credit has been duly filed with the Secretary...."); 28 U.S.C. § 2501 ("Every claim of which the United States p.1066 Court of Federal Claims has jurisdiction shall be barred unless the petition thereon is filed within six years after such claim first accrues."); 28 U.S.C. § 2107(a) ("Except as otherwise provided in this section, no appeal shall bring any judgment, order or decree in an action, suit or proceeding of a civil nature before a court of appeals for review unless notice of appeal is filed, within thirty days after the entry of such judgment, order or decree."); 28 U.S.C. § 2409a(g) ("Any civil action under this section, except for an action brought by a State, shall be barred unless it is commenced within twelve years of the date upon which it accrued."). Like the first category of statutes discussed *supra,* these statutes speak in mandatory terms. They do not, however, merely require that parties take actions at specified times. Instead, these statutes require the courts to respond in a certain way to a party's failure to timely act by making the *consequences* of noncompliance, rather than just the acts, mandatory.

It is clear, then, that there are two different kinds of mandatory provisions: (1) those that make certain actions mandatory on the parties but do not specify the consequences of noncompliance, and (2) those that also provide mandatory consequences for failures to act according to their prescriptions. The Court has mentioned the importance of this distinction in the past. *See Henderson,* 131 S.Ct. at 1204 (holding a statute nonjurisdictional in part because its language did "not suggest, let alone provide clear evidence, that the provision was meant to carry jurisdictional consequences"); *Holland,* 130 S.Ct. at 2560 (noting that the nonjurisdictional statute did "not set forth an inflexible rule requiring dismissal whenever its clock has run" (internal quotation marks and citations omitted)). I agree with the majority that not all mandatory prescriptions are properly categorized as jurisdictional. *See* Op. at 1039. But I also believe that, to determine which mandatory prescriptions are jurisdictional, we must pay close attention to precisely *what* Congress has made mandatory (i.e. a party's action or the consequences for a party's failure timely to act). Thus, when Congress has mandated that a particular consequence will accompany a party's noncompliance with statutory timing provisions, courts are not free to impose other consequences or, as the majority does in this case, to fail to impose any consequence at all.

The reason is simple: When Congress mandates that a particular *consequence* be imposed, it limits the court's power to act. When the consequence is that the claim "shall be barred" or the case "shall not be maintained," Congress has spoken in jurisdictional terms.[14] *Cf. John R. Sand & Gravel,* 552 U.S. at 134, 128 S.Ct. 750 (holding that 28 U.S.C. § 2501, which includes "shall be barred" language, is jurisdictional); *Dalm,* 494 U.S. at 609, 110 S.Ct. 1361 (holding that 26 U.S.C. § 6511(a), which, when read with 26 U.S.C. § 7422(a), includes "may not be maintained" language, is jurisdictional). The majority holds that *John R. Sand & Gravel* and *Bowles* "did not hold [the statutes at issue] jurisdictional based on the consequential language of the statute" but because p.1067 of "a century's worth of precedent and practice in American courts." Op. at 1040, n. 3. But what was that "century's worth of precedent" based on? The Court's ancient recognition that some statutes of limitations have *consequences. Kendall v. United States,* 107 U.S. 123, 125, 2 S.Ct. 277, 27 L.Ed. 437 (1883) (statute of limitation "forever barred" "*every claim*"); *Finn v. United States,* 123 U.S. 227, 233, 8 S.Ct. 82, 31 L.Ed. 128 (1887) (holding that the express words of the act of 1863—stating claims were "forever barred"—was a condition to the right to a judgment against the United States and the court *must* dismiss the petition if the condition was not satisfied). Such consequences speak to "the courts' statutory ... power to adjudicate the case." *Steel Co. v. Citizens for Better Env't,* 523 U.S. 83, 89, 118 S.Ct. 1003, 140 L.Ed.2d 210 (1998). To illustrate this point, one asks: What statutory power does a court have to adjudicate a claim which, according to congressional mandate, "shall be barred" or "shall not be maintained?" The answer is simple: None.[15] It seems natural, then, to conclude that when a statute includes such language, it speaks in jurisdictional terms. *See Landgraf v. USI Film Prods.,* 511 U.S. 244, 274, 114 S.Ct. 1483, 128 L.Ed.2d 229 (1994) ("[J]urisdictional statutes speak to the power of the court rather than to the rights of obligations of the parties." (citation omitted)).[16]

Section 2401(b) falls into the second category identified above. It does not merely specify what a party must do; it specifies the consequences of a failure to act according to its time limit. If action is not begun p.1068 within six months after the agency mailed its final denial of the claim, such claim "shall be forever barred." *See* 28 U.S.C. § 2401(b). Because the court has no statutory power to adjudicate such a claim, I would hold that, unlike the statute considered in *Holland,* § 2401(b) "set[s] forth an inflexible rule requiring dismissal whenever its clock has run." *Holland,* 130 S.Ct. at 2560. In that manner, and unlike the statute considered in *Henderson,* the language of § 2401(b) "provide[s] clear evidence[] that the provision was meant to carry jurisdictional consequences." *Henderson,* 131 S.Ct. at 1204. Thus, its pronouncement "speak[s] in jurisdictional terms" or, at the very least, "refer[s] in any way to the jurisdiction of the district courts." *Reed Elsevier,* 559 U.S. at 165, 130 S.Ct. 1237.[17]

The majority calls my delineation of statutes of limitations a "grand theory". Op. at 1039. I appreciate their praise, but I humbly submit there is nothing "grand" about following the "clear evidence" provided by Congress and the Supreme Court.

C. The Importance of the Term "Forever."

The majority escapes this rather straightforward conclusion with the assertion that " § 2401(b) merely states what is always true of statutory filing deadlines: once the limitations period ends, whether extended by the application of tolling principles or not, a plaintiff is 'forever barred' from presenting his claim to the relevant adjudicatory body." Op. at 1038 (citing *Kubrick*, 444 U.S. at 117, 100 S.Ct. 352).[18] The majority has simply written the term "forever" out of the statute, ascribing it no meaning nor importance at all. It is a mere "vestige of mid-twentieth-century congressional drafting conventions,"[19] Op. at 1039, and adds nothing that the statute would not say without it, because all statutes of limitations, if applicable, bar claims "forever," *see* Op. at 1038-39.

p.1069 But the majority fails to consider the standard canon of statutory construction that requires courts to give meaning, if possible, to *each* of a statute's terms. *See Lowe v. SEC.*, 472 U.S. 181, 208 n. 53, 105 S.Ct. 2557, 86 L.Ed.2d 130 (1985) ("[W]e must give effect to every word that Congress used in the statute."); *see also* Antonin Scalia & Bryan A. Garner, *Reading Law: The Interpretation of Legal Texts* 174 (2012) (explaining that "[t]he surplusage canon holds that it is no more the court's function to revise by subtraction than by addition."). To the majority, the term "forever" is tautological; it has no meaning whatsoever. But that is not the view of well-established dictionaries at the time the statute was drafted. *See, e.g.,* Webster's New International Dictionary 990 (2d ed.1943) (defining the adverb "forever" as "1. For a limitless time or endless ages; everlastingly; eternally," and "2. At all times; always; incessantly," and identifying "invariably" and "unchangeably" as synonyms).

Usage of the term "forever," as in "forever barred," connotes something that obtains under any and all circumstances, something that is invariably so. But this is nothing new. In *Kendall v. United States,* the Supreme Court interpreted a statute of limitations which included the phrase "forever barred" and stated: "What claims are thus barred? The express words of the statute leave no room for contention. *Every claim*-except those specially enumerated-is forever barred unless asserted within six years from the time it first accrued." 107 U.S. at 125, 2 S.Ct. 277 (emphasis added). Forever, as in "forever barred", has an inclusionary meaning—"every claim"—as well as a temporal meaning—for all time. *Kendall* has continued to be cited approvingly in *Soriano v. United States,* 352 U.S. at 273, 77 S.Ct. 269,[20] and *John R. Sand & Gravel,* 552 U.S. at 134, 128 S.Ct. 750, on the way to holding statutes of limitations "jurisdictional."

As used in § 2401(b), then, the term "forever" means that an FTCA claim is invariably barred unless a civil action is commenced within the six-month period following final denial of the administrative claim. Moreover, according to the majority's theory, the fact that Congress included "forever barred" language in "various other statutes enacted in the mid-twentieth century," *see* Op. at 1039, must mean that Congress merely plugged boilerplate language into these provisions, without thinking or assigning any special meaning to the words it chose to employ. But the fact that Congress included the term in *various* limitations periods, and not *all* limitations periods, suggests the exact opposite is true: On the occasions when

Congress used the term "forever barred," it did so intentionally and for a reason. It is especially telling that Congress did not adhere to the majority's claimed "drafting convention" when, in 1948, it drafted § 2401(a), the very section that precedes the one here in issue. *See* Act of June 25, 1948, chap. 646, 62 Stat. 971 (June 25, 1948) ("Every civil action commenced against the United States shall be barred unless the complaint is filed within six years after the right of action first accrues."); *see also Russello v. United States,* 464 U.S. 16, 23, 104 S.Ct. 296, 78 L.Ed.2d 17 (1983) ("[W]here Congress includes particular language in one section of a statute but omits it in another section of the same Act, it is generally presumed that Congress acts intentionally and purposely p.1070 in the disparate inclusion or exclusion" (citations omitted)).

The majority finally holds that *if* "forever" does mean anything, it merely focuses on time and emphasizes that "once barred, [a FTCA claim] is precluded permanently, not temporarily or until some later event occurs" and that "the word 'forever' cannot bear [the] weight" that I give it. Op. at 1041, n. 4. However, our canons of construction cannot bear the *lack* of weight the majority gives it, see *Lowe,* 472 U.S. 181 at n. 53, 105 S.Ct. 2557, and neither can our history. *See Kendall,* 107 U.S. at 125, 2 S.Ct. 277.

I do not subscribe to the facile construct that we can read "forever barred" to mean nothing more than "barred." Nor do I believe "forever" is a non-cipher. "We are not free to rewrite the statutory text." *McNeil,* 508 U.S. at 111, 113 S.Ct. 1980. By providing that claims not presented within the time prescribed "shall be forever barred," Congress clearly expressed its intention that "every claim" (*Kendall,* 107 U.S. at 125, 2 S.Ct. 277) would be *invariably* barred, not *sometimes* barred so that equitable considerations might be held to extend the time in which to begin actions on such claims.

D. Ninth Circuit Precedent

The majority relies on three of this court's previous opinions to support its conclusion that § 2401(b)'s "shall be forever barred" language does not mean that the statute's time limit is jurisdictional.[21] *See* Op. at 1038-39. It first relies on *Cedars-Sinai Medical Center v. Shalala,* 125 F.3d 765, 770 (9th Cir.1997), which held that § 2401(a) is not jurisdictional. In fairness, the majority notes that this opinion's continued vitality was called into question by *Aloe Vera of America, Inc. v. United States,* 580 F.3d 867, 872 (9th Cir. 2009) ("To the extent that *Cedars-Sinai* is still valid after *John R. Sand,* the holding in *Cedars-Sinai* does not dictate the jurisdictional nature of section 7431(d)." (citation omitted)). It dismisses that statement, however, because it "was made without the benefit of the Supreme Court's most recent decisions clarifying the distinction between jurisdictional and nonjurisdictional rules." Op. at 1038 n. 2. Of course, this claim gets us nowhere, because *Cedars-Sinai* was also decided without the benefit of those decisions. Thus, we cannot blindly rely on *Cedars-Sinai;* instead, we must examine whether it accords with the Supreme Court's most recent guidance.[22]

p.1071 *Cedars-Sinai's* analysis of the jurisdictional question is simple and brief. *See Cedars-Sinai,* 125 F.3d at 770. The court held: "Because the statute of limitations codified at 28 U.S.C. § 2401(a) makes no mention of jurisdiction but erects only a procedural bar, ... we hold that § 2401(a)'s six-year statute of limitations is not jurisdictional, but is subject to waiver." *Id.* (citations omitted). Two problems with *Cedars-Sinai's* analysis lead me to conclude that it is no longer good law.

First, *Cedars-Sinai* appears to erect an absolute rule that a statute of limitations is jurisdictional only when it specifically mentions the term "jurisdiction." *See Cedars-Sinai*, 125 F.3d at 770. Since *Cedars-Sinai* was decided, however, the Supreme Court has advised that Congress "need not incant magic words ... to speak clearly [about jurisdiction]." *Sebelius*, 133 S.Ct. at 824.[23] A requirement that Congress use the term "jurisdiction" runs afoul of this instruction. Moreover, the Court has clarified that a statute of limitations may be jurisdictional when it "speak[s] in jurisdictional terms or refer[s] *in any way* to the jurisdiction of the district courts." *Reed Elsevier*, 559 U.S. at 165, 130 S.Ct. 1237 (emphasis added). As previously discussed, one way to refer to the courts' jurisdiction is to "suggest ... that the provision was meant to carry jurisdictional consequences." *Henderson*, 131 S.Ct. at 1204. *Cedars-Sinai* failed to appreciate that, by providing that any claim not filed within the time specified "shall be barred," § 2401(a) limited the courts' power to act and, thus, referred to the courts' jurisdiction.

Second, *Cedars-Sinai* relied heavily on *Irwin's* quotation of 28 U.S.C. § 2501, which the Court had deemed jurisdictional in *Soriano v. United States*, 352 U.S. 270, 77 S.Ct. 269, 1 L.Ed.2d 306 (1957).[24] After *Irwin*, there was initially good reason to believe *Soriano* had been overruled. *See Irwin*, 498 U.S. at 98, 111 S.Ct. 453 p.1072 (White, J., concurring in part and concurring in the judgment) ("Not only is the Court's holding inconsistent with our traditional approach to cases involving sovereign immunity, it directly overrules a prior decision by this Court, *Soriano v. United States*." (citation omitted)). Because it seemed *Irwin* had overruled *Soriano*, it also seemed the terms "shall be barred" were insufficient to make a statute jurisdictional. If that had been true, *Cedars-Sinai* may have been correct. But the Court has since clarified *Irwin* and reaffirmed *Soriano's* vitality. *See John R. Sand & Gravel*, 552 U.S. at 137, 128 S.Ct. 750 ("[T]he Court [in *Irwin*], while mentioning a case that reflects the particular interpretive history of the court of claims statute, namely *Soriano*, says nothing at all about overturning that or any other case in that line. Courts do not normally overturn a long line of earlier cases without mentioning the matter." (citations omitted)). Given this clarification, and *Cedars-Sinai's* tension with intervening Supreme Court decisions, I would hold that it was incorrectly decided and is of no precedential value on this issue. *See Oregon Natural Desert Ass'n v. U.S. Forest Serv.*, 550 F.3d 778, 782-83 (9th Cir.2008) (explaining that circuit precedent is "effectively overruled" when its "reasoning or theory ... is clearly irreconcilable with the reasoning or theory of intervening higher authority." (internal quotation marks and citations omitted)).

The majority then cites *Partlow v. Jewish Orphans' Home of Southern California*, 645 F.2d 757, 760-61 (9th Cir.1981), *abrogated on other grounds by Hoffmann-La Roche, Inc. v. Sperling*, 493 U.S. 165, 110 S.Ct. 482, 107 L.Ed.2d 480 (1989), and *Mt. Hood Stages, Inc. v. Greyhound Corp.*, 616 F.2d 394, 396-407 (9th Cir.1980), as instances where this court has held that the language "shall be forever barred" did not render a statute jurisdictional. *See Op.* at 1039. Of course, these cases pre-date all of the Supreme Court's recent guidance as well. For that reason, we should once again take a critical look at their reasoning before relying on them.

The *Partlow* court held that equitable tolling could be applied to 29 U.S.C. § 255, the statute of limitations applicable to actions brought under the Fair Labor Standards Act. *See Partlow*, 645 F.2d at 760-61. Interestingly, the court did not conduct any in-depth analysis of the statute's text, context, or historical treatment. Indeed, the *Partlow* opinion does not once quote the statute's text or even mention the phrase "shall be forever barred." *See id.* at 757-61. Instead, the court relied on opinions from two of our sister circuits, each of which held that § 255 could be equitably tolled. *See id.* at 760 (citing *Ott v. Midland-Ross Corp.*, 523 F.2d 1367, 1370 (6th Cir.1975), and *Hodgson v. Humphries*, 454 F.2d 1279, 1283-84 (10th Cir. 1972)). It then noted that "courts have often stated that equitable tolling is read into *every* federal statute of limitations." *Id.* (citation omitted) (emphasis added). It then concluded that the statute should be tolled in the circumstances of that case. *See id.* at 760-61.

If it were unclear at the time *Partlow* was decided, it has since become abundantly clear that equitable tolling is not to be read into *every* federal statute of limitations. *See John R. Sand & Gravel*, 552 U.S. at 133-34, 128 S.Ct. 750 (explaining that some federal statutes of limitations— such as 28 U.S.C. § 2501, for instance—must be treated as jurisdictional, so that courts are forbidden to "consider whether certain equitable considerations warrant extending [the] limitations period[s]" they contain). Moreover, *Partlow* fails to conduct the kind of analysis required by the Court's more recent decisions. *See Reed Elsevier*, 559 U.S. at 166, 130 S.Ct. 1237 (providing that "the jurisdictional analysis p.1073 must focus on the 'legal character' of the requirement, which we discern[] by looking to the condition's text, context, and relevant historical treatment" (citations omitted)). For these reasons, I would hold that *Partlow* is today flat wrong, and of no precedential value on the question presently before the court.

In *Mt. Hood Stages,* this court held that equitable tolling could be applied to 15 U.S.C. § 15b. *See Mt. Hood Stages*, 616 F.2d at 396. It is once again telling that the court did not conduct any in-depth analysis of the statute's text or even mention the statute's phrase "shall be forever barred." *See id.* at 396-406. It is clear, then, that the decision was not based on a determination that the statute did not refer in any way to the courts' jurisdiction. In a word, *Mt. Hood Stages* skipped the first, Court-required step of textual analysis for a consideration of the statute's purpose in a regulatory scheme. *See Reed Elsevier*, 559 U.S. at 166, 130 S.Ct. 1237.[25] Instead, the decision was based on the court's conclusion that "tolling the running of limitations serves the important federal interest in accommodating enforcement of the Sherman Act with enforcement of the Interstate Commerce Act, and is not inconsistent with the purposes of the Clayton Act's limitation period." *Id.* at 396.

In particular, the *Mt. Hood Stages* court found that tolling would "contribute[] to a reasonable accommodation of the [Interstate Commerce Commission]'s responsibility for furthering the national transportation policy with the responsibility of the courts to effectuate the national antitrust policy." *Id.* at 397. Because the case "involved subject matter Congress ha[d] given the Commission jurisdiction to regulate," it "created a dispute *only* the Commission could resolve." *Id.* (emphasis added). The court noted that, "[i]f Mt. Hood had filed [its] antitrust suit ... prior to the Commission determination [of a particular factual issue]," accommodation of the Clayton and Interstate Commerce Acts would have compelled "the court ... to dismiss or stay the suit pending the necessary administrative determination." *Id.* at 399. Thus, "[c]ongressional purposes under the two statutory regimes would be served by tolling the statute of limitations during the Commission proceeding." *Id.* at 400. For that reason, the court held that the statute of limitations could be "tolled pending resort to an administrative agency for a preliminary determination of issues within its primary jurisdiction." *Id.* at 405; *see also Pace Indus., Inc. v. Three Phoenix Co.*, 813 F.2d 234, 241 (9th Cir.1987) ("[O]ur decision [in *Mt. Hood Stages*] rested on considerations of federal policy and primary jurisdiction which are not present here.").

Contrary to the majority's implication, *see* Op. at 1038, *Mt. Hood Stages* does not stand for the proposition that "shall be forever barred" does not refer to the courts' jurisdiction. Indeed, a statute may *refer* to the courts' jurisdiction and yet not be jurisdictional, much like a statute which does not speak in jurisdictional terms may still be jurisdictional. *See United States v. Brockamp*, 519 U.S. 347, 352, 117 S.Ct. 849, 136 L.Ed.2d 818 (1997) (holding that the timing requirements of 26 U.S.C. § 6511 are jurisdictional, even though the statute does not refer to the courts' jurisdiction, because of the provision's "detail, its technical language, the iteration of the limitations in both procedural and substantive forms, and the explicit listing of exceptions"). In short, even a statute that refers in some way to the courts' jurisdiction may not be jurisdictional when, for example, Congress has created dual statutory regimes, such as those involved in *Mt. Hood Stages,* that essentially require tolling p.1074 for their accommodation. Of course, there are no such dual regimes at issue in this case, nor does this case involve the sort of federal policy and primary jurisdiction considerations that animated the court's opinion in *Mt. Hood Stages.* Thus, I would hold that *Mt. Hood Stages* offers no useful guidance on the question whether § 2401(b)'s language refers to the courts' jurisdiction.

In defense of *Partlow* and *Mount Hood Stages,* the majority states that these cases still "undermine the notion that Congress intended through the use of magic words... to establish jurisdictional bars in statutes allowing for civil suits against private parties." Op. at 1041, n. 5. Of course, this argument is merely a straw man; we all agree that Congress never uses "magic words" to establish jurisdiction. *See supra*, Bea Dissent at 1068, n. 17.

III. The Statute's Purpose

As earlier noted, in *John R. Sand & Gravel,* the Court identified the kinds of goals that make statutes of limitations jurisdictional: "[Jurisdictional] statutes of limitations ... seek not so much to protect a defendant's case-specific interest in timeliness as to achieve a broader system-related goal, such as facilitating the administration of claims, limiting the scope of a governmental waiver of sovereign immunity, or promoting judicial efficiency." 552 U.S. at 133, 128 S.Ct. 750. Consideration of each of the goals outlined in *John R. Sand & Gravel* illustrates that § 2401(b)'s broad, system-related purposes require us to find that its timing provisions are indeed jurisdictional.

A. Section 2401(b) Facilitates the Administration of Claims

The Court has held that § 2401(b)'s "obvious purpose" is to "encourage the prompt presentation of claims." *See United States v. Kubrick,* 444 U.S. 111, 117, 100 S.Ct. 352, 62 L.Ed.2d 259 (1979).[26] The requirement that a civil action be filed within six months of a denial of an administrative claim guarantees that the civil action will commence while the denial of the claim is relatively fresh. For actions filed within that time period, the Department of Justice, which will defend the cases, will be able to access the relatively fresh memories of the administrators who denied the claim. It is also more likely that those administrators will be on the job six months after the denial of the claim than would be the case if the denial had taken place years before.

p.1075 B. Section 2401(b) Limits a Waiver of Sovereign Immunity

The Court has held that § 2401(b) limits the waiver of sovereign immunity expressed in the FTCA. *See Kubrick,* 444 U.S. at 117-18, 100 S.Ct. 352. In particular, the Court has stated:

> "We should ... have in mind that the [FTCA] waives the immunity of the United States and that in construing the statute of limitations [expressed in § 2401(b)], *which is a condition of that waiver,* we should not take it upon ourselves to extend the waiver beyond that which Congress intended."

Id. (emphasis added). This passage clearly identifies § 2401(b) as a provision "limiting the scope of a governmental waiver of sovereign immunity," which is exactly the kind of broader, system-related goal that makes a statute's time limit "more absolute." *See John R. Sand & Gravel,* 552 U.S. at 133, 128 S.Ct. 750; Op. at 1046.

The majority agrees that the FTCA "is predicated on a sovereign immunity waiver." Op. at 1046. Further, the majority admits that many of the cases upon which they rely—*Auburn Regional Medical Center, Gonzalez, Henderson, Holland,* and *Bowles*—do *not* involve issues of government immunity and therefore "may not raise precisely parallel sovereign immunity concerns" as are now before us. *See* Op. at 1046 n. 12. The majority is unable to deny that (1) the FTCA limits waiver of sovereign immunity and therefore meets a goal that makes statutes of limitations jurisdictional under *John R. Sand & Gravel,* or (2) this difference distinguishes the FTCA and § 2401(b) from other cases on which the majority tries to rely.

C. Section 2401(b) Promotes Judicial Efficiency

First, like all statutes of limitations, § 2401(b) "protect[s] ... the courts from having to deal with cases in which the search for truth may be seriously impaired by the loss of evidence, whether by death or disappearance of witnesses, fading memories, disappearance of documents, or otherwise." *See Kubrick,* 444 U.S. at 117, 100 S.Ct. 352. By promoting the prompt presentation of claims, § 2401(b) seeks to limit the amount of evidence lost to time and ensure that courts will adjudicate cases with complete records. *See id.*

Second, when read together with § 2675, it is clear that § 2401(b) was intended to protect against the burdens of claims filed outside of its time prescriptions. In *McNeil v. United States,* the Court held that § 2675's administrative exhaustion requirement was jurisdictional. 508 U.S. 106, 111-12, 113 S.Ct. 1980, 124 L.Ed.2d 21 (1993). There, the petitioner filed a complaint in federal district court alleging that the United States Public Health Service had injured him while conducting experimentation on prisoners in the custody of the Illinois Department of Corrections. *See id.* at 108, 113 S.Ct. 1980. Four months later, he submitted a claim for damages to the Department of Health and Human Services. *See id.* at 109, 113 S.Ct. 1980. After the Department denied the claim, the petitioner sent the district court a letter and asked that it permit him to commence his legal action. *See id.* The court held that it lacked jurisdiction to entertain an action commenced before satisfaction of § 2675's administrative exhaustion requirement. *See id.* The Seventh Circuit affirmed and held that the petitioner had filed his action too early. *See id.*

The Supreme Court affirmed and held that § 2675's administrative exhaustion requirement was a jurisdictional prerequisite to filing suit under the FTCA. *See id.* at 112-13, 113 S.Ct. 1980. As relevant here, it noted that "every premature filing of an action under the FTCA imposes some burden on the judicial system...." *Id.* at 112, p.1076 113 S.Ct. 1980. Similar burdens are imposed on the judicial system when actions are filed late, accompanied by claims that the court should toll the running of the statute of limitations for equitable reasons which may or may not justify the plaintiff's tardiness. As was the case for premature filings in *McNeil,* "the burden may be slight in the individual case." *Id.* But § 2401(b) "governs the processing of a vast multitude of claims." *Id.* For that reason, "adherence to the straightforward statutory command" is the best way to promote "[t]he interest in orderly administration of this body of litigation." *Id.*

Because § 2401(b) serves each of the three system-related purposes identified in *John R. Sand & Gravel* as making statutory time limits "more absolute," equitable tolling should not be applied here. Instead, we should hold that § 2401's time limits are jurisdictional in nature.

IV. The Statute's Context

Section 2401(b)'s context includes its placement in the larger statutory scheme, as well as any relevant exceptions Congress may have legislated. It also includes the Supreme Court's "interpretation of similar provisions in many years past." *Reed Elsevier,* 559 U.S. at 168, 130 S.Ct. 1237.

A. The Supreme Court's Interpretation of Similar Provisions

The majority correctly notes that "there has not been ... a venerable, consistent line of [Supreme Court] cases treating the FTCA limitations period as jurisdictional" and, indeed, that "there is no Supreme Court precedent on the question."[27] Op. at 1045. Still, the Supreme Court has examined similar provisions and offered guidance useful here. As previously stated, *Kubrick* and *John R. Sand & Gravel,* taken together, strongly suggest that § 2401(b)'s time limits are jurisdictional.

The Court's analysis in *McNeil* only bolsters this conclusion. There, the Court held that 28 U.S.C. § 2675(a) "bars claimants from bringing suit in federal court [under the FTCA] until they have exhausted their administrative remedies." *McNeil*, 508 U.S. at 113, 113 S.Ct. 1980. This requirement is jurisdictional. Courts cannot entertain a suit brought before exhaustion of administrative remedies, even if the claimant exhausts those remedies before "substantial progress [is] made in the litigation," because such a suit was filed too early. *Id.* at 110-11, 113 S.Ct. 1980. Here, there is no dispute that, like the petitioner in *McNeil*, Wong filed her action before denial of her administrative claim and was similarly premature.

The majority emphasizes that § 2675(a) is located in chapter 171 and that Congress expressly conditioned the district courts' jurisdiction upon plaintiffs' compliance with the provisions of that chapter. *See* Op. at 1042. In *McNeil*, however, the Court did not even mention this fact. Instead, it based its decision on two considerations: (1) the statutory text is unambiguous and expresses Congress's intent to require complete exhaustion of administrative remedies, and (2) "[e]very premature filing of an action under the FTCA imposes p.1077 some burden on the judicial system and on the Department of Justice which must assume the defense of such actions." *McNeil*, 508 U.S. at 111-12, 113 S.Ct. 1980. With respect to the premature filing, the Court noted that, "[a]lthough the burden may be slight in an individual case, the statute governs the processing of a vast multitude of claims," such that "[t]he interest in orderly administration of this body of litigation is best served by adherence to the straightforward statutory command." *Id.*

The Court's language suggests once again that the FTCA's timing requirements fit into the jurisdictional category. *See John R. Sand & Gravel*, 552 U.S. at 133, 128 S.Ct. 750 (identifying "facilitating the administration of claims" as one of the broader, system-related goals that makes a statutory time limit "more absolute"). In *McNeil*, the Court took a systemic view of its decision; it was concerned with the "orderly administration of this body of litigation" precisely because § 2675(a) "governs the processing of a vast multitude of claims." *McNeil*, 508 U.S. at 112, 113 S.Ct. 1980. Because the same is true of § 2401(b), our analysis should feature the same concern. And, when one takes this more systemic view of § 2401(b), one will surely find that every premature—or late—filing imposes a burden on the judicial system and on the Department of Justice and agree with the Court that "strict adherence to the procedural requirements specified by the legislature is the best guarantee of evenhanded administration of the law." *Id.* at 113, 113 S.Ct. 1980.[28]

B. Placement

Seeking another interpretive tool to support its position, the majority emphasizes the fact that § 2401(b) is located in a provision separate from the FTCA's jurisdiction-granting provision. *See* Op. at 1042. With respect, this fact is irrelevant. As the Court has explained, "some time limits are jurisdictional even though expressed in a separate statutory section from jurisdictional grants, while others are not, even when incorporated into the jurisdictional provisions." *Barnhart*, 537 U.S. at 159 n. 6, 123 S.Ct. 748 (citations omitted). "Formalistic rules do not account for the difference, which is explained by contextual and historical indications of what Congress meant to accomplish." *Id.*

Even more problematic to the majority's analysis of the FTCA's reorganization in 1948, *see* Op. at 1043, is the inconvenient enactment of a law rejecting placement in the Act as a valid interpretive tool. The majority acknowledges that, before 1948, Congress had expressly conditioned the grant of jurisdiction over tort claims against the United States upon plaintiffs' compliance with, among other things, the FTCA's original limitations provision. *See* p.1078 Op. at 1043. In 1948, however, Congress reorganized the FTCA and placed the limitations provision in chapter 161 and other provisions, such as § 2675, in chapter 171. *See* Op. at 1043. It appears the majority would conclude from this fact that Congress intended to separate jurisdictional requirements (§ 2675) from non-jurisdictional ones (§ 2401). Congress, however, expressly rejected this possible reading of its reorganization efforts by an enactment of law. *See* Pub.L. No. 773, 62 Stat. 869, 991 (1948) ("No inference of a legislative construction is to be drawn by reason of the chapter in Title 28, Judiciary and Judicial Procedure, ... in which any section is placed."). The majority simply ignores this Act of Congress, perhaps because it cuts directly against the majority's desired result: interpretive value based on the statute's placement.

Congress clearly stated that the placement of § 2401 in chapter 161 was not intended to change the way it should be interpreted. If Congress intended to condition the grant of jurisdiction over tort claims against the United States on compliance with the limitations period, the recodification in 1948 should not be read to alter that intent. That Congress later amended the jurisdiction-granting provision to provide that the district courts would have exclusive jurisdiction over FTCA actions "[s]ubject to the provisions of chapter 171 of this title," 28 U.S.C. § 1346(b)(1), says nothing about the jurisdictional status of a provision located in chapter 161.

C. The Significance of § 2401(a)'s Exceptions

"[A]s a general rule, ... Congress's use of certain language in one part of [a] statute and different language in another can indicate that different meanings were intended." *Sebelius,* 133 S.Ct. at 825. As relevant here, § 2401(b) enumerates no exceptions, while § 2401(a) provides that "action of any person under legal disability or beyond the seas at the time the claim accrues may be commenced within three years after the disability ceases." 28 U.S.C. § 2401(a). The relevant meaning to be inferred from *Sebelius'* interpretive canon quoted above is that Congress did not intend for any exceptions to be applied to § 2401(b). The majority is correct that this canon, standing alone, does not constitute a "clear statement" by Congress. *See* Op. at 1044. The canon can, however, "tip the scales when a statute could be read in multiple ways." *Sebelius,* 133 S.Ct. at 826. I would not hold that consideration of this canon alone dictates a conclusion that § 2401(b)'s time limit is jurisdictional, but it reinforces that conclusion when considered with the statute's text and context.

V. Conclusion

Congress clearly expressed its intent that § 2401(b) would have "jurisdictional" consequences. Jurisdictional treatment accords with the statute's text and the Supreme Court's analysis of similar provisions. For these reasons, equitable tolling should not be applied to the time limits contained in § 2401(b). I respectfully dissent.

[1] *Marley* dismissed *Alvarez-Machain I* as having "no precedential value" because the panel opinion in that case was vacated and the case was taken en banc. *See Marley,* 567 F.3d at 1037-38 (citing *Alvarez-Machain v. United States (Alvarez-Machain III),* 284 F.3d 1039 (9th Cir.2002)). But the opinion that was vacated by *Alvarez-Machain III* was not *Alvarez-Machain I.* Rather, it was a different opinion in the same case: *Alvarez-Machain v. United States (Alvarez-Machain II),* 266 F.3d 1045 (9th Cir.2001). Thus, *Alvarez-Machain I* was still good law when *Marley* was decided. The result was an intracircuit conflict, which we can resolve only through en banc proceedings. *See Atonio v. Wards Cove Packing Co.,* 810 F.2d 1477, 1478-79 (9th Cir. 1987) (en banc).

[2] *Aloe Vera of America, Inc. v. United States,* 580 F.3d 867, 872 (9th Cir.2009), called into question *Cedars-Sinai's* continued vitality following the Supreme Court's decision in *John R. Sand & Gravel Co.,* 552 U.S. 130, 128 S.Ct. 750, 169 L.Ed.2d 591 (2008). That statement was made without the benefit of the Supreme Court's most recent decisions clarifying the distinction between jurisdictional and nonjurisdictional rules.

[3] Contrary to Judge Bea's assertion, *John R. Sand & Gravel* did not hold 28 U.S.C. § 2501 "jurisdictional" based on the "consequential" language of the statute. Rather, it held *Irwin's* presumption of equitable tolling rebutted based on the fact that "the Court had ... previously provided a definitive interpretation" of § 2501. 552 U.S. at 137, 128 S.Ct. 750. Nor did *Bowles* hold that the limitations provision in 28 U.S.C. § 2107 was jurisdictional solely based on its "consequential" language; like *John R. Sand & Gravel, Bowles* rested largely on the "century's worth of precedent and practice in American courts" ranking "time limits for filing a notice of appeal" jurisdictional. 551 U.S. at 209 n. 2, 127 S.Ct. 2360.

[4] It is unclear how much weight the Bea dissent accords the term "forever." For the most part, the dissent categorizes statutes that simply use "shall be barred" terminology as within its self-created "consequence" category. *See* Bea Dissent at 1066-68. But Judge Bea then devotes an entire section to the word "forever," and writes that "[i]t is especially telling" that Congress included the term "forever barred" in § 2401(b), but did not do so in § 2401(a), "the very section that precedes the one here in issue." Bea Dissent at 1068-70.

In fact, as we have noted, § 2401(a) does provide that an FTCA claim "shall be barred" unless it is filed within six years after the right of action accrues. *See* 28 U.S.C. § 2401(a); *see also* Act of June 25, 1948, chap. 646, 62 Stat. 971 (1948). Thus, the dissent seems to rest, at least in part, on the proposition that it is the word "forever" that transforms limitations language into the "consequential" variety. For reasons discussed in the text, the word "forever" cannot bear that weight.

[5] Judge Bea also takes issue with *Partlow* and *Mount Hood Stages, supra,* which, as discussed above, held statutes of limitation containing language similar to § 2401(b) subject to equitable tolling. Judge Bea questions the value of these precedents because they preceded the Court's more recent cases distinguishing between jurisdictional and nonjurisdictional rules. Bea Dissent at 84-87. As noted, however, later decisions by this Court and the Supreme Court affirm the availability of equitable tolling under 15 U.S.C. § 15b, the statute at issue in *Partlow. See Hexcel Corp.,* 681 F.3d at 1060-61; *Rotella,* 528 U.S. at 561, 120 S.Ct. 1075. More fundamentally, these precedents undermine the notion that Congress intended through the use of magic words in the Clayton Act Amendments and FLSA limitations provisions to establish jurisdictional bars in statutes allowing for civil suits against private parties.

[6] Judge Bea's reference to *Kendall v. United States,* 107 U.S. 123, 2 S.Ct. 277, 27 L.Ed. 437 (1883), as support for attributing jurisdictional meaning to the phrase "forever barred," Bea Dissent at 1068-69, is misplaced. Though *John R. Sand & Gravel* did rely on *Kendall,* it did so not because of *Kendall's* logic, but out of deference to "[b]asic principles of *stare decisis," John R. Sand & Gravel,* 552 U.S. at 139, 128 S.Ct. 750, as the statute in *John R. Sand & Gravel* was the same court of claims statute that *Kendall* (and *Finn v. United States,* 123 U.S. 227, 8 S.Ct. 82, 31 L.Ed. 128 (1887), and *Soriano v. United States,* 352 U.S. 270, 77 S.Ct. 269, 1 L.Ed.2d 306 (1957)) had already interpreted. *Id.* at 134-35, 128 S.Ct. 750. Indeed, *John R. Sand & Gravel* recognized that the older cases on which it relied were out of step with *Irwin,* but justified that reliance on "Justice Brandeis['s]... observ[ation] that 'in most matters it is more important that the applicable rule of law be settled than that it be settled right.'" *Id.* at 139, 128 S.Ct. 750 (quoting *Burnet v. Coronado Oil & Gas Co.,* 285 U.S. 393, 406, 52 S.Ct. 443, 76 L.Ed. 815 (1932) (dissenting opinion)).

[7] The fact that this statute "produce[d] an intracircuit split, several en banc dissents, and dozens of pages of analysis by the majority," Tashima Dissent at 1058, does not mean that the cross reference to chapter 171 is *itself* ambiguous. While reasonable jurists may certainly debate the general equitable tolling question this case presents, the cross reference to chapter 171, and not to chapter 161, is plain as day.

[8] The original limitations provision in Section 420 of the Act provided:

Every claim against the United States cognizable under this title shall be forever barred, unless within one year after such claim accrued ... it is presented in writing to the Federal agency out of whose activities it arises, if such claim is for a sum not exceeding $1,000; or unless within one year after such claim accrued ... an action is begun pursuant to part 3 of this title. In the event that a claim for a sum not exceeding $1,000 is presented to a Federal agency as aforesaid, the time to institute a suit pursuant to part 3 of this title shall be extended for a period of six months from the date of mailing of notice to the claimant by such Federal agency as to the final disposition of the claim or from the date of withdrawal of the claim from such Federal agency pursuant to section 410 of this title, if it would otherwise expire before the end of such period.

60 Stat. 812, 845. As originally enacted, the FTCA did not *require* claimants to exhaust their administrative remedies. That requirement was added in 1966. *See* 28

U.S.C. § 2401(b) (1994); H.R.Rep. No. 89-1532 at 6-7 (1966); S.Rep. No. 89-1327 at 2-3 (1966).

[9] We note as well that the proposition that *any* requirement that the FTCA's jurisdictional grant is "subject to" is automatically a jurisdictional prerequisite is a questionable one. The fact that § 1326(b) requires plaintiffs to comply with certain requirements to file a claim against the United States does not mean that each and every one of those requirements concern "a tribunal's power to hear a case." *Union Pac. R.R.*, 558 U.S. at 81, 130 S.Ct. 584. Indeed, "subject to" originally encompassed section 411 of Title IV, which made the Federal Rules of Civil Procedure applicable in FTCA cases; under Judge Tashima's approach, compliance with the Federal Rules would have thus been a jurisdictional requirement. "Subject to" is more sensibly read to mean that litigants have to follow the prescribed procedures, not that each and every one of those procedures, if not followed, gives rise to the "drastic" consequences that follow from lack of subject matter jurisdiction. *See Gonzalez*, 132 S.Ct. at 648. We have never held otherwise. And where the Supreme Court has held a specific provision in chapter 171 jurisdictional, it has not done so because *every* rule in chapter 171 is a jurisdictional requirement. *See McNeil v. United States,* 508 U.S. 106, 111-13, 113 S.Ct. 1980, 124 L.Ed.2d 21 (1993); *Smith v. United States,* 507 U.S. 197, 199, 113 S.Ct. 1178, 122 L.Ed.2d 548 (1993).

[10] Aside from our holdings in *Brady v. United States,* 211 F.3d 499, 502-03 (9th Cir.2000), and *Lesoeur v. United States,* 21 F.3d 965, 967 (9th Cir.1994), which held, respectively, that the administrative exhaustion requirement in § 2675(a) and discretionary function exception in § 2680(a) are jurisdictional, we have not addressed whether any of the other provisions in chapter 171 of the FTCA set forth jurisdictional requirements. In holding § 2401(b) nonjurisdictional, we express no views as to whether the other provisions located in chapter 171 are jurisdictional.

[11] *Blain, Mann,* and *Augustine,* cited in *Marley,* addressed the two-year administrative claim limitation period in § 2401(b), not the six-month post-exhaustion period. *See Blain,* 552 F.2d at 291; *Mann,* 399 F.2d at 673; *Augustine,* 704 F.2d at 1077.

[12] The Court's other recent cases discussing the distinction between jurisdictional and nonjurisdictional statutes, including *Auburn Regional Medical Center,* ___ U.S. ___, 133 S.Ct. 817, *Gonzalez,* ___ U.S. ___, 132 S.Ct. 641, *Henderson,* ___ U.S. ___, 131 S.Ct. 1197, *Holland,* 560 U.S. 631, 130 S.Ct. 2549, and *Bowles,* 551 U.S. 205, 127 S.Ct. 2360, also involve lawsuits against governmental entities. But they were not lawsuits in federal court against the federal government, and so may not raise precisely parallel sovereign immunity concerns.

[13] In *Munoz,* for example, we held that section 203 of the Nicaraguan Adjustment and Central American Relief Act, Pub.L. No. 105-100, 111 Stat. 2160 (1997), was a statute of repose, because it contained "fixed, statutory cutoff date[s]" requiring an alien to file an application for relief by April 1, 1990 or December 31, 1991. The statute did "'not await a specific event to start the deadline clock,'" but "'[r]ather ... served as the endpoint of the definite time period in which Congress would permit [applicants] to file applications.'" 339 F.3d at 957 (quoting *Iacono v. Office of Pers. Mgmt.,* 974 F.2d 1326, 1328 (Fed.Cir.1992) (emphasis omitted)).

[14] The Supreme Court has, at times, indicated that equitable considerations are less likely to apply to limitations provisions limiting the scope of a governmental waiver of sovereign immunity. *See John R. Gravel & Sand,* 552 U.S. at 133-34, 128 S.Ct. 750; *Soriano,* 352 U.S. at 275-77, 77 S.Ct. 269. Most notably, *Soriano* declined to equitably toll the statute of limitations for filing a claim in the Court of Claims, 28 U.S.C. § 2501, explaining "that limitations and conditions upon which the Government consents to be sued must be strictly observed and exceptions thereto are not to be implied." *See* 352 U.S. at 275-76, 77 S.Ct. 269.

Noting that the Court's "previous cases dealing with the effect of time limits in suits against the Government have not been entirely consistent," *Irwin* discussed the result in *Soriano,* and concluded that its holding did not apply to the thirty-day time limit in Title VII of the Civil Rights Act, 42 U.S.C. § 2000e-16(c). *Irwin,* 498 U.S. at 94-95, 111 S.Ct. 453. Instead, *Irwin* explained, "this case affords us an opportunity to adopt a more general rule to govern the applicability of equitable tolling in suits against the Government," namely, the rebuttable presumption in favor of tolling. *Id.* at 95-96, 111 S.Ct. 453. In announcing this "general prospective rule," *John R. Sand & Gravel,* 552 U.S. at 137, 128 S.Ct. 750, *Irwin* did not expressly overrule *Soriano,* but made clear that *Soriano* is not to be read to proscribe the application of equitable doctrines to limitations on waivers of sovereign immunity in every case.

[15] For example, the revisions of the Federal Employees Liability Reform and Tort Compensation Act of 1988 (the "Westfall Act"), Pub.L. No. 100-964, §§ 5-6, 102 Stat. 4563, 4564-65 (1988), to 28 U.S.C. § 2679(d)(5), provide that an action dismissed under the exhaustion requirement in 28 U.S.C. § 2675(a) is considered timely under 28 U.S.C. § 2401(b) if the administrative claim would have been timely had the claim been filed on the date of commencement of the civil action. *See* 28 U.S.C. § 2679(d)(5).

[16] As noted, Wong's initial motion seeking leave to amend sought to treat the INS's inactivity regarding her claim as the agency's final decision under § 2675(a), but preceded the INS's denial of her claim on December 3, 2001. *See supra* part I.B.

[1] Of course, this logic dictates that the requirements of Chapter 171 are also jurisdictional. At least two Circuit Courts have so held in accord with this reasoning. *See Mader v. United States,* 654 F.3d 794, 807 (8th Cir.2011) (en banc) (relying on the "[s]ubject to" language of § 1346(b) in finding the presentment requirements of 28 U.S.C. § 2675(a) jurisdictional); *White-Squire v. U.S. Postal Serv.,* 592 F.3d 453, 457-58 (3d Cir.2010) (relying on the same in finding the sum certain requirement of 28 U.S.C. § 2675(b) jurisdictional). *But see Parrott v. United States,* 536 F.3d 629, 634-35 (7th Cir.2008) (holding that the statutory exceptions of 28 U.S.C. § 2680 are not jurisdictional, notwithstanding the language of § 1346(b)).

[2] In a footnote, the majority suggests that the phrase "'[s]ubject to' is more sensibly read to mean that litigants have to follow the prescribed procedures, not that each and every one of those procedures, if not followed, gives rise to the 'drastic' consequences that follow from lack of subject matter jurisdiction." Maj. Op. at 1044 n. 9. This interpretation not only ignores the ordinary meaning of "subject to," but it would render the opening clause of § 1346(b) surplusage. The very existence of the "prescribed procedures," as standalone statutory provisions, "means that litigants have to follow [them]." Thus, the "[s]ubject to" clause of § 1346(b) would have no substantive import under the majority's reading.

[3] The Supreme Court has repeatedly relied on the Reviser's Notes in determining whether a substantive change was intended through the 1948 Act. *See, e.g., John R. Sand & Gravel,* 552 U.S. at 136, 128 S.Ct. 750; *Newman-Green, Inc. v. Alfonzo-Larrain,* 490 U.S. 826, 831, 109 S.Ct. 2218, 104 L.Ed.2d 893 (1989).

[4] The same purpose was carried out with respect to the jurisdiction-granting provision, which was consolidated in § 1346 with the other provisions of Title 28 granting jurisdiction in civil actions against the government. *See* 1948 Act, § 1, 62 Stat. at 933; *see also* William W. Barron, The Judicial Code: 1948 Revision, 8 F.R.D. 439, 445 (1949) ("The statutes conferring jurisdiction ... are consolidated into a single section. The revised section consolidates and clarifies three widely separated provisions of the former code.").

[5] As described below, the legislative history is particularly probative of congressional intent in the instant case given that the focus is on the statutory scheme as *enacted* by Congress, and given that this enactment occurred only two years prior to the adoption of the current statutory language.

[6] The majority contends that, under my treatment of the legislative history, the limitations period would remain jurisdictional regardless of "what Congress wrote into the FTCA's jurisdictional grant in 1948." Maj. Op. at 1044. Hardly the case. If Congress truly intended to alter the provision's jurisdictional status, it could have provided an affirmative statement to this effect in the text of the 1948 Act, in the Reviser's Notes, or elsewhere in the legislative history. *See* Barron, *supra,* at 446 ("Congress... includ[ed] in its reports the complete Reviser's Notes to each section in which are noted all instances where change is intended and the reasons therefor."). The requirement that Congress affirmatively express such an intent is not one I have created, but one that is mandated as a matter of Supreme Court doctrine. *See Keene Corp.,* 508 U.S. at 209, 113 S.Ct. 2035.

[1] In *Irwin,* the petitioner was fired from his job by the Veterans' Administration ("VA"). *See id.* at 90, 111 S.Ct. 453. He filed a complaint with the VA, alleging that it had unlawfully discharged him on the basis of race and physical disability. *See id.* at 91, 111 S.Ct. 453. The VA dismissed the complaint, and the Equal Employment Opportunity Commission ("EEOC") affirmed that decision. *See id.* The petitioner had the right to file a civil action in district court but was required to do so within 30 days of the EEOC's affirmance. *See id.* (citing 42 U.S.C. § 2000e-16(c)). The petitioner filed a complaint in district court 44 days after his attorney's office received the EEOC's notice, which was only 29 days after the date on which he claimed to have received the notice. *See id.* The district court held that the limitations period began when the attorney's office received the notice and granted the VA's motion to dismiss for lack of jurisdiction. *See id.* The Fifth Circuit affirmed and held that compliance with § 2000e-16(c)'s time limit was a jurisdictional requirement. *See id.* The Supreme Court held that § 2000e-16(c)'s time limit was not jurisdictional; instead, the Court held that "the same rebuttable presumption of equitable tolling applicable to suits against private defendants should also apply to suits against the United States." *Id.* at 95-96, 111 S.Ct. 453. Because the principles of equitable tolling did "not extend to what is at best a garden variety claim of excusable neglect," however, the Court affirmed the dismissal. *See id.* at 96, 111 S.Ct. 453.

[2] In *John R. Sand & Gravel*, the petitioner filed an action in the Court of Federal Claims, asserting that various Environmental Protection Agency activities on land it leased for mining purposes amounted to an unconstitutional taking of its leasehold rights. *See id.* at 132, 128 S.Ct. 750. The Government initially asserted that the claims were untimely under 28 U.S.C. § 2501, which provides that "[e]very claim of which the United States Court of Federal Claims has jurisdiction shall be barred unless the petition thereon is filed within six years after such claim first accrues." *See id.* (quoting 28 U.S.C. § 2501). The Government later conceded that certain claims were timely, and subsequently won on the merits. *See id.* On appeal, the Court of Appeals for the Federal Circuit held that the action was untimely filed and should have been dismissed for that reason. *See id.* at 133, 128 S.Ct. 750. The Supreme Court affirmed and held that compliance with § 2501's time limit is a jurisdictional requirement. *See id.* at 138-39, 128 S.Ct. 750. As noted below, the Court also explained the difference between jurisdictional statutes of limitations and those to which *Irwin's* presumption can be applied. *See id.* at 133-34, 128 S.Ct. 750.

[3] The majority ignores the simple truth contained in the aphorism ascribed, perhaps apocryphally, to Abraham Lincoln: "If you call a tail a leg, how many legs has a dog? Five? No, calling a tail a leg don't make it a leg."

[4] In *Henderson*, the petitioner, a veteran of the Korean War who had been given a 100-percent disability rating for paranoid schizophrenia, filed a claim with the Department of Veterans Affairs ("VA") for supplemental benefits based on his need for in-home care. *See id.* at 1201. The VA regional office and Board of Veterans' Appeals denied the petitioner's claim. *See id.* The petitioner filed a notice of appeal with the Veterans Court, but he missed the 120-day filing deadline by 15 days. *See id.* (citing 38 U.S.C. § 7266(a)). The Veterans Court dismissed the appeal for lack of jurisdiction, treating compliance with the 120-day deadline as a jurisdictional requirement. *See id.* at 1202. The Federal Circuit affirmed. *See id.* Because § 7266(a) "provide[d] no clear indication that Congress wanted the provision to be treated as having jurisdictional attributes," the Supreme Court reversed and held that the 120-day limitation period was not jurisdictional. *Id.* at 1205-06.

[5] In *Reed Elsevier*, authors, some of whom had registered copyrights for their works and others who had not, sued publishers and electronic databases for copyright infringement. *See id.* at 158, 130 S.Ct. 1237. The parties settled and filed a motion in federal district court to certify a class for settlement and approve the settlement agreement. *See id.* at 159, 130 S.Ct. 1237. Ten freelance authors ("the Muchnick respondents") objected. *See id.* The district court overruled those objections, certified a settlement class of freelance authors, approved the settlement, and entered final judgment. *See id.* The Muchnick respondents appealed, and the Second Circuit held that the district court lacked jurisdiction to certify a class of claims arising from the infringement of unregistered works. *See id.* at 159-60, 130 S.Ct. 1237 (citing 17 U.S.C. § 411(a), which provides, in relevant part, that "no civil action for infringement of the copyright in any United States work shall be instituted until preregistration or registration of the copyright claim has been made"). The Supreme Court reversed and held that § 411(a) imposed a non-jurisdictional precondition to suit. *See id.* at 166, 130 S.Ct. 1237.

[6] In *Dalm,* the respondent had been appointed administratrix of her employer's estate. *See id.* at 598, 110 S.Ct. 1361. In return for her services, she received fees from the estate and two payments from the employer's surviving brother. *See id.* at 599, 110 S.Ct. 1361. The respondent reported the latter payments as gifts and paid the appropriate gift tax. *See id.* The Internal Revenue Service ("IRS") audited the respondent's income tax returns and determined that the payments should have been reported as income. *See id.* The respondent petitioned the Tax Court for a redetermination but subsequently settled the case. *See id.* After she agreed to the settlement, the respondent immediately filed an administrative claim for return of the gift tax she had paid. *See id.* When the IRS failed to act on her claim within six months, she filed suit in district court, seeking a refund of "overpaid gift tax." *Id.* at 600, 110 S.Ct. 1361. The district court granted the Government's motion to dismiss the suit for lack of jurisdiction, because the respondent's suit was untimely under the applicable statute of limitations: 26 U.S.C. § 6511(a). *See id.* The Sixth Circuit reversed and held that the doctrine of equitable recoupment should be applied to permit the respondent's suit to proceed. *See id.* The Supreme Court reversed and held that the district court did not have jurisdiction to entertain the untimely action. *See id.* at 610, 110 S.Ct. 1361.

[7] In *Dalm,* there were two such provisions. *See id.* at 601-02, 110 S.Ct. 1361 (stating that 26 U.S.C. § 7422, which provides that "[n]o suit or proceeding shall be maintained in any court for the recovery of any internal revenue tax alleged to have been erroneously or illegally assessed or collected ... until a claim for refund or credit has been duly filed with the Secretary," and 26 U.S.C. § 6511(a), which provides that, if a taxpayer is required to file a return with respect to a tax, the "[c]laim for refund or credit ... shall be filed by the taxpayer within 3 years from the time the return was filed or 2 years from the time the tax was paid, whichever of such periods expires the later," were both relevant qualifications on a taxpayer's right to bring a refund suit). Because both provisions established conditions on a taxpayer's right to bring suit, the Court read them together. *See id.* at 602, 110 S.Ct. 1361 ("Read together, the import of these sections is clear: unless a claim for refund of a tax has been filed within the time limits imposed by § 6511(a), a suit for refund... may not be maintained in any court." (citations omitted)); *see also* Antonin Scalia & Bryan A. Garner, Reading Law: The Interpretation of Legal Texts 167 (2012) ("Perhaps no interpretive fault is more common than the failure to follow the whole-text canon, which calls on the judicial interpreter to consider the entire text, in view of its structure and of the physical and logical relation of its many parts.").

[8] In *Bowles,* an Ohio jury convicted the petitioner of murder and sentenced him to 15-years-to-life imprisonment. *See id.* at 207, 127 S.Ct. 2360. The petitioner unsuccessfully challenged his conviction and sentence on direct appeal, and then filed a federal habeas corpus petition. *See id.* The district court denied habeas relief. *See id.* After the entry of final judgment, the petitioner had 30 days to file a notice of appeal. *See id.* (citing 28 U.S.C. § 2107(a)). He failed to do so. *See id.* Instead, he later filed a motion to reopen the period in which to file a notice of appeal under 28 U.S.C. § 2107(c), which allows district courts to extend the filing period for 14 days. *See id.* The district court granted the motion to reopen, but "inexplicably gave [the petitioner] 17 days," instead of the 14 days permitted by statute. *See id.* The

petitioner filed his notice of appeal after the 14-day period allowed by statute but within the 17 days allowed by the district court. *See id.* The Sixth Circuit held that it lacked jurisdiction to entertain the appeal, because the notice of appeal was untimely filed. *See id.* The Supreme Court affirmed and held that "the timely filing of a notice of appeal in a civil case is a jurisdictional requirement." *Id.* at 214, 127 S.Ct. 2360.

[9] Unfortunately, the Court has not yet analyzed whether § 2401(b) is or is not jurisdictional. We must therefore use what tools the Court has given us in its discussions of similar statutory provisions and reason by analogy.

[10] In *Barnhart,* the Court addressed 26 U.S.C. § 9706(a)'s requirement that the Commissioner of Social Security assign, before October 1, 1993, each coal industry retiree eligible for benefits to an operating company or related entity, which would then be responsible for funding the assigned beneficiary's benefits. *See id.* at 152-53, 123 S.Ct. 748. The Commissioner did not complete all the assignments by the statutory date, and several coal companies challenged the Commissioner's by then tardy assignments. *See id.* at 156, 123 S.Ct. 748. The companies obtained summary judgments in each case, and the Sixth Circuit affirmed. *See id.* at 157, 123 S.Ct. 748. The Supreme Court held that it was "unrealistic to think that Congress understood unassigned status as an enduring 'consequence' of uncompleted work, for nothing indicates that Congress even foresaw that some beneficiaries matchable with operators still in business might not be assigned before October 1, 1993." *Id.* at 164-65, 123 S.Ct. 748. Thus, it read the statutory deadline as "a spur to prompt action, not as a bar to tardy completion of the business of ensuring that benefits are funded ... by those identified by Congress as principally responsible." *Id.* at 172, 123 S.Ct. 748.

[11] In *Holland,* the petitioner was convicted of first-degree murder and sentenced to death. *See id.* at 2555. The Florida Supreme Court affirmed that judgment, and, on October 1, 2001, the Supreme Court denied the petition for certiorari. *See id.* On that date, 28 U.S.C. § 2244(d)'s one-year statute of limitations for filing a habeas petition began to run. *See id.* On September 19, 2002 (i.e. 12 days before the one-year limitations period expired), a state-appointed attorney filed a motion for post-conviction relief in the state court, which automatically stopped the running of the limitations period. *See id.* In May 2003, the state trial court denied relief. *See id.* By February 2005, when the Florida Supreme Court heard oral argument in the case, the petitioner and his appointed attorney rarely communicated. *See id.* Indeed, the petitioner asked the Florida Supreme Court to remove the attorney from his case because of a "complete breakdown in communication," including a failure to keep him informed of the case's status. *See id.* The Florida Supreme Court denied the petitioner's request. *See id.* at 2556. The petitioner subsequently wrote the attorney several times and emphasized the importance of filing a timely petition for habeas corpus in federal court once the Florida Supreme Court ruled against him. *See id.* In November 2005, the Florida Supreme Court affirmed the denial of post-conviction relief. *See id.* On December 1, 2005, it issued its mandate, and the federal habeas clock began again to tick. *See id.* Twelve days later, the one-year limitations period expired, with the petitioner never having been informed that the Florida Supreme Court had made a ruling. *See id.* at 2556-57. When the petitioner learned of the adverse ruling on January 18, 2006, he immediately wrote a pro se habeas petition

and mailed it to the district court. *See id.* at 2557. The district court held that equitable tolling was unwarranted because the petitioner did not seek help from the court system to determine when the mandate issued. *See id.* The Eleventh Circuit affirmed and held that the attorney's negligence could never constitute an "extraordinary circumstance" sufficient to toll the limitations period. *See id.* The Supreme Court rejected the district court's erroneous determination that the petitioner had not been diligent and the Eleventh Circuit's rigid, categorical approach. *See id.* at 2565. It then held that § 2244(d)'s time limit was subject to equitable tolling and remanded for further proceedings. *See id.* at 2565.

[12] In *Kontrick,* a creditor objected to a debtor's discharge in a liquidation proceeding. *See id.* at 446, 124 S.Ct. 906. The applicable rule provided that such an objection had to be made within "60 days after the first date set for the meeting of creditors." *Id.* (quoting Fed. R. Bkrtcy. P. 4004(a)). The creditor's objection was untimely under this rule. *See id.* The debtor did not file a motion to dismiss the objection as untimely, however, until after the Bankruptcy Court decided that the discharge should be refused. *See id.* The Bankruptcy Court held that the time limit was not jurisdictional, and the Seventh Circuit affirmed. *See id.* at 447, 124 S.Ct. 906. The Supreme Court affirmed and held that Rule 4004(a) was not jurisdictional, so that "a debtor forfeits the right to rely on Rule 4004 if the debtor does not raise the Rule's time limitation before the bankruptcy court reaches the merits of the creditor's objection to discharge." *Id.*

[13] Of course, if the court finds that the presumption has been rebutted or that no equitable considerations justify tolling the statute, it should dismiss the complaint for failure to comply with the statute of limitations. The key consideration here is that, when a statute does not specify mandatory consequences for failure timely to act, the court is permitted to rely on *Irwin's* presumption that equitable tolling applies. Nothing in the text of that statute suggests that the presumption should not apply.

[14] I acknowledge that such a holding may conflict with *Cedars-Sinai Medical Center v. Shalala,* 125 F.3d 765, 770 (9th Cir.1997), but, for reasons discussed *infra* at 1069-72, I believe that case is inconsistent with subsequent Supreme Court cases and is no longer good law.

Further, by giving examples of when Congress has spoken in jurisdictional terms I am not relying on "magic words" that must be included. Op. at 1040. These phrases are merely examples of terms which mandate that a particular consequence must be imposed, and that *consequence* is what makes the statute jurisdictional.

[15] This fact separates the two kinds of statutes of limitations. When a statute does not specify a mandatory consequence, the operation of *Irwin's* presumption makes sense (i.e. courts can generally assume Congress intended equitable tolling to apply unless something suggests otherwise). When Congress specifies a mandatory consequence, however, courts should assume Congress meant what it said (i.e. that the consequence is mandatory and applicable in every case).

[16] Unfortunately, while the Court has stated, on several occasions, that a particular statute does not speak in jurisdictional terms, *see ante* at 1064, it has not clarified exactly when a statute does speak in jurisdictional terms. Still, the Court has held that the statutes in the second category above are jurisdictional. *See John R.*

Sand & Gravel, 552 U.S. at 134, 128 S.Ct. 750 (holding that 28 U.S.C. § 2501, which provides that "[e]very claim of which the United States Court of Federal Claims has jurisdiction shall be barred unless the petition is filed within six years after such claim first accrued," is jurisdictional); *Bowles,* 551 U.S. at 213, 127 S.Ct. 2360 (holding that 28 U.S.C. § 2107(a) and (c), which provide that "no appeal shall bring any judgment, order or decree in an action, suit or proceeding of a civil nature before a court of appeals for review unless notice of appeal is filed, within thirty days after entry of such judgment, order, or decree," except that a court may "extend the time for appeal upon a showing of excusable neglect or good cause," is jurisdictional); *Dalm,* 494 U.S. at 609, 110 S.Ct. 1361 (holding that 26 U.S.C. § 6511(a), which, when read with 26 U.S.C. § 7422(a), provides that "unless a claim for refund of a tax has been filed within the time limits ..., a suit for refund ... may not be maintained in any court," is jurisdictional). It has also mentioned the kind of language that would speak in jurisdictional terms. *See Henderson,* 131 S.Ct. at 1204 (implying that jurisdictional language would include a suggestion "that the provision was meant to carry jurisdictional consequences"); *Holland,* 130 S.Ct. at 2560 (implying that a statute would speak in jurisdictional language if it "set forth an inflexible rule requiring dismissal whenever its clock has run" (internal quotation marks and citations omitted)). In any event, as the majority acknowledges, the Court has instructed that Congress "need not incant magic words ... to speak clearly." Op. at 1036 (quoting *Sebelius v. Auburn Reg'l Med. Ctr.,* ___ U.S. ___, 133 S.Ct. 817, 824, 184 L.Ed.2d 627 (2013)). Thus, Congress need not explicitly state that a time limit is jurisdictional; it is free to specify consequences that relate to a court's power to adjudicate cases and trust that the court will understand what those consequences mean.

[17] While a statute that specifies mandatory consequences is jurisdictional, the reverse is not necessarily true. *See, e.g., McNeil,* 508 U.S. at 111-12, 113 S.Ct. 1980 (holding 28 U.S.C. § 2675, which does not specify mandatory consequences for noncompliance, jurisdictional). This dissent does not imply that the specification of mandatory consequences is the *only* way for Congress to express its intent that a statute be jurisdictional. Congress may express its intent that a statute be jurisdictional in other ways (i.e. it need not incant magic words), and, indeed, a statute may be jurisdictional for reasons other than the text. *See Reed Elsevier,* 559 U.S. at 166, 130 S.Ct. 1237 (2010) (instructing courts, in determining whether a statute is jurisdictional, to look to the statute's "text, *context and relevant historical treatment*" (emphasis added)).

[18] I must confess that I have struggled to find which portion of the Court's opinion in *Kubrick* supports the majority's position about what is "ordinarily true of statutory filing deadlines." Op. at 1038. Surely it is not this portion: "Section 2401(b), the limitations provision involved here, is the balance struck by Congress in the context of tort claims against the Government; and we are not free to construe it so as to defeat its obvious purpose, which is to encourage the prompt presentation of claims." *Kubrick,* 444 U.S. at 117, 100 S.Ct. 352. And surely it is not this portion: "We should also have in mind that the Act waives the immunity of the United States and that in construing the statute of limitations, which is a condition of that waiver, we should not take it upon ourselves to extend the waiver beyond

that which Congress intended." *Id.* at 117-18, 100 S.Ct. 352. I simply see no support for the majority's position in *Kubrick*.

[19] The majority's deprecatory labelling is off by about 100 years. In *Kendall v. U.S.,* 107 U.S. at 124, 2 S.Ct. 277, the term "forever barred" in the act of March 3, 1863, was definitively interpreted.

[20] *John R. Sand & Gravel* held that *Soriano* is still good law. 552 U.S. at 137, 128 S.Ct. 750.

[21] The majority also cites out of circuit authority—*Arteaga v. United States,* 711 F.3d 828, 832-33 (7th Cir.2013); *Santos ex rel. Beato v. United States,* 559 F.3d 189, 194-98 (3d Cir.2009); *Perez v. United States,* 167 F.3d 913, 916-17 (5th Cir.1999)—for the proposition that § 2401(b) is subject to tolling. However, these cases are not persuasive. *Arteaga* holds that because 28 U.S.C. § 2674 meant to hold the government liable in the same way as a private individual, and equitable tolling is available to private individuals, equitable tolling is available under the FTCA. *Arteaga,* 711 F.3d at 833. However, the *Arteaga* court ignores the plain language of § 2401(b) which states "to the agency to which it was presented." A private individual may not be held liable for an agency claim. Further, *Santos* ignores *Congress'* clear intent when it concludes that "the placement of the separate statutory savings provision does not suggest that Congress intended it to preclude equitable tolling." *Santos,* 559 F.3d at 196. See Pub.L. No. 773, 62 Stat. 869, 991 (1948) ("No inference of a legislative construction is to be drawn by reason of the chapter in Title 28, Judiciary and Judicial Procedure, ... in which any section is placed."). Finally, *Perez* discussed the use of the phrase "forever barred" and found it was irrelevant, but failed to consider and attempt to distinguish prior cases interpreting the term, such as *Perez v. U.S.,* 167 F.3d at 915-18, and *Finn v. U.S.,* 123 U.S. at 233, 8 S.Ct. 82.

[22] The Court's "recent guidance" includes *John R. Sand & Gravel Co. v. United States,* 552 U.S. 130, 128 S.Ct. 750, 169 L.Ed.2d 591 (2008), *Reed Elsevier, Inc. v. Muchnick,* 559 U.S. 154, 130 S.Ct. 1237, 176 L.Ed.2d 18 (2010), *Holland v. Florida,* 560 U.S. 631, 130 S.Ct. 2549, 177 L.Ed.2d 130 (2010), *Henderson v. Shinseki,* ___ U.S. ___, 131 S.Ct. 1197, 179 L.Ed.2d 159 (2011), and *Auburn Regional Medical Center,* ___ U.S. ___, 133 S.Ct. 817.

[23] In *Sebelius,* the governing statute allowed health care providers to file, within 180 days, an administrative appeal to the Provider Reimbursement Review Board from an initial determination of the reimbursement owed for inpatient services rendered to Medicare beneficiaries. *See id.* at 821 (citing 42 U.S.C. § 1395*oo* (a)(3)). The Secretary of the Department of Health and Human Services, by regulation, authorized the Board to extend the 180-day limitation, for good cause, up to three years. *See id.* The Court held that the 180-day limitation period was not jurisdictional and that the regulation permitting a three-year extension was a permissible construction of the statute. *See id.* at 821-22. It further held that equitable tolling "does not apply to administrative appeals of the kind here at issue." *Id.* at 822.

[24] In *Soriano,* the petitioner, a resident of the Philippines, filed suit in the Court of Claims to recover "just compensation for the requisitioning by Philippine guerilla forces of certain foodstuffs, supplies, equipment, and merchandise during the Japanese occupation of the Philippine Islands." *Id.* at 270-71, 77 S.Ct. 269. The

relevant statute of limitations provided that "[e]very claim of which the Court of Claims has jurisdiction shall be barred unless the petition thereon is filed ... within six years after such claim first accrues." *Id.* at 271 n. 1, 77 S.Ct. 269 (quoting 28 U.S.C. § 2501). The petitioner filed suit more than six years after the alleged requisition claiming his delay was caused by World War II conditions in the Philippines. *See id.* at 271, 77 S.Ct. 269. The Court of Claims dismissed the suit without reaching the limitation question. *See id.* at 272, 77 S.Ct. 269. The Supreme Court affirmed and held that, by the time the petitioner filed suit, "his claim ... was barred by statute." *Id.* at 277, 77 S.Ct. 269.

[25] This dissent analyzes § 2401(b)'s purposes in Part III, *infra.*

[26] In *Kubrick,* the respondent, a veteran, was admitted to a VA hospital for treatment of an infected femur in April 1968. *See id.* at 113, 100 S.Ct. 352. Medical personnel irrigated the infected area with neomycin, an antibiotic, until the infection cleared. *See id.* Six weeks later, the respondent noticed some hearing loss. *See id.* at 114, 100 S.Ct. 352. In January 1969, doctors informed the respondent that it was "highly possible" that the neomycin treatment caused his hearing loss. *See id.* In 1972, the respondent filed suit under the FTCA, alleging he had been injured by negligent treatment at a VA hospital. *See id.* at 115, 100 S.Ct. 352. The VA denied the respondent's administrative claim, which he presented after he filed suit, in April 1973. *See id.* at 116 n. 4, 100 S.Ct. 352. The Government then filed a motion to dismiss the suit as time-barred under 28 U.S.C. § 2401(b)'s two-year statute of limitations, on the theory that the respondent's claim accrued in January 1969, when doctors told the respondent that his hearing loss was likely caused by the neomycin treatment. *See id.* at 115, 100 S.Ct. 352. The district court rejected this defense and rendered judgment for the respondent. *See id.* The Third Circuit affirmed. *See id.* at 116, 100 S.Ct. 352. The Supreme Court reversed and held that claims accrue when the individual "knows both the existence and the cause of his injury." *See id.* at 113, 124-25, 100 S.Ct. 352.

[27] The majority's focus is—jurisprudentially speaking—far too narrow. *See Reed Elsevier,* 559 U.S. at 168, 130 S.Ct. 1237 ("[T]he relevant question here is not ... whether [the statute] itself has long been labeled jurisdictional, but whether the type of limitation that [the statute] imposes is one that is properly ranked as jurisdictional absent an express designation."). Section 2401(b) expresses the same "type of limitation" the Court held jurisdictional in *Soriano* and *John R. Sand & Gravel. See* 28 U.S.C. § 2501 ("Every claim of which the United States Court of Federal Claims has jurisdiction shall be barred unless the petition thereon is filed within six years after such claim first accrues.").

[28] The majority notes that § 2675 is silent as to the deadline for filing a properly exhausted claim in the district court and concludes that "there is no contextual reason to think that the limitations period provisions are also jurisdictional." Op. at 1044. But § 2675 does not require only that individuals exhaust their administrative remedies; instead, it specifies that individuals must exhaust their administrative remedies first (i.e. before they file complaints in federal court). *See* 28 U.S.C. § 2675(a). Thus, the statute requires a particular timing of administrative exhaustion, and the *McNeil* Court found this timing requirement significant. *See McNeil,* 508 U.S. at 111, 113 S.Ct. 1980 (noting that the "petitioner's complaint was filed too early"); *id.* at 112, 113 S.Ct. 1980 (addressing the burdens premature filings impose on the

judicial system and the Department of Justice). Just as in *McNeil,* appellant Wong's complaint was filed "too early" and imposed a burden on the judicial system and Department of Justice. Because late filings impose similar burdens on the courts and the Department of Justice, there is good reason to believe that the limitations period expressed in § 2401(b) is also jurisdictional.

Tenth Circuit Decisions
Federal Tort Claims Act

ROGER GARLING; SHERYL GARLING; R AND D ENTERPRISES, INC.,
Plaintiffs-Appellants,
v.
UNITED STATES ENVIRONMENTAL PROTECTION AGENCY, Defendant-
Appellee.

No. 16-8028.

United States Court of Appeals, Tenth Circuit.

Filed March 7, 2017.

Appeal from the United States District Court for the District of Wyoming; (D.C. No. 1:15-CV-00036-SWS).

Christopher S. Pugsley (Anthony J. Thompson, with him on the briefs), Thompson & Pugsley, Washington, D.C., appearing for Appellants.

C. Levi Martin, Assistant United States Attorney (Christopher A. Crofts, United States Attorney, with him on the brief), Office of the United States Attorney for the District of Wyoming, Cheyenne, Wyoming, appearing for Appellee.

Before MATHESON, McKAY, and MORITZ, Circuit Judges.

MATHESON, Circuit Judge.

Roger Garling, Sheryl Garling, and their business, R and D Enterprises, Inc., (collectively, "the Garlings") sued the United States for damages arising from an Environmental Protection Agency ("EPA") raid and investigation of their laboratory. The district court held the Garlings' action time-barred under the Federal Tort Claims Act ("FTCA"). The Garlings appeal, arguing the EPA's conduct was a continuing tort or, alternatively, that they were entitled to equitable tolling.

Exercising jurisdiction under 28 U.S.C. § 1291, we conclude that sovereign immunity barred the Garlings' claims and the district court thus lacked subject matter jurisdiction. We therefore reverse the district court's judgment and remand with directions to dismiss this action for lack of jurisdiction.

I. BACKGROUND

In reviewing a district court's dismissal under Rule 12(b)(1) or 12(b)(6), "[w]e accept as true all well-pleaded factual allegations in the complaint and view them in the light most favorable to the [plaintiff]." *SEC v. Shields,* 744 F.3d 633, 640 (10th Cir. 2014) (quotations omitted) (Rule 12(b)(6)); *see Ruiz v. McDonnel,* 299 F.3d 1173, 1180 (10th Cir. 2002) (Rule 12(b)(1)). We therefore recite the facts as alleged in the Garlings' Second Amended Complaint, the operative complaint here.

A. *Factual Background*

Roger and Sheryl Garling owned and operated the Casper, Wyoming branch of Energy Laboratories, Inc. ("ELI"), a commercial laboratory business.[1] The EPA initiated an investigation after an ELI employee told the EPA that ELI was submitting false water quality reports. On October 30, 2007, agents from the EPA's Criminal Investigation Division ("EPA-CID") and other federal officers executed an armed raid of the ELI facilities pursuant to a search warrant.

On February 25, 2008, as a result of the raid, ELI forced the Garlings to resign. In February 2009, the Garlings met with Jack Rychecky, the EPA officer in charge of implementing the Safe Drinking Water Act ("SDWA") program in the region covering Wyoming. He informed them that he had advised EPA-CID, based on his belief that the agency lacked a sufficient factual basis, against conducting the raid. In September 2009, Assistant U.S. Attorney ("AUSA") James Anderson confirmed to the Garlings' attorney that they were the targets of the EPA's investigation.

From June 2011 to March 2013, the Garlings filed several Freedom of Information Act ("FOIA") requests with the EPA about the investigation. The EPA terminated its investigation on October 18, 2012, without filing charges.

B. *Procedural History*

On May 12, 2013, the Garlings filed an FTCA administrative claim with the EPA seeking damages "due to EPA's 2007 raid and subsequent investigation." Aplt. App. at 18. The EPA denied the claim.[2] The Garlings requested reconsideration, which the EPA denied.

On March 9, 2015, the Garlings filed an FTCA action in the United States District Court for the District of Wyoming. Their Second Amended Complaint alleged injuries as a result of "EPA officials' reckless and grossly negligent conduct." *Id.* at 8. The Garlings attempted to assert seven claims: (1) "reckless and/or gross negligence in the form of criminal investigation" ("tortious investigation"), (2) false imprisonment, (3) false arrest, (4) abuse of process, (5) defamation, (6) intentional infliction of emotional distress, and (7) conspiracy. *Id.* at 23.

The United States moved to dismiss under Federal Rule of Civil Procedure 12(b)(6), arguing the Garlings failed to meet the FTCA's two-year statute of limitations to file their administrative claim. *See* 28 U.S.C. § 2401(b). It also moved to dismiss the tortious investigation and defamation claims under Rule 12(b)(1) for lack of subject matter jurisdiction because the FTCA does not waive the United States' sovereign immunity for those claims.

The district court dismissed the Garlings' entire FTCA action as time-barred. It determined the Garlings' claims accrued on the date of the EPA's armed raid (October 30, 2007) or, at the latest, the date their ELI employment ended (February 25, 2008)—more than five years before they filed their administrative claim. The court did not address subject matter jurisdiction. The Garlings now appeal.

II. JURISDICTION

The district court's ruling that the Garlings' claims were time-barred was a non-jurisdictional basis for dismissal. *See United States v. Kwai Fun Wong,* 135 S. Ct. 1625, 1638 (2015) (holding "the FTCA's time bars are nonjurisdictional"). To reach the issue of timeliness, however, the district court needed to have had subject matter jurisdiction. *See Steel Co. v. Citizens for a Better Env't,* 523 U.S. 83, 94 (1998) ("Without jurisdiction the court cannot proceed at all in any cause." (quotations omitted)). Thus, although the Garlings do not address this issue on appeal, we must first consider whether the district court had subject matter jurisdiction over their claims. *See Bender v. Williamsport Area Sch. Dist.,* 475 U.S. 534, 541 (1986) (providing that federal appellate courts have an independent obligation to examine subject matter jurisdiction).

Because we resolve this issue based on the complaint, we must accept its factual allegations as true, *see Ruiz,* 299 F.3d at 1180, but not its legal conclusions, *see Ashcroft v. Iqbal,* 556 U.S. 662, 678 (2009). Mere "labels and conclusions" do not count. *See Bell Atl. Corp. v. Twombly,* 550 U.S. 544, 555 (2007).[3]

A. FTCA Waiver of Sovereign Immunity and Exceptions to Waiver

Sovereign immunity precludes federal court jurisdiction. *FDIC v. Meyer,* 510 U.S. 471, 475 (1994). "[T]he United States can be sued only to the extent that it has waived its immunity." *United States v. Orleans,* 425 U.S. 807, 814 (1976); *see United States v. Mitchell,* 463 U.S. 206, 212 (1983) ("It is axiomatic that the United States may not be sued without its consent and that the existence of consent is a prerequisite for jurisdiction."); *Aviles v. Lutz,* 887 F.2d 1046, 1048 (10th Cir. 1989) (stating that, where Congress had not authorized suit under the FTCA, the district court was "without subject matter jurisdiction").

Through 28 U.S.C. § 1346(b)(1), the FTCA waives sovereign immunity for certain state law tort claims against the United States. This provision is subject to 28 U.S.C. § 2680(h), which lists exceptions to waiver for various intentional torts. But § 2680(h) also includes language that restores waiver for some of those torts. The ensuing overview attempts to make this clearer. We then apply this framework to this case.

1. Waiver of Sovereign Immunity — § 1346(b)(1)

The FTCA "is a limited waiver of sovereign immunity, making the Federal Government liable to the same extent as a private party for certain torts of federal employees acting within the scope of their employment." *Orleans,* 425 U.S. at 814. Subject to the exceptions listed in § 2680, the FTCA permits:

> civil actions on claims against the United States, for money damages . . . for injury or loss of property, or personal injury or death caused by the negligent or wrongful act or omission of any employee of the Government while acting within the scope of his office or employment, under circumstances where the United States, if a private person, would be liable to the claimant in accordance with the law of the place where the act or omission occurred.

28 U.S.C. § 1346(b)(1). "State substantive law applies to suits brought against the United States under the FTCA." *Hill v. SmithKline Beecham Corp.,* 393 F.3d 1111, 1117 (10th Cir. 2004).

2. Exceptions to Waiver — § 2680

Title 28 U.S.C. § 2680 lists exceptions to the FTCA's waiver of sovereign immunity. *Id.* § 2680(a)-(n). When an exception applies, sovereign immunity remains, and federal courts lack jurisdiction. *Aviles,* 887 F.2d at 1048; *see Franklin v. United States,* 992 F.2d 1492, 1495 (10th Cir. 1993) (stating that whether the FTCA exception in § 2680(h) applies was a "question of subject matter jurisdiction"); *see also Milligan v. United States,* 670 F.3d 686, 692 (6th Cir. 2012) ("Because the FTCA is a jurisdictional statute, if a case falls within the statutory exceptions of 28 U.S.C. § 2680, the court lacks subject matter jurisdiction. . . ." (brackets and quotations omitted)); *Hydrogen Tech. Corp. v. United States,* 831 F.2d 1155, 1161 (1st Cir. 1987) ("[B]ecause 28 U.S.C. § 1346(b) provides that federal courts shall have jurisdiction over FTCA claims '*subject to*' . . . section 2680 [and] the exceptions found in that section define the limits of federal subject matter jurisdiction in this area.").

Two of the § 2680 exceptions are relevant here: (1) claims involving discretionary functions, § 2680(a), and (2) claims involving intentional torts, including defamation, § 2680(h).

a. *Discretionary function exception — § 2680(a)*

Under § 2680(a), the United States is not liable for:

> Any claim . . . based upon the exercise or performance or the failure to exercise or perform a discretionary function or duty on the part of a federal agency or an employee of the Government, whether or not the discretion involved be abused.

28 U.S.C. § 2680(a).

This discretionary function exception "marks the boundary between Congress' willingness to impose tort liability upon the United States and its desire to protect certain governmental activities from exposure to suit by private individuals." *United States v. S.A. Empresa de Viacao Aerea Rio Grandense,* 467 U.S. 797, 808 (1984).

Whether the exception applies depends on the nature of the agency's conduct. *See United States v. Gaubert,* 499 U.S. 315, 322 (1991). To determine whether agency conduct falls within the exception, we apply a two-part test. *See Garcia v. U.S. Air Force,* 533 F.3d 1170, 1176 (10th Cir. 2008) (citing *Berkovitz v. United States,* 486 U.S. 531, 536 (1988)). First, we determine whether the conduct was discretionary— whether it was "a matter of judgment or choice for the acting employee." *Id.* (quotations omitted). "Conduct is not discretionary if a federal statute, regulation, or policy specifically prescribes a course of action for an employee to follow. In this event, the employee has no rightful option but to adhere to the directive." *Id.* (quotations omitted). Second, if the conduct was discretionary, we consider whether it required the "exercise of judgment based on considerations of public policy." *Id.* If both elements are met, the governmental conduct is protected as a discretionary function, and sovereign immunity bars a claim that involves such conduct. *Id.*

b. *Intentional tort exception — § 2680(h)*

Sections 2680(b)-(n) list claims that are excluded from FTCA's waiver of sovereign immunity in § 1346(b)(1). The first clause of § 2680(h) excludes:

Any claim arising out of assault, battery, false imprisonment, false arrest, malicious prosecution, abuse of process, libel, slander, misrepresentation, deceit, or interference with contract rights[.]

28 U.S.C. § 2680(h). This provision is known as the "intentional tort exception." *Millbrook v. United States,* 133 S. Ct. 1441, 1442 (2013).

i. Exceptions to the intentional tort exception

Although § 2680(h)'s first clause preserves sovereign immunity for eleven enumerated torts, its second clause waives sovereign immunity for six of those torts when they arise from the "acts or omissions" of federal "law enforcement officers." *See* 28 U.S.C. § 2680(h). This clause states:

Provided, [t]hat, with regard to acts or omissions of investigative or law enforcement officers of the United States Government, the provisions of this chapter and section 1346(b) of this title shall apply to any claim arising, on or after the date of the enactment of this proviso, out of assault, battery, false imprisonment, false arrest, abuse of process, or malicious prosecution.

As the Supreme Court explained, Congress carved out an exception to § 2680(h)'s preservation of the United States' sovereign immunity for intentional torts "by adding a proviso covering claims that arise out of the wrongful conduct of law enforcement officers." *Millbrook,* 133 S. Ct. at 1443. "Known as the 'law enforcement proviso,' this provision extends the waiver of sovereign immunity to claims for six intentional torts"—assault, battery, false imprisonment, false arrest, abuse of process, and malicious prosecution. *Id.*

B. *Analysis*

Sovereign immunity bars all of the Garlings' seven claims and precludes federal court jurisdiction. First, the discretionary function exception in § 2680(a) bars the tortious investigation, intentional infliction, false arrest, false imprisonment, and abuse of process claims. Second, the intentional tort exception in § 2680(h) precludes the defamation claim. Third, § 1346(b)(1) does not waive sovereign immunity for the conspiracy claim because it would not be recognized under Wyoming law.

1. Discretionary Function Exception

The discretionary function exception under § 2680(a) bars the Garlings' claims for tortious investigation, intentional infliction, false arrest, false imprisonment, and abuse of process.

a. *Tortious investigation*

Applying part one of the test described above to the tortious investigation claim, we conclude the EPA's conduct was discretionary. If a "federal statute, regulation, or policy [had] specifically prescribe[d] a course of action" for EPA-CID employees to follow in conducting their SDWA investigation, the employees may have had "no rightful option but to adhere to the directive." *See Berkovitz,* 486 U.S. at 536. If there were "no discretion in the conduct for the discretionary function exception to protect," the EPA-CID employees' conduct here could possibly have opened the United States to an FTCA suit. *See id.* But that was not the case here.

Congress delegated broad authority to the EPA to implement and enforce the SDWA. *See* 42 U.S.C. §§ 300f, 300g-2, 300g-3; 18 U.S.C. § 3063 (granting EPA officers law enforcement authority for the investigation of criminal violations); *Hydro Res., Inc. v. EPA,* 608 F.3d 1131, 1166 (10th Cir. 2010) (noting the EPA's "considerable discretion under the SDWA"). We have not found statutes, regulations, or policies prescribing a specific course of action for EPA employees to follow in investigating potential SDWA violations that would foreclose the discretionary function exception and permit the Garlings' tortious investigation claim.

The second part of the discretionary function test is satisfied because the EPA's investigation required the exercise of judgment based on public policy considerations, such as ensuring safe drinking water.

The Garlings raised two arguments in district court attempting to show the tortious investigation claim falls outside the discretionary function exception. Both lack merit.

First, the Garlings argued a 1994 memorandum written by Earl E. Devaney, Director of the EPA Office of Criminal Enforcement, (the "Devaney Memo") removed the EPA's conduct from the protections of the discretionary function exception. In fact, it does the opposite. The Devaney Memo, titled "The Exercise of Investigative Discretion," discusses the EPA's significant discretion in identifying misconduct worthy of investigation and pursuing potential wrongdoers. *See* Aplt. App. at 110, 112. The Memo does not issue a specific directive that EPA employees must follow. Instead, it acknowledges the EPA's "full range of enforcement tools," *id.* at 115, and offers general recommendations on allocating EPA resources to focus on the most serious offenders, *see id.* at 112 (identifying "significant environmental harm and culpable conduct" as important factors in EPA's discretionary case selection).

Second, the Garlings contended in district court that the EPA lacked discretion because the agency had delegated primary SDWA enforcement authority to Wyoming. But they provided no source for this contention, and EPA regulations published on October 10, 2007, just before the EPA's raid here, say the opposite: "EPA has [SDWA] primacy [in] . . . Wyoming." *See* National Primary Drinking Water Regulations for Lead and Copper, 72 Fed. Reg. 57,782-01, 57,797 (Oct. 10, 2007) (parenthesis omitted). The websites for the EPA and the Wyoming Department of Environmental Quality ("DEQ") also state that the EPA—not Wyoming—has primary SDWA enforcement authority.[4] And the Garlings cited nothing in support of their argument that agency policy requires that "the EPA, states, and local agencies work closely together" to share information and conduct investigations. *See* Aplt. App. at 20-21. Even if the Garlings' contentions were correct, they still have not shown how the EPA's discretion in conducting SDWA investigations is so limited as to bar application of the discretionary function exception.

The Garlings' tortious investigation claim thus falls within the discretionary function exception to the FTCA. The district court lacked jurisdiction to consider this claim because the United States has not waived sovereign immunity.

b. *Intentional infliction*

The Garlings' intentional infliction claim also falls under the discretionary function exception because it stems from the same conduct as the tortious investigation claim—the EPA's raid and investigation. *See Sydnes v. United States*, 523 F.3d 1179 (10th Cir. 2008) (holding intentional infliction claim barred under discretionary function exception when the conduct giving rise to the claim was discretionary). The district court therefore lacked jurisdiction over this claim.

c. *False arrest, false imprisonment, and abuse of process*

The district court also lacked jurisdiction over the Garlings' claims for false arrest, false imprisonment, and abuse of process. As discussed above, § 2680(h) at first excludes these claims from § 1346(b)(1)'s waiver but then the law enforcement proviso in § 2680(h) waives sovereign immunity for these claims when they arise from alleged misconduct by federal law enforcement.

In determining whether the Garlings' claims fall within the law enforcement proviso, we look to the substance of their claims and not how they labeled them in their complaint. The Sixth Circuit put it well: a plaintiff may not "recast a negligence tort as an intentional tort to take advantage of the law enforcement exception to § 2680(h)." *Milligan*, 670 F.3d at 696; *see also Lambertson v. United States*, 528 F.2d 441, 443 (2d Cir. 1976) ("In determining the applicability of the [§] 2680(h) exception, a court must look, not to the theory upon which the plaintiff elects to proceed, but rather to the substance of the claim which he asserts."); *Johnson v. United States*, 547 F.2d 688, 691-92 (D.C. Cir. 1976) ("[S]urely a litigant cannot circumvent the [FTCA] by the simple expedient of drafting in terms of negligence a complaint that in reality is a claim as to which the United States remains immunized.").

The Garlings' complaint attempts to bring intentional tort claims without alleging intentional tort facts. As to the false arrest claim, the complaint never alleges the Garlings were arrested. Similarly, as to the false imprisonment claim, it never alleges the Garlings were detained. Finally, the complaint never alleges facts showing that EPA had the required "ulterior purpose" for an abuse of process claim in Wyoming. *See Bosler v. Shuck*, 714 P.2d 1231, 1234 (Wyo. 1986). Indeed, the complaint conflates abuse of process with its tortious investigation claim. *See, e.g.*, Aplt. App. at 8 (complaint alleging that "EPA officials acted with reckless and grossly negligent disregard when conducting the armed raid and, but for this abuse of process, the plaintiffs" would not have been injured).

These three claims stem from the EPA's raid and investigation, and the facts alleged at most amount to negligence or recklessness. As discussed above, the discretionary function exception precludes the claim for negligent or reckless investigation. The Garlings attempt to ascribe the labels of "false arrest," "false imprisonment," and "abuse of process" to these allegations to fit the law enforcement proviso in § 2680(h). But considering, as we must, the substance of the allegations and not the labels, we conclude the district court lacked jurisdiction over these claims.[5]

2. Defamation

The district court lacked jurisdiction over the Garlings' defamation claim because § 2680(h) excludes "libel" and "slander" from the FTCA's waiver of sovereign immunity. *See* 28 U.S.C. § 2680(h); *Aviles,* 887 F.2d at 1047-48. Defamation claims are the "equivalent" of "libel" and "slander" and thus exempt from the waiver of sovereign immunity under the intentional tort exception. *Cooper v. Am. Auto. Ins. Co.,* 978 F.2d 602, 613 (10th Cir. 1992).

3. Conspiracy

Finally, as to the Garlings' conspiracy claim, an FTCA claim must be recognized as a tort under the "law of the place where the act or omission occurred." 28 U.S.C. § 1346(b)(1); *see Hill,* 393 F.3d at 1117. The Wyoming Supreme Court has recognized tort claims for conspiracy provided there is an underlying cause of action in tort. *See White v. Shane Edeburn Constr., LLC,* 285 P.3d 949, 958 (Wyo. 2012). Because the Garlings have no underlying causes of action remaining that overcome sovereign immunity, the FTCA does not waive sovereign immunity for their conspiracy claim because it would fail under Wyoming law.

III. CONCLUSION

We reverse the district court's judgment and remand with directions to dismiss this action for lack of jurisdiction.[6]

[1] Roger and Sheryl Garling own R and D Enterprises, Inc., which owned the properties ELI leased for its Casper, Wyoming business operations.

[2] Although the EPA's denial cited the Garlings' "fail[ure] to state a claim . . . for which relief is available," *see* Aplt. App. at 18, an agency is not required to state a reason for denying an FTCA administrative claim, *see* 28 C.F.R. § 14.9(a) (stating the notice of denial "may include a statement of the reasons for the denial").

[3] *Iqbal* and *Twombly* addressed how a complaint should be analyzed in response to a Rule 12(b)(6) motion to dismiss for failure to state a claim, rather than a Rule 12(b)(1) motion to dismiss for lack of subject matter jurisdiction. We agree with the Fourth Circuit, which said that "when a defendant asserts that the [FTCA] complaint fails to allege sufficient facts to support subject matter jurisdiction, the trial court must apply a standard patterned on Rule 12(b)(6) and assume the

truthfulness of the facts alleged." *Kerns v. United States,* 585 F.3d 187, 193 (4th Cir. 2009).

[4] The EPA website states, "Wyoming is the only State that has not applied to the [EPA] for authority to administer the public water supply program," and thus EPA Region 8 "directly implements the [SDWA]" in the state, including "[l]aboratory certification" and "[f]ormal enforcement." EPA Region 8 Drinking Water Program, *Wyoming Drinking Water Program,* EPA, https://perma.cc/L7HG-UYBZ (last visited Feb. 24, 2017). Wyoming's DEQ website states, "EPA Region 8 has primary enforcement authority . . . for all [SDWA] regulatory programs," except for several programs not relevant here. Wyo. Dep't of Envtl. Quality, *What is Primacy?,* DEQ, https://perma.cc/73YH-ZT6Z (last visited Feb. 24, 2017).

These sources permit judicial notice of the EPA's primary SDWA enforcement authority in Wyoming. *See* Fed. R. Evid. 201(b); *New Mexico ex rel. Richardson v. Bureau of Land Mgmt.,* 565 F.3d 683, 702 & n.22 (10th Cir. 2009) (taking judicial notice of facts on government websites and observing, "It is not uncommon for courts to take judicial notice of factual information found on the world wide web" (quotations omitted)); *see also United States v. Windsor,* 133 S. Ct. 2675, 2690 (2013) (citing state government website for results of citizens' initiatives concerning same-sex marriage); *Denius v. Dunlap,* 330 F.3d 919, 926-27 (7th Cir. 2003) (taking judicial notice of information from government website).

[5] We recognize the disagreement among the circuits regarding the interaction between § 2680(a) and § 2680(h). *Compare Nguyen v. United States,* 556 F.3d 1244, 1257 (11th Cir.2009) ("[I]f a claim is one of those listed in the proviso to subsection (h), there is no need to determine if the acts giving rise to it involve a discretionary function; sovereign immunity is waived in any event."), *with Medina v. United States,* 259 F.3d 220, 224-26 (4th Cir. 2001) (holding that intentional tort claims under § 2680(h) must also clear the discretionary function hurdle under § 2680(a)). Because the Garlings fail to allege facts showing they were falsely arrested, falsely imprisoned, or subject to an intentional abuse of process, they cannot use § 2680(h) to avoid sovereign immunity, and we need not reach this issue.

[6] Because this action must be dismissed for lack of subject matter jurisdiction, we do not address the Garlings' arguments on appeal that their claims are not time-barred or that equitable tolling should apply.

823 F.3d 970 (2016)

Leonard E. LOPEZ, Plaintiff-Appellant,
v.
UNITED STATES of America, Defendant-Appellee.

No. 15-1169.

United States Court of Appeals, Tenth Circuit.

May 23, 2016.

Lopez v. US, 823 F. 3d 970 (10th Cir. 2016)

Appeal from the United States District Court for the District of Colorado; (D.C. No. 1:12-CV-02259-RPM).

Benjamin I. Sachs (Jim Leventhal with him on the briefs), of Leventhal & Puga, P.C., Denver, CO, for Plaintiff-Appellant.

Robert Mark Russel, Assistant United States Attorney (John F. Walsh, United States Attorney, with him on the brief), Denver, CO, for Defendant-Appellee.

Before BRISCOE, McKAY and BALDOCK, Circuit Judges.

BRISCOE, Circuit Judge.

p.971Plaintiff Leonard Lopez appeals following a bench trial on his medical negligence claims. Lopez underwent lower back surgery at the Veterans Administration Medical Center of Denver, Colorado (VA Hospital), in order to alleviate longstanding sciatic pain. Immediately following surgery, however, Lopez began experiencing excruciating pain in his left foot. Lopez has since been diagnosed with neuropathic pain syndrome and has to rely on a combination of prescription pain medicine and a surgically-placed peripheral nerve stimulator to deal with the pain.

Lopez filed suit against the United States pursuant to the Federal Tort Claims Act alleging, in pertinent part, that (1) Dr. Samuel Waller was negligent in performing the surgery, and (2) that the hospital was negligent in credentialing and privileging Dr. Glenn Kindt, the supervising physician involved in the surgery. The case proceeded to a bench trial, and at the conclusion of the trial the district court found in favor of the government on both claims. Lopez now appeals. Exercising appellate jurisdiction pursuant to 28 U.S.C. § 1291, we affirm the district court's judgment in favor of the United States on Lopez's claim of medical negligence involving Waller, but reverse the district court's judgment on the negligent credentialing and privileging claim and remand with directions to dismiss that claim for lack of jurisdiction.

I

Factual background

Lopez, a resident of Pueblo, Colorado, served as a military policeman and was stationed with the National Guard in Iraq between 1989 and 1991. While on duty in Iraq, Lopez injured his lower back. After returning home and leaving the service, Lopez continued to have lower back pain. In particular, he suffered from intermittent sciatic pain on his left side that ran from his buttocks to his foot.

Lopez also experienced a "pins and needles" sensation in his left foot from time to time. To relieve the symptoms, Lopez had to sit down and stretch out his leg.

In early 2010, Lopez met with Kindt, a neurosurgeon employed by the University of Colorado who had surgical privileges at the VA Hospital, but was not a federal employee. Kindt, who was approximately 79 years old at the time, told Lopez that he could surgically relieve Lopez's sciatic pain and symptoms. Kindt also allegedly told Lopez that he had performed thousands of similar surgeries without issue.

On March 5, 2010, Lopez underwent a surgical decompression of the lumbosacral nerve root and disc excision at L5-S1. The surgery was performed at the VA Hospital by Kindt, who was assisted by Waller, a second-year surgical resident at the VA Hospital. The goal of the surgery was to remove bulging disc material and thereby decompress the nerve root and alleviate the sciatic pain Lopez had been experiencing. During the course of the procedure, as Kindt was removing pieces of disc material with a surgical instrument called a Kerrison, Kindt pulled out a small piece of tissue approximately an inch in length that, according to Waller, "looked a little bit like a piece of angel hair pasta or something along those lines." App., Vol. 4 at 455. Kindt allegedly remarked to Waller that the tissue "must be nerve" and expressed his intention to send the tissue to pathology for examination.[1] *Id.* According p.972 to Waller, "the tone of the operation changed a little bit" at that point and Kindt "started looking for [a] cerebrospinal fluid leak." *Id.* at 455-56. No such fluid was found by Kindt and Waller. Consequently, Kindt completed the removal of the bulging disc material and, together, Kindt and Waller closed the incision. Due to the concerns raised during the surgery, Kindt directed that Lopez lie flat overnight in order to prevent or reduce any symptoms that might arise from a possible cerebrospinal fluid leak.

When Lopez awoke following the surgery, he experienced a significant amount of pain in his left foot. According to Lopez, the bottom of his left foot felt like "pins and needles," and he felt a severe burning sensation in the rest of his left foot. *Id.*, Vol. 3 at 399. When asked by hospital staff to rate his pain on a scale of 1 to 10, with 10 being the worst, Lopez responded that his pain was a "20." *Id.* at 396-97. The pain in his left foot was so severe that Lopez could not put a sock or shoe on that foot. Lopez was classified as having allodynia.[2]

Lopez was discharged from the VA Hospital with a prescription for pain medication. After using all of his available sick and annual leave, Lopez returned to his job as a government security guard. The pain in his left foot had not subsided, however, and Lopez eventually quit his job because he felt that he could not perform the tasks required of him. In particular, the pain in his left foot made it difficult for Lopez to walk.

Due to the continuing pain and his reliance on prescription medications, Lopez saw Dr. Giancarlo Barolat, a neurosurgeon with a private practice in Denver. Barolat diagnosed Lopez with "Neuropathic Pain Syndrome caused by damage to the L5 and S1 nerve roots" that occurred at some point during the surgery. *Id.*, Vol. 6 at 836. To help alleviate some of the pain, Barolat surgically placed a peripheral nerve stimulator on the sciatic nerve in the back of Lopez's left thigh (the device is powered by a battery that was placed in the front of Lopez's left thigh). The stimulator helps to reduce Lopez's pain by fifty to sixty percent, lessens his dependence upon prescription painkillers, and increases his ability to function. That said, Lopez still relies on prescription painkillers to help deal with the pain in his left foot.

Procedural background

On August 24, 2012, Lopez filed a complaint in federal district court against Kindt and Waller. The complaint alleged that Lopez was seeking relief under the Federal Tort Claims Act (FTCA), 28 U.S.C. § 2671, et seq., and "ha[d] satisfied the jurisdictional prerequisite of 28 U.S.C. § 2675(a) by timely filing an administrative claim against the United States," which was denied on August 15, 2012. App., Vol. 1 at 13. The complaint further alleged that Kindt and Waller were both employees of the United States who were acting within the course and scope of their employment at the time of the events in question. More specifically, the complaint alleged that both Kindt and Waller performed each aspect of the operation on Lopez. The complaint in turn alleged claims for medical negligence arising from p.973 the conduct of both Kindt (Claim One) and Waller (Claim Two).

The United States filed an answer substituting itself as defendant in place of Waller and denying that Kindt was a federal employee. Kindt filed an answer on his own behalf also denying that he was an employee of the United States.[3] Kindt admitted that "he was the attending surgeon for the procedure being performed on ... Lopez, and was assisted during this surgery by ... Waller." *Id.* at 23. Kindt alleged "that during the removal of the disc material following the exposure and retraction of the dura and other surrounding tissue, a small piece of nerve root was found to be contained within the disc material after it was removed by the surgeons, and that this aberrant anatomical finding was not visible or otherwise known to them prior to removal." *Id.*

On June 17, 2013, Lopez moved to amend his complaint "to add claims against the United States ... for negligent credentialing and privileging related to ... Kindt ... at the [VA Hospital]." *Id.* at 63. In support, Lopez alleged that "Kindt's credentialing file produced by the United States in discovery reveal[ed] the [VA Hospital] failed to follow its own bylaws in failing to ensure ... Kindt was competent to continue performing neurosurgical procedures." *Id.* at 64.

The district court granted Lopez leave to amend on July 11, 2013, and Lopez's first amended complaint was filed that same day. The first amended complaint alleged three claims for relief: Count One alleged a claim of medical negligence arising from the conduct of Kindt; Count Two alleged a claim of medical negligence arising from the conduct of Waller; and Count Three (misnamed in the first amended complaint as the "Fourth Claim") alleged a claim of negligent privileging and credentialing.[4] *Id.* at 110.

On August 12, 2013, Lopez and Kindt filed a joint stipulation dismissing all claims against Kindt with prejudice; this action was the result of a settlement between Lopez and Kindt. App., Vol. 2 at 148. This left two surviving claims: the medical negligence claim arising from the conduct of Waller and the negligent credentialing and privileging claim relating to Kindt.

The case proceeded to a multi-day bench trial beginning on December 15, 2014. On March 6, 2015, the district court issued a written memorandum of decision concluding that Lopez "ha[d] failed to prove his claims by a preponderance of the evidence." App., Vol. 9 at 1237. In reaching this conclusion, the district court stated:

> The reasonable probability is that the angel hair pasta sized tissue that came out with disc material was one of the fibers that coalesce into the L-5 nerve root but was not in the nerve root itself. Removal of it was accidental given the patient's anatomy and it is not probable that it would have been seen and avoided even with greater illumination and magnification. The unfortunate outcome of this surgery has not been shown to be caused by a failure to perform this surgery within the standard of care expected of a neurosurgeon in 2010.
>
> p.974 Assuming that negligence has been shown, liability of the Government depends upon finding that the removal of nerve tissue was done by Dr. Waller. The testimony of Dr. Waller on this issue [i.e., that Dr. Kindt performed the surgery and removed the nerve tissue and that Dr. Waller simply assisted Dr. Kindt] is accepted as more credible than that of Dr. Kindt, who, in the end [of his deposition testimony] said he would accept what Dr. Waller said. The attempt to impeach Dr. Waller by suggesting medical reports showing him as the surgeon was not persuasive.
>
> The plaintiff has attempted to show that the VA should not have permitted Dr. Kindt to be the attending surgeon in this case. There has been post-trial briefing on the applicability of negligent credentialing as a claim under the FTCA. Assuming that there may be such liability, the evidence does not support that claim. This was not a complex surgical procedure and this Court is persuaded by the testimony of Dr. Brega [an associate professor of neurosurgery at the University of Colorado] that Dr. Kindt was competent to perform it. The failure of the VA to follow proper protocol in 2009 does not establish a claim that Dr. Kindt was not competent to perform this type of surgery in 2010.

Id. at 1236.

Judgment in the case was entered on March 6, 2015. Lopez filed a postjudgment motion asking the district court to reconsider its conclusion that Lopez "failed to meet his burden of proving his claim involving the negligent removal of the L5 nerve root," and in turn asking the district court to "make additional findings, and award damages to [Lopez] on his negligent credentialing claim." *Id.* at 1317. The district court summarily denied Lopez's motion.

II

The medical negligence claim arising from the conduct of Waller

In his first issue on appeal, Lopez challenges the district court's resolution of his medical negligence claim arising from the conduct of Waller. Specifically, Lopez argues that the district court erred (a) in relying on the testimony of the government's expert witness, neurosurgeon Dr. Jeffrey Arle, regarding the precise cause of Lopez's injury, (b) in relying on Arle's testimony to reject Lopez's claim that Waller was negligent for failing to use a loupe (a small magnification device, essentially a microscope, that is worn on the head) or a headlight during the surgery, and (c) by making inadequate findings on Lopez's claim that Waller failed to properly mitigate the nerve injury suffered by Lopez. We agree with the government, however, that these claims are moot.

Lopez's medical negligence claim arising from the conduct of Waller rested on the theory that it was Waller, a federal employee, who actually performed all or most of the surgery, under the supervision of Kindt, and damaged Lopez's nerve roots. Indeed, Lopez's counsel emphasized this issue during his opening statement to the district court: "One of the issues and the Court is well aware of this is who did the surgery. And so what we have is significant evidence, overwhelming evidence that the procedure was performed by Dr. Waller." App., Vol. 3 at 237. At the conclusion of the trial proceedings, the district court found in its written memorandum of decision that it was Kindt, who was not a federal employee, who actually performed the surgery and removed the nerve tissue. App., Vol. 9 at 1236. In making this finding, the district court stated that it found Waller's trial testimony on this issue "more credible" than the deposition testimony p.975 of Kindt. *Id.* On appeal, Lopez has not challenged as clearly erroneous the district court's finding on this fundamental point.[5] Consequently, it is unnecessary for us to address the other challenges that Lopez has mounted to the district court's resolution of his medical negligence claim pertaining to the conduct of Waller.

The negligent credentialing and privileging claim

Lopez also challenges the district court's resolution of his negligent credentialing and privileging claim. The district court addressed and rejected this claim on the merits, and Lopez now argues that the district court erred in failing to grant relief on the claim. We agree with the government, however, that the district court lacked jurisdiction over the claim.

The administrative claim that Lopez filed with the government described the "Basis of Claim" in the following manner:

> This is a claim for medical malpractice arising from substandard medical care provided to Leonard Lopez during a surgical procedure on March 5, 2010 at the VA Medical Center. During the left L5-S1 decompression/discectomy procedure, Glenn W. Kindt, M.D., and Samuel Waller, M.D., cut and removed part of a nerve. Dr. Kindt's and Dr. Waller's cutting and removal of this nerve was a breach of the standard of care and caused Mr. Lopez injuries, damages and losses.
>
> As a result of Dr. Kindt's and Dr. Waller's cutting and removal of the nerve from Mr. Lopez's body, he developed permanent injuries including CRPS Type II and exacerbation of his post-traumatic stress disorder.

App., Vol. 1 at 78.

When Lopez sought to amend his complaint to include a claim for negligent credentialing and privileging, the government opposed that request, arguing that Lopez's administrative claim did not include such a claim. The district court rejected the government's argument, stating:

> It is apparent that counsel for the plaintiff had no information about the competence of Dr. Kindt at the time of the filing of the administrative claim and first obtained that information through the discovery process in this civil

action. The amendment does not present a new claim and is based on information known to the VA hospital and is well within the scope of the claim that the surgery was performed negligently causing damage to the plaintiff.

App., Vol. 2 at 124.

In its appellate response brief, the government argues that the district court erred in making this ruling and asserting jurisdiction over the negligent credentialing and privileging claim.[6] "Whether the district court has subject matter jurisdiction over a claim is a question of law we review de novo." *Estate of Trentadue ex rel. Aguilar v. United States,* 397 F.3d 840, 852 (10th Cir.2005).

"The [FTCA] is a limited waiver of sovereign immunity, making the Federal Government liable to the same extent as a private party for certain torts of federal employees acting within the scope of their p.976 employment." *United States v. Orleans,* 425 U.S. 807, 813, 96 S.Ct. 1971, 48 L.Ed.2d 390 (1976). "This unequivocal waiver of immunity must be construed narrowly and the 'limitations and conditions upon which the Government consents to be sued must be strictly observed and exceptions thereto are not to be implied.'" *Miller v. United States,* 463 F.3d 1122, 1123 (10th Cir.2006) (quoting *In re Franklin Savings Corp.,* 385 F.3d 1279, 1289-90 (10th Cir.2004)).

"The FTCA bars claimants from bringing suit in federal court until they have exhausted their administrative remedies." *McNeil v. United States,* 508 U.S. 106, 113, 113 S.Ct. 1980, 124 L.Ed.2d 21 (1993). Specifically, the FTCA states, in pertinent part, that

> [a]n action shall not be instituted upon a claim against the United States for money damages for injury or loss of property or personal injury or death caused by the negligent or wrongful act or omission of any employee of the Government while acting within the scope of his office or employment, unless the claimant shall have first presented the claim to the appropriate Federal agency and his claim shall have been finally denied by the agency in writing and sent by certified or registered mail.

28 U.S.C. § 2675(a). This exhaustion requirement is "jurisdictional and cannot be waived."[7] *Bradley v. United States by Veterans Admin.,* 951 F.2d 268, 270 (10th Cir.1991). "In other words, the FTCA bars would-be tort plaintiffs from bringing suit against the government unless the claimant has previously submitted a claim for damages to the offending agency, because Congress wants agencies to have an opportunity to settle disputes before defending against litigation in court." *Smoke Shop, LLC v. United States,* 761 F.3d 779, 786 (7th Cir.2014) (citing *McNeil,* 508 U.S. at 112 & n. 7, 113 S.Ct. 1980).

We have stated that the jurisdictional statute can be satisfied by a claimant "filing (1) a written statement sufficiently describing the injury to enable the agency to begin its own investigation, and (2) a sum certain damages claim." *Trentadue,* 397 F.3d at 852 (quoting *Bradley,* 951 F.2d at 270). That is, we have effectively construed the term "claim," as employed in § 2675, as encompassing two requirements: (1) a written statement describing the injury in sufficient detail to allow the agency to begin an investigation into the possibility of potentially tortious conduct, and (2) a request for a sum certain in damages. That pragmatic interpretation is consistent with Form SF95, the form typically used for filing administrative claims. As the Seventh Circuit noted long ago, "no statement of legal theories is required" by Form SF95, "only facts plus a demand for money." *Murrey v. United States,* 73 F.3d 1448, 1452 (7th Cir.1996). Thus, the "claim" asserted "encompasses any cause of action fairly implicit in the facts." *Id.*

Applying these principles to the case at hand, we conclude that the facts alleged in Lopez's administrative claim were not sufficient to encompass and give the government notice of his negligent credentialing and privileging claim. To be sure, a negligent p.977 credentialing and privileging claim under Colorado law requires proof that the plaintiff was injured by the negligent acts of the improperly credentialed and privileged physician. *See Braden v. Saint Francis Hosp.,* 714 P.2d 505, 507 (Colo. App.1985) ("In extending staff privileges to a doctor, a hospital does not generally expose itself to liability *for the doctor's negligence* unless it knows or should know of a propensity on the doctor's part to commit negligent acts.") (quoting *W. Ins. Co. v. Brochner,* 682 P.2d 1213 (Colo.App. 1983) (emphasis added)). But such a claim also requires proof that the hospital/employer breached a legal duty by credentialing and privileging the physician. *See id.* Nothing in Lopez's administrative claim provided the government with notice that it needed to investigate whether the VA Hospital was negligent in credentialing and privileging Kindt, and it was in turn deprived of any opportunity to settle this potential claim without litigation. Consequently, we conclude that Lopez's administrative claim did not reasonably encompass his negligent credentialing and privileging claim.

In concluding otherwise, the district court focused primarily on irrelevant factors. Specifically, rather than examining whether Lopez's administrative claim provided the government with notice of the relevant facts, the district court instead noted that Lopez's counsel "had no information about the competence of Dr. Kindt at the time of the filing of the administrative claim," and that the claim was "based on information known to the VA hospital." App., Vol. 2 at 124. While both of these facts may be true, nothing in Lopez's administrative claim would have caused the government to investigate whether Kindt was properly credentialed. Further, simply because an agency is in possession of information relevant to a claim does not mean that the agency is aware of the claim itself. To excuse a claim from the FTCA's administrative exhaustion requirements for the reasons stated by the district court would undermine the very purpose of those exhaustion requirements (i.e., to give the agency notice of the claim, an opportunity to investigate, and a chance to settle the claim prior to litigation), and could effectively and improperly extend the FTCA's statute of limitations.

For these reasons, we conclude that the district court lacked subject matter jurisdiction over Lopez's negligent credentialing and privileging claim.

III

We AFFIRM the district court's entry of judgment in favor of the United States on Lopez's claim of medical negligence involving Waller. We REVERSE the district court's judgment in favor of the United States on Lopez's negligent credentialing and privileging claim and REMAND with directions to dismiss that claim for lack of jurisdiction.

[1] According to the evidence in the record, Kindt placed the piece of tissue in a cup along with multiple pieces of disc fragments. Although the cup and its contents were sent to the pathology department, there is no evidence that Kindt or anyone else involved in the surgery notified the pathologist of the possibility of nerve tissue in the cup. The resulting pathology report mentioned only the existence of disc tissue.

[2] Allodynia is commonly defined as "[p]ain from stimuli which are not normally painful." Definition of Allodynia, MedicineNet.com, http://www.medicinenet.com/script/main/art. asp?articlekey=25197 (last visited on May 9, 2016).

[3] It was ultimately determined that Kindt was not a federal employee, but rather an employee of the University of Colorado. Consequently, the district court exercised supplemental jurisdiction pursuant to 28 U.S.C. § 2671 over Lopez's negligence claim against Kindt. App, Vol. 9 at 1217.

[4] Lopez subsequently filed a second amended complaint revising his negligent privileging and credentialing claim. App., Vol. 2 at 196, 204-05.

[5] Having carefully examined the record on appeal, we are doubtful that Lopez could establish that the district court's finding on this issue was clearly erroneous in any event.

[6] Although the government did not file a cross-appeal, we can consider this issue because it concerns the district court's subject matter jurisdiction. *See Sebelius v. Auburn Reg. Med. Ctr.,* ___ U.S. ___, 133 S.Ct. 817, 824, 184 L.Ed.2d 627 (2013) ("Objections to a tribunal's jurisdiction can be raised at any time.").

[7] The FTCA also includes a statute of limitations that states:

A tort claim against the United States shall be forever barred unless it is presented in writing to the appropriate Federal agency within two years after such claim accrues or unless [the] action is begun within six months after the date of mailing, by certified or registered mail, of notice of final denial of the claim by the agency to which it was presented.

28 U.S.C. § 2401(b).

776 F.3d 1134 (2015)

Larry Wayne BARNES, Sr.; Linda Sue Barnes, Plaintiffs-Appellants,

v.

UNITED STATES of America; John Doe, sued as: John Does 1-30, unknown individuals of the Tulsa Police Department and/or Batf and John Does 31-40, unknown supervisors and/or policy makers for the Tulsa Police Department and/or BATF, Defendants-Appellees.

No. 13-5014.

United States Court of Appeals, Tenth Circuit.

January 21, 2015.

Barnes v. US, 776 F. 3d 1134 (10th Cir. 2015)

p.1136 Art Fleak, Tulsa, OK (J. Derek Ingle, E. Terrill Corley & Associates, Tulsa, OK, and E. Anthony Mareshie, E. Anthony Mareshie, P.L.L.C., Tulsa, OK, with him on the briefs), for Plaintiffs-Appellants.

Zakary Toomey, Civil Division, U.S. Department of Justice, Washington, D.C. (Stuart F. Delery, James G. Touhey, Jr., and Lawrence Eiser, Civil Division, U.S. Department of Justice, Washington, D.C., with him on the brief), for Defendants-Appellees.

Before KELLY, GORSUCH, and HOLMES, Circuit Judges.

HOLMES, Circuit Judge.

Larry and Linda Barnes appeal from the dismissal of their Federal Tort Claims Act ("FTCA") suit. The district court dismissed p.1137 the case for lack of subject-matter jurisdiction pursuant to Federal Rule of Civil Procedure 12(b)(1), based on its finding that the Barneses' claims were time-barred under the six-month statute of limitations in 28 U.S.C. § 2401(b). The Barneses now seek reversal of this order, arguing that the district court misinterpreted the statute of limitations and further erred by failing to afford the Barneses the benefit of the doctrines of relation back, equitable tolling, and equitable estoppel. Exercising jurisdiction under 28 U.S.C. § 1291, we affirm.

I

In August 2007, a federal grand jury of the United States District Court for the Northern District of Oklahoma returned a two-count indictment against Larry Barnes, charging him with crimes relating to the possession and distribution of methamphetamine.[1] After a three-day trial, a jury convicted Mr. Barnes on both counts, and Mr. Barnes was sentenced to sixty-six months' incarceration on each count, to run concurrently, as well as a lengthy period of supervised release.

While Mr. Barnes's direct appeal was pending, the government acquired evidence indicating that material testimony offered at trial by a Bureau of Alcohol, Tobacco, Firearms, and Explosives ("BATF") special agent, an officer of the Tulsa Police Department, and a confidential informant had been fabricated. The government responded to the newly acquired evidence by asking the court to vacate Mr. Barnes's conviction, to dismiss the indictment against him, and to release him from incarceration. On July 2, 2009, the district court entered an order effectuating this request and directed the Bureau of Prisons to immediately release Mr. Barnes.

Following his release, Mr. Barnes desired redress related to his prosecution and imprisonment. He and his wife, Linda Barnes, began the process of seeking it on May 20, 2010, by filing administrative tort claims with the BATF. About a year later, on May 13, 2011, the Barneses filed a civil lawsuit against the BATF in Oklahoma state court ("Lawsuit # 1"), asserting various claims sounding in tort. The BATF removed this suit to the United States District Court for the Northern District of Oklahoma pursuant to 28 U.S.C. § 1442(a)(1), which permits "[t]he United States or any agency thereof" to remove any "civil action or criminal prosecution" against it to federal district court.

On September 23, 2011, less than two weeks after removing the case to federal court, the BATF filed a motion to dismiss for lack of subject-matter jurisdiction. The agency's argument proceeded as follows: (1) because 28 U.S.C. § 1346(b) vests exclusive jurisdiction over FTCA suits in the federal district courts; and (2) removal jurisdiction under 28 U.S.C. § 1442(a) is derivative and cannot vest jurisdiction in a federal court where the state court had none; then (3) the state court and, perforce, the district court, lacked jurisdiction to hear the case.

On October 25, 2011, while the motion to dismiss Lawsuit # 1 remained pending before the district court, the BATF provided p.1138 notice via certified mail to the Barneses (through their counsel) of its formal denial of their administrative claims. In apparent contemplation of 28 U.S.C. § 2401(b)'s statute of limitations,[2] the BATF's notice expressly informed the Barneses of a deadline for filing any subsequent lawsuit: "If your clients are dissatisfied with this action, a lawsuit must be filed in an appropriate United States district court not later than *six months* after the date of the mailing of this notification." Aplt.App. at 37 (Letter to J. Derek Ingle, Esq., from Eleaner R. Loos, Assoc. Chief Counsel, Litig. Div., U.S. Dep't of Justice, dated Oct. 24, 2011) (emphasis added). Approximately five months later, on March 23, 2012, the district court granted the BATF's motion to dismiss Lawsuit # 1 for lack of jurisdiction and dismissed that case without prejudice.[3]

On August 22, 2012, the Barneses filed their second lawsuit ("Lawsuit # 2"), the action now before us on appeal. Notably, this action was filed approximately five months after the district court dismissed Lawsuit # 1 *and* nearly ten months after the BATF gave the Barneses notice of its formal denial of their administrative claims. More specifically, with regard to the BATF's formal denial, the Barneses filed Lawsuit # 2 nearly four months *after* the six-month deadline (i.e., April 25, 2012) that the BATF communicated to the Barneses in the formal denial.

The government filed a motion to dismiss Lawsuit # 2 for lack of jurisdiction under Federal Rule of Civil Procedure 12(b)(1). This time, the government argued that the Barneses' claims were barred by the FTCA's statute of limitations, 28 U.S.C. § 2401(b), because by the time the Barneses filed Lawsuit # 2, the statute's six-month limitations period had run.

The district court agreed, finding the Barneses' claims time-barred. It rejected the Barneses' arguments regarding the doctrines of relation back and equitable estoppel, finding these doctrines inapplicable under the pleaded facts. Finally, the court found that the Barneses' claims were not saved by equitable tolling, because "[t]he

Tenth Circuit has repeatedly referred to the FTCA's timeliness requirement as being jurisdictional," and thus, the statutory limitations period was "not subject to equitable tolling." Aplt.App. at 102 (Order, filed Jan. 14, 2013).

Based on these conclusions, the district court granted the government's motion and dismissed the Barneses' claims with prejudice. The Barneses timely filed this appeal, and we now exercise jurisdiction pursuant to 28 U.S.C. § 1291.

II

A

First, we conclude that the district court soundly analyzed whether Lawsuit # 2 was time-barred and properly determined that it was. Consequently, we find that the Barneses' action was properly dismissed as time-barred. *See Jones v. Bock,* 549 U.S. p.1139 199, 215, 127 S.Ct. 910, 166 L.Ed.2d 798 (2007) ("If the allegations ... show that relief is barred by the applicable statute of limitations, the complaint is subject to dismissal for failure to state a claim...."); *accord Vasquez Arroyo v. Starks,* 589 F.3d 1091, 1096 (10th Cir.2009).

1

In assessing the district court's ruling that Lawsuit # 2 was barred by the statute of limitations, we turn first to the court's interpretation and application of the statute of limitations itself, which we review de novo. *See Braxton v. Zavaras,* 614 F.3d 1156, 1159 (10th Cir.2010).

We start by observing that the FTCA has both an administrative-exhaustion requirement, set forth in 28 U.S.C. § 2675(a), and a statute of limitations, set forth in 28 U.S.C. § 2401(b). Combined, these provisions act as chronological bookends to an FTCA claim, marking both a date before which a claim may not be filed and a date after which any filing is untimely.

The Barneses conflate these two distinct features of the statutory scheme when they argue that compliance with the administrative-exhaustion requirement under § 2675(a)'s "deemed denial" provision effectively exempted them from § 2401(b)'s six-month limitations period. To the contrary (as the district court correctly found), the six-month limitations period in § 2401(b) is triggered by an agency's formal denial of a potential plaintiff's administrative claims—regardless of whether that plaintiff has filed a claim pursuant to § 2675(a)'s "deemed denial" provision.

The administrative-exhaustion requirement applicable to FTCA claims "bars claimants from bringing suit in federal court until they have exhausted their administrative remedies." *McNeil v. United States,* 508 U.S. 106, 113, 113 S.Ct. 1980, 124 L.Ed.2d 21 (1993). Section 2675(a) provides:

> An action shall not be instituted upon a claim against the United States for money damages for injury or loss of property or personal injury or death caused by the negligent or wrongful act or omission of any employee of the Government while acting within the scope of his office or employment, unless the claimant shall have first presented the claim to the appropriate Federal

agency and his claim shall have been finally denied by the agency in writing and sent by certified or registered mail. The failure of an agency to make final disposition of a claim within six months after it is filed shall, at the option of the claimant any time thereafter, be deemed a final denial of the claim for purposes of this section. 28 U.S.C. § 2675(a). In other words, to meet the threshold requirement of administrative exhaustion, plaintiffs must either (1) have their administrative claims finally denied by the relevant federal agency; or (2) if the agency fails to act on their administrative claims within six months of presentment, they may thereafter deem the claims (constructively) denied.

If § 2675(a)'s exhaustion requirement establishes a date *before* which a claim cannot be filed, § 2401(b)'s limitations period establishes the date *after* which any claim is barred. Recall, this provision states: "A tort claim against the United States shall be forever barred unless... action is begun within six months after the date of mailing, by certified or registered mail, of notice of final denial of the claim by the agency to which it was presented." 28 U.S.C. § 2401(b). The issue—one of first impression in this circuit—is simply how these two provisions relate to one another.

To resolve this issue, we begin by looking at the statutory text. *See First* p.1140 *Nat'l Bank of Durango v. Woods (In re Woods)*, 743 F.3d 689, 694 (10th Cir.2014) (noting that statutory interpretation "must begin ... with the language of the statute itself" (internal quotation marks omitted)). In doing so, our analysis is guided by the fact that, "[l]ike a waiver of [sovereign] immunity itself, which must be unequivocally expressed[,] [the Supreme] Court has long decided that limitations and conditions upon which the Government consents to be sued must be strictly observed and exceptions thereto are not to be implied." *Franklin Sav. Corp. v. United States (In re Franklin Sav. Corp.)*, 385 F.3d 1279, 1289-90 (10th Cir.2004) (third and fourth alterations in original) (quoting *Lehman v. Nakshian*, 453 U.S. 156, 160-61, 101 S.Ct. 2698, 69 L.Ed.2d 548 (1981)) (internal quotation marks omitted). We bear in mind, moreover, that "[s]tatutes of limitations... represent a pervasive legislative judgment that it is unjust to fail to put the adversary on notice to defend within a specified period of time and that the right to be free of stale claims in time comes to prevail over the right to prosecute them." *Id.* at 1291 (quoting *United States v. Kubrick*, 444 U.S. 111, 117, 100 S.Ct. 352, 62 L.Ed.2d 259 (1979)) (internal quotation marks omitted).

Turning to the text, we ask whether § 2401(b)'s six-month statute of limitations may operate to bar an FTCA claim that has been filed after exhaustion pursuant to the "deemed denial" provision of § 2675(a). More specifically, the question is whether, notwithstanding a plaintiff's proper exercise of the option of deeming an administrative claim denied, an agency still retains the ability to issue a formal denial, thereby triggering § 2401(b)'s six-month statute of limitations and barring the plaintiff's claim, if tardy.

In textual terms, the Barneses' best argument relates to the use in both § 2401(b) and § 2675(a) of the phrase "final denial." They assert that because there can only be one "final denial," the use of this term in both provisions should be read to imply that what is "deemed a final denial of the claim" under § 2675(a) precludes a future "final denial of the claim" under § 2401(b). The fundamental problem with this reading is that it ignores the express language in § 2675(a) saying that an agency's failure to act on a claim may be deemed a final denial "for purposes of this section." That is, the plain language of the statute suggests that a deemed denial is final only for purposes of satisfying the exhaustion requirement, and not for other purposes, such as satisfying a limitations period in a *different* section of the statute. *See Lehman v. United States,* 154 F.3d 1010, 1014 (9th Cir.1998) (noting that "a 'deemed' final denial under section 2675(a) has no effect beyond what is stated in *that* section"); *accord Ellison v. United States,* 531 F.3d 359, 363 (6th Cir.2008).

Ignoring this limiting language would lead to a bizarre result. Generally, courts have concluded that § 2675(a) provides no independent limitation on when plaintiffs may file in federal court after deeming their administrative claims denied.[4] In other words, courts are virtually of one mind in ruling that (at least until there has been a final denial by the relevant agency) there is no limit on when a plaintiff may file a lawsuit predicated on a deemed denial. *See, e.g., Ellison,* 531 F.3d at 363 (noting that the statute does not restrict when a claimant can exercise the p.1141 "option to 'deem' a claim constructively denied," though that option "evaporates once the agency actually denies the claim"); *Pascale v. United States,* 998 F.2d 186, 193 (3d Cir.1993) ("[T]here is no limit... on a claimant's time to deem the claim denied."); *Taumby v. United States,* 919 F.2d 69, 70 (8th Cir.1990) ("[T]here is no time limit for the filing of an FTCA action when an administrative claim is deemed to be denied...."); *cf. Anderson ex rel. Anderson v. United States,* 803 F.2d 1520, 1522 (9th Cir.1986) ("Six months after the submission of the administrative claim, the claimant may either deem it denied and file suit in district court at any time prior to final agency action or the claimant may await final agency action and file suit within six months thereafter.").

Consequently, if the statutory provisions were read to prevent agencies from triggering § 2401(b)'s six-month limitations period through final denial of administrative FTCA claims after a "deemed denial," then plaintiffs would effectively have an indefinite statute of limitations for such claims. "[A] claimant theoretically could file an action, voluntarily dismiss it, and then re-file years later," *Lehman,* 154 F.3d at 1015, if this were true. Such an indefinite limitations period would be plainly contrary to § 2401(b)'s statutory objective of "requir[ing] the reasonably diligent presentation of tort claims against the government." *Plaza Speedway Inc. v. United States,* 311 F.3d 1262, 1266 (10th Cir.2002) (quoting *Arvayo v. United States,* 766 F.2d 1416, 1418 (10th Cir.1985)) (internal quotation marks omitted).

We reject the Barneses' implausible reading of § 2675(a) and § 2401(b) and instead adopt the position that these two provisions act independently of one another. In doing so, we join the Sixth Circuit in *Ellison* and the Ninth Circuit in *Lehman.* Particularly persuasive is *Lehman,* which addressed a scenario strikingly similar to the one before us. In that case, as in this one, the plaintiffs filed an administrative tort claim with an agency (there, the U.S. Postal Service), and after six months had elapsed, deemed the claim denied and filed a lawsuit. *See Lehman,* 154 F.3d at 1012. As in the present case, the agency mailed its final denial of the plaintiffs' claim while the plaintiffs' original lawsuit was still pending and, as in the present case, the lawsuit was subsequently dismissed without prejudice. *See id.*

As here, the *Lehman* plaintiffs subsequently refiled, but did so more than six months after the final agency denial of their administrative claim, and the district court dismissed the second lawsuit as untimely under § 2401(b). *See* 154 F.3d at 1012-13. Affirming the *Lehman* district court, the Ninth Circuit explained:

> Neither section 2401(b) nor section 2675(a) nor any other provision of the FTCA contains anything to suggest that an agency's authority to issue a notice of final denial is terminated, or even temporarily suspended, when a claimant brings an action that is timely under section 2675(a). To the contrary, the wording of sections 2401(b) and 2675(a) suggests that they are functionally distinct. Section 2675(a) expressly states that a claim may be deemed denied only "for purposes of this section." Thus, a "deemed" final denial under section 2675(a) has no effect beyond what is stated in *that* section....
>
> Further, our reading of the statutes [i.e., § 2401(b) and § 2675(a)] finds contextual support. Triggering the statute of limitations by an *actual* denial after a claim has been "deemed" denied serves an important function: It provides an agency with *certainty* that it will not be subject to an action to establish liability after a definite date. That function is particularly important under the FTCA, p.1142 because the statute contains *no time limit* for commencing an action when an administrative claim has been deemed denied under section 2675(a), in the absence of an actual denial.

Id. at 1014-15.

In *Ellison,* which differed factually from this case in that the plaintiff there never filed a timely first action, the Sixth Circuit endorsed substantially the same reading of § 2675(a) and § 2401(b) as the Ninth Circuit:

> [E]ven if a claimant somehow could deem a claim constructively denied "any time []after" six months of agency dormancy (notwithstanding later agency action), that power would trigger only a claimant's option to *initiate* a claim and would have no bearing on when the Act bars the filing of a claim. Section 2675(a) allows a party to deem a claim constructively denied only "for the purposes of [that] section," a section that determines nothing more than when a claim may "be instituted" in the district court. In a different section, the Act "forever bar[s]" a court claim "unless action is begun within six months after... notice of final denial of the claim by the agency." 28 U.S.C. § 2401(b).

531 F.3d at 363 (second, third, and fourth alterations in original) (omission in original).

Our own independent reading of the text of § 2675(a) and § 2401(b) comports with the analyses of this issue found in *Lehman* and *Ellison.* In a nutshell, § 2675(a) articulates an administrative-exhaustion requirement that dictates when a potential plaintiff's opportunity to initiate a claim begins; it has no bearing on the point at which that opportunity ceases. To the extent that § 2675(a) permits a party to "deem" an administrative claim denied, the statute makes clear that this constitutes a "final denial" *only* for purposes of determining whether the administrative-exhaustion requirement is satisfied, i.e., whether it is still too *early* to file a claim.

By contrast, § 2401(b) describes the time at which it is too *late* to file. The six-month window described by this provision opens only upon the "mailing ... of notice of final denial of the claim *by the agency* to which it was presented." 28 U.S.C. § 2401(b) (emphasis added). Ordinarily, this means that, regardless of whether plaintiffs have already "deemed" their administrative claims denied and commenced a suit against the government under the FTCA, a formal denial of those claims triggers the six-month limitations period described in § 2401(b).

2

Having clarified the operation of § 2401(b), it is a fairly straightforward matter to conclude that the Barneses' Lawsuit # 2 was untimely. The Barneses filed their administrative claims on May 20, 2010. A year later, the agency had not yet acted on their claims, so the Barneses invoked § 2675(a), "deemed" their claims denied for purposes of exhaustion, and filed Lawsuit # 1 on May 13, 2011. While Lawsuit # 1 was still pending, the BATF formally denied the Barneses' claims, effective October 25, 2011, triggering the six-month statute of limitations period of § 2401(b), which would expire on April 25, 2012.

On March 23, 2012, the district court granted the government's pending motion to dismiss Lawsuit # 1. Although the Barneses at this point had roughly a month remaining in which to refile within the statute of limitations, they did not do so. Instead, they waited until August 22, 2012, to file Lawsuit # 2—*viz.,* nearly four months *after* the statute of limitations had run. It is plain from this chronology of events that the district court correctly ruled that, "absent some basis for avoiding the FTCA's limitations period, [the p.1143 Barneses'] claims [in Lawsuit # 2 were] time-barred." Aplt.App. at 100.

3

The Barneses disagree, arguing that Lawsuit # 2 is actually timely because it relates back to Lawsuit # 1 under Federal Rule of Civil Procedure 15(c). That is, under their view, the filing date of Lawsuit # 1 should be deemed the operative date for the FTCA limitations analysis. Specifically, as relevant here, "[a]n amendment to a pleading relates back to the date of the original pleading when ... the amendment asserts a claim or defense that arose out of the conduct, transaction, or occurrence set out—or attempted to be set out—in the original pleading." Fed. R.Civ.P. 15(c)(1)(B); *accord Full Life Hospice, LLC v. Sebelius,* 709 F.3d 1012, 1018 (10th Cir.2013). We review the district court's ruling on the relation-back doctrine de novo. *See Garrett v. Fleming,* 362 F.3d 692, 695 (10th Cir.2004).

We may dispose of the Barneses' relation-back argument in summary fashion; by its plain terms, the rule is inapposite. As the district court ably explained, the doctrine of relation back "applies to an amendment to a pleading in the *same* action." Aplt.App. at 100 (emphasis added); *see Marsh v. Soares,* 223 F.3d 1217, 1219 (10th Cir.2000) ("[A] separately filed claim, as opposed to an amendment or a supplementary pleading, does not relate back to a previously filed claim." (alteration in original) (quoting *Benge v. United States,* 17 F.3d 1286, 1288 (10th Cir.1994)) (internal quotation marks omitted)); *accord Neverson v. Bissonnette,* 261 F.3d 120, 126 (1st Cir.2001). In light of the Barneses' concession that Lawsuit # 2 "was refiled rather than one where their claim was asserted through amendment," Aplt. Opening Br. at 29, we are hard-pressed to endorse the idea that the relation-back doctrine applies here. The district court did not abuse its discretion in rejecting the Barneses' relation-back challenge.

Therefore, the Barneses' instant action is time-barred under § 2401(b).

B

With some circumspection, we ultimately conclude that the district court was correct in determining that, under our precedent, the ineluctable consequence of the Barneses' action being time-barred was that the court lacked subject-matter jurisdiction. The district court therefore properly dismissed the action under Federal Rule of Civil Procedure 12(b)(1).

The government cites to a number of cases indicating that this court "has repeatedly held that '[a]s a threshold matter, timeliness is one of the conditions of the government's waiver of sovereign immunity under the FTCA,'" and, accordingly, "[a federal] court lacks subject matter jurisdiction to proceed under the FTCA if a plaintiff fails to satisfy the FTCA's timing requirements set forth in § 2401(b)." Aplee. Br. at 18-19 (alterations in original) (quoting *Harvey v. United States,* 685 F.3d 939, 947 (10th Cir.2012)) (internal quotation marks omitted). For many years, our cases have indeed reflected precisely this view. *See, e.g., Harvey,* 685 F.3d at 947; *In re Franklin Sav. Corp.,* 385 F.3d at 1287; *see also Dahl v. United States,* 319 F.3d 1226, 1228 (10th Cir.2003) ("[I]f a litigant does not satisfy the timing requirement of § 2401(b), the district court must dismiss for lack of subject matter jurisdiction." (citing *Casias v. United States,* 532 F.2d 1339, 1340 n. 1 (10th Cir.1976))).

We must acknowledge, however, that our decisions in this area have not involved rigorous analysis.[5] In light of significant p.1144 developments in the Supreme Court's jurisdictional jurisprudence, we question whether our caselaw accurately reflects the current state of the law. *See, e.g.,* Gregory C. Sisk, *The Continuing Drift of Federal Sovereign Immunity Jurisprudence,* 50 Wm. & Mary L.Rev. 517, 553 (2008) ("[F]or nearly two decades, the Supreme Court has repeatedly turned aside the government's insistence that time limitations should be treated as jurisdictional conditions on the waiver of sovereign immunity."); *id.* at 559 ("[T]he statute of limitations governing FTCA claims, which is not included within the general section waiving sovereign immunity and simultaneously conferring district court jurisdiction, presumably would not be given a jurisdictional read and would not constitute a nonwaivable constraint on judicial authority." (footnotes omitted)). In particular, we are given pause by the Court's seminal decisions in *Irwin v. Department of Veterans Affairs,* 498 U.S. 89, 111 S.Ct. 453, 112 L.Ed.2d 435 (1990), and *Sebelius v. Auburn Regional Medical Center,* ___ U.S. ___, 133 S.Ct. 817, 184 L.Ed.2d 627 (2013).

In *Irwin,* the Court recognized that 42 U.S.C. § 2000e-16(c)'s filing deadline for Title VII claims "is a condition to the waiver of sovereign immunity and thus must be strictly construed." 498 U.S. at 94, 111 S.Ct. 453. However, the Court also noted that "previous cases dealing with the effect of time limits in suits against the Government ha[d] not been entirely consistent" and had left "open the general question whether principles of equitable tolling, waiver, and estoppel apply against the Government when it involves a statutory filing deadline." *Id. Irwin's* acknowledgment of this open question is significant because such doctrines as equitable tolling and equitable estoppel ordinarily would not apply if statutory filing deadlines are jurisdictional. *See Nat'l R.R. Passenger Corp. v. Morgan,* 536 U.S. 101, 121, 122 S.Ct. 2061, 153 L.Ed.2d 106 (2002) (contrasting "jurisdictional prerequisite[s] to filing" with "requirement[s] subject to waiver, estoppel, and equitable tolling"); *accord Zipes v. Trans World Airlines, Inc.,* 455 U.S. 385, 393, 102 S.Ct. 1127, 71 L.Ed.2d 234 (1982). Thus, at least arguably, the question that *Irwin* recognized as open was whether statutory filing deadlines in suits against the government are jurisdictional. *See* Sisk, *supra,* at 554 ("Because the Supreme Court 'has no authority to create equitable exceptions to jurisdictional requirements,' the Court's presumptive allowance of equitable tolling of statutes of limitations on claims against the government removes such provisions from the category of jurisdictional commands." (footnote omitted) (quoting *Bowles v. Russell,* 551 U.S. 205, 214, 127 S.Ct. 2360, 168 L.Ed.2d 96 (2007))).

Notably, the Court clarified that where Congress has created a waiver of sovereign immunity, filing deadlines related p.1145 to the waiver are presumptively subject to such doctrines as equitable tolling:

> Once Congress has made such a waiver, we think that making the rule of equitable tolling applicable to suits against the Government ... amounts to little, if any, broadening of the congressional waiver.... We therefore hold that the same rebuttable presumption of equitable tolling applicable to suits against private defendants should also apply to suits against the United States. Congress, of course, may provide otherwise if it wishes to do so.

Irwin, 498 U.S. at 95-96, 111 S.Ct. 453.

In the FTCA context, *Irwin* has caused some courts—including our sister circuits—to seriously question and, in some instances, discard their previous view that § 2401(b)'s limitations provisions are jurisdictional. *See, e.g., Hughes v. United States,* 263 F.3d 272, 278 (3d Cir.2001) (relying on *Irwin* and noting that "the FTCA's statute of limitations is not jurisdictional"); *Glarner v. U.S. Dep't of Veterans Admin.,* 30 F.3d 697, 701 (6th Cir. 1994) ("[T]he VA first argues that the doctrine of equitable tolling cannot apply to § 2401(b) because the latter is a jurisdictional statute of limitations that cannot be equitably tolled. This assertion is incorrect."); *see also State v. Sharafeldin,* 382 Md. 129, 854 A.2d 1208, 1217 (2004) ("Most of the lower Federal courts have given credence to that language [of *Irwin*], however, have shifted their previously-held view, and have applied equitable tolling principles to untimely claims made to the administrative agency or to untimely lawsuits after denial of the claim."); Jacob Damrill, Note, *Waves of Change Towards a More Unified Approach: Equitable Tolling and the Federal Torts Claims Act,* 50 Tulsa L.Rev. 271, 276 (2014) ("Prior to *Irwin,* federal courts consistently and unanimously held that equitable tolling did not apply to the FTCA because section 2401(b)'s two-year limitations provision was a jurisdictional bar to untimely claims. In the wake of *Irwin,* federal courts reversed course and immediately began to apply equitable tolling to [the] FTCA two-year limitation period." (italics added) (footnotes omitted)).[6]

In *Auburn Regional,* in 2013, the Court adopted a new analytical framework for assessing whether statutory conditions on lawsuits against the United States were jurisdictional. The Court recognized that through a series of cases it had "'tried ... to bring some discipline to the use' of the term 'jurisdiction.'" *Auburn Reg'l,* 133 S.Ct. at 824 (quoting *Henderson ex rel. Henderson v. Shinseki,* 562 U.S. 428, 131 S.Ct. 1197, 1202, 179 L.Ed.2d 159 (2011)). In these opinions the Court had, in particular, explained time and again that statutes of limitations are not always—and, indeed, presumptively are *not*—jurisdictional. The touchstone standard laid out in these cases "for determining whether to classify a statutory limitation as jurisdictional" is a "readily administrable bright p.1146 line" rule. *Id.* (quoting *Arbaugh v. Y & H Corp.,* 546 U.S. 500, 516, 126 S.Ct. 1235, 163 L.Ed.2d 1097 (2006)) (internal quotation marks omitted); *see also Utah ex rel. Utah Dep't of Envtl. Quality v. U.S. EPA,* 765 F.3d 1257, 1258 (10th Cir.2014) ("Filing deadlines can be jurisdictional or non[-]jurisdictional. To decide which deadlines are jurisdictional, we apply a 'bright-line' rule.").

Fundamentally, this framework "focuses on Congress's stated intention." *Utah,* 765 F.3d at 1258; *see Hobby Lobby Stores, Inc. v. Sebelius,* 723 F.3d 1114, 1157 (10th Cir.2013) (en banc) (Gorsuch, J., concurring) ("T[he] rule requires us to 'inquire whether Congress has clearly stated that the rule is jurisdictional; absent such a clear statement ... courts should treat the restriction as nonjurisdictional in character.'" (omission in original) (quoting *Auburn Reg'l,* 133 S.Ct. at 824)), *aff'd sub nom. Burwell v. Hobby Lobby Stores, Inc.,* ___ U.S. ___, 134 S.Ct. 2751, 189 L.Ed.2d 675 (2014).

In applying this bright-line test, "we focus on the legal character of the deadline, as shown through its text, context, and historical treatment." *Utah,* 765 F.3d at 1258; *see Hobby Lobby Stores, Inc.,* 723 F.3d at 1158 (Gorsuch, J., concurring) ("In addition to [consulting the] statutory text, we may when necessary consider as well 'context, including [the Supreme] Court's interpretation of similar provisions in many years past.'" (second alteration in original) (quoting *Reed Elsevier, Inc. v. Muchnick,* 559 U.S. 154, 168, 130 S.Ct. 1237, 176 L.Ed.2d 18 (2010))). "Statutes that speak clearly to 'the courts' statutory or constitutional *power* to adjudicate the case' must of course be treated as jurisdictional and given their full effect," *Hobby Lobby Stores, Inc.,* 723 F.3d at 1157-58 (Gorsuch, J., concurring) (quoting *Steel Co. v. Citizens for a Better Env't,* 523 U.S. 83, 89, 118 S.Ct. 1003, 140 L.Ed.2d 210 (1998)), "[b]ut statutes that speak to the rights or obligations of parties to a lawsuit establish 'claim-processing rules,'" and "should not be treated as 'jurisdictional prescriptions,'" *id.* at 1158 (quoting *Reed Elsevier,* 559 U.S. at 161, 130 S.Ct. 1237).

Our research has unearthed three decisions of our sister circuits that have addressed the jurisdictional status *vel non* of the FTCA's limitations provisions (specifically, § 2401(b)) since *Auburn Regional.*[7] p.1147 In two of those decisions, separate circuits—the Ninth (en banc) and the Seventh—concluded, in explicit reliance on *Auburn Regional,* that the limitations provisions were not jurisdictional. *See Kwai Fun Wong v. Beebe,* 732 F.3d 1030, 1047 (9th Cir.2013) (en banc) ("In short, nothing in the text, context, or purpose of § 2401(b) clearly indicates that the FTCA's six-month limitations period implicates the district courts' adjudicatory authority. We therefore hold that § 2401(b) is a nonjurisdictional claim-processing rule subject to the presumption in favor of equitable tolling...."), *cert. granted,* ___ U.S. ___, 134 S.Ct. 2873, 189 L.Ed.2d 831 (2014); *Arteaga v. United States,* 711 F.3d 828, 833 (7th Cir.2013) ("With regard to the Federal Tort Claims Act, the presumption that the deadline for exhausting remedies is not jurisdictional, far

from being rebutted by clear statutory language, is confirmed by such language....
[W]e think the answer is that [the FTCA statute of limitations] can be tolled—and
we doubt that the contrary approach has survived the Supreme Court's decision in
the *Auburn Regional Medical Center* case." (citations omitted)).

And in the third decision, in light of *Auburn Regional* and its progeny, the First
Circuit has cast doubt on the correctness of its caselaw that has concluded that §
2401(b)'s limitations provisions are jurisdictional. Specifically, the First Circuit
acknowledged that it had "previously opined that the FTCA's timeliness
requirements are jurisdictional." *Sanchez v. United States*, 740 F.3d 47, 54 (1st Cir.),
cert. denied, ___ U.S. ___, 135 S.Ct. 54, 190 L.Ed.2d 30 (2014). However, surveying
the post-*Auburn Regional* jurisprudential landscape, the court stated as follows: "The
Supreme Court's most recent guidance on what is 'jurisdictional' suggests that we
may have erred in presuming that subject matter jurisdiction hinged on compliance
with the FTCA's deadlines for presenting claims." *Id.*

Thus, in light of *Irwin* and *Auburn Regional*, we harbor some reservations regarding
whether our existing precedent relating to the jurisdictional status *vel non* of §
2401(b)'s time limitations is good law. However, "[w]e are bound by the precedent
of prior panels absent en banc reconsideration or *a superseding contrary decision by the
Supreme Court*." *In re Smith*, 10 F.3d 723, 724 (10th Cir.1993) (per curiam) (emphasis
added); *see, e.g.*, *Berry v. Stevinson Chevrolet*, 74 F.3d 980, 985 (10th Cir.1996) (noting
that, "[a]bsent an *intervening Supreme Court* or en banc decision justifying such action,
we lack the power to overrule [prior Tenth Circuit precedent]" (emphasis added)).
With due respect for existing precedent, we cannot conclude that the collective
message of *Irwin* and *Auburn Regional* is so indisputable and pellucid in the FTCA
context that it constitutes intervening (i.e., superseding) law that would permit us to
hold (without en banc consideration) that § 2401(b)'s limitations provisions—and,
in particular, the six-month provision—are *non* jurisdictional.

Neither *Irwin* nor *Auburn Regional* involved § 2401(b), nor did these cases construe
its terms. Furthermore, if the judicial reception of *Irwin* and the related Supreme
Court cases that followed on its heels is any indication, we can be confident of at
least one thing: the collective direction p.1148 of *Irwin* and *Auburn Regional* is likely
to be the subject of judicial debate and confusion in the FTCA context. In this
regard, we note that *Irwin* and the related cases of the Court issued relatively soon
thereafter have even generated intra-circuit inconsistencies. *Compare, e.g.*, *Perez v.
United States*, 167 F.3d 913, 915-16 (5th Cir.1999) (holding § 2401(b)'s limitations
provisions nonjurisdictional after observing that *Irwin* "undid the old rule that
equitable tolling was never available against the government, and thus placed the
jurisdictional nature of the FTCA statute of limitations into doubt"), *Glarner*, 30
F.3d at 701 (holding on behalf of the Sixth Circuit that the FTCA's limitations
provisions are not jurisdictional and subject to equitable tolling), *and Schmidt v.
United States*, 933 F.2d 639, 640 (8th Cir.1991) ("Because the FTCA's statute of
limitations is not jurisdictional, failure to comply with it is merely an affirmative
defense which the defendant has the burden of establishing."), *with Jackson v. United
States*, 751 F.3d 712, 719 (6th Cir.2014) (citing *Glarner* and noting that "whether the
time limitations in the FTCA are jurisdictional in nature" is an issue that "has
prompted some variance within this circuit," and noting that it "need not decide the
issue of whether the time limitations in the FTCA are jurisdictional in nature"), *In re*

FEMA Trailer Formaldehyde Prods. Liab. Litig., 646 F.3d 185, 189, 191 (5th Cir.2011) (per curiam) (without citing *Irwin* or *Perez*, holding that "[t]he FTCA's statute of limitations is jurisdictional" and that the plaintiff's claim thus "should not be equitably tolled"), *and T.L. ex rel. Ingram v. United States*, 443 F.3d 956, 961 (8th Cir.2006) (distinguishing but not clearly overruling *Schmidt* in concluding that "there is no inconsistency between viewing compliance with the statute of limitations as a jurisdictional prerequisite and applying the rule of equitable tolling"). In short, "[n]ot all of the Federal courts" in *Irwin's* wake have taken the same approach on the jurisdictional question. *Sharafeldin*, 854 A.2d at 1217; *see id.* at 1217-18 & n. 6 (collecting cases).[8]

Thus, we ultimately adhere to our existing precedent and hold that the district court properly dismissed the Barneses' FTCA lawsuit on jurisdictional grounds after correctly determining that the action was time-barred.

C

Because the six-month statute of limitations is jurisdictional, the Barneses cannot, as a matter of law, avail themselves of the doctrines of equitable estoppel or equitable tolling in seeking to excuse the otherwise tardy lawsuit. *See, e.g., Nat'l R.R. Passenger Corp.*, 536 U.S. at 121, 122 S.Ct. 2061; *Zipes*, 455 U.S. at 393, 102 S.Ct. 1127. However, like the district court, we feel constrained to observe that, even if these doctrines were available to the Barneses, they could secure no relief under them. "We review the district court's refusal to apply the doctrine of equitable estoppel for abuse of discretion." *Haynes Trane Serv. Agency, Inc. v. Am. Standard, Inc.*, 573 F.3d 947, 957 (10th Cir.2009) (quoting *Spaulding v. United Transp. Union*, 279 F.3d 901, 911 (10th Cir.2002)) (internal quotation marks omitted). Likewise, "[w]e review the district court's refusal p.1149 to apply equitable tolling for an abuse of discretion." *Alexander v. Oklahoma*, 382 F.3d 1206, 1215 (10th Cir.2004) (quoting *Garrett*, 362 F.3d at 695).

1

The "doctrine[ ] of equitable estoppel ... may bar a defendant from enforcing a statute of limitation when its own deception prevented a reasonably diligent plaintiff from bringing a timely claim." *Auburn Reg'l*, 133 S.Ct. at 830 (Sotomayor, J., concurring). However, "winning an equitable estoppel argument against the government is a tough business." *Wade Pediatrics v. Dep't of Health & Human Servs.*, 567 F.3d 1202, 1206 (10th Cir.2009). In this circuit, four basic elements are necessary to obtain equitable estoppel against the government:

> (1) the party to be estopped must know the facts; (2) he must intend that his conduct will be acted upon or must so act that the party asserting the estoppel has the right to believe that it was so intended; (3) the latter must be ignorant of the true facts; and (4) he must rely on the former's conduct to his injury.

Tsosie v. United States, 452 F.3d 1161, 1166 (10th Cir.2006) (quoting *Lurch v. United States*, 719 F.2d 333, 341 (10th Cir.1983)) (internal quotation marks omitted).

In addition to these four basic elements, we have required plaintiffs to make a showing of "affirmative misconduct" on the part of the government. *See Wade Pediatrics,* 567 F.3d at 1206; *Tsosie,* 452 F.3d at 1166. We need not address each of the four elements at length, because in any event, the Barneses have patently failed to establish "affirmative misconduct" by the government here. In this regard, even if we were to assume that the government failed to clearly indicate its intention to invoke § 2401(b)'s six-month statute of limitations, and that the Barneses relied upon this failure in electing not to file Lawsuit # 2 earlier, the Barneses have not even alleged, let alone made any showing, that the government's failure was an act of "affirmative misconduct."[9] Consequently, the district court did not abuse its discretion in rebuffing the Barneses' equitable-estoppel argument.

2

We now turn to the Barneses' argument that the statute of limitations in this case should have been equitably tolled. The district court, operating on the belief that the timeliness requirement was jurisdictional, found that tolling was unavailable. However, it noted in the alternative that even "if the doctrine of equitable tolling was applicable, the court would still find plaintiffs' claims time-barred." Aplt. App. at 102-03. We agree with the district court that the Barneses' claims here would be time-barred even assuming the availability of equitable tolling.

The Supreme Court has recently reiterated that "the general purpose of p.1150 statutes of limitations [is] 'to protect defendants against stale or unduly delayed claims.'" *Credit Suisse Sec. (USA) LLC v. Simmonds,* ___ U.S. ___, 132 S.Ct. 1414, 1420, 182 L.Ed.2d 446 (2012) (quoting *John R. Sand & Gravel Co. v. United States,* 552 U.S. 130, 133, 128 S.Ct. 750, 169 L.Ed.2d 591 (2008)). And, under "long-settled equitable-tolling principles[,] '[g]enerally, a litigant seeking equitable tolling bears the burden of establishing two elements: (1) that he has been pursuing his rights diligently, and (2) that some extraordinary circumstances stood in his way.'" *Id.* at 1419 (emphasis omitted) (quoting *Pace v. DiGuglielmo,* 544 U.S. 408, 418, 125 S.Ct. 1807, 161 L.Ed.2d 669 (2005)). The Court has "held that 'a garden variety claim of excusable neglect,' such as a simple 'miscalculation' that leads a lawyer to miss a filing deadline, does not warrant equitable tolling." *Holland v. Florida,* 560 U.S. 631, 651-52, 130 S.Ct. 2549, 177 L.Ed.2d 130 (2010) (citations omitted) (quoting *Irwin,* 498 U.S. at 96, 111 S.Ct. 453, and *Lawrence v. Florida,* 549 U.S. 327, 336, 127 S.Ct. 1079, 166 L.Ed.2d 924 (2007)).

Furthermore, as particularly pertinent to these facts, in *Pfannenstiel v. Merrill Lynch, Pierce, Fenner & Smith,* 477 F.3d 1155 (10th Cir.2007), we held that equitable tolling was unavailable where a plaintiff had "ample opportunity"—one month—to file a motion to vacate in a timely fashion, even though "he had no way of knowing about" the grounds for this motion until two months of the applicable three-month time limit had already elapsed. *Id.* at 1158; *see Impact Energy Res., LLC v. Salazar,* 693 F.3d 1239, 1247 (10th Cir.2012) (citing with approval D.C. Circuit precedent "den[ying] equitable tolling unless a delay in notification 'makes it impossible reasonably for the party to comply with the filing statute'" (quoting *Gardner v. FCC,* 530 F.2d 1086, 1091 n. 24 (D.C.Cir.1976))).

Similarly, in *Impact Energy Resources,* we held that, where the plaintiffs had more than eighty days in which to timely file their claims and did not claim that the delay "meaningfully limited their ability to comply with the ... statute of limitations," equitable tolling was unmerited. 693 F.3d at 1247-48. Indeed, we noted that even forty-five days (the amount of time the plaintiffs claimed was available to them) was "longer than the thirty days approved in *Pfannenstiel.*" *Id.* at 1248.

In the present case, the district court explained why, in its view, equitable tolling could not save the Barneses:

> [The Barneses] had a month after the dismissal of their claims against the government (until April 25, 2012) to refile their claims, but instead waited until August 22, 2012, to file their lawsuit, more than four months later. While plaintiffs may have been unaware that the government would argue their claims were untimely, they were aware, from the time the case was removed, that the government had taken the position that the court lacked subject matter jurisdiction over their FTCA claims. If plaintiffs had researched the issue when it was first raised and proceeded to dismiss and then refile their claims against the United States, their claims would not have been barred.

Aplt.App. at 103. Reviewing this aspect of the court's order, it is plain that the district court did not abuse its discretion.

The Barneses essentially ask the court to toll the statute of limitations in this case due to their misunderstanding of the law. They assail as "unfair[ ]" the district court's "suggest[ion] that the Appellants were being inattentive in refiling" when they did, and they explain that "the Appellants had every reason to believe there was no statute of limitation issue." Aplt. Opening Br. at 22-23. Such arguments p.1151 amount to no more than a contention of excusable neglect, and that is not good enough. *See Holland,* 560 U.S. at 651-52, 130 S.Ct. 2549.

Significantly, the Barneses plainly failed to pursue their rights diligently, as required by our caselaw. Just like the plaintiffs in *Pfannenstiel* and *Impact Energy Resources,* the Barneses had ample opportunity in which to timely file, but failed to do so. After Lawsuit # 1 was dismissed without prejudice on March 23, 2012, they had more than thirty days (the threshold identified in *Impact Energy Resources,* 693 F.3d at 1248) during which they could have refiled in compliance with § 2401(b). Instead, they did not do so for five months.[10]

The Barneses' only response to any of this appears to be that they did not believe there was any urgency to refile, based on their belief that, having deemed their administrative claims denied and having filed Lawsuit # 1, they were no longer subject to *any* statute of limitations. But, as we have explained, this belief reflects a wholly unjustified and unprecedented interpretation of § 2401(b) and § 2675(a). Moreover, the BATF's final denial of the Barneses' administrative claims in this case expressly advised the Barneses that they had six months thereafter in which to file a lawsuit in an appropriate federal court, putting the Barneses on notice that, whatever their own understanding of the law, the *government* believed that the six-month statute of limitations began to run on October 25, 2011.

In sum, the Barneses had at least a full month after the district court dismissed Lawsuit # 1 during which they could have timely refiled. They did not do so, nor have they alleged any other extraordinary circumstances that would have prevented them from doing so. Consequently, even if it were available to them, the Barneses could have gained no succor from the equitable-tolling doctrine. The district court thus did not abuse its discretion in refusing to toll the statute of limitations on the Barneses' claims.

III

For the reasons set forth above, the district court correctly held that the Barneses' claims in this matter were time-barred under the six-month statute of limitations in 28 U.S.C. § 2401(b) and properly dismissed the action for lack of subject-matter jurisdiction under Federal Rule of Civil Procedure 12(b)(1). We observe, however, that the district court dismissed the lawsuit *with* prejudice. Jurisdictional dismissals ordinarily should be entered *without* prejudice. *See Brereton v. Bountiful City Corp.*, 434 F.3d 1213, 1218 (10th Cir.2006) ("[O]ur prior, long-standing line of cases requir[es] that a dismissal for lack of jurisdiction be without prejudice."); *Albert v. Smith's Food & Drug Ctrs., Inc.*, 356 F.3d 1242, 1249 (10th Cir.2004) ("In cases where the district court has determined that it lacks jurisdiction, dismissal of a claim must be without prejudice."). Accordingly, in our ultimate disposition, we remand to the district court to correct the judgment by entering a *without*-prejudice dismissal.

p.1152 IV

For the foregoing reasons, we AFFIRM the judgment of the district court dismissing the Barneses' action for lack of subject-matter jurisdiction. We REMAND the case with instructions to the district court to enter a dismissal *without* prejudice.

KELLY, Circuit Judge, concurs in the result.

[1] In describing the factual background to this case, we rely in part on the records from Mr. Barnes's earlier criminal and civil cases, of which we take judicial notice. *See United States v. Ahidley*, 486 F.3d 1184, 1192 n. 5 (10th Cir.2007) ("[W]e may exercise our discretion to take judicial notice of publicly-filed records in our court and certain other courts concerning matters that bear directly upon the disposition of the case at hand."); *St. Louis Baptist Temple, Inc. v. FDIC*, 605 F.2d 1169, 1172 (10th Cir.1979) ("[F]ederal courts, in appropriate circumstances, may take notice of proceedings in other courts, both within and without the federal judicial system....").

[2] The relevant statutory provision states, in pertinent part: "A tort claim against the United States shall be forever barred ... unless action is begun within six months after the date of mailing, by certified or registered mail, of notice of final denial of the claim by the agency to which it was presented." 28 U.S.C. § 2401(b).

[3] Although the Barneses' initial complaint had improperly named the BATF as defendant instead of the United States, which the FTCA requires, *see Franklin Sav. Corp. v. United States*, 180 F.3d 1124, 1142 (10th Cir. 1999), the amended complaint in Lawsuit # 1 remedied this defect so that the district court's dismissal without prejudice regarded properly pleaded claims against the United States.

[4] Though we have not specifically addressed this issue, it is not contested here. Thus, for purposes of this appeal, we will assume without deciding that, absent final agency action, plaintiffs ordinarily may deem their administrative claims denied and file suit at any time after the six-month period referred to in § 2675(a).

[5] *Harvey*, for example, simply recites (without analysis) language from *In re Franklin Savings Corp.* to the effect that because "timeliness 'is one of the conditions of the government's waiver of sovereign immunity under the FTCA,'" it is a jurisdictional prerequisite to suit. 685 F.3d at 947 (quoting *In re Franklin Sav. Corp.*, 385 F.3d at 1287). *In re Franklin Savings Corp.* itself provides no greater elaboration, simply stating the same conclusion, supported by a citation to our 2003 opinion in *Dahl. See* 385 F.3d at 1287. *Dahl* reflects more of the same, explaining briefly that § 2401(b) is a condition on the government's waiver of sovereign immunity and, "[t]hus, if a litigant does not satisfy the timing requirement of § 2401(b), the district court must dismiss for lack of subject matter jurisdiction." 319 F.3d at 1228 (citing *Casias*, 532 F.2d at 1340 n. 1). Our decision in *Casias* is apparently the first case in which we described § 2401(b)'s statute of limitations as jurisdictional. It also engages in no analysis whatsoever, simply referring to the jurisdictional nature of the limitations provision in a footnote that cites a Ninth Circuit case, *Caton v. United States*, 495 F.2d 635 (9th Cir.1974). *See Casias*, 532 F.2d at 1340 n. 1.

[6] Indeed, one commentator has gone so far as to assert that "every court of appeals to address the question has concluded or suggested that the FTCA provision is not jurisdictional and instead falls within the presumption of *Irwin v. Department of Veterans Affairs*—that statutes of limitations in federal government cases are subject to equitable tolling." Sisk, *supra*, at 559 (italics added) (footnote omitted). However, we are cautious of such broad statements and decline to undertake here a precise jurisprudential headcount regarding the positions of the various courts with respect to the jurisdictional status *vel non* of § 2401(b) and the related issue of equitable tolling. As suggested in text *infra*, the courts' holdings after *Irwin* are not uniform and reflect some confusion, even within circuits, regarding these issues. It is clear, however, that *Irwin* caused several courts to rethink their historical position that the FTCA's limitations provisions are jurisdictional.

[7] Although we have not applied *Auburn Regional's* bright-line rubric in the FTCA context, we have employed it in other settings. For example, in *United States v. McGaughy*, 670 F.3d 1149 (10th Cir.2012), we applied the test to the fourteen-day time limit in Federal Rule of Criminal Procedure 35(a). There, we noted that "[t]o be jurisdictional, the restriction on the court's authority not only must be specified by Congress—it must also express a clear Congressional intent to be jurisdictional," and wrote that the Supreme Court's decision in *Gonzalez v. Thaler*, ___ U.S. ___, 132 S.Ct. 641, 181 L.Ed.2d 619 (2012), "suggests courts must look to a restriction's 'textual, contextual, and historical backdrop.'" *McGaughy*, 670 F.3d at 1156 (quoting *Gonzalez*, 132 S.Ct. at 652 n. 8). The statutory provision underpinning Rule 35(a) used overtly jurisdictional language. It provided that "*[t]he court* may not modify a term of imprisonment once it has been imposed except that... *the court* may modify an imposed term of imprisonment to the extent otherwise expressly permitted by ... Rule 35." 18 U.S.C. § 3582(c)(1)(B) (emphases added). Accordingly, we held that Rule 35(a)'s deadline was "given jurisdictional force by the very provision authorizing courts to correct errors." *McGaughy*, 670 F.3d at 1158. Similarly, in

Emann v. Latture (In re Latture), 605 F.3d 830 (10th Cir.2010), we concluded that Federal Rule of Bankruptcy Procedure 8002(a)'s time limit for filing an appeal in a bankruptcy matter was jurisdictional largely because the statutory provision imposing this time limit, 28 U.S.C. § 158(c)(2), was "located in the same section [of the statute] granting ... jurisdiction to hear appeals." 605 F.3d at 837. Most recently, in *Utah ex rel. Utah Department of Environmental Quality v. U.S. EPA,* we applied the bright-line rule in concluding that the sixty-day deadline for filing a petition for judicial review under the Clean Air Act is a jurisdictional limit. *See* 765 F.3d at 1258. Citing *Auburn Regional,* we examined "the textual, contextual, and historical treatment" of the statutory deadline and concluded that all of these factors supported that conclusion. *Utah,* 765 F.3d at 1262.

[8] We are cognizant in any event that the Supreme Court has granted certiorari in the Ninth Circuit's *Kwai Fun Wong* case, where the question presented relates to whether the FTCA's limitations provisions are jurisdictional. *See* Resp't Br., *United States v. Kwai Fun Wong,* No. 13-1074, 2014 WL 5804278, at i (Nov. 4, 2014) ("Is the six-month limit for filing suit under the Federal Tort Claims Act, 28 U.S.C. § 2401(b), jurisdictional?"). Presumably, the Court will shed some light on the matter.

[9] At most, the Barneses accuse the government of being sloppy with language. However, the undisputed text of the letter the BATF sent the Barneses denying their administrative claims referred directly to the sixth-month limitation: "If you[ ] ... are dissatisfied with this action, a lawsuit must be filed in an appropriate United States district court not later than six months after the date of the mailing of this notification." Aplt.App. at 37. Nevertheless, the Barneses argue that this letter was unclear, complaining that "[i]f the [government] intended the Appellants to have 'originated' or 'instituted[,'] and not merely 'filed' an action, ... they ... could have used those words expressly enumerating a first-time commencement." Aplt. Opening Br. at 28. In light of the Barneses' failure to allege any affirmative misconduct on the part of the government, advancing this grievance cannot secure them relief.

[10] We note, moreover, that the fact that the Barneses had only a month in which to refile was a result of their own failure to take reasonably diligent steps. As the district court noted, the Barneses knew as early as September 2011, when Lawsuit # 1 was removed to federal district court, that there was at least potentially a jurisdictional issue with that first lawsuit due to their having filed in state court. At any point thereafter, the Barneses could have voluntarily dismissed their claim and refiled, thereby avoiding the entire problem now before us.

728 F.3d 1239 (2013)

Delbert INGRAM, Plaintiff-Appellant,

v.

Hashib D. FARUQUE, M.D.; Yan Feng, M.D.; David Wood, Donna Delise; Kyle Inhofe; Lt. Michael Stevenson; Captain Tim Collins; Department of Veteran Affairs, Defendants-Appellees.

No. 11-6341.

United States Court of Appeals, Tenth Circuit.

September 6, 2013.

Ingram v. Faruque, 728 F. 3d 1239 (10th Cir. 2013)

p.1240 Eric D. Cotton, The Cotton Law Firm, PLLC, Edmond, OK, for Plaintiff-Appellant.

Suzanne Mitchell, Assistant United States Attorney (Sanford C. Coats, United States Attorney, and Laura M. Grimes, Assistant United States Attorney, with her on the brief), Oklahoma City, OK, for Defendants-Appellees.

Before MATHESON, EBEL, and MURPHY, Circuit Judges.

EBEL, Circuit Judge.

INTRODUCTION

Plaintiff-Appellant Delbert Ingram appeals from a district court's dismissal of his claims against Defendants-Appellees ("Defendants"). Mr. Ingram sued Defendants-Appellees—Dr. Hashib D. Faruque, Dr. Yan Feng, Donna Delise, Kyle Inhofe, Lt. Michael Stevenson, and Captain Tim Collins[1]—claiming that Defendants had violated his rights under the Fourth and Fifth Amendments of the U.S. Constitution by holding him in a psychiatric ward for over twenty-four hours without his consent. Defendants filed motions to dismiss, arguing that, among other things, the district court lacked subject matter jurisdiction over the action, because the Federal Tort Claims Act ("FTCA") provided the sole remedy for Mr. Ingram's claims, and that the court therefore should not authorize a judicial remedy under *Bivens v. Six Unknown Named Agents,* 403 U.S. 388, 91 S.Ct. 1999, 29 L.Ed.2d 619 (1971). Fed. R.Civ.P. 12(b)(1).

The district court agreed that it lacked subject matter jurisdiction over Mr. Ingram's claims, and therefore granted Defendants' motions to dismiss. Specifically, the court concluded that Mr. Ingram had a remedy available under 38 U.S.C. § 7316 ("VA Immunity Statute"), which applies the remedy available against the United States under the FTCA to damages arising from the provision of medical services by health care employees of the Veteran's Administration ("VA"). Because of the availability of a remedy under the VA Immunity Statute, it concluded that Mr. Ingram did not have a cause of action under *Bivens.*

Having jurisdiction under 28 U.S.C. § 1291, we affirm on the basis that Mr. Ingram has, or has had, an adequate alternative remedy available through the VA Immunity Statute and the FTCA,[2] and it is therefore not appropriate to authorize a p.1241 *Bivens* remedy for Mr. Ingram. Accordingly, the district court did not err in ruling that it lacked subject matter jurisdiction over Mr. Ingram's claims.

BACKGROUND

I. Factual Background

Mr. Ingram is an employee at the Oklahoma City Department of Veterans Affairs Medical Center ("VAMC"). At the time of the incidents resulting in this appeal, VAMC police received a report from one of Mr. Ingram's coworkers, stating that Mr. Ingram had said that he had been thinking about killing his supervisor. Defendant Captain Collins (VAMC's Assistant Chief of Police) reported the threat to Dr. Nasreen Bukhari (not a party to this action), who recommended that Mr. Ingram receive a psychiatric assessment. Dr. Bukhari informed Defendant Inhofe (VAMC's Chief of Human Resources) and Defendant Delise (VAMC's Acting Assistant Director) of the situation. Mr. Inhofe and Ms. Delise decided to talk to Mr. Ingram about the reported threat and ask him to go to the Emergency Room for evaluation, in accordance with Dr. Bukhari's instructions. Mr. Ingram agreed to go to the emergency room with Mr. Inhofe and Ms. Delise. Captain Collins directed Defendant Lt. Stevenson (a VAMC police officer) to escort Mr. Inhofe, Ms. Delise, and Mr. Ingram to the emergency room.

In the emergency room, Mr. Inhofe and Ms. Delise accompanied Mr. Ingram to a padded isolation room. Subsequently, another physician, Dr. Karunesh Singhal (not a party to this action) filled out an affidavit stating that Mr. Ingram "has threatened to assault his supervisor and in my evaluation is having homicidal ideation," and that on that basis, Mr. Ingram was sufficiently ill "that immediate emergency action [was] necessary." Aplt.App. at 78. When Mr. Ingram attempted to leave the emergency room, Lt. Stevenson informed him that, although he was not under arrest, he was not free to leave the emergency room. Mr. Ingram asserts that Lt. Stevenson said this "with his hand on his firearm," and that after making this statement, Lt. Stevenson shut and locked the door to the isolation room. Aplt. Br. 4.

Mr. Inhofe and Ms. Delise waited with Mr. Ingram until Defendant Dr. Faruque (a VAMC staff psychiatrist) arrived. After Dr. Faruque arrived, he examined Mr. Ingram. During the examination, Mr. Ingram admitted saying something about "doing foolish things to [his supervisor]," but denied having the intent to hurt or kill her. Aplt.App. at 104. Dr. Faruque's report following the examination recommended "[i]npatient admission to provide safe environment and further assessment."[3] Aplt.App. at 104. Mr. Ingram p.1242 agreed to be admitted for further evaluation. Dr. Faruque's report states that he shared this plan with Dr. Singhal, and that he "emphasized that [Mr. Ingram] is not to leave [the] ER except for transfer to [the psychiatric ward]," and "suggested that [Mr. Ingram] be transferred from [the] ER to [the psychiatric ward] under police escort." *Id.* at 105.

After arriving in the psychiatric ward, Defendant Dr. Feng (another VAMC staff psychiatrist) interviewed Mr. Ingram for the inpatient admission evaluation. Mr. Ingram denied making threats about his supervisor and stated that he wished to leave the hospital. But Dr. Feng informed Mr. Ingram that "because of the report of the threat and the Third Party Affidavit [signed by Dr. Singhal], [she] was obligated to conduct an investigation to determine whether he and other people would be safe if he were discharged from the hospital." *Id.* at 106. She told Mr.

Ingram that he could voluntarily sign himself in for assessment, or that she would initiate the paperwork to obtain an Emergency Order of Detention.

After this conversation, Mr. Ingram agreed to admit himself to the hospital, and signed a voluntary consent form. But subsequently, although he repeatedly requested to leave, Mr. Ingram was held in the psychiatric ward for over twenty-four hours before being medically cleared and released.

II. Procedural Background

Mr. Ingram subsequently filed an action against Defendants in their individual capacities. He asserted that they had collectively violated his rights under the Fourth and Fifth Amendments by detaining him against his will, and he sought a remedy. Defendants filed motions to dismiss, arguing that, among other things, the court lacked subject matter jurisdiction over Mr. Ingram's claims. *See* Fed.R.Civ.P. 12(b)(1).

A primary argument of the Defendants was that Mr. Ingram should not be permitted to pursue a cause of action under *Bivens v. Six Unknown Named Agents,* 403 U.S. 388, 91 S.Ct. 1999, 29 L.Ed.2d 619 (1971), because under the VA Immunity Statute, the FTCA provided the sole remedy for his claims. The district court agreed, concluding that Mr. Ingram's claims fell under the VA Immunity Statute, and that he therefore could not bring an action under *Bivens.* Accordingly, it ruled that it lacked subject matter jurisdiction over Mr. Ingram's claims, and dismissed the claims against all Defendants without prejudice. Within thirty days, Mr. Ingram filed a motion for reconsideration, which was denied by the district court. Mr. Ingram timely appeals.

STANDARD OF REVIEW

Rule 12(b)(1) motions can take the form of either a "facial" or a "factual" attack on the court's subject matter jurisdiction. *Stuart v. Colo. Interstate Gas Co.,* 271 F.3d 1221, 1225 (10th Cir.2001). Where the party challenging subject-matter jurisdiction mounts a facial attack, "the district court must accept the allegations in the complaint as true." *Id.* But if the challenging party brings a factual attack by "go[ing] beyond allegations contained in the complaint and challeng[ing] the facts upon which subject matter jurisdiction is based ... [the] court has wide discretion to allow affidavits, other documents, and a limited evidentiary hearing to resolve disputed jurisdictional facts." *Id.* (internal quotation marks omitted). Here, the district court determined that it would "consider the materials appended to the parties' briefs," Aplt.App. at 166; thus, we will treat this as a factual attack and likewise consider the materials presented by the parties to the district court.

p.1243 "We review de novo ... the district court's determination of subject-matter jurisdiction...." *Rio Grande Silvery Minnow (Hybognathus amarus) v. Bureau of Reclamation,* 599 F.3d 1165, 1175 (10th Cir.2010). Moreover, "[w]e review the [district] court's findings of jurisdictional facts for clear error," and "[a] finding is clearly erroneous when although there is evidence to support it, the reviewing court on the entire evidence is left with the definite and firm conviction that a mistake has been committed." *Id.* (second alteration in original) (internal quotation marks omitted). But we will "view the evidence in the light most favorable to the district court's ruling." *Id.* (internal quotation marks omitted). Thus, "[i]f the district court's account of the evidence is plausible in light of the record viewed in its entirety, the court of appeals may not reverse." *Id.* (internal quotation marks omitted).

DISCUSSION

In *Bivens v. Six Unknown Named Agents of Federal Bureau of Narcotics,* 403 U.S. 388, 91 S.Ct. 1999, 29 L.Ed.2d 619 (1971), the U.S. Supreme "Court recognized for the first time an implied private action for damages against federal officers alleged to have violated a citizen's constitutional rights." *Ashcroft v. Iqbal,* 556 U.S. 662, 675, 129 S.Ct. 1937, 173 L.Ed.2d 868 (2009) (internal quotation marks omitted). In *Bivens,* the Court "held that a victim of a Fourth Amendment violation by federal officers may bring suit for money damages against the officers in federal court." *Corr. Servs. Corp. v. Malesko,* 534 U.S. 61, 66, 122 S.Ct. 515, 151 L.Ed.2d 456 (2001) (citing *Bivens,* 403 U.S. 388, 91 S.Ct. 1999). Following *Bivens,* the Supreme Court has authorized actions under *Bivens* on only two occasions: first, the Court authorized a cause of action under *Bivens* to redress a violation of the equal protection component of the Due Process Clause of the Fifth Amendment, *see Davis v. Passman,* 442 U.S. 228, 99 S.Ct. 2264, 60 L.Ed.2d 846 (1979), and second, the Court authorized a *Bivens* remedy for the estate of a prisoner who had allegedly died as the result of government officials' deliberate indifference to his medical needs, in violation of his rights under the Eighth Amendment, *see Carlson v. Green,* 446 U.S. 14, 100 S.Ct. 1468, 64 L.Ed.2d 15 (1980).

But since the Supreme Court's last decision to authorize a *Bivens* remedy in 1980, the Court has "refused to extend *Bivens* liability to any new context or new category of defendants." *Malesko,* 534 U.S. at 68, 122 S.Ct. 515. Indeed, even though the "Court has had to decide in several different instances whether to imply a *Bivens* action[,] ... in each instance it has decided against the existence of such an action." *Minneci v. Pollard,* ___ U.S. ___, 132 S.Ct. 617, 622, 181 L.Ed.2d 606 (2012).

The standards for determining whether a *Bivens* remedy is appropriate have evolved over time. In *Green,* the Court explained that a *Bivens* action is available unless (1) "defendants demonstrate special factors counseling hesitation in the absence of affirmative action by Congress," or (2) "defendants show that Congress has provided an alternative remedy which it explicitly declared to be a substitute for recovery directly under the Constitution and viewed as equally effective." 446 U.S. at 18-19, 100 S.Ct. 1468 (emphasis omitted). But since *Green,* the Supreme Court has relaxed these requirements, and has declined to fashion a *Bivens* remedy, even where statutory remedies may not be equally effective.

For instance, in *Bush v. Lucas,* the Court explained that the question whether a *Bivens* cause of action is available "cannot be answered simply by noting that existing remedies do not provide complete relief for the plaintiff." 462 U.S. 367, 388, 103 S.Ct. 2404, 76 L.Ed.2d 648 (1983). In p.1244 *Bush,* even though the Court "assum[ed]... a federal right ha[d] been violated and Congress ha[d] provided a less than complete remedy for the wrong," *id.* at 373, 103 S.Ct. 2404, the Court declined to fashion a *Bivens* remedy for a federal employee who claimed that his superior had violated his rights under the First Amendment, *id.* at 368, 103 S.Ct. 2404. The Court held that because the claim at issue "ar[o]se out of an employment relationship that [was] governed by comprehensive procedural and substantive provisions giving meaningful remedies against the United States, it would be inappropriate for [the] Court to supplement that regulatory scheme with a new nonstatutory damages remedy." *Id.* at 367, 103 S.Ct. 2404.

Similarly, in *Schweiker v. Chilicky,* the Court stated that "[t]he absence of statutory relief for a constitutional violation ... does not by any means necessarily imply that courts should award money damages against the officers responsible for the violation." 487 U.S. 412, 421-22, 108 S.Ct. 2460, 101 L.Ed.2d 370 (1988). Indeed, the Court held that "the concept of 'special factors counseling hesitation in the absence of affirmative action by Congress' has proved to include an appropriate judicial deference to indications that congressional inaction has not been inadvertent." *Id.* at 423, 108 S.Ct. 2460. Accordingly, it declined to authorize a *Bivens* remedy to address the improper denial of Social Security disability benefits, *id.* at 414, 91 S.Ct. 1999, even though the Court acknowledged that "Congress ha[d] failed to provide for 'complete relief,'" *id.* at 425, 91 S.Ct. 1999, and "[t]he creation of a *Bivens* remedy would obviously offer the prospect of relief for injuries that must now go unredressed," *id.*

Consistent with *Bush* and *Schweiker,* in its recent jurisprudence, the Supreme Court has generally prescribed two steps to apply when determining whether to recognize a *Bivens* remedy. *See Wilkie v. Robbins,* 551 U.S. 537, 550, 127 S.Ct. 2588, 168 L.Ed.2d 389 (2007); *accord Minneci,* 132 S.Ct. at 623. First, "[t]here is the question whether any alternative, existing process for protecting the interest amounts to a convincing reason for the Judicial Branch to refrain from providing a new and freestanding remedy in damages." *Wilkie,* 551 U.S. at 550, 127 S.Ct. 2588, Second, "even in the absence of an alternative, a *Bivens* remedy is a subject of judgment;" and therefore "the federal courts must make the kind of remedial determination that is appropriate for a common-law tribunal, paying particular heed ... to any special factors counseling hesitation before authorizing a new kind of federal litigation." *Id.*

In determining whether there is a *Bivens* remedy available to Mr. Ingram, we will first consider whether the VA Immunity Statute provides an alternative, existing process that amounts to a convincing reason to refrain from creating a new *Bivens* remedy. We conclude that it does; specifically, we hold that the text of the VA Immunity Statute creates an exclusive remedy that precludes a *Bivens* claim. We then consider whether Mr. Ingram's claims fall within the scope of the VA Immunity Statute, such that he is precluded from bringing a cause of action under *Bivens.* We conclude that they do. Mr. Ingram therefore may not pursue a cause of action under *Bivens.* Accordingly, we need not consider whether there are other "special factors counseling hesitation before authorizing" a *Bivens* remedy. *See id.*

I. The VA Immunity Statute Provides an Alternative, Existing Process That Precludes a *Bivens* Remedy

Mr. Ingram argues that he should be allowed to pursue a cause of action under p.1245 *Bivens,* because he contends that Defendants held him against his will in violation of his rights under the Fourth and Fifth Amendments to the U.S. Constitution. But the district court determined that the VA Immunity Statute provided Mr. Ingram with a remedy for his claims, such that he did not have available a cause of action under *Bivens.* This section will first set out the legal framework for analyzing the VA Immunity Statute, and will then consider whether the Statute precludes a cause of action under *Bivens.*

A. The VA Immunity Statute

As context for analyzing the VA Immunity Statute, "[t]he doctrine of sovereign immunity prohibits suits against the United States except in those instances in which it has specifically consented to be sued." *Fent v. Okla. Water Res. Bd.,* 235 F.3d 553, 556 (10th Cir.2000) (internal quotation marks omitted). "The FTCA constitutes a limited waiver of the federal government's sovereign immunity from private suit." *Estate of Trentadue ex rel. Aguilar v. United States,* 397 F.3d 840, 852 (10th Cir.2005). "When federal employees are sued for damages for harms caused in the course of their employment, the [FTCA] generally authorizes substitution of the United States as the defendant." *Hui v. Castaneda,* 559 U.S. 799, 130 S.Ct. 1845, 1848, 176 L.Ed.2d 703 (2010) (citation omitted). And "[t]he prerequisite for liability under the FTCA is a 'negligent or wrongful act or omission of any employee of the [Government] while acting within the scope of his office or employment, under circumstances where the United States, if a private person, would be liable to the claimant in accordance with the law of the place where the act or omission occurred.'" *Id.* at 1853 n. 38 (quoting 28 U.S.C. § 1346(b)). In other words, the FTCA allows the United States to be sued for claims arising out of negligent or wrongful acts or omissions of its employees, when such employees are acting within the scope of their duties. 28 U.S.C. § 1346(b)(1).

The VA Immunity Statute applies the remedy available against the United States under the FTCA to damages arising from the provision of medical services by health care employees of the VA. *See* 38 U.S.C. § 7316(a)(1), (f). Section 7316(a)(1) states:

> The remedy ... against the United States provided by sections 1346(b) and 2672 of title 28 ... for damages for personal injury, including death, allegedly arising from malpractice or negligence of a health care employee of the Administration in furnishing health care or treatment while in the exercise of that employee's duties in or for the Administration shall be exclusive of any other civil action or proceeding by reason of the same subject matter against the health care employee (or employee's estate) whose act or omission gave rise to such claim.

38 U.S.C. § 7316(a)(1).

There are some exceptions to the FTCA's waiver of sovereign immunity. Specifically, 28 U.S.C. § 2680(h) states that the provisions of the FTCA

> shall not apply to ... [a]ny claim arising out of assault, battery, false imprisonment, false arrest, malicious prosecution, abuse of process, libel, slander, misrepresentation, deceit, or interference with contract rights....

28 U.S.C. § 2680(h). Thus, under the general provisions of the FTCA, the United States cannot be sued for claims arising out of these enumerated intentional torts. *See id.* But in the context of the VA Immunity Statute, § 7316(f) states:

> The exception provided in section 2680(h) of title 28 shall not apply to any claim arising out of a negligent or p.1246 wrongful act or omission of any person described in subsection (a) in furnishing medical care or treatment (including medical care or treatment furnished in the course of a clinical study or investigation) while in the exercise of such person's duties in or for the Administration.

38 U.S.C. § 7316(f). In other words, "§ 2680(h) does not bar application of the FTCA to [intentional] tort claims arising out of the conduct of VA medical personnel within the scope of" 38 U.S.C. § 7316(f). *Franklin v. United States,* 992 F.2d 1492, 1502 (10th Cir.1993).[4]

B. The VA Immunity Statute Provides an Exclusive Remedy

We now consider whether the VA Immunity Statute provides an alternative, existing process that amounts to a convincing reason to refrain from creating a new *Bivens* remedy. We conclude that the Statute provides an exclusive remedy that precludes the creation of a remedy under *Bivens.*

In our analysis, there are two relevant provisions of the VA Immunity Statute at issue—§ 7316(a)(1) and § 7316(f). We will consider each in turn.

1. Section § 7316(a)(1)

The Supreme Court has determined that language similar to that contained in § 7316(a)(1) creates an exclusive cause of action that precludes a *Bivens* remedy. In *Hui,* the Supreme Court concluded that 42 U.S.C. § 233(a) precluded a *Bivens* action against U.S. Public Health Service ("PHS") personnel. 130 S.Ct. at 1848. In relevant part, § 233(a) provides:

> The remedy against the United States provided by sections 1346(b) and 2672 of Title 28 ... for damage for personal injury, including death, resulting from the performance of medical, surgical, dental, or related functions, including the conduct of clinical studies or investigation, by any commissioned officer or employee of the Public Health Service while acting within the scope of his office or employment, shall be exclusive of any other civil action or proceeding by reason of the same subject-matter against the officer or employee (or his estate) whose act or omission gave rise to the claim.

42 U.S.C. § 233(a).

As background, in *Hui,* a man was detained by U.S. Immigration and Customs Enforcement at the San Diego Correctional Facility. 130 S.Ct. at 1848. While there, he sought a biopsy for a lesion, but a biopsy was never provided. *Id.* at 1848-89. After his release from prison, later biopsy results confirmed that the detainee was suffering from cancer, and after unsuccessful treatment, he died. *Id.* at 1849.

Before his death, the detainee brought a cause of action under *Bivens,* suing PHS personnel for a violation of his constitutional rights. *Id.* at 1849. PHS personnel moved to dismiss on the grounds that " § 233(a) g[a]ve[] them absolute immunity from *Bivens* actions by making a suit against the United States under the FTCA the exclusive remedy for harms caused by PHS personnel in the course of their medical or related duties." *Id.* at 1849-50. The district court denied the motion, and the Ninth Circuit affirmed. *Id.* at 1850. p.1247 Among other things, the Ninth Circuit applied the holding in *Green* that "a *Bivens* remedy is unavailable only when an alternative remedy is both expressly declared to be a substitute and can be viewed as equally effective," and concluded that " § 233(a) d[id] not expressly make the remedy under the FTCA a substitute for relief under *Bivens*." *Id.* Moreover, "[f]or essentially the reasons given in [*Green,*] the [Ninth Circuit] Court of Appeals also determined that the FTCA remedy is not equally effective as a *Bivens* remedy." *Id.* (citation omitted).

The Supreme Court reversed the Ninth Circuit's decision, holding that the text of § 233(a) precluded a *Bivens* action against petitioners. *Id.* at 1855. Specifically, the Court concluded that § "233(a) makes the FTCA remedy against the United States 'exclusive of any other civil action or proceeding' for any personal injury caused by a PHS officer or employee performing a medical or related function 'while acting within the scope of his office or employment,'" and it held that "[b]ased on the plain language of § 233(a) ... PHS officers and employees are not personally subject to *Bivens* actions for harms arising out of such conduct." *Id.* at 1848.

In this case, the language of 38 U.S.C. § 7316(a)(1) mirrors the language of § 233(a). Both 38 U.S.C. § 7316(a) and 42 U.S.C. § 233(a) state that, under these provisions, "[t]he remedy against the United States provided by sections 1346(b) and 2672 of title 28 ... shall be *exclusive* of *any* other civil action or proceeding by reason of *the same subject-matter* against the ... employee ... whose act or omission gave rise to [the] claim." 38 U.S.C. § 7316(a)(1) (emphases added); *accord* 42 U.S.C. § 233(a). In *Hui,* the Court stated:

> By its terms, § 233(a) limits recovery for such conduct to suits against the United States. The breadth of the words "exclusive" and "any" supports this reading, as does the provision's inclusive reference to all civil proceedings arising out of "the same subject-matter."

130 S.Ct. at 1851. The same is true here; the wording of § 7316(a)(1) indicates that the VA Immunity Statute is an exclusive remedy.

Mr. Ingram argues the Supreme Court's holding in *Carlson v. Green* requires that he be allowed to proceed with a cause of action under *Bivens*. In *Green,* a respondent sued on behalf of her deceased son's estate, alleging that he had died from injuries inflicted by federal prison officials in violation of his rights under the Eighth Amendment. 446 U.S. at 16, 100 S.Ct. 1468. In authorizing a cause of action under *Bivens,* the Court rejected prison officials' argument that the remedy available under the FTCA precluded respondent's *Bivens* claim. *Id.* at 19-20, 100 S.Ct. 1468. Although both *Green* and Mr. Ingram's case involve the question whether the remedy available under the FTCA precludes a *Bivens* claim, *Green* does not control this case.

Green's claim against federal prison officials for alleged violations of his Eighth Amendment rights did not implicate the VA Immunity Statute. Thus, the Court in *Green* was not considering the VA Immunity Statute when it determined that the

FTCA did not foreclose a cause of action under *Bivens.* And, the Supreme Court recognized in *Hui* that some statutory provisions may make the FTCA an exclusive remedy, such that it is not appropriate for courts to authorize a cause of action under *Bivens.* 130 S.Ct. at 1848. Thus, although there may be circumstances where the availability of a remedy under the FTCA may not foreclose a *Bivens* action, *Green,* 446 U.S. at 19-20, 100 S.Ct. 1468, other statutory provisions relating to the FTCA do preclude such a remedy. The Supreme Court has held that one such provision is p.1248 42 U.S.C. § 233(a). *Hui,* 130 S.Ct. at 1855. Similarly, we hold that § 7316(a)(1) makes the VA Immunity Statute an exclusive remedy and therefore precludes a claim under *Bivens.*

2. Section § 7316(f)

Section 7316(f) expands § 7316(a)(1) to provide a remedy under the FTCA for intentional torts arising in the context of VA health care employees providing medical care or treatment. *See* 38 U.S.C. § 7316(f). This provision was added to the VA Immunity Statute in 1988.[5] Pub.L. 100-322. Under § 7316(f), the exception to the waiver of sovereign immunity for certain intentional torts that is contained in 28 U.S.C. § 2680(h) does not apply to "any claim arising out of a negligent or wrongful act or omission of any ... [health care employee of the VA] in furnishing medical care or treatment ... while in the exercise of such person's duties in or for the Administration." 38 U.S.C. § 7316(f). Thus, § 7316(f) allows the United States to be sued under the FTCA for certain intentional torts committed by VA health care employees in the context of providing medical care. *See Franklin,* 992 F.2d at 1502.

In *Franklin,* we previously considered the purpose and effect of subsection (f). Specifically, we explained that, prior to the amendment of the VA Immunity Statute to include subsection (f), "in circumstances where the government's waiver of sovereign immunity was excluded by § 2680(h) and, therefore, the injured party had no possible remedy under the FTCA, a cause of action against the responsible health worker could be maintained." *Id.* at 1500.

This had created a difficulty, because, depending on state law, malpractice actions might be based on a theory of negligence or a theory of battery. *See id.* And unless a statutory exception applies, a person cannot bring a claim for battery under the FTCA. 28 U.S.C. § 2680(h). Thus, under the FTCA generally, "[i]f the negligence theory [of malpractice] applies, redress against the government under the FTCA is available, while if the battery theory controls, the action is specifically excluded from the government's waiver of sovereign immunity under the FTCA." *Franklin,* 992 F.2d at 1496 (citations omitted). Before the enactment of § 7316(f), this was true under the VA Immunity Statute. But "[e]ventually, Congress recognized this situation—and, specifically, the example of medical battery—as a problem to be corrected." *Id.* at 1500. To illustrate this point, we quoted in *Franklin* the following legislative history for § 7316(f):

> For many years, VA medical personnel have been protected from personal liability in medical malpractice actions arising out of allegedly negligent conduct in the furnishing of medical care or treatment to veterans. However, the Government does not extend this immunity to actions arising out of intentional

conduct—so-called "intentional torts." In some instances, State law characterizes an act of medical malpractice as an intentional tort, leaving VA medical personnel potentially liable for an action for which the law intends the Government to assume liability. As an example, if a patient consents to an operation on his left elbow, but the physician mistakenly operates on the right elbow, responsibility for this action would lie with the United States. However, if the suit was based on a theory that a battery occurred, which is defined as any contact with a person without that person's consent, p.1249 the Government is not allowed to assume the employee's liability. In essence, State law, which controls the character of the action brought against VA medical personnel, could defeat the intent of the Federal law to provide such employees with immunity.

Id. at 1500 (quoting H.R.Rep. No. 100-191, 100th Cong., 2d Sess. 19 (1988), *reprinted in* 1988 U.S.C.C.A.N. 432, 450).

Although Congress was specifically concerned with medical battery, the remedy available under § 7316(f) is not limited to battery. Instead, by rendering 28 U.S.C. § 2680(h) inapplicable, § 7316(f) allows the United States to be sued for "assault, battery, false imprisonment, false arrest, malicious prosecution, abuse of process, libel, slander, misrepresentation, deceit, or interference with contract rights," 28 U.S.C. 2680(h), when such claims arise in the context of VA health care employees providing medical care or treatment, 38 U.S.C. § 7316(f). As we noted in *Franklin,* Congress could have resolved the problem in a variety of ways, and it need not have waived sovereign immunity for all of the intentional torts listed in 28 U.S.C. § 2680(h), but "Congress chose ... *'to expand the circumstances under which the Federal government accepts liability* for the acts of its employees acting within the scope of their employment *so as to cover actions of VA health-care employees that are characterized as intentional torts* under the laws of various states.'" *Franklin,* 992 F.2d at 1500 (emphasis in original) (quoting 1988 U.S.C.C.A.N. at 502-03). Thus, in the context of VA health care employees providing medical care or treatment, § 7316(f) provides a remedy under the FTCA for claims of intentional torts, including false arrest and false imprisonment.

In sum, § 7316(f) provides alternative, existing process for protecting the interests implicated in this appeal, *see Wilkie,* 551 U.S. at 550, 127 S.Ct. 2588, by expanding the scope of § 7316(a)(1) and providing a remedy under the FTCA for intentional torts arising in the context of VA health care employees providing medical care or treatment. 38 U.S.C. § 7316(f). Section 7316(f) therefore "insulate[s] the individual government employee by nullifying § 2680(h) and thereby expanding the injured party's remedy against the government under the FTCA." *Franklin,* 992 F.2d at 1501.

For the foregoing reasons, we conclude that there is an adequate alternative remedy available under the VA Immunity Statute; indeed, the Statute provides an exclusive remedy that precludes a cause of action under *Bivens* for claims that fall within the scope of the Statute. Accordingly, we now consider whether Mr. Ingram's claims fall within the scope of the VA Immunity Statute.

II. Mr. Ingram's Claims Fall Within the Scope of the VA Immunity Statute

Mr. Ingram argues that his claims do not fall within the scope of the VA Immunity Statute for two reasons. First, he contends that the VA Immunity Statute is not implicated, because his claims do not arise from malpractice or negligence. Specifically, he "alleges that his confinement was not the result of medical evidence, evaluation or opinion, but instead was a result of intentional acts of Defendants unrelated to any medical opinion of physicians." Aplt. Br. at 13. Second, he also argues that Defendants are not qualified for immunity under the Statute because they do not fall within the definition of "other supporting personnel."

As background, Mr. Ingram alleges in his complaint that he was "wrongfully and unlawfully detained and held in the psychiatric ward as a result of the actions of p.1250 Defendant Furuque [sic], Defendant Feng,... Defendant DeLise [sic], Defendant Inhofe, Defendant Lt. Stevenson, and Defendant Captain Collins, who were acting within the course and scope of their employment with [the VA]." Aplt.App. at 12. He goes on to argue that: "Defendants conducted an objectively unreasonable and insufficient investigation to determine whether there was a sufficient basis for holding Plaintiff against his will in the psychiatric ward," and that "[b]ased upon the actions, assertions, and statements of Defendants, Plaintiff was coerced into signing the consent for admission form against his will." *Id.* He also contends that "[t]he conduct of Defendants resulted in Plaintiff Delbert Ingram being falsely, maliciously, and unlawfully detained and held in the psychiatric ward." *Id.* And finally, he asserts that "Defendants Furuque [sic], Feng, ... DeLise [sic], Inhofe, Lt. Stevenson, and Captain Collins' actions were [done with] willful, wanton, intentional, and ... reckless disregard." *Id.* at 15.

As to Mr. Ingram's first argument, it is plain that his claims fall within the scope of the VA Immunity Statute. As discussed above, the VA Immunity Statute immunizes VA health care employees for "damages ... allegedly arising from malpractice or negligence of a health care employee of the [VA]," 38 U.S.C. § 7316(a)(1), as well as claims for "assault, battery, false imprisonment, false arrest, malicious prosecution, abuse of process, libel, slander, misrepresentation, deceit, or interference with contract rights," 28 U.S.C. § 2680(h), that "aris[e] out of a negligent or wrongful act or omission of any ... [health care employee] in furnishing medical care or treatment," 38 U.S.C. at § 7316(f). Mr. Ingram's claims arise from the medical care he received at the VAMC. Specifically, his claims indicate either that Defendants' actions were negligent and fell below an objective standard of care, which would implicate a claim of malpractice, *see Id.* § 7316(a)(1), or that they were wrongful acts or omissions that would implicate a claim for an intentional tort, within the context of providing medical care or treatment, *see* 28 U.S.C. § 2680(h) & 38 U.S.C. § 7316(f). And because he argues that he was unlawfully detained and held as a result of Defendants' "willful, wanton, intentional, and ... reckless disregard," Aplt. App at 15, it is evident that he is arguing that Defendants committed an intentional tort—specifically, false arrest or false imprisonment—for which a remedy under the FTCA is provided by § 7316(f). Thus, his claims fall within the scope of the VA Immunity Statute.

As to Mr. Ingram's second argument, we conclude that the district court did not err in determining that the Defendants were immune to suit as "health care employee[s]" within the meaning of the VA Immunity Statute. Section 7316(a)(2) provides:

> the term "health care employee of the Administration" means a physician, dentist, podiatrist, chiropractor, optometrist, nurse, physician assistant, expanded-function dental auxiliary, pharmacist, or paramedical (such as medical and dental technicians, nursing assistants, and therapists), or other supporting personnel.

38 U.S.C. § 7316(a).

Mr. Ingram argues that Defendants are not "other supporting personnel," but we need not consider that argument as to Defendants Dr. Faruque and Dr. Feng, because both doctors are "physicians"— specifically, VAMC staff psychiatrists. The district court found that the actions of both Dr. Faruque and Dr. Feng

> were actions relevant to the provision of medical care[,].... that each action was undertaken based on decisions and information pertinent to Defendants as a p.1251 result of their specialized education and training in the field of medicine/psychology[,].... [and] that their contact with Plaintiff arose as a result of the need for an evaluation by a medical professional.

Aplt.App. at 167. We agree. Because both doctors are physicians and their interactions with Mr. Ingram were in the scope of their duties and in the course of furnishing medical care, *see* 38 U.S.C. § 7316(a), (f), they are entitled to immunity under the VA Immunity Statute.

As to the other Defendants, the district court determined that they were acting as supporting personnel to medical providers in their interactions with Mr. Ingram. Section 7316(a)(2) does not provide a definition for "other supporting personnel." But the phrase is not limited to "medical personnel"—in other words, it is not necessary under the statute that "other supporting personnel" must themselves be qualified to practice medicine or be regularly employed as medical personnel. *See* 38 U.S.C. § 7316(a)(2). Instead, the statute defines "health care employee" as

> physician, dentist, podiatrist, chiropractor, optometrist, nurse, physician assistant, expanded-function dental auxiliary, pharmacist, *or* paramedical (such as medical and dental technicians, nursing assistants, and therapists), *or other supporting personnel.*

Id. (emphases added). Thus, employees of the VA may be "health care employee[s]" under the statute if they are employed as one of the listed types of medical personnel, *or* if they are providing support to such medical personnel. *See id.* And for other supporting personnel to qualify for immunity under § 7316(a)(1) or § 7316(f), they must provide support for medical personnel, *id.* § 7316(a)(2), "in furnishing medical care or treatment ... while in the exercise of [their] duties in or for the Administration," *id.* § 7316(f); *accord Id.* § 7316(a)(1).

Here, the district court found that "[b]ut for the perceived need to provide medical care to Plaintiff in the form of psychiatric care, neither Defendants Stevenson nor Collins would have had any contact with Plaintiff." Similarly, it found that "Defendants DeLise's [sic] and Inhofe's interaction with Plaintiff arose solely at the behest of or in support of the medical personnel who were evaluating

Plaintiff's condition." Aplt.App. at 170. Viewing the evidence in the light most favorable to the district court's ruling, the court's findings regarding the interactions between Mr. Ingram and Defendants Delise, Inhofe, Stevenson, and Collins were not clearly erroneous. *Rio Grande Silvery Minnow,* 599 F.3d at 1175. Each of these Defendants testified that he or she was acting within the scope of his or her duties and pursuant to instructions from medical personnel. Accordingly, the record before the district court supports that these Defendants interacted with Mr. Ingram only to provide support to medical personnel in furnishing medical care to Mr. Ingram.

Mr. Ingram's sole argument as to why Defendants could not have been other "supporting personnel," is that they were acting under the direction of Dr. Bukhari, and Mr. Ingram contends that Dr. Bukhari did not "t[ake] any action that could give rise to a malpractice claim."[6] Aplt. Br. at 16. Mr. Ingram misses the point. Dr. Bukhari is not a party to this action, and it is irrelevant whether Mr. Ingram's allegations would give rise to a cause of action p.1252 against Dr. Bukhari under the VA Immunity Statute. The only relevant question to consider in determining whether the four Defendants are other "supporting personnel" is whether they were providing support to medical personnel in furnishing health care or treatment. *Id.* Because their interactions with Mr. Ingram took place solely in the context of providing support to medical personnel in furnishing medical care to Mr. Ingram, we agree that they are "other supporting personal" under the VA Immunity Statute.

In sum, Mr. Ingram's claims fall within the scope of the VA Immunity Statute, and the Defendants fall within the Statute's definition of health care employees. And because we hold that the FTCA provides an alternative, existing process for addressing Mr. Ingram's interests that is exclusive of any other cause of action arising from the same subject matter, Mr. Ingram may not pursue a cause of action under *Bivens.* For that reason, the district court did not err in concluding that it lacked subject-matter jurisdiction to consider Mr. Ingram's claims.

CONCLUSION

Mr. Ingram has an alternative, existing process for protecting his interests available through the VA Immunity Statute. And the language of the Statute provides for an exclusive remedy that precludes Mr. Ingram from pursuing a cause of action under *Bivens.* Because Mr. Ingram's claims fall within the scope of the VA Immunity Statute, we AFFIRM the district court's decision concluding that it lacked subject matter jurisdiction and dismissing Mr. Ingram's claims without prejudice.

[1] Mr. Ingram also initially named as defendants David Wood, director of the Oklahoma City Department of Veterans Affairs Medical Center, in his official capacity, and the Department of Veteran Affairs, but he later voluntarily dismissed these two parties.

[2] Plaintiff did not assert a claim under the FTCA and therefore the district court did not express any opinion whether Mr. Ingram's potential FTCA claim might now be barred for procedural or timeliness reasons, or otherwise. Likewise, we do not address that issue.

[3] Mr. Ingram claims that Dr. Faruque informed Mr. Ingram that even though he "found that Plaintiff's thought content had no suicidal, violent or paranoid ideations, Defendant Faruque informed Plaintiff 'in order to save my job and clear your name, I am going to have to commit you to the psychiatric ward.'" Aplt.App. at 10. Mr. Ingram further contends that Dr. Faruque told him that "[a]s of this moment you have no say in this matter, you have no rights," and that "[y]ou are either going voluntarily or by force." *Id.* at 10-11. While Dr. Faruque's report following the examination did state that Mr. Ingram's "[t]hought content has no suicidal, violent or paranoid ideations," the report also recommended intake for further assessment, *Id.* at 104, and his affidavit before the district court stated that he "determined that, because of the severity of the reported threats and his obvious agitation, Mr. Ingram required a more thorough psychiatric evaluation than I could perform in the limited time available to me in the Emergency Room setting," *id.* at 102.

[4] In *Franklin*, we analyzed 38 U.S.C. § 4116, which is the precursor to the statute at issue in this case (38 U.S.C. § 7316). 992 F.2d at 1500 n. 8, 1502 (explaining that " § 4116 was repealed and reenacted as § 7316," and that "[t]he version set out under the new designation includes no pertinent substantive changes"). But the relevant language that was formerly contained in § 4116(a) is substantially similar to the language currently contained in § 7316(a); thus, our holding in *Franklin* applies equally to 38 U.S.C. § 7316.

[5] At the time subsection (f) was added, the VA Immunity Statute was codified at 38 U.S.C. § 4116.

[6] Mr. Ingram does not make any other arguments as to why Defendants Inhofe, Delise, Stevenson, and Collins are not "other supporting personnel" under the VA Immunity Statute, and "[t]his court ... will not craft a party's arguments for him," *Perry v. Woodward,* 199 F.3d 1126, 1141 n. 13 (10th Cir. 1999).

ELEVENTH CIRCUIT DECISIONS
Federal Tort Claims Act

781 F.3d 1315 (2015)

Carlos ZELAYA, individually, and George Glantz, individually and as trustee of the George Glantz Revocable Trust, for themselves and on behalf of all those persons similarly situated, Plaintiffs-Appellants,

v.

UNITED STATES of America, Defendant-Appellee.

No. 13-14780.

United States Court of Appeals, Eleventh Circuit.

March 30, 2015.

Zelaya v. US, 781 F. 3d 1315 (11th Cir. 2015)

p.1318 Gaytri Kachroo, Rebecca P. McIntyre, John H. Ray, III, Kachroo Legal Services, PC, Cambridge, MA, Brandon Ross Levitt, Hall Lamb & Hall, PA, Sean R. Santini, Santini Law Firm, Miami, FL, for Plaintiffs-Appellants.

Steve Frank, Phil MacWilliams, U.S. Department of Justice, Washington, DC, Wifredo A. Ferrer, Kathleen Mary Salyer, U.S. Attorney's Office, Miami, FL, for Defendant-Appellee.

Before TJOFLAT, JULIE CARNES, and GILMAN,[*] Circuit Judges.

JULIE CARNES, Circuit Judge:

The plaintiffs in this case, Carlos Zelaya and George Glantz, are victims of one of the largest Ponzi schemes in American history: the much-publicized Ponzi scheme orchestrated by R. Allen Stanford. All Ponzi operations eventually unravel, and when the scheme that had victimized Plaintiffs was publicly revealed to have been a fraud, Plaintiffs were taken by surprise. Yet, according to Plaintiffs, the federal agency entrusted with the duty of trying to prevent, or at least reveal, Ponzi schemes was not all that surprised. To the contrary, this agency, the United States Securities and Exchange Commission ("SEC"), had been alerted over a decade before that Stanford was likely running a Ponzi operation. According to Plaintiffs, notwithstanding its knowledge of Stanford's likely nefarious dealings, the SEC dithered for twelve years, content not p.1319 to call out Stanford and protect future investors from his fraud. And even though the SEC eventually roused itself to take action in 2009, by then, of course, the money was long gone, and many people lost most of their investments.

Pursuant to the Federal Tort Claims Act, Plaintiffs sued the United States in federal court, alleging that the SEC had acted negligently. The federal government moved to dismiss, arguing that it enjoyed sovereign immunity from the lawsuit. The district court agreed, and dismissed Plaintiffs' case. Plaintiffs now appeal that dismissal to this Court. In reviewing the district court's dismissal, we reach no conclusions as to the SEC's conduct, or whether the latter's actions deserve Plaintiffs' condemnation. We do, however, conclude that the United States is shielded from liability for the SEC's alleged negligence in this case. We therefore affirm the district court's dismissal of the Plaintiffs' complaint.

I. *Factual Background*

As noted, this action arises from one of the largest Ponzi schemes in history.[1] In the 1990s and 2000s, financier R. Allen Stanford ("Stanford" or "Allen Stanford") engineered investments in his Antiguan-based Stanford International Bank Ltd. ("Stanford Bank") through a network of entities: Stanford Bank itself; Stanford Group, with more than twenty-five offices across the United States; Louisiana-based Stanford Trust Company; and Miami, Houston, and San Antonio-based Stanford Fiduciary Investor Services. Through this network, Stanford Bank issued high-interest certificates of deposit ("CDs") to tens of thousands of investors across the globe, ultimately accumulating billions of dollars. Unbeknownst to these investors, however, Stanford Bank never invested this money in securities, as it had promised to do. Instead, the Bank funneled new infusions of cash to earlier investors and to Allen Stanford himself.

As early as 1997, the SEC had been alerted that Stanford was conducting a Ponzi scheme through the above companies. One of these companies, Stanford Group, had been registered with the SEC since 1995 as a broker-dealer and investment advisor, which meant that it was subject to SEC reporting requirements. Yet, despite four investigations between 1997 and 2004, the SEC took no action to stop the fraud until 2009.

In its first investigation, begun in 1997, the SEC discovered that Stanford had contributed $19 million in cash to Stanford Group, which caused the SEC "concern[] that the cash contribution may have come from funds invested by customers at [Stanford Bank]." The Branch Chief of the Fort Worth, Texas SEC office conducting the investigation considered the purported returns on Stanford Bank's CDs to be "absolutely ludicrous" and believed that they were not "legitimate CDs." The Assistant District Administrator heading the investigation warned the Branch Chief to "keep your eye on these people [referencing Stanford] because this looks like a Ponzi scheme to me and someday it's going to blow up." The following year, the successor of that Assistant District Administrator stated, "[A]s far as I was concerned at that period of time[,] . . . we all thought it was a Ponzi scheme to start with. Always p.1320 did." The investigating group concluded, "[P]ossible misrepresentations. Possible Ponzi scheme." Still, the SEC took no action against Stanford.

In the SEC's second investigation, begun in 1998, the investigators decided that "Stanford was operating some kind of fraud" through Stanford Group. They noted that Stanford Group was "extremely dependent upon [Stanford Bank's very generous commission] compensation to conduct its day-to-day operations." Despite this, the SEC did nothing.

In 2002, the SEC investigated Stanford a third time, determining that Stanford Group should be assigned the SEC's highest risk rating because of the SEC's "suspicions the international bank [Stanford Bank] was a Ponzi scheme" and because Stanford Bank's "consistent above-market reported returns" were likely illegitimate. Notwithstanding this concern, the SEC, once again, did nothing.

In 2004, the SEC conducted a fourth investigation of Stanford, again reaching the conclusion that Stanford Bank "may in fact be a very large Ponzi scheme." Sitting on this information for five more years, the SEC finally took enforcement action against Stanford and his various business entities in 2009.[2] By then though, most of the investors' money was gone, and the SEC has been able to recover only $100 million of the $7 billion invested in Stanford Bank.

Plaintiffs Zelaya and Glantz were two of the many investors who thought they were purchasing legitimate securities. Zelaya invested $1 million and Glantz invested approximately $650,000. Both plaintiffs have lost almost their entire investments.

II. *Procedural Background*

Pursuant to the Federal Tort Claims Act ("FTCA"), and alleging one count of negligence based on the SEC's failure to act upon its knowledge of Stanford Group's participation in the Stanford Bank Ponzi scheme, Plaintiffs filed suit in 2011 against the United States ("the Government") in the United States District Court for the Southern District of Florida. In their initial complaint, Plaintiffs identified two separate statutory duties that the SEC had allegedly breached through its inaction. First, Plaintiffs asserted a "notification claim" pursuant to the Securities Investor Protection Act of 1970, 15 U.S.C. §§ 78aaa-*lll*. Specifically, Plaintiffs relied on § 78eee(a)(1), which provides that "[i]f the [SEC] is aware of facts which lead it to believe that any broker or dealer subject to its regulation is in or is approaching financial difficulty, it shall immediately notify SIPC." SIPC is an acronym for the Securities Investor Protection Corporation, which is a nonprofit corporation with which Stanford Group, as a registered broker-dealer, was required to maintain membership. Plaintiffs note that although Stanford Group was subject to regulation by the SEC and the SEC had allegedly concluded that Stanford Group was involved in a Ponzi scheme, the SEC failed to notify SIPC, as required by § 78eee(a)(1).

p.1321 Second, Plaintiffs also raised a "registration claim" pursuant to 15 U.S.C. § 80b-3(c). Plaintiffs contend that § 80b-3(c) required the SEC to revoke the registration of Stanford Group, but the SEC failed to do so.

The Government responded with a motion to dismiss. As discussed below, while the FTCA, as a general matter, waives what would otherwise be the federal government's sovereign immunity from legal actions for torts committed by its employees, there are exceptions to that general waiver. In its motion to dismiss, the Government argued that one of those exceptions, the "discretionary function exception," barred Plaintiffs' claims based on the alleged breach of both of the above statutory duties. Given the application of this exception, the Government contended that the district court lacked subject matter jurisdiction.

The district court granted the Government's motion to dismiss with regard to the registration claim, holding that the discretionary function exception applied and therefore preserved the Government's sovereign immunity on that claim. The district court, however, denied the Government's motion to dismiss with regard to Plaintiffs' notification claim.

Plaintiffs then filed an amended complaint, re-alleging the surviving notification claim as the sole basis for their negligence action. The Government again moved to dismiss, this time raising the "misrepresentation exception" as a bar to its capacity to be sued under the FTCA. Although it had earlier rejected the application of the discretionary function exception to the notification claim, the district court agreed that the misrepresentation exception did apply and that it precluded this claim. As a result, the court concluded that it likewise lacked subject matter jurisdiction on the notification claim and therefore granted the Government's motion to dismiss. With no remaining claims, the court entered a final judgment for the Government. Plaintiffs filed the present appeal, contending that the district court should not have dismissed either the registration claim or the notification claim.

III. *Discussion*

A. Sovereign Immunity, Subject Matter Jurisdiction, and the Federal Tort Claims Act—Generally

The district court dismissed Plaintiffs' claims based on an absence of subject matter jurisdiction. We review a district court's dismissal of an action for lack of subject matter jurisdiction *de novo. Motta ex rel. A.M. v. United States,* 717 F.3d 840, 843 (11th Cir.2013).

It is well settled that the United States, as a sovereign entity, is immune from suit unless it consents to be sued. *Christian Coal. of Fla., Inc. v. United States,* 662 F.3d 1182, 1188 (11th Cir.2011) (citing *United States v. Dalm,* 494 U.S. 596, 608, 110 S.Ct. 1361, 108 L.Ed.2d 548 (1990)); *accord Alden v. Maine,* 527 U.S. 706, 758, 119 S.Ct. 2240, 144 L.Ed.2d 636 (1999) ("To the extent Maine has chosen to consent to certain classes of suits while maintaining its immunity from others, it has done no more than exercise a privilege of sovereignty concomitant to its constitutional immunity from suit."). Through the enactment of the FTCA, the federal government has, as a general matter, waived its immunity from tort suits based on state law tort claims. *Millbrook v. United States,* ___ U.S. ___, 133 S.Ct. 1441, 1443, 185 L.Ed.2d 531 (2013) (citing *Levin v. United States,* ___ U.S. ___, 133 S.Ct. 1224, 1228, 185 L.Ed.2d 343 (2013)). But in offering its consent to be sued, the United States has the power to condition a waiver of its immunity as broadly or narrowly p.1322 as it wishes, and according to whatever terms it chooses to impose. *United States v. Sherwood,* 312 U.S. 584, 586, 61 S.Ct. 767, 85 L.Ed. 1058 (1941) ("[T]he terms of [the government's] consent to be sued in any court define that court's jurisdiction to entertain the suit."). That being so, a court must strictly observe the "limitations and conditions upon which the Government consents to be sued" and cannot imply exceptions not present within the terms of the waiver. *Soriano v. United States,* 352 U.S. 270, 276, 77 S.Ct. 269, 1 L.Ed.2d 306 (1957). If there is no specific waiver of sovereign immunity as to a particular claim filed against the Government, the court lacks subject matter jurisdiction over the suit. *See F.D.I.C. v. Meyer,* 510 U.S. 471, 475-76, 114 S.Ct. 996, 127 L.Ed.2d 308 (1994).

But that which the Sovereign gives, it may also take away, and the Government has done so through statutory exceptions in 28 U.S.C. § 2680, including the § 2680(a) discretionary function exception and the § 2680(h) misrepresentation exception, which serve to block the waiver of sovereign immunity that would otherwise occur under the FTCA. *See* 28 U.S.C. § 2680. These exceptions "must be strictly construed in favor of the United States," and when an exception applies to neutralize what would otherwise be a waiver of immunity, a court will lack subject matter jurisdiction over the action. *JBP Acquisitions, LP v. United States ex rel. FDIC,* 224 F.3d 1260, 1263-64 (11th Cir.2000) (internal quotation marks omitted).

B. Interplay Between 28 U.S.C. §§ 1346(b)(1), 2674(b)(1), and 2680

Any plaintiff seeking to sue the United States under the FTCA must satisfy two initial statutory burdens to establish jurisdiction. *Clark v. United States,* 326 F.3d 911, 912 (7th Cir.2003). First, as with all suitors in federal courts, the plaintiff must identify an explicit statutory grant of subject matter jurisdiction, which in the case of the FTCA is 28 U.S.C. § 1346(b)(1). *Id.* This statute provides:

> Subject to the provisions of chapter 171 of this title [i.e., 28 U.S.C. §§ 2671-2680], the district courts . . . shall have exclusive jurisdiction of civil actions on claims against the United States, for money damages, accruing on and after January 1, 1945, for injury or loss of property, or personal injury or death caused by the negligent or wrongful act or omission of any employee of the Government while acting within the scope of his office or employment, under circumstances where the United States, if a private person, would be liable to the claimant in accordance with the law of the place where the act or omission occurred.

28 U.S.C. § 1346(b)(1) (emphasis added). Translated, any time the federal government is sued based on the act of an employee performed within the scope of his employment duties, federal district courts will have exclusive jurisdiction of such claims. In addition, § 1346(b)(1) sets, as a predicate, a requirement that the circumstances be such that a private person would be liable under the law of the state where the federal employee's act or omission occurred, had a private person so acted.

Because the United States is a sovereign entity, the second jurisdictional requirement is a statute that waives its sovereign immunity. *Clark,* 326 F.3d at 912; *see also Meyer,* 510 U.S. at 475, 114 S.Ct. 996 ("Sovereign immunity is jurisdictional in nature."). This waiver of sovereign immunity is provided in chapter 171 of Title 28, which chapter includes §§ 2671-2680. The waiver is most directly referenced in § 2674.

p.1323 As the texts of the two statutes indicate, jurisdiction depends on both statutes being satisfied. Indeed, § 1346(b)(1) explicitly makes its grant of jurisdiction subject to the conditions of chapter 171, with its introductory phrase declaring that the subsection is "[s]ubject to the provisions of chapter 171 of this title." Two provisions found in chapter 171 are pertinent in this case. Section 2674 affirmatively establishes the Government's liability for tort claims, but reiterates § 1346(b)(1)'s requirement conditioning liability by the Government on a showing that a private individual would be liable under like circumstances.[3] Finally, § 2680, the final section of chapter 171, lists exceptions to the United States' waiver of sovereign immunity, under which "[t]he provisions of this chapter and section 1346(b)(1) of this title shall not apply." *See* 28 U.S.C. § 2680.

Thus, between § 1346(b)(1) and chapter 171, there are numerous prerequisites to, and limitations on, the grant of jurisdiction over tort suits against the United States. In the present case, two obstacles potentially block Plaintiffs' efforts to use the FTCA to sue the Government based on the SEC's alleged negligence in this case. First, as noted, there are exceptions, found within the FTCA itself, that preclude use of that statute by a plaintiff to sue the Government for tort claims. And it is the applicability of those exceptions on which the district court and parties focused below, with the court ultimately determining that two statutory exceptions blocked Plaintiffs' efforts to use the FTCA to pierce the Government's sovereign immunity.

But there is another obstacle that was largely ignored by the district court and the parties. Specifically, even when no applicable exception exists, the FTCA does not provide an open field for a litigant to sue the federal government for the alleged torts of its agents. Instead, the particular statute granting subject matter jurisdiction over such claims—28 U.S.C. § 1346(b)(1)—constrains a litigant as to the type of claims that can properly be brought pursuant to the statute. That is, both §§ 1346(b)(1) and 2674 preclude liability of the federal government absent a showing by the plaintiff that a private individual who had acted as did the federal employee, in like circumstances, would be liable for the particular tort under governing state law where the tort occurred.

We address first the impact of the above requirement on this litigation, after which we discuss the applicability of statutory exceptions in this case.

C. The Federal Tort Claims Act's Requirement of a State Law Analogue

1. The Need for a State Tort Analogue

The FTCA was enacted to provide redress to injured individuals for ordinary torts recognized by state law but committed by federal employees. *Ochran v. United States,* 273 F.3d 1315, 1317 (11th Cir.2001) *("Ochran II"); Sellfors v. United States,* 697 F.2d 1362, 1365 (11th Cir. 1983) (Congress "was concerned primarily with providing redress for the garden variety common law torts recognized by state law."). Indeed, the reference in § 1346(b)(1) to "the law of the place where the act or omission occurred" means the law of the state where the alleged tort occurred. *Stone v. United States,* 373 F.3d 1129, 1130 (11th Cir.2004).

p.1324 As a corollary of that principle, it is well established that a federal statute cannot constitute the "law of the place" because "[t]he FTCA was not intended to redress breaches of federal statutory duties." *Sellfors,* 697 F.2d at 1365. Stated another way, the fact that a federal employee has failed to perform duties imposed by federal law is insufficient by itself to render the federal government liable under the FTCA. *Pate v. Oakwood Mobile Homes, Inc.,* 374 F.3d 1081, 1084 (11th Cir.2004). Instead, a state tort cause of action is a *sine qua non* of FTCA jurisdiction, and we have dismissed FTCA suits that have pleaded breaches of federal duties without identifying a valid state tort cause of action. *See, e.g., Ochran II,* 273 F.3d at 1317.

Yet notwithstanding their inability to support an FTCA suit, federal statutes and regulations can still be important. First, they "may provide evidence that the government has assumed duties analogous to those recognized by local tort law." *Art Metal-U.S.A., Inc. v. United States,* 753 F.2d 1151, 1158 (D.C.Cir.1985). Similarly, they "may provide the standard of care against which the government's conduct should be assessed." *Id.* at 1159. Accordingly, the negligent performance of duties set out in federal statutes and regulations may shore up a claim under the FTCA, "but *only* if there are analogous duties under local tort law." *Id.* at 1157 (emphasis in original). In short, while a federal employee's breach of a federally-imposed duty may bolster a FTCA claim, it cannot, on its own, create the duty that gives rise to that claim. That task falls to the applicable state jurisdiction.

When the complaint involves one of the "garden variety common law torts," this requirement of a state tort cause of action can be easily met. *Sellfors*, 697 F.2d at 1365. For example, a plaintiff suing based on an automobile accident caused by a federal employee would readily find a comparable state-law tort to buttress his FTCA claim. Difficulties arise, however, when the activities at issue are "uniquely governmental functions" with unique duties that suggest no obvious analogue among private actors. *Indian Towing Co. v. United States*, 350 U.S. 61, 64, 76 S.Ct. 122, 100 L.Ed. 48 (1955). Without question, it can be difficult to imagine how a private person could be liable for breaches of such quintessentially governmental functions as the regulation of air travel, prisoners, drugs, and livestock because no private person has such duties under state law.[4] *See, e.g., Smoke Shop, LLC v. United States*, 761 F.3d 779, 780 (7th Cir.2014) (drug enforcement regulations); *Alfrey v. United States*, 276 F.3d 557, 559 (9th Cir. 2002) (regulation of prison inmates); *Dorking Genetics v. United States*, 76 F.3d 1261, 1262 (2d Cir.1996) (cattle inspections); *Howell v. United States*, 932 F.2d 915, 916 (11th Cir.1991) (airline safety regulations).

Notwithstanding these conceptual difficulties, the Supreme Court long ago made clear that there is no exception from FTCA liability solely because the particular tort arose from the performance of uniquely governmental functions. *Indian Towing*, 350 U.S. at 64, 76 S.Ct. 122. So, the question arises, how should the FTCA be applied when uniquely governmental functions are at issue? We have recognized that "[n]ormally, the most analogous p.1325 approach in determining whether the government is liable in the regulator-enforcer context under state law is the [G]ood [S]amaritan doctrine." *Pate*, 374 F.3d at 1086; *see also Indian Towing*, 350 U.S. at 64-65, 76 S.Ct. 122 ("[T]he statutory language [of 28 U.S.C. § 2674] is 'under like circumstances,' and it is hornbook tort law that one who undertakes to warn the public of danger and thereby induces reliance must perform his '[G]ood Samaritan' task in a careful manner."). Thus, in cases where the plaintiff points to the violation of a federal statutory or regulatory duty, we generally look to the applicable state's Good Samaritan doctrine to decide if the plaintiff has alleged a state tort claim that satisfies the § 1346(b)(1) requirement and thereby opens the door for a claim under the FTCA. *See, e.g., Sellfors*, 697 F.2d at 1367; *Howell*, 932 F.2d at 918; *Pate*, 374 F.3d at 1086.

2. The Plaintiffs' Negligence Claim

Here, Plaintiffs' first amended complaint alleged only the tort of negligence, without specifying which state's law of negligence applied and in apparent ignorance of the fact that identifying an analogous state tort cause of action is required for an FTCA cause of action. Instead, Plaintiffs alleged generally that the SEC breached "the duty of care owed to investors" as a result of violations of its federal statutory duties to revoke Stanford Group's registration and to notify SIPC of Stanford Group's financial hazard. But, as explained, mere breaches of federal statutory duties are, as a threshold matter, insufficient to support a cause of action. *Sellfors*, 697 F.2d at 1365. Unless Plaintiffs can identify corresponding state law duties, they have, at the least, failed to state a claim, and arguably their lapse deprives the court of even subject matter jurisdiction over the action. *Ochran II,* 273 F.3d at 1317; *Bennett v. United States,* 102 F.3d 486, 488-89 & n. 1 (11th Cir.1996); *Lawrence v. Dunbar,* 919 F.2d 1525, 1528 (11th Cir.1990) (per curiam) ("State law . . . governs the question of whether the United States has waived its sovereign immunity against liability. . . ."); *see also Glade ex rel. Lundskow v. United States,* 692 F.3d 718, 723 (7th Cir.2012) (determining that the specific state law cause of action is "a threshold issue" upon which subject matter jurisdiction depends); *Gould Elec. Inc. v. United States,* 220 F.3d 169, 179 (3d Cir.2000).

Although the Government did not raise this issue in its first motion to dismiss, it did so in its second motion. The Government noted that, based on Plaintiffs' factual allegations, any state tort on which it relied would have to exist either under the laws of Texas (where the alleged investigative failures occurred) or the District of Columbia (where the SEC is headquartered). The Government also noted that, absent some special relationship between the parties, "neither jurisdiction recognizes any duty on the part of a private individual to act for the protection of another or to prevent harm by a third person."

Notwithstanding this argument by the Government, the district court did not address this matter in its order dismissing Plaintiffs' notification claim. Nor do the parties address the state law cause of action requirement in this appeal. But to the extent that the failure to provide a pertinent state tort analogue robs a plaintiff of subject matter jurisdiction under the FTCA, it appears that Plaintiffs would face some uphill sledding in trying to find such an analogue here.

First, adopting the approach of the Restatement (Second) of Torts, neither Texas nor the District of Columbia requires a person to act to prevent harm to others, absent some special relationship. *Torrington* p.1326 *Co. v. Stutzman,* 46 S.W.3d 829, 837 (Tex.2000) (citing Restatement (Second) of Torts § 314 (1965)); *Feirson v. Dist. of Columbia,* 506 F.3d 1063, 1068-69 (D.C.Cir.2007) (same).[5] Again following the Restatement, neither jurisdiction generally requires a person to prevent a third party from causing harm. *Greater Houston Transp. Co. v. Phillips,* 801 S.W.2d 523, 525 (Tex.1990) (citing Restatement (Second) of Torts § 315 (1965)); *Skeen v. Federative Republic of Brazil,* 566 F.Supp. 1414, 1419 (D.D.C.1983) (same).[6] Also in line with the Restatement, neither jurisdiction permits recovery through a negligence action for purely economic losses absent some special relationship between the parties. *Jones v. Hartford Life and Acc. Ins. Co.,* 443 F.Supp.2d 3, 7 n. 4 (D.D.C.2006) (requiring an "intimate nexus" between the parties); *Express One Int'l, Inc. v. Steinbeck,* 53 S.W.3d 895, 898 (Tex.Ct.App. 2001); *see also* Restatement (Second) of Torts § 323 (1965). Moreover, with regard to liability arising from voluntary ("Good Samaritan") undertakings, Texas requires that the plaintiff establish both reliance and an increased risk of harm. *Torrington Co.,* 46 S.W.3d at 838 n. 7; *see also Colonial Sav. Ass'n v. Taylor,* 544 S.W.2d 116, 119-20 (Tex.1976) (noting that Texas follows the Restatement (Second) of Torts § 323 (1965) on voluntary-undertaking liability). Plaintiffs here have expressly denied reliance in their notification claim.

It therefore seems questionable whether Plaintiffs could show, for either Texas or the District of Columbia, the existence of a tort cause of action against a private person under the circumstances alleged by Plaintiffs here. We are reluctant to decide the case on this ground, however because neither party has briefed the matter. Accordingly, were the absence of a state tort analogue the only potential obstacle to the existence of subject matter jurisdiction here, we would be inclined to remand the case to the district court for the latter to rule, in the first instance, on this question. But that is not necessary because the district court did find the absence of subject matter jurisdiction based on a second ground that the parties have litigated. And because we agree with the district court that the discretionary function exception and the misrepresentation exception do apply here to negate the waiver of sovereign immunity that might otherwise arise from the FTCA, we resolve the case on that ground. We turn to these § 2680 exceptions now.

D. Exceptions to Waiver of Sovereign Immunity

As noted, when either the discretionary function exception or the misrepresentation exception applies, there is no waiver of sovereign immunity under the FTCA. *See* 28 U.S.C. § 2680(a), (h). These exceptions "must be strictly construed in favor of the United States" and, when an exception applies, a court will lack subject matter p.1327 jurisdiction over the action. *JBP Acquisitions,* 224 F.3d at 1263-64. We turn now to examine whether the above exceptions apply here.

1. Plaintiffs' Registration Claim

In support of their registration claim, Plaintiffs argue that 15 U.S.C. § 80b-3(c) imposed on the SEC a duty to revoke Stanford Group's registration as a broker-dealer once it had determined that Stanford Group was involved in a Ponzi scheme. The district court rejected this claim on two grounds. First, it concluded that Plaintiffs had misread § 80b-3(c). The court held that, although this statute may impose certain duties on the SEC in its review and approval of an *initial* registration application by a broker-dealer, it did not impose those same duties with regard to a broker-dealer's subsequent registration amendments. Because only registration amendments, not the initial registration, were at issue here, the district court concluded that Plaintiffs had failed to articulate an applicable duty of the SEC. Second, the district court held that, even assuming a duty by the SEC to similarly review registration amendments, any actions taken, or not taken, after that review would be discretionary and therefore barred by the discretionary function exception.

a. Duties Pertaining to Registration Amendments

Analysis of the merits of the district court's first ground for dismissal focuses on the question whether 15 U.S.C. § 80b-3(c) imposes not only a duty to disallow initial registration by a broker-dealer who makes a material misstatement or is otherwise disqualified, but also a duty to take adverse action against an advisor at a later time when the latter amends his registration.[7] Because Plaintiffs allege nothing amiss about the Stanford Group's initial 1995 registration, the registration claim was properly dismissed if the statutory duty applies only to an initial registration. If, on the other hand, the duty also applies to registration amendments, then Plaintiffs have potentially made out a registration claim, and we would then have to determine whether the discretionary function exception would apply to that claim.

So, as to the question whether 15 U.S.C. § 80b-3(c) imposes on the SEC the duty that Plaintiffs attribute to it, the answer is no. The title of § 80b-3(c) is "Procedure for registration; filing of application; effective date of registration; amendment of registration." It has two subsections. The first, § 80b-3(c)(1), sets out the documentation an applicant must submit to the SEC when applying for broker-dealer registration. The second, § 80b-3(c)(2), mandates that, within 45 days of filing, the SEC must either grant a registration application or institute proceedings on that application. The provision further sets out the criteria that the SEC should use in determining whether to grant or deny registration:

> The Commission shall grant such registration if the Commission finds that the requirements of this section are satisfied and that the applicant is not prohibited from registering as an investment advisor under section 80b-3a of this title. The Commission shall deny such registration if it does not make such a finding or if it finds that if the applicant were so registered, its registration would be subject to suspension or revocation under subsection (e) of this section.

p.1328 15 U.S.C. § 80b-3(c)(2). Spelled out, the statute tells the SEC that it should grant the applicant's registration if all requirements under the section are satisfied and if the applicant is not otherwise prohibited on grounds set out in § 80b-3a. Conversely, the SEC should deny registration if it does not make the findings necessary to grant the application or if the registration would be subject to suspension or revocation under § 80b-3(e), had it already been granted.

The problem with Plaintiffs' argument that § 80b-3(c)(2) imposes upon the SEC certain duties at the time of the amendment of an existing registration is the absence of any mention of that fact in its text. It is true that the phrase "amendment of registration" is in the title of § 80b-3(c), but that isolated reference is the only time the phrase is used. The language of the section consistently refers to "granting" or "denying" registration, which are words that imply an initial application, rather than an amendment to an existing application. Further, the text contains no discussion of procedures or duties assigned to the SEC were it required to consider suspension or revocation at the time of the filing of an amended registration. Indeed, the only time that § 80b-3(c) mentions suspension or revocation of an existing registration is when it refers to a different statute, § 80b-3(e), as the statute that sets the standard for such action.[8]

With the absence of any reference to revocation or suspension of an entity's registration at the time of an amendment of that registration, Plaintiffs are left with only a policy argument: that this Court should nonetheless expand the SEC's responsibilities under § 80b-3(c) to impose, with regard to a registration amendment, the same duties that the SEC is directed to perform at the time of initial registration. Failure to do so, Plaintiffs argue, would mean that "investment advisors that the SEC knew were in violation of Federal securities laws [could] remain registered, virtually indefinitely."

Leaving aside the fact that a court has no power to rewrite a statute in response to a persuasive policy argument, Plaintiffs' concerns are nonetheless overstated because, as § 80b-3(c)(2) clearly contemplates, the SEC maintains the authority to suspend or revoke an existing registration under § 80b-3(e) if it is "in the public interest."[9] In addition, the SEC has discretionary authority to pursue violations of the securities laws under other statutory provisions and regulations.[10] Thus, the p.1329 SEC's power to suspend reckless or dishonest broker-dealers does not depend on the forced reading of § 80b-3(c) advocated by Plaintiffs.

But even if we could assume that the duties described in § 80b-3(c) were deemed to apply to amendments to registration, we would still have to determine whether the discretionary function exception would apply to shield the SEC from liability. Unfortunately for Plaintiffs, the description of the SEC's duties in § 80b-3(c) falls short of the specificity that would be required to escape the discretionary function exception. To understand why this is so, an explanation of that exception is necessary.

b. Impact of the Discretionary Function Exception on Plaintiffs' Registration Claim

As noted, while the FTCA, as a general matter, waives the federal government's immunity from suit as to certain tort claims, Congress has created exceptions to that general waiver of immunity. One of those exceptions, known as the discretionary function exception, provides that the provisions of the FTCA shall not apply to:

> (a) Any Claim based upon an act or omission of an employee of the Government, exercising due care, in the execution of a statute or regulation, whether or not such statute or regulation be valid, or based upon the exercise or performance or the failure to exercise or perform a discretionary function or duty on the part of a federal agency or an employee of the Government, whether or not the discretion involved be abused.

28 U.S.C. § 2680(a) (emphasis added).

In short, the discretionary function exception serves to preserve sovereign immunity for any claim that is based on a federal agency or employee's performance or nonperformance of a discretionary task, even if, in so acting, the agency employee may have abused his discretion. *See* 28 U.S.C. § 2680(a); *Nguyen v. United States,* 556 F.3d 1244, 1251 (11th Cir.2009). Thus, this exception "marks the boundary between Congress' willingness to impose tort liability upon the United States and its desire to protect certain governmental activities from exposure to suit by private individuals." *United States v. S.A. Empresa de Viacao Aerea Rio Grandense (Varig Airlines),* 467 U.S. 797, 808, 104 S.Ct. 2755, 81 L.Ed.2d 660 (1984); *accord Marbury v. Madison,* 5 U.S. (1 Cranch) 137, 170, 2 L.Ed. 60 (1803) ("The province of the court is . . . not to enquire how the executive, or executive officers, perform duties in which they have a discretion.").

In guiding the courts' application of the discretionary function exception, the Supreme Court has formulated a two-part test. First, the conduct that forms the basis of the suit must involve an element of judgment or choice by the employee. *Berkovitz v. United States,* 486 U.S. 531, 536, 108 S.Ct. 1954, 100 L.Ed.2d 531 (1988); *Autery v. United States,* 992 F.2d 1523, 1526-28 (11th Cir.1993). In determining whether judgment or choice is present in the particular conduct at issue, the inquiry focuses on "whether the controlling statute or regulation mandates that a government agent perform his or her function in a specific manner." *Hughes v. United States,* 110 F.3d 765, 768 (11th Cir.1997) (internal quotation marks omitted). If a federal statute, regulation, or policy specifically prescribes a course of action for an employee to follow, the Government will have failed to show that the action at issue allowed for the employee's p.1330 exercise of judgment or choice because, in that case, "the employee ha[d] no rightful option but to adhere to the directive." *United States v. Gaubert,* 499 U.S. 315, 322, 111 S.Ct. 1267, 113 L.Ed.2d 335 (1991) (internal quotation marks omitted). Conversely, unless a "federal statute, regulation, or policy specifically prescribes a course of action embodying a fixed or readily ascertainable standard," it will be presumed that the particular act involved an element of judgment or choice. *Autery,* 992 F.2d at 1529 (internal quotation marks, citation, and emphasis omitted).

If the Government has met this first element of the test for applying the exception, then the second part of the test requires the court to "determine whether that judgment is of the kind that the discretionary function exception was designed to shield." *Berkovitz,* 486 U.S. at 536, 108 S.Ct. 1954. A particular decision will be of the kind protected by the exception if it is the type of decision that one would expect to be inherently grounded in considerations of policy. *Autery,* 992 F.2d at 1530-31. Indeed, when a government agent is permitted to exercise discretion in making a particular decision—whether that permission is express or implied—"it must be presumed that the agent's acts are grounded in policy when exercising that discretion." *Gaubert,* 499 U.S. at 324, 111 S.Ct. 1267; *accord OSI, Inc. v. United States,* 285 F.3d 947, 951 (11th Cir.2002). Finally, in examining whether an employee's discretion is of the type grounded in public policy, one uses an objective test, and the employee's subjective intent is irrelevant. *Gaubert,* 499 U.S. at 325, 111 S.Ct. 1267; *accord Mid-S. Holding Co., Inc. v. United States,* 225 F.3d 1201, 1207 (11th Cir.2000); *Reynolds v. United States,* 549 F.3d 1108, 1112 (7th Cir.2008) ("Those labels [of 'malicious and bad faith conduct'] do nothing for [plaintiff's] cause, though . . . [because] subjective intent is irrelevant to our analysis.").

We now apply the above standard to the case before us. We agree with the district court that even if one could somehow intuit from § 80b-3(c) the existence of some undescribed duties imposed on the SEC with regard to amended registration submissions, the discretionary function exception would immunize the Government from liability based on a faulty performance of those duties. First, because the decision whether to deny an original registration application involves an element of judgment or choice, likewise so would a decision regarding the appropriate response to an amended registration. Second, Plaintiffs have identified no federal statute, regulation, or policy that sets a "fixed or readily ascertainable standard" by which to gauge the adequacy of the employee's rendering of this decision. To the contrary, the language of § 80b-3(c) provides no standard at all by which the SEC should make findings that underpin a decision to deny an application at the time an amended registration is filed. The language provides that the Commission "shall grant such registration if the Commission finds that the requirements of this section are satisfied and that the applicant is not prohibited from registering as an investment advisor under section 80b-3a of this title" and the Commission "shall deny such registration if it does not make such a finding." 15 U.S.C. § 80b-3(c)(2).[11] Here, p.1331 the Commission made no finding at all on either score because it was understandably not on notice that this section even authorized it to take a particular action on an amended registration submission.[12] Thus, there was no "fixed or readily ascertainable standard" that would have guided it on this matter.

The SEC having met the first prong of the test for applying the exception, we proceed to the second prong: whether the employee's duties were of the type that the discretionary function exception was intended to protect. As set out above, the exception is intended to protect any decision grounded in public policy, and all discretionary decisions are presumed to be grounded in public policy.

As the Supreme Court explained in the context of the regulation of savings and loan associations:

> Where Congress has delegated the authority to an independent agency or to the Executive Branch to implement the general provisions of a regulatory statute and to issue regulations to that end. . . the actions of Government agents involving the necessary element of choice and grounded in the social, economic, or political goals of the statute and regulations are protected [by the discretionary function exception.]

Gaubert, 499 U.S. at 323, 111 S.Ct. 1267 (emphasis added).

The SEC is an independent agency, created by the Securities Exchange Act of 1934 to regulate the securities markets and protect investors through its enforcement of that and other statutes. *See* 15 U.S.C. § 78d.[13] Its regulation of the securities markets clearly involves the kinds of decisions "we would expect inherently to be grounded in considerations of policy." *Autery,* 992 F.2d at 1530-31 (internal quotation marks omitted); *Baer v. United States,* 722 F.3d 168, 175 (3d Cir.2013) (noting that "there is a strong presumption that the SEC's conduct is susceptible to policy analysis"); *see also Schmidt v.* p.1332 *United States,* 198 F.2d 32, 36 (7th Cir. 1952) (holding that SEC's investigations are "clearly within the scope of its discretionary authority"); *Sprecher v. Von Stein,* 772 F.2d 16, 18 (2d Cir.1985) (same). Indeed, as the Supreme Court has recognized, the legislative history of the discretionary function exception indicates that it was "designed to preclude application of the [FTCA] to a claim based upon an alleged abuse of discretionary authority by a regulatory or licensing agency—for example, the Federal Trade Commission, the Securities and Exchange Commission, the Foreign Funds Control Office of the Treasury, or others." *Varig Airlines,* 467 U.S. at 809, 104 S.Ct. 2755 (quoting the statement of Assistant Attorney General Francis M. Shea) (internal quotation marks omitted). That being so, investigatory decisions by the SEC are the types of decisions that the discretionary function exemption would be expected to shield.

Agreeing on this point, two of our sister circuits have recently applied the discretionary function exception to preclude claims based on the SEC's failure to discover, investigate, and dissolve other Ponzi schemes. In *Dichter-Mad Family Partners, LLP v. United States,* 709 F.3d 749, 750-51 (9th Cir.2013), the Ninth Circuit affirmed the dismissal of a complaint made by plaintiffs who lost money in the Bernard Madoff Ponzi scheme. Laying out a long history of SEC failures to identify and upset Madoff's scheme, the plaintiffs alleged a breach of the SEC's duties to investigate violations of the securities laws. *Id.* at 756-60. The Ninth Circuit rejected the plaintiffs' argument on the ground that the discretionary function exception covered the actions taken (and not taken) in the course of the investigation. *Id.* at 787. The court noted that, despite the presence of some statutory duties couched in mandatory language, the weight of the complaint involved poor performance of discretionary actions. *Id.* at 751 (quoting *Sabow v. United States,* 93 F.3d 1445, 1453

(9th Cir.1996) ("[T]he presence of a few, isolated provisions cast in mandatory language does not transform an otherwise suggestive set of guidelines into binding agency regulations.")).

Similarly, in *Baer,* the Third Circuit dismissed a suit by plaintiffs injured in the Madoff scheme that was premised on the incompetence of the SEC's investigations. 722 F.3d at 171-72. As in *Dichter-Mad,* the *Baer* plaintiffs identified various regulatory duties framed in mandatory language, and contended that those constituted a mandatory directive. *Id.* at 173-74. The court pointed out:

> The regulations identified . . . do not prescribe any particular course of action for the SEC to follow. At most, these regulations attempt to limit the scope of discretion afforded the SEC during the course of an investigation. While a violation of these regulations may amount to an abuse of discretion, that is not sufficient to waive the federal government's sovereign immunity. . . .

Id. at 175 (citation omitted). On that basis, the Third Circuit also held that the discretionary function exemption applied. *Id.* at 177.

As *Dichter-Mad* and *Baer* emphasize, the duties that Plaintiffs' registration identify as being breached are duties that fall with the discretion of the SEC. As such, we hold that, in the unlikely event that § 80b-3(c) authorized the SEC to revoke a registration based on a subsequent amendment, the discretionary function exception would apply, and Plaintiffs' registration claim would fall.

2. Plaintiffs' Notification Claim

a. *The SEC's Statutory Duty to Notify SIPC of Stanford Group's Financial Difficulties*

Plaintiffs also claim that the SEC was required by statute to notify SIPC that p.1333 Stanford Group was in financial difficulty. SIPC is a non-profit corporation with which Stanford Group, as a registered broker-dealer, was required to maintain membership. Once notified that a member is in financial difficulty, SIPC can, among other things, file an application for a protective decree against that member in a court of competent jurisdiction. *See* Securities Investor Protection Act of 1970, 15 U.S.C. §§ 78aaa-*lll;* 15 U.S.C. §§ 78eee(a)(3)-(4), (b). The specific statutory duty upon which Plaintiffs rely provides:

> If the Commission or any self-regulatory organization is aware of facts which lead it to believe that any broker or dealer subject to its regulation is in or is approaching financial difficulty, it shall immediately notify SIPC, and, if such notification is by a self-regulatory organization, the Commission.

15 U.S.C. § 78eee(a)(1) (emphasis added). As noted, despite indications that Stanford Bank was running a Ponzi scheme, the SEC let twelve years pass before taking any public action. Plaintiffs contend that had the SEC earlier notified SIPC, the latter might have taken action to protect existing and future investors. It is from this failure to act, in alleged violation of § 78eee(a)(1), that Plaintiffs have derived their notification claim.

b. Interplay Between the SEC's Duty to Notify and the Misrepresentation Exception

Whether or not the SEC violated § 78eee(a)(1)'s provision requiring it to notify SIPC of Stanford's financial issues, the Government contends that it is protected from liability through the misrepresentation exception. Like the discretionary function exception, the misrepresentation exception preserves the United States' sovereign immunity and thereby protects the Government from tort liability that it might otherwise face under the FTCA. The district court concluded that the misrepresentation exception applies, and it dismissed Plaintiffs' notification claim. We agree.

The misrepresentation exception is set out in 28 U.S.C. § 2680(h). That section provides a list of torts for which there can be no waiver of sovereign immunity. Specifically,

> The provisions of this chapter [Chapter 171] and section 1346(b) of this title shall not apply to—
>
> . . . .
>
> (h) Any claim arising out of assault, battery, false imprisonment, false arrest, malicious prosecution, abuse of process, libel, slander, misrepresentation, deceit, or interference with contract rights. . . .

28 U.S.C. § 2680(h) (emphasis added).

The phrase "arising out of" is interpreted broadly to include all injuries that are dependent upon one of the listed torts having been committed. *United States v. Shearer*, 473 U.S. 52, 55, 105 S.Ct. 3039, 87 L.Ed.2d 38 (1985) ("Section 2680(h) does not merely bar claims *for* assault or battery; in sweeping language it excludes any claim *arising out of* assault or battery.") (emphasis in original). So, a claim will be deemed to have arisen from a § 2680 excepted tort if the governmental conduct that is essential to the plaintiff's cause of action is encompassed by that tort. And this is so even if the plaintiff has denominated, as the basis for the cause of action, a tort not found within § 2680(h)'s list of excepted torts. *See Metz v. United States*, 788 F.2d 1528, 1534 (11th Cir.1986); *accord O'Ferrell v. United States*, 253 F.3d 1257, 1266 (11th Cir.2001); *Atorie Air, Inc. v. Fed. Aviation Admin.*, 942 F.2d 954, 958 (5th Cir.1991); *see also Shearer*, 473 U.S. at 55, 105 S.Ct. 3039 (noting, in discussing the battery exception, p.1334 that "[n]o semantical recasting of events can alter the fact that the battery was the immediate cause of Private Shearer's death and, consequently, the basis of respondent's claim").

Accordingly, it is "the substance of the claim and not the language used in stating it which controls." *Gaudet v. United States*, 517 F.2d 1034, 1035 (5th Cir.1975).[14] And if the governmental conduct that is essential to proving a plaintiff's claim would be covered by the misrepresentation exception, then the Government is shielded from liability by sovereign immunity, no matter how the plaintiff may have framed his claim or articulated his theory. In other words, "a plaintiff cannot circumvent the misrepresentation exception simply through the artful pleading of its claims." *JBP Acquisitions*, 224 F.3d at 1264. Instead, the misrepresentation exception applies "when the basis for the . . . action is an underlying claim for misrepresentation." *Id.*

So, then how does one define a claim of misrepresentation for purposes of determining whether the misrepresentation exception applies? The Supreme Court has characterized "misrepresentation" as being a breach of the "duty to use due care in obtaining and communicating information upon which [another] may reasonably be expected to rely in the conduct of his economic affairs." *United States v. Neustadt*, 366 U.S. 696, 706, 81 S.Ct. 1294, 6 L.Ed.2d 614 (1961). Accordingly, "the essence of an action for misrepresentation, whether negligent or intentional, is the communication of misinformation on which the recipient relies." *Block v. Neal*, 460 U.S. 289, 296, 103 S.Ct. 1089, 75 L.Ed.2d 67 (1983). Collapsing the above guidance into one inquiry, we therefore examine Plaintiffs' notification claim to determine if the latter is based on the communication or miscommunication of information upon which others might be expected to rely in economic matters. If it does, and if a flawed communication caused the Plaintiffs' injury, then Plaintiffs' claim will be construed as a misrepresentation claim for which the analogous exception under § 2680(h) applies, and sovereign immunity will therefore bar the claim.

c. Application to Plaintiffs' Notification Claim

As the statutory basis for their notification claim, Plaintiffs rely on 15 U.S.C. § 78eee(a)(1), which states that "[i]f the [SEC] is aware of facts which lead it to believe that any broker or dealer subject to its regulation is in or is approaching financial difficulty, it shall immediately notify SIPC." The Plaintiffs allege that the SEC was aware that Stanford Group was in or approaching financial difficulty and that, through its longstanding silence, the SEC violated its statutory duty to notify SIPC of this fact. Thus, Plaintiffs do not fault the SEC for a miscommunication regarding Stanford Group's solvency; they fault the SEC for its non-communication of information regarding that issue.

But unfortunately for Plaintiffs, miscommunication and non-communication yield the same result for purposes of the misrepresentation exception, because the misrepresentation exception "encompasses failure to communicate as well as miscommunication." *JBP Acquisitions*, 224 F.3d p.1335 at 1265 n. 3 (citing *Neustadt*, 366 U.S. at 706-07, 81 S.Ct. 1294); *Muniz-Rivera v. United States*, 326 F.3d 8, 13 (1st Cir.2003) (citing *JBP Acquisitions*, 224 F.3d at 1265) ("The case law makes manifest that the prophylaxis of the misrepresentation exception extends to failures of communication."); *Lawrence v. United States*, 340 F.3d 952, 958 (9th Cir.2003) (citing *Neustadt*, 366 U.S. at 705-06, 81 S.Ct. 1294) ("The misrepresentation exception shields government employees from tort liability for failure to communicate information, whether negligent, or intentional.").

Therefore, because Plaintiffs' claim is focused on non-communication of financial information by the SEC, the misrepresentation exception springs into action to prevent a waiver of the Government's sovereign immunity. Resisting this seemingly straightforward application of the misrepresentation exception, however, Plaintiffs attempt to analogize their facts to cases in which courts have refused to apply the misrepresentation exception even when there has been a miscommunication or non-communication by the governmental actor. As we explain, Plaintiffs' cited cases are distinguishable.

Addressing first those cases in which courts have refused to apply the misrepresentation exception to claims asserting pecuniary loss, even when a misrepresentation by the governmental agency has occurred, it is true that the misrepresentation exception "does not bar negligence actions which focus not on the Government's failure to use due care in communicating information, but rather on the Government's breach of a different duty." *Block v. Neal,* 460 U.S. 289, 297, 103 S.Ct. 1089, 75 L.Ed.2d 67 (1983); *JBP Acquisitions,* 224 F.3d at 1265 (same). In *Block,* a governmental agency oversaw the construction of the plaintiff's house, but the construction turned out to be shoddy. *Block,* 460 U.S. at 297, 103 S.Ct. 1089. The agency conducted three inspections throughout the project and represented that the construction met appropriate standards, but the agency's statement was wrong. *Id.* at 292, 296, 103 S.Ct. 1089. Eventually learning that she had purchased a lemon, the plaintiff-homeowner sued.

Holding that the misrepresentation exception did not apply, the Supreme Court acknowledged that the governmental agency had made misrepresentations to the plaintiff when it provided inaccurate inspection reports. Yet, the Court noted, the plaintiff was proceeding under a state law Good Samaritan cause of action on a claim that the agency had voluntarily undertaken supervision of the construction. *Id.* at 297, 103 S.Ct. 1089. Such a claim does not fall within the tort of misrepresentation. Further, while the agency may have made misrepresentations to the plaintiff, through erroneous inspection reports, it was the negligent oversight of the construction of the home that allegedly caused the injury, and such a claim is not barred by the misrepresentation exception. *Id.* at 298, 103 S.Ct. 1089.

The Supreme Court contrasted the facts in *Block* with those at issue in *United States v. Neustadt,* 366 U.S. 696, 81 S.Ct. 1294, 6 L.Ed.2d 614 (1961), a home construction case in which the Court had held that the misrepresentation exception did apply. In *Neustadt,* the plaintiffs had relied on a federal agency's erroneous appraisal of a house, and, as a result, paid more than it was worth. *Id.* at 700-01, 81 S.Ct. 1294. Although plaintiffs alleged that the basis of their claim was the agency's negligent inspection of the house, the Supreme Court concluded that the claim actually arose from a contention that the agency had made a misrepresentation. As such, the claim was barred by the misrepresentation p.1336 exception. *Id.* at 711, 81 S.Ct. 1294.

Reconciling its holding in *Block* with its earlier holding in *Neustadt,* the Supreme Court noted that the only basis for the *Neustadt* action was a claim that the federal agency had made a misstatement. With only a misstatement claim, the misrepresentation exception necessarily applied. But the claim in the *Block* action had rested not on the agency's duty to make accurate communications, but instead on a different duty: its duty to use due care in supervising a construction project. Accordingly, the misrepresentation exception did not apply in *Block. Block,* 460 U.S. at 296-97, 103 S.Ct. 1089.

In short, if a plaintiff can show that the Government has breached a duty distinct from the duty not to make a misrepresentation and if that breach has caused the plaintiff's injury, the fact that the Government may have also made a misrepresentation will be insufficient to trigger the misrepresentation exception to a waiver of sovereign immunity. As the Ninth Circuit has explained, "[t]he Government is liable for injuries resulting from negligence in performance of operational tasks even though misrepresentations are collaterally involved. It is not liable, however, for injuries resulting from commercial decisions made in reliance on government misrepresentations." *Guild v. United States,* 685 F.2d 324, 325 (9th Cir. 1982).

Relying on the reasoning of *Block,* Plaintiffs liken their claim to cases in which courts have refused to apply the misrepresentation exception to bar claims of economic loss. But in those cases, as with *Block,* courts have identified some separate duty—usually referred to as an "operational" duty—that is both distinct from the duty to communicate and essential to the plaintiff's claim. For example, in *JM Mechanical Corporation v. United States,* 716 F.2d 190, 191 (3d Cir.1983), the plaintiff, a construction subcontractor, was left unpaid when the general contractor had failed to secure performance bonds required by the Department of Housing and Urban Development ("HUD"). After learning that the contractor had failed to acquire the bonds, HUD then failed in its own duty to obtain such bonds, and it also misrepresented to the subcontractor that the contractor had acquired the bonds. *Id.* at 191-92. The Third Circuit held that the essence of the claim was "the failure of the government to secure new bonds, not. . . the government's failure to tell [the subcontractor] of the failure of the original bonds." *Id.* at 195. That is, like *Block,* the sufficient cause of the injury was the breach of a duty that was distinct from the duty not to miscommunicate. A subsequent and collateral misrepresentation that merely aggravated the injury did not suffice to invoke the misrepresentation exception.

Along similar lines are cases cited by Plaintiffs that involve the mishandling of records. In these cases, a plaintiff was denied a benefit because the government misdelivered or misfiled some essential document. *See, e.g., Metro. Life Ins. Co. v. Atkins,* 225 F.3d 510, 511-13 (5th Cir. 2000) (plaintiff was denied insurance benefits because the government incorrectly filed an insurance beneficiary form that lacked the proper signature to make it effective); *Devlin v. United States,* 352 F.3d 525, 527-28 (2d Cir.2003) (Postal Service failed to forward an employee's life insurance beneficiary form to the Office of Personnel Management, a failure that subsequently deprived the beneficiary of the policy benefits). Yet, in both *Atkins* and *Devlin,* the cause of the plaintiff's injury was the clerical error itself, which "operational" act did not trigger application of p.1337 the misrepresentation exception. The agency's subsequent failure to disclose its error to the plaintiff did not change the fact that it was the "operational" act that was the basis for the plaintiff's claim.[15]

The cases cited by Plaintiffs are therefore distinguishable from this case. The poor supervision of the construction project in *Block,* the failure to secure construction bonds in *JM Mechanical,* and the filing errors in *Atkins* and *Devlin* were all *acts* of the governmental agency and it was these acts that caused the injuries the plaintiffs suffered. Even though subsequent failures to notify the plaintiffs of the agency's misdeeds may have aggravated the problems, the economic injuries suffered by the plaintiffs in those cases did not "arise out of" any misrepresentation by the agency.

In contrast, Plaintiffs' injuries here arose precisely from the SEC's failure to notify SIPC. As Plaintiffs allege, it was this notification that "would have set in motion a process through which the [Plaintiffs] would have learned of the Ponzi scheme and been able to avoid or mitigate their damages." Thus, it was the SEC's failure to communicate particular information to SIPC that led to Plaintiffs' economic injuries. And, to repeat, a miscommunication or failure to communicate, in this context, gives rise to the misrepresentation exception.

Faced with this grim reality, Plaintiffs attempt to transform the SEC's duty to notify SIPC into an "operational" task devoid of any communicative aspect. Plaintiffs argue that they are not faulting the SEC for the substance, or absence of substance, of any particular communication. In fact, Plaintiffs go so far as to assert that "the content of the communication [to be sent to the SIPC] is immaterial to the claim." Instead, Plaintiffs argue that, as in *Atkins* and *Devlin*, where the mere presence of the right form in the right place would have sufficed to prevent the plaintiffs' injuries, the SEC merely had to complete the physical act of sending something, anything, to SIPC. Accordingly, Plaintiffs argue, the SEC's failure to perform this "operational" act takes this case outside of the misrepresentation exception.

But this argument makes no sense at all. Obviously, it is the content of any writing sent to SIPC that would be critical to that corporation's determination of the appropriate action to take, not the fact that SIPC's mailroom may have happened to log in some undescribed communication from the SEC. The district court rejected Plaintiffs' effort to end-run the misrepresentation exception with this semantical sleight-of-hand, and so do we.[16]

Finally, Plaintiffs also try to analogize their case to cases where courts have held p.1338 that the duty to warn is not covered by the misrepresentation exception. However, the misrepresentation exception did not apply in these "duty to warn" cases cited by Plaintiffs cite because the injuries involved in those cases did not arise from the plaintiffs' commercial decisions based on the governments' misrepresentations. *See, e.g., Mandel v. United States,* 793 F.2d 964, 967 (8th Cir.1986) (park ranger recommended a body of water for swimming, but negligently failed to warn the swimmer of submerged rocks, upon which the swimmer then suffered a serious head injury); *McNeil v. United States,* 897 F.Supp. 309, 310-11 (E.D.Tex.1995) (plaintiffs injured in a fire when the Farmer's Home Administration ("FmHA") failed to inform them that an inspection of a house the plaintiffs were purchasing had discovered a faulty smoke alarm and FmHA had failed to repair the alarm); *Lemke v. City of Port Jervis,* 991 F.Supp. 261, 263-64 (S.D.N.Y.1998) (negligent home-safety inspectors failed to identify lead pipes, which poisoned the plaintiff).

As *Neustadt* explained, the misrepresentation exception applies to the breach of the "duty to use due care in obtaining and communicating information upon which that party may reasonably be expected to rely in the conduct of his economic affairs." 366 U.S. at 706, 81 S.Ct. 1294. The injury Plaintiffs suffered here was the loss of their investment money, which is an economic injury arising from a commercial decision that Plaintiffs may not have made had the SEC notified SIPC of Stanford Group's financial frailty. Thus, the failure-to-warn cases, which involve non-economic injuries, are not on point.

For all the above reasons, we conclude that the § 2680(h) misrepresentation exception applies and the Government enjoys sovereign immunity from this claim. Therefore, we affirm the district court's dismissal of the notification claim, as well as the registration claim.

IV. *Alternative Ground For Dismissal Under Rule 12(b)(6)*

We affirm the district court's dismissal of Plaintiffs' claims for lack of subject matter jurisdiction under Rule 12(b)(1) under the assumption that the applicability of a § 2680 exceptions deprives a court of jurisdiction over tort claims made against the Government. This conclusion is consistent with the language of § 2680 and § 1346(b), which make the jurisdictional grant of the latter section inapplicable when one of the former section's exceptions to the FTCA's waiver of sovereign immunity applies. The Supreme Court has also expressly stated that sovereign immunity, which the § 2680 exceptions preserve, is "jurisdictional in nature." *Meyer,* 510 U.S. at 475, 114 S.Ct. 996. Finally, this Court has consistently treated the § 2680 exceptions as jurisdictional, as evidenced by the fact that we have considered their existence before reaching other statutory prerequisites that likewise could be said to enjoy some claim to jurisdictional status. *See, e.g., Powers v. United States,* 996 F.2d 1121, 1123 n. 2 (11th Cir.1993) (deciding that the discretionary function exception applied, and thus not addressing the argument that "the plaintiffs cannot bring this suit, because a private party would not be liable under like circumstances"); *Mesa v. United States,* 123 F.3d 1435, 1439 n. 6 (11th Cir.1997) ("In light of our conclusion that the appellants' claim is barred by the discretionary function exception, we need not address the United States' argument that the appellants have failed to allege facts sufficient to support recovery under Florida law."); *Ochran v. United States,* 117 F.3d 495, 504 n. 6 (11th Cir.1997) *("Ochran I")* (noting that the discretionary function exception is jurisdictional and stating that the Court had not yet considered p.1339 the question of a valid state law claim). Other circuits have expressly agreed with this approach. *See Lesoeur v. United States,* 21 F.3d 965, 967 (9th Cir. 1994) ("[F]ederal courts do not have subject matter jurisdiction over tort actions based on federal defendants' performance of discretionary functions."); *White-Squire v. U.S. Postal Service,* 592 F.3d 453, 457-58 (3d Cir.2010) (chapter 171 provisions are jurisdictional).

For these reasons, we affirm the district court's dismissal of these claims based on its lack of subject matter jurisdiction. That said, we also recognize that in its recent jurisprudence, the Supreme Court has become more reluctant, when sanctioning the dismissal of some claims, to base its rejection on jurisdictional grounds, as opposed to a deficiency in the merits of the claim. For example, in reversing the Second Circuit, the Supreme Court explained that the Copyright Act's requirement that copyright holders register their works before suing for infringement was not a jurisdictional prerequisite, but rather "a precondition to filing a claim that does not restrict a federal court's subject-matter jurisdiction." *Reed Elsevier, Inc. v. Muchnick,* 559 U.S. 154, 157, 130 S.Ct. 1237, 176 L.Ed.2d 18 (2010). Explaining the distinction in *Morrison v. National Australia Bank Ltd.,* 561 U.S. 247, 254, 130 S.Ct. 2869, 177 L.Ed.2d 535 (2010), the Court noted that whereas jurisdictional questions go to the court's "power to hear a case," merits questions ask "whether the allegations the plaintiff makes entitle him to relief." (internal quotation marks omitted). This is a distinction with a difference, because:

> Branding a rule as going to a court's subject-matter jurisdiction alters the normal operation of our adversarial system. . . . Courts do not usually raise claims or arguments on their own. But federal courts have an independent obligation to ensure that they do not exceed the scope of their jurisdiction, and

therefore they must raise and decide jurisdictional questions that the parties either overlook or elect not to press.

Henderson ex rel. Henderson v. Shinseki, 562 U.S. 428, ___, 131 S.Ct. 1197, 1202, 179 L.Ed.2d 159 (2011). That is, classifying a prerequisite to suit as jurisdictional makes it the court's responsibility to raise the issue *sua sponte* even if the parties do not address it themselves.

The FTCA has not been immune to the recent debate concerning which side of the jurisdiction/merits pendulum a particular statutory defect in a claim should lie. Relying on the Supreme Court's holding in *Kontrick v. Ryan,* 540 U.S. 443, 455, 124 S.Ct. 906, 157 L.Ed.2d 867 (2004), a case involving bankruptcy procedure, the Seventh Circuit "no longer treats § 2675(a) [which requires exhaustion of administrative claims before commencing suit under the FTCA] as a jurisdictional prerequisite." *Smoke Shop, LLC v. United States,* 761 F.3d 779, 786-87 (7th Cir.2014). We, however, have characterized this provision as jurisdictional. *Dalrymple v. United States,* 460 F.3d 1318, 1324 (11th Cir.2006). More recently, the Ninth Circuit has held that the statute of limitations applicable to the FTCA, 28 U.S.C. § 2401(b), is not jurisdictional. *Kwai Fun Wong v. Beebe,* 732 F.3d 1030, 1044 (9th Cir.2013) (en banc), *cert. granted sub nom. United States v. Kwai Fun Wong,* ___ U.S. ___, 134 S.Ct. 2873, 189 L.Ed.2d 831 (June 30, 2014) (decision pending).

In *Kwai Fun Wong,* the Ninth Circuit made clear that it was expressing no view on the jurisdictional status of the chapter 171 provisions of Title 28. *Id.* at 1044 n. 10. However, in the wake of this general jurisprudential shift, the Seventh Circuit has taken the position that the statutory p.1340 exceptions to the United States' waiver of sovereign immunity, found in § 2680(a)-(n), "limit the breadth of the Government's waiver of sovereign immunity, but they do not accomplish this task by withdrawing subject-matter jurisdiction from the federal courts." *Parrott v. United States,* 536 F.3d 629, 634 (7th Cir.2008). Instead, the applicability of these exceptions goes to the plaintiff's entitlement to relief. As a result of this conclusion, the Seventh Circuit held that it is now "the Government's burden to assert these exceptions if and when it seeks to defeat a claim because of them." *Id.* at 634-35.

Nonetheless, given the texts of the applicable statutes, the general admonition by the Supreme Court that sovereign immunity is jurisdictional, and our own precedent, we will treat the § 2680 exceptions as jurisdictional in this case. We can comfortably do so because we conclude that the result of this case would be the same whether the absence of a § 2680 exception operates as a jurisdictional prerequisite or instead as a question going to the merits of Plaintiffs' claims. In *Morrison,* the Supreme Court concluded that the Second Circuit had mistakenly treated a provision of federal securities laws as jurisdictional, when it affirmed a Federal Rule of Civil Procedure 12(b)(1) dismissal. Instead, the Supreme Court concluded that, based on the same defect in the complaint, the case should have been dismissed pursuant to Rule 12(b)(6) for failure to state a claim. 561 U.S. at 253-54, 130 S.Ct. 2869. The Supreme Court held that remand was unnecessary, however, because "a remand would only require a new Rule 12(b)(6) label for the same Rule 12(b)(1) conclusion." *Id.* at 254, 130 S.Ct. 2869.

We believe the same approach applies here. Should the § 2680 exceptions someday be interpreted as going to the merits of a plaintiff's claim, rather than the district court's jurisdiction to hear the case, then for the same reasons that we affirm the dismissal for lack of subject matter jurisdiction, we would also affirm for failure to state a claim upon which relief could be granted.

V. *Conclusion*

For the above reasons, we AFFIRM the district court's dismissal of Plaintiffs' claims.

[*] Honorable Ronald Lee Gilman, United States Circuit Judge for the Sixth Circuit, sitting by designation.

[1] The facts considered on this appeal are taken from the allegations set out in the Plaintiffs' amended complaint. In reviewing the grant of a motion to dismiss, we "accept[] the allegations in the complaint as true and constru[e] them in the light most favorable to the nonmoving party." *Kizzire v. Baptist Health Sys., Inc.,* 441 F.3d 1306, 1308 (11th Cir. 2006).

[2] In February 2009, the SEC filed civil proceedings against Stanford Group. *See* Complaint at 1, *SEC v. Stanford Int'l Bank, Ltd.,* No. 3:09-cv-298-N (N.D. Tex. Feb. 17, 2009). Stanford was ordered to disgorge $6.7 billion to the SEC and he received a $5.9 billion penalty. *See* Order at 17, *SEC v. Stanford Int'l Bank, Ltd.,* No. 3:09-cv-298-N (N.D. Tex. Apr. 25, 2013). On June 18, 2009, Stanford was indicted on mail fraud, wire fraud, conspiracy to commit securities fraud and money laundering, and conspiracy to obstruct an SEC investigation. He was convicted in 2012 and sentenced to 110 years in prison. *See* Judgment at 3, *United States v. Stanford,* No. 4:09-cr-00342-01 (S.D. Tex. June 14, 2012), *appeal docketed,* No. 12-20411 (5th Cir. June 19, 2012).

[3] "The United States shall be liable, respecting the provisions of this title relating to tort claims, in the same manner and to the same extent as a private individual under like circumstances. . . ." 28 U.S.C. § 2674.

[4] Further, the analogy that must be made is one between the federal government and a private person, and thus a state law that permits tort claims against the state or local government does not suffice. *United States v. Olson,* 546 U.S. 43, 44, 126 S.Ct. 510, 163 L.Ed.2d 306 (2005); *Maradiaga v. United States,* 679 F.3d 1286, 1292 (11th Cir.2012).

[5] Under the Restatement, the recognized "special relations" arise between (1) common carriers to passengers, (2) innkeepers to guests, (3) possessors of land held open to members of the public, and (4) custodians to their wards. Restatement (Second) of Torts § 314A (1965). The relationship of the SEC to investors does not appear to fit into any of these classes.

[6] Under the Restatement, there is a duty to prevent another from causing harm in these relationships: (1) parents and children, (2) masters and servants, (3) possessors of land or chattels and their licensees, (4) those in charge of persons with dangerous propensities and those dangerous persons, and (5) custodians and wards. Restatement (Second) of Torts §§ 316-320 (1965). Again, none of these appear analogous to the relationship between the SEC and Stanford Group.

[7] Once registered, a broker-dealer is required to submit an annual, amended update to the Form ADV submitted at the initial registration. 17 C.F.R. § 275.204-1 (2011).

[8] Section 80b-3(e) bears the title "Censure, denial, or suspension of registration; notice and hearing." It requires the SEC to take action up to and including the revocation of registration if "it finds, on the record after notice and opportunity for hearing, that such censure, placing of limitations, suspension, or revocation is in the public interest." 15 U.S.C. § 80b-3(e).

Notably, Plaintiffs have not proceeded under this § 80b-3(e), which is the subsection that addresses revocation of an entity's registration.

[9] Plaintiffs do not contend that § 80b-3(e) has been violated. Nor do their pleadings offer any basis for concluding that the SEC failed in any duty set by § 80b-3(e), because the latter predicates suspension or revocation on a finding, made after notice and opportunity for hearing, that such adverse action would be in the public interest. Plaintiffs' allegations here concern internal, non-public determinations of the SEC, not findings made after a hearing.

[10] *See, e.g.,* 15 U.S.C. § 78u(a)(1) ("The Commission may, in its discretion, make such investigations as it deems necessary to determine whether any person has violated, is violating, or is about to violate [securities laws]."); 17 C.F.R. § 202.5(a) ("The Commission may, in its discretion, make such formal investigations . . . as it deems necessary to determine whether any person has violated, is violating, or is about to violate . . . the federal securities laws. . . .").

[11] Even the use of "shall" in the statutory text is not sufficient to take the action out of the discretionary function exception. *See Ochran v. United States,* 117 F.3d 495, 500-01 (11th Cir.1997) *("Ochran I")* ("We agree with the Government that the use of the word 'shall' in describing the responsibilities of the AUSA does not necessarily mean that the Guidelines left no room for the AUSA to exercise judgment or choice" because the Guidelines did not specify how, when, or under what circumstances action was necessary.); *Powers v. United States,* 996 F.2d 1121, 1125 (11th Cir. 1993) (holding that "shall" not dispositive where "Congress has not specifically prescribed a course of action.").

[12] Plaintiffs did not proceed on the statutory section that actually authorizes the SEC to suspend the registration of a broker-dealer: § 80b-3(e). Perhaps they declined to so proceed because the latter section permits suspension only when the Commission has made the required findings on the record after notice and an opportunity for a hearing. Because the decision to convene a hearing is obviously a discretionary judgment that would trigger application of the discretionary function exception, Plaintiffs' reluctance to rely on what would seem to be the apt statutory provision for purposes of suspension of a registration is perhaps understandable. In any event, during the time period in question, no hearing was ever held by the SEC to consider suspension of Stanford Group.

[13] As Congress explained in that statute:

[T]ransactions in securities as commonly conducted upon securities exchanges and over-the-counter markets are effected with a national public interest which makes it necessary to provide for regulation and control of such transactions and of practices and matters related thereto, . . . to require appropriate reports to remove impediments to and perfect the mechanisms of a national market system for securities and a national system for the clearance and settlement of securities transactions and the safeguarding of securities and funds related thereto, and to impose requirements necessary to make such regulation and control reasonably complete and effective, in order to protect interstate commerce, the national credit, the Federal taxing power, to protect and make more effective the national banking system and Federal Reserve System, and to insure the maintenance of fair and honest markets in such transactions[.]

15 U.S.C. § 78b.

[14] In *Bonner v. City of Prichard, Ala.,* we held "that the decisions of the United States Court of Appeals for the Fifth Circuit (the 'former Fifth' or the 'old Fifth'), as that court existed on September 30, 1981, handed down by that court prior to the close of business on that date, shall be binding as precedent in the Eleventh Circuit, for this court, the district courts, and the bankruptcy courts in the circuit." 661 F.2d 1206, 1207 (11th Cir.1981).

[15] Indeed, in *Atkins,* the Fifth Circuit held that the evidence, in the light most favorable to the plaintiff, suggested that the deceased had signed the designation of beneficiary form and that the personnel department of the federal agency had simply misplaced that form. A breach of that duty constituted the breach of an operational task. The court indicated that if instead the evidence had indicated that there was no signed form, but the personnel department had failed to communicate to the deceased the need to sign the form, then the case might well be covered by the misrepresentation exception. *Metro. Life Ins. Co. v. Atkins,* 225 F.3d 510, 512-13 (5th Cir.2000).

[16] The district court noted in its order granting dismissal:

The crucial element in the Plaintiffs' chain of causation is the alleged failure to communicate information about Stanford's company. The Plaintiffs cannot disguise the essence of their negligent misrepresentation claim by repackaging the SEC's alleged negligence from having failed to 'notify' or 'report' . . . to having failed to send the required notification.

785 F.3d 1384 (2015)

Ronald COLBERT, Jerri Colbert, Plaintiffs-Appellees,
v.
UNITED STATES of America, Defendant-Appellant,
Kandis Martine, et al., Defendants.

No. 14-12007.

United States Court of Appeals, Eleventh Circuit.

May 7, 2015.

Colbert v. US, 785 F. 3d 1384 (11th Cir. 2015)

p.1385 Charles A. Sorenson, Matthew Nichols Posgay, David Maxwell Milton, Coker, Schickel, Sorenson & Posgay, PA, Jacksonville, FL, Bryan S. Gowdy, Creed & Gowdy, P.A., Jacksonville, FL, for Plaintiffs-Appellees.

Stuart F. Delery, Asst. Atty. Gen., A. Lee Bentley, III, U.S. Atty., Barbara C. Biddle, Jeffrica Jenkins Lee, Attorneys, Appellate Staff, Civil Div., Washington, DC, for Defendant-Appellant.

Before WILSON and ANDERSON, Circuit Judges, and VOORHEES,[*] District Judge.

VOORHEES, District Judge:

I.

The United States challenges subject matter jurisdiction, namely, the district court's partial summary judgment ruling that, under the Federal Tort Claims Act ("FTCA"), 28 U.S.C. § 1346 *et seq.*, and pursuant to the self-determination contract entered into between the United States Department of Interior, Bureau of Indian Affairs ("BIA") and the Navajo Nation Tribe, 25 U.S.C. § 450f[1], Navajo Nation Department of Justice ("NNDOJ") Attorney Kandis Martine was "deemed" an employee of the BIA and afforded the full protection and coverage of the FTCA. The district court determined that given Martine's role in connection with the Navajo Nation Child & Family Services Program ("NNCFS"), and its efforts to oppose the adoption of a Navajo child by a non-Navajo family in Florida state court, Martine was entitled to protection under the FTCA. As a result, the district court dismissed Martine from the lawsuit and held that the United States was the proper party-defendant, 28 U.S.C. § 2679(d)(3). On appeal, the United States contends the district court erred in finding as a factual matter that Martine was "carrying out" work under the self-determination contract. The United States asserts that the decision to afford Martine FTCA coverage, allegedly based upon erroneous factual findings, constitutes an impermissible extension of the Government's waiver of sovereign immunity.

Pursuant to the Indian Self Determination and Education Assistance Act ("Self-Determination Act" or "ISDEAA"), codified principally at 25 U.S.C. § 450, *et seq.*, Congress created a mechanism for Indian tribes and tribal organizations to enter into agreements with the United States providing for the tribe or organization to assume responsibility for programs or services to Indian populations that otherwise would be provided by the Federal government.[2] *See* Pub.L. No. 93-638, 88 Stat. 2203 (1975).

p.1386 In 2006, the BIA and the Navajo Nation entered into a three-year self-determination contract (or '638 contract), effective January 1, 2006 through December 31, 2008, which generally provides for the Navajo Nation to deliver an array of social services to Navajo children and their families. Prior to 2006, these social services were administered by the BIA under the Indian Child Welfare Act ("ICWA"), 25 U.S.C. §§ 1901-1963. ICWA's objective is "to protect the best interests of Indian children and to promote the stability and security of Indian tribes and families ... by providing for assistance to Indian tribes in the operation of child and family service programs." *Id.* § 1902. Of particular relevance here is ICWA's goal "to prevent the breakup of Indian families and, in particular, to insure that the permanent removal of an Indian child from the custody of his parent or Indian custodian shall be a last resort." *Id.* § 1931(a). In connection with the '638 contract at issue here, the Navajo Nation established the Navajo Nation Child & Family Services Program and charged NNCFS with the delivery of social services to Navajo families in compliance with ICWA.

In or around March 2007, the Navajo Nation was notified of a potential adoption of a Navajo child by a non-Navajo family and a related hearing scheduled for April 2, 2007 in Jacksonville, Florida.[3] The Navajo Nation referred the case to the NNCFS ICWA Unit, which was advised that the presiding state court judge was not following ICWA's placement preference. The Navajo Nation objected to the proposed adoptive placement. During NNCFS's staffing of cases with the NNDOJ, the Director of the NNCFS Program, Regina Yazzie, elected to involve NNDOJ Attorney Kandis Martine.

As an attorney for the NNDOJ, Martine serves as "the legal representative for the NNCFS Program." According to Martine, she dedicates more than half of her time working for the NNCFS and approximately twenty percent of her time working alongside the ICWA Unit at NNCFS. Martine, described by Yazzie as an "expert on ICWA," was asked to attend the state court adoption hearing along with a NNCFS ICWA Unit social worker. Martine obtained approval from her immediate supervisor, Assistant Attorney General, at the NNDOJ to travel to Jacksonville for the adoption hearing. The funds used for Martine's travel were provided by the NNCFS. The Navajo Nation, through Martine, also retained a Florida adoption lawyer, Attorney Jodi Seitlin, to represent its interests in the state proceeding. Although not licensed to practice law in the State of Florida, Martine was expected to educate Seitlin about ICWA and monitor the state court adoption proceeding relative to ICWA compliance.

On the morning of April 2, 2007, while in Jacksonville, Florida for the hearing, Martine and NNCFS social worker, Lucy Laughter-Begay, were in a car accident. At the time of the accident, Martine and p.1387 Laughter-Begay were traveling to Seitlin's downtown office prior to the 10:00 a.m. hearing. Martine, the driver of the rental car, traveled the wrong direction on a one-way street and caused a car occupied by Ronald and Jerri Colbert to rear-end another vehicle, injuring both of the Colberts and precipitating the instant civil action.

On October 2, 2009, after waiting six months for a response from the United States to the Colberts' administrative claims, the Colberts commenced litigation in the United States District Court, Middle District of Florida, against the United States, Martine, and P.V. Holding Corporation, d/b/a "Budget Rent-A-Car System, Inc." ("Budget").[4] The Colberts' complaint alleged negligence and loss of consortium claims against the United States and Martine, and negligence, loss of consortium, and dangerous instrumentality claims against Budget.

The Colberts named the United States as a party-defendant based upon the Navajo self-determination contract. *See* 25 U.S.C. § 450f(a)(1)(b). Inclusion of the United States as a party was premised on the theory that Martine is considered a federal employee for purposes of the FTCA when performing work under the self-determination contract. § 450f(c)(1).

After the lawsuit was filed, the BIA denied both administrative claims on grounds that Martine was not a federal employee. Similarly, the United States Attorney for the Middle District of Florida declined to certify that Martine was an "employee of the Government" acting within the scope of her employment under 28 U.S.C. § 2679(d)(1).[5]

On October 25, 2010, the United States moved to dismiss the claims brought against the government pursuant to Rule 12(b)(1) of the Federal Rules of Civil Procedure. The Colberts and Martine moved for partial summary judgment the same day, asking the Court to rule as a matter of law that FTCA coverage was available to Martine.

During the pendency of these motions, Ronald Colbert died and his wife became the designated personal representative for his estate. On March 29, 2011, a Second Amended Complaint was filed adding a p.1388 wrongful death claim and, alternatively, a survival action pursuant to Florida law.

On May 13, 2011, the district court denied the United States' motion to dismiss and the Colberts' and Martine's motions for partial summary judgment. With respect to subject matter jurisdiction, the district court found that whether Martine could properly be deemed a federal employee required an analysis of the merits and further development of the record. *See* Fed.R.Civ.P. 12(b)(1). The court also found that, at that stage of the case, genuine issues of material fact precluded decision on the FTCA coverage issue. *See* Fed.R.Civ.P. 56.

In the fall of 2012, following discovery, the Colberts renewed the motion for partial summary judgment on the same FTCA issue and Martine joined in the motion. Martine's motion also encompassed a request that the district court find and certify under 28 U.S.C. § 2679(d)(3) that Martine is entitled to FTCA coverage.[6] Although the motion was styled as a summary judgment motion, the court construed it as a petition for certification under § 2679(d)(3). On a more developed evidentiary record, the district court reconsidered its May 13, 2011 decision that summary judgment disposition was precluded and held on November 21, 2012 that subject matter jurisdiction was present pursuant to the FTCA, 28 U.S.C. § 1346(b). Martine was dismissed from the case and the United States was substituted as contemplated by 28 U.S.C. § 2679(d)(3). The claims against Budget were dismissed at summary judgment.

The district court presided over a five-day bench trial held June 10, 2013 through June 14, 2013 to determine liability and damages. On November 20, 2013, the court issued findings of fact and conclusions of law. The trial judge found the

United States eighty percent at fault and Mr. Colbert twenty percent at fault. The United States was ordered to pay the Colberts more than 2.6 million dollars in damages. On March 6, 2014, upon a Rule 59(e) motion filed by the Government, the damages award was subsequently reduced, resulting in a final judgment against the United States in the amount of $2,599,691.20.

On appeal, the United States challenges the applicability of the FTCA under these facts. The district court's findings concerning liability and damages are not at issue.

On March 12, 2015, the Navajo Nation was granted leave of this Court to participate as *amicus curiae*. The Navajo Nation urges the Court to affirm in recognition of the objective of the ISDEAA and implications for future tribal employees performing '638 contract functions.

II.

This Court "review[s] *de novo* a district court's determination of whether it p.1389 has subject-matter jurisdiction." *Gupta v. McGahey,* 709 F.3d 1062, 1064-65 (11th Cir.2013). The district court's interpretation or construction of a statute is also subject to *de novo* review. *Bankston v. Then,* 615 F.3d 1364, 1367 (11th Cir.2010).

III.

Having conducted a *de novo* review, we conclude that the district court's decision concerning subject matter jurisdiction is consistent with ISDEAA's statutory scheme, the terms of the governing self-determination contract, and the record evidence. We begin by considering the origin of ISDEAA.

The Congressional statement of findings present in 25 U.S.C. § 405 provides that:

> The Congress, after careful review of the Federal government's historical and special legal relationship with, and resulting responsibilities to, American Indian people, finds that—the prolonged Federal domination of Indian service programs has served to retard rather than enhance the progress of Indian people and their communities by depriving Indians of the full opportunity to develop leadership skills crucial to the realization of self-government, and has denied to the Indian people an effective voice in the planning and implementation of programs for the benefit of Indians which are responsive to the true needs of Indian communities.

25 U.S.C. § 450(a)(1). Based upon these Congressional findings, the United States declared as policy "the obligation of the United States to respond to the strong expression of the Indian people for self-determination by assuring maximum Indian participation in the direction of ... Federal services to Indian communities...." *Id.* § 450a(a). Likewise, the Congress declared its commitment to "establish[] a meaningful Indian self-determination policy which will permit an orderly transition from the Federal domination of programs for, and services to, Indians to effective and meaningful participation by the Indian people in the planning, conduct, and administration of those programs and services." *Id.* § 450a(b).

The Indian Self Determination and Education Assistance Act implements this policy. However, as originally enacted, ISDEAA failed to account for the problem of liability insurance for tribal employees who "step into the shoes" of the federal government pursuant to these self-determination contracts. *See FGS Constructors, Inc. v. Carlow*, 64 F.3d 1230, 1234 (8th Cir.1995) ("Congress acknowledged that the tribal governments, when carrying out self-determination contracts, were performing a federal function and that a unique legal trust relationship existed between the tribal government and the federal government in these agreements."); *see also* S.Rep. No. 107-324, at 2 (2002), *available at* 2002 WL 31474281 ("The Self Determination Act authorizes Indian tribes and tribal consortia to 'step into the shoes' of the United States and assume responsibility and managerial control of services and programs previously administered by the Federal government."). As a result, tribal employees performing what would otherwise be "federal" work did not enjoy FTCA protection.

In 1990, Congress took additional measures and amended ISDEAA by requiring the BIA to obtain liability insurance "for Indian tribes, tribal organizations, and tribal contractors carrying out" self-determination contracts. 25 U.S.C. § 450f(c)(1). Section 314 of the ISDEAA provides in pertinent part:

> With respect to claims resulting from the performance of functions ... under a contract ... authorized by the [ISDEAA]..., an Indian tribe, tribal organization p.1390 or Indian contractor is deemed hereafter to be part of the Bureau of Indian Affairs in the Department of the Interior ... while carrying out any such contract ... and its employees are deemed employees of the [BIA] ... while acting within the scope of their employment in carrying out the contract.... [A]fter September 30, 1990, any civil action or proceeding involving such claims brought hereafter against any tribe, tribal organization, Indian contractor or tribal employee covered by this provision shall be deemed to be an action against the United States and will be defended by the Attorney General and be afforded the full protection and coverage of the Federal Tort Claims Act....

See Pub.L. No. 101-512, § 314, 104 Stat. 1915 (1990) (codified at 25 U.S.C. § 450f notes). Therefore, as a result of the 1990 Amendment to ISDEAA (commonly referred to as "Section 314"), Congress provided that Indian tribes, tribal organizations, Indian contractors, and their employees, may be deemed employees of the BIA for purposes of the FTCA when they are carrying out functions authorized in or under a self-determination contract. *Id.*

Federal regulations confirm the intended breadth of ISDEAA's FTCA protection. In addition to offering FTCA protection to tribal employees paid directly pursuant to '638 contracts, FTCA coverage is available to tribal employees who are paid from funding derived from a source other than self-determination contract funding "*as long as the services out of which the claim arose were performed in carrying out the self-determination contract.*" *See* 25 C.F.R. § 900.197 (emphasis added).[7]

IV.

As a matter of first impression, we consider the plain meaning of Section 314 of the Self-Determination Act and hold that the statutory language is unambiguous.

See Lowery v. Alabama Power Co., 483 F.3d 1184, 1199 (11th Cir.2007) (internal citations omitted). Accordingly, to the extent not already defined by statute, we assign all terms their ordinary meaning.[8] *Id.*

p.1391 Section 314 expressly provides FTCA coverage to "an Indian tribe, tribal organization or Indian contractor ... and its employees" that are engaged in "carrying out" functions authorized in or under a self-determination contract. 25 U.S.C. § 450f notes. The ISDEAA defines the terms "Indian tribe," "tribal organization," and "Indian."[9] 25 U.S.C. § 450b. For purposes of ISDEAA, "Indian contractor" necessarily refers to a member of an Indian tribe, or "a tribe-related organization that may itself enter into a self-determination contract" as opposed to a private party. *See FGS Constructors, Inc.,* 64 F.3d at 1234-35 ("Indian contractor" is "limited to a tribe-related organization that may itself enter into a self-determination contract, not a private party ... that has been retained to work on a project funded by a self-determination contract."); *see also Demontiney v. United States,* 54 Fed.Cl. 780, 786 (Fed.Cl.2002).

Next, we consider the meaning of "carrying out" in the context of Section 314.[10] The phrase "to carry out" has been defined as "to put into execution," "to bring to a successful issue," or "[t]o conduct duly to completion or conclusion; to carry into practice or to logical consequences or inferences." *Shirk v. United States,* 773 F.3d 999, 1005 (9th Cir.2014) (internal citations omitted) (relying on dictionaries for the ordinary meaning of the term at or around the time of the statute's enactment). Therefore, "carrying out" a self-determination contract simply means to act or perform under the contract.

The term "employee" is defined in part by the contours of the FTCA, which we acknowledge is an exception to the general rule that the United States enjoys sovereign immunity unless that immunity is expressly waived. *See Means v. United States,* 176 F.3d 1376, 1378-79 (11th Cir. 1999); *see also Suarez v. United States,* 22 F.3d 1064, 1065 (11th Cir.1994) ("The FTCA is a specific, congressional exception to the general rule of sovereign immunity."). In *Means,* we explained:

> Congress has authorized a limited waiver of sovereign immunity under the FTCA
>
> for injury or loss of property, or personal injury or death caused by the negligent or wrongful act or omission of any employee of the Government *while acting within the scope of his office or employment,* under circumstances where the United States, if a private person, would be liable to the claimant in accordance with the law of the place where the act or omission occurred.

Means, 176 F.3d at 1378-79 (quoting 28 U.S.C. § 1346(b)) (emphasis added); *see also United States v. Orleans,* 425 U.S. 807, 813, 96 S.Ct. 1971, 48 L.Ed.2d 390 (1976). "Whether an individual is an employee p.1392 of the United States for purposes of the FTCA is determined by federal law." *Means,* 176 F.3d at 1379 (internal citations omitted).

Notwithstanding the United States' contrary position, ISDEAA's Section 314 means exactly what it says. Section 314 expands the United States' waiver of sovereign immunity to Indian tribes, tribal organizations, Indian contractors, and their employees as a means of advancing the "long-standing federal policy of encouraging Indian self-determination, giving Indian tribes control over the administration of federal programs benefitting Indians." *FGS Constructors, Inc.,* 64 F.3d at 1234; *see also Allender v. Scott,* 379 F.Supp.2d 1206, 1218 n. 15 (D.N.M.2005) (responding to policy arguments of the government agencies and noting that Congress settled the question in favor of providing insurance coverage).

In addition, the parties agree that, if properly "deemed" a BIA employee, Martine was acting within the scope of her employment under Florida law and as contemplated within Section 314. Therefore, the sole issue presented for this Court is whether Martine was, in fact, carrying out the Navajo self-determination contract when the car accident occurred and, therefore, properly "deemed" a BIA employee falling within the protection of the FTCA.

In seeking to apply ISDEAA to the facts of this case, we next turn to the Navajo self-determination contract.[11] *See, e.g.,* 25 U.S.C. § 450l. The first matters addressed by the self-determination contract are "Authority and Purpose." (Contract, § A). At the outset, the self-determination contract states that it "is entered into by the Secretary of the Interior [BIA] ... for and on behalf of the United States pursuant to [ISDEAA] and *by the authority of the Navajo Nation* (referred to in this agreement as the 'Contractor')." (Contract, § A, 1) (emphasis added). To be clear, the Navajo Nation is the contracting authority—not the NNCFS. In the following paragraph, the purpose of the self-determination contract is explained:

> Each provision of the [ISDEAA] and each provision of this Contract shall be liberally construed for the benefit of the Contractor to transfer the funding and the following related functions, services, activities and programs (or portions thereof), that are otherwise contractible..., including all related administrative functions, from the Federal Government to the Contractor: *Navajo Children and Family Services Program (ICWA).*

(Contract, § A, 2). Thus, the Navajo self-determination contract effectively transfers the BIA's responsibility for ensuring adherence to ICWA to the Navajo Nation. To that end, the Navajo Nation created and funded NNCFS.

The Navajo self-determination contract incorporates by reference an Annual Funding Agreement ("AFA"), which itself is comprised of multiple funding-related documents, including "Attachment A," entitled "Scope of Work." The AFA addresses its "Program, Functions, Services and Activities":

> The Navajo Nation shall administer and perform those portions of the [BIA's] *Navajo Children & Family Services Program* identified in the Scope of Work, ... in accordance with its own laws and policies and the terms, provisions, and conditions of the Contract and this AFA and any attachments thereto...."

p.1393 (AFA, § A, ¶ 1).[12]

The Scope of Work attachment identifies the specific goals and tasks to be undertaken by the Navajo Nation under the contract. Indeed, consistent with ICWA, the Navajo Nation's goals are: "to prevent the break up of Navajo families, to protect the best interest of Navajo children and to promote the stability of Navajo families." (AFA, Attach. A). The means for achieving these goals are specifically outlined as eleven enumerated functions within the Scope of Work. Here, the relevant contract functions are:

5. Request coordination of legal services from the Navajo Nation Department of Justice on behalf of Navajo children and families, when applicable.

9. Provide education and training on the provisions of ICWA.

11. Monitor the efforts made by the State to comply with the ICWA, such as, placement preference and whether active efforts are being provided.

(AFA, § A, ¶¶ 5, 9, 11).

In addition to setting out the boundaries of the self-determination contract, the AFA speaks directly to application of the FTCA. Under the "Federal Tort Claims Act" section of the AFA:

> For purposes of Federal Tort Claims Act coverage, *the Navajo Nation and its employees* are deemed to be employees of the Federal government while performing work under the contract. This status is not changed by the source of the funds used by the Navajo Nation to pay the *employees* [*sic*] salary and benefits unless the employee receives additional compensation for performing covered services from anyone other than the Navajo Nation.

(AFA, § O) (emphases added); *see* 25 C.F.R. § 900.186(a) (model FTCA clause). The AFA speaks broadly in terms of FTCA coverage being available for *all Navajo Nation employees* assuming the other statutory criteria are met. *Id.* Consistent with Section 314 of ISDEAA, the AFA does not limit FTCA coverage to employees of the NNCFS.

In this case, Martine works for the NNDOJ, which in and of itself is not a party to, nor designated beneficiary of, any '638 contract.[13] However, Martine is a member and employee of the Navajo Nation, a recognized eligible Indian tribe as defined by ISDEAA. *See* 25 U.S.C. § 450b(e). In sum, given the aims of ISDEAA, and the terms of the Navajo self-determination contract, we conclude that, for purposes of the debated FTCA coverage, the relevant limiting principle is the alleged tortfeasor's performance of identifiable '638 contract functions—"carrying out" the self-determination contract. Thus, the *actual work performed* by Martine is the focus of our factual inquiry.

V.

The district court properly found as a fact that Martine was "carrying out" the self-determination contract by performing functions identifiable in, and expressly authorized by or under, the contract, namely, Scope of Work Functions 9 and 11. According to the Government, Martine's licensure as an attorney, including p.1394 her purported performance of "legal services" in connection with the Jacksonville, Florida adoption proceeding, is dispositive of the issue and precludes FTCA coverage. Given that Martine performed at least two other identifiable functions under the Navajo self-determination contract, we need not decide whether Martine actually performed legal services.[14]

In this instance, Martine testified that her work for the NNCFS was consistent with, and in furtherance of, the prescribed '638 contract goals:

> "To assist our contract attorney on an adoption case in the state court of Florida."

> "[T]elling [the contract attorney] what ICWA is, providing her guidance on how the case should go, but leaving it to her as the legal representative."

"I was present in the state of Florida for an Indian child welfare case that fell under the federal law of the Indian Child Welfare Act, in that a mother relinquished her rights to her child and requested that the child be adopted by a nonnative family. Navajo Nation objected to that. And we wanted the state court, as well as the adoptive family to realize that under the federal law, the placement preferences are that the child be placed with a Navajo family.

So my intention as a representative— a legal representative of Navajo Child & Family Services was to assist them by, first of all, locating a contract attorney to represent us in the court and to assist that contract attorney with the complexities of the Indian Child Welfare Act...."

In other words, consistent with Scope of Work Function 9, Martine made herself available to the Navajo Nation's contract attorney, Jody Seitlin, to educate and train Seitlin (and possibly others involved in the adoption proceeding) on ICWA. Similarly, Martine's physical presence at the adoption hearing enabled Martine to monitor first-hand the State's efforts to comply with ICWA as outlined by Scope of Work Function 11. The evidentiary record supports the district court's finding that, at the time of the accident, Martine was carrying out work falling squarely within the Navajo self-determination contract.

Likewise, the district court properly found that Martine was sufficiently qualified to perform Scope of Work Functions 9 and 11, and eligible for FTCA protection, despite her professional status as an attorney. The Government argues that attorneys are not contemplated by the '638 contract that governs here. Appellees, on the other hand, argue that under ISDEAA, the Indian tribe must be allowed discretion to determine who is needed to carry out the '638 contract.

There is no support within Section 314, or the Navajo self-determination contract itself, for the proposition that a tribal attorney is *ipso facto* not *qualified* to perform p.1395 traditional social work tasks. The Government points to the "Personnel Management" section within the AFA that reads in part:

> [A]ll personnel employed by the Navajo Nation to carry out the Contract and this AFA shall meet the qualifications set forth by the Navajo Nation Department of Personnel Management....

(AFA § I.2). The Government argues that, in light of the need to strictly construe waiver of its sovereign immunity, the proper construction of the '638 contract is to require a staffing plan that identifies "key personnel" and their qualifications in order to limit employee eligibility for FTCA protection. *See* 25 C.F.R. § 23.23(b)(6)(i)-(ii).[15] More specifically, the United States contends that for purposes of FTCA, "key personnel" should be limited to those positions set out within the Program Budget and Description of Positions attachments to the AFA. The Government relies on the *Shirk* decision for this proposition, which we find unpersuasive. *See, Shirk,* 773 F.3d at 1006-07 (observing in dictum that "[i]f a court determines that the relevant federal [self-determination] contract does not encompass the activity that the plaintiff ascribes to the employee, or if the agreement covers that conduct, *but not with respect to the employee in question,* there is no subject matter jurisdiction.") (emphasis added).

Admittedly, the AFA does not include the position of "attorney" within its listing of budgeted NNCFS personnel. However, "guidance, legal representation, and advice to Indian families" involved in child custody proceedings is precisely the type of child and family program envisioned by ICWA. *See* 25 U.S.C. § 1931(a); 25 C.F.R. §§ 23.13(a)-(f) and 23.22(a)(6)(2014).[16] In fact, the evidence tends to show that the NNCFS and NNDOJ often worked in tandem to accomplish these and other ICWA objectives on behalf of the Navajo Nation. Most importantly, to accept the Government's proposed construction would require the Court to ignore the more specific AFA FTCA clause, which expressly states that coverage under the FTCA is available to *"any Navajo Nation employee"* carrying out work under the '638 contract.[17]

p.1396 **VI.**

Finally, we also hold that provision of FTCA coverage to Martine and the substitution of the United States under 28 U.S.C. § 2679(d)(3), does not constitute an improper extension of the waiver of sovereign immunity. First, as previously discussed, Section 314 of ISDEAA is unambiguous and plainly extends the United States' waiver of sovereign immunity to Indian tribes, tribal organizations, Indian contractors and their employees that are engaged in "carrying out" functions authorized in or under a self-determination contract. Secondly, because Martine's work fell squarely within the identifiable functions of the Navajo self-determination contract, the district court's application of the law to these facts comports with the above-referenced sovereign immunity principles, including the FTCA.

AFFIRMED.

[*] Honorable Richard Voorhees, United States District Judge for the Western District of North Carolina, sitting by designation.

[1] All citations to the United States Code and the Code of Federal Regulations are to the most recent edition, unless otherwise noted.

[2] A "self-determination contract" is "a contract... between a tribal organization and the appropriate Secretary for the planning, conduct and administration of programs or services which are otherwise provided to Indian tribes and their members pursuant to Federal law." 25 U.S.C. § 450b(j). The self-determination contracts provide for the allocation of federal funds to the tribe or organization assuming responsibility for these programs or services. *Id.* § 450j-1.

[3] A Navajo mother relinquished her parental rights and the Navajo child was being placed up for adoption. *See in re: The Adoption Of: Baby Boy Billy, A Minor,* Fourth Judicial Circuit, Duval County, Florida. (Supp. App. 005). ICWA provides Indian tribes the right to intervene "[i]n any State court proceeding for the foster care placement of, or termination of parental rights to, an Indian child...." 25 U.S.C. § 1911(c)(1978).

[4] On November 24, 2008, as a prerequisite to filing a claim under the FTCA, the Colberts submitted administrative claims with the BIA pursuant to 28 U.S.C. § 2675(a). Title 28, United States Code, Section 2675(a) reads:

An action shall not be instituted upon a claim against the United States for money damages for injury or loss of property or personal injury or death caused by the negligent or wrongful act or omission of any employee of the Government while acting within the scope of his office or employment, unless the claimant shall have first presented the claim to the appropriate Federal agency and his claim shall have been finally denied by the agency in writing and sent by certified or registered mail. The failure of an agency to make final disposition of a claim within six months after it is filed shall, at the option of the claimant any time thereafter, be deemed a final denial of the claim for purposes of this section....

28 U.S.C. § 2675(a).

[5] Title 28, United States Code, Section 2679 provides for the exclusiveness of remedies against the United States for claims cognizable under the FTCA, 28 U.S.C. § 1346(b). Title 28, United States Code, Section 2679(d)(1) reads in pertinent part:

Upon certification by the Attorney General that the defendant employee was acting within the scope of his office or employment at the time of the incident out of which the claim arose, any civil action or proceeding commenced upon such claim in a United States district court shall be deemed an action against the United States under the provisions of this title and all references thereto, and the United States shall be substituted as the party defendant.

28 U.S.C. § 2679(d)(1).

[6] When the Attorney General elects not to certify that the defendant was an employee, or was acting within the scope of office or employment under § 2679(d)(1), § 2679(d)(3) permits certification by the U.S. District Court. Subsection 2679(d)(3) reads in pertinent part:

In the event that the Attorney General has refused to certify scope of office or employment under this section, the employee may at any time before trial petition the court to find and certify that the employee was acting within the scope of his office or employment. Upon such certification by the court, such action or proceeding shall be deemed to be an action or proceeding brought against the United States under the provisions of this title and all references thereto, and the United States shall be substituted as the party defendant....

28 U.S.C. § 2679(d)(3).

[7] Title 25, Section 900.197 of the Code of Federal Regulations, asks and answers the question:

Does FTCA cover employees of the contractor who are paid by the contractor from funds other than those provided through the self-determination contract?

Yes, as long as the services out of which the claim arose were performed in carrying out the self-determination contract.

25 C.F.R. § 900.197. Section 900.197 was promulgated after public notice and comment and has the force and effect of law. *See Perez v. Mortgage Bankers Ass'n*, ___ U.S. ___, 135 S.Ct. 1199, 1203, 191 L.Ed.2d 186 (2015) ("Rules issued through the notice-and-comment process are often referred to as 'legislative rules' because they have the 'force and effect of law.'") (quoting *Chrysler Corp. v. Brown*, 441 U.S. 281, 302-03, 99 S.Ct. 1705, 60 L.Ed.2d 208 (1979)).

[8] The district court aptly noted competing canons of construction advanced by the parties. First, the "principle of statutory construction that statutes passed for the benefit of dependent Indian tribes are to be liberally construed, with doubtful expressions being resolved in favor of the Indians." (M & O, 23-24) (citations omitted). Secondly, "[a] waiver of the Federal Government's sovereign immunity

must be unequivocally expressed in statutory text, and will not be implied. Moreover, a waiver of the Government's sovereign immunity will be strictly construed, in terms of its scope, in favor of the sovereign." (M & O, 24-25) (citations omitted). Because the district court found Section 314, ISDEAA's FTCA provision, unambiguous, neither of these canons was found to control the analysis.

[9] "'Indian tribe' means any Indian tribe, band, nation, or other organized group or community, ... which is recognized as eligible for the special programs and services provided by the United States to Indians because of their status as Indians." 25 U.S.C. § 450b(e). "'[T]ribal organization' means the recognized governing body of any Indian tribe; any legally established organization of Indians which is controlled, sanctioned, or chartered by such governing body or which is democratically elected by the adult members of the Indian community to be served by such organization and which includes the maximum participation of Indians in all phases of its activities." *Id.* § 450b(*l*). "'Indian' means a person who is a member of an Indian tribe." *Id.* § 450b(d).

[10] We observe that this "carrying out" limitation qualifies the group of '638 tribal actors (i.e., "Indian tribe, tribal organization or Indian contractor ... and its employees") including the potentially eligible tortfeasor-employee, Martine.

[11] The Navajo self-determination contract is based on a "model" '638 contract.

[12] Again, although the NNCFS is the designated beneficiary, the signatories to the AFA are the Navajo Nation and the BIA.

[13] As already noted, the fact that Martine's salary was not paid directly via '638 contract funds is not determinative. *See* 25 C.F.R. § 900.197. The NNDOJ receives federal funding indirectly for its employees' '638 contract work. There is also provision within ISDEAA for "contract support costs" for funding activities necessary to ensure compliance with the '638 contract goals. 25 U.S.C. § 450j-1(a)(2).

[14] Martine's primary role did not entail the performance of "legal services." Rather, separate counsel was retained to represent the interests of the Navajo Nation in the Jacksonville, Florida adoption proceeding. Although licensed as an attorney in the States of New Mexico, Washington, and within the Navajo Nation, Martine was not licensed to practice law in the State of Florida. Martine was not admitted *pro hac vice* and did not enter an appearance on the record as counsel. Beyond answering questions posed to her by the Court, Martine did not make legal arguments, present legal briefs, or address the Court for purposes of representing NNCFS. Moreover, even if Martine was engaged in helping to develop the NNCFS legal strategy with the Florida adoption attorney, there is no provision within ISDEAA, the Navajo self-determination contract, or any other statute or applicable regulation that purports to restrict Martine from performing legal services while contemporaneously carrying out the '638 contract.

[15] Section 23.23 of the Code of Federal Regulations prescribes mandatory tribal applications requirements for '638 contracts, including:

A staffing plan that is consistent with the implementation of the above-described program plan of operation and the procedures necessary for the successful delivery of services.

The plan must include proposed key personnel; their qualifications, training or experience relevant to the services to be provided; responsibilities; Indian preference criteria for employment; and position descriptions.

25 C.F.R. § 23.23(b)(6)(i). Here, the Navajo self-determination contract includes a staffing plan in the Scope of Work and other AFA attachments.

[16] Section 23.22 of Title 25 of the Code of Federal Regulations identifies the purpose of tribal government grants to Indian Tribes under ICWA as for the establishment and operation of tribally designed Indian child and family service programs. Section 23.22 reads in part:

The objective of every Indian child and family service program shall be to prevent the breakup of Indian families and to ensure that the permanent removal of an Indian child from the custody of his or her Indian parent or Indian custodian shall be a last resort. Such child and family programs may include, but need not be limited to: (8) *Guidance, legal representation and advice to Indian families involved in tribal, state, or Federal child custody proceedings....*

25 C.F.R. § 23.22(a)(8) (emphasis added).

[17] Advancing the same sovereign immunity argument in a different manner, the United States contends that Congress did not intend for FTCA coverage to extend to tribal employees acting in roles not traditionally filled by the BIA. The United States claims that because the BIA would not have hired a federal lawyer to represent the interests of the Navajo Nation Tribe (as opposed to the interests of Navajo children and families), Martine cannot be entitled to FTCA coverage. The United States attempts to draw a distinction between the respective interests of the Navajo Nation and Navajo children and families that does not exist. The United States' argument cannot be reconciled with ICWA, which expressly and unequivocally aligns the Navajo Nation's interests with the interests of its members—Navajo children and families. *See* 25 U.S.C. § 1931(a). The Tribe's ideal to preserve the Navajo family unit to the extent possible is merely one example of their common interests. *See id.* § 1902 (ICWA's objective is "to protect the best interests of Indian children and to promote the stability and security of Indian tribes and families....").

Made in the USA
Las Vegas, NV
24 June 2023

73851474R00321